International Business Law and the Legal Environment

The fifth edition of *International Business Law and the Legal Environment: A Transactional Approach* gives business and law students a clear understanding of the legal principles that govern international business. This book goes beyond compliance by emphasizing how to use the law to create value and competitive advantage.

DiMatteo's transactional approach walks students through key business transactions—from import and export, contracts, and finance to countertrade, dispute resolution, licensing, and more—giving them both context and providing real-world applications. This new edition also features:

- Added coverage of new technologies, such as smart contracts, digital platforms, and blockchain technology, artificial intelligence, market for non-fungible tokens, and the metaverse
- Discussion of businesses and sustainability, climate change, and creating a circular economy
- International perspective and use of a variety of national and international law materials
- Greater coverage of EU substantive law including the new Artificial Intelligence Act.

Upper-level undergraduate and postgraduate students of business law and international business will appreciate DiMatteo's lucid writing style, and professionals will find this book to be a comprehensive resource. Online resources include an instructor's manual, PowerPoint slides, and test bank.

Larry A. DiMatteo is Huber Hurst Professor of Contract Law & Legal Studies at the Warrington College of Business and Levin College of Law, and Affiliate Professor, Center for European Studies, at the University of Florida, USA. He is the author or editor of 20 books and 170 publications.

"This is an excellent source for students, academics, and practitioners alike interested in legal, ethical, and strategic issues in international business transactions. The author carries out a detailed analysis of important pieces of legislation, and provides a number of useful examples of different types of transactions."

Douglas Cumming, *York University, Canada*

"Professor DiMatteo's text provides a well-organized, comprehensive tour of international business law. The up-to-date text is sufficiently detailed for the advanced student, but works equally well as an introduction to numerous topics in international law. Clearly written, the text provides both an overview of international business issues and strategies, as well as detailed summaries and highlights of international agreements. The instructor has a wealth of exceptionally detailed case studies and questions to explore with students. An internationally recognized expert in international contract, Professor DiMatteo has included information on the rise of China in global trade, including the attendant economic and ethical implications. Legal issues involving sustainability, including environmental ethics, climate change, and human rights raise some of the most pressing issues of our times for students."

Stephanie M. Greene, *Boston College, USA*

"In a globalized world, success of any market player depends on adhering to the complex market rules. DiMatteo's textbook provides a helpful guide. Offering a comprehensive overview of international business transactions through the assessment of applicable theories, supported with practical examples and relevant judicial decisions, this text would be of particular use to both students and practitioners."

Pavel Repyeuski, *Leeds Beckett University, UK*

"DiMatteo advances an original approach to the relationship between international law and business. The textbook provides an authoritative account of the rules in an accessible and user-friendly structure to ensure that chapters are easy to navigate, and key information can be readily broken down and retained. It is a valuable resource for educators and researchers alike with an interest in international business law."

T. Leigh Anenson, *University of Maryland, USA*

International Business Law and the Legal Environment

A Transactional Approach

5th Edition

Larry A. DiMatteo

Routledge
Taylor & Francis Group
NEW YORK AND LONDON

Designed cover image: Getty Images

Fifth edition published 2025
by Routledge
605 Third Avenue, New York, NY 10158

and by Routledge
4 Park Square, Milton Park, Abingdon, Oxon, OX14 4RN

Routledge is an imprint of the Taylor & Francis Group, an informa business

First edition published by Thompson/South-Western 2003
Fourth edition published by Routledge 2021

ISBN: 978-1-032-74444-5 (hbk)
ISBN: 978-1-032-74446-9 (pbk)
ISBN: 978-1-003-46923-0 (ebk)

DOI: 10.4324/9781003469230

Typeset in Sabon
by Deanta Global Publishing Services, Chennai, India

Access the Instructor Resources: www.Routledge.com/9781032744469

To my Colleagues and Friends who have inspired me to pursue my international and comparative law interests.

Contents in Brief

Contents in Full

Tables

Figures

Images

Preface to the Fifth Edition

Supplemental Materials

The following materials are available online for the fifth edition:

(1) Instructor's Manual and Test Bank
(2) PowerPoint Presentations (each chapter)

Coverage Changes

Emphasis has been placed on updating EU law including coverage of the General Directive on Privacy Rights (GDPR) and the 2024 Artificial Intelligence Act (AI Act).

Additional Coverage

New chapters are dedicated to "Sustainability and the Circular Economy" (Chapter 3) and the "Digital Economy and Acceleration of Technology" (Chapter 19).

International Perspective

The fifth edition continues to take an "International Perspective" instead of a purely "American View." But it is important that there are standard "templates" for transacting business internationally: exporting–importing (standard contract clauses, INCOTERMS 2020, UCP 600, and so forth). Because of this, the variation between the International View and the American View is minor. More than one view over another, the book uses a comparative law approach in presenting the various topics.

It has been said that all business now is international business. Smaller and smaller companies, including "mom and pop" businesses or the European notion of small and medium-sized enterprises (SMEs), are actively involved in exporting and importing goods and services. The Internet and advanced technologies, government assistance programs, low trade barriers, as well as dependable transport, financial, and payment structures have opened access to foreign markets and lowered the risks of doing business internationally. The continued outsourcing of manufacturing inputs (raw materials and component parts) and of services, such as contact centers have increased business opportunities and the growth of international trade. This book examines the means and practices developed in law and business to facilitate transborder trade and mitigate the risks of doing business internationally. The book also notes more recent pushbacks against free trade in the name of protecting local economies and national security.

Legal, International, Transactional, and Practical Perspectives

Creating a "generalist" book on international business law seems an exceptional challenge because there is no single body of international business law as such. International business law is at most a compilation of different national systems and a few international conventions. This book deals with this abundance of law through its transactional orientation. The text presents international business transactions with an emphasis on rules and practice. It is the author's belief that it is these practical legal aspects of international business that are most relevant to today's business and law students.

This transactional approach is the book's distinctive characteristic. It draws from a broad variety of law, economic, and sociological sources, and above all it deals with international business transactions in the context of their real settings. This grounding of the legal aspects of international business is evident in the numerous practical bits of information that are not a reflection of law but are related to law. The practices and techniques discussed are directed at fully utilizing the facilitative nature of law and are directed at avoiding the regulatory side of law, such as litigation, corruption, and violations of laws and regulations.

Use of the case method is retained to expose students to the legal reasoning of courts. The case selection avoids the American-only perspective as the cases are drawn from a variety of legal systems. Each case is followed by a synopsis of "Case Highlights" that summarize the key legal points of the case to aid student understanding.

As noted above, the book is much more than a recitation of black letter law. It takes a more practical approach to international business law, focusing on a great range of information taken from business practice, providing material which is of use to legal and business practitioners (or students aiming to practice). This more technical approach equips students with the practical skills of negotiating an international sales contract and drafting the supporting documents. To this end, the book provides students with a plentiful supply of practical examples of disputes, checklists, and practice notes. The book is interested in how the law impacts business decisions and strategy. In that way, its legal focus blends with managerial and contract-based focuses. The subtitle, *A Transactional Approach*, is captured in more than 180 "figures" or capsules that provide additional commentaries, legal forms, checklists, practical examples, and legal analyses. These figures come in three types: *Comparative Law*, *Doing Business Internationally*, and *Focus on Transactions*. Along with the figures, there are numerous tables and images inserted to keep the attention of students.

The Global Marketplace

The international marketplace offers great opportunities for domestic enterprises seeking to expand. It is also a place where the risks of loss are unique in character. Accordingly, the businessperson must become an astute manager of international business risk in order to minimize the chances of financial loss. This book illuminates the risks of doing business internationally and at the same time provides tools for their minimization. The legal issues relevant to international business transactions can be seen as a due diligence checklist. The sophisticated international entrepreneur directly addresses the legal issues discussed in this book before transacting international business. The tremendous expansion of international business is a testament to the fact that the legal issues in international business transactions are easily discernible. Furthermore, the real world provides solutions to the risks associated with those issues. The expansion of international trade began at the end of World War II with the establishment of the World Bank, the International Monetary Fund, the United Nations, and the evolution of the General Agreement on Tariffs and Trade (GATT). The trend continued to accelerate with the establishment of the World Trade Organization (WTO). At the regional level, we saw the evolution of the European Economic Community into the European Union (EU). North America saw the adoption of the United States–Mexico–Canada Agreement (USMCA) in 2020. New markets opened as shown by Poland's transition from an emerging economy to a developed economy. However, the Russia–Ukraine War, beginning in February 2022, has had severe repercussions for the world economy with the isolation of the Russian economy from the Western economies.

Despite the backlash against free trade and the increased splintering of the world economy, small to medium-sized companies continue to develop "international business strategies," aided by the Internet and digital platforms, in order to stay competitive. This book introduces the legal issues relating to international business transactions in order to better equip the reader in formulating such a strategy.

Law as Risk Management

A major theme of this book is that businesses can "go international" without incurring a great deal of risk if the businessperson understands the legal mechanisms that have developed to minimize, and in many cases eliminate, such risks. The nature of the free trade era is that small and medium-sized companies, along with large companies, may and should enter the international marketplace. The aim of this book is to clearly explain how business is conducted internationally, with a strong emphasis on the exporting–importing of goods and the licensing of intellectual property, and how the law is used as a facilitator, not an obstacle, to doing business internationally. What distinguishes this textbook from the other textbooks in the field, as noted above, is that it provides a transactional-practical focused approach to the topic of international business law. It provides the necessary legal material but always in the context of real-world transactions.

The perspective and presentation of the materials in the book move beyond complying with the "law," to using the law to create value and competitive advantage. That is, international business law should be applied proactively to encourage international business transactions by being used creatively to keep parties from breaching contracts, resolving disputes amicably, and preserving the contracting parties' relationship. This perspective necessitates teaching lawyers and business managers the basics of international business law as a vital part in doing business and minimizing the unique risks of transborder transactions. This is especially true for small and medium-sized businesses.

Coverage

The *new* edition provides additional materials on contracting law with an emphasis on comparative contract and sales law and European private law. The book is divided into five parts: Part I on legal environment of international business including risks of doing business internationally, ethics, creating a sustainable and circular international economy, strategies for doing business, international commercial dispute resolution, and international and national trade regulation; Part II on doing business in the European Union and China; on comparative legal systems, international contract and sales law; Part III on exporting, importing, trade finance; employment and sale of services; Part IV on intellectual property rights and licensing; and Part V on foreign direct investment, e-commerce, and the digital economy.

Managerial Perspective: Capsules

Throughout the book capsules and materials will be provided to illustrate the law of international business transactions *as practiced*. A variety of methods will be utilized to provide the student with a "real world" perspective. These methods include case studies, checklists, forms, tables, and summaries.

Text Boxes

Learning the terminology of international business is an important part of any international business law course. Text boxes provide definitions of key legal and nonlegal terminology, as well as additional information on the material covered in the text.

Case Highlights

At the end of each case, instead of asking a set of generic questions, a summation of "case highlights" are provided. These capsules list principles of law, concepts, and business practices presented in the case. Some of the highlights summarize the reasons why the case was inserted into the textbook. Other highlights alert the student to the fact that most legal disputes involve multiple issues. The intent of the "highlights capsules" is to make sure the reader clearly understands the key issues presented by the case. The instructor may also use these as a starting point for more in-depth discussions of the issues of the case.

Chapter Summaries, Key Terms, Problems, and Internet Sources

At the end of each chapter, there are chapter summaries, lists of key terms, problems, and Internet sources. A number of Internet exercises are provided throughout the book. These provide important websites that students can use for reference or to answer a question or project posed. These projects can be used in individual or group assignments. In addition, at the end of each chapter are important Internet addresses that can be used for extended study and research projects.

Ethics Coverage

There is expanded coverage of ethics in Chapter 2 and ethical issues are raised throughout the book, some explicitly and others implicitly, that can be mined by instructors wanting to discuss ethical issues that arise in various contexts. These contexts include the ethics of negotiations, disclosure of information, dealing with foreign governments, corruption, and the divergence between home country and host country laws. The student will be encouraged to form a mindset in which ethical behavior will become an inherent part of their approach to international business. The ethics coverage has expanded to include a separate chapter on environmental ethics, namely, the need for "Sustainability and a Circular Economy."

International and Foreign Sources

The text reflects an earnest attempt to expose the student to a sampling of foreign and international laws. National laws from approximately two dozen countries are referenced and used for purposes of illustration. There are numerous references throughout the text to a number of primary sources, such as American law, Chinese law, Russian law, EU law, and the law of individual European countries. The reader may refer to the endnotes for the proper citations.

Style and Structure

A premium has been placed upon readability by the use of clear narrative, carefully edited case summaries and articles, and concise use of tangential materials. Also, in the spirit of the practical-managerial focus of the book, more in-depth insight is offered in certain areas so that the student is exposed not only to *why* a given rule of law has evolved, but also *how* it is applied in practice.

Acknowledgments

I would like to thank my lovely and legally educated wife Colleen for her editorial assistance, as well as the editorial staff at Routledge, especially my editors.

Acronyms

Agreement on Technical Barriers to Trade (TBT)
Agreement on the Application of Sanitary and Phytosanitary Measures (SPS)
Agreement on Trade-Related Aspects of Intellectual Property Rights (TRIPS)
Agreement on Trade-Related Investment Measures (TRIMs)
Alien Tort Claims Act (ATCA)
American Arbitration Association (AAA)
American Institute of Marine Underwriters (AIMU)
American Law Institute (ALI)
Anti-Cybersquatting Consumer Protection Act (ACPA)
Artificial Intelligence Act (AI Act)
Asia-Pacific Economic Cooperation (APEC)
Automated Export System (AES)
Bilateral Investment Treaties (BITs)
Brazil, Russia, India, and China (BRIC)
British Pounds Sterling (GBP)
Business Software Alliance (BSA)
Business-to-Business (B2B)
Business-to-Consumer (B2C)
Carriage of Goods by Sea Act (COGSA)
Central America–Dominican Republic FTA (CAFTA-DR)
China International Economic and Trade Arbitration Commission (CIETAC)
Chinese Contract Law (CCL)
Comité Maritime International (CMI)
Common European Sales Law (CESL)
Convention on Contracts for the International Sale of Goods (CISG)
Customary Freight Unit (CFU)
Department of Commerce (DOC)
Digital Content Directive (DCD)
Digital Services Act (DSA)
Directorates Generals (DG) (EU)
Dispute Resolution Understanding (DSU)
Dispute Settlement Body (DSB)
Economic Espionage Act of 1996 (EEA) (U.S.)
Electronic Data Interchange (EDI)

European Central Bank (ECB)
European Convention on Human Rights (ECHR)
European Court of Human Rights (ECtHR)
European Court of Justice (ECJ)
European Union General Data Protection Regulation (GDPR)
European Patent Convention (EPC)
European Union (EU)
Export Administration Regulations (EAR)
Export Control Classification Number (ECCN)
Export-Import Bank (Eximbank)
Export Management Company (EMC)
Export Trading Company (ETC)
Federal Trade Commission (FTC) (U.S.)
Federal Trademark Dilution Act (FTDA)
Foreign Corporation Insurance Agency (FCIA)
Foreign Corrupt Practices Act (FCPA)
Foreign Direct Investment (FDI)
Foreign or Free Trade Zones (FTZ)
Foreign Sovereign Immunities Act (FSIA)
Free Trade Agreement (FTA)
General Agreement on Tariffs and Trade (GATT)
General Agreement on Trade in Services (GATS)
General Data Protection Regulation (GDPR)
General Usage for International Digitally Ensured Commerce (GUIDEC)
Generalized System of (Tariff) Preferences (GSP)
Genetically Modified Organisms (GMOs)
German Civil Code or Bürgerliches Gesetzbuch (BGB)
Gross Domestic Product (GDP)
Harmonized Tariff Schedule (HTS)
Institute of London Underwriters (ILU)
Intellectual Property Rights (IPR)
International Accounting Standards (IAS)
International Bar Association (IBA)
International Centre for Settlement of Investment Disputes (ICSID)
International Chamber of Commerce (ICC)
International Institute for the Unification of Private Law (UNIDROIT)
International Labour Organization (ILO)
International Monetary Fund (IMF)
International Organization for Standardization (ISO)
International Organization of Securities Commissions (IOSCO)
International Patent Searching Authorities (ISA)
International Standard Banking Practice (ISBP)
International Standby Practices (ISP 98)
International Trade Commission (ITC)
Just-in-Time Contracting (JIT)
Korea–U.S. Free Trade Agreement (KORUS FTA)
Least-Developed Countries (LDCs)

Measure Equivalent to a Quantitative Restriction (MEQR)
Members of the European Parliament (MEPs)
Ministry of Foreign Trade and Economic Cooperation (MOFTEC) (China)
Multilateral Investment Guarantee Agency (MIGA)
Multimodal Transport Operators (MTOs)
Mutual Recognition Agreement (MRA)
Nongovernmental Organizations (NGOs)
Nontariff Barriers (NTBs)
North American Free Trade Agreement (NAFTA)
Organisation for Economic Co-Operation and Development (OECD)
Overseas Private Insurance Corporation (OPIC)
Pacific Bridge Initiative (PBI)
Patent Cooperation Treaty (PCT)
Principles of European Contract Law (PECL)
Protection and Indemnity Policy (P & I)
Qualified Majority Voting (QMV) (EU)
Rules of Origin (ROO)
Sanitary and Phytosanitary Standards (SPS)
Shipper's Export Declaration (SED)
Small and Medium-Sized Enterprises (SMEs)
Small Business Administration (SBA)
Society for Worldwide Interbank Financial Telecommunication (SWIFT)
Special Administrative Region (SAR) (Hong Kong)
Special Drawing Rights (SDR)
Special Import Measures Act (SIMA) (Canada)
State-Owned Enterprises (SOEs) (China)
Supreme People's Court (SPC) (China)
Technical Barriers to Trade (TBT)
Trade and Investment Cooperation Agreement (TICA)
Trade and Investment Framework Agreement (TIFA)
Transatlantic Trade and Investment Partnership (T-TIP)
Trans-Pacific Partnership (TPP)
Treaty of the European Union (TEU) (Maastricht Treaty)
Treaty on the Functioning of the European Union (TFEU) (Treaty of Rome)
Unfair Commercial Practices Directive (UCPD)
UNIDROIT Principles of International Commercial Contracts (PICC)
Uniform Commercial Code (UCC) (U.S.)
Uniform Computer Information Transactions Act (UCITA)
Uniform Customs and Practice for Documentary Credits (UCP 600)
Uniform Electronic Transactions Act (UETA)
United Nations Commission on International Trade Law (UNCITRAL)
United Nations Conference on Trade and Development (UNCTAD)
United Nations Convention on the Recognition and Enforcement of Foreign Arbitral Awards (New York Convention)
United Nations Educational, Scientific, and Cultural Organization (UNESCO)
United States International Trade Commission (ITC)
United States Trade and Development Agency (USTDA)

U.S. Customs and Border Protection (CBP)
U.S. Trade Representative (USTR)
Value-Added Tax (VAT)
World Customs Organization (WCO)
World Intellectual Property Organization (WIPO)
World Trade Organization (WTO)

Part I

Legal Environment of International Business

Chapter 1

Introduction to International Business Transactions

The purpose of this chapter is to briefly review some of the major topics and issues involved in international business transactions. The remaining chapters of the book will expand on the topics outlined in this chapter. The first part of Chapter 1 will note the tremendous growth in international business transactions. One factor that has aided the expansion of international trade is the development of a supranational trade law and the recognition of customary international law.

We will examine the ways that international business is transacted. The concepts of direct and indirect exporting, licensing, and foreign direct investment (FDI) will be introduced. This discussion will provide a basic understanding of the advantages and disadvantages of each method of transacting international business. These methods will be explored further in Chapter 3, along with hybrid ways of **transacting** business, such as **franchising** and joint venturing.

The second half of Chapter 1 will focus on the risks involved in international business transactions. Some risks are the same as those in purely domestic transactions; others are more unique to the international business environment. First, we will analyze how companies evaluate such risks. Second, a review of the generic risks associated with international business transactions will be undertaken. These include risks associated with cultural and language differences, currency risks, legal risks, and political risks. Finally, we will briefly explore the tools that have been developed to minimize and manage such risks. The chapter concludes by discussing strategies for managing international business risks, including the development of an export plan, the use of intermediaries, and a form of international business known as **countertrade**.

DOI: 10.4324/9781003469230-2

Ultimately, the goal of teaching international business law is to sensitize future entrepreneurs and lawyers to ways to manage such risks. A savvy entrepreneur is adept at analyzing risk and knowledgeable about the techniques to minimize risk. Chapter 1 will serve as an introduction, while the rest of the textbook will explore more fully how risks are minimized in the areas of exporting, foreign direct investment, and intellectual property licensing.

Global and Regional Marketplace

The post-World War II (WWII) era has seen the rapid expansion of international trade. The expansion of cross-border transactions has occurred in all areas of business: exporting–importing, sale of services, licensing of technology, and FDI. Exporting enables small and medium-sized enterprises (SMEs) to diversify their portfolios and insulates them against periods of slower growth in their domestic markets. In a similar way, companies wanting to remain competitive need to extend their supply chains into foreign channels by outsourcing some of their functions.

A number of factors have decreased the obstacles to international trade. The most important factor is the success of the **World Trade Organization (WTO)**, and its predecessor the **General Agreement on Tariffs and Trade** (GATT), in lowering tariffs and **nontariff barriers** to trade; the almost complete removal of the threat of **expropriation** as countries have moved to privatize their industries; and the proliferation of **free trade agreements** (**FTAs**) that have further opened foreign markets. Other factors resulting in the growth of international trade include the disintegration of the Soviet Union, the advent of "emerging economies," dramatic advances in telecommunications and information technology, and the development of vibrant international capital markets. The result of these developments has been the creation of global supply chains, as well as an economically and financially interdependent world.

International trade has resulted in the fragmentation of the manufacturing process that includes the selling and transporting of finished products, as well as transborder movements of raw materials and the assembly of products crossing national borders. The fragmentation of the manufacturing process is known as the **global supply chain**, which includes numerous intermediary steps in the production of goods in different countries. For example, the manufacture of consumer electronics includes the importation of a majority of inputs (raw material, such as precious metals and component parts) from Brazil and China.[1] Specialization achieved by the export-import of materials and services is efficient and leads to economic growth, but also makes the countries economically vulnerable to international economic downturns.

The WWII free trade era has resulted in significant increases in cross-border trade in manufacturing goods and services, international joint ventures, mergers, acquisitions, strategic alliances and affiliations, infrastructure projects, **privatization**, and international direct investment. The liberalization of trade and investment rules has created a "world of opportunities" for the international entrepreneur.[2] The mobility of goods and services has allowed domestic companies to search the world for new markets to sell their products or to procure component parts used in the manufacture of products. The producer of goods and services, or the innovator of technology, can maximize profits with a global business strategy including, developing foreign markets for a company's products and outsourcing materials, labor, and component parts. Even a company that takes a more isolated domestic sales strategy is likely to be affected by international developments.

One measure of globalization has been the tremendous growth in the international **trade in goods**. This growth has been accelerated by reductions in trade barriers, including the evolution of free trade unions, such as the European Union's common market and the United States–Mexico–Canada Agreement (USMCA).[3] A negative development in free trade areas and customs unions was the withdrawing of the United Kingdom (UK) from the European Union (EU) known as Brexit.

Another measure of globalization is the **foreign direct investment** (**FDI**). FDI represents the capital investments made by companies in other countries. This includes the purchase of real estate, manufacturing plants, service and distribution centers, or foreign businesses. See Chapter 17's coverage of FDI. The dramatic increase in world FDI has, much like trade, occurred mostly in the three major regional trade areas of Europe, the Americas, and East Asia.

Political and economic stability is a key factor in attracting FDI. An example of how decisions of a country can have disastrous consequences for its economy, even in times of growth, is seen in the collapse of the economy of the Russian Federation, beginning in 2014 and the stalling of its economy following the invasion of Ukraine in 2022. Some of the repercussions included an outflow of FDI, closing of Western enterprises in Russia, inflation, collapse of the ruble, freezing of sovereign capital held abroad, and an outflow of young adults. This demonstrates that national economies are highly interconnected and that national decisions can have dramatic consequences on FDI and a country's economic stability.

Despite the rise of nationalism and the Trump trade wars of 2016 to 2020, globalization is likely to continue to expand, both at the regional level and at the global level. The causes of this expected growth include the advance of global telecommunications and the increased transferability of services and intellectual property. The service and knowledge industries, such as entertainment, education, and health care, have benefited from the reduction of trade barriers in non-sale of goods areas. The greatest concern is that unilateralism as represented by recent trade wars (raising of tariff rates) between China and the United States (U.S.) and the EU and the U.S. has weakened the role of the WTO as the enforcer of economic free trade rules.

While tariff rates remain at historical lows, an International Chamber of Commerce Report shows that the number of trade restrictions, known as non-tariff measures (NTMs), has increased since the 2008 financial crisis, and most of them have come from the developed economies (G-20). Many of these restrictions relate to anti-dumping measures to prevent the importation of goods being sold below their cost of production or the sale of lower-priced goods due to illegal government subsidies.

G-20 Countries include Argentina, Australia, Brazil, Canada, China, France, Germany, India, Indonesia, Italy, Japan, Mexico, Russian Federation,* Saudi Arabia, South Africa, South Korea, Turkey, the UK, the U.S., and the EU as a whole.

*Expelled due to its invasion of Ukraine, as well as the Group of 8.

The WTO's 2013 **Ninth Ministerial Conference** in Bali focused on improving market access for least-developed countries (LDCs) and new rules for the exporting of agricultural goods. The end result was a **Trade Facilitation Agreement (TFA)** that reduces mostly bureaucratic barriers to the flow of products through global supply chains. The TFA aims at streamlining customs and border procedures and infrastructure communications. The ultimate goal is greater access ("duty free and quota free") to foreign markets for LDCs.

Law of International Business Transactions

International law generally refers to the historically developed transnational rules and norms that national courts use to regulate three primary relationships: (1) the relationship between two nations; (2) the relationship between a nation and an individual; and (3) the relationship between private persons or entities from different countries. This book is primarily concerned with the person-to-person relationship between parties transacting business across national borders. The first two types of relationships will be reviewed, at times, because of their effect upon private business relationships. Thus, the regulations promulgated by the WTO will be studied in Chapter 6 because of their direct impact on the export and import of goods, services, and intellectual property rights.

There are numerous sources of international business law. **Article 38 of the Statute of the International Court of Justice**[4] lists the sources of international public law, which can be applied by analogy to transborder private law. In order of superiority, they are: (1) international conventions and treaties; (2) international custom or general practice; (3) general principles of law recognized by civilized nations; and (4) judicial decisions and scholarly writings. These are the same sources of law often used by private parties in international litigation or arbitration proceedings.

The term *convention* is used in connection with multilateral agreements, as opposed to bilateral arrangements. The Vienna Convention on the Law of Treaties defines a treaty as "an international agreement between States and governed by international law." Under U.S. law a treaty becomes federal law and is binding on federal, state, and local governments.

The primary source of law in international business transactions is the private contract entered into by the parties. The contract is the primary source of law in case of a dispute. At times, however, the contract may fail to provide a solution either because it does not deal with the issue in dispute or because the parties interpret the contract differently. "No written contract is ever complete; even the most carefully drafted document rests on volumes of assumptions that cannot be explicitly expressed."[5] This quote illustrates that a substantial core of norms or practices in international business transactions is nonlegal in nature. Businesspersons prefer the language of business and are often unconcerned with the legal language of formal contract documents.

Despite this informal attitude, the language of business is viewed as a type of soft law through legal recognition of business custom and trade usage. This transformation of practice into law is a tradition that dates back to the medieval ***lex mercatoria***.[6] The *lex mercatoria*, or law of merchants, provides the mechanism in which courts and arbitral tribunals recognize day-to-day trade usage and business practices as **customary international law**. The latter half of the twentieth century saw a broad expansion of international practices, codes, and rules emanating from public and private organizations. This transformation has resulted in a radical expansion of international business law.

> The original *lex mercatoria* (Latin for "merchant law") is the body of commercial law used by merchants throughout Europe during the medieval period. It evolved as a system of custom and best practices, which were enforced through a system of merchant courts along the main trade routes. In modern international commercial disputes, arbitrators often apply *lex mercatoria* principles.

Businesspersons and lawyers should incorporate the modern *lex mercatoria* into their international business transactions because such "neutral" (non-national) sources are a good way of overcoming cultural, language, and legal differences in cross-border transactions.

Most international business disputes stem from poorly written contracts or the parties' failure to recognize key substantive issues. Given the universal nature of business transactions and the globalization of the marketplace, contractual failures attributable to inherent linguistic and cultural differences have significantly diminished but they can still lead to contract damages. Another cause of legal disputes is the existence of fundamental differences in national rules relating to the interpretation of contracts. Thus, a primary way to understand the legal risk of international business transactions is to research cases and arbitral decisions dealing with key issues.

Customary International Law

Businesspersons can avoid misunderstandings by following standard practices, custom, and trade usage to minimize the risks of legal disputes. These sources of international business law can be divided into two groups. The first includes international conventions or regional initiatives aimed at harmonizing rules relating to cross-border transactions. Examples include the Hague Rules[7] on the liability of international carriers of goods by sea and the WTO's Agreement on Trade-Related Aspects of Intellectual Property Rights (TRIPS). Regional efforts generally revolve around major free trade areas noted above (USMCA and EU), and broader-based institutions such as the Organisation for Economic Co-operation and Development (OECD).

The second source is the *lex mercatoria* or customary international law which has developed to bridge language, cultural, and legal differences between businesspersons throughout the world. The materials produced by the **International Chamber of Commerce (ICC)** illustrate the evolution of the *lex mercatoria*. The ICC was created in 1919 to promote free trade and private enterprise and to represent business interests at the international level. Members include national councils from more than 60 countries. Headquartered in Paris, France, the ICC is a nongovernmental organization that works to promote world trade, harmonize trade practices, and provide practical services to

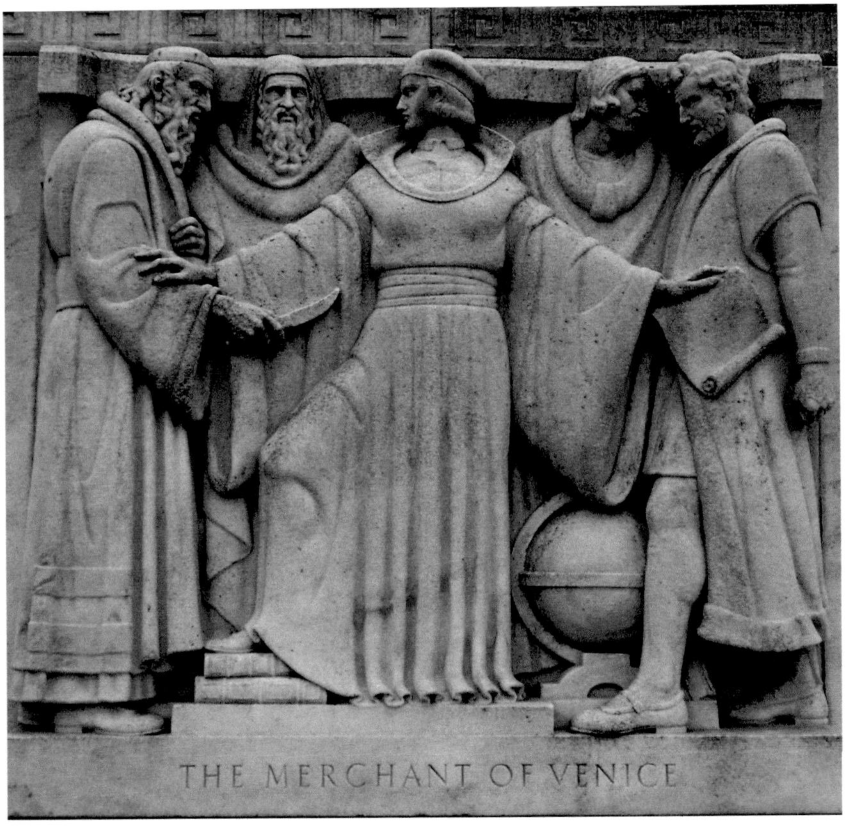

Image 1.1 Merchant of Venice.
Source: Smallbones, WikiCommons.

businesspersons. These services include the International Court of Arbitration in Paris, the Centre for Maritime Cooperation in London, the Counterfeiting Intelligence Bureau in London, and the Institute of International Business Law and Practice in Paris. The ICC's UCP 600 (Uniform Customs and Practice for Documentary Credits)[8] (see Chapter 13) and its INCOTERMS 2020 manual (trade terms) (see Chapter 12) are examples of international trade customs that have risen to universal acceptance in the international banking and business communities.

Businesspersons doing business internationally require an understanding of the particular laws of the countries in which they do business. All countries have mandatory rules that vary in type and content. For example, a clearly written, principal-friendly termination clause in an agency agreement will not survive the **evergreen laws** found in numerous European countries. Evergreen laws are statutory pre-emptions of the termination clauses found in private agency contracts. Therefore, a disclaimer of liability clause enforceable in the U.S. would not be enforceable under EU law. Evergreen laws will be discussed in Chapter 14's coverage of agency and distribution contracts.

The Written Contract

A clear and properly written contract remains the international entrepreneur's best protection in minimizing the risks of doing international business. In practice, many business transactions are characterized by a high degree of informality. As an English court noted: "One has to bear in mind that commercial men and women do not look at things from the lawyer's point of view."[9] Despite the informal nature of business contracting and the common use of standard forms, sophisticated businesspersons base their agreements on at least semi-formal writings. This seems especially prudent given the obstacles of foreign languages and cultures, including differences in negotiating styles. These factors, and the potential difficulty and expense of obtaining a legal remedy in a foreign country, justify the additional time spent in negotiating and writing a contract. Negotiating a written contract will often highlight the latent differences of language and law while there is time to reconcile differences before the execution of the contract. Differences in foreign legal systems and national contract laws will be examined in Chapter 9. The **United Nations Convention on Contracts for the International Sale of Goods** (CISG),[10] as the major international sales contracts law, will be reviewed in Chapter 10.

Behind every business transaction is the fear of nonperformance requiring one of the parties to seek a legal remedy. Understanding international contract dispute resolution is important in order to negotiate and draft an effective contract. Just as prenuptial agreements are written in anticipation of a possible divorce, contracts should be written in anticipation of possible contract disputes. The issue of dispute resolution, including minimizing the costs of disputes, will be addressed in Chapter 5 on "International Commercial Dispute Resolution."

Scope of International Business Transactions

The essence of being a businessperson or entrepreneur is a willingness to confront loss in search of profits. Profit-seeking and risk-taking underscore the capitalistic, free-market system. The most consistently successful entrepreneurs are those who take steps to avoid or minimize risk. Risk-aversion techniques and strategies have been developed to provide stability and security to international business transactions.

The "**basket of risks**" associated with an international transaction is different in many ways from that of a purely domestic transaction. Businesses' efforts to minimize risk differ, too. Many international risk management devices, although long-standing, are likely to be unfamiliar to businesspersons on their initial foray into exporting, licensing, or foreign direct investment. International dealings are further complicated by the fact that the basket of risks is constantly fluctuating, depending on the type of business entity, the type of good or service being sold, the country of the other party, the country of performance, and the means of transportation.

At the broadest level of analysis, the risk characteristics will depend largely on the type of transaction. Transactions are categorized under four general groupings: (1) exporting–importing (sale of goods); (2) **sale of services** (consulting, distribution, transportation, marketing, sales); (3) licensing (technology, intellectual property transfer); and (4) foreign direct investment (foreign operations). There are also numerous hybrid forms of doing business like franchising and joint venturing that will be discussed in Chapter 4 ("Strategies for International Business") and Chapter 17 ("Foreign Direct Investment"). The **franchise** transaction, for example, involves the contractual transfer or licensing of a bundle of intellectual property rights, know-how, trade secrets, and, in some cases, the sale of goods or services. The **joint venture** is closely associated with foreign direct investment, but may also involve the transfer of goods, services, technology, and capital. A third hybrid form, discussed later in this chapter, is countertrade, which is a form of exporting used to overcome the risks of currency inconvertibility, local participation requirements, and restrictions against the repatriation of capital (profits). Countertrade can also be used within the framework of a joint venture or technology transfer transaction.

Direct and Indirect Exporting

The most popular method of transacting business internationally is the exporting of goods, which can be divided into indirect and direct exporting. Direct exporting is when a company exports goods on its own account—dealing directly with a foreign customer and sending its goods to that customer in exchange for payment. **Indirect exporting** involves the use of an intermediary firm to facilitate the exporting of a company's goods. The principal advantage of indirect exporting for a smaller company is that it provides a way to penetrate foreign markets without the complexities, costs, and risks of direct exporting. A company uses **commission agents** or **buying agents** who find foreign firms that want to purchase a company's products. Such agents seek to obtain the desired items at the lowest possible price and are paid a commission by their foreign clients. The agents may be representing foreign government agencies empowered to locate and purchase desired goods.

Indirect exporting often involves the use of an **export management company (EMC)** or **export trading company (ETC)**. An EMC acts much like the export department for one or several producers of goods or services. As a private business, it solicits and sells goods in the name of the producers it represents for a commission. Some EMCs offer immediate payment for products either by arranging financing or by directly purchasing products for resale. The best EMCs know the products and markets through well-established networks of foreign distributors. This immediate access to foreign markets is one of the principal reasons for using an EMC. One disadvantage of using an EMC is that a manufacturer loses control over foreign sales.

> **Export Management Companies (EMCs)** develop personalized services promoting their client's products to international buyers and distributors. The main reason for a manufacturer using an EMC is that an EMC can provide immediate access to foreign markets. The process of directly developing a relationship with foreign buyers can be lengthy and costly.

A manufacturer can eliminate foreign transaction risk by selling its goods to a domestic ETC. An ETC takes title to the product and exports on its own account. For the manufacturer, the transaction is essentially a domestic sale.

> **Export Trading Company (ETC)** is an independent distributor. As opposed to representing a given manufacturer in a foreign market, the ETC determines what U.S. products are desired in a given market and then works with U.S. producers to satisfy the demand.

Specialized ETCs are organized and operated by producers. These types of ETCs are organized along multiple or single-industry lines and can represent producers of competing products.

An indirect exporting method similar to an ETC is selling goods to an export agent or **remarketer**. Export agents or remarketers purchase products directly from the manufacturer, and then pack and mark the products according to their own specifications. The remarketers sell overseas through their contacts in their own names and assume all account risks. Finally, a hybrid type of exporting is **consignment**. Consignment involves the delivery of merchandise to a foreign party, whereby the exporter retains title to the goods that it transfers when the consignment company sells the goods. The consignee gets paid a commission upon the sale of the goods and payment to the exporter. Retaining ownership of the goods until they are sold provides protection to the exporter.

Direct Exporting

The most common form of international trade is direct exporting or importing. A company new to direct exporting often treats export sales no differently than domestic sales, using existing personnel and organizational structures. However, to be successful requires the separation of international from domestic business, including focusing marketing efforts through a separate international sales department. Regardless of how a company organizes its exporting, it should ensure that the structure facilitates the marketer's job. Experience shows that a company's success in foreign markets depends less on the attributes of its products than on its marketing methods. It should be noted that this has not created a major barrier for the exporting of goods by small companies. See Figure 1.1 *Doing Business Internationally*: "Myths of the Risks of Exporting by Small Companies."

The key decision of an exporting company is determining the proper channel of distribution in each market. These channels include sales representatives, agents, distributors, retailers, and end-users. A **foreign sales representative** is a manufacturer's representative in a foreign country that uses the company's product literature and samples to present to potential buyers. A representative is often an independent company that handles complementary lines of products from different manufacturers. The sales representative usually works on a commission basis, assumes no risk or responsibility, and is under contract for a definite period of time. The contract defines territory, terms of sale, method of compensation, and reasons and procedures for terminating the agreement. In contrast, a foreign agent normally has authority to make commitments on behalf of the firm he or she represents. The **commercial agency** contract should state whether the representative or agent does or does not have legal authority to bind the firm to contracts.

MYTH 1: EXPORTING IS TOO RISKY: Different international markets have different levels of risks. Risks are identifiable, and there are numerous low-cost ways of minimizing such risks. See Chapter 7 ("Free Trade Agreements"), Chapter 13 ("Transport of Goods"), Chapter 14 ("Documentary Transactions"), Chapter 15 ("International Trade Finance"), and Chapter 17 ("Hiring Agents and Distributors").

MYTH 2: GETTING PAID IS DIFFICULT: Trade finance and global banking have evolved to the point where buying and selling things internationally is routine, safe, and efficient. Reliable payment collection methods are numerous and include letters of credit through banks, credit cards, and online payments. See Chapter 15 ("International Trade Finance").

MYTH 3: EXPORTING IS TOO COMPLICATED: Most exporting requires minimal paperwork. Researching markets and finding buyers can in many instances be done from your computer using free or low-cost information. Third-party export facilitators, such as e-commerce platforms, can remove much of the complexity and risk.

MYTH 4: STAYING DOMESTIC IS A SOUND STRATEGY: U.S. businesses are involved in or affected by international business, whether they realize it or not. Small and medium-size companies need an international strategy that includes diversifying markets.

MYTH 5: COMPANIES CAN BE TOO SMALL TO GO INTERNATIONAL: No company is too small to go global. In fact, nearly 30 percent of all U.S. exporters in 2005 had fewer than 19 employees, and many had fewer than five.

MYTH 6: AMERICAN PRODUCTS ARE LESS MARKETABLE ABROAD: If your product or service sells well in the United States, there's a good chance an overseas market can be found. For some markets, you may have to make some modifications because of cultural or regulatory differences.

MYTH 7: I AM NOT LIKELY TO SUCCEED BECAUSE OF A LACK OF FOREIGN LANGUAGE SKILLS: The English language will take you a very long way, and help is readily available for situations in which interpreters and translators are necessary. Some basic knowledge of cultural and business etiquette can be learned and is very helpful, despite language difficulties.

Figure 1.1 Doing Business Internationally: Myths of the Risks of Exporting by Small Companies.

Source: David Lingelbach.

The **foreign distributor** is a merchant who purchases merchandise from an exporter, resells it at a profit, and generally provides after-sales support and service. The distributor usually carries an inventory of products and spare parts and maintains adequate facilities and personnel for normal servicing operations. An exporter must carefully screen all potential representatives, agents, or distributors. The following information should be obtained and reviewed: (1) current status and history, including background of principal officers; personnel and other human resources (salespeople, warehouse, and service facilities); (2) sales territory covered; (3) current sales volume; (4) typical customer profiles; (5) methods of introducing new products into the sales territory; (6) names and addresses of domestic firms it currently represents; (7) trade and bank references; and (8) the foreign company's view of the in-country market potential for the exporter's products. To protect itself against possible conflicts of interest, the exporter should learn about other product lines that the foreign firm currently represents.

Evaluating Risks Through Market Research

International entrepreneurs and exporters must assess foreign markets through market research. Exporters engage in market research primarily to identify marketing opportunities and constraints and also to identify and find prospective customers. A company's market research should determine the largest foreign markets for its products and identify trends, outlook, conditions, practices, and competitors in those markets.

In conducting primary market research, a company collects data directly from the foreign marketplace through interviews, surveys, and other direct contact with representatives and potential buyers. Primary market research has the advantage of being tailored to a company's needs, but it is time-consuming and expensive. Because of the expense of primary market research, most firms rely on secondary data sources that are publicly available online, often produced by government agencies or international organizations.

Secondary market research is conducted in three ways. First, keeping abreast of world events that influence the international marketplace, watching for announcements of specific projects, or visiting foreign markets. Second, analyzing trade and economic statistics. Trade statistics are compiled by product category and by country. Government agencies compile statistics with information about shipments of products over specified periods of time; demographic and economic statistics such as population size and makeup, per capita income, and production levels by industry, which are important indicators of the market potential for a company's products. Third, obtaining the advice of experts, including contacting experts at government agencies; attending seminars, workshops, and international trade shows; hiring an international trade and marketing consultant; talking with successful exporters of similar products; and contacting trade and industry association staff. The use of secondary research is a valuable and easy first step for a company to take. See Figure 1.2 *Doing Business Internationally*: "A Step-by-Step Approach to Market Research."

1. **Screen potential markets**

   Step 1. Obtain export statistics that indicate product exports to various countries. The more specific the information the better; it should be based on "Commodity by Country" statistics.
   Step 2. Identify five to ten large and fast-growing markets for the firm's products. Examine them over the past three to five years. Has market growth been consistent year to year? Did import growth occur even during periods of economic recession? If not, did growth resume with economic recovery?
   Step 3. Identify some smaller but fast-emerging markets that may provide ground-floor opportunities. If a market is just beginning to open up, there may be fewer competitors. Growth rates should be substantially higher in these countries to qualify as up-and-coming markets.
   Step 4. Target three to five of the most statistically promising markets for further assessment. Consult with government agencies, business associates, freight forwarders, and others to refine analysis of targeted markets.

2. **Assess targeted markets**

   Step 1. Examine trends for company products as well as related products that could influence demand. Calculate overall consumption of the product and the amount filled by imports. Industry Sector Analyses (ISAs), alert reports, and country marketing plans give economic backgrounds and market trends for each country. Demographic information (population, age) can easily be obtained online.
   Step 2. Ascertain the sources of competition, including domestic industry production and countries of origin of the major competitors.
   Step 3. Analyze factors affecting marketing and use of the product, such as end user sectors, channels of distribution, cultural idiosyncrasies, and business practices.
   Step 4. Identify any foreign barriers (tariff or nontariff) to the product being imported into the country. Identify any barriers (such as export controls) affecting exports to the country.
   Step 5. Identify any home country or foreign government incentives to promote exporting of the product or service.

3. **Draw conclusions**

   After analyzing the data, the company may conclude that its resources would be applied more effectively to a few countries. In general, efforts should be directed to fewer than ten markets if the company is new to exporting; one or two countries may be enough at the beginning. The company's internal resources should help determine its level of effort.

Figure 1.2 Doing Business Internationally: A Step-by-Step Approach to Market Research.

Some businesses enlist private companies that specialize in risk assessment.

Risks of International Business Transactions

The risks associated with international business transactions vary depending on the method of transaction. They will also vary depending on where the business parties are located and in the country where the transaction is to be performed. The country where a party is a citizen or national is its **home country**. If a party is transacting business in a foreign country, then that country is referred to as the **host country**. This section will analyze four categories of international business risks: cultural and language, currency, legal, and political, as well as methods used to minimize each of these risks. See Table 1.1 for risks of doing business internationally.

The types of risks that an international businessperson faces depend on a number of variables. Two of the most fundamental variables, noted above, are the identity of the host country and the type of transaction. The level of risk escalates when moving from exporting–importing to licensing and from licensing to foreign direct investment. The importance of assessing host country risk is highlighted by a review of three comparative scenarios presented below in "International Business Scenarios." In each scenario, representatives of a company must weigh the risks of doing business in two countries using one of three basic market entry strategies. The *italicized* words represent key concepts that will be defined and explored throughout the textbook. These three scenarios highlight the complexity of risks involved in international business transactions.

Risk in Developing Countries

The level of risk in transacting business in many developing countries is considerably higher than in developed countries. Some countries are characterized by arbitrary government actions, excessive taxation, ineffective dispute resolution systems, and a high degree of corruption. These countries find it difficult to attract foreign investment. Some countries have passed laws to reassure foreign investors and businesspersons by attempting to reduce the risks of doing business. Mexico passed the Foreign Investment Act of 1993 in order to attract and protect foreign investment. The Act provides expedited procedures to obtain governmental approvals.

Table 1.1 Risks of Doing Business Internationally.

Type of Risk	*Description*	*Mitigation of Risks*
Generic Risk: Method of Doing Business	Foreign Direct Investment (FDI) Riskier Than Licensing; Licensing Riskier than Exporting	There are numerous ways of mitigating risk depending on the method of business
Generic Risk: Foreign Country	Different Countries Have Different Risk Characteristics	A risk assessment should be performed to determine a foreign country's political and economic stability
Generic Risk: Non-Delivery of Goods	Buyer Makes Payment, But Never Receives Goods	On-Account Transaction Documentary Collection Transaction Standby Letter of Credit
Generic Risk: Non-Payment (Exporter)	Seller Sends Goods, But Never Receives Payment	Cash in Advance Letter of Credit Retention of Title Consignment
Language Risk	Misunderstanding of Oral Communications and Written Contract	Translation Contract in Both Languages
Cultural Risks	Risk of Offending Other Party Different Negotiation Styles	Etiquette Building Trust
Currency Risks	Fluctuation, Convertibility, and Repatriation Risks	Payment in Own Currency Hedging Countertrade
Political Risks	Expropriation Change in Regulations ("creeping" expropriation)	Political Risk Insurance Bilateral Investment Treaties (BITs) Concession Agreement
Legal Risks	Differences in Law, Enforcement of Law, and Legal Remedies Enforceability of Judgments	Foreign Lawyer Contract Remedies Choice of Law Forum Selection Arbitration Clause (New York Convention)
Special Import Laws	Local Participation and Content Requirements Standards Termination Laws ("evergreen laws")	Market Selection Use of Independent Contractors
Transportation Risks	Damage of Goods in Transit and Misdelivery	Cargo Insurance Trade Term

International Business Scenarios

Scenario 1: Sale of Goods to Nigeria and Canada

Nigeria has been rated near the top of the *Corruption Index* published by Transparency International, a nongovernmental organization (NGO). It may be difficult to undertake business in Nigeria without being asked to give a bribe. In order to best understand the risks of doing business in such a country, it would be prudent to order a *political risk report* from a professional risk assessment company. It is also advisable to contact domestic government agencies for information. It is imperative to fully investigate the foreign private party, including credit and reference checks. A strong *ethics compliance program* will need to be in place in order to prevent the giving of bribes in violation of national anti-bribery laws and the OECD Anti-Bribery Convention. Also, the Nigerian currency is not *convertible* to a hard currency (U.S. dollar, European euro, Swiss franc, or English pound). Payment in one of these hard currencies is unlikely because of government restrictions against the *repatriation* of such currencies. Thus, the risk of doing business, even in the relatively risk-free method of exporting, may be too great.

Any exporting to such a country needs to be supported by a *confirmed letter of credit* from a reputable international bank. The currency convertibility and repatriation problems could be overcome through a *countertrade* transaction in which goods are exchanged for each other (barter) or an export transaction is linked to an import transaction (counter-purchase). Another device to eliminate risks is finding an *export trading company* willing to perform the transaction on its own account. Finally, the costs and feasibility of obtaining political and credit risk insurance should be investigated.

Exporting to Canada offers a low level of risk. *Country* and *currency risks* are minimal given that Canada is a stable, industrialized country, with a stable currency that is easily convertible. Currency fluctuation risk may be a concern in a long-term transaction, but parties can manage such risk through a variety of *hedging* techniques. A foreign exporter can eliminate all currency risk simply by requiring payment in its home country's currency.

Scenario 2: Licensing Technology to the People's Republic of China and France

The licensing of technology and the transfer of *intellectual property rights* (IPR) presents the next level of risk in international business transactions. Any time a company discloses confidential information and trade secrets to a third party, there is always a risk that the information may be improperly used or further disclosed to unauthorized parties. The risk is compounded when that disclosure is made in a foreign country that is not protective of intellectual property (IP).

China has acceded to numerous IPR conventions, such as the Berne Convention, but the level of trademark, copyright, and patent infringement through piracy and counterfeiting has been relatively high. The cost and time of legal action to prevent the importation (exportation from China) of illegally produced goods is the only effective countermeasure. In recent times, China's record for protection of IPR has improved as it transitions from a factors-based economy to an innovation-driven economy. Nonetheless, the *licensor* needs to negotiate a *transfer agreement* that includes contractual protections against the misuse of the licensed information. The problem remains whether such protections will be enforced. In order to reduce the cost of enforcement and increase the likelihood of success, the licensor should consider alternative dispute resolution methods such as *mediation* and *arbitration*. It is also important for the licensor to understand that the licensing agreement may not be a totally private affair. Some countries, including China, require government approval and registration of licensing agreements. The contract is likely to be reviewed and pro-licensor clauses modified. Clauses most susceptible to revision include *royalty*, *confidentiality*, *termination*, and *grant-back* clauses.

In contrast to China, France has an established record of IP protection. It is important for IP owners to register their rights under the patent, copyright, and trademark laws of France before entering any transfer agreement. The license or transfer agreement is generally enforced as written under French law. Certain provisions, such as territorial restrictions, may be illegal under EU law, especially in the area of *competition* (antitrust) *law*.

Scenario 3: Purchasing or Establishing a Company in Germany and India

The riskiest of all international business transactions is foreign direct investment (FDI), which can range from opening a branch office to purchasing an existing company or building a manufacturing facility. FDI is risky primarily because it makes a company susceptible to a wide range of *host country laws*. These laws cover the areas of employment and labor, environmental, health and safety, product liability, and taxation. In considering FDI, the first decision is what type of legal vehicle should be chosen to operate the foreign enterprise. The most popular way of doing business is to establish an independent subsidiary under the laws of the host country.

India is a country where the use of *joint ventures* with established Russian partners is advantageous. A joint partner can share the risks and provide capital or offer necessary government contacts and distribution systems.

In contrast, purchasing a company in Germany is much the same as buying in most Western European countries. There is little likelihood of government *expropriation* or *nationalization*. Germany's pro-worker labor laws, however, prohibit an acquiring firm from ignoring existing collective bargaining agreements. German employment is viewed as a *property right* that must be respected. Any substantial changes in the workforce, such as layoffs or plant closings, must be submitted to a *works council* made up of employees. Finally, the corporation laws in both India and Germany need to be researched. The limited liability protection provided by different business forms is not absolute. Foreign legal systems vary in the degree that they will allow the *piercing of the corporate veil* to hold a parent company or a joint venture partner liable for the debts of the entity.

A major advantage to investing in India for companies from common law countries, such as the U.S., UK, and the other 60 countries of the British Commonwealth of Nations, is that India is a common law country and English is a national language. Communications and knowledge of Indian law and its legal system are easier to understand.

Pricing Risks

For the exporter of goods, it is vital to internalize all the additional costs of international trade within your product's price. A domestic company cannot assume that the appropriate price of its goods in the domestic market is the appropriate price for a foreign market. Depending on the type of transaction and the trade term inserted into the contract, there will be a number of costs unique to international sales that will need to be incorporated into the price charged for the goods. Assume you are an exporter of goods and enter into a documentary transaction and the trade term is **CIF (cost, insurance, and freight)** (see Chapter 12), which means that the costs of transport and insurance to the place of destination need to be incorporated into the price. In a documentary credit transaction (see Chapter 13), the exporter must obtain a list of documents. Some of these documents will cost money to obtain, such as an inspection certificate, standby letter of credit, and certificate of origin. The exporter also has to obtain an export license, meet all marking and labeling requirements, as well as any necessary product or marketing modifications to comply with the laws of the country of import. If the seller is being paid in a foreign currency, it may want to buy a hedge or insurance against a detrimental currency fluctuation, such as a **currency option**. All such costs need to be internalized in the price if the exporter wants to maintain its profit margins. A checklist of questions to be considered in formulating an export plan and in the setting of the price of the exported goods includes:

- Do the products need to be modified or tailored to the foreign market?
- What products and product prices are the best fits for a given market?
- Have you determined the time and costs of each phase of the export plan?
- Have you determined the costs unique to international sales, such as the costs of insurance, obtaining documentation, and compliance with customs regulations?
- Have you researched the need to obtain the services of experts, such as freight forwarders, custom brokers, and foreign legal counsel?
- Have you determined how to provide warranty and after-sales services?
- Have you allotted sufficient time to implement the plan and to determine its long-term profitability?
- Do the products and accompanying marketing materials need to be modified due to different standards and requirements in the country of import? Do advertising materials have to be adjusted to conform to the cultural and legal differences found in foreign markets?
- Is an export license required?
- How do you plan on distributing the goods in the foreign country?
- Have you allocated enough resources to help ensure success?
- Who will have the authority to modify the plan to improve its effectiveness?

If the good being exported is ready to sell to the ultimate purchaser, the exporter must determine whether the price for the product (with all the internalized costs) is marketable in the foreign country. The price may make the product cost prohibitive in a country with a low per capita GDP. The exporter is left to decide not to export to that country, modify the product to make it less costly, or license the right to produce the product to a company in the foreign country. A foreign company (licensee) may be able to produce the product more cheaply because of the lower costs of labor, regulatory compliance, and materials in its country. The exporter (licensor) would then collect royalties.

The importer also has additional expenses in an international transaction that need to be factored in determining the actual costs of the goods. Using the above scenario (documentary credit transaction and CIF trade term), the buyer is obligated to pay the costs of obtaining a letter of credit from a commercial bank and of unloading the ship. Other trade terms assign the following costs to the importer: warehousing costs at the port of import, clearing goods through customs, paying import tariffs, and transporting the goods from the port to another location. If the payment is in the exporter's currency, the costs of buying a currency option, future, or forward contract need to be factored into the costs.

Legal Risks

One of the primary risks in international business transactions is the application and enforcement of foreign laws. Host country (foreign) laws may include restrictions on currency conversion and repatriation of profits. If a company is deemed to be doing business in a foreign country it will become subject to the legal jurisdiction of that country's court system. Companies that establish a presence in a foreign country must comply with local employment laws. Many countries impose restrictions on the termination of employees or agents (evergreen laws), such as requiring lengthy notice requirements and substantial severance payments. Other host country laws include labeling, marketing, and advertising regulations; income and sales tax laws; environmental laws; product and consumer liability protection; health and safety laws; and antitrust or competition laws. In order to decrease the uncertainty of the risks of complying with foreign laws, countries enter into **bilateral investment treaties** (**BITs**; see Chapters 6 and 17). These treaties provide the basic legal framework for a company investing in a foreign country. They generally address issues of convertibility of currency, repatriation of profits, compensation for expropriation, protection of IP, and nondiscriminatory treatment of foreign investors.

Because of differences in language, culture, and legal systems, the intentions of the parties in an international transaction may not be easily understandable from their agreement. Therefore, it is imperative for the parties to carefully express intended rights and obligations in a written contract. At the time of execution, it is important that the parties, with the assistance of their lawyers, review each contract clause to make sure all the parties understand their meanings. However, vagueness or ambiguity in contractual language is employed to cover up conflicts in the negotiation in order to achieve the illusion of agreement. Another reason for misunderstandings is the common scenario where the principals (companies) negotiate the general framework for an agreement and then turn the task of writing the contract to their attorneys. Businesspersons often do not use lawyers in the negotiation stage of contracting, viewing them as obstacles, rather than facilitators of agreement. In international contracting, the businessperson, especially one new to international dealings, should hire an astute international transactional lawyer, knowledgeable in that particular industry or business, in order to obtain a clearly written agreement.

Of course, such a model approach to contract review is often not practical. For example, in the typical export transaction there is no single agreement that both parties read and sign. The parties exchange their own forms in order to conclude a contract—one form being the offer and the other the acceptance. Nonetheless, each party should take the time to carefully review the terms and conditions found in the other party's form before entering into the contract. This is especially important if it is the first transaction between the contracting parties. It is also important, in large transactions with a corporation or partnership, to verify the other person's authority to bind their company to the contract.

Legal systems can differ in substantive laws, procedures, remedies, and levels of enforcement. Although the fundamental legal concepts dealing with business transactions are similar in civil and common law countries (see Chapter 8), differences in the rules can result in unexpected legal liabilities. For example, in Germany, the civil law system recognizes the notion of *nachfrist* notice[11] in the area of sale of goods. *Nachfrist* notice implies that delivery dates should not be strictly enforced. A request for additional time should be granted unless the nonbreaching party can give a commercially viable reason for not granting the requested extension. At common law, a party has the right to strictly enforce the delivery date stated in the contract and summarily reject a request for more time (see Chapter 10).

Suppose that an Indian businessperson enters a contract with a German supplier for the delivery of goods on June 1. On May 25, the German supplier sends a letter requesting an extension for delivery to June 15. Under Indian law, the buyer may simply reject the request and hold the German supplier in breach of contract if the goods are not delivered on June 1. On June 1, the goods are not delivered, and the Indian buyer obtains substituted goods from another supplier. On June 15, goods are received from the German supplier. The Indian buyer responds by rejecting the "late" delivery. Under *nachfrist* notice, it is the Indian buyer and not the German supplier who has breached the contract. Because the Indian buyer failed to give a commercially viable reason for not granting the additional time, the civil law automatically awards the time extension. Therefore, the delivery on June 15 was timely and the German party is able to sue for full contract damages if the applicable law is German law.

In other instances, the rules of law may be similar, but the procedures and remedies available may differ significantly. In some countries, there is a cultural abhorrence to litigation. In these countries, the discovery of evidence may be restricted.[12] The U.S. Federal Rules of Civil Procedure provide a liberal set of rules that allow for full discovery of the other party in search of evidence. Such sweeping discovery techniques are not available in other countries. Also, the remedies available to the plaintiff may be of a different order. The American concept of punitive (extra) damages is not found in foreign legal systems, and the common law's resistance to grant the remedy of specific performance is not found in civil law countries.

Finally, similarities in the substantive laws of a country mask differences in the enforcement of those laws. This can be seen in the areas of IP protection and corruption. A number of countries have ratified the primary IPR conventions, such as the Paris and Berne Conventions, but are lax in their enforcement. Lax enforcement has resulted in high levels of counterfeiting and piracy of trademarks, patents, and copyrights. Also, even though all countries prohibit the bribing of government officials, lack of enforcement in some countries has resulted in cultures of corruption.

Some countries limit the amount of equity ownership that a foreign company may hold in a host country enterprise. These **local participation** requirements often result in the foreign company creating a partnership or joint venture with nationals of the host country. Because of the limited amount of hard currency in some countries, other laws restrict a foreign investor or exporter from withdrawing or repatriating profits or royalties from the country.

Another common area of host country intervention is in the area of technology transfer (licensing). In some countries, private licensing agreements must be registered and approved by the government. Pro-licensor clauses involving royalty payments, termination, and training may be rewritten to be more favorable to the licensee. These types of specialized host country laws need to be analyzed to determine their impact on a potential foreign investment, export transaction, or intellectual property transfer.

Language and Cultural Risk

In the past, a major obstacle to international business transactions involved the differences in language and cultural backgrounds of the transacting parties. Language difficulties have diminished significantly due to the rise in foreign language proficiency, especially in the use of English. Nonetheless, even when dealing with a foreign counterpart who speaks English, it is important to understand that misunderstandings still occur. One device to overcome language differences is to have the contract drawn in the languages of both parties. The *Falcoal, Inc. v. Kurumu* case illustrates that even this precaution may fail to overcome inconsistencies in translation. The language problem in this case revolves around the issues of where the parties may bring a claim under the contract's forum selection clause and whether a court has **personal jurisdiction** over the foreign defendant, as well as determining the law applicable to the case.

Falcoal, Inc. v. Kurumu

660 F. Supp. 1536 (S.D. Tex. 1987)

Judge. Plaintiff Falcoal, Inc. is an American corporation and Defendant Kurumu (TKI) is a commercial entity, owned and controlled by the Turkish government. TKI decided to import a portion of Turkey's coal supply. In an attempt to solicit bids, TKI issued a notice announcing a *sartname* (terms and conditions). The sartname distributed by TKI was issued in Turkish and provided by its terms that any conflicts as to its terms would be settled by reference to the Turkish language version of the contract. Falcoal submitted the bid that was ultimately accepted by TKI. Falcoal's bid was signed and submitted by its authorized agent, Zihni, a Turkish company. The negotiation of the contract took place in Ankara, Turkey.

After the parties had agreed to the terms, Zihni prepared two copies of the contract, an English version and a Turkish version. The English and Turkish contracts contained forum selection clauses, which directly contradicted each other. The Turkish-language version provides that "the final jurisdiction for the settlement of any disputes, in the case of the PURCHASER [TKI] submitting a claim, lies within the jurisdiction of the Houston commercial courts and, in the case of the SUPPLIER [Falcoal] submitting a claim it lies within the jurisdiction of the Ankara commercial courts." The English-language contract stated the opposite: "claims shall be settled in Houston and submitted to the jurisdiction of the Courts of the U.S.A. if the claim is put forward by Supplier [Falcoal] and in Ankara, Turkey, and submitted to the Turkish Courts if the claim is put forward by Buyer [TKI]."

Pursuant to the contract, Falcoal was to deliver 100,000 tons of coal to a shipper of TKI's choice. Falcoal agreed to post a performance bond in an amount equal to 10 percent of the contract price. Citibank International-Ankara issued a performance bond in favor of TKI. The bond was secured by a letter of credit opened by Falcoal at Citibank International-Dallas. The contract further provided that, to secure payment for the coal, TKI was to open a letter of credit in New York. TKI failed to open this letter of credit. When the coal was not shipped, TKI drew on Falcoal's performance bond. Falcoal subsequently brought this suit, alleging breach of contract for failing to open the New York letter of credit, conversion and fraud for wrongfully drawing on Falcoal's performance bond, and injury to Falcoal's business reputation. TKI has moved to dismiss, alleging lack of **subject matter jurisdiction** and lack of **personal jurisdiction**.

Subject Matter Jurisdiction

TKI asserts that this Court lacks subject matter jurisdiction because TKI, as an entity of the Turkish government, has sovereign immunity. However, Falcoal contends that TKI waived sovereign immunity by agreeing to a forum selection clause and further that the contract falls within the commercial exception. The waiver and commercial exceptions are described in American law as follows:

> *Foreign Sovereign Immunity Act, Section 1605 (a) A foreign state shall not be immune from the jurisdiction of courts of the United States or of the States in any case—*
>
> 1. *in which the foreign state has waived its immunity either explicitly or by implication;*
> 2. *in which the action is based upon a commercial activity carried on in the United States by the foreign State; or upon an act performed*

in the United States in connection with a commercial activity of the foreign state elsewhere; or upon an act outside the territory of the United States in connection with a commercial activity of the foreign state elsewhere and that act causes a direct effect in the United States.

Under the facts of this case where, as here, there are two contradictory forum clauses and where the issue of which forum clause should control is vigorously contested, the English-language clause cannot be said to constitute a waiver of sovereign immunity. The next issue is whether the TKI contract comes within the commercial activity exception. Courts have taken two approaches. Some have held that an effect cannot reach the level of "direct" effects described in the statute and thus sovereign immunity cannot be overcome unless the effect fulfills the minimum contacts requirement. Other courts have given "direct effect" its literal meaning and found such an effect when an American corporation has suffered a direct financial injury due to a foreign sovereign's conduct. This Court finds the latter approach to be the most reasonable. The Court holds that the conduct of TKI in drawing on Falcoal's performance bond was an action, which caused a direct effect in the U.S., and thus TKI cannot claim sovereign immunity from this suit. Subject matter jurisdiction, therefore, exists. Furthermore, this case involved the sale of coal from a private party therefore, a U.S. court has subject matter jurisdiction under the commercial activity exception.

Personal Jurisdiction

TKI asserts, and Falcoal has not shown otherwise, that it has had no contacts with the Texas forum, or in fact with the U.S., other than its involvement in the contract which is the subject of this suit. That contract was solicited, negotiated, drafted, and executed in Turkey and in the Turkish language. The contract itself does not establish minimum contacts with the Texas forum. Nor does TKI's agreement to pay through a letter of credit in New York create personal jurisdiction. Thus, in the instant case, the constitutional requirements (minimum contacts) for exercise of *in personam* (personal) jurisdiction are lacking.

Constitutionally, this Court cannot exercise personal jurisdiction over TKI unless TKI has taken some action that may be construed as an expression of waiver or implied consent to the exercise of such jurisdiction. Falcoal contends that such an implied consent is found in the forum selection clause of the English-version contract. However, such consent could only apply if the Turkish-language clause is unenforceable and the English version valid. Because the contract was solicited, negotiated, and executed in Turkey, Turkish law must apply. Both parties agree that, were Texas law to apply, the existence of contradictory clauses would evidence a lack of meeting of the minds and both clauses would be stricken. However, in the absence of a determination of similar Turkish law, the clauses cannot be eliminated from the contract. Although this Court finds that TKI has been divested of its sovereign immunity to this suit by its actions in Turkey having a direct effect in the U.S. and, thus, subject matter jurisdiction exists, the Court finds that it lacks personal jurisdiction over TKI. TKI's Motion to Dismiss is GRANTED.

Case Highlights

- Importance of the forum selection clause in international contracts
- Use of letters of credit and performance bonds to secure payments and performances
- Defense of sovereign immunity, along with the waiver and "commercial activity" exceptions
- Determining if a court has personal jurisdiction over the defendant through the "minimum contacts" or "direct effects" standards
- Importance of determining the appropriate law to be applied
- Importance of selecting the language that controls when more than one language contract is executed.

The importance of religious practices should not be underestimated; religious and cultural differences impact a foreign entrepreneur directly in the negotiation of a contract. The *Kern v. Dynalectron Corp.* case illustrates the challenges faced by an organization in conducting its business in a foreign country.

Kern v. Dynalectron Corp.

577 F. Supp. 1196 (N.D. Tex. 1983)

Judge. Kern filed this religious discrimination suit pursuant to the American Civil Rights Act of 1964, against Dynalectron Corporation. Kern entered into a written contract of employment with the Defendant, Dynalectron, to perform duties as a helicopter pilot. The work to be performed in Saudi Arabia consisted of flying helicopters over crowds of worshippers making their pilgrimage to Mecca. Pilots stationed at Jeddah would be required to fly into Mecca. Saudi Arabian law, based upon the tenets of the Islamic religion, prohibits the entry of non-Muslims into the holy area, Mecca, under penalty of death. Thus, Dynalectron, in accordance with its employment contract, requires all pilots stationed at Jeddah to become Muslim. Kern would, therefore, have to convert from being a Baptist to a Muslim. Defendant later offered Kern a job as a member of the air crew, a position not requiring his conversion. However, Kern declined to take that job. Kern filed a complaint based on discrimination against him because of his religious beliefs.

Dynalectron argued that the discrimination was not unlawful since religion was a **bona fide occupational qualification (BFOQ)**.

> *It shall not be an unlawful employment practice for an employer to hire and employ employees on the basis of religion, sex, or national origin in those certain instances where religion, sex, or national origin is a bona fide occupational qualification reasonably necessary to the normal operation of that particular business or enterprise.*

The use of the word "necessary" requires the application of a business necessity test, not a business convenience test. There can be no question that non-Muslim pilots stationed in Jeddah are not safe compared to Muslim pilots. Therefore, Dynalectron's discrimination against Kern is not unlawful since religion "is a bona fide occupational qualification reasonably necessary to the normal operation of that particular business." Notwithstanding the religious discrimination, in this case, the Court holds that the BFOQ exception is properly applicable. Thus, Kern voluntarily and unilaterally rescinded his agreement to work for Defendant and thus breached his obligation under the contract.

Case Highlights

A written employment contract, in this case, helped limit the employer's liability because it expressly stated the business necessity of conversion to Islam.

- Bona Fide Occupational Qualification (BFOQ) is a defense to an employment discrimination claim
- Religion can be a BFOQ in some international business situations
- In contrast to *Kern v. Dynalectron*, another case involved a female plaintiff who sued her employer for discriminatorily not promoting her to a higher-level job because she was female.[13] The job would have required her to deal with South American businessmen who prefer not to do business with women. The Court reasoned that the mere fact that it was an international case did not distinguish it from other cases where mere customer preference would not justify the use of the BFOQ exception.

Business executives who hope to expand abroad should learn about the history, culture, and customs of the countries to be visited. Business manners and methods, religious customs, dietary practices, humor, and acceptable dress vary widely from country to country. For example, never touch the head of a Thai or pass an object over it—the head is considered sacred in Thailand. Avoid using triangular shapes in Hong Kong, Korea, and Taiwan—where it is considered to be negative. The number seven is considered bad luck in Kenya and good luck in the Czech Republic, and it has magical connotations in Benin. The number ten is bad luck in Korea, and four means death in Japan. Red is a positive color in Denmark, but it represents witchcraft and death in many African countries. A nodding up and down means "no" in Bulgaria and shaking the head from side to side means "yes." The "OK" sign commonly used in the U.S. means zero in France and carries a vulgar connotation in Brazil.

Understanding and heeding cultural variables such as these is critical to success in international business. Some of the cultural distinctions that firms face most often include differences in business styles, attitudes toward development of business relationships, negotiating styles, gift-giving customs, greetings, the significance of gestures, meanings of colors and numbers, and customs regarding personal titles. In some countries, businesspersons have a very direct style, while in others they have a subtle style and value creating a personal relationship. For example, in the Middle East, engaging in small talk before engaging in business is standard practice. Attitudes toward punctuality vary from one culture to another. Romanians, Japanese, and Germans are very punctual, whereas people in some Latin countries have a more relaxed attitude toward time. The Japanese consider it rude to be late for a business meeting, but acceptable, even fashionable, to be late for a social event.

Proper use of names and titles is often a source of confusion in international business relations. In many countries (UK, France, and Denmark), it is appropriate to use titles until use of first names is suggested. First names are seldom used when doing business in Germany. Visiting businesspeople should use the surname preceded by a title. Titles such as "Herr Direktor" are used to indicate prestige, status, and rank. In Thailand, people address one another by first names and reserve last names for very formal occasions and written communications. In Belgium, it is important to address French-speaking business contacts as "Monsieur" or "Madame."

Customs concerning gift giving vary. In some cultures, gifts are expected, and failure to present them is considered an insult, whereas in other countries offering a gift is considered offensive. Business executives also need to know when to present gifts, where to present gifts, what type of gift to present, what color the gift should be, and how many to present. Gift giving is an important part of doing business in Japan, where gifts are usually exchanged at the first meeting. In sharp contrast, gifts are rarely exchanged in Germany and are usually considered inappropriate.

Customs concerning the exchange of business cards vary, too. Although these customs may seem less important, it remains important to observe a country's card-giving customs. In Japan, the Western practice of accepting a business card and pocketing it immediately is considered rude. The proper approach is to look carefully at the business card after accepting it, observe the title and organization, and acknowledge the importance of the information.

Currency Risks

Currency risks are a concern in cross-border transactions when different currencies exist. There are three separate risks that relate to currency: convertibility, repatriation, and currency rate fluctuation. Payment is usually made in either the buyer's or the seller's currency or in a mutually agreed-on currency that is foreign to both parties. Currency **convertibility** is whether one currency is convertible into another currency. Other than the world's hard currencies, such as the U.S. dollar, English pound, European euro, Swiss franc, Japanese yen, and, more recently, the Chinese yuan, many national currencies are not easily convertible. An exporter or investor can overcome convertibility problems by requiring payment in a hard currency or its home currency. However, businesses in countries with soft currencies may find it difficult to obtain hard currencies. That leaves the businessperson from a hard currency country with limited options—reinvest the soft currency in the host country or find an alternate means of payment, such as countertrade (see Figure 1.4 on "Countertrade"). The currency risk of **repatriation** occurs when a foreign country bars removal of hard currency from the country. Some countries have limited hard currency reserves and do not allow them to be used for the purchase of private goods. Once again, countertrade may be the only option available to overcome a repatriation risk.

The most common currency risk is the devaluation of the currency of payment (**currency rate fluctuations**). The relative value of a currency may change between the time the deal is made and the time payment is received. If the exporter is being paid in a foreign currency, a devaluation of that currency could cause the exporter to lose money in the transaction. One of the simplest ways for an exporter to avoid this type of risk is to quote prices and require payment in its home currency. Then, the burden and risk are placed on the buyer to make the currency exchange. The *Bernina Distributors v. Bernina Sewing Machines* case illustrates how a party did not anticipate the risk of a currency rate fluctuation. In this case, a poorly written *open price term* resulted in significant losses due to an unanticipated currency fluctuation.

Bernina Distributors, Inc. v. Bernina Sewing Mach.

646 F.2d 434 (10th Cir. 1981)

Defendant Bernina Sewing Machine Co. (Importer), a Utah corporation, imports and supplies Bernina sewing machines to plaintiff Bernina Distributors (Distributor). The problem arises from the fluctuations of exchange rates and decreases in the value of the U.S. dollar versus the Swiss franc. The case involves a long-term supply contract for seven years. The contract contained an open price term in which "prices are automatically subject to change when factory costs are increased." The importer is required to pay in Swiss francs.

The open price term allowed Importer to increase prices as follows: "(a) To the extent of increase of factory invoice costs to Importer. (b) any increase in duty charges. (c) increases in insurance, freight, handling, broker and port fees, or similar charges. Increases in factory invoice costs shall be adjusted as they occur. Increases to all other charges shall be adjusted at the commencement of each calendar year." But with the precipitous decline of the dollar in relation to the Swiss franc, Importer's costs nearly doubled.

Judge. Importer maintains that the risk of currency fluctuations had not been allocated in the contract and that, under the Uniform Commercial Code, an "open price term" should be what the court finds to be reasonable. We (court) believe that the contract provisions are quite comprehensive and, hence, the statutory provision is inapplicable to this case. Thus, we believe the contract places the risk of a diminishing profit margin on Importer and that Importer bears the risk of currency fluctuations.

Importer also asserts that the court's interpretation makes the contract impracticable under § 2-615 of the Uniform Commercial Code. The UCC excuses performance under a contract when performance "has been made impracticable [hardship] by the occurrence of a contingency the nonoccurrence of which was a basic assumption on which the contract was made." In our view, the instant contract is not one made impracticable by the contingency of the devalued dollar. Comment 8 to § 2-615 states that this excuse does "not apply when the contingency in question is sufficiently foreshadowed at the time of contracting." Also, cost increases alone do not render a contract impracticable. Importer was aware of the possibility of a reduction in profits due to exchange rate fluctuations and could have guarded against this contingency. For example, a cost-plus formula for determining the price could have been utilized.

To grant relief on this issue would be to disturb an agreed-upon allocation of risk between commercial equals. Furthermore, the contract was not rendered impracticable due to the increase in costs to the Importer related to currency fluctuation.

Case Highlights

- Common practice of entering into long-term supply contracts
- Use of open price or price escalation clauses to adjust the contract price over the term of the contract
- A determination that a risk has been allocated to one of the parties defeats a demand for a contract adjustment
- Contract law allows for an excuse from not fulfilling a contract. In the sale of goods, the Uniform Commercial Code § 2-615 grants an excuse for commercial impracticability. The law also allows the parties to write an express excuse or *force majeure* clause
- An excuse for commercial impracticability will not be granted if the risk was foreseeable or where the burden on a party is not unduly severe
- Since currency fluctuations are foreseeable, courts are likely to view them as allocated risks and are unlikely to grant an excuse
- It is important to write clear and detailed clauses, especially in long-term contracts. The Court suggested the use of a "cost-plus" formula in the open price term.

A foreign importer or exporter can minimize the risk of a negative currency rate change through techniques of **hedging**. This is accomplished by entering into **forward**, **futures**, or **option contracts**. A forward contract requires two parties to exchange specified amounts of two currencies at some future time. The problem with a forward contract is that if the underlying deal falls through, the party is still required to purchase the other currency. However, futures contracts are like negotiable bonds that can be sold prior to maturity. A party can avoid their obligations under a futures contract by selling it in the secondary market. A well-developed futures market provides a high level of liquidity, but, just as in the bond market, the value of futures contracts will fluctuate depending on the underlying values of the currencies. A futures contract is based on standardized forms, while in forward contracts the parties are free to negotiate custom terms.

In the *Bernina* case, the importer could have hedged by entering a forward or futures contract or by buying a currency option to purchase Swiss francs for a fixed amount of U.S. dollars. This would have protected it against the subsequent devaluation of the dollar. In fact, if the importer had purchased a future contract its value would have increased since the contract gives a right to buy Swiss francs at a lower price than the market price.

A currency option is the most common form of hedging. The right to sell a currency in the future is a *put option*, while the right to buy is a *call option*. A party pays a fee for the right to buy a foreign currency at a rate fixed in the option contract. The owner of the option is under no obligation to exercise the option. For a seller-exporter, the option fee needs to be internalized into the sales contract price (see above section on "Pricing Risks"). The purchaser may choose to exercise or pass on the option, thus limiting the risk of unfavorable exchange rate fluctuation and preserving the benefits from a favorable currency fluctuation.

Political Risk

Political or country risk broadly refers to the negative consequences that stem from a change in government policies. In the area of import–export, **trade barriers** represent the most common risk. Trade barriers are classified into seven general categories:

- Import policies including tariffs and other import charges, quantitative restrictions (quotas and embargoes), and import licensing
- Standards, labeling, testing, and certification
- Government procurement restrictions
- Export subsidies
- Lack of intellectual property protection
- Service barriers
- Investment barriers.

The **WTO Agreements** commit countries to reduce and eliminate all categories of trade barriers. Nontariff barriers include import quotas and other quantitative restrictions, import licensing, customs charges and fees, customs procedures, export subsidies, unreasonable standards, discriminatory labeling, and discriminatory government procurement policies. The WTO and its role in international trade will be examined in Chapter 6.

The WTO Agreements target trade barriers through the Agreement on Import Licensing, Agreement on Technical Barriers, Agreement on the Application of Sanitary and Phytosanitary Measures, Agreement on Customs Valuation, and the Agreement on Pre-shipment Inspection. Restrictions on government procurement are the subject of the Agreement on Government Procurement. Illegal export subsidies were addressed in the 1947 Agreement in Article VI (Anti-dumping and Countervailing Duties), Article XXIII (Nullification and Impairment), and the 1994 Anti-Dumping Agreement.

Intellectual property protection, barriers to trade in services, and barriers to foreign investment are dealt with in separate agreements: Agreement on Trade-Related Investment Measures (TRIMs), General Agreement on Trade in Services (GATS), and the Agreement on Trade-Related Aspects of Intellectual Property Rights (TRIPS). The TRIMs Agreement prohibits countries from requiring their governmental agencies to purchase only domestically produced products, conditioning the importation of products on a company's agreement to export an equal value of domestic products, and restricting access to foreign exchange. The GATS Agreement prohibits the use of qualification and licensing requirements as disguised barriers to the establishment of a business or practicing of a profession by a foreign party. Any such requirements are to be based upon "objective and transparent criteria" and must include "adequate procedures to verify the competence of professionals" from foreign countries. The scope and content of GATS will be reviewed in Chapter 14. The TRIPS Agreement is a comprehensive framework that covers intellectual property, including copyright, trademark, country of origin indicators, patent, industrial designs, and trade secrets. This TRIPS Agreement will be reviewed in Chapter 15.

A prevalent form of political risk involves changes in government regulation of foreign business activity, referred to as **creeping expropriation**. This includes changes in regulations, licensing procedures, increasing taxes, and the enactment of price controls. Creeping expropriation also includes the extortion of bribes, arbitrary changes in standards and inspection requirements, and the nonenforcement of intellectual property laws. A change in tax rates, denial of a tax credit, or a change in accounting rules can be used to manipulate corporate income taxes. Other types of revenue taxes, related to import and export of goods, can also be manipulated, such as the value-added tax,[14] sales tax, excise tax, and tariffs.

Expropriation and Nationalization

The most extreme form of political risk is expropriation and nationalization. **Expropriation** is a government seizure of a foreign business and assets. **Nationalization** refers to the seizure of all businesses, foreign and domestic, in a particular industry. Under international law, both require prompt, adequate, and effective compensation to the foreign investor. Fortunately, the threats of a foreign government nationalizing an industry or expropriating a foreign company's assets have diminished. The free trade era has made it clear that countries need to attract foreign investment and trade in order to continue to develop. In fact, the opposite of nationalization and expropriation, the privatization of government-owned industries has been the dominant trend.

The key area of dispute is not whether a country has the legal right to nationalize or expropriate, but the amount of compensation to be paid. Often, foreign governments are willing to pay only the cost paid by the foreign investor instead of the real or current value of the investments. Bilateral Investment Treaties (BITs) are another avenue by which countries safeguard the foreign investments of their companies from expropriation and other investment risks. BITs provide that a host country must not discriminate against foreign investors and must agree to pay prompt, adequate, and effective compensation in case of expropriation. They also provide for alternative dispute resolution by way of arbitration with the **International Centre for Settlement of Investment Disputes (ICSID)**. See Chapter 17 on "Foreign Direct Investment."

Risk Management

In large projects, a company's management should meet with government officials of the foreign country to discuss the company's goals. If possible, a formal **concession agreement** should be negotiated outlining the duties of the foreign government and the rights of the company. It should specify the level of tariffs to be charged, the right of the company to repatriate profits, the host country's commitment to intellectual property protection, the applicable level of taxation, and the government's transfer pricing policy.[15] It is also prudent to require the use of mediation and arbitration in case of a dispute.

Managing Risk Through Insurance and Government Assistance Programs

The internationally based investment insurance company (MIGA) was established by the World Bank. MIGA encourages investment in developing countries through the mitigation of noncommercial investment barriers. It provides insurance against expropriation, war, and other noncommercial risks and offers investment guarantees for FDI, as well as licensing, franchising, and transfers of technology. The determination of whether political (government intervention) or commercial risk (contacting party fails to perform) insurance will be needed should be made when negotiating the underlying contract. Insurance procurement may be subject to foreign government regulation. In China, for example, insurance in conjunction with a joint venture must be obtained through a Chinese insurance company. The decision to obtain commercial insurance may be required by a commercial lender. Choice of law clauses should be reviewed to determine if there are laws that preclude the insured from making a claim under its insurance policy.

The application for insurance, like the application for a letter of credit, is contractual in nature. The general rule is that the applicant must disclose any information that would "materially" influence the insurance company's decision to grant the requested insurance.[16] In the related area of marine insurance, a court stated that: "an applicant for a marine insurance policy is bound to reveal every fact within its knowledge that is material to the risk."[17] In that case, an owner of a company failed to disclose that she had previously filed claims for more than two dozen losses at sea. The court found that there was sufficient evidence for fraud in intentionally concealing material facts and allowed rescission (voiding) of the insurance policy.

Typical provisions found in most insurance contracts include a description of the insured property, a definition of an act of expropriation, waiting period, notice, warranties, recoveries, duty to minimize loss, and definition and computation of loss. An investor should closely scrutinize the definition of expropriation in its insurance policy. Does the policy cover partial and total loss due to expropriation? A "waiting period" is often required between the loss and collecting on the insurance policy. In large projects the waiting period can be as long as a year. The duties of the insured regarding the preservation of the investment and any claims pertaining to the loss should be clearly defined. A warranty provision often requires the insured to take steps in order to preserve its coverage. For example, the insured may have to certify that it will comply with relevant host country laws and that an uninsured portion of the investment will remain uninsured. The later requirement is to incentivize the insured to take steps to protect the insured property.

Many countries have government agencies and programs that assist domestic companies wanting to do business internationally. For example, the U.S. promotes exporting through: (1) Commercial Service (trade promotion in the Department of Commerce's International Trade Administration or ITA); (2) Trade and Development Agency (USTDA) (grants for feasibility studies for doing business in developing countries); (3) Small Business Administration (SBA) (finance programs); (4) International Buyer Program (IBP) (connect exporters at trade shows with foreign buyers); (5) Agency for International Development (USAID) (procures goods and services from U.S. companies for use in developing countries); and (6) Trade Fair Certification Program (TFC) (certifies international trade events). There are also international institutions whose purpose is to assist exporting–importing in all countries, such as the **Multilateral Development Bank** (**MDB**) (provides development-related financing and professional advising) and the **Multilateral Investment Guarantee Agency** (**MIGA**).

Managing Risk Through Intermediaries

Using professional consultants and agents reduces exporting, licensing, and FDI risks. International specialists such as commercial banks, freight forwarders, customs brokers, political risk analysts, international lawyers, and commercial insurance companies all offer expertise and services. **Customs brokers** assist importers with the entry of goods into foreign countries. They are licensed pursuant to national law to transact business with the country's customs service. Customs brokers provide a variety of services including advising the importer on the formalities, regulations, and tariffs (taxes or duties) for the specific country of import.

Under some trade terms, such as DDP (see Chapter 12), the "importer" might actually be the exporter. Under the DDP term, the exporter has the obligation to clear the goods through customs and pay tariff fees at the country of import. The customs broker advises the importer on selecting the correct HTS classification number describing the goods to be imported (see Chapter 6) in the hope of paying a lower tariff rate. It also prepares and reviews customs documents, including the Application for Import License, Import Declaration, and Special Customs Invoice, delivers them to the customs authorities, and obtains the document releasing the goods for importation. Additional services provided by customs brokers include arranging for the warehousing of the goods at the port of importation (after the goods clear customs).

Commonly, the seller or exporter hires a **freight forwarder**, while the customs broker is the agent for an importer or purchaser. Freight forwarders must be certified to handle ocean freight. The freight forwarder often arranges documentation needed to move a shipment from origin to destination and assembles documents for presentation to the bank (for payment) in the exporter's name. The forwarder arranges for cargo insurance, notifies the buyer of the shipment, and advises the shipper of marking and labeling requirements. In exchange, the forwarder is paid a fee and may receive a percentage of the freight charge from the common carrier (railroad, ship).

International bankers offer financing assistance, provide guarantees of payment, and facilitate the movement of documents between the parties. Another important third-party service is the **ATA Carnet**. The ATA Carnet is a standardized international customs document used to obtain duty-free temporary admission of certain goods. The abbreviation ATA is derived from the French phrase *admission temporaire* and the English words *temporary admission*. Under the ATA Convention, commercial and professional travelers may temporarily take commercial samples, tools of the trade, advertising material, and cinematographic, audio-visual, medical, scientific, or other professional equipment into member countries without paying customs duties and taxes or posting a bond at the border of each country. Carnets are generally valid for 12 months.

Countertrade

Countertrade is used to overcome currency convertibility and repatriation problems or the capital shortcomings of a foreign buyer.[18] The common forms of countertrade include barter, **buy-back**, and **counter-purchase**. A **barter transaction** involves an exchange of goods or services, and not payment by currency. A form of countertrade known as counter-purchase is an economic transaction in which one party sells goods to a foreign party and, in return, the first party agrees to purchase goods of equal value from a seller in that foreign country so as to achieve a balance of trade. A variant is the **offset agreement**: "Offsets constitute an agreement by the foreign seller to include as part of the sale in the foreign nation the use of parts or services from local suppliers." An offset satisfies local content requirements where the host country mandates that a certain percentage of a good includes local materials and labor. In buy-back or compensation transactions, exporters of heavy equipment, technology, or entire manufacturing facilities enter into an agreement with the foreign company or government to purchase a certain percentage of the output at a reduced price. See Figure 1.3's explanations of the different types of countertrade. Again, countertrade are cashless transactions that are used to avoid currency risks or when one of the parties lacks financial means. See Figure 1.3 *Doing Business Internationally* for a review of countertrade terminology.

The **United Nations Commission on International Trade Law's (UNCITRAL)** *Legal Guide on International Countertrade Transactions* provides information on how best to structure a countertrade transaction. It also discusses the types of clauses generally found in countertrade contracts. The clauses discussed in the *Guide* include type, quality, and quantity of goods; pricing of goods; participation of third parties; payment; restrictions on resale; liquidated damages;

security for performance; failure to perform; choice of law; and settlement of disputes.

Because of the difficulty in finding marketable goods in a foreign country to fulfill a countertrade commitment, certain clauses take on added importance. First, an extended period of time should be allotted to the exporter to obtain host country goods to satisfy its countertrade obligations. Second, a broad list of countertrade goods should be negotiated to enhance the exporter's chances of finding marketable goods. Third, the costs and uncertainty of the countertrade arrangement may warrant the granting of a *disagio* (discount) on the amount of goods to be purchased to fulfill countertrade commitments.

Another provision included in countertrade contracts is the penalty clause for nonperformance of the countertrade commitment. In some cases, paying a penalty instead of purchasing unmarketable goods may make better economic sense for the exporter. Of course, the penalty clause should make clear that payment of the penalty releases the exporter from any further liability.

It is important to note that the counter-purchase arrangement is more of a currency transaction than a sale of goods. When a foreign government releases hard currency to one of its nationals to purchase imported goods, the government wants to be assured that an equal amount of hard currency is returned to the country. An exporter of goods may satisfy its counter-purchase obligations not only by purchasing goods from the foreign country, but also through a currency transaction. For example, if a company has no interest in purchasing foreign goods it may make a deal to purchase soft currency from the buyer's country. For example, if a Mexican company purchases goods from Chile and gets paid in Chilean pesos, the American, European, or Japanese company who happens to buy goods from Chile could agree to buy the Chilean pesos from Mexico with dollars, euros, or yen. This arrangement satisfies the American company's counter-purchase obligation—hard currency flows back into Mexico, and the American company can immediately buy Chilean goods with the acquired pesos.[19]

Developing an Export Plan

Before attempting to export, a firm should develop an export plan. It should provide short-term and long-term objectives and milestones. Figure 1.4 provides an outline of a generic export plan. The export plan determines whether the firm should export directly or indirectly.

The direct exporting approach is more ambitious and difficult, since the exporter handles every aspect of the exporting process from market research and planning to foreign distribution and collections. This approach is the best way to achieve maximum profits and long-term growth. With appropriate help and guidance from third-party experts including freight forwarders and international banks, small or medium-sized firms can export directly. A company may instead take a multifaceted approach to exporting. For example, it may elect to export directly to nearby markets, while letting an export management company handle sales to distant foreign markets. An exporter may also choose to gradually increase its level of direct exporting, after it has gained experience and sales volumes to justify added investment.

16 *Law & Policy Int'l Bus.* 1 (1984)

Countertrade frequently is confused with the concept of barter. Barter is an exchange of goods effectuated without the use of currency. Barter transactions is a subcategory of countertrade. The two most common types of countertrade are known as counter-purchase and compensation (buy-back) transactions.

Counter-purchase

In a counter-purchase arrangement, a private firm agrees to sell products to a foreign company and agrees to purchase the same value of goods from that country at a later time. For example, in a series of transactions between a major French manufacturer of commercial aircraft and the government of Serbia, the French company sold jet aircraft to Serbia and agreed to purchase substantial quantities of Serbian crystal glassware, cutting tools, leather coats, and canned hams.

In a counter-purchase transaction, each party is paid in a hard currency upon the delivery of its products to the other party. It is common in such transactions for a private firm to be allowed a period of time following the delivery of the goods in which to fulfill its counter-purchase obligation. Periods of from three to five years are not uncommon. Often, the parties agree upon a list of goods from which the private firm later will be able to select items to purchase.

Private firms resort to a variety of methods to dispose of goods which they are forced to purchase, but most frequently resell the goods to trading companies or directly to end users, often at a *disagio* (discount). The discount is a loss since it is below the price paid by the firm but is offset by factoring the discount into the price of the goods that it sold in the initial transaction.

Compensation

The most common form of countertrade is "compensation" or "buy-back." In a compensation transaction, a private firm will supply equipment, technology, or sometimes an entire plant to a foreign nation or company in exchange for the right to purchase a portion of the output produced from the use of the equipment or technology. For example, in a $20 billion Occidental Petroleum ammonia countertrade transaction with Russia, Occidental assisted Russia in constructing and financing ammonia plants and agreed to purchase quantities of ammonia produced in these plants over a 20-year period (at a discounted price).

Compensation transactions frequently involve significantly longer periods of time during which the private firm will be permitted to fulfill its purchase obligation than in counter-purchase. In addition, compensation transactions are generally of larger monetary value than counter-purchase transactions. Unlike counter-purchase transactions, the products, which the private firm purchases are frequently of marketable quality and in demand in the international marketplace. Firms supplying capital, equipment, technology,

Figure 1.3 Doing Business Internationally: Thomas B. McVey, "Countertrade: Commercial Practices, Legal Issues, and Policy Dilemmas."

and expertise are able to negotiate a purchase price for their share of the output that is below the market price, allowing them to earn a profit in reselling the product, and receiving a return on their investments.

Barter

Barter, swap, and other types of noncurrency transactions are viewed as forms of countertrade. In many cases, the sovereign nation will impose a barter requirement in a coercive fashion for purposes of disposing of surplus or low-quality goods, which it otherwise cannot sell. Barter transactions are frequently utilized in crude oil transfers as a means of conveying crude below official OPEC prices. Similarly, barter is used as a means of "liberating" blocked currencies or otherwise circumventing foreign exchange controls.

Clearing Agreements

Countertrade arrangements also occur between and among nations. Nations have historically entered into bilateral or multilateral "clearing agreements" under which they agree to purchase equal values of each other's products over a specified period of time. This is a form of reciprocal trading used when an imbalance develops in an account that a nation cannot rectify: private companies known as "switch trading" firms offer to assist the parties in disposing of the goods, which it is required to purchase, usually for a fee.

Framework Agreements

In a countertrade "framework agreement" a private firm establishes a formal, long-term "crediting" mechanism with the host nation under which exports generated by the private firm are routinely credited to the countertrade commitments of numerous third-party firms on an ongoing basis. The key to a framework agreement is that the "crediting" of the offsetting purchases or the escrowing and payment of funds is undertaken on a routine and ongoing basis under a prearranged contract, rather than on a case-by-case basis.

"Positive" or "Reverse" Countertrade

In "positive" or "reverse" countertrade, private firms view the goods that it will be required to purchase as more valuable than hard currency. This is most often the case when a firm seeks to establish a guaranteed supply of a valuable commodity or production component. For example, in one of the proposed East–West "gas-for-pipes" transactions, a group of private firms negotiated with Russia to transfer equipment and technology for the transportation and production of natural gas in return for guarantees of quantities of natural gas produced through the use of the equipment and technology.

Performance Requirements

A performance requirement is a condition imposed by a sovereign government that requires foreign parties that invest in the country to agree to take certain

Figure 1.3 (Continued)

steps to increase exports from the nation. Such steps include the agreement by the foreign investors to export a certain percentage of the output from the investment project, to employ a certain level of local workers in the project, to use a predetermined level of locally produced components in the manufactured product, and to transfer certain technology to the host nation. Performance requirements and most other types of countertrade involve intervention by the host nation into the free market process.

Collection-through-Export Transactions

A major problem for firms doing business abroad is the collection of overseas funds, which have been restricted from repatriation due to foreign exchange controls. In a collection-through-export transaction, the firm uses the local currency to purchase locally produced goods, export the goods, and sell the goods overseas for convertible currency.

Figure 1.3 (Continued)

Is your company's management committed to pursuing export operations? The following areas of concerns should be covered in the export plan:

Part I. Situation/Background Analysis

- background data on target countries and market
- basic market statistics: historical and projected
- benefits from existing Free Trade Agreements
- export compliance
- classification of products under the Harmonized Tariff Schedule
- personnel and export organization
- resources of the firm
- evaluation of industry structure, competition, and demand.

Part II. Marketing Component

- identifying, evaluating, and selecting target markets
- product selection and pricing: product pricing including costs associated to seller, such as freight, insurance, and import costs; additional costs, such as foreign advertising and web site development
- distribution methods
- terms and conditions: selection of proper trade term(s) (*Incoterms*) to determine additional costs to be internalized in product pricing
- sales goals: profit and loss forecasts.

Part III. Tactics: Action Steps

- determining primary target countries and secondary target countries (Test primary market first and then target secondary markets.)
- Consider use of indirect exporting at first to test market before moving to direct exporting based upon marketability of product.
- selection and use of a foreign distributor
- Devise and implement strategy for protecting intellectual property and confidential information (before exporting goods or hiring a foreign distributor).

Part IV. Export Budget

- pro forma financial statements

Part V. Implementation Schedule

- follow-up: periodic operational and management review (measuring results against plan)

Figure 1.4 Focus on Transactions: Sample Outline for an Export Plan.

Chapter Summary

1. The intent of Chapter 1 is to provide the framework for the coverage of the book's remaining 18 chapters by highlighting the reasons for doing business internationally, the methods of doing business internationally, the risks of doing business internationally, and the means of mitigating those risks. Finally, Chapter 1 exposes the student to much of the terminology used in international trade and throughout the rest of this book, as can be seen on the list below of "Key Terms."

2. There are three generic methods of doing business internationally: (a) exporting–importing of goods and services; (b) licensing of technology and intellectual property rights; and (c) foreign direct investment. Another means of doing business is the sale of services.
3. In the sale of goods there are a number of direct ways of selling in foreign markets. The generic division is between direct exporting and indirect exporting. There are a number of methods of direct exporting: (a) direct sales to foreign customers; (b) sales to foreign distributors; and (c) consignment sales. Indirect exporting is often done through a third-party export management consultant (EMC), an exporting trading company (ETC), or a remarketer.
4. The risks associated with international business include: (a) pricing risks; (b) legal risks; (c) cultural and language risks; (d) currency risks; and (e) political risks.
5. There are three types of currency risks: (a) convertibility; (b) fluctuation; and (c) repatriation. Hedging is a common way of mitigating currency risks and includes the use of currency options, futures contracts, and forward contracts.
6. Another form of minimizing currency risks and the risks of entering a venture with an undercapitalized foreign entity is countertrade. The common forms of countertrade include: (a) barter; (b) counter-purchase; and (c) buy-back or compensation.
7. There are a number of third parties that provide necessary services for the exporting–importing of goods, including: (a) commercial banks; (b) insurance companies; (c) common carriers; (d) customs brokers; (e) freight forwarders; and (f) ATA Carnet.

Key Terms

Arbitrage
Article 38 of the Statute of the International Court of Justice
ATA Carnet
Barter Transaction
Basket of Risks
Bilateral Investment Treaty (BIT)
Buy-Back
Buying Agent
Commission Agent
Concession Agreement
Consignment
Convertibility
CIF (Cost, Insurance, and Freight)
Counter-Purchase
Countertrade
Currency Option
Currency Rate Fluctuation
Customary International Law
Customs Broker
Disagio
Evergreen Laws
Export Management Company (EMC)
Export Trading Company (ETC)
Exporting–Importing
Expropriation
Foreign Direct Investment (FDI)
Foreign Distributor
Foreign Sales Representative
Forward Contract
Franchise; Franchising
Free Trade Agreement (FTA)

Freight Forwarder
Futures Contract
Global Supply Chain
Hedging
Home Country
Host Country
Indirect Exporting
International Centre for Settlement of Investment Disputes (ICSID)
International Chamber of Commerce (ICC)
International Court of Justice
Joint Venture
Jurisdiction, Personal Jurisdiction, Subject Matter
Lex Mercatoria
Licensing
Multilateral Development Bank (MDB)
Multilateral Investment Guarantee Agency (MIGA)
Nationalization
Nontariff Barriers
United States-Mexico-Canada Agreement (USMCA)
Offset Agreement
Option Contract
Privatization
Remarketer
Repatriation
Sale of Services
Technical Barriers
Trade Barriers
Trade Facilitation Agreement (TFA)
Trade in Goods
Transfer Pricing
United Nations Commission on International Trade Law (UNCITRAL)
United Nations Convention on Contracts for The International Sale of Goods (CISG)
Uruguay Round
World Trade Organization (WTO)
WTO Agreements

Chapter Problems

1. You are a manager at a U.S. company that manufactures moderately priced personal computers. The company is contemplating expanding overseas with an initial emphasis on exporting to Latin America. You have been assigned the task of preparing a preliminary market analysis for the country of Brazil. Conduct market research and prepare a report that focuses on the opportunities and pitfalls of exporting to Brazil and offer recommendations.
2. As Vice President for Foreign Operations of a multinational corporation, you have been asked to prepare a report for the board of directors regarding "doing business" in Germany and Nigeria. Please discuss the following in your report: (1) the different ways of "doing business" in foreign countries; (2) the way you would recommend for each of the two countries mentioned; (3) the risks of doing business in these countries; and (4) the ways of minimizing those risks.
3. Your company is contemplating exporting goods to the following countries: France, Hungary, and Nigeria. Research the following: (1) the currency of each country and the current conversion rate into euros; and (2) restrictions in each country pertaining to the conversion of the national currency into U.S. dollars and any repatriation limitations. If the currency risks are severe for any of these countries, what alternatives should you explore in order to do business in these countries?

Internet Exercises

1. Review the website of the International Court of Justice for information on current court cases: http://www.icj-cij.org.
2. Review the online catalog of materials published by International Chamber of Commerce Publishing, SA: http://www.iccbooks.com.
3. Review the website of the World Intellectual Property Organization at http://www.wipo.org for materials that would be of assistance to someone contemplating the international licensing of intellectual property rights.
4. Search the web for sites of international law firms that aid companies undertaking international business transactions. Some of these sites provide interesting articles and links to current developments in the law of international business transactions.
5. Using the template "A Step-by-Step Approach to Market Research" provided earlier in the chapter, write a market research report for a small American electronics company that produces portable radios and MP3 players, using the following readily available resources:

   - U.S. Commercial Services at export.gov
   - Trade Stats Express at tse.export.gov
   - United Nations Statistical Yearbook at unstats.un.org/unsd/syb
   - World Bank Atlas of Global Development at data.worldbank.org/products/atlas
   - World Development Indicators at data.worldbank.org/products/wdi
   - International Monetary Fund (IMF) Data and Statistics at imf.org/external/data.htm.

Other Internet Sources

World Bank: http://www.worldbank.org (provides statistics and information on international trade and finance).

Links to *Lex Mercatoria* Developments: http://www.jus.uio.no/lm. This website describes itself as a monitor for developments in customary international law and Internet infrastructure.

American Society of International Law: http://www.asil.org (provides information on current developments in international law, along with links to international documents and analysis).

World Trade Organization: http://www.wto.org (provides links to all WTO Agreements).

Notes

1 ICC, *Rethinking Trade and Finance 2014* at 23.

2 See generally, Ward Bower, "The Future Structure of the Global Legal Marketplace," *The Metropolitan Corporate Counsel* (1999).

3 The United States–Mexico–Canada Agreement of 2019 replaced the 1992 North American Free Trade Agreement (NAFTA).

4 The International Court of Justice (ICJ) or World Court is located at The Hague in the Netherlands. Its Statute, a part of the United Nations Charter, dictates the jurisdiction and powers of the court.

5 Arthur Rosett, "Critical Reflections on the CISG," 45 *Ohio State Law Journal* 265, 287 (1984).

6 See generally, Roy Goode, "Usage and Its Reception in Transnational Commercial Law," 46 *International & Comparative Law Quarterly* 1 (1997); Lord Mustill, "The New Lex Mercatoria: The First Twenty-Five Years," 4 *Arbitration International* 86 (1988).

7 The Hague Rules were codified in the U.S. as the 1936 Carriage of Goods by Sea Act (COGSA), which applies to an international export or import shipment involving a bill of lading for transport from or to a U.S. port.

8 The UCP was first published in 1933 and subsequently revised in 1951, 1962, 1974, 1983, and 1993. The UCP 600 came into effect on July 1, 2007.

9 Hugh Beale and Tony Dugdale, "Contracts Between Businessmen: Planning and the Use of Contractual Remedies," 2 *British Journal of Law & Society* 45, 49 (1975).

10 United Nations Convention on Contracts for the International Sale of Goods (April 11, 1980), U.N. Doc. A/CONF.97/18, Annex I, reprinted in 19 I.L.M. 668.

11 *Nachfrist* notice is the requirement that a party grant an extension of time to perform the contract upon the request of the other party. *Nachfrist* notice will be examined in Chapter 10.

12 Discovery is the pretrial process whereby the litigants uncover evidence by questioning the other party either in writing (interrogatories) or in person (depositions) and by examining documents provided by the other party to the litigation.

13 *Fernandez v. Wynn Oil Co.*, 653 F.2d 1273 (9th Cir. 1981).

14 Value-added tax (VAT) is a popular method of taxation in Europe. It imposes a tax on goods and services at each stage of the production process equal to the value added to the product at each stage. It is similar, but not identical, to a sales tax.

15 Transfer pricing is the price that an affiliated company, such as a subsidiary, charges another affiliated company. Manipulation of transfer prices can be used to move profits and costs from a high-tax to a low-tax country.

16 See New York Insurance Law §3105 (McKinney's).

17 *Cigna Property & Casualty Insurance Co. v. Polaris Pictures Co.*, 1998 WL 734391 (9th Cir. 1998).

18 See generally, John Grabow, "Negotiating and Drafting Contracts in International Barter and Countertrade Transactions," 9 *North Carolina Journal of International Law & Commercial Regulation* 255 (1984).

19 Source: International Trade Administration, *Trade Finance Guide* (November 2012).

Chapter 2

Ethics of International Business

This textbook's primary focus is on the *legal* implications of doing business internationally. This chapter will emphasize some of the important *ethical* implications of international business dealings and will explore how a multinational business confronts the issues of transnational ethics. The importance of ethics pervades all areas of business, government, and society. This chapter will focus on a few areas most related to doing business internationally: (1) differences between host–home country standards (health, environmental, quality, workplace safety); (2) bribery and corruption; and (3) sustainability and environmental ethics.

Most international business decisions have both legal and ethical implications—how to address differences between host and home countries' laws and ethics is an example. The legal answer to this dilemma is quite clear—since the business activity transpires within the jurisdiction of the host country, then the businessperson need only comply with the standards of the host country, assuming no extraterritorial application of home country laws. The ethical answer is much more complicated. If the host country's standards are lower than those of the home country, is complying with the lesser standards ethical? Most companies from the developed world face this question when starting business operations in lesser-developed countries. Answering this question becomes more difficult if the lesser standards are likely to result in harm to people or the environment. Ultimately a multinational company (MNC) may be *ethically* required to apply standards higher than those required by the host country's laws.

Ethical assessments are complicated by differing cultural and national views on what is ethically appropriate, which are influenced by the nuances of culture, religion, and economics. **Ethical or cultural relativism** holds that because different countries or cultures have different ethical belief systems there is no

DOI: 10.4324/9781003469230-3

supranational way of determining whether an action is right or wrong, and that ethical beliefs are only determinable at the national level. Ethical relativism asserts that the correctness of an action is to be measured by whatever a majority of people within a society believe is morally correct. The alternative belief system to ethical relativism is *absolutism*, which holds that certain moral and ethical principles should be upheld in all cultures and countries. Human rights documents provide examples of core principles that should be followed by all civilized countries. Recognition of basic principles of civilized societies does not mean that local religious and ethical rules should be disrespected if in conflict with those principles.

Business Ethics

Business managers often do not recognize the ethical implications of their decisions; therefore, they need ethical tools that can guide them in making ethically correct decisions. From the perspective of corporate profits and credibility, a good reputation in the global marketplace has become paramount for most multinational enterprises, partly because bad ethical practices are readily apparent in an increasingly transparent global economy. Multinational companies are often the target of surveillance by the media, government agencies, competitors, private watch groups, and their own employees. Public relations disasters resulting from unethical practices can be catastrophic.

To better sensitize employees to ethical issues, there must be agreement on basic assumptions regarding the rightness of certain practices. For example, the issue is not whether bribery is wrong, but whether most civilized nations believe that bribery is wrong. A review of the traditional schools of ethics provides a starting point for the businessperson's approach to ethical decision-making. The ethical schools to be reviewed include utilitarianism, rights and duties, virtue, and ethics of care.

Utilitarianism

The **utilitarian** or teleological approach to ethics looks to the consequences of a decision or an action to determine if it was ethically appropriate. There are many different formulations of this approach. The most basic or crude form of utilitarianism is **hedonism** or egoism, which simply determines the rightness of an action based on whether it produces greater good for the individual decision-maker. In the area of business, egoism is often associated with the economics of Adam Smith, an eighteenth-century Scottish philosopher and the father of modern economics. His masterwork, *The Wealth of Nations*, which was published in 1776, provides the rationalization for free market economics: Individuals should be allowed to make decisions based upon their own narrow self-interests. If not interfered with, such rational self-interest will produce an efficient economy that benefits society as a whole. Smith's view of self-interest and the free market has largely been misunderstood, however. Smith's moral philosophy as described in his other masterwork, *A Theory of Moral Sentiments*, saw *rational* self-interest as incorporating many altruistic factors not normally associated with rational self-interest.

A simplified version of utilitarianism is the **cost-benefit analysis**, which attempts to monetize the ethical decision-making by placing a value on the benefits and costs of an action from the narrow perspective of the decision-maker. But, again, this is not the basis of utilitarianism as an ethical school of thought. A true utilitarian analysis attempts to weigh all direct and indirect effects from the perspectives of all parties or stakeholders affected and not just from the perspective of the decision-maker. It is imperative for the decision-maker to continuously expand the utilitarian analysis to consider as many effects and stakeholders as possible.

A weakness of utilitarianism is that it fails to consider how the net benefit of an action is distributed. Thus, a multinational company decision that creates a net benefit is unlikely to be ethical if the company retains the entire net benefit or it is shared by only a few government leaders and their associates. Critics of utilitarianism argue that it should be the first stage in a two-stage process. A second stage would analyze how the net benefits are distributed. This process is associated with the notion of **distributive justice**. Another approach is to argue that the utilitarian approach is inappropriate in certain situations, for example, if a net benefit results in the diminishment of basic human rights, then the action is unethical. In essence, certain concerns or **dominant considerations**, such as human rights, would take priority over the results of a purely utilitarian analysis.

After determining the outcome of a decision on all those affected, utilitarianism requires a second step. It is also important to seek out alternatives that would minimize costs (harm) and increase the net benefit. If alternatives are found, then the decision-maker should ask some fundamental questions in comparing the alternatives: Which alternative best promotes the common good? Which alternative best respects the rights of the individual?

Rights and Duties

While the utilitarian approach focuses upon the net benefits to society, a rights and duties approach views morality from the perspective of the individual. A **moral right** of someone creates a correlative **moral duty** on others not to interfere in the exercise of that right. John Locke championed the notion of inalienable rights or social contract that binds people together in a society and binds a government to the people. These inalienable rights, as enunciated in the U.S. Constitution and the French *Rights of Man*, recognize the sanctity of individual autonomy and equality in the pursuit of personal interests. The **United Nations Declaration of Human Rights** adopts a basic rights approach to the international realm. The United Nations' **Declaration on the Right to Development**[1] places responsibility on individual nations and the international community to ensure that everyone shares in the benefits of development. Article 3 of the Declaration states that countries have "the duty to cooperate in ensuring development and eliminating obstacles to development," including the formulation of international development policies that promote the "more rapid development of developing countries."

The developmental benefits of a foreign investment must be weighed against the need to protect the rights of the individual. The **Theory of Relative Development**[2] questions the appropriateness of applying standards from the home country of a multinational company to a less developed country (LDC), where food production is more important in the short-term than the consequences of pollution. Instead, it suggests in determining the appropriate standards the company should use the perspective of what would have been acceptable at the time the home country was at a similar stage of development. However, some host country standards can be considered inadequate for any level of development. This is the issue in the ethics of wage determination. It is generally agreed that workers have a right to a living wage.

A form of a rights approach to ethics is **Kantian ethics**. Like the rights approach, this school is deontological in nature. It is premised on the belief that there are absolute duties (or rights) that can never be broken. Immanuel Kant constructed an ethical system that recognized the existence of absolute moral duties or laws that he referred to as **categorical imperatives**. Unlike utilitarianism, which looks at the consequences of a decision, Kantian ethics applies pre-determined moral principles (*a priori*) before the decision is made. One common formulation of the categorical imperative is that human beings can never be used as a "means to an end." All individuals are to be recognized as equal, rational persons. It is thereby wrong to subject anyone to a risk without their informed consent. An MNC that constructs a hazardous chemical plant in a developing country has a moral duty to fully disclose the health risks to its host country, the local community, and its foreign workers. The problem with disclosure is that a low level of economic development and per capita income may render the information meaningless. Does the foreign company have to do more than disclose and obey whatever host country regulations apply? Kantian ethics would hold that we have a universal duty not to intentionally harm one another.

Virtue Ethics

Virtue ethics focuses not upon the morality of an action but on the moral character or motivation of the actor. Aristotle saw virtues as acquired moral traits that allow a person to act according to right and practical reason. This approach is useful in understanding the importance of corporate culture. Clearly a corporate culture that emphasizes profit at any cost is not conducive to encouraging moral business virtues among the company's employees. Virtue ethicists argue that developing morally desirable virtues lead to moral actions when decisions need to be made. In contrast to virtue ethics, utilitarianism looks to the consequences of a decision or action to determine if the decision is an ethical one. In deontology or Kantian ethics, moral principles are developed and then applied whatever the situation. In virtue ethics, moral principles are not determined beforehand, each situation is taken individually, and a decision is made generally guided by the desire to be virtuous or benevolent. In this way, it is similar to situation ethics, where the determination of an ethical decision depends on context. Each case is unique and deserves a unique solution and, therefore, flexible guidelines rather than absolute rules are needed.

Ethics of Care

The **ethics of care**[3] approach focuses on the importance of preserving a *web of relationships*. A company's weighing of the benefits and costs of a decision should consider certain *concrete relationships*. It is ethically appropriate for example, for a company to place greater weight on the benefits and costs of a decision to its workers and home community. Utilitarian and deontological approaches to ethics emphasize the impartiality and equality of all parties. The ethics of care allows for the recognition that we owe more of an obligation to some than to others.

The potential influence of this approach can be illustrated by the typical case of plant relocation. The board of directors must decide whether to relocate a long-established and aging plant in its country to a more economically friendly location in a developing country. A utilitarian approach would justify the move purely on financial concerns. The rights perspective would recognize the right of an owner to move its business in order to maintain the financial viability of his company. Under the employment-at-will doctrine, prevalent in the U.S., an employer owes no duty of continued employment to its workers. In contrast, the ethics of care would recognize the special obligation a company has to its workers and community. Thus, the cost of the relocation to the company's workers and community may override the determinations made under the other approaches.

Integrative Approach to International Business Ethics

The different ethical approaches to business decision-making all offer insight into how to decide or act. An **integrative ethics approach**, incorporating the best of each, is especially prudent in international business dealings given the problem of ethical and cultural relativism. Such an approach would weigh the benefits and harms of a decision and compare them to alternatives (utilitarian). It would consider whether a given action would disrespect the basic rights of persons (rights/duties). It would also judge the distributive effects of the decision and see how the benefits and burdens are ultimately distributed (justice). Finally, it would weigh the impact of the decision upon those who have a concrete relationship with the company (care). Such an approach can be found in many **corporate codes of conduct**. An examination of Motorola's approach to ethical conduct illustrates the uses of the various approaches to ethics. The reader can see in its mandates the influences of utilitarian, rights, justice, and virtue-based approaches to ethical decision-making.

Motorola's Approach to Ethical Decision-Making

Code's Language	*Ethical Approach*
"Look carefully at the consequences of the action"	Utility Calculation
"*All* parties are to be considered—not just an individual or company and includes both monetary and *nonmonetary* variables"	Expanded Utilitarian Analysis (direct & indirect effects)
"The action produces more overall good to *compensate* for harm done"	Utilitarianism
"Give each person his due"	Justice & Fairness
"Respect human and civil rights"	Rights (Deontology)
"Duties are found in law, contracts, policies, and religions, but they are always subject to interpretation"	Duties/Relativism (Respect for Local Culture)
"It is important to recognize the influence of admirable behavior in decision-making such as honesty and courage."	Virtues

Figure 2.1 Doing Business Internationally: Motorola's Corporate Code.

Motorola's corporate code (see Figure 2.1 *Doing Business Internationally*: "Motorola's Corporate Code") states that "employees of Motorola will respect the laws, customs, and traditions of each country in which they operate, but will, at the same time, engage in no course of conduct which, even if legal, customary, and accepted in any such country, could be deemed to be in violation of the accepted business ethics of Motorola or the laws of the home country relating to business ethics."[4] The problem is that abstract terms, such as *human rights* or *bribery*, have various connotations that depend upon cultural values and local customs. The Motorola Code directly addresses the notion of ethical relativism. Nonetheless, it firmly obligates its employees to be guided by home country and not host country beliefs.

Amoral International Businessperson

Nobel laureate Milton Friedman wrote in 1970 that the only social responsibility of business is to increase profits.[5] Under Friedman's analysis, corporations have no social conscience and should not be concerned with being good "corporate citizens." In his view, it is wrong for a corporation to spend corporate profits on social or charitable concerns since the practice of social responsibility applies only to individuals and not to corporations. From an ethical perspective, corporations need conform only to the **moral minimum** by obeying the law.

An argument against the rejection of corporate social responsibility advocated by Friedman asserts that good ethics is consistent with the pursuit of profits (long-run profitability). Francis Fukuyama in his study of why some societies were more prosperous than others isolated the notion of trust as the crucial factor.[6] Under his notion of trust, business is essentially a cooperative venture whose very existence requires ethical behavior. In fact, the nature of business shows that even people motivated solely by self-interest still have good reason to be ethical in their business dealings. In the era of branding (distinguishing your brand or product), reputation for ethical behavior, quality, and environmental friendliness are seen as creating competitive advantages.

Organizational Ethics

Organizational ethics is a crucial issue for the multinational enterprise. Assuming that organizations are morally responsible, what individuals within the organization should be held accountable for violations of the corporation's moral duties? The traditional view is that those who *knowingly* partake in unethical actions should be held accountable. The problem is the fragmentation of responsibility in large organizations. An unethical action may be produced by many loosely connected actors. Some may be unaware of the outcome of their contribution to the process; their ignorance may absolve them of moral responsibility.

The *problem of* ***subordinate responsibility*** was a central issue in the 1963 work *Eichmann in Jerusalem: A Report on the Banality of Evil*. Adolf Eichmann was a typical middle-level bureaucrat in charge of delivering the trains carrying Jews to the death camps. His response to the morally reprehensible nature of his behavior was that he was "just following orders." His "inability to think [ethically]" was as dangerous as someone acting with evil intent. Viewing an action from the perspectives of different stakeholders inside and outside of the organization will sensitize corporate decision-makers to ethically relevant issues. The stakeholder approach is found in the **Caux Round Table Principles for International Business:**

- Principle 1 makes it the responsibility of business to go *beyond shareholders toward stakeholders*. Businesses should take into consideration not only the well-being of their shareholders (owners) but also that of their customers, employees, suppliers, competitors, and communities.
- Principle 2 deals specifically with companies transacting business in a foreign country. It requires that the social and economic impact of business be directed at advancing *innovation, justice, and world community*. Businesses in foreign countries should create productive employment and raise the standard of living of its citizens.
- Principle 3, *Business Behavior: Beyond the Letter of Law toward a Spirit of Trust*, admonishes that it may not be appropriate for a company to enforce its rights strictly under the law. In the area of intellectual property rights, disclosure of information demonstrates a concern for the long-term development of an impoverished country.
- Principle 6 makes *respect for the environment* a moral minimum for all international businesses. Environmental protection includes improving the environment, promoting sustainable development, and avoiding the wasteful use of natural resources.
- Principle 7, *Avoidance of Illicit Operations*, targets bribery and corruption and their damaging effect on a country's development.

The assumption that corporations have social and environmental responsibilities is further recognized in the United Nations Global Impact Program. The Global Impact initiative is a voluntary program that invites companies to commit themselves to protecting the environment, abolishing child labor, and supporting free-trade unions.[7]

Corruption and Bribery

Transparency International Corruption Perceptions Index[8] rates countries numerically and also scores each country individually on levels of corruption. Corruption at some level exists in all countries but when contemplating whether to do business in a foreign country, the level of corruption should be weighed in the decision. The country with the lowest level of corruption is Denmark, with a score of 90 (100 being the least corrupt), and the country with the highest level of corruption is Somalia (180th) with a score of 11. Sampling of countries (ranking and scores), one from each of the tiers, shows these results: Singapore (5th, 83); Canada and Estonia (12th, 76); UK (20th, 71); U.S. (24th, 69); Spain (36th, 60); Botswana (39th, 59); Slovakia (54th, 47); Argentina (66th, 45); China (76th, 42); India (93rd, 39); Brazil (104th, 36); Ukraine (104th, 36); Panama (108th, 35); Turkey (115th, 34); Russia (141st, 26); Nigeria (145th, 25). Unfortunately, improvements on the Corruption Index have been minor. Ukraine has made significant gains moving from a five-way tie at 126th (score of 30) in 2019 to 104th (score of 36), but still has a long way to go in its fight against corruption.

Countries feel more and more pressure to rid corruption from international business transactions. The stronger economies have increasingly recognized the harm that corruption has on their countries' well-being, such as the ability to attract foreign direct investment. To combat bribery of foreign officials, a number of laws have been enacted including, the U.S. Foreign Corrupt Practices Act in 1978 (FCPA) and the UK Bribery Act of 2010.

The **Organisation for Economic Co-operation and Development** (**OECD**) adopted an Anti-Bribery Convention in 1997. A few of the harms inflicted by

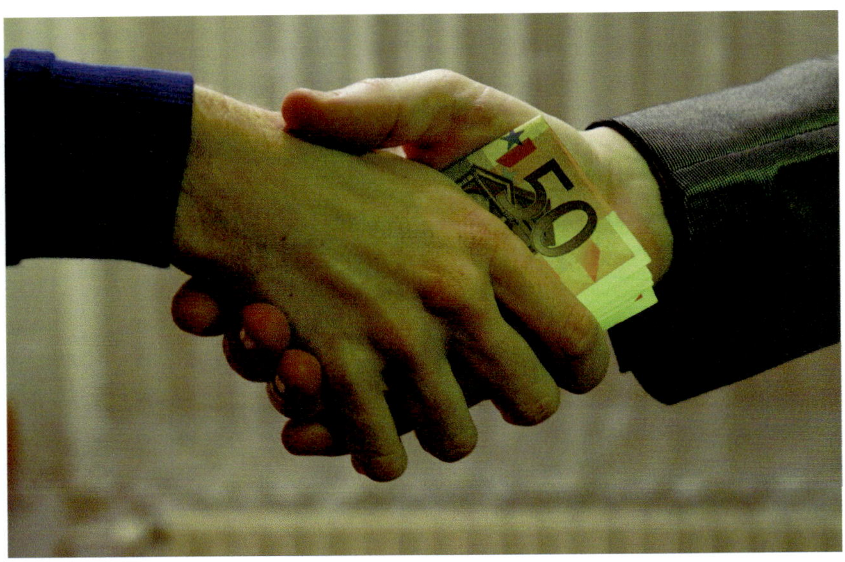

Image 2.1 Handshake Bribe.

Sources: Kiwiev and Eugene Pivovarov, WikiCommons.

corruption include inefficient government contracting, delays in receiving necessary government licenses and approvals, inequality of wealth, damage to the political legitimacy of the government, and slower economic growth.[9] The following coverage of anti-bribery laws starts with a detailed review of the U.S. FCPA since it has been around the longest and the provisions of the OECD Convention and UK Bribery Act are similar in nature to the FCPA. All three cover the issues of what is a bribe, who are government officials, what is third-party bribery, and what is the required *mens rea* (state of mind)—intentionally, knowingly, or acting with reckless disregard to be convicted of a crime?[10]

Foreign Corrupt Practices Act

The FCPA prohibits U.S. individuals, residents, companies, and foreign subsidiaries of U.S. companies from offering, promising, or paying anything of value to any foreign government official in order to obtain or retain business. Since the passage of the FCPA, numerous firms convicted of bribing foreign officials have been subject to criminal and civil enforcement actions, resulting in large fines, exclusion from bidding on federal government contracts, and jail terms for employees and officers. The FCPA also requires companies to meet strict accounting provisions. These provisions require corporations to keep books and records that accurately reflect the transactions of the corporation, as well as devising an adequate system of internal accounting controls. The FCPA provides three exceptions from liability in bribing a foreign government official: (1) payments for **routine governmental action**; (2) **bona fide expenditure** paid for additional services (potable water supply, extra police security, travel and lodging expenses for officials related to the promotion, demonstration, or explanation of products or services); (3) payments that are **lawful under the written laws** and regulations of the foreign country. See Figure 2.2 for an example of a company's activities held to be illegal under the FCPA.

The joint 2008 DOJ/SEC penalty of $1.6 billion to resolve corruption-related charges is the largest ever paid. The SEC's complaint alleges that between March 12, 2001 and September 30, 2007, Siemens violated the FCPA by engaging in a widespread and systematic practice of paying bribes to foreign government officials to obtain business. Siemens created elaborate payment schemes to conceal the nature of its corrupt payments, and the company's inadequate internal controls allowed the conduct to flourish. The misconduct involved employees at all levels, including former senior management, and revealed a corporate culture long at odds with the FCPA. During this period, Siemens made thousands of payments to third parties in ways that obscured the purpose for, and the ultimate recipients of, the money. At least 4,283 of those payments, totaling approximately $1.4 billion, were used to bribe government officials in return for business to Siemens around the world. Among others, Siemens paid bribes on transactions to design and build metro transit lines in Venezuela; metro trains and signaling devices in China; power plants in Israel; mobile telephone networks in Bangladesh; telecommunications projects in Nigeria; national identity cards in Argentina; traffic control systems in Russia; refineries in Mexico; and mobile communications networks in Vietnam. An additional 1,185 separate payments to third parties totaling approximately $391 million were not properly controlled and were used for illicit purposes, including commercial bribery. The company's tone at the top was inconsistent with an effective FCPA compliance program and created a corporate culture in which bribery was tolerated and even rewarded at the highest levels of the company. Employees obtained large amounts of cash from cash desks, which were sometimes transported in suitcases across international borders for bribery. Authorizations for payments were placed on post-it notes and later removed to eradicate any permanent record. Siemens used numerous slush funds, off-books accounts maintained at unconsolidated entities, and a system of business consultants and intermediaries to facilitate the corrupt payments. Siemens failed to implement adequate internal controls to detect and prevent violations of the FCPA.[15]

Figure 2.2 Focus on Transactions: Siemens FCPA Settlement. (Criminal Fines of over $1.6 Billion.)

The international entrepreneur should always be cautious about activities that may involve the corruption of foreign officials. National laws outlaw the payment of bribes in order to obtain a service, contract, license, approval, or other regulatory consideration from a government official. Unfortunately, anti-corruption laws in some countries are not enforced, and bribes are openly solicited.[11] The court in *Lamb v. Philip Morris, Inc.*[12] ruled that the FCPA does not provide a private right of action. Thus, a businessperson cannot bring a lawsuit against a competitor for obtaining a contract in violation of the FCPA. The businessperson is limited to bringing the alleged violation to the attention of the Justice Department.

FCPA Amendments state that minor payments made to "any employee of a foreign government or any department, agency, or instrumentality thereof whose duties are essentially ministerial or clerical" are not a bribe under the FCPA. The exception for minor payment or expenditures has been narrowly construed by the courts. Two other important definitional changes were made by the 1988 Amendments. First, the definition of "foreign official" was broadened to include "any officer or employee of a public international organization." Second, the "knowing" requirement for criminal liability under the FCPA was substantially modified. Actual knowledge of a bribe is not required. Instead, the government needs to only prove that a party had reason to know that some of its money would be used to bribe a foreign official. A party can be found guilty of bribery if the party is aware that another person is "engaging in such conduct, that such circumstance exists, or that such result is *substantially certain* to occur." When knowledge of the existence of a particular circumstance is required for an offense, such knowledge is established if a person is "aware of a *high probability* of the existence of such circumstance."

The type of circumstantial evidence that can be used to satisfy the "reason to know" (criminal intent) requirement was illustrated in *SEC v. Tesoro Petroleum Corp.*[13] In that case, a company was prosecuted even though it did not directly pay or authorize bribes. It hired a foreign agent to obtain contracts from a foreign government. The evidence included the payment of a commission considerably larger than the market rate, a disproportionately small contract price compared to the commission paid, and a large degree of secrecy including the use of Swiss bank accounts and when no written contract is entered into with the foreign agent. These facts showed the company did not exercise *due diligence* and take steps to ensure they formed a business relationship with a reputable partner or representative. Third-parties must be investigated to determine if they are qualified, whether they have ties to the government, the number and reputation of their clients, and their reputation with local bankers and other business associates.

The *Tesoro* and *Liebo* cases show that a number of red flags (indicates or draws attention to a problem or irregularity) need to be addressed in any company's anti-corruption compliance program. Investigating signs and "red flags" are especially important where express and direct bribery is not present. Red flags include paying a commission substantially higher than the going rate, the existence of family or business ties between an agent and government officials, and commission payments made in a third country. These red flags indicate the potential for third-party bribery. A company's compliance program should require potential agents to disclose past or current ties to government officials, a report on the agent's character (reference checks), and the use of a carefully worded written agreement with the agent. The written agreement should expressly state that the agent is working as an independent agent and is not authorized to make any illicit payments on behalf of the principal. The agreement should include a clause that requires the agent to comply with all laws and regulations of both the home and host countries.

The standards of "substantial certainty" or "high probability" of **third-party bribery** are illustrated in the *Liebo* case. Third-party bribery exists when a company hires another party and has "reason to know" that a portion of the money paid would be used to bribe. A third-party may be a joint venture partner or an agent. The court found that illegal bribery can be proven circumstantially. In *Liebo*, the court held that giving airline tickets as a "gift" to a cousin of a foreign official was sufficient to sustain a conviction, where approval of the foreign official was necessary to obtain contracts. This case shows that third-party bribery is just as illegal as "direct" bribery.

Anti-bribery law does not distinguish between violations involving direct bribery, third-party bribery, and bribery committed by a controlled subsidiary. Whether a parent company is liable for the acts of a foreign subsidiary depends on the degree of ownership and control exerted by the parent over its subsidiary. If it is a majority owner, then it is vicariously (secondarily) liable for the violations of its subsidiary. If it owns less than 50 percent, then it need only make a good-faith effort to have its subsidiary comply with anti-bribery law.

United States v. Liebo

923 F.2d 1308 (8th Cir. 1991)

Judge. Liebo appeals convictions for violating the bribery provisions of the Foreign Corrupt Practices Act and making a false statement to a government agency. The background leading to Liebo's conviction has all the earmarks of a modern fable. Liebo was vice-president in charge of the Aerospace Division of NAPCO International. NAPCO's primary business consisted of selling military equipment and supplies. Liebo flew to Niger to get the President of Niger's approval of a supply contract and met with Ali Tiemogo. Tiemogo was the chief of maintenance for the Niger Air Force. Liebo told him that his company would make "some gestures" if he helped get the contract approved. When asked whether this promise played a role in deciding to recommend approval of the contract, Tiemogo stated, "I can't say 'no,' I cannot say 'yes,' at that time," but "it encouraged me." Following Tiemogo's recommendation, the President signed the contract.

Tahirou Barke, Tiemogo's cousin, testified that he returned to Niger to get married. After the wedding, he and his wife honeymooned in Paris, Stockholm, and London. He testified that before leaving for Niger, he informed Liebo of his honeymoon plans, and Liebo offered to pay for his airline tickets which cost $2,028, as a gift.

Over a two-and-a-half-year period, NAPCO made payments totaling

$130,000 to three "commission agents." The practice of using agents and paying them commissions on international contracts are common and accepted business practices in third-world countries. NAPCO issued commission checks to "agents," identified as Amadou Mailele, Tiemogo's brother-in-law and Fatouma Boube, Tiemogo's sister-in-law. Mailele and Boube set up bank accounts in Paris. A superior of Liebo approved the "commission payments." To obtain foreign military sales financing, NAPCO was required to submit a Contractor's Certification and Agreement. In the Contractor's certification, Liebo certified that "no rebates, gifts or gratuities have been given to officers, officials, or employees" of the Niger government. Following a three-week trial, the jury acquitted Liebo on all charges except the count concerning NAPCO's purchase of Barke's honeymoon airline tickets and the related false statement count.

Liebo contends that there was insufficient evidence to show that the airline tickets were "given to obtain or retain business." Second, he argues that there was no evidence to show that his gift of honeymoon tickets was done "corruptly." This court believes that there is sufficient evidence that the airplane tickets were given to obtain or retain business. The relationship between Barke and Tiemogo allowed a reasonable jury to *infer* that Liebo made the gift to Barke intending to buy Tiemogo's help in getting the contracts approved. Accordingly, a reasonable jury could conclude that the gift was given "to obtain or retain business."

Next, Liebo contends that his conviction should be reversed because the court erred in the giving of jury instructions distinguishing a "gift or gratuity" from a bribe. Here, the court instructed the jury that the term "corruptly" meant that "the offer, promise to pay, payment or authorization of payment must be intended to induce the recipient to misuse his official position or to influence someone else to do so," and that "an act is 'corrupt' if done voluntarily and intentionally, and with a bad purpose of accomplishing either an unlawful end or result, or a lawful end or result by some unlawful method or means." We agree.

Case Highlights

- Third-party bribery includes the use of agents to make payments to government officials and indirect payments to persons associated with a government official
- Merely classifying something as a gift or a donation is not conclusive in assessing whether it constitutes a bribe. Intent may be inferred from circumstantial evidence
- Despite the multimillion-dollar size of the government contracts, the purchase of two airline tickets meet the threshold of "anything of value" requirement and is not considered a "minor expense."

Accounting Provisions

The FCPA requires companies doing international business to "make and keep records in *reasonable* detail, that accurately and fairly reflect the transactions and dispositions of assets." Failure to do so subjects that person or company to the same types of fines as imposed under the bribery provisions. Thus, a company can violate the law without committing any acts of bribery. The problem with the accounting requirements is that the law does not define what is meant by "reasonable." It does not provide a materiality standard to assist in the determination of what needs to be reported.

Reasonableness was subsequently determined not to require a company to show an unrealistic degree of exactitude. Implied in the notion of the prudent businessperson is the use of a benefit–cost approach. Therefore, the accounting requirements are satisfied if the system of internal accounting controls is sufficient to provide reasonable assurance that (1) transactions are executed in accordance with management's specific authorizations; (2) transactions are recorded to permit preparation of financial statements in conformity with generally accepted accounting principles; (3) access to assets is permitted only with specific management authorization; and (4) accountability for assets is reviewed at reasonable intervals. Criminal liability under the accounting provisions is limited to those who *knowingly* falsify records.

OECD Convention on Combating Bribery

The magnitude of foreign bribery has resulted in movement at the international and regional levels. The OECD Convention on Combating Bribery of Foreign Public Officials in International Business Transactions[14] went into effect in 1999. The OECD Convention sets forth the following goals:

- to achieve the highest sustainable economic growth and employment and a rising standard of living in member countries, while maintaining financial stability, and to contribute to the development of the world economy;
- to contribute to the expansion of world trade on a multilateral and nondiscriminatory basis in accordance with international obligations.

The Convention provides a framework and guidance to signatories regarding the steps to be taken to combat bribery of public officials. It defines public officials broadly to include public agencies, public enterprises, and public international organizations. Like the FCPA, it adopts an extraterritorial approach to the international bribery of foreign government officials. It mandates that countries prosecute their nationals for offenses committed abroad. In the accounting area, it requires that each signatory enact "dissuasive civil, administrative, or criminal penalties for omissions and falsifications in respect of books, records, accounts, and financial statements." Companies will be required to disclose, on their financial statements, any potential liabilities under the Convention that rise to the level of a material contingent liability. The Convention provides a four-phase process: (1) design of anti-bribery law; (2) legislative and practical implementation; (3) enforcement; and (4) analysis. The OECD performs individual reviews of countries. In 2017, it did a Phase IV review of the Czech Republic for compliance with the Convention, making 17 recommendations. In 2019, it issued a "Phase IV Two-Year Follow-up Report," finding that the country fully implemented four recommendations, partially implemented 10 recommendations, and did not implement three recommendations. Figure 2.3 provides a summary of the OECD Report. It illustrates the many facets found in an anti-corruption scheme or programme.

Positive Comments

- Detection of foreign bribery by Financial Intelligence Unit;
- prosecuting its first case of foreign bribery;
- Czech anti-money laundering (AML) system was expanded to include more areas subject to suspicious transaction reports (STRs);
- additional training to uncover bribery through tax audits;
- introduced an exemption from liability for legal persons that have made "all efforts that can be justly required to prevent the commission of an unlawful act" and published a Guide on what constitutes an efficient compliance management system (CMS);
- Supreme Public Prosecutor's Office has conducted roundtables on "criminal liability of legal entities and compliance" to raise public awareness.

Shortcomings

- Measures have not been adopted to guarantee greater independence to prosecutors;
- absence of appropriate protection from discriminatory or disciplinary action especially for private sector employees who report suspected acts of foreign bribery;
- insufficient staff allocated to media monitoring;
- no law providing comprehensive whistleblower protections;
- has not adopted legislative measures to protect foreign bribery investigations and prosecutions from undue interference;
- judgments (including agreements on guilt and punishment) concerning foreign bribery are not automatically published;
- have not ensured that penalties for false accounting are effective, proportionate, and dissuasive.

Neutral Comments

- No training on how the payments to foreign public officials are laundered, although there is a plan to deliver such training;
- Czech National Bank employees obligated to report all suspicions of foreign bribery, but insufficient training to identify red flags for foreign bribery;
- Czech Republic plans to increase operational resources of National Organised Crime Agency with six positions specialized in foreign bribery and money laundering is positive, but analytics do not serve the detection and investigation of foreign bribery, and nothing indicates that investigating foreign bribery has become a priority;
- have not increased the confiscation of proceeds of crime in foreign bribery cases to raise awareness to ensure a wider use of monetary sanctions;
- extensive efforts to provide training to prosecutors and judges have not included training on calculating appropriate penalties in foreign bribery cases;
- the number of money laundering convictions has increased, but there is an absence of money laundering convictions related to foreign bribery.

Figure 2.3 Summary of OECD Report on Czech Republic.

UK Bribery Act 2010

The UK Bribery Act covers four distinct "categories of offenses": (1) bribing another person; (2) taking bribes; (3) bribing foreign public officials; and (4) the failure of a commercial organization to prevent bribery."[15] The UK Bribery Act "applies extraterritorially, reaching any individual 'closely connected' with the United Kingdom and, with respect to the corporate offense of failing to prevent bribery, any commercial organization that carries on a business or part of a business in the United Kingdom." The UK Ministry has provided six guiding principles:

1. *Proportionate Procedures*: "A commercial organisation's procedures to prevent bribery by persons associated with it are proportionate to the bribery risks it faces and to the nature, scale, and complexity of its activities."
2. *Top-Level Commitment*: "The top-level management of a commercial organisation is committed to preventing bribery by persons associated with it. They foster a culture within the organisation in which bribery is never acceptable."
3. *Risk Assessment*: "The commercial organisation assesses the nature and extent of its exposure to potential external and internal risks of bribery on its behalf by persons associated with it. The assessment is periodic, informed, and documented."
4. *Due Diligence*: "The commercial organisation applies due diligence procedures, taking a proportionate and risk-based approach, in respect of persons who perform or will perform services for or on behalf of the organisation, in order to identify and mitigate bribery risks."
5. *Communication and Training*: "The commercial organization seeks to ensure that its bribery prevention policies and procedures are embedded and understood throughout the organisation through internal and external communication, including training that is proportionate to the risks it faces."
6. *Monitoring and Review*: "The commercial organisation monitors and reviews procedures designed to prevent bribery by persons associated with it and makes improvements where necessary."

The UK Serious Fraud Office is assigned the tasks of investigation and enforcement, as well as providing additional guidelines and policy statements. Its policy is that facilitation payments are bribes. It gives as an example where a government official is given money or goods to speed up the performance of an existing duty, which is not illegal under the routine "government expenditure exception" of the FCPA. However, the UK Act recognizes "business expenditure" as excusable payments, such as bona fide hospitality or promotional or other legitimate business expenditure, which is similar to the FCPA's "bona fide expenditure" exception.

Corporate self-reporting can benefit the company accused of violating the Bribery Act and may prevent a prosecution of their violations: "The fact that a corporate body has reported itself will be a relevant consideration to the extent set out in the *UK Guidance on Corporate Prosecutions*." In order to receive credit for self-reporting, the Guidance requires that the self-report must form part of a "genuinely proactive approach adopted by the corporate management team when the offending conduct is brought to their notice."[16]

Anti-Corruption Clause

The ICC (International Chamber of Commerce) Anti-Corruption Clause[17] incorporates ICC Rules on Combating Corruption. Inclusion in a contract demonstrates a party's commitment to maintaining a corporate anti-corruption compliance program. The corruption clause and an anti-corruption program are important given the global supply chain. This is especially important when a company's home country prohibits the giving of bribes, as does the American FCPA or countries that have adopted the OECD Convention, which prohibits third-party bribery. The corruption clause allows a party to terminate a contract if the other party allegedly violates the ICC Rules on Combating Corruption and does not remedy the situation or does not take adequate anti-corruption preventive measures.

Corrupt practices include bribery in connection with public or private procurement contract awards, regulatory permits, taxation, customs, and judicial and legislative proceedings; extortion and solicitation; trading in influence; and laundering the proceeds from corrupt practices. On the issue of gifts and hospitality, the ICC recommends that enterprises establish procedures to ensure that any gift giving: (1) comply with the law; (2) are reasonable and bona fide; (3) do not affect (or appear to affect) the recipient's independence of judgment toward the giver; (4) are not contrary to the known provisions of the recipient's code of conduct; and (5) are offered or received neither too frequently nor at an inappropriate time.

Article 2 of the ICC rules applies to the issue of third-party bribery. Companies often hire third parties, such as agents, consultants, sales representatives, customs agents, resellers, subcontractors, franchisees, lawyers, accountants, or similar intermediaries. The company should instruct third parties with which they are engaged: (1) not to commit any act of corruption on behalf of the company; (2) not to use the company as a conduit for any corrupt practice; (3) that the third party's hiring is only to the extent appropriate for the regular conduct of the company's business; and (4) that the company will not pay them more than what is appropriate for their legitimate services.

Sentencing Guidelines for Organizations and Importance of Effective Compliance Programs

Organizations are subject to fines, probation, ordered to make restitution and issue public notices of conviction, and exposed to applicable forfeiture statutes. Under the guidelines, the corporate or organizational entity can be held vicariously liable for the criminal acts of its employees. The guidelines also allow for the mitigation or reduction of fines for those companies that demonstrate **due diligence** in attempting to prevent misconduct. They provide for more lenient treatment of corporate executives who implemented an ethics program. Criminal liability can attach to an organization whenever an employee of the organization commits an act within the apparent *scope of employment*, even if the employee acted directly contrary to company policy and instructions. An entire organization, despite its best efforts to prevent wrongdoing in its ranks, can still be held criminally liable for its employees' illegal actions. Factors used by countries to determine criminal penalties for bribery, fraud, and other types of misconduct include aggravating (increased penalties) and mitigating (decreased penalties) factors. Mitigating credit is generally contingent upon *prompt reporting* to the authorities and the *noninvolvement of high-level personnel*[18] in the actual offensive conduct.

Federal Sentencing Guidelines for Organizations[19] of the U.S. determines criminal penalties by using six factors that the sentencing court must consider. The four factors that increase the ultimate punishment of an organization are: (1) the involvement in or tolerance of criminal activity; (2) prior history of the organization; (3) violation of an order; and (4) obstruction of justice. The two factors that mitigate the ultimate punishment of an organization are (5) the existence of an effective compliance and ethics program and (6) self-reporting, cooperation, or acceptance of responsibility. It provides for calculating a culpability score to determine the appropriate penalty. The calculation begins at five, and then points are added based upon a five-point scale for the six factors. It also allows penalties to be lessened if the company provides substantial assistance in the investigation or prosecution of another organization or in the investigation or prosecution of an individual not directly affiliated with the company. See Figure 2.4 *Focus on Transactions*: "Case Example: Fines under the Federal Sentencing Guidelines for Organizations."

The penalties can be reduced if the company has an existing compliance program, along with exhibiting due diligence in policing the program. It is in a company's best interest to develop a compliance program in such areas as bribery, export regulations, environmental compliance, and health and safety laws (see Figure 2.5 *Doing Business Internationally*: "Seven Criteria for an Effective Compliance Program").

Again, the levels of base fines are based upon two calculations: the seriousness of the offense and the culpability of the organization. Offenses in which penalties can widely vary based on the above factors include customs violations,

	Maximum	*Minimum*
Existence of compliance program, self-reporting crime, cooperation with government investigation	\$2.74 million	\$685,000
Compliance program only	\$10.96 million	\$5.48 million
No program, reporting, or cooperation	\$27.4 million	\$13.7 million
No program, reporting, or cooperation, and involvement by high-ranking personnel	\$54.8 million	\$27.4 million

Figure 2.4 Focus on Transactions: Case Example: Fines under the Federal Sentencing Guidelines for Organizations.

Establish Standards and Procedures to Prevent and Detect Criminal Conduct

***

Oversight by High-Level Personnel

***

Due Care in Delegating Discretionary Authority

***

Effective Communications at all Levels

***

Reasonable Steps to Achieve Compliance (systems for monitoring, auditing, and reporting wrongdoing without fear of reprisal)

***

Consistent Enforcement and Disciplinary Mechanisms

***

Reasonable Steps to Prevent Recurrence of a Violation

Figure 2.5 Doing Business Internationally: Seven Criteria for an Effective Compliance Program.

bid rigging, fraud, antitrust violations, transportation of hazardous materials, environmental crimes, commercial bribery, and copyright infringement.

Human Rights Violations

This section begins with the central premise that it is always unethical to violate an individual's human rights. Issues include whether there are differences between "human rights" and "fundamental rights." There is general agreement on a set of "core" human rights, such as freedom of religion, right to due process when accused of a crime, and the equality of all human beings. Modern "rights" documents have expanded the list of human rights to include broader fundamental rights, such as the right to work and the right to a living wage. The

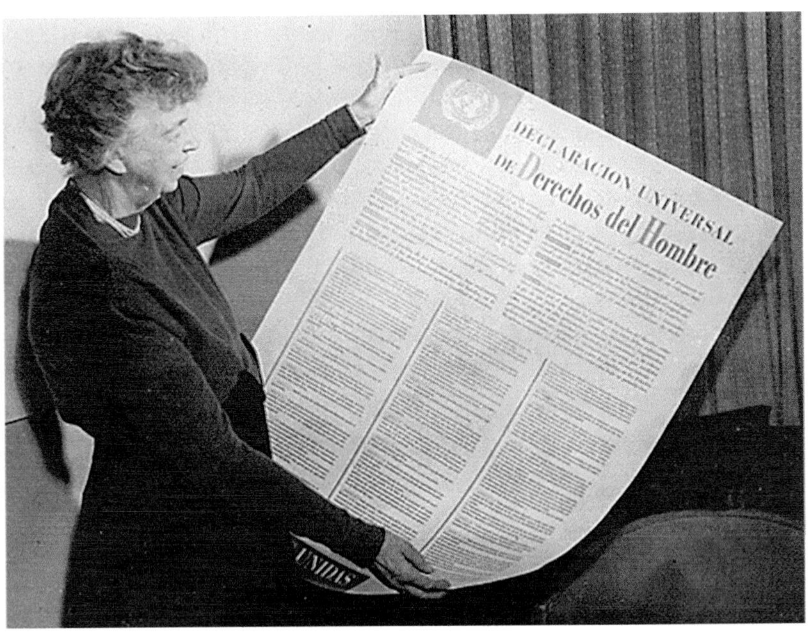

Image 2.2 Eleanor Roosevelt.
Source: UN Human Rights, WikiCommons.

United Nations Universal Declaration of Human Rights is considered a fundamental human rights document that sets the scope of human rights and issues relating to human rights violations.

Universal Declaration of Human Rights

(Adopted by the United Nations General Assembly on December 10, 1948)

Article 2 states that "everyone is entitled to certain rights and freedoms, without distinction of any kind, such as race, color, sex, language, religion, political or other opinion, national or social origin, property, birth, or other status." This nondiscrimination principle applies to the enumerated rights listed in the declaration. Article 3 provides the general recognition that "everyone has the right to life, liberty, and security of person." Other articles provide specific rights, including the right against torture or degrading treatment (Article 5), right to recognition everywhere as a person under the law (Article 6), right to an effective remedy for acts violating fundamental rights (Article 8), right to a fair and public hearing by an impartial tribunal (Article 10), freedom of movement (Article 13), right to own property (Article 17), freedom of religion (Article 19), right to take part in government (Article 21), and the right to social security, including "economic, social, and cultural rights indispensable for his dignity" (Article 22). In the area of nondiscrimination, Article 7 states that: "all are entitled to equal protection against discrimination." Article 23 provides that "everyone, without any discrimination, has the right to equal pay for equal work." Quality of life and a living wage are considered fundamental human rights. Article 23 states that everyone has a right to work, to just and favorable working conditions, to a just remuneration ensuring for himself and his family "an existence worthy of human dignity." Article 25 further defines just remuneration as one that provides a "standard of living adequate for health and well-being, including food, clothing, housing and medical care and necessary social services, and the right to security in the event of unemployment, sickness, disability, or old age."

For information on another fundamental human rights doctrine, the EU **Charter of Fundamental Rights**, which was enacted as EU law in 2009, see Chapter 6, "European Union." Compare the 1948 United Nations Declaration with the 2009 EU Charter to see the broadening of the scope of human or fundamental rights.

Bhopal Disaster

The Union Carbide India Limited (UCIL) pesticide plant in Bhopal, India exploded, exposing a half-million people to toxic gases and chemicals. The large size of the number of people exposed was due to the construction of "shanty towns" next to and around the plant. It is estimated that about 16,000 people died due to gas-related illnesses, and more than 100,000 have experienced serious medical conditions. The parent company, Union Carbide Corporation

(UCCorp) of the U.S., owned 50.9 percent, with the Indian government and Indian nationals owning 49.1 percent. UCCorp chairman Warren Anderson, together with a technical team, immediately traveled to India. Upon arrival, Anderson was placed under house arrest. UCCorp organized a team of international medical experts, as well as supplies and equipment, to work with the local Bhopal medical community.

UCIL's plant was managed by an entirely Indian workforce and was subject to safety inspections by Indian government agencies. The Indian government enacted the Bhopal Gas Leak Act to gain status as the legal representative of all the victims.

India brought a lawsuit against UCCorp in the U.S. The court dismissed the complaint by holding that Bhopal, India was the proper venue. The Bhopal disaster has become a classic ethics case study and variation of the facts is useful in developing additional hypothetical case studies. A number of "facts" are provided here to encourage discussion of legal and ethical issues related to the disaster.

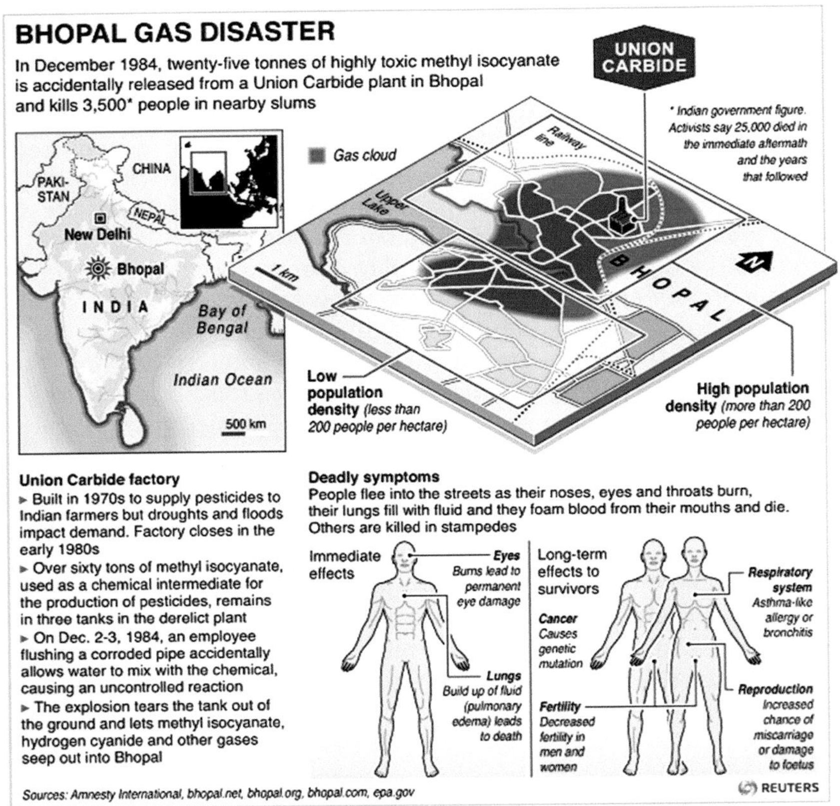

Image 2.3 Bhopal.

- Fact 1: The plant was under-maintained with decaying facilities, a weak attitude toward safety, and an undertrained workforce.
- Fact 2: Management and the local government underinvested in safety and allowed for a dangerous working environment.
- Fact 3: "Serious communication problems and management gaps between Union Carbide and its Indian operation," characterized by "the parent company's hands-off approach to its overseas operation" and "cross-cultural barriers."
- Fact 4: There was no disaster plan in place at the time of the disaster.
- Fact 5: The UCCorp chairman was released within 24 hours of his arrest on bail of $2,100 and was flown out on an Indian government plane.
- Fact 6: Chemicals abandoned at the plant continue to leak and pollute the groundwater; whether the chemicals pose a health hazard is disputed.

The above facts should be applied to the issues listed in Figure 2.6.

Ethics requires that MNCs do more than merely disclose or comply with host country regulations. UCCorp argued that it was not morally responsible for the Bhopal disaster[20] is difficult to support under the duty not to harm. Union Carbide argued that it lacked sufficient control over the safety and operations of the Indian plant. It argued that its independent subsidiary, which was 49 percent owned by the Indian government and citizens, was responsible for the plant. Furthermore, it argued that it had no responsibility for the safety of the plant because all management and safety personnel were Indian and the Indian government controlled safety inspections and standards. In fact, the blueprints for the Bhopal plant provided by UCCorp were rejected in favor of an Indian-designed alternative. Does the forced abdication of all control by UCCorp to the Indian government absolve it of moral responsibility for the accident, or is it simply an excuse used by the parent company to avoid liability? Critics would argue that such companies have a moral responsibility not to locate hazardous plants in a foreign country unless they retain sufficient control. Should the fact that the pesticides produced by the Bhopal plant helped feed millions of Indians be entered into this ethical calculation?

- To what extent should multinational companies maintain identical standards at home and abroad, regardless how lax the laws are in the host country?
- How wise are laws that require plants to be staffed entirely by local employees?
- What is the responsibility of corporations and governments in allowing the use of otherwise safe products that become dangerous because of local conditions (e.g., proximity of residences in Bhopal)?
- Should certain kinds of plants not be located in developing nations? Was the true moral responsibility for Bhopal that of the Indian government because of its local participation and management requirements (which reduce parent company control and the flow of technical expertise)?
- Did the parent company have an ethical responsibility to protect workers and the public? Does this responsibility have priority over the duty to earn a profit?
- Does the absence of sufficient government regulations excuse the parent company from any legal responsibility?
- Did the parent company have a social responsibility not to locate a plant in a foreign country where it did not have sufficient control? Should a parent company be held liable as parents are held liable for the damage done by their children?

Figure 2.6 Focus on Transactions: Ethical Issues Raised by Bhopal Disaster.

International Standards

Standards refer to government regulations pertaining to labor, health, safety, and environmental concerns. A variety of "voluntary standards" also exist, advanced by either trade associations or nongovernmental organizations (NGOs). The **International Labour Organization** is an example of an NGO that publishes standards for the workplace. Standards to ensure adequate levels of quality, labor, and environmental sensitivity in the production and marketing of goods and services are important and evolving. The wide variety of national standards in these areas produces a number of problems. First, it promotes the lowest common denominator in the production of goods. Companies motivated by short-term profits will attempt to cut costs by searching for countries with weak environmental and labor laws. Second, a company seeking to market its products internationally has to contend with differing standards that may act as barriers to importing a company's goods into various countries.

One solution to both problems has been the development of international standards, which can reduce barriers to trade and ensure minimum levels of quality, labor, and environmental compliance. However, each country has the sovereign right to set their own environmental, health, quality, and safety standards. So, since the goal of complete harmonization is unrealistic, countries will continue to have different levels of standards. An important trend is the voluntary adoption of standards that will be recognized as socially responsible. Companies are incentivized to obtain standards certifications to satisfy social responsibility codes, increase the marketability of their goods, and to satisfy national standards requirements or to smoothly import goods into different countries.

Examples of international standards are those issued by the **International Organization for Standardization (ISO)**. The ISO was established in 1947 and has 165 member countries. Companies who want to be ISO-certified voluntarily apply their standards and some countries have adopted ISO standards as national law. Companies have a number of purposes for obtaining ISO certifications including: (1) the World Trade Organization requires members to adhere to international standards of the type developed by the ISO; (2) standards help companies save on costs; (3) standards reassure customers about the trustworthiness of the company and its products; and (4) standards have been shown to contribute to economic growth.[21] Figure 2.7 lists the different types of ISO standards that are available.

The mission of the ISO is to promote the development of standardization in order to facilitate the international exchange of goods and services and to develop cooperation in the spheres of intellectual, scientific, technological, and

ISO 9000: Quality Management	ISO 26000: Social Responsibility
ISO 14000: Environmental Management	ISO 27001: Information Security
ISO 19600: Compliance Management	ISO 50001: Energy Management
ISO 22000: Food Management	ISO 31000: Risk Management

Figure 2.7 ISO Standards.

economic activity. International standardization is well-established for many technologies in such diverse fields as information processing and communications, textiles, packaging, distribution of goods, energy production and utilization, shipbuilding, banking, and financial services.

The ISO has been successful in raising the level of awareness in areas of product quality and the environment. Its certifications under ISO 9000 and ISO 14000 provide both practical and ethical benefits to companies. From a practical perspective, products with these certifications are likely to find fewer obstacles in the area of the importation of goods. Most countries recognize the significance of ISO certifications. From a business perspective, ISO certifications can be used by companies for branding purposes as evidence of their commitment to producing quality products and being an environmentally conscious company.

The most recognized international standard is the **ISO 9000** (Quality Management). The purpose of the ISO 9000 Standard is to facilitate international commerce by providing a single set of quality standards that people everywhere recognize and respect. The ISO 9000 Standard applies to all types of organizations. The ISO provides guidelines for developing quality management systems. To become certified, an independent auditor must verify that the company's factory, laboratory, or office meets ISO quality standards. They issue an official certificate and record the company's name in their registry. The company can then promote the quality of its products and services as ISO 9000 certified.

ISO 14000 (Environmental Management) is a series of international, voluntary environmental management standards. ISO 14000 standards effectively address the needs of organizations worldwide by providing a common framework for managing environmental issues. ISO 14000 standards require a company to establish an environmental management system (EMS). An EMS enables an organization of any size or type to control the impact of its activities, products, or services on the natural environment. The benefits of installing an EMS include: (1) assuring customers of a commitment to demonstrable environmental management; (2) maintaining good public and community relations; (3) obtaining insurance at reasonable cost; (4) reducing incidents that result in liability; and (5) facilitating the attainment of permits and authorizations. The ISO 14000 includes organization-oriented standards and product-oriented standards. Organization-oriented standards provide comprehensive guidance for establishing, maintaining, and evaluating an EMS. Product-oriented standards are concerned with determining the environmental impact of products and services over their life cycles and include environmental labeling and disclosures. Product-oriented standards help an organization communicate specific environmental information to consumers.

ISO 26000's (Social Responsibility) intent is to use corporate social responsibility to improve lives of workers, natural environments, and communities. It lays the basis for a common understanding of social responsibility, as well as promoting communication, transparency, and trust among stakeholders. The seven principles of ISO 26000 include: accountability; transparency; ethical behavior; respect and consideration of all stakeholders; respect for the rule of law; international norms of behavior; and human rights. Over 60 countries have adopted the Standard.

The Council on Economic Priorities Accreditation Agency has used the ISO model to develop a **Social Accountability Standard.** The SA 8000 standard ensures that a company and its suppliers provide an equitable and safe workplace for their employees. The SA 8000 certification requires a company to forbid child or forced labor, to respect the right of workers to unionize, limit the working week to 48 hours, provide a safe working environment, and pay a living wage. The SA 8000 allows companies to demonstrate a commitment to international human rights standards. Firms that wish to avoid bad publicity should adopt the SA 8000 standards as a preventive measure.

The ISO has also developed hundreds of codes besides the ones listed in Figure 2.7. For example, the ISO has developed international codes for country names, currencies, and languages that have helped to eliminate duplication and incompatibilities in the collection, processing, and dissemination of information. Universally understandable codes play an important role in both automated and manual documentation.

The activities of the EU deserve special attention. EU requirements include the placement of a **CE mark** by the manufacturer on all regulated products. Importers who obtain the CE mark will be able to gain access to the markets of all EU members. The CE mark asserts that the product meets mandatory health, safety, and environmental requirements of the EU. The EU also developed the **EU Ecolabel.** Products without the Ecolabel may still enter the EU, but the label, if used, replaces the existing national equivalents. In order to obtain an Ecolabel, the manufacturer must show that its products are less harmful to the environment than other similar products.

Ethics of Advertising

How a company markets its products internationally plays a major role in whether it is successful. Failure to consider the differences in national cultural and legal approaches to advertising is a recipe for failure. Internationally, the development of supranational rules of advertising has been sporadic. The best example of a multinational effort is the Marketing Supervision Network. About 20 other countries have agreed to cooperate in resolving advertising disputes that cross national boundaries.[22] At the regional level, the EU has enacted two directives aimed at harmonizing European law on misleading and **comparative advertising.**[23] Before the enactment of Directive 97/55/EC on Comparative Advertising, such advertising was banned in Italy, Belgium, and Luxembourg, and was highly restricted in such countries as Germany and France. In contrast, in the U.S. comparative advertising is legal.[24]

The Directive legalizes the use of comparative advertising that is defined as "any advertising, which explicitly or by implication identifies a competitor or goods or services offered by a competitor." However, comparative advertising is permitted only if: (1) it does not mislead; (2) it compares goods or services meeting the same needs or serving the same purpose; (3) it objectively compares one or more material, relevant, verifiable, and representative features of the goods and services; (4) it does not create confusion in the marketplace between the advertiser and a competitor or with the competitor's trademarks or trade names; (5) it does not discredit or denigrate the trademarks, trade names, goods, or services of a competitor; (6) for products with designation of origin, it relates in each case to products with the same designation; and (7) it does not present goods or services as imitations or replicas of trademarked goods or services.

The EU Directive also requires that the advertiser demonstrate promptly the accuracy of its comparative claim. "Comparison on the basis of subjective factors, and opinion-based puffery" are therefore prohibited under the Directive. The use of "objectively" administered consumer preference tests are not permitted. An exporter should not assume that its comparative advertisements are automatically legal under the new Directive. This is especially true in countries that have traditionally prohibited such advertisements.

Professional Standards of International Advertising

The ICC has sponsored a number of ethical codes relating to international advertising and marketing, including the International Code of Advertising Practice, International Code of Sales Promotion, International Code of Practice on Direct Marketing, Code on Environmental Advertising, Code on Sponsorship, and the International Code of Marketing and Social Research Practice. The ICC International Code of Advertising Practice (see Figure 2.8 *Doing Business Internationally*: "ICC International Code of Advertising Practice") was first issued in 1937. The ICC code applies to advertising in *any* medium for the sale of goods *or* services.

Article 2: Decency

Should not offend prevailing standards of decency.

Article 3: Honesty

Should not exploit consumers' lack of experience or knowledge.

Article 4: Social Responsibility

Should not condone any form of discrimination, play on fear, or play on superstition.

Article 5: Truthful Presentation

Should not mislead with regard to characteristics, value, terms of guarantee, intellectual property rights, or official recognition or approval and should not misuse research results.

Article 6: Comparisons

Comparison to other products should be based on facts that can be substantiated and should not be unfairly selected.

Article 7: Denigration

Should not denigrate any firm, organization, profession, or product.

Article 8: Testimonials

No use of personal testimonials or endorsements unless genuine, verifiable, relevant, and based upon personal experience or knowledge. Testimonials that have become obsolete should not be used.

Article 10: Exploitation of Goodwill

Should not infringe upon intellectual property or goodwill.

Article 11: Imitation

Should not imitate other advertisements or unduly imitate others' advertising campaigns in other countries.

Article 12: Identification

Should not be made to appear as an editorial or news item. Should be presented so that it is readily recognized as an advertisement.

Article 14: Children

Applies to children as defined as minors under applicable national laws. Should not exploit their inexperience or give unreal perception of the true value of the product. For example, the use of the word *only* should be avoided. Should not directly appeal to children to persuade their parents to buy the advertised products.

Article 15: Guarantees

Should not contain any reference to a guarantee that does not provide the consumer with rights additional to those provided by law.

Figure 2.8 Doing Business Internationally: ICC International Code of Advertising Practice.

The introduction to the Code describes it as a voluntary, self-regulating ethical code but noted its use in a legal proceeding: "The Code is designed primarily as an instrument of self-discipline, but it is also intended for the use of courts as a reference document within the framework of applicable law."[25] The underlying principle of the Code is that "all advertising should be legal, decent, and truthful."

Articles 3 through 17 provide details regarding the meaning of "decent and truthful." Article 18 allots responsibilities to professional advertising agencies and any firm or company that advertises. Furthermore, anyone employed within these companies or agencies shall be liable to "a degree of responsibility commensurate with their positions." Liability can be levied against both the selling company and its advertising agency, along with responsible officers and employees.

Chapter Summary

1. Three common areas of ethical concern when doing business internationally include: (a) differences between host–home country standards, (b) bribery and corruption, and (c) sustainability and environmental ethics.
2. Two views of international ethics are ethical relativism (culturally determined) and absolutism (universal ethical or moral principles).
3. Schools of ethical thought include: (a) utilitarianism, (b) deontology (Kantian Ethics), (c) ethics of care, (d) virtue ethics, and (e) situation ethics. An integrative approach to ethics holds that if properly applied, the different schools of ethics should produce the same decision or outcome.
4. There are two schools of thought regarding the role of companies in society: (a) the theory of the amoral businessperson that states that a company's only ethical obligation other than to make profits is to obey the law (moral minimum) and (b) corporate social responsibility that states companies are obligated to be good citizens by acting charitably and not harming the environment.
5. The *Caux Round Table Principles for International Business* blend the Western concept of the dignity of all human beings with the Japanese concept of *kyosei*—that a primary value of society is working together for the common good.
6. The Rio Declaration established world standards and goals for environment protection and sustainability.
7. Penalties for criminal misconduct by an organization are sometimes set by sentencing guidelines. Three factors mitigate against the severity of the penalties assessed: (a) effective compliance program; (b) self-reporting; and (c) cooperation in investigation.
8. There is a trend in developing harmonized or international standards relating to goods, services, and employment. Some of the important international standards have been developed by the: (a) International Labor Organization; (b) International Organization for Standardization; and (c) the EU with its CE mark and Ecolabel.

Key Terms

Attorney General Opinion
Benefit–Cost Analysis
Categorical Imperatives
Caux Round Table Principles for International Business
CE Mark
Charter of Fundamental Rights
Comparative Advertising
Conflict of Cultural Traditions
Corporate Codes of Conduct
Cultural Relativism
Declaration on the Right to Development
Distributive Justice
Dominant Considerations
Due Diligence
Ethical Relativism
Ethics of Care
EU Ecolabel
Federal Sentencing Guidelines for Organizations
Foreign Corrupt Practices Act (FCPA)
Hedonism
Incommensurability
Integrative Ethics Approach
International Labour Organization
International Organization for Standardization (ISO)
ISO 9000
ISO 14000
ISO 19600
ISO 26000
Kantian Ethics
Moral Duty
Moral Minimum
Moral Right
Myth of the Amoral Businessperson
Organisation for Economic Co-Operation and Development (OECD)
Organizational Ethics
Routine Government Expenditures
Social Accountability Standard
Subordinate Responsibility
Sustainable Development Goals (SDGs)
Theory of Relative Development
Third-Party Bribery
Transparency International
United Kingdom Bribery Act
United Nations Declaration of Human Rights
Utilitarian Ethics
Virtue Ethics

Chapter Problems

1. How can a parent company insulate itself from liability under the Foreign Corrupt Practices Act for acts of its foreign subsidiaries, affiliates, and partners? See Brown, "Parent-Subsidiary Liability Under the Foreign Corrupt Practices Act," 50 *Baylor Law Review* 1 (1998).
2. Devise a program for your company to ensure compliance with the Foreign Corrupt Practices Act. What is the importance of *corporate culture* to any such compliance program? See Goelzer, "Designing an FCPA Compliance Program: Minimizing the Risks of Improper Foreign Payments," 18 *Northwestern Journal of International Law & Business* 282 (1998). See also Head, "The Development of Compliance Programs: One Company's Experience," 18 *Northwestern Journal of International Law & Business* 535 (1998).

3. What is the difference between a bribe and a facilitation fee? Does it make a difference if payments or bribes are a crime in a foreign country, but such crimes are not enforced? From an ethical point of view, should anti-bribery laws be read broadly or narrowly? Is giving a bribe a victimless crime? Does bribe-giving affect the free-market system?
4. Your company has been trying for more than a year to obtain the assets of a formerly government-owned petroleum business. However, the approval process and review of the contract documents have been held up for months in the government bureaucracy. A government official approaches the Vice President of Acquisitions and suggests that if your company pays the expenses for a ten-day "negotiating" trip for himself and his family to Disney World and Miami, the approval process could be completed within one week. Should your company authorize the expenditure? Would your answer be different if it were a $200 "fee" to expedite the importation of your company's products into the country?
5. You have obtained a government grant to help train physicians in a developing country on new techniques for fighting AIDS. While working within the developing country's Ministry of Disease Control you have uncovered evidence that certain monies received through the International Red Cross had been misappropriated by certain officials in the Ministry. The money was to be used to test and ensure the safety of the country's blood supply. Instead, it seems that the money was used to buy new ambulances for some of the country's hospitals. Should you report this transgression? Do you have any legal duty to report? Do you have an ethical duty to report? If so, to whom? Does the fact that such reporting may jeopardize your relationship with members of the Ministry and the agency that hired you enter into your decision? How can materials on "whistleblowing" be applied to this hypothetical? Do you have an obligation to obtain a sufficient amount of evidence before reporting?
6. Your company transfers you to a foreign subsidiary as an assistant manager of operations. The purpose of the assignment is to be trained by one of the company's "top managers." Soon after arriving you discover that the manager had instituted an unusual accounting system. You have no real evidence, but the talk around the office is that the manager's success is due to his payments to his government connections. It is also rumored that some of the hidden transactions have profited the manager personally. The subsidiary remains one of the most profitable of your company's foreign operations. What do you do?
7. Lord Coke had this to say about bribery: "Though the bribe be small, yet the fault is great." Do you agree that the size of the bribe is important in determining legal or ethical wrongdoing?
8. What are the elements of an effective ethics or environmental compliance program? How would you develop an ethics or environmental compliance program that would satisfy the dictates of the Federal Sentencing Guidelines for Organizations? See Paul Fiorelli, "Fine Reductions through Effective Ethics Programs," 56 *Albany Law Review* 403 (1992); Paul Fiorelli, "The Environmental Sentencing Guidelines for Business Organizations," 22 *Boston College Environmental Affairs Law Review* 481 (1995).

9. It is currently estimated that only 15 percent of middle managers posted overseas by U.S. companies are women, even though women make up nearly half of the middle managers at these companies. What do you think are the reasons for such an imbalance? At the same time, a poll of human resources executives shows that 80 percent of them believed that global work experience was essential for advancement. Can this be seen as the potential for creating a global glass ceiling (ability to be promoted to high management positions)? What can companies do to overcome such bias?
10. In 1971, John Rawls published his masterwork, *A Theory of Justice*. Simply stated, he equated justice with notions of procedural fairness. Rawlsian justice judges a decision or rule on whether it was arrived at through a process of procedural fairness. Thus, a decision is just or ethical if it was fairly made. A decision or rule is fairly made if each person affected by it is given the most extensive basic liberties compatible with the similar rights of others. Furthermore, social and economic inequalities are arranged to the greatest benefit of the least advantaged persons, and such inequalities are attached to positions open to all under conditions of fair equality of opportunity. Although Rawls' approach is targeted at political and not moral theory, its use in dealing with the least advantaged countries of the world may be productive. These rules are to be applied behind a *veil of ignorance* where the parties are unaware of their status or positions (the negotiating parties are unaware of whether they are acting as representatives of the developed or the lesser developed country). How can this approach be used to ethically judge dealings between developed and developing countries? If these rules were applied behind such a veil, then would such dealings likely result in more equitable transactions?
11. One of the negative by-products of the corporate ethics movement is a decrease in employee privacy. In order to ensure ethical compliance in the workplace, employers will feel pressure to monitor employee activities. To discourage employee misbehavior, employers have begun to monitor employee use of the company's e-mail system to discourage its use for personal purposes and as a vehicle of sexual harassment. Some companies have installed video cameras to monitor employee movements. How should companies balance their ethics monitoring with employee privacy concerns? Need they fully disclose to their employees the extent of their monitoring practices?
12. Define and give an example of each of the following concepts:
    1. Ethical Relativism
    2. Distributive Justice
    3. Dominant Consideration
    4. Ethics of Care
    5. Problem of Subordinate Responsibility
    6. Theory of Relative Development
    7. Routine Government Expenditure
    8. Bona Fide Expenditure
    9. Third-Party Bribery
    10. Anti-Corruption Clause

Business Ethics Quiz

1. You are an office manager, and one upper-level manager has repeatedly used the company credit card for personal expenses. How do you handle the situation?
   (a) You do nothing because the person is higher up in the organization.
   (b) You confront the person and hope that it will not affect your job.
   (c) You confront the person and report your finding to a higher-level manager in human resources.
2. You are a middle-level manager with no accounting experience, and a new company policy requires you to sign the balance sheet and tax information for your department. What do you do?
   (a) You sign it because it is required and you are not expected to know whether it is accurate.
   (b) You ask someone more knowledgeable to review the material with you.
   (c) You sign it with the hope of taking an accounting course for future purposes.
3. You are on the hiring committee for a key position at your company. A woman interviews for the job and, although you do not ask, it comes out that she wants to start a family. Can you factor in that there is a likelihood she may leave or take a maternity leave in the near future?
   (a) Yes, you can factor the information into the hiring decision because she volunteered the information.
   (b) No, it is discrimination if you do not hire her based on that information.
   (c) If another candidate has the same record, you can use the information to "break the tie."
4. You have been asked to work with the publications team on a press release for a new product that you worked to develop. However, the product did not turn out as well as promised in earlier press releases. How much do you reveal in the press release?
   (a) You do not reveal the new information, in order to protect the image of your company.
   (b) You write a more mildly enthusiastic, but honest, press release.
   (c) You write a brutally honest press release thinking it will earn the respect of your customers.
5. You are in charge of preparing a budget report for a project that will be presented to the board of directors. Just before the board meeting, the president of the company asks you to leave something negative out of the report and just add it to the next report as a favor. What do you do?
   (a) Yes, since holding the information to the next meeting shouldn't do any harm.
   (b) Yes, but only if the president agrees to return the favor in your year-end bonus.
   (c) No, because one exception to the rule may lead to future exceptions.

Internet Exercises

1. Review the Corruption Perception Index published by Transparency International at http://www.transparency.org.
2. Review the website of *Sweatshop Watch* for recent developments involving the problem of low labor standards in the international production of goods: http://www.sweatshopwatch.org.
3. Review the OECD Anti-bribery Convention and see if and how it has been implemented over the past two decades: http://www.oecd.org/corruption/oecdantibriberyconvention.htm.

Other Internet Sources

Markkula Center for Applied Ethics: www.scu.edu/ethics (database of nearly one thousand links on ethics including business and environmental ethics); see also, **Caux Round Table:** www.cauxroundtable.org (social corporate responsibility). **International Society for Environmental Ethics** at http://www.cep.unt.edu/ISEE.html.

Transparency International: http://www.transparency.org.

OECD Convention on Combating Bribery of Foreign Public Officials: http://www.oecd.org/corruption/oecdantibriberyconvention.htm.

Answers to Business Ethics Quiz

Question 1: (c) Need to report to upper-level officer in human resources to make sure the improper conduct won't continue.

Question 2: (b) Ask someone with expertise to review the financial and accounting materials.

Question 3: (b) Deciding not to hire an applicant because she or he is planning on starting a family is illegal discrimination.

Question 4: (b) It is reasonable to expect that a press release will put a positive spin on the subject of the release. An optimistic press release that is honest should be sufficient, unless the withholding of the information would have major negative consequences.

Question 5: (c) Withholding information from the board of directors is a form of misrepresentation. This may lead to the development of a bad habit, which is a slippery slope toward white-collar crime.

Notes

1 United Nations General Assembly Resolution 41/128 (December 16, 1986).

2 Thomas Donaldson, "Values in Tension: Ethics Away from Home," *Harvard Business Review* (September–October 1996).

3 Carol Gilligan, *In a Different Voice: Psychological Theory and Women's Development* (1982).

4 See R. Moorthy, Richard DeGeorge, Thomas Donaldson, William Ellos, Robert Solomon, and Robert Textor, *Uncompromising Integrity: Motorola's Global Challenge* (1998).
5 Milton Friedman, "The Social Responsibility of Business Is to Increase Profits," *New York Times Magazine* (1970).
6 Francis Fukuyama, *Trust: The Social Virtues and the Creation of Prosperity* (1995).
7 "Dark smoke arising from factories are symbols of our nation's growth and prosperity." Hong Sik Cho, "An Overview of Korean Environmental Law," 29 *Environmental Law* 501 (1999).
8 See https://www.transparency.org/cpi2019.
9 Nicholas Lord, *Regulating Corporate Bribery in International Business* 19 (2014).
10 For a "real world" exercise on bribery and environmental ethics see "Choosing Values: Public–Private Relationships in a Global Economy" in the supplemental materials.
11 See M. Cecilia Arruda, "Business Ethics in Latin America," 16 *Journal of Business Ethics* 1597 (1997) ("deception, bribery, fraud, and dishonest negotiations are means to succeed in private and public organizations in Latin American countries").
12 915 F.2d 1024 (6th Cir. 1990).
13 2 FCPA Rep. (1980).
14 See http://www.oecd.org/corruption/oecdantibriberyconvention.htm.
15 Lawrence Trautman and Kara Altenbaumer-Price, "Lawyers, Guns, and Money: The Bribery Problem and the UK Bribery Act," 47 *The International Lawyer* 482 (2013).
16 Ibid
17 ICC, *Anti-Corruption Clause* (2012) (ICC Publication No. 740E).
18 "High-level personnel of the organization" means an individual who has substantial control over the organization or who has a substantial role in the making of policy within the organization. The term includes: a director; an executive officer; an individual in charge of a major business or functional unit of the organization, such as sales, administration, or finance; and an individual with a substantial ownership interest.
19 Paula Desio, "An Overview of the Organizational Guidelines," U.S. Sentencing Commission at http://www.ussc.gov/guidelines-manual/guidelines-manual.
20 *In re Union Carbide Corp. (Gas Plant Disaster at Bhopal)*, 809 F.2d 195 (1987).
21 See Jennifer Sawayda, "Introduction to ISO," University of New Mexico's Daniel Ethics Initiative at http://e-businessethics.com.
22 Allyson L. Stewart, "International Marketing Police Resolve Trading Disputes," *Marketing News* 15 (June 7, 1993).
23 Directive 84/450/EEC (1984) ("Misleading Advertising Directive").
24 Paul Spink and Ross Petty, "Comparative Advertising in the European Union," 47 *International & Comparative Law Quarterly* 855 (1998).
25 ICC, *International Code of Advertising Practice*, Introduction (1997 edition).

Chapter 3

Sustainability and the Circular Economy

Sustainability, Environment, and Circular Economy

Rapid economic development and industrialization comes at a price: harm to the local and world environments. It is important to balance the goals of industrialization with environmental protection. The current issue is whether a sufficient amount of the monies produced by a country's economic expansion will be used to modernize its environmental laws and their enforcement.

The notion of **sustainability** is used in multiple contexts. For example, short-termism refers to a company's management seeking to improve profits in the short term and not to the sustainability of profits in the long term. Sustainability has also become intimately connected with the preservation of the environment and protection of human rights in the long term. Environmental issues have now become human rights issues. This section explores the notion of sustainability in the context of the environment and human rights.

The United Nations has established a set of **Sustainable Development Goals** (SDGs) intended to be universal in the sense of embodying a shared common global vision of progress toward a safe, just, and sustainable space for all human beings. They reflect the moral principle that every country is responsible for protecting the planet especially the human-made problem of climate change. The **Rio Principles** espoused in a 2012 Resolution of the United Nations provides an outline of the various issues related to environmental protection (see Figure 3.1 *Doing Business Internationally*: "Selected Principles of Rio Declaration").

The Rio Principles are a bit dated but many of its central tenets hold true today. For example, it recognizes a basic **transgenerational human right** to a clean and natural environment. The article argues that any solution requires a public and private law focus (Principle 3). Principle 6 notes the needs of the

DOI: 10.4324/9781003469230-4

Selected Provisions of Rio Principles

Principle 3

The right to development must be fulfilled so as to equitably meet developmental and environmental needs of present and future generations.

Principle 4

In order to achieve sustainable development, environmental protection shall constitute an integral part of the development process and cannot be considered in isolation from it.

Principle 6

The special situation and needs of developing countries, particularly the least developed and those most environmentally vulnerable, shall be given special priority.

Principle 7

The developed countries acknowledge the responsibility that they bear in the international pursuit of sustainable development in view of the pressures their societies place on the global environment and of the technologies and financial resources they command.

Principle 8

To achieve sustainable development and a higher quality of life for all people, States should reduce and eliminate unsustainable patterns of production and consumption.

Principle 10

At the national level, each individual shall have appropriate access to information concerning the environment that is held by public authorities, including information on hazardous materials and activities in their communities.

Principle 15

In order to protect the environment, the precautionary approach shall be widely applied by States according to their capabilities.

Principle 17

Environmental impact assessment, as a national instrument, shall be undertaken for proposed activities.

Principle 24

Warfare is inherently destructive of sustainable development. States shall therefore respect international law providing protection for the environment in times of armed conflict and cooperate in its further development, as necessary.

Figure 3.1 Doing Business Internationally: Selected Principles of Rio Declaration.

developing world and their financial limitations. The importance of individual and consumer knowledge of environmental concerns is stated in Principle 10. Principle 15 restates the long-established **precautionary principle** that where there are threats of serious or irreversible damage, lack of full scientific certainty shall not be used as a reason for postponing cost-effective measures to prevent environmental degradation. Simply put, when in doubt of the environmental consequences of an activity it is best not to pursue that activity until it can be shown to be environmentally safe. Principle 17 relates to the precautionary principle in that it requires countries to perform **environment impact assessments** before approving significant projects. Civil society needs to continue to pressure national governments and large corporations to reverse course and dramatically move away from a fossil fuel-based economy to a circular, no waste economy.

> **Precautionary principle** states that if an action or policy has a suspected risk of causing harm to the environment or human beings in the absence of scientific consensus of whether or not the action or policy is harmful, the burden of proof that it is *not* harmful falls on those taking an action.

Sustainable Development and Climate Change

The climate change crisis and its noticeable effects on the quality of life have falsified the assumption that economic development at any cost is beneficial. Environmental pollution and **climate change** cannot be contained within national boundaries. Since the health of the planet affects all countries, there must be a coordinated effort by all nations to reduce global warming. The **Paris Agreement** was an attempt to lower carbon emissions to reduce climate warming. Unfortunately, it has not been successful as indicated by increased instances of extreme heat throughout the world. The U.S., along with China and India remain the top emitters of carbon in the world.

But not all is lost, and a number of automobile manufacturers are voluntarily complying with higher mileage standards. The key point of contention is not whether drastic preventive measures need to be taken, but whether developed countries have a moral obligation to fund initiatives to reduce carbon emissions in less-developed countries.

This section will review international law that forward the goals of sustainable development, with a focus on how private or business law can be utilized to meet sustainability goals. Given the urgency of climate change, international sustainable development law has developed at the intersection between international economic, environmental, and social law. New bilateral, regional, and global treaties have been negotiated in the areas of trade, environment, and development over the past two decades, unfortunately the implementation of their rules and goals has been slow. At the same time, disputes over human rights, environmental protection, and economic development are increasingly common.

The three primary goals of sustainable development are: to minimize the depletion of natural resources when creating economic development; to create a development strategy that can be maintained and sustained without causing further harm to the environment; and to provide methods for retrofitting existing industries to make them more environmentally friendly.

> **Sustainable development** is the organizing principle for meeting human development goals while simultaneously sustaining the ability of natural systems to provide natural resources upon which the economy and society depend, as well as preserving existing ecosystems. The desired result is a state of society where living conditions and resources are used to continue to meet human needs without undermining the integrity and stability of the natural system.

Sustainable Development as International Law

Weather patterns are changing and becoming more extreme, sea levels are rising, and greenhouse gas emissions continue at high levels. As a result, the growth of international conventions and national laws relating to sustainable development has resulted in sustainable development goals becoming a part of public and private customary international law. In the recent decisions of international courts and tribunals, the concept of sustainable development has been used to resolve conflicting interests, such as economic growth, environmental harm, and human rights. The International Court of Justice in the *Gabčíkovo-Nagymaros Project (Hungary v. Slovakia)* stated:

> Throughout the ages, mankind has, for economic and other reasons, constantly interfered with nature. In the past, this was often done without consideration of the effects upon the environment. Owing to new scientific insights and to a growing awareness of the risks for mankind—for present and future generations of pursuit of such interventions at an unconsidered and unabated pace, new norms and standards have been developed, set forth in a great number of instruments. Such new norms have to be taken into consideration, and such new standards given proper weight, not only when States contemplate new activities but also when continuing with activities begun in the past. This need to reconcile economic development with protection of the environment is aptly expressed in the concept of sustainable development.

The Permanent Court of Arbitration reaffirmed this reasoning in its arbitral award regarding the *Iron Rhine (Ijzeren Rijn) Railway (Belgium v. Netherlands).* In this case, the Netherlands, which had created nature reserves along the path of the historic 'Iron Rhine' railway line, sought to prevent its reactivation by Belgium. Belgium wanted to reopen the railway and shift from road to rail transportation, assisting in the reduction of greenhouse gases and contributing to sustainable development. The Tribunal balanced environmental protection against economic development and held that the environmental measures taken by the Netherlands were not grounds to deny Belgium's transit rights:

> Environmental law and the law on development stand not as alternatives but as mutually reinforcing, integral concepts, which require that where development may cause significant harm to the environment, there is a duty to prevent, or at least mitigate such harm. … This duty, in the opinion

of the Tribunal, has now become a principle of general international law. This principle applies not only in autonomous activities but also in activities undertaken in implementation of specific treaties between the Parties.

Interrelated with the issue of sustainability are the areas of fairness, justice, human rights, and intellectual property rights. These issues often relate to one another both directly and indirectly. For example, something may be sustainable but also cause injustice from a distributive justice perspective when sustainability improvements do not benefit a majority of the population. Human rights and intellectual property rights conflict in cases where a company's intellectual property rights prevent medicines or scientific innovation from reaching people most in need. The two types of rights are at times complementary in nature. From the perspective of sustainability, innovation is essential to develop means to use natural resources, reduce waste, and protect the environment more effectively. Failure to recognize intellectual property rights in these areas will limit the development of new means to sustainability.

European New Green Deal

The European Commission published a developmental strategy on December 11, 2019, known as **The European Green Deal.** It self-describes itself as a "new growth strategy that aims to transform the EU into a fair and prosperous society, with a modern, resource-efficient and competitive economy where there are no net emissions of greenhouse gases by 2050 and where economic growth is decoupled." See Image 3.1 on "The European Green Deal."

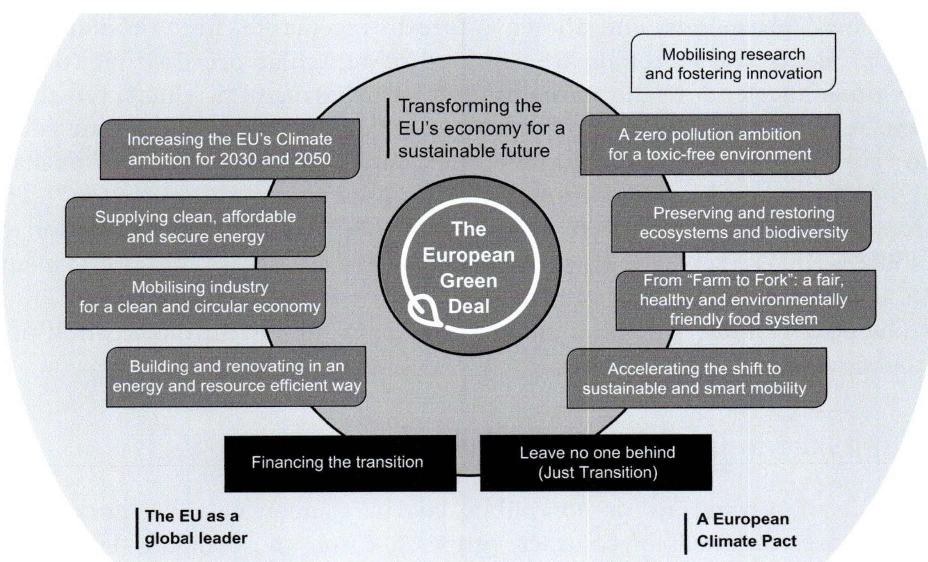

Image 3.1 Brussels, 11.12.19 COM (2019) 40 final: The European Green Deal.

The elements of the Green Deal include the creation of effective **carbon pricing** throughout the economy. This will encourage changes in consumer and business behavior and facilitate an increase in sustainable public and private investment. The plan also requires the transition to climate neutrality and requires **smart infrastructure**. The new infrastructure includes the deployment of innovative technologies, such as smart electric grids; hydrogen networks; carbon capture, storage, and utilization; and energy storage. The creation of a **circular economy** is the ultimate goal of the Green Deal, which is discussed below.

Sustainability and Business Law

Many consumers are motivated to purchase goods that were produced by environmentally friendly processes and that advance the goals of sustainability. For example, the **EU Ecolabel** criteria take a lifecycle approach that assesses the entire production cycle—extraction of natural resources, production, products lifecycle (durability), recycling of reusable materials, and reducing waste. These concerns are reflected in the idea of converting the current linear economy to a **circular economy** (no waste economy). A circular economy results in an efficient use of natural resources and decreases environmental pollution. See Image 3.2 "Linear versus Circular Economy."

The longstanding model of development has been characterized as a linear economy, that begins with the extracting of raw materials from nature, turning them into products, and then discarding used products as waste. It is estimated that only 7.2 percent of used materials are cycled back into the world's economy. The circular economy is a system that eliminates most waste, conserves precious metals, and allows nature to regenerate. In a circular economy, products and materials are captured in a circular process that consists of maintenance and the durability of products, sharing of products, refurbishment, remanufacture, and recycling. "In a circular economy, electronic goods are refurbished, water-soluble, recyclable, and truly biodegradable packaging becomes the norm, and animal waste is used as natural fertilizers."[1] The circular economy disconnects economic activity from the consumption of resources. Image 3.3 "The Circular Economy Model" shows the core elements in the creation of a circular economy.

The next sections will examine the role of private law in the creation of a circular economy.

Private Law in Creating a Circular Economy

The role of private law or non-public law in combatting the climate crisis encompasses the areas of contract, property, torts, and company law. These areas may be viewed from the micro to the macro. Contract law can be viewed from the perspective of a single export-import transaction to the global supply chain. Property law can be viewed from the transfer of a single home in a residential subdivision to syndication of hundreds of millions of dollars of high-rise

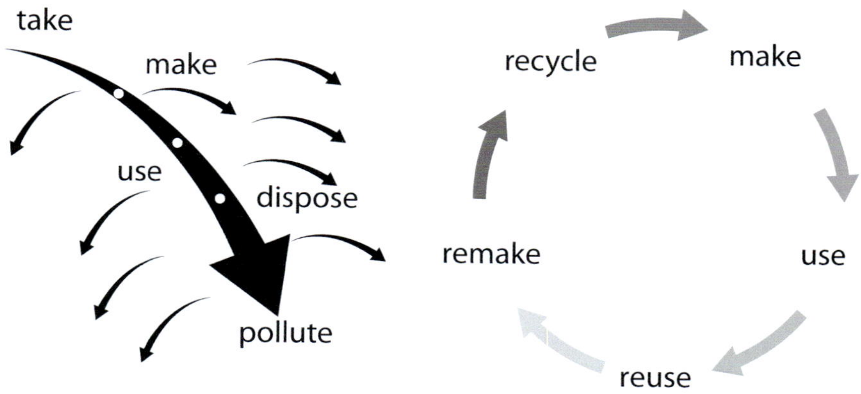

Image 3.2 Linear versus Circular Economy.

Source: Wikimedia Commons, https://commons.wikimedia.org/wiki/File:Linear_ versus_circular.jpg.

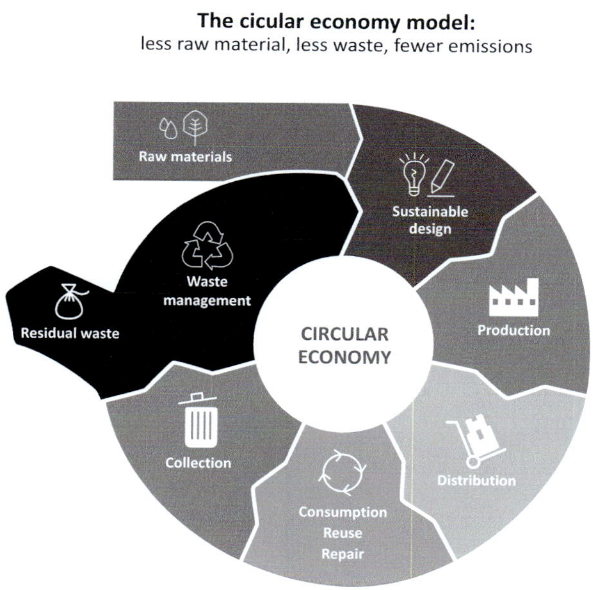

Image 3.3 The Circular Economy Model.

Source: https://www.europarl.europa.eu/topics/en/article/20151201STO05603/circular-economy-definition-importance-and-benefits

apartment and commercial buildings. Tort law can be viewed from the perspective of a personal injury lawsuit to the catastrophic event leading to toxic tort litigation.

In the present context effective information disclosure must include posting or marking the expected period of usability of products. In this sense, effective information would allow buyers interested in purchasing durable products to make informed decisions. Arguably the most effective strategy is using durability labels that follow the example of EU ecolabels.[2] The **European CE Mark** also aims to construct a circular economy. CE seeks the efficient use of products to preserve them as long as possible in the economy through product-life extension, redistribution/reuse, remanufacturing, and recycling.

Contract and Warranty Law

The idea of a general contract duty to protect the environment and decrease greenhouse emissions is seen in the 2021 Chinese Civil Code. Article 300 states that: "The parties shall abide by the principle of good faith, and perform obligations of notification, assistance, confidentiality, *saving resources and reducing pollution*, in accordance with the nature and purpose of the contract and the transaction practice." Article 348 states that "after the termination of credit and debt, the parties shall observe the principle of honesty and good faith and perform the obligations of notification, assistance, confidentiality, and discarded product recovery (recycle)." A more direct approach would be to expand the scope of warranty law to include an implied warranty of durability, which is discussed below.

Planned Obsolescence and Implied Warranty of Durability

A key component in creating a circular economy is to deter **planned obsolescence** and increase the durability of products.[3] The best approach should be measured on two parameters—providing an adequate remedial structure for purchasers of products and secondly, to deter manufacturers from producing goods with unnecessarily short lifespans. It should be the goal of an expanded warranty regime to incentivize producers to manufacture goods with longer lifespans and greater durability. The battle against environmental pollution and climate change requires that natural resources be used efficiently. This includes the production of goods that have sufficient durability. In July 2011, the European Commission issued the following statement:

> The Commission considers that 'planned obsolescence' ... can have negative impacts on consumers' interests, on the environment, and on fair competition. European legislation provides means to combat such practices. Firstly, Directive 99/44/EC on the sale of consumer goods and associated guarantees [Consumer Sales Directives or CSD] offers to consumers' minimum rights against sellers of faulty products, i.e. of products whose quality and performance are not normal in goods of the same type and cannot be reasonably expected by the consumers. These rights include the right to have a faulty product repaired or replaced free of charge or to obtain, under certain conditions, a refund or a price reduction within a period of two years from the delivery of the product. Member States may adopt

> more stringent provisions, i.e. longer guarantee periods, in their national legislations. Planned obsolescence clearly runs counter to the objectives set out by the Commission in its Europe 2020 strategy to achieve resource-efficient growth. An important element of resource efficiency is sustainable materials management.[4]

Environmental labeling of products has become common and the concerns over climate change have become so widespread as to justify the creation of an implied warranty of durability or sustainability.

Planned Obsolescence should be understood in multifaceted ways. Vance Packard in his 1960 book, *The Waste Makers*, differentiated types of obsolescence strategies—"obsolescence of desirability," "obsolescence of function," and "obsolescence of quality." In the obsolescence of quality, the lifetime of a product ends prematurely because of quality or technical issues. In cases of obsolescence of desirability and function, the good still runs flawlessly. Users choose to stop using the still usable item because they feel the need for a follow-up product influenced by marketing strategies (desirability) or because the newer product has additional or enhanced technical functions. Larry A. DiMatteo and Stefan Wrbka, "Planned Obsolescence and Consumer Protection: The Unregulated Extended Warranty and Service Contract Industry" (2019) 28 *Cornell Journal of Law & Public Policy* 483, 494–495.

Commercial and consumer law provides a number of implied in law warranties. The American Uniform Commercial Code provides for an Implied Warranty of Merchantability, which under English law is referred to as the Implied Warranty of Satisfactory Quality, as well as the Implied Warranty for a Particular Purpose.[5] It has been suggested that contract law should recognize an Implied Warranty of Sustainability. Christine Hottinger argues that:

The **implied warranty of sustainability**, though simple in application, would have far-reaching positive impacts for consumers and the sustainable production of [goods]. The implied warranty of sustainability would (a) increase information available to consumers, leading to (b) consumers exerting greater pressure on producers and stores. The implied warranty would also (c) give stores an incentive to stock sustainable [products].[6]

Another approach would be to recognize planned obsolescence as a patent defect. This way it would come within the scope of existing implied warranties (merchantability, satisfactory quality, for a particular purpose), as well as come under product liability law. Unfortunately, the limited express warranty given by most manufacturers would preclude a breach of warranty if the planned obsolescence defect appeared after the express warranty period. To prevent this from happening, warranty law should be changed to require that the commencement of express warranty periods start upon the detectability of the defect and not from the time of delivery of the product.

Finally, another approach would be simply to lengthen the warranty periods fixed by law. This approach can be found in Ireland and the UK, which adopted six-year warranty periods, and Belgium, which has a prescription period (period for bringing a legal claim) of ten years from the discovery of the latent defect (failure of the product).[7] Products that do not reach a **reasonably expected lifetime** are considered to be defective. For example, the Finnish Consumer Disputes Board has the authority to issue (non-binding) lifespan standard ranges for different product categories. If a product falls significantly short of the applicable target, a durable defect is presumed.

Sustainability Clauses

There are many sustainability standards and goals that can be used to construct contract **sustainability clauses**. This is an important method to convert soft law standards to enforceable law. An analogy can be found in intellectual property protection. Some countries are notorious for failing to enforce intellectual property laws. This incentivizes licensors of technology to write pro-licensor licensing contracts, which include transplanting protections provided by intellectual property law into their contracts, the logic being that some national courts may not be able to deal with the nuances of intellectual property law, but they are capable of handling breach of contract litigation (see Chapter 16: "Licensing of Technology"). Although damages may be difficult to prove in breaching contractual sustainability clauses, the breach does allow the non-breaching party to terminate the contract and such breaches cause negative reputational effects on the breaching party.

Sustainability clauses are especially needed in supply contracts given the growth of global supply chains. It is important for sustainability clauses to use words of obligation such as the supplier "will," "is required to," or "must" and avoid merely referential language ("according to the UN Global Compact"), as well as avoiding aspirational language, such as "you should strive to comply." Enforceability increases when the obligations of the other contracting party are detailed in concrete terms, instead of using a simple recital of general principles (incorporation by reference). In sum, placement of the clauses in the body of the contract and not in the general conditions (standard terms), use of specifically worded clauses, and use of words of promise or obligation increase the likelihood of enforceability.

Duty to Repair and Consumers' Right to Repair

Most product warranties allow the manufacturer to choose the appropriate remedy of repair or replace.[8] If the consumer has the choice, then in most instances they will choose the replacement option. The replacement option should be deterred since it creates considerably greater amounts of waste than does repair. Considering the difference in environmental or sustainability costs between repair and replacement, national warranty laws should be reformed to prioritize the remedy of repair over that of replacement. In order to prevent waste, an attempt to repair should be required before the replacement option is used. In cases where replacement is unavoidable, post-replacement obligations of a manufacturer should include the duty to "mine" or recycle reusable materials from the goods being replaced.

The law should also recognize a **consumer's right to self-repair**. Consumers should be allowed to repair their own products rather than be forced to pay the higher costs of repair in manufacturer-certified repair shops or to purchase a new replacement product. Four parts of a model law recognizing the consumer's right to self-repair include: "(1) mandating disclosure of information that will allow repairs; (2) mandating the availability of parts and tools to facilitate repairs; (3) mandating disclosure of information to allow security protections to be reset; and (4) forbidding any contracting-around of such provisions in contract terms between authorized repair providers and the original equipment manufacturers."[9] Examples of designs that make self-repair difficult include affixed or glued batteries in electronic products and the Apple screw that prevents opening and repairing of Apple products with ordinary types of screwdrivers. In order to make self-repair possible, companies should be required to make available the manuals needed to effectuate self-repair, along with maintaining an inventory of repair parts.

Circular Economy and Servitization

Sustainability depends on the efficient use and re-use of sources and materials. A circular economy focuses on the **dematerialization** of the economy by the diminishment of dependency on scarce resources. This process involves numerous techniques and approaches to material use and the production of waste. Examples include the changing of perspectives from the purchase of new products with the sharing of products. The **share economy** allows people to share their homes (Airbnb) and to share rides (Uber). The next generation of sustainability products would involve the conversion from buying basic goods to sharing or leasing of goods. **Servitization** seeks to replace ownership of things with the leasing or sharing of things. This would entail converting purchase contracts to service contracts. For example, Philips, a lighting manufacturer, offers a program that instead of buying their light bulbs a company may enter into a service contract in which Philips maintains, repairs, and replaces the company's lighting system. Servitization incentivizes a manufacturer to make longer lasting products. When selling light bulbs, a company is incentivized to limit their lifespans so as to generate additional sales in the future. In a service contract scenario, the incentives are reversed in that the company wants to reduce the costs of servicing by producing longer lasting bulbs.

EU Corporate Sustainability Due Diligence Directive

On 15 March 2024, a qualified majority of the member states of the EU voted in favor of the Corporate Sustainability Due Diligence Directive (CSDDD). The CSDDD requires companies to screen and manage their suppliers to determine if the activities of the suppliers show a high probability of risk of negative impact on the environment. Negative impact includes damage to biodiversity and the illegal handling of waste. The CSDDD would cover companies with more than 1,000 employees and more than EUR 450 million in revenues. Companies must make environmentally-friendly changes in their supply chains. If their due diligence finds that suppliers are unlikely to make required changes, then the company must suspend or terminate the supply relationship. Violations of the CSDDD would be punishable of penalties up to 5 percent of a company's global consolidated revenues.

The CSDDD defines suppliers as a value chain or chain of activities (supply chain) that includes: (1) a company's own suppliers (upstream suppliers) and direct or indirect partners, (2) as supplier a company is responsible for downstream activities such as distribution, transport, and storage, (3) although not directly liable, financial service providers should take the negative environmental impact of a customer's activities into account when considering a financial relationship.

From a legal, ethical, and public reputation perspective companies should implement a **due diligence** system for risk-based screening of suppliers to determine negative impacts on the environment. It should have an **ESG Policy** that includes a **climate transition plan**. ESG stands for environmental, social, and governance. ESG standards are used to rate businesses on how well they monitor emissions, pursue sustainable governance, protect human rights, and other factors. There are numerous rating companies that grade other companies on how well their ESG policies are working. ESG ratings or a company's overall reputation on these issues have substantial business consequences. It's typically used by investors in making investment decisions (purchase stocks or bonds of the company), as well as customers, suppliers, employees, and the general public. Climate transition plans assert a company's commitment to work to reduce carbon emissions and to transition to a net-zero carbon or greenhouse emissions. Companies should also adopt a **Supplier Code of Conduct** to communicate the values found in their ESG Policy. The CSDDD, whether or not treated as mandatory law in the EU, should be voluntarily used (principles and requirements) as good company policy.

Chapter Summary

1. With the advent of climate change the world is now faced with an existential threat to maintaining a livable planet. There have been long-standing instruments, such as the Rio Principles that have established general principles to lower carbon emissions (greenhouse gases) to prevent the warming of the planet but they have not led to sufficient commitments or the honoring of commitments by countries.
2. Environmental protection is best served from shifting from a linear to a circular economy. The circular economy maximizes the use of materials in the economy through the production of durable products and reducing waste.
3. The European Green Deal sets an agenda to combat climate change through the implementation of carbon pricing and the creation of a circular economy.

4. Business law and private companies need to play an important role in slowing the effects of climate change.
5. A key target is to incentivize the manufacture of durable products and to limit the phenomenon known as planned obsolescence (premature failure of functionality of products). An initial step would be to require the labelling of products to indicate estimated lifetimes.
6. Changes in private law would include the use of warranty law to impose obligations on manufacturers to produce goods with long lifespans. This could include extending the minimum length of warranty periods relating to the quality of goods and by recognizing a failure of a product to function for a reasonably expected lifetime as a latent defect.
7. Another approach would be to create a new warranty of durability or sustainability, which would incentivize manufacturers and retailers to produce and stock more durable products.
8. Contract law or government regulation is needed to make repair of goods the preferred remedy for warranty claims. The manufacturer should be required to repair a faulty product before choosing the option of replacement. In addition, after the expiration of a warranty, the law should recognize a consumer right to self-repair.
9. The reuse or sharing of goods and materials to prevent unnecessary waste should be encouraged. One example of such a strategy is the conversion of sale contracts to service contracts known as servitization.
10. The EU Corporate Sustainability Due Diligence Directive requires companies to screen and monitor suppliers and partners for processes that have a negative impact on the environment.
11. Companies must vigorously enforce ESG Policies that should include a climate transition plan and a supplier's code of conduct.

Key Terms

Circular Economy
Climate Change
Climate Transition Plan
Consumer's Right to Self-Repair
Due Diligence
Duty to Repair
Dematerialization
Environment Impact Assessments
ESG Policy
EU CE Mark
EU Ecolabel
EU Corporate Sustainability Due Diligence Directive
European Green Deal
Implied Warranty of Durability
Implied Warranty of Sustainability
Paris Agreement
Planned Obsolescence
Reasonably Expected Life
Precautionary Principle
Rio Principles
Servitization
Share Economy
Smart Infrastructure
Supplier Code of Conduct
Sustainable Development
Sustainable Development Goals
Sustainability
Sustainability Clauses

Chapter Problems

1. You are a manager of a large manufacturing company that relies primarily on fossil fuels or electricity mostly generated by the burning of fossil fuels. You are tasked with the job of writing a climate transition plan for your company. Write such a plan using the information provided by the American Environmental Protection Agency (EPA). See EPA Center for Corporate Climate Leadership, "Climate Transition Planning" at https://www.epa.gov/climateleadership/climate-transition-planning.
2. Review the "principles" found in the Rio Principles on Environment and Development at https://www.cbd.int/doc/ref/rio-declaration.shtml.
3. What are the core elements of transitioning to a circular economy? See European Commission, "Circular Economy" at https://www.europarl.europa.eu/topics/en/topic/circular-economy.
4. Review a company's Environment, Sustainability and Governance (ESG) Policy. See, for example, https://www.ibm.com/topics/environmental-social-and-governance.
5. What are the essential elements of a Supplier Code of Conduct and its application? See United Nations Global Compact Database of suppliers codes of conduct at https://unglobalcompact.org/search?search%5Btype%5D=all&search%5Bkeywords%5D=supplier+code+of+conduct.

Internet Sources

United Nations Global Compact: Guide for General Counsel on Corporate Sustainability at https://www.unglobalcompact.org/docs/publications/GuideforGeneralCounsel.pdf.

Markkula Center for Applied Ethics: www.scu.edu/ethics (database of nearly one thousand links on ethics including business and environmental ethics); see also, **Caux Round Table:** www.cauxroundtable.org (social corporate responsibility).

International Society for Environmental Ethics at http://www.cep.unt.edu/ISEE.html.

Transparency International: http://www.transparency.org.

European Consumer Centres Network (**ECC-Net**) at https://www.eccnet.eu/european-consumer-centres-network.

Notes

1 UNDP, "Climate Promise," https://climatepromise.undp.org/news-and-stories/what-is-circular-economy-and-how-it-helps-fight-climate-change.

2 See Regulation (EU) 2017/1369 of the European Parliament and of the Council of 4 July 2017 Setting a Framework for Energy Labelling and Repealing Directive 2010/30/EU, 2017 O.J. (L 198) 1.

3 Stefan Wrbka and Larry DiMatteo, "Comparative Warranty Law: Case of Planned Obsolescence" (2019) 21 *University of Pennsylvania Journal of Business Law* 907.

4 Joint answer given by Janez Potočnik on behalf of the Commission written questions: E-001284/11, E-002875/11, E-004273/11, 8 July 2011.
5 See, Chapter 10 (International Sales Law), "Warranty Provisions."
6 Christine Hottinger, "For an Implied Warranty of Sustainability: Come Mr. Tallyman, Tally My Banana's Environmental Impact" (2014) 26 *Georgetown Int'l Environmental L. Rev.* 303, 318–319.
7 Article 1641 of the Belgian Civil Code.
8 Larry A. DiMatteo and Stefan Wrbka, "Planned Obsolescence and Consumer Protection: The Unregulated Extended Warranty and Service Contract Industry" (2019) 28 *Cornell Journal of Law & Public Policy* 483.
9 Leah Chan Grinvald and Ofer Tur-Sinai, "Intellectual Property Law and the Right to Repair" (2019) 88 *Fordham L. Rev.* 63.

Chapter 4

Strategies for International Business

Companies should develop a strategy or business plan when deciding to establish foreign business operations. A foreign business strategy encompasses activities like hiring foreign employees, establishing a foreign office, and acquiring foreign assets, including the acquisition of companies or establishment of a subsidiary. The factors that affect planning foreign operations, like the risks of international business transactions, vary depending on the country, type of industry, size of the operation, and legal issues such as foreign regulations and taxation.

The most indirect form of foreign entry is through exportation of goods or the licensing of technology. These transactions can involve little direct contact or the use of surrogates or agents within host countries. Companies will often hire foreign agents to help market, sell, and distribute their products. These agents are generally hired as independent contractors and not as direct employees.

Strategies for Doing Business: Creating a Business Entity

Most countries offer equivalent forms of doing business in order to limit the liability of their owners. The establishment of a business organization in most foreign countries is done under national and local laws that regulate businesses once established,[1] as well as registration with various levels of government. The entities reviewed in this area include: the branch office, partnerships and joint ventures, limited liability companies, and corporations.

Alternatively, a foreign company may elect to operate one of a number of independent entities, including the joint venture, general partnership, corporation,

DOI: 10.4324/9781003469230-5

and limited liability companies. The **joint venture** is a hybrid that forms either as a partnership or as a new corporation. A joint venture can be loosely defined as an association between two or more parties with an agreement to share the profits and often the management of a particular project. The joint venture is a common method for international business investment, in which a foreign company seeks out a domestic company in order to penetrate the host country's market. The advantages of joint venturing will be discussed in greater detail later in the chapter.

In a **general partnership**, the partners are "jointly and severally" (wholly) liable for partnership debts. Unlike in a joint venture, a partnership mandate is more flexible and ongoing. A joint venture is established to accomplish more narrow business objectives, while a general partnership generally envisions a long-term evolution of the business, including the development of goals not contemplated by the partners at the time of inception. In a partnership, as in the partnership-style joint venture, the losses and profits of the business *pass through* directly to the partners for purposes of taxation.

A newer form of business that has become popular is the **social enterprise company**. Such entities apply commercial strategies to maximize improvements in human and environmental well-being, as well as making profits for its owners. However, making money for shareholders is considered secondary to maximizing social impact. Social enterprises can be structured as for-profit or not-for-profit businesses and may take different forms depending on the country where it is established, such as a cooperative, benefits corporation, or charitable organization. Many corporations take their social responsibilities seriously and invest company money in charitable causes, while the social enterprise company's charitable commitment is central to the mission of the business. These forms of doing business are part of a general movement or trend toward **social entrepreneurship**, which in many cases is international in nature.

One of the more famous early examples of social entrepreneurship is Grameen Bank. What makes Grameen Bank different is that it pioneered the concept of *microcredit* for small or start-up businesses in developing or improvised countries in Asia, Africa, and Latin America. It provides loans to persons or businesses that do not qualify for mainstream loans due to lack of a credit or employment history, assets, or collateral. These high-risk loans have proved not to be that risky. Grameen Bank reported that repayment rates were a stunning 98 percent. The United Nations declared 2005 as the International Year of Microcredit. Bangladeshi social entrepreneur Muhammad Yunus, the founder of Grameen Bank, won the 2006 Nobel Peace Prize.

The microfinance movement supports entrepreneurship with the ultimate purpose of alleviating poverty, as well as empowering women and raising the standard of living for entire communities. Microfinance includes providing loans, but also provides a wider range of financial services, such as establishing savings for the poor. In many communities, women lack stable employment histories that traditional lenders tend to require. Many are illiterate and therefore unable to get conventional loans. See Figure 4.1 *Doing Business Internationally*: "Real World Stories from the Grameen Foundation."

Microlending. A poor Indonesian couple barely survives by running a food stand in front of their home. They attended a microloan informational meeting and subsequently obtained a $100 loan that they used to purchase materials and equipment, allowing them to produce more food in a shorter period of time. There daily profits increased by 33 percent. Their dream is to someday own their own restaurant.

Microsavings Accounts. An aunt and her niece in the Philippines save for their children's future. Every day, a savings officer visits their home and collects about 50 cents from Elsa and other members of her savings group. On good days, Elsa deposits even more money. Her goal is to save about $200 to pay future tuition fees for her children.

Figure 4.1 Doing Business Internationally: Real World Stories from the Grameen Foundation.[2]

Another source for raising funds is ***crowdfunding***. Crowdfunding usually entails a person or entity who proposes a project to be funded, individuals or groups who support the idea, and a moderating organization or platform that acts as a conduit between the parties. Crowdfunding is an old idea. For example, in 1885, France gave the famous Statue of Liberty to the U.S. The problem was the American government failed to provide funding for building the pedestal to place the Statue. Instead, a private fundraising effort resulted in donations by more than 120,000 contributors. Crowdfunding was used again in the 1980s to finance the restoration of the Statue. The Internet has made crowdfunding easier and has resulted in tremendous growth and diversity in its use. An estimated $5.3 billion was raised in 2013. In 2019, the global amount raised by crowdfunding was $34 billion. Other varieties of crowdfunding have

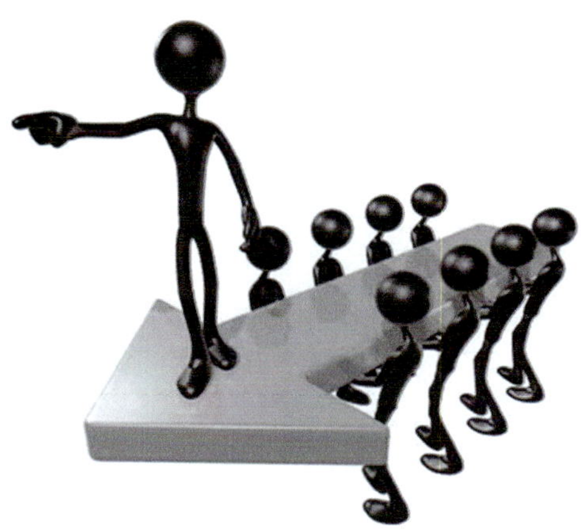

Image 4.1 Strategy.

also grown rapidly, including $25 billion in *peer-to-peer lending*, $5.5 billion in *donation crowdfunding*, and $2.5 billion in *equity crowdfunding* (money for promise of a share of the company).[3]

Strategies for Entering a Foreign Market

As noted above, a company that wants a direct foreign presence has a number of options, including establishing a representative office, a joint venture with an established company, setting up a branch office, or forming a full-scale foreign subsidiary. Forming a foreign subsidiary requires deeper business and legal involvement than establishing a representative office.

The least costly way of starting a business in a foreign country is through a **branch** or **representative office**. Generally, the only formal procedure required to establish a branch is to register to do business with the appropriate government regulatory agency. The branch is considered simply an extension of the foreign corporation, and the corporation remains liable for the debts of the branch office.

A branch office is established for limited purposes, such as undertaking a market analysis and product promotion. Host country laws dictate what types of activities a representative office may pursue. For example, a representative office may obtain leads of potential customers but cannot negotiate or enter into contracts, tasks reserved for the parent company. The advantage of operating a representative office is that the company is not considered to be *doing business* in the foreign country, so it will avoid host country regulations and will not be subject to taxation.

In order to have a full-time presence and to transact business, a company will need to establish an operation in a foreign country. The joint venture vehicle allows a company to share expertise and risks with a local partner, who often brings benefits such as customer and distribution networks, existing contacts with important government officers, and knowledge of the host country's legal and regulatory system. A joint venture may also be the only option in a country that prohibits wholly owned foreign subsidiaries. A joint venture can be undertaken by creating an independent entity under the laws of the host country. These types of enterprises are referred to as **equity joint ventures**. Another option is a **contractual joint venture** where the parties agree to perform certain tasks without forming a new entity.

A company may elect to establish an **independent foreign subsidiary** or **affiliate**. An affiliate is a business enterprise located in one country that is directly or indirectly owned or controlled by a foreign company. Companies with foreign subsidiaries often attempt to reduce the enterprise's overall tax liability through **transfer pricing**, where one subsidiary of an enterprise charges another for goods or services. Companies manipulate these transfer prices in order to move profits to countries with lower tax rates. Such transfer pricing is considered illegal under international tax conventions. The crucial advantage of a foreign subsidiary over the branch office is the parent company has limited liability and is able to carry on a broad range of business activities.

Foreign Corporation Law

The roles and duties played by different constituent groups, such as the shareholders and board of directors, vary under foreign corporation laws (see Figure 4.2 *Comparative Law*: "Corporate Governance in the United States, Germany, and Japan"). Japanese corporate law is strikingly similar to American corporate law: The shareholders elect the board of directors, and the directors owe the traditional duties of loyalty (no conflicts of interest) and care (to act competently) to the corporation and its shareholders.

In China, approval of the shareholders is the dominant form of corporate decision-making. Unlike in the U.S., shareholder power pervades the day-to-day operation of the company. Chinese Company Law requires large companies to establish a supervisory committee of shareholders, which has the power

Corporate Goals and Objectives

What differentiates the governance structures in the U.S., Japan, and Germany are the roles the various stakeholders play in monitoring and controlling the firm. For example, in the United States, the primary stakeholder is the shareholder (owners), whereas in Japan and Germany, employees have a strong voice. The American Law Institute asserts that a corporation's primary objective should be "corporate profit and shareholder gain." Traditionally, Japanese corporations have operated to benefit a small group of owners, rather than to maximize shareholder value. Its corporate governance system emphasizes the protection of employees and creditor interests as much as shareholder interests. The German corporation statute states that: "the managing board, on its own responsibility, is to manage the corporation for the good of the enterprise and its employees, society, and the State." German law dictates that managers operate the firm for the benefit of multiple stakeholders, not just shareholders.

Management Structure

In the United States and Japan, shareholders typically elect directors at annual shareholder meetings. Labor or employee representations are rarely involved in the corporate governance system. The system used in Germany is significantly different from those in either the United States or Japan. In large German firms, employees select half the board of directors. This practice is known as *co-determination*. German corporations with over 500 employees have a two- tiered board structure. A **supervisory board** performs the strategic oversight role, while a **management board** performs the day-to-day management role. In firms with over 2,000 employees, employees must comprise half of the supervisory board; shareholder representatives make up the other half. The German board structure ensures that major strategic decisions are not made without the consent of employees and their representatives.

Figure 4.2 Comparative Law: Corporate Governance in the United States, Germany, and Japan.[4]

to investigate and supervise the financial affairs of the company. Furthermore, shareholders are authorized to pass their own resolutions that must be implemented by the board of directors. Business plans and investment decisions are formulated by the board of directors but must be submitted to the shareholders for approval.

French corporate law is unique because it provides alternate governance structures for the public corporation, or *S.A.* The articles of incorporation may select a management structure that is headed by a board of directors or one that consists of a management committee or executive board and **shareholders' council.** The latter form acts in many ways like the two-tiered system found in Germany.

Piercing the Corporate Veil

The corporate form of doing business provides limited liability protection for the owners (shareholders), directors, officers, and parent companies relative to their subsidiaries. Thus, a corporation may use an independently incorporated subsidiary to shield itself from liability. However, in narrow circumstances, courts have allowed the **piercing of the corporate veil**. Piercing can be used to hold owners of a company directly liable to the creditors of the corporation and to hold a parent company liable for the debt of a subsidiary.

The case of *Raven Metal Products v. McGann*[5] illustrates some of the factors a court assesses when deciding if a corporate entity should be disregarded and the entity's owners exposed to personal liability. Raven Metal brought suit for breach of contract for nonpayment for materials delivered to Northeast Trailer, Inc. Brenda McGann was the sole director, officer, and shareholder of Northeast Trailer. Northeast held no corporate meetings and no corporate records existed. McGann used corporate funds to pay personal expenses. The court stated that there are two general elements that must be met in order to pierce the corporate veil. First, the owners must exercise complete domination of the corporation. Second, such domination is used to commit a fraud or wrong against another party. However, the court refused to pierce the corporate veil, despite the domination of McGann over Northeast, because there was no evidence of fraud. This case illustrates the U.S. view in favor of upholding the limited liability of the corporate form.

The *Finnish Fur Sales v. Shulof* case below shows that the presumption against piercing the corporate veil is not held as strongly in some countries.

Establishing a Business in a Foreign Country

Finnish Fur Sales Co., Ltd. v. Juliette Shulof

770 F. Supp. 139 (S.D.N.Y. 1991)

Leisure, District Judge. This is an action to collect sums allegedly owed in connection with furs purchased at two auctions in Vantaa, Finland. Plaintiff Finnish Fur Sales Co., Ltd. (FFS), asserts its claim of failure to pay for 2,469 fox pelts against defendants Juliette Shulof Furs, Inc. (JSF), and George Shulof. Plaintiff Okobank asserts its claim of failure to honor a bill of exchange (draft or cheque) against defendants JSF and Juliette Shulof. FFS sell fur pelts raised by Finnish breeders at public auctions. The auctions are conducted under certain Conditions of Sale ("Conditions"), which are listed in the auction catalog, a copy of which is given to each prospective bidder in advance of the auction. A one-page English translation of the Conditions appears on the inside cover of the catalog.

JSF is a New York corporation that has conducted a fur business for approximately 15 years. George Shulof, an officer of JSF, has been in the fur business for fifty years. Mr. Shulof attended the FFS auctions held in Vantaa, Finland and purchased over $1.2 million of furs. A partial payment was made by a bill of exchange for the furs. FFS claims that, in addition to the liability of JSF, Mr. Shulof is personally liable, based on Finnish law, the custom and practice of the fur trade, and the provisions of section 4 of the Auction Conditions. Section 4 provides: "Any person bidding at the auction shall stand as a surety (guarantor) as for the debt until full payment is made for purchased merchandise." George Shulof denies any personal liability on the grounds that the provision is unenforceable under both New York and Finnish law. Later, FFS endorsed (transferred) the bill of exchange to Okobank and was denied payment by the bank. The bill of exchange was signed "Juliette A. Shulof" above the printed name "Juliette Shulof Furs Inc."

Liability of George Shulof

The New York court elected to enforce the choice of law clause in the contract, which stated that Finnish law would be the governing law. Mr. Shulof argued that, under New York law, his personal liability under Section 4 of the contract should be invalidated as contravening New York's policy against imposing personal liability on corporate officers.

It is also well established under New York law, as under Finnish law, that "the owner of property offered for sale at auction has the right to prescribe the manner, conditions and terms of sale." Shulof further argued that the personal liability provision was unconscionable (too one-sided to be enforced). The court rejected this argument, reasoning that a New York court would enforce such a provision since it was in an arm's-length commercial transaction involving sophisticated parties. The court held that Mr. Shulof was "jointly and severally liable" with JSF for any damages owed to FFS for the furs purchased at its auctions.

Liability of Juliette Shulof

The parties do not dispute that the bill of exchange is a negotiable instrument, and therefore subject to the provisions of Article 3 of the New York Uniform Commercial Code. The relevant section of the Code is § 3-403, which governs signatures by authorized representatives. Under subsection (2), an authorized representative who signs his own name to an instrument:

a *is personally obligated if the instrument neither names the person represented nor shows that the representative signed in a representative capacity;*

b *except as otherwise established between the immediate parties, is personally obligated if the instrument names the person represented but does not show that the representative signed in a representative capacity, or if the instrument does not name the person represented but does show that the representative signed in a representative capacity.*

In the case, Mrs. Shulof signed as "Juliette A. Shulof" above a typed name of "Juliette Shulof Furs Inc.," which had been typed in by the preparer of the instrument, FFS. New York has a policy against imposing personal liability on corporate officers. However, this policy gives way before the policy considerations underlying N.Y.U.C.C. § 3-403, which "aims to foster certainty and definiteness in the law of commercial paper (negotiable instruments), as to the party obligated to pay." Okobank, as a *holder in due course*, never dealt directly with either of the Shulofs or JSF. Accordingly, the Court finds that Mrs. Shulof's signature on the bill of exchange did not give notice that she signed in a representative capacity only, and therefore she is personally liable for the amount of the bill.

Case Highlights

There is a strong public policy in corporate law against imposing personal liability on corporate officers for actions performed on behalf of the corporation.

- It is customary under Finnish law for an agent to be held personally liable as a surety for goods purchased at an auction
- A corporate officer who signs a bill of exchange or draft must state she signs *only* in a representative capacity in order to avoid personal liability
- The public policy underlying negotiable instrument law is that a *holder in due course* may collect against the signer of the instrument
- A choice of law clause in a contract will be enforced if there is a reasonable connection between the choice and the transaction, unless a strong public policy of the forum court is threatened
- Owners at an auction have the right to prescribe the manner, conditions, and terms of sale.

The requirements to establish a business or an office in a foreign country vary dramatically from one country to the next. For example, some countries limit foreign companies to hiring nationals as sales representatives or agents. The foreign exporter, however, can exert substantial control over its agents through **management agreements.** With a branch office, the parent company can establish different types of operations. The branch office generally operates under the trade name of the parent company. Advantages of such an operation include ease in establishment, central management, and fewer required disclosures of confidential information to third parties. The major disadvantages are the risk of host country taxation and unlimited liability for the activities of the branch office, such as product liability. In some countries, branch office activities may also be limited.

Companies planning a permanent presence in a foreign country may choose to establish an independent subsidiary or purchase an existing company. As noted previously, most countries recognize a variety of limited liability entities. For example, the French Civil Code recognizes the individual partnership (general and limited), *limited liability company* (LLC) (ordinary or additional liability), joint stock company (corporation) (open and closed), and the industrial enterprise (state or municipal).

The corporate entity is recognized in almost all countries in the world, but names and abbreviations for corporations vary in different legal systems. In the U.S., a corporation is signified by the use of "Inc." after the company's name to indicate that it is an "incorporated" entity. The term "Limited" or "Ltd." is used in Canada and Great Britain. "S.A." for *Sociedad Anonyme* is the corporate designation in France and Spain. "SpA" or *Societa per Azioni* is the Italian symbol for corporation, and "Y.K." or *Yugen-Kaisha* is the Japanese designation for a corporation. In Germany, a public corporation is designated by the abbreviation "AG" (*Aktiengesellschaft*) and the private corporation is referred to as "GmbH" (*Gesellschaft mit beschränkter Haftung*). Another variation not found in U.S. law is the LLC *with additional liability*. The standard Russian LLC, like those in the U.S., limits the owners' liability for the debts of the company to the value of their contributions. The LLC with additional liability makes the owners liable for a *pro rata* share of the company's debts in bankruptcy. This form is intended to provide additional security to creditors. The **joint stock company** is a form of corporation. The closed version is limited to no more than 50 shareholders, under Russian law, who can maintain their ownership interests through a preemptive right to purchase a *pro rata* share of any subsequent issuance of stock.[6]

Foreign Competition Law

If the market entry strategy decided upon is the purchase of an existing foreign company, then the law of the host country must be thoroughly researched, especially its antitrust or **competition law.** The EU provides one example of an advanced competition law system. In order to purchase a company situated in an EU country, a purchaser must obtain clearance from Directorate Competition of the European Commission. The following *Commission Decision of 17/11/1999* provides insight into the nuances of European competition law.

Commission Decision of 17/11/1999

1999 OJ C 357 (Case No IV/M.1652)

The Commission received a notification of proposed concentration (large market share or monopoly) involving the acquisition by the Belgian company, SA D'Ieteren NV (D'Ieteren), of sole control of the South African company Plate Glass & Shatterprufe Industries Limited (PGSI). Following examination of the notification, the Commission concluded that the notified operation falls within the scope of Council Regulation (EEC) No. 4064/89 (exemption) and does not raise serious doubts as to its compatibility with the common market and the European Economic Area Agreement (EEA).

D'Ieteren is involved in a range of business activities in the automotive sector, comprising broadly: (i) wholesale and retail motor vehicle distribution, (ii) servicing and repair and the supply of spare parts for motor vehicles, (iii) short-term car rental, and (iv) long-term car rental and financing. D'Ieteren has practically no activities outside the EU, and within the EU some 70 percent of its turnover is in Belgium. PGSI is a group involved in the manufacture, distribution, repair, and replacement of glass and board products. It has activities in South Africa, Central Africa, U.S., Australia, New Zealand, and Brazil, as well as in the EU.

The transaction consists of a number of steps through which D'Ieteren will acquire sole control of PGSI. D'Ieteren will carry out these steps through a joint venture company, SA Dicobel (Dicobel), in which it will hold 70 percent of the shares. The remaining 30 percent is to be held by SA Copeba Novo (Copeba), a Belgian holding company. In the Shareholders' Agreement of Dicobel, Copeba's role is stated to be that of "financial partner," and provision is made for a majority representation by D'Ieteren on the Board. Dicobel will, in turn, acquire the majority shareholding of each of three companies, namely, Old Belron, Rest of the World, Hold Co Southern Africa, and Glass SA, which between them comprise the PGSI group of companies. Through its majority presence on the Boards of these companies, Dicobel will enjoy sole control over PGSI. Thus D'Ieteren, through its sole control of Dicobel, will have sole control of PGSI.

Concentration of a Community Dimension

The operation constitutes an acquisition by D'Ieteren of sole control of PGSI, and is, therefore, a concentration within the meaning of Article 3.1.b. of the Merger Regulation. D'Ieteren and PGSI have a combined aggregate worldwide turnover in excess of €2,500 million. In each of three EU Member States, their combined aggregate turnover is over €100 million. The operations have, therefore, a Community dimension.

Relevant Product Markets

The activities of D'Ieteren and PGSI, through its subsidiary, Belron International overlap in two areas, vertically related, (i) supply of automotive glass to the independent aftermarket, consisting of independent car dealerships, garages, and body shops (IAM), which the Commission has already considered to constitute a product market in itself; and (ii) the repair and replacement of automotive glass, which would constitute another product market.

Relevant Geographic Markets

The IAM market has already been considered to be of a Community-wide geographic scope by the Commission, and this definition is retained in the present case. With regard to the repair and replacement of automotive glass, D'Ieteren submitted that the existence of national distribution networks with national pricing and single (free call) telephone numbers indicated a national geographic scope for this market. Other characteristics, such as different suppliers in different EU Member States and price differences from one EU Member State to another, can be considered further indicators of a national scope for the market for these services. However, given that the operation (merger) does not raise any serious concerns, either at a national or wider level (D'Ieteren does not have these activities outside of Belgium), the Commission does not need to define the geographic scope of the market for the repair and replacement of automotive glass more precisely.

Assessment—Repair and Replacement of Automotive Glass

The repair and replacement of automotive glass would constitute an affected market in Belgium. Although the merger (acquisition) strengthens D'Ieteren's market share, the actual change brought about in the overall structure of supply in the market is very small, given D'Ieteren's very limited share. Furthermore, D'Ieteren has indicated that it will be confronted with competition from a variety of competitors, including: (i) independent service providers (5 to 15 percent of the market); (ii) independent car dealerships (25 to 35 percent); and (iii) body shops and garages (15 to 25 percent). Under these circumstances, the Commission considers that the operation will not lead to the creation or strengthening of a dominant position in the repair and replacement of automotive glass in Belgium.

For the above reasons, the Commission has decided not to oppose the notified operation and to declare it compatible with the common market.

Case Highlights

- Directorate Competition of the European Commission is responsible for the enforcement of EU competition law
- Before acquiring a European company, a foreign investor should *notify* (consult) with Directorate Competition
- Factors used to determine whether an acquisition or merger will create a *dominant position* (monopoly) subject to abuse include whether the acquisition has a community dimension, the relevant product markets, the geographic scope of the market, and the market shares of the companies.

For more information on EU competition law, see Chapter 7, "European Union and People's Republic of China."

Foreign Trade Zones

A foreign or free trade zone can minimize legal exposure in a foreign country. Foreign and domestic merchandise may enter the designated foreign trade zones without a formal customs entry. Therefore, importation and subsequent re-exportation are not subject to customs duties or excise taxes. While in the trade zone, the merchandise may be stored, sampled, labeled, repaired, assembled, processed, tested, displayed, repackaged, and manufactured. A foreign exporter may ship unsold goods into a trade zone for storage purposes without incurring the costs of duties or formal entry into the country. The goods may be trans-shipped without penalty, or prospective buyers can inspect goods and rejected goods can be transferred out or destroyed duty-free.

If the final product is exported, no customs duty, or excise tax is levied. If the final product is imported into the country, then customs duties and excise taxes are due at the *time of transfer* from the foreign trade zone to formal entry into the country. The fact that duties are due only at the time of formal entry of the merchandise can be used by foreign exporters to improve their cash flow. Foreign trade zones are found in many countries in the world and conform to the free trade principles of the World Trade Organization (WTO).

Joint Ventures and Franchising

International joint venture or franchising arrangements are attractive for a number of reasons.[7] They allow a party to utilize the partners' or franchisees' local expertise, marketing skills, and established lines of distribution. Joint ventures and franchising are well suited for entry into a foreign market through the use of a host country national familiar with the local language, law, and culture. It should be noted that the term "joint venture" is not legally defined in some foreign legal systems. Joint ventures in many countries will be governed by general partnership law, while in other countries there are specialized joint venture laws. It is important to research foreign law to familiarize oneself with the forms of doing business recognized under national law that can be utilized to approximate the joint venture concept.

Joint Ventures

International joint ventures are used in a wide variety of manufacturing, mining, and service industries and are frequently undertaken in conjunction with technology licensing. Companies find it desirable to enter into a joint venture with a foreign firm in order to share high capital costs and risks frequently associated with foreign operations. Moreover, the local partner brings to the joint venture its knowledge of the customs and tastes of the people, an established distribution network, government connections, and valuable business contacts.

There are, of course, disadvantages to international joint ventures. A major drawback to joint ventures, especially in countries that limit foreign companies to 49 percent or less participation, is the loss of effective managerial control. A loss of effective managerial control can result in reduced profits, inferior product quality, and exposure to product liability and environmental litigation and fines. Like technology licensing agreements, joint ventures can raise competition (antitrust) issues, particularly when the prospective joint venture partners are existing or potential competitors in the affected national markets.

Companies contemplating international joint ventures should consider retaining experienced legal counsel in the host country. Qualified foreign counsel (lawyers) can be very helpful in obtaining government approvals and providing ongoing advice regarding the host country's patent, trademark, copyright, tax, labor, corporate, commercial, antitrust, and exchange control laws.

Joint Venture Agreement

A simple definition of joint venture is "a contract that creates a partnership for the purpose of performing some kind of business operation."[8] It is a business collaboration in which the joint venture participants share resources, risks, and profits. Joint ventures often involve joint management and are established for specific objectives and sometimes for a fixed duration. In order for a joint venture to succeed, it must be carefully thought out by all the prospective partners. The parties must move cautiously in order to gain the trust of other participants, the parties' capacities, motives, prior relationships, and project objectives should be fully discussed during the preliminary stage of the negotiations.

A joint venture is an elastic vehicle for doing business and can take numerous forms. For example, the parties can enter into an agreement to work together, or they can agree to create an entirely separate entity, such as a corporation, in order to transact business. Two forms of joint ventures are the *single project* and *business alliance* joint ventures.[9] The single project venture aims to develop specific business opportunities with a single, identifiable goal. These single project joint ventures generally have a relatively short life span. An example would be a joint venture for a single construction project. The business alliance venture envisions a more fluid, long-term business relationship.

In negotiating and structuring joint ventures, proper attention should be given to the issues of share allocation, financing, protecting minority interests, confidentiality, and the transfer or continuation of the business. Shares may be allocated based upon each party's contribution, or joint venturers may authorize different classes or types of shares in order to attract other investors such as venture capitalists. Investors may structure their contributions as either equity contributions or loans and should consider all accounting and tax ramifications, such as the EU's 1 percent duty on company capital. The following list explains some of the key provisions in the joint venture agreement:

- The **purpose clause**, which maps the scope and goals of the business enterprise, is crucial for maintaining the long-term viability of the joint venture arrangement. Scope relates to geography, products and services, and duration. In order to allow for the venture to move in different directions to take advantage of unforeseen opportunities, an **exceptions clause** that allows for adjustments to the purpose clause along prescribed parameters should be included.

- Joint venturers must also establish the initial level of capitalization, including the amount and type of currency to be invested by each partner. If non-currency contributions are contemplated, the agreement should specify a valuation method. Also, the parties should expressly agree to the adoption of accounting standards such as American or EU accounting standards and practices. The agreement should also specify the level of indebtedness by establishing an acceptable debt-to-equity ratio.
- A successful joint venture agreement provides the means to make future funding decisions. If external funding is likely to be sought in the future, an agreement is needed as to whether the joint venture partners will provide guarantees in order to procure external financing.
- If the joint venture is between numerous parties, then provisions to protect minority interests may be necessary. One way to protect minority interests is to categorize decisions as "ordinary" or "extraordinary." Extraordinary decisions would require a supermajority vote for approval such as a two-thirds or 75 percent vote. Extraordinary decisions include capital expenditures in excess of a certain amount; borrowings in excess of a certain amount; admittance of a new joint venture partner; appointment or removal of directors; material changes in the business operation; sale or transfer of assets; contracting with principals of the joint venture; and approval of budgets.

Other provisions should address the transfer or sale of ownership by partners. Strict confidentiality and noncompetition provisions are also necessary. The partners may be prohibited from competing with the joint venture by stipulations that include being unable to hire employees of the joint venture for a period of time, maintaining the secrecy of all confidential information, and not soliciting customers of the joint venture. Of course, these restrictions must be reasonable, or they may be subject to challenge as illegal restraints of trade under common law or EU competition law.

Another crucial set of provisions to ensure the ongoing viability of the venture is management provisions. *Double parenting* is a pervasive problem in which both joint venturers attempt to assert independent control over the joint venture. The degree of managerial control allocated to the different joint venturers should be carefully defined such as whether the owner of the greater share will have greater managerial control or whether veto power is to be given to the partners, including minority partners, for particular classes of important decisions, as well as designating the partner for selecting a management team and the reporting and information systems that will be used by the joint venture.[10] Ultimately, these provisions will reflect the essential nature of the joint venture as one controlled by a dominant parent or as one with a shared management structure.

Finally, the joint venture should have a detailed termination provision stating the events that allow the parties to terminate their involvement such as failure of a participant to obtain necessary government approvals; failure of the venture to reach a pre-agreed level of profitability; management deadlock; and an adverse and debilitating change in the law. The termination clause should also describe how unforeseeable or *force majeure* events will affect termination of the joint venture.

Ancillary (Collateral) Agreements

Secondment agreements are used to require the "lending" of employees of the joint venture partners to the joint venture. It is important to determine whether these employees are to be treated as independent contractors or employees of the joint venture. Service contracts between the partners and their joint venture could also be utilized in the management of the joint venture enterprise.

Often one of the contributions of a joint venture partner is its expertise in its home country regarding the distribution of goods or services. An express **distribution agreement** should be entered into between that partner and the joint venture. The distribution agreement's termination provisions should be tied to those in the joint venture agreement.

International joint ventures may include the use of the know-how or intellectual property rights of one of the joint venture partners. In such a situation, an independently negotiated **intellectual property transfer** or licensing agreement is necessary and should deal with the withdrawal of the licensor-partner. The licensor-partner may demand that the licensing of intellectual property rights be dependent on the licensor's continued involvement in the joint venture.

Foreign Government Regulation

Foreign governments commonly regulate joint venture transactions. The most common restrictions are foreign participation requirements in which control of the enterprise must vest in a local company. Unique types of government regulations can be found on a country-by-country basis. For example, the People's Republic of China enacted Regulations on Labor Management in Foreign Joint Ventures. It requires that a labor contract, approved by the Chinese government, be entered into between the joint venture and a trade union. It further provides that all workers of the joint venture "shall be selected for employment through examinations conducted by the joint venture." The joint venture's ability to discharge employees is also restricted: "Punishment by discharge must be reported to the department in charge of enterprises and the labor management department for approval." China's more generic law on joint ventures, the Law on Chinese-Foreign Cooperative Joint Ventures, should be carefully reviewed before beginning any negotiations. It provides that the parties should agree in a *cooperative venture contract* on the terms and conditions of cooperation, the distributions of earnings or products, the sharing of risks and losses, the form of operation and management, and the ownership of property. All such contracts need to be approved by the relevant examination and approval authorities.

Chinese law states that "matters such as employment, discharge, remuneration, welfare, labor protection, and labor insurance should be stipulated through the making of contracts in accordance with the law." Therefore, a foreign investor is required to enter into a labor contract as a condition for joint venture approval. The labor contract must be submitted to the municipal or provincial government for approval. Finally, any discharge of an employee must be reported to the labor management department for approval. When contemplating a joint venture in China it is good practice to consult with the Chinese Ministry of Foreign Economic Relations and Trade (MOFERT) to expedite foreign trade contracts.

Franchising

There are different types of franchising arrangements, including: (1) production or manufacturing; (2) distribution; (3) developer agreements; and (4) master franchise agreements. In production franchises the franchisor licenses its trademark to the licensee, who is then authorized to manufacture according to the franchisor's specifications and to market the product. In a distribution franchise, the franchisor produces the goods and sells them to the distributor franchisee for resale to the final consumer. In area developer agreements, also known as territorial franchises, the franchisor gives the franchisee the right to develop an entire territorial area. The master franchise agreement allows the franchisee to sub-franchise, meaning the franchisee may assign rights to other parties. Such an arrangement creates a chain of relationships: master franchisor to master franchisee/sub-franchisor to sub-franchisee.

The allocation of exclusive franchise territories is susceptible to attack under foreign competition or antitrust laws. In Europe, an EU **block exemption** provides a general exception for franchise arrangements. The EU block exemption has resulted in the franchise industry in Europe being primarily self-regulated. The European Franchise Federation acts as an umbrella organization for the different national franchise associations, guiding franchisors promoting franchise operations. At the national level, the German Franchise Association publishes Pre-Contract Disclosure Requirements.

Other areas of interest for those contemplating franchising, licensing, or joint venturing in a foreign country include the protection of intellectual property rights (IPR), the use of local attorneys, transferability of ownership interests, and expropriation and dispute settlement policies. Intellectual property laws are not always enforced in some countries, which requires creative strategies to protect IPR, such as identifying counterfeiters and then signing them as legal licensees. Using a local partner is the best way to defend against the infringement of IPR.

Franchise Law

The advantage of franchising is that it is an efficient method for facilitating the transfer of know-how and expertise to other companies, while simultaneously allowing the franchisor to quickly establish a presence in foreign countries. In typical franchise agreements, the franchisor receives royalties and fees in exchange for the franchisee's use of the franchisor's IPR and confidential information to sell services or produce products. The franchisor typically provides training and guidance.

Some franchise agreements provide for a pool of funds contributed by franchisees that the franchisor uses to place advertisements. The franchise agreement should detail how advertising monies are to be spent by the franchisor. The franchisees should negotiate a clause allocating monies between national or international advertising campaigns and local advertisement. The *Broussard v. Meineke Discount Muffler Shops* case involves a dispute over such an advertisement provision.

Broussard v. Meineke Discount Muffler Shops

155 F.3d 331 (4th Cir. 1998)

Judge. This case is a study in the tensions that can beset the franchisor–franchisee relationship. Ten owners of Meineke Discount Muffler franchises sued franchisor Meineke Discount Muffler Shops, Inc. (Meineke), Meineke's in-house advertising agency New Horizons Advertising, Inc. (New Horizons), three officers of Meineke, and Meineke's corporate parents GKN and GKN Parts Industries Corporation (PIC). Plaintiffs claimed that Meineke's handling of franchise advertising breached the Franchise and Trademark Agreements (FTAs) that Meineke had entered into with each of the franchisees. Plaintiffs won a $390 million judgment against Meineke and its affiliated parties.

Under all versions of the FTA, each franchisee was to pay Meineke an initial franchise fee and thereafter some percentage of its weekly gross revenue (generally 7 to 8 percent) as a royalty. Franchisees also paid Meineke 10 percent of weekly revenues to fund national and local advertising. Initially, franchisees made these advertising contributions directly to a third-party advertising agency, M&N Advertising (M&N), which placed ads on a commission basis. In 1982, franchisees paid their 10 percent contributions to a central account maintained by Meineke, the Weekly Advertising Contribution (WAC) account.

Franchise advertising is addressed in two sections of the FTAs. All versions of the FTA oblige Meineke "to purchase and place from time to time advertising promoting the products and services sold by FRANCHISEE." At a dealers' meeting in April 1993, a Meineke official read from a December 1992 Uniform Franchise Offering Circular (UFOC) that disclosed New Horizons' 5 percent to 15 percent commission rates (essentially taking money from the advertising account for itself).

The jury returned a verdict against Meineke for breach of contract and against Meineke and New Horizons for breach of fiduciary duty, negligence, and unjust enrichment. The jury found that GKN and PIC had utilized Meineke and New Horizons as mere instrumentalities, and that PIC was merely an instrumentality of GKN, which justified piercing the corporate veil and imposing vicarious liability on GKN. Meineke, New Horizons, GKN, PIC, and three officers of Meineke were found to have committed fraud, and of making negligent misrepresentations. The jury awarded plaintiffs $196 million in compensatory damages, as well as $150 million in punitive damages (penalties).

However, the lower court erred by allowing plaintiffs to advance claims for breach of fiduciary duty when there is no such duty under North Carolina law between franchisee and franchisor. Though plaintiffs would portray franchisees as helpless Davids to the franchisor's Goliath, size, as that story teaches, is not a reliable indicator of strength or influence. Instead, courts in many other jurisdictions refuse to superimpose fiduciary duties on a franchisor–franchisee relationship. REVERSED.

Case Highlights

- Note that the reversal related to the claim of breach of fiduciary duties, but not the claims for breach of contract, negligence, and unjust enrichment
- The franchise arrangement is contractual in nature; however, regulations require certain disclosures through the use of a Uniform Franchise Offering Circular (UFOC)
- Because of the contractual nature of the franchise arrangement, the franchisor does not owe a fiduciary duty to its franchisees
- Note the size of the punitive damage component of the jury's award. Punitive damages are unique to American law and are not found in other legal systems
- Note also that the corporate veil will only be pierced to hold shareholders or a parent corporation vicariously liable when the shareholders or parent exercises complete *domination* over the corporation or its subsidiary, or if they fail to observe corporate formalities.

The franchise relationship is an American creation.[11] The U.S. has developed an extensive body of law regulating the franchise agreement and relationship: A large number of states regulate the offer and sale of franchises; many state laws require franchisors to register a detailed offering statement before being able to solicit franchisees; some statutes provide the franchisee with a right to cure any of its defaults under the franchise agreement and grant a minimum notice period prior to termination by the franchisor. The next section will review some of the clauses commonly found in the franchise agreement.

The Franchise Agreement

The following commonly used clauses place various obligations upon the franchisor and the franchisee. These clauses should be completely understood when negotiating a franchise agreement. A **site selection clause** delineates the franchisor's responsibilities in the site selection process. Such clauses range from placing an affirmative duty on the franchisor to find an appropriate site to simply requiring the franchisor's approval. An approval clause should state the criteria for the franchisor's disapproval of a site. In *Brennan v. Carvel Corp.*,[12] the court went outside the boundaries of the franchise site selection clause in finding that the franchisor had failed to meet its obligations in the site selection process. The court found the franchisor's Deposit Agreement stated that the franchisor would expend a "substantial amount of time and effort in seeking, surveying, and showing locations available for a store." This case illustrates the importance in reviewing all franchise documentation for consistency. A merger or entire agreement clause (excluding the use of evidence outside the written agreement) in the final franchise agreement is unlikely to prevent courts from reviewing preliminary agreements, ancillary agreements, promotional materials, and governmental filings for purposes of clarification or to substantiate a claim of misrepresentation.

Physical layout and signage, along with operational standards, are important areas of control for the franchisor. Clauses relating to these matters are essential to maintain system-wide integrity and uniformity of standards. Most retail franchises utilize layouts that maintain the uniformity of appearance at all franchise locations. The appearance (design or display) of the franchise location may be protected by a separate trademark (trade dress) or be composed of a variety of trademarks, service marks, and copyrights. Failure of the franchisee to adhere to these and other operational standards provides the franchisor with good cause for termination of the franchise operation. Most layout clauses give the franchisor the absolute right of approval.

An **operational standards clause** provides a detailed description of quality standards and operational goals. It generally refers to an operating manual provided by the franchisor. An associated concern is the training of the franchisee and its employees, since training and consultation provided by the franchisor are at the heart of many franchise arrangements. A franchisor's failure to provide adequate training and consultation under these clauses would be grounds for a lawsuit by the franchisee. Most franchise systems are premised on uniform treatment between the franchisor and all its franchisees. However, franchisors sometimes incorporate a clause in their franchise agreements that allows them to vary contractual terms among their different franchisees. Such clauses have been grounds for claims of discriminatory treatment.

Territorial clauses grant the franchisee an exclusive territory within which the franchisor is barred from competing. The problem with such clauses is that the franchisor and franchisee may disagree regarding the scope of expansion of franchise operations within the territory. After the expiration of a certain period of time, the franchisor may then be allowed to further develop the territorial market.

The termination of the franchise by the franchisor, either for cause or nonrenewal is the action most likely to lead to litigation. Most franchise agreements contain a clause that allows the franchisor to terminate for any violation. However, termination for a minor breach will not be viewed favorably in most courts. Likewise, the **renewal clause** often provides an absolute right of the franchisor not to renew. Instead of absolute rights to terminate or not to renew, termination or nonrenewal clauses should specify the violations that are considered material for termination and grounds for nonrenewal. Appropriate grounds for termination or nonrenewal include the loss of a lease, franchisee insolvency, denial of franchisor access to inspect, and repeated violations of quality standards. Internationally, termination without good cause or without a reasonable period to correct deficiencies is vulnerable to legal challenge.

The franchise agreement commonly requires that an initial fee be paid for the right to obtain a franchise and then payment of **royalties** based upon a percentage of gross or net sales. It is prudent for the franchisor, especially in the international setting, to require the franchisee to maintain certain types and amounts of insurance including specific amounts of comprehensive general liability and products liability insurance. The contract should provide that the franchisor will be an "additional endorsee" on all such policies. The **insurance clause** should be coupled with a hold harmless clause that requires the franchisee to defend the franchisor against any liability claims arising from or related to its operation of the franchise.

Since most franchise arrangements include the transfer of IPR, the agreement should expressly retain the title to those rights to the franchisor. See Figure 4.3 *Comparative Law*: "Intellectual Property Transfer Clause," which illustrates a franchise clause dealing with the transfer of trade secrets and intellectual property. The clause makes clear that the franchisor owns the intellectual property being licensed and that on the franchise's termination all of the property rights return to the franchisor.

UNIDROIT Guide to International Master Franchising

One way to avoid entering multiple franchise agreements with individual franchisees in a foreign country is the **master franchise** arrangement. In the master franchise arrangement, the franchisor enters into an agreement with a sub-franchisor (master franchisee) in order to develop a franchise territory. The sub-franchisor is entitled to establish individual franchise locations or to find sub-franchisees to operate within its territory: Franchisor >>> Master Franchise (Sub-Franchisor) >>> Sub-Franchisees. Master franchise agreements are defined in the EU Franchise Regulations as those in which "the relationship between franchisor and franchisees is made through a third undertaking, the master franchisee." In this way, the franchisor can directly exercise control over the individual franchise operations.

The International Institute for the Unification of Private Law's *UNIDROIT Guide to International Master Franchise Arrangements* provides an array of information, along with standard clauses to be used in the drafting of a franchise contract. Some of the issues addressed include the types of franchising

FRANCHISEE acknowledges that ownership of all right, title, and interest to the ABC franchise system and its marks are and shall remain vested solely in the franchisor, and the FRANCHISEE disclaims any right or interest therein or the goodwill derived therefrom. FRANCHISEE agrees that all materials loaned or otherwise made available to him by the franchisor at any time before or during the term of this Agreement relating to the franchise system, including, without limitation, the Manual in its entirety, financial information, marketing strategy, and programs are to be considered trade secrets of the franchisor and shall be kept confidential and used by FRANCHISEE only in connection with the franchise operation. FRANCHISEE agrees not to divulge any of the trade secrets to any person other than its employees and then only to the extent necessary for the operation of the franchise and, specifically, that FRANCHISEE will not, nor permit anyone to, reproduce, copy, or exhibit any portion of the Manual or any other trade secrets of the franchisor. FRANCHISEE shall immediately notify franchisor of all infringements or limitations of franchisor's marks, which come to its attention.

Figure 4.3 Comparative Law: Intellectual Property Transfer Clause.

arrangements available, the relationship between the franchising agreement and other types of agreements (commercial agency, license, technology transfer, distribution), and the differences in the franchisor–franchisee and sub-franchisor–sub-franchisee relationships.

International Franchising

EU regulations define franchising as "a gathering of industrial or intellectual property rights relative to trademark, commercial denominations, insignia, utility models, designs, copyrights, know-how, or patents to be utilized for the resale of goods or services to a final user."[13] The franchise agreement generally requires a common and uniform presentation of franchise operations, the transfer of expertise and know-how from the franchisor to the franchisee, and the supplying of technical assistance by the franchisor. The court in *McAlpine v. AAMCO Automatic Transmission, Inc.*[14] described the synergy of franchising and the inherent seeds of its own destruction:

> The franchise arrangement starts as a mutually advantageous business relationship. Both the franchisor and the franchisee contribute to this arrangement in order to obtain benefits they could not obtain independently. The franchisor's contribution is a combination of factors: trademark, recognized product or service, experience, advertising, and management support. The franchisee's contribution is capital, day-to-day management and the payment of franchise fees. The franchisor benefits from the use of franchisee capital, fees, and lower-level management, for it allows the franchise organization to expand more rapidly. As the franchise becomes successful, the partnership arrangement, which seemed reasonable at its inception, and then begins to appear burdensome to the franchisee who comes to regard the payment of franchise fees as restricting its profitability.

To further illustrate this point, the *Dayan v. McDonald's Corp.* case below exemplifies the two major risks of international franchising; namely, loss of control over franchise operations and the inability to terminate the franchise relationship under some national laws.

Another issue especially important when franchising in a foreign country is to provide the appropriate means of termination and the protection of **trade secrets**. There is no generally accepted definition of trade secrets. It is a much broader concept than statutorily protected IPR (patent, copyright, trademark). The Uniform Trade Secrets Act offers this definition:

> "Trade Secret" means information, including a formula, pattern, compilation, program, device, method, technique, or process, that: (i) derives independent economic value, actual or potential, from not being generally known to, and not being readily ascertainable by proper means by other persons who can obtain economic value from its disclosure or use, and (ii) is the subject of efforts that are reasonable under the circumstances to maintain its secrecy.[15]

Raymond Dayan v. McDonald's Corp.

466 N.E.2d 958 (Ill. App. 1984)

This appeal arises out of a suit brought to enjoin (prevent) McDonald's Corporation from terminating Raymond Dayan's restaurant franchise in Paris, France. Other issues relating to this controversy have been considered twice before by the court. After a 65-day trial, the Circuit Court of Cook County denied plaintiff's request for a permanent injunction. The trial court issued a 114-page memorandum and an order terminating plaintiff's franchise to operate McDonald's restaurants in and around Paris.

The unique character of the 1971 license agreement was a key factor at trial. Dayan insisted upon paying a lower royalty of 1 percent for a developmental license. Nonetheless, maintaining the Quality, Safety, and Cleanliness (QSC) standards of McDonald's Corp. was explicitly recognized in the Master License Agreement (MLA). It recites the rationale for maintaining QSC standards: "departure of Restaurants anywhere in the world from these standards impedes the successful operation of Restaurants throughout the world and injures the value of its [McDonald's] Patents, Trademarks, Trade name, and Property." The individual operating license agreements (OLA) included the following termination provision:

> *Licensee acknowledges that uniform quality and taste of food, excellence of service, cleanliness, appearance, and general performance are of the utmost importance to the successful operation of the business venture of the Licensee and of all other Licensees using said System. The Licensee agrees that any violation of this paragraph shall be deemed to be a substantial breach of this Agreement and shall give the Licensor the right to terminate the Agreement.*

Witnesses called by McDonald's testified as to the deplorable condition of Dayan's restaurants. In particular, their testimony revealed that Dayan was not using approved products; used no pickles; charged extra for catsup (ketchup) or mustard; hid straws and napkins under the counter; refused to take a refresher course at McDonald's "Hamburger University"; the stores were filthy and without many items of necessary equipment; the store crews were poorly trained and frequently out of uniform; and customer complaints were numerous. Barnes, the president of McDonald's international division, testified that in June 1976 he informed Dayan that he would be given six months to bring his restaurants up to standard and at the end of this period McDonald's would exercise its right to formal inspection. The inspectors found gross violations of McDonald's QSC standards at all the stores they visited. In July 1977, a stern warning letter was sent to Dayan advising him that the number, variety, and severity of QSC deficiencies justified a default declaration but that such declaration would be held in abeyance (delayed) for six months to "give you an opportunity to take immediate corrective action." Ultimately, McDonald's brought suit in Paris to terminate the MLA, which resulted in Dayan filing the present suit in Illinois to enjoin termination.

In America (as well as other countries), a *covenant of good faith* and *fair dealing* is implied in every contract absent express disavowal. Problems relating to good faith performance typically arise where one party to the contract is given broad discretion in performance. It remains to be seen, however, what limitation the implied covenant of good faith imposes on franchisor discretion in terminating a franchise agreement. Another court stated that: "when parties enter into a contract of this character, and there is no express provision that it may be cancelled without cause, it seems fair and reasonable to assume that both parties entered into the arrangement in good faith, intending that if the service is performed in a satisfactory manner it will not be cancelled arbitrarily." These cases reflect judicial concern over longstanding abuses in franchise relationships, particularly contract provisions giving the franchisor broad unilateral powers of termination at will. The plaintiff argues that even if McDonald's had good cause for termination, it also had an improper motive (recapture the lucrative Paris market) thus breaching the implied covenant of good faith. We cannot agree. As a general proposition of law, it is widely held that where good cause exists, motive is immaterial. Our review of the evidence shows the trial court properly resolved this issue in favor of McDonald's. To characterize the condition of Dayan's restaurants as being in substantial noncompliance with McDonald's QSC standards is a profound understatement. Witnesses used terms describing the uncleanliness—such as "indescribable," "extremely defective sanitary conditions," "filthy, grimy, cruddy," "deplorable," "significantly unsanitary," "contaminated," "unsanitary," "very dirty," "very, very dirty," "disgusting," "abundance of filth," and "pig pens." Dayan also argues that McDonald's was obligated to provide it with operational assistance necessary to enable him to meet the QSC standards. As the trial court correctly realized: "It does not take a McDonald's trained French speaking operational man to know that grease dripping from kitchen vents must be stopped and not merely collected in a cup hung from the ceiling, that dogs are not permitted to defecate where food is stored, that insecticide is not blended with chicken breading, that past-dated products should be discarded, that a potato peeler should be somewhat cleaner than a tire-vulcanizer and that shortening should not look like crank case oil."

The judgment of the trial court denying plaintiff's request for a permanent injunction and finding that McDonald's properly terminated the franchise agreement is AFFIRMED.

Case Highlights

- Note the length and complexity, and ultimately the costs, of the litigation pertaining to the termination of a franchise agreement
- A master license agreement (MLA) is often used to develop an entire territory, while each franchise location is also governed by individual operating license agreements (OLA)
- The franchisor's right to terminate a franchise is limited by the duty of good faith and fair dealing, and in some cases, specific franchise termination laws
- Standards relating to quality, safety, and cleanliness (QSC) are vital to maintaining the integrity and reputation of the franchise system as a whole.

Trade Secrets and Confidential Information

The franchisor should determine if the information being given is a trade secret. If so, it should expressly list in the franchise agreement the information that it intends to treat as trade secrets. The agreement may list information not generally considered trade secrets and expressly state that the information is to be deemed "secret and confidential." For example, customer lists provided by the franchisor have been held to be legally protected trade secrets. A trade secret designation in the agreement is enhanced if: (1) the information is not readily obtainable through alternative sources and (2) the franchisor treats the lists as "secret and confidential." The agreement can further protect the franchisor with a separate confidentiality clause and a noncompetition clause. Overly restrictive noncompetition clauses are likely to be reviewed and modified by most courts. A franchise agreement that provides for a large amount of franchisor control may create problems under host country laws and regulations.[16] If viewed as a dependent agency relationship, the franchisor may become susceptible to the tax and labor laws of the host country, as well as being vulnerable to lawsuits such as products liability claims.

EU Franchise Regulations

EU competition law places limits on franchising. **EU Regulation of Franchise Agreements** provides an exemption from the application of EU competition law found in Article 85 of the Treaty of Rome.[17] Commission Regulation 4087/88 pertains to franchise agreements involving the distribution of goods or services, along with master franchise agreements. The Regulation expressly exempts from its coverage industrial franchises that generally include the manufacture of products through the transfer of intellectual property rights. It notes that those types of franchises may make use of the block exemptions pertaining to patent and know-how licensing.

EU Regulations recognize that some restrictions on the rights of the franchisee are needed in order to maintain the "homogeneity of the network and the constant cooperation between the franchisor and the franchisees [in order to] ensure a constant quality of the products and services" being provided. Article 2 provides a list of enforceable seemingly anti-competitive clauses:

- Allow for the development of exclusive franchise territories and prohibit franchisees actively seeking customers outside their designated franchise territories;
- Master franchisee can be prohibited from entering a sub-franchise agreement with an entity outside the territory of the master franchise;
- Prohibit the franchisee from selling goods or services of a competitor;
- Clauses mandating that the franchisee only sell goods or services that match "minimum objective quality specifications;"
- Generally, the franchisee cannot be restricted in determining its sources of supply; however, an exemption from this prohibition is given if requirements to purchase supplies from the franchisor or other designated third-party suppliers are necessary in order to meet "objective quality specifications;"

- Other clauses that are expressly permitted include best efforts, minimum sales quotas, customer service and warranty requirements, advertising requirements, confidentiality (including post-termination confidentiality), training requirements, rights to improvements made by franchisee to franchisor's intellectual property, location restrictions, nonassignment without prior consent, notice of infringement, and sales restricted to end users, other franchisees and resellers.

Prohibited clauses include those that restrict a franchisee from purchasing from another franchisee, from filling orders from parties outside its territory that were not actively sought, unduly limiting the franchisee's choice of suppliers or customers, and restrictions on pricing. These prohibited restrictions relate to a stated purpose of the Regulation that ensures that parallel imports and cross deliveries between franchisees remain possible. These prohibitions are aimed to limit the territorial restrictions for the benefit of consumers, allowing them to obtain products at lower prices.

Chapter Summary

1. There are numerous methods or strategies of doing business in foreign countries, some more risky and costly than others. Common methods used to gain a presence in a foreign country include opening a branch office, joint venturing with another company, or establishing a separate foreign subsidiary company (corporation, limited liability company, or social enterprise).
2. Foreign corporation law is different across countries. American corporation law focuses on the role of the shareholder, while in other countries corporate law sees shareholders and employees as equal stakeholders and, therefore, provides a wide array of employee protections. German corporations have two boards, the top board being the Supervisory Board with one-half of the members elected by shareholders and one-half by employees. The lower board is called the Management Board.
3. Some countries recognize entities that provide limited liability by different names such as the corporation, limited liability company, and joint stock company.
4. Some countries are more willing to "pierce the corporate veil" and hold shareholders liable for corporate debt than is found under American law.
5. European competition (antitrust) law is in certain areas stricter and places greater weight on consumer benefit than is found in the U.S. Before buying or merging with a European company, a company should seek the clearance or approval of Directorate General (DG) for Competition of the European Commission.
6. Joint ventures are a common means of expanding into foreign markets. In the common scenario, a company outside of a country partners with a company inside the country. This allows the outside company the ability to use the existing distribution network, knowledge of the foreign law, and government connections of its partner.

7. The key document in joint venturing is the joint venture agreement. This contract should be carefully negotiated and drafted. It is important that the joint venture agreement be strategic in nature in order to increase the chances of the joint venture being successful. Some of the important clauses in an international joint venture agreement include purpose, exception, and cross-indemnity clauses.
8. The joint venture agreement is generally accompanied by a number of ancillary contracts, such as distribution, intellectual property transfer or licensing, and secondment contracts.
9. Some countries, such as China, have specific laws that regulate joint ventures or certain types of ventures, such as technology joint ventures.
10. Franchising has become a method of quickly expanding overseas through direct, master, regional development, and distribution franchise arrangements. Franchising benefits from a block exemption under EU competition law.
11. A substantial body of franchise law has developed in the U.S. and has begun to evolve in other countries, such as countries in Europe and in China.
12. Some of the key clauses in the franchise agreement include site selection; operational standards; territorial royalties; intellectual property transfer; and renewal clauses. However, certain versions of these clauses may be unenforceable under EU Franchise Regulations.

Key Terms

Affiliate
Benefit Corporation
Block Exemption
Branch Office
Business Review Letter
Competition Law
Contractual Joint Venture
Corporation
Counter-Indemnity Clause
Crowdfunding
Distribution Agreement
Enterprise Liability
Equity Joint Venture
EU Regulations of Franchise Agreements
Exceptions Clause
Export Trade Certificate of Review
Foreign Subsidiary
Franchisee Review Clause
General Partnership
Insurance Clause
Intellectual Property Transfer
Joint Stock Company
Joint Venture
Limited Liability Company (LLC)
Limited Partnership
Management Agreements
Management Board
Master Franchise
Operational Standards Clause
Piercing the Corporate Veil
Purpose Clause
Renewal Clause
Representative Office
Royalties Clause
Secondment Agreement
Shareholders' Council
Site Selection Clause
Social Enterprise Company
Social Entrepreneurship
Supervisory Board
Supervisory Committee
Territorial Clause
Trade Secrets
Transfer Pricing

Chapter Problems

1. Select two of the following countries: China, U.S., Japan, Germany. Compare and contrast corporate law in the two countries you have selected. Discuss how corporate law reflects society's fundamental view of the role of the corporation.
2. What does the phrase "piercing the corporate veil" mean? When might the corporate veil be pierced? How does this philosophy compare with that of many of the U.S.'s trading partners?
3. What are some of the issues that potential joint venture partners need to discuss in detail before entering into an agreement? Discuss some of the contractual clauses that can be incorporated into an agreement in order to minimize potential conflict.

Internet Exercises

1. Research a foreign country or countries for opportunities and restrictions on the different ways of transacting business discussed in this chapter using the U.S. Department of State's Country Commercial at http://www.state.gov.
2. Research the status of franchising in a foreign country. A good place to start is the website for the International Franchise Association at http://www.franchise.org. A growing number of national franchise associations, along with the European Franchise Federation, can also be accessed.

Other Internet Sources

Cornell Legal Information Institute at http://www.law.cornell.edu/topics/ corporations.html (overview of corporation law).

UNIDROIT Guide to International Master Franchise Arrangements (2nd ed. 2007): http://www.unidroit.org/instruments/franchising/guide/second-edition-2007.

International Franchise Association: http://www.franchise.org.

Notes

1 Unlike the U.S., where most business organization or enterprise law is found at the level of the 50 different states.

2 See http://www.grameenfoundation.org/our-impact/personal-stories.

3 See Fundly at https://blog.fundly.com/crowdfunding-statistics.

4 Excerpted from Timothy L. Fort and Cindy A. Schipani, "Corporate Governance in a Global Environment: The Search for the Best of All Worlds," 33 *Vanderbilt Journal of Transnational Law* 829 (2000).

5 699 N.Y.S.2d 503 (1999).

6 See Edward C. Vandenberg, "The Evolution of Russian Forms of Business Enterprise," 28 *Ottawa Law Review* 343 (1997).
7 See generally Karen J. Hladik, *International Joint Ventures* (1985).
8 William F. Fox, Jr., *International Commercial Agreements: A Primer on Drafting, Negotiating and Resolving Disputes* 79 (1992).
9 Mark Perry-Knox-Gore, "Joint Ventures" in *Structuring International Contracts* 87 (ed. Dennis Campbell 1997).
10 Steven R. Salbu and Richard A. Brahm, "Strategic Considerations in Designing Joint Venture Contracts," *Columbia Business Law Review* 253 (1992).
11 Robert W. Emerson, "Franchise Contract Clauses and the Franchisor's Duty of Care Toward its Franchisees," 72 *North Carolina Law Review* 905, 909 (1994) (the article is the source of much of the material covered in this section).
12 929 F.2d 801 (S.D. Fla. 1992).
13 Commission Regulation (EEC) No. 4087/88 of 30 November 1988 on the Application of Article 85(3) of the Treaty to Categories of Franchise Agreements.
14 461 F. Supp. 1232, 1238-39 (E.D. Mich. 1978).
15 Uniform Trade Secrets Act § 1(4), 14 U.L.A. 541 (1980).
16 Ralph H. Folsom and Michael W. Gordon, *International Business Transactions* 428 (1995).
17 Commission Regulation (EEC) No. 4087/88 of 30 November 1988 on the Application of Article 85(3) of the Treaty to Categories of Franchise Agreements.

Chapter 5

International Commercial Dispute Resolution

The cost and uncertainty of potential litigation with a foreign citizen or company act as a deterrent to entering into international business transactions. The prospect of having to pursue or defend a claim in a foreign court using foreign law may prove too risky for some businesspersons. Anyone contemplating a business transaction with a foreign entity should ask the following questions: (1) What are the alternatives to transnational litigation? (2) Where will a future dispute be argued or settled? (3) What country's law would be applied to such a dispute? (4) Will a settlement or decision be enforceable in a foreign country? These questions should be discussed during the earlier stages of contract negotiation. The response to Question (1) is the recognition that international commercial arbitration has been a longstanding and popular alternative to international litigation. The contractual devices represented by choice of law and forum selection clauses provide the avenue for dealing with Questions (2) and (3). Finally, a review of national laws and international conventions will help answer Question (4).

International Litigation

Anyone seeking to undertake international litigation faces three areas of concern. First, how does one properly begin a lawsuit against a foreign company? Second, once the litigation begins, how do the parties gather evidence? Third, if successful in the litigation, how does one enforce a judgment in another country?

DOI: 10.4324/9781003469230-6

Starting Litigation: Service of Process and Jurisdiction

To bring a lawsuit against a foreign company, one must properly serve process. **Service of process** is the formal notification of the defendant to defend itself in court.[1] Proper service of process is necessary in order for a court to obtain **personal jurisdiction** over the defendant. Failure to obtain legally sufficient service of process is likely to result in the non-enforceability of any *default judgment* obtained in the event that the defendant fails to appear. In order to require a foreign party to defend itself in a suit brought in another country, the service of process should meet the requirements of both the country of the party being served and the country where any judgment will need to be enforced. Service of process requirements vary widely throughout the world. Some national *rules of civil procedure* allow service in a foreign country "by any form of mail, requiring a signed receipt." In contrast, service by mail is not recognized by a majority of foreign court systems.

The Convention on the Service Abroad of Judicial and Extrajudicial Documents in Civil or Commercial Matters, or **Hague Service Convention** provides for international service of process. The signatory countries to the Convention are required to establish a Central Authority for processing foreign plaintiffs' service of process requests. The Central Authority serves the defendant directly or arranges to have it served by the appropriate government agency. A number of important trading countries have adopted it, including the U.S., Japan, China, France, Germany, UK, Italy, Spain, and Canada. In countries not party to the Convention, **dual service** of process is recommended. Dual service aims to satisfy the service requirements of the country of the forum court and the country of the defendant in order to enhance the enforceability of any future judgment. The issues of personal jurisdiction over a foreign defendant are discussed in *Alpine View Co., Ltd. v. Atlas Copco AB*.

Alpine View Co., Ltd. v. Atlas Copco AB

205 F.3d 208 (5th Cir. 2000)

Judge. This case arises out of a breach of an Agreement between Alpine View Company (Alpine View) and Uniroc AB (Uniroc), a wholly-owned subsidiary of a Swedish holding company, and Atlas Copco AB (ACAB). Bjorn Hansen, the president of Alpine View, was granted exclusive worldwide rights for the distribution and sale of offshore drill bits manufactured by Shanghai Machinery & Equipment Import-Export Corporation (SMEC), a Chinese company.

To facilitate the sale of these products, Hansen sought an established distributor, and entered into the Agreement with Uniroc. Under the Agreement, Uniroc was to purchase drill bits from Hansen, and eventually become the exclusive distributor of the products. Uniroc was to pay Alpine View a commission based on net sales to users and distributors outside the Atlas Copco Group, which comprises ACAB and its 71 subsidiaries. To enhance its ability to deal directly with SMEC, Uniroc entered into a separate distributorship agreement. The existence of the separate distributorship agreement was a precondition for the effectiveness of the Agreement. Alpine View is incorporated under the laws of the British Virgin Islands and Hansen is a resident of Norway.

Dismissal for Lack of Personal Jurisdiction

We review the lower court's dismissal for want of personal jurisdiction. The Due Process Clause of the U.S. Constitution permits the exercise of personal jurisdiction over a nonresident defendant when (1) defendant has purposefully availed himself of the benefits and protections of the forum state by establishing *minimum contacts* with the forum state and (2) exercise of jurisdiction over that defendant does not offend traditional notions of fair play and substantive justice. Minimum contacts can be established either through contacts sufficient to assert specific jurisdiction, or contacts sufficient to assert general jurisdiction. *Specific jurisdiction* over a nonresident corporation is appropriate when that corporation has purposefully directed its activities at the forum state and the "litigation results from alleged injuries that arise out of or relate to those activities." *General jurisdiction* attaches where the nonresident defendant's contacts with the forum state, although not related to the plaintiff's cause of action, are "continuous and systematic."

Specific Jurisdiction and Stream-of-Commerce Theory

The Supreme Court stated that the "foreseeability that is critical to due process analysis is that the defendant's conduct and connection with the forum State are such that he should reasonably anticipate being hauled into court there." Plaintiffs rely heavily on the *stream-of-commerce theory*. In support of their argument that the stream-of-commerce theory is applicable to cases other than those involving products liability, plaintiffs point to courts applying the theory to cases arising in antitrust or intellectual property related claims.

When a nonresident's contact with the forum state stems from a product, sold or manufactured by the foreign defendant which has caused harm in the forum state, the court has specific jurisdiction if it finds that the defendant delivered the product into the stream of commerce with the expectation that it would be purchased by or used by consumers in the forum state. However, delivery of products into the stream of commerce does not support the assertion of specific jurisdiction over ACAB and Robbins. Plaintiffs argue that putting products into the stream of commerce with the expectation that Texans will purchase or use those products suffices to establish jurisdiction with respect to "any claims." This is more akin to a general jurisdiction argument than to a specific jurisdiction argument. Plaintiffs make no attempt to link defendants' contacts with Texas and the current litigation. This is a link that specific jurisdiction requires. Plaintiffs have not asserted that the alleged misdeeds occurred in Texas, or that the Agreement was negotiated or executed in Texas. Neither Alpine View nor Hansen is considered a Texas resident.

General Jurisdiction and Alter-Ego Theory

Plaintiffs also challenge the lower court's conclusion that they had failed to prove its assertion that the court had general jurisdiction over the defendants. To make a *prima facie* case showing general jurisdiction, plaintiffs must produce evidence that shows that ACAB's and Robbins' contacts with Texas that are unrelated to the litigation, are sufficient to satisfy due process requirements. Those unrelated contacts must be substantial, continuous, and systematic. It is clear that plaintiffs have not demonstrated that Robbins' direct contacts with Texas during the relevant period were sufficient to establish general jurisdiction. The evidence shows that Robbins sold on isolated occasions products to entities located in Texas and that Robbins' personnel made field service visits to Texas. These contacts are neither substantial, continuous, nor systematic. The same conclusion applies to ACAB. Plaintiffs rely on evidence that indicates that the products of ACAB's subsidiaries are sold in Texas. However, "a foreign parent corporation is not subject to the jurisdiction of a forum state merely because its subsidiary is doing business there; the mere existence of a parent-subsidiary relationship is not sufficient to warrant the assertion of jurisdiction over the foreign parent." Plaintiffs must show that ACAB so controls the other organizations that the activities of those organizations may be fairly attributed to ACAB. Under Texas law, the *alter-ego doctrine* applies when there is such unity between the parent corporation and its subsidiary that the separateness of the two corporations has ceased. However, "100% stock ownership and commonality of officers and directors are not alone sufficient to establish an *alter-ego* relationship between two corporations." Instead, "the degree of control exercised by the parent must be greater than that normally associated with common ownership and directorship." Such control has not been indicated here. The existence of inter-corporate loans does not establish the requisite dominance, and in fact, interest-bearing loans suggest separation of corporate entities. We conclude that the lower court was correct in dismissing plaintiffs' claims against Robbins and ACAB for lack of personal jurisdiction.

Case Highlights

- International litigation is often complex due to the diversity of the parties. In this case, the parties were from China, Sweden, Norway, the British Virgin Islands, and the states of New York, Massachusetts, Washington, and Delaware
- The due process clause of the U.S. Constitution requires that personal jurisdiction over a defendant must be based on either "minimum contacts" for purposes of gaining specific jurisdiction or "substantial, continuous, and systematic" contacts for purposes of gaining general jurisdiction
- Specific jurisdiction requires a nexus between the minimum contacts and the injuries claimed, while general jurisdiction allows for lawsuits on even unrelated claims
- The "stream-of-commerce" theory is only applicable if the defendant delivers a product into the stream of commerce with the expectation that it would be purchased in the forum state

- A foreign parent company does not become subject to the jurisdiction of a foreign court simply because its subsidiary is amenable to that state's jurisdiction
- "Alter-ego theory" allows for jurisdiction over a parent company if the parent company "dominates" the activities of a subsidiary that has sufficient contacts with the forum court.

Personal jurisdiction means that a court has power over the defendant in a dispute. If the defendant fails to appear at the appointed time the judge may issue a directed verdict (meaning that the plaintiff automatically wins and may collect on the damages without a court trial). There are two types of personal jurisdiction: general and specific. General personal jurisdiction means a defendant can be sued in the foreign court for any types of claims, whether or not connected to the court's geographical jurisdiction. For a foreign company this type of personal jurisdiction is based on the fact that the company is "doing business" in a given country; in essence doing business means the company is a resident of all countries that it does business in a "substantial, continuous, or systematic" way. Specific personal jurisdiction means that a company can only be sued on claims specifically connected to the foreign country or court. There are two bases for specific personal jurisdiction: (1) the claims against the defendant are connected to the foreign country ("minimum contacts," which is something less than doing business in an ongoing way); (2) a foreign company or person commits a tort (delict) in the foreign country or commits a tort outside of the country that has direct effects in the foreign country.

Litigation Defenses: Immunity of Foreign Governments and Officials

There are a number of defenses to a foreign court's exercise of jurisdiction even when such an exercise would be proper under the requirements of due process (court has jurisdiction over the claims). Sovereign immunity prevents a sovereign state from being subjected to suit without its consent. The **doctrine of sovereign immunity** stands for the principle that a nation is immune from suit in the courts of another country. Some countries recognize an exception of foreign sovereign immunity called the commercial activities exception. The doctrine of sovereign immunity protects foreign governments only from governmental activities and not from *commercial* activities. The problem with this type of categorization of activities is that government procurement has become increasingly commercialized, making the distinction between sovereign and commercial activities difficult to draw. The gravity of this problem becomes apparent in developing countries where almost by necessity a governmental entity is involved with international transactions. For example, a government partners with private entities in a joint venture undertaking. For the private company, it is important in such dealings to negotiate a contract clause in which the government entity *waives* its potential sovereign immunities defenses. Another type of immunity is the *foreign official immunity*. The Supreme Court limited the reach of this type of immunity in *Samantar v. Yousuf*.

Samantar v. Yousuf

(130 S. Ct. 2278 2010)

Justice Stevens. Respondents, who were persecuted by the Somali government during the 1980s, filed a damages action alleging that petitioner, who then held high-level government positions, exercised command and control over the military forces committing the abuses. The District Court granted petitioner's motion to dismiss the suit, resting its decision on the foreign sovereign immunities doctrine. The Fourth Circuit reversed, holding that sovereign immunity does not apply to officials of a foreign state.

Under the common-law doctrine of foreign sovereign immunity, there is nothing to suggest that "foreign state" should be read to include an official acting on behalf of that state. A foreign state "includes a political subdivision or an agency or instrumentality" of the state. "Entity" typically refers to an organization. This does not suggest that officials are included. Though a foreign state's immunity may, in some circumstances, extend to an individual for official acts. In this case, respondents have sued petitioner in his personal capacity and seek damages from his own pockets. The court noted that the petitioner had necessarily acted beyond the scope of his official authority by allegedly violating international law.

Therefore, petitioner's claim of immunity is DENIED.

Case Highlights

- The foreign sovereign immunity doctrine provides a defense from litigation against foreign countries in national courts
- The immunity from suits relates to the foreign sovereign's "public acts"
- The immunity does not automatically attach to foreign government officials. It does not apply in this case because the former official is being sued in his personal capacity and the plaintiff is seeking damages from the official and not the foreign government
- Foreign sovereign immunity does not apply to a foreign government official acting beyond the scope of its official authority in violation of international law.

Diplomatic Immunity

There is a rich jurisprudential and statutory history surrounding the international practice of diplomatic immunity. Article 31 of the Vienna Convention on Diplomatic Immunity provides that, with certain exceptions, a diplomatic agent shall be immune from the civil jurisdiction of the "receiving" state's courts and shall "not be obliged to give evidence as a witness."

Forum Non Conveniens *Doctrine*

Some courts have developed a general discretionary principle known as the ***forum non conveniens* doctrine.** *Forum non conveniens* doctrine is Latin for "a forum which is not convenient." It can be applied to any case if the court determines that there is another more convenient forum to hear the case. This doctrine is employed when the court chosen by the plaintiff is inconvenient for witnesses or poses an undue hardship on the defendants. In such situations, the defendants would petition the court for an order dismissing the case or transferring it to a more convenient court. The *Capital Currency Exchange v. National Westminster Bank* case examines some of the nuances of this doctrine.

Capital Currency Exchange v. National Westminster Bank

155 F.3d 603 (2d Cir. 1998)

Judge. Capital Currency Exchange (CCE) is a financial company organized under the laws of the Netherlands Antilles. CCE and its affiliates are engaged in two kinds of international financial transactions: (1) retail currency exchange and (2) money transfers from the U.S. to England. CCE and its affiliates had a longstanding banking relationship with Barclays UK. CCE, on behalf of Worldcash, sought a New York State money transmission license. To qualify for this license, Worldcash posted a $500,000 bond with the New York State banking authorities. CCE arranged with Barclays UK's New York office to issue an irrevocable letter of credit as security for the bond. Subsequently, for reasons that the parties dispute, Barclays UK told CCE to find another banker. NatWest UK declined to provide CCE with banking services. CCE maintains that NatWest UK and Barclays UK conspired to drive CCE out of the money transfer business by depriving it of banking services in violation of antitrust (competition) law. CCE brought suit in New York. Defendants moved to dismiss the complaint under the *forum non conveniens* doctrine.

In a *forum non conveniens* analysis, a court must determine that an adequate alternative forum exists. An alternative forum is adequate if: (1) the defendants are subject to service of process there (personal jurisdiction exists in the alternative forum); and (2) the forum permits "litigation of the subject matter of the dispute." We believe there is an adequate, alternative forum. Plaintiffs may challenge defendants' allegedly anticompetitive actions under Articles 85 and 86 of the Treaty of Rome, which English courts are bound to enforce. It is also well established that the unavailability of treble or triple damages (available under American Sherman Antitrust Act) does not render a forum inadequate. Thus, this lawsuit is subject to dismissal under the *forum non conveniens* doctrine.

Case Highlights

- In order for a court to dismiss a case under the *forum non conveniens* doctrine, it must determine that an adequate alternative forum exists
- The unavailability of certain remedies under the laws of the alternative forum does not render that forum inadequate.

Alien Tort Claims Act

Another issue is whether a foreign party may sue in tort or delict in the national courts of a person or company for acts committed outside of that country. The U.S. **Alien Tort Claims Act (ATCA)** provides standing to sue in U.S. courts to foreign parties for torts committed outside the U.S. in certain situations. The ATCA is an old U.S. law enacted in 1789 that states: "The U.S. courts shall have jurisdiction of any civil action by an alien (foreign party) for a tort, committed in violation of the law of nations or a treaty of the United States." Numerous suits have been brought under the ATCA for human rights abuses, including cases brought against private corporations as "aiding and abetting" foreign governments in committing human rights violations.

It is also clear that the ATCA extends to American companies that commit tort acts outside the U.S. and allows foreign citizens to seek remedies in U.S. courts for torts committed outside the U.S. The U.S. Supreme Court, in *Kiobel v. Royal Dutch Petroleum Co.*, had to decide the issue of whether persons legally in the U.S. could bring a tort action in the U.S. courts against foreign companies for torts committed in Nigeria.[2] The Court invoked the "presumption against extraterritoriality" in dismissing the claim.

Kiobel v. Royal Dutch Petroleum Co.

133 Sup. Ct. 1659 (2013)

Twelve Nigerian citizens obtained political asylum in the U.S. and then sued Dutch and British oil companies. The plaintiffs alleged that the defendants, through their Nigerian subsidiary, had aided and abetted human rights violations including forced exile and murder. The claimants assert that the defendants provided transportation to Nigerian forces; allowed their property to be utilized as a staging ground for attacks; provided food for soldiers involved in the attacks; and provided compensation to those soldiers.

Chief Justice Roberts. The Supreme Court unanimously affirms the dismissal of the claim but disagreed about the reason. The majority opinion applied the "presumption against extraterritoriality" to protect against unintended clashes between our laws and those of other nations, which could result in international discord. Indeed, the danger of unwarranted judicial interference in the context of foreign policy is magnified in the context of the ATCA. The Court expressed concern that applying the ATCA to foreign conduct has the potential to exacerbate rather than alleviate friction with foreign countries.

Justice Breyer, concurring and joined by Justices Ginsburg, Sotomayor, and Kagan. Instead of applying the presumption against extraterritoriality, the Court should limit ATCA litigation to three circumstances: (1) the alleged tort occurs on American soil, (2) the defendant is an American national, or (3) the defendant's conduct substantially and adversely affects an important American national interest, including not to be a safe harbor for a torturer or other common enemy of mankind. Breyer noted that acts of piracy were commonly brought under the ATCA involved conduct not only outside the

U.S. but also on foreign-flagged vessels (effectively on foreign territory). Nevertheless, the court agreed that this particular case should be dismissed given the defendants' minimal and indirect American presence.

Case Highlights

- The ATCA does not extend jurisdiction to foreign parties wanting to bring suit against a foreign corporation unless there is a close connection to American territory
- This decision of the Supreme Court is interesting because it was a unanimous decision, but the reasons for the decision were varied among the majority opinion and three concurring opinions
- The majority opinion rested on the presumption against the extraterritorial application of American law. The concurring opinion rejected the presumption argument. Instead, it argued the closeness of the claim to American territory should not prevent jurisdiction to hear suits against "a torturer or other common enemy of mankind."

The *Kiobel* decision is likely to lead to a significant reduction in international human rights litigation in U.S. courts under the ATCA. However, plaintiffs will be able to bring claims against individual defendants for foreign acts of torture and extrajudicial killings under the Torture Victim Protection Act.[3]

International Discovery

Once the defendant is properly served and personal jurisdiction is obtained, the next issue is the ability to pursue **discovery**. Discovery is the process of gathering evidence from one's adversary and other third parties. Discovery is often the most difficult and costly part of international litigation. The purpose of the Convention on the Taking of Evidence Abroad in Civil or Commercial Matters (**Hague Evidence Convention**) is to facilitate the discovery of foreign parties. This Convention provides for the use of "Letters of Request" that require foreign courts to perform the discovery process. It also provides for the "taking of evidence by diplomatic officers, consular agents and commissioners."

A number of factors limit the effectiveness of the Convention. First, few countries outside of the U.S. and Western Europe have adopted the Convention. Second, a foreign court may reject a letter of request if the court deems it to be in violation of its national laws. Nonetheless, a plaintiff having problems with foreign discovery should seek the help of its government in gathering evidence through the Hague Evidence Convention.

Enforceability of Judgments

After obtaining a judgment in an international litigation, the winning party will at times have to enforce the judgment in a foreign country (when the foreign defendant does not have enough assets in the forum court to satisfy the judgment). Court judgments are more difficult to enforce than arbitral awards.

A number of international conventions have been promulgated to help enforce judgments internationally. Three are regional in nature: Members of the EU can use the **Brussels Convention on Jurisdiction and the Enforcement of Judgments in Civil and Commercial Matters**. The **Lugano Convention** applies to all countries in the European Free Trade Area. Finally, the **Inter-American Convention on the Extraterritorial Validity of Foreign Judgments** applies to members of the Organization of American States.

The only truly "international" convention is the **Hague Convention on International Jurisdiction and Foreign Judgments in Civil and Commercial Matters.** The Hague Convention was updated on July 2, 2019 (2019 Enforcement Convention).[4] Article 4 provides: "a judgment given by a court of a Contracting State (State of origin) shall be recognized and enforced in another Contracting State in accordance with the Convention." Additionally, the 2019 Enforcement Convention sets out in Article 7(1) the exclusive bases on which recognition and enforcement may be refused, which include improper service, fraud, and incompatibility with the public policy of the state being asked to enforce the judgment. Some countries, however, routinely refuse to enforce foreign court judgments. For example, France and Switzerland refuse to enforce a foreign judgment against their nationals unless there is a clear indication that the national voluntarily intended to submit to the jurisdiction of the foreign court. Faced with such obstacles, a party is better served by filing suit directly in the country of the defendant or to arbitrate the claim.

Choice of Law

How do courts determine which national laws apply in a given case? Generally, absent a **choice of law clause** in which the parties to a contract expressly state the law that will govern any disputes, the law of the country most *closely connected* to the agreement will govern. Sometimes the courts may apply the principle of ***dépeçage*** to apply different governing laws to different parts of the contract. In short, different parts of the contract may have closer connections to different countries. The country of closest connection will often be the country of the residence of the performing party. Courts have fashioned **conflict of law rules** to assist them in making choice of law decisions. These rules are essentially a list of factors used to determine the country with the closest connection to the case.

Under the *Restatement (Second) of Conflict of Laws*,[5] the law of the jurisdiction with the "most significant contacts" governs both tort and contract claims. In evaluating tort claims, the following four factors are relevant: (1) the domicile, place of incorporation, and place of business of the parties; (2) the place where the tort occurred; (3) the place where the relationship of the parties is centered; and (4) the place where the injury occurred. With respect to contract claims, the factors are: (1) the place of contracting; (2) the place of negotiation; (3) the place of performance; (4) the location of the subject matter of the contract; and (5) the domicile, place of incorporation, and place of business of the parties. Another factor that is considered is the location where the breach of contract occurred. The Restatement also states that if the place of negotiating the contract and the place of performance are in the same country, the law of that country will usually be applied. If a specific contract clause or issue is invalid in a country with a close connection to the contract, then that country's laws may be deferred to because of its strong interest in enforcing its laws and public policies.

The **doctrine of *renvoi*** is when a court uses another country's conflict of law rules that direct the court to apply its own country's law (in sum, the foreign conflict of law rules that direct the forum court to the forum court's law are preferred over the application of the forum court's conflict of law rules that direct the forum court to foreign law). A related principle used in determining the law to be applied by the forum court is that absent sufficient proof to establish with reasonable certainty the substance of the foreign law, the court could apply the law of the forum. A court is not expected to decide a case based on incomplete and frequently confusing explanations of foreign law. Before drafting a contract and a choice of law clause, the conflict of law rules in the national law of the other party should be researched. This will help determine whether an express choice of law clause is needed and, if so, the factors the foreign country will use in assessing the enforceability of the choice of law selection.

Judicial Abrogation of Choice of Law Clauses

Internationally, courts and arbitration tribunals generally enforce contractual choice of law clauses. Courts, however, will usually require that the choice of law have some connection to the parties to the contract. Arbitration tribunals, on the other hand, are more likely to enforce a reasonable choice of law selection even if the choice is not connected to the contract or the transaction, especially when the law chosen is considered neutral. Arbitrators may see an unconnected choice of law selection as a fair compromise given the international nature of the transaction. This is especially true if the parties' choice is one of the more popular neutral country laws, such as the UK, U.S., Switzerland, and Germany. At times, statutory mandates may pre-empt this reasonableness inquiry. For example, the UK Unfair Contract Terms Act 1977 voids any choice of law clause whose purpose is the avoidance of the restrictions found in the Act.

Courts have used a number of factors in scrutinizing choice of law clauses. The following excerpts from the *Restatement (Second) of Conflict of Laws* provide the rationale for the need for such rules and the factors that courts review in deciding whether to honor a choice of law selection.

> *Section 1*: Reason for the Rules of Conflict of Laws
>
> The world is composed of territorial states having separate and differing systems of law, making necessary a special body of rules and methods for their ordering and resolution.
>
> *Section 6: Choice-of-Law Principles*
>
> *The factors relevant to the choice of law include:*

> *needs of the international system, relevant policies of the forum,*
> *relevant policies of other interested states and the relative interests of those states in determination of the particular issue,*
> *protection of justified expectations,*
> *basic policies underlying the particular field of law, certainty, predictability, and uniformity of result, and*
> *ease in the determination and application of the law to be applied.*

In weighing these factors, the modern judicial trend is to give great deference to the contracts' choice of law clauses: "In the area of contracts, where choice-of-law rules are uncertain, some measure of predictability and certainty is achieved by allowing the parties, within broad limits, to select the law to govern the validity and effect of their contract."[6] This deference also advances the policy goal of protecting "the justified expectations" of the contracting parties.

The *Restatement* provides two grounds for abrogating the parties' choice of law clause. First, the chosen law has no substantial relationship to the parties or the transaction, and there is no reasonable basis for the parties' choice. Second, application of the law of the chosen state would be contrary to a fundamental policy of the forum country. Thus, the forum court is unlikely to enforce a choice of law that would be contrary to its country's law and policy.

International Commercial Arbitration

A common feature in international contracts is the arbitration clause. The arbitration rules that apply to the arbitral proceeding are those stated in the arbitration clause. When there is no arbitration clause, then the rules would need to be agreed upon by the parties through a voluntary submission for arbitration. The enforcement of arbitration awards of one country in other countries has been made much easier due to the fact that 160 countries have ratified the **New York Convention**. Since arbitration awards are considered final and binding, the losing party cannot fight their enforcement by arguing the arbitration panel wrongfully decided the case. However, the New York Convention allows for the nonenforcement of an arbitration award on narrow grounds unrelated to the substance of the case:

(1) the award has been stayed by another court; (2) the characteristics of the arbitrators or the arbitration procedures were in conflict with the arbitration agreement; (3) the losing party was not given proper notice or opportunity to present its case; (4) the arbitration decided issues not within the scope of the arbitration agreement; and (5) the arbitration agreement was invalid.

The costs, inefficiency, and unpredictability of national court systems have made international arbitration the preferred means of dispute resolution in international business transactions. Civil procedure (litigation) rules vary greatly among national legal systems. A party may be comfortable when litigating within its domestic court system, but wary of having to sue in a foreign court system. Also, well-recognized national and international arbitration tribunals provide the aura of neutrality that parties seek in resolving their disputes.

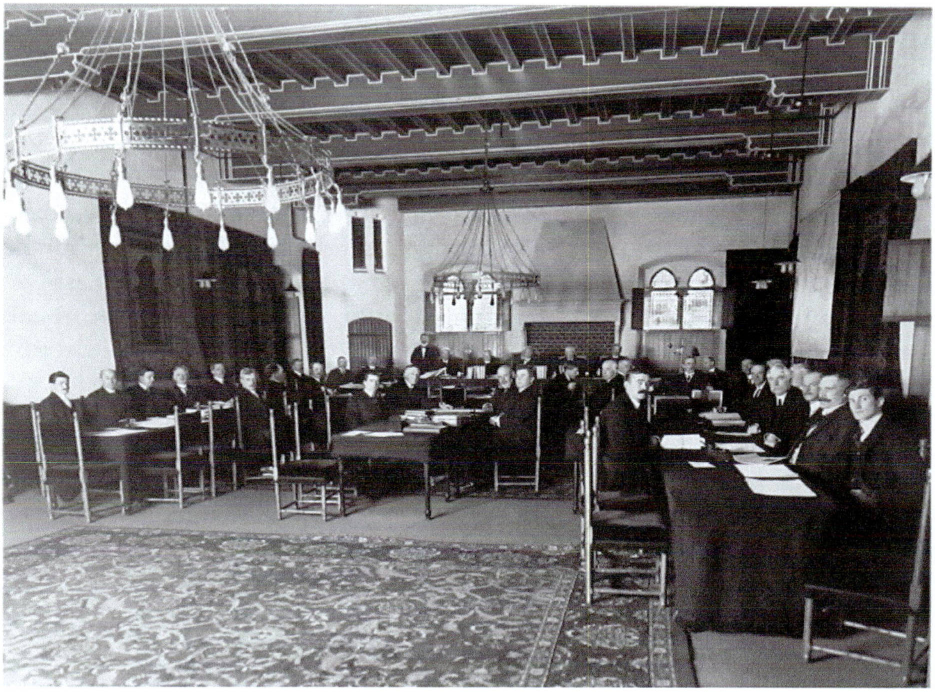

Image 5.1 1910 North Atlantic Fisheries Arbitration at The Hague.

Source: Law Society of Upper Canada Archives, at www.lsuc.on.ca/PDC/Archives/Archives-Collection/. "All images from the Law Society Archives featured on The Commons are free of copyright restrictions, either because the term of copyright has expired or the Law Society of Upper Canada owns the copyright."

International commercial arbitration can be institutionalized through the use of standard rules provided by such organizations as the **International Chamber of Commerce** (**ICC**) or by using the Model Rules published by UNCITRAL. Arbitration offers the potential for a shortened, cost-effective, confidential, and hopefully more amicable means to resolve a dispute than litigation. It allows the parties to select arbitrators with the necessary expertise to understand the technicalities of the issues in dispute. Also, an unusual choice of law is more likely to be enforced by a panel of arbitrators than by national courts of law. Unlike courts, arbitrators' primary mandate comes from the contractual arbitration clause and not national public policy concerns. The confidentiality of arbitration, especially in disputes involving sensitive information, is another reason why arbitration is a preferred means of dispute resolution. The largest area of growth in international arbitration has been in East Asia. The total number of arbitration cases received by major international arbitration institutions located in East Asia—the China International Economic and Trade Arbitration Commission (CIETAC), Japan Commercial Arbitration Association (JCAA), Hong Kong International Arbitration Centre (HKIAC), Kuala Lumpur Regional Center for Arbitration (KLRCA), Singapore International Arbitration Centre (SIAC), and the Korean Commercial Arbitration Board (KCAB)—now surpass the cases arbitrated in Western nations, including the American Arbitration Association (AAA), the International Chamber of Commerce's International Court of Arbitration (ICC), the London Court of International Arbitration (LCIA), and the international arbitration centers in Stockholm, Vienna, and Vancouver.[7]

China International Economic and Trade Arbitration Commission (CIETAC) has become one of the busiest arbitration venues for international commercial contract disputes (700 or more cases per year).[8] The rise of China as a major arbitration venue is understandable due to its rise as an economic power. Despite East–West cultural differences, CIETAC has proven its ability in reaching fair and reasonable outcomes using Western-style hard and soft commercial laws. In fact, it has proven itself to be a model arbitral forum by showing high regard for the amicability, confidentiality, voluntary compliance, and efficiency of international arbitration.

Litigation is the less-preferred method of dispute resolution for international and domestic disputes in many countries. It is seen in some countries, most notably in Japan, as a failure of both the business parties. (See Figure 5.1 *Doing Business Internationally*: "Role of Alternative Dispute Resolution in Japan.") In "some cultures arbitration may prove a 'face-saving' approach to dispute resolution."[9] From a more practical perspective, litigation is an expensive process likely to permanently damage the business relationship and is inherently unpredictable as to results.

The uncertainty of dispute resolution in a foreign country is generally more manageable through arbitration than through the national court system. This is especially true in former Soviet-bloc countries and developing countries where the enforcement of Western-style substantive law is uncertain and uneven. Furthermore, even when a judgment is enforced, the remedies granted may be insufficient to fully protect the contract and property rights of the foreign party. For an international arbitration to work effectively, the national courts in the countries of both parties to the dispute must recognize and support arbitration. By acceding to the UN Convention on the Recognition and Enforcement of Foreign Arbitral Awards (New York Convention), countries have undertaken international legal obligations to recognize and enforce foreign arbitral awards. The key provisions of the New York Convention are provided in Figure 5.2 *Comparative Law*: "Convention on the Recognition and Enforcement of Foreign Arbitral Awards." The New York Convention is by far the most important private international law agreement and is credited for much of the explosive growth of arbitration in international business disputes.

The Japanese have characteristically been reluctant to litigate disputes. There is a cultural aversion to conflict based on ingrained notions of *wa* or peace and harmony. Informal resolution usually preserves the relationship between the parties. It removes the stigma of blame or fault associated with one who is found liable. The Japanese attitude toward compromise, conciliation, and arbitration is discussed below.

Figure 5.1 Doing Business Internationally: Role of Alternative Dispute Resolution in Japan.[10]

Compromise. Compromise or *wakai* differs from out-of-court settlement negotiations in that it involves a judge. In *benron-ken wakai*, the parties present their cases orally before the judge and, with the judge, explore areas of compromise. In *soshjno wakai* or "compromise before the court," after thorough discussions with both parties, the judge generates compromise proposals. Compromise offers obvious benefits not found in traditional litigation. A compromise may preserve peace and the status quo between the parties; unlike in a court of law, the judge in compromise proceedings is free to disregard the legal merits and standing of the parties in order to settle the dispute equitably and restore a sense of harmony between the parties. Under Confucian principles, the judge is bound to act with compassion and benevolence. The compromise proceedings are confidential. The compromise agreement represents a voluntary contract; parties are always free to refuse a judicially sponsored settlement, however the same judge presiding over the compromise proceedings would also hear the case at trial.

Conciliation. Conciliation or *chtei* may be initiated by application of the parties or by the court and may occur while a lawsuit is pending. Unlike court-sponsored compromise, a court appoints a conciliation committee. A conciliation commissioner must be a lawyer, must have expert knowledge and experience useful in settling disputes, and must possess "rich knowledge and experience in public life." There is, however, no guarantee that the outcome will reflect the legal merits of the case. Indeed, it has been described as "OK, OK (*maamaa*)" or "fifty/fifty (*seppan*)" conciliation because of the overriding emphasis placed on settling the dispute and restoring harmony.

Arbitration. Japanese arbitration or *chsai* can be divided into two categories: arbitration conducted between two Japanese parties, and arbitration conducted between a Japanese party and a foreign party. Arbitration has not been favored as a method of dispute resolution among the Japanese because, like litigation, arbitration involves the "imposition" of a settlement by a third party and therefore cannot restore harmony between the disputants. Arbitration has, however, gained widespread acceptance as a means of resolving disputes in international business transactions between Japanese and foreign parties. Arbitration allows Japanese parties to negotiate "equitable positions as opposed to purely legal technicalities" and to avoid extensive pretrial discovery battles that serve only to "exacerbate the conflict."

Figure 5.1 (Continued)

The Convention provides for the full recognition of contract arbitration clauses and outlines a narrow set of grounds for the nonenforcement or vacating of an arbitration award. These include: (1) where an award was procured by corruption, fraud, or undue means; (2) where there was evident partiality or corruption in the arbitrators; (3) where the arbitrators were guilty of misconduct in refusing to postpone the hearing or in refusing to hear evidence pertinent and material to the controversy; (4) where the arbitrators exceeded their powers; (5) where there was evident miscalculation of figures; and (6) where the arbitrators have awarded upon a matter not submitted to them. The *Iran Aircraft*

Article I

When signing, ratifying or acceding to this Convention any State may on the basis of reciprocity declare that it will apply the Convention to the recognition and enforcement of awards made in the territory of another Contracting State.

Article II

Each Contracting State shall recognize an agreement in writing under which the parties undertake to submit to arbitration all or any differences which have arisen or which may arise between them in respect of a defined legal relationship, whether contractual or not, concerning a subject matter capable of settlement by arbitration. The term "agreement in writing" shall include an arbitral clause in a contract or a standalone arbitration agreement.

Article III

Each Contracting State shall recognize arbitral awards as binding and enforce them in accordance with the rules of procedure of the territory where the award is relied upon.

Figure 5.2 Comparative Law: Convention on the Recognition and Enforcement of Foreign Arbitral Awards (1958).

Industries v. Avco Corporation case below examined the issue of the enforceability of a foreign arbitration award.

Arbitration is an alternative to the court system but at the same time is dependent on the court system.[11] At least in two instances the court system is crucial to the vitality of the arbitration process. The first is the most obvious—the arbitration award must be enforced through the court system. An unenforceable award renders the arbitration process an empty exercise. Fortunately, the New York Convention has provided security of enforcement in many national jurisdictions. A second role for the court system is in granting injunctive relief pending the outcome of the arbitration. The arbitration clause may provide that the parties can apply to the arbitrators for injunctive relief or other "interim measures," but the arbitrator's ability to restrain the parties may be legally ineffective. Thus, the clause should also allow the parties to resort to the court system. This provision is especially important in the area of intellectual property, where judicial injunctions are needed to restrain the release of confidential information and trade secrets, as well as to prevent the continuing infringement of IP rights.

Iran Aircraft Industries v. Avco Corporation

980 F.2d 141 (2d Cir. 1992)

Circuit Judge. The lower court declined to enforce an award of the Iran-United States Claims Tribunal, which resulted in an award of $3,513,086 due from Avco to the Iranian parties. The Iranian parties contend that the Award is enforceable under the "New York Convention."

New York Convention

The New York Convention, however, provides for nonenforcement where: "The party against whom the award is invoked was not given proper notice of the appointment of the arbitrator or of the arbitration proceedings or was otherwise unable to present its case." In this case, Avco was not made aware that the Tribunal required actual invoices to substantiate its claim. We believe that by so misleading Avco the Tribunal denied Avco the opportunity to present its claim in a meaningful manner. AFFIRMED.

Cardamone, Circuit Judge, dissenting. The specific defense with which we deal in the case appears in Article V(1)(b). That section states that enforcement of an arbitral award may be denied if the court is satisfied that the party against whom the award is sought to be enforced was unable to present its case before the arbitration panel. Avco was not denied due process. Avco had a full opportunity to present its claims and was on notice that there might be a problem with its proof. I dissent and vote to enforce the award.

Case Highlights

- The New York Convention requires courts to enforce foreign arbitration awards
- Enforcement of an arbitration award may be withheld if the losing party was denied due process
- Due process requires that the defendant be given proper notice and an opportunity to be heard.

Applicable Law

When deciding upon the applicable law, factors to consider include: (a) selecting a legal system that has a well-developed body of law relating to the specific issues likely to arise; (b) whether only the laws that regulate the subject-matter (substance) of the dispute should apply, or if the applicable law of a country also includes international law rules within that country that may, in turn, refer the dispute to the law of another country (conflict of law rules or private international law); and (c) whether the chosen governing law considers the subject matter of the contract to be arbitrable. In some countries, for example, copyright, patent, and antitrust matters do not qualify as arbitrable matters.

If there is no choice of law clause the arbitration panel will use conflict of law rules to determine the applicable law. Some arbitration rules will provide guidance, such as the International Centre for Settlement of Investment Disputes (ICSID), which states that the law of the host state shall apply. However, most arbitration rules are silent, giving the arbitration panel wide discretion in choosing the law to apply to the dispute.

The *severability principle* recognizes the arbitration clause in a contract as a separate agreement independent of the contract. Therefore, a law is needed to determine the validity of the arbitration clause. If viewed as a separate agreement, then it can be enforced even if the underlying contract is determined to be invalid or unenforceable. The New York Convention states the law of the location of the arbitration applies, thus denying the use of conflict of law rules.

No Law Alternative

The parties may choose a law but may also allow the arbitration panel some leeway in not having to strictly apply the chosen law. Alternatively, they may select no law at all and instruct the arbitration panel to simply make a fair and equitable award. The traditional terms of *ex aequo et bono* (according to what is equitable and good) and *amiable compositor* (arbitrators being empowered to modify or moderate the consequences of the contractual provisions based on equity) refer to the ability of the arbitration panel to use any source of law, including customary international law (business customs and trade usage) to render a fair and equitable decision.

Arbitration Rules

The selection of a set of arbitration rules to govern the dispute between the contracting parties provides a general framework for the arbitration. The benefit of this system is that it gives the parties the ability to select arbitration rules and at the same time tailor them to their specific needs. Unfortunately, contracting parties and their lawyers often do not spend the time to negotiate a customized clause. The arbitration clause selects a set of institutional, ad hoc arbitration or a hybrid of rules from different sources to cover different dispute resolution procedures (mediation, conciliation, arbitration) or different issues (tort claims, contract claims, claims against a government, and so forth). For example, the parties may choose the UNCITRAL (United Nations Commission on International Trade Law) Model Law on International Commercial Arbitration as the rules governing their arbitration and at the same time adopt the rules of the International Bar Association on the Taking of Evidence. See Table 5.1 for a list of important arbitration rules and conventions.

Other important arbitration forums include the Arbitration Association of Stockholm; Cairo Regional Centre for International Commercial Arbitration (CRCICA); China International Economic and Trade Arbitration Commission (CIETAC); Hong Kong International Arbitration Commission (HKIAC); Moscow Arbitration Court; and the Vienna International Arbitration Centre (VIAC). The Panama Arbitration Convention has been adopted by 17 countries in Central and South America, as well as Mexico and the U.S. The Washington Convention is important in that it allows private individuals to sue a foreign government directly in suits involving foreign direct investment. It also provides a process for one country to sue another country for violation of a bilateral investment treaty.

There are a number of methods of conducting arbitration, such as *last offer arbitration*. In this form of arbitration, each party provides a single "best offer" and the arbitrator selects one of the two offers. The parties are incentivized to provide reasonable offers (somewhere between their original positions and the position of the other party). If a party makes an unreasonable offer to settle,

Table 5.1 Important Conventions, Sets of Arbitration Rules, and Forums.

Conventions	*Arbitration Rules*	*Arbitration Forums*
1958 UN Convention on the Recognition and Enforcement of Foreign Arbitral Awards (New York Convention)	International Chamber of Commerce (ICC)	International Court of Arbitration (ICC)
Inter-American Convention on International Arbitration (Panama Convention)	UN Model Law on International Commercial Arbitration (UNCITRAL Arbitration Rules)	London Court of International Arbitration (LCIA)
European Convention on International Commercial Arbitration	American Arbitration Association (AAA)	International Center for Dispute Resolution (AAA)
Convention on the Settlement of Investment Disputes (Washington Convention)	ICSID Arbitration Rules	International Centre for Settlement of Investment Disputes (ICSID)

then it is likely to lose since the arbitrator will select the more reasonable offer. The benefit of this approach is that the arbitration process moves quickly.

Ad Hoc versus Institutional Arbitration

In negotiating an arbitration clause, the contracting parties must first decide their preference for ad hoc arbitration or institutional arbitration. *Institutional arbitration* is dispute settlement proceedings supervised by an organization or institution, in accordance with the rules of arbitration established or approved by that institution. Institutional arbitration has the benefit of providing a well-drafted, unbiased set of arbitration rules, a list of expert arbitrators, and the award will be considered to be highly credible given the prestige of the institution. As a general proposition, the arbitration clause used should be coordinated with and reflect the arbitral rules of the institution. If institutional arbitration is chosen, the institution chosen need not be located in the place of arbitration. For example, the ICC administers arbitrations throughout the world.

Ad hoc arbitration means there is no formal administration of the arbitration or dispute settlement process by any established arbitral organization. Instead, the parties create their own procedures for the arbitration. This can be accomplished, for example, either by: (1) drafting a set of ad hoc procedures in a contract; (2) referring to a set of generally accepted ad hoc arbitration rules, such as the UNCITRAL Model Arbitration Rules; or (3) allowing the arbitration tribunal to produce its own procedures. Ad hoc arbitration can sometimes be less expensive, but it places more of a burden on the parties to organize and administer the arbitration.

UNCITRAL Model Arbitration Rules

The UNCITRAL Model Arbitration Rules provide a comprehensive set of procedural rules for conducting an arbitration. The Rules cover all aspects of the arbitral process, providing a model arbitration clause, setting out procedural rules regarding the appointment of arbitrators and the running of arbitral proceedings, and establishing rules in relation to the form, effect, and interpretation of the award.

The revised UNCITRAL Arbitration Rules became effective on August 15, 2010. They include provisions dealing with multiple-party arbitration and a procedure to object to experts appointed by the arbitral tribunal. A number of innovative features contained in the Rules aim to enhance procedural efficiency, including revised procedures for the replacement of an arbitrator, the requirement for setting reasonable costs, and a review mechanism regarding the costs of arbitration. They also include more detailed provisions on interim measures. Table 5.2 provides excerpts from the UNCITRAL Model Arbitration Rules and shows some issues relating to commercial arbitration.

Table 5.2 UNCITRAL Model Arbitration Rules.

Article and Title	*Excerpts from the Rules*
Article 7: Number of Arbitrators	If the parties have not previously agreed on the number of arbitrators, then three arbitrators shall be appointed.
Article 9: Selection of Arbitrators	If three arbitrators are to be appointed, each party shall appoint one arbitrator. The two arbitrators will then choose the third arbitrator who will act as the presiding arbitrator of the arbitral tribunal.
Article 12: Challenge an Arbitrator	Any arbitrator may be challenged if circumstances exist that give rise to justifiable doubts as to the arbitrator's impartiality or independence.
Article 17: Arbitration Hearing	The arbitral tribunal may conduct the arbitration in such manner, as it considers appropriate, provided that the parties are treated with equality and each party is given a reasonable opportunity to present its case.
Article 23: Jurisdiction of Arbitrators	The arbitral tribunal shall have the power to rule on its own jurisdiction, including any objections with respect to the existence or validity of the arbitration agreement. For that purpose, an arbitration clause that forms part of a contract shall be treated as an agreement independent of the other terms of the contract. A decision by the arbitral tribunal that the contract is void does not automatically invalidate the arbitration clause.
Article 26: Interim Measures	The arbitral tribunal, at the request of a party, may grant interim measures (orders or injunctions).
Article 27: Evidence	1. Witnesses, including expert witnesses, may be presented by the parties. 2. The arbitral tribunal may require the parties to produce documents, exhibits, or other evidence.

(*Continued*)

Table 5.2 (Continued)

Article and Title	Excerpts from the Rules
Article 29: Experts	After consultation with the parties, the arbitral tribunal may appoint one or more independent experts to report to it on specific issues.
Article 34: Form of Award	The arbitral tribunal shall state the reasons upon which the award is based.
Article 35: Applicable Law	1. The arbitral tribunal shall apply the rules of law designated by the parties as applicable to the substance of the dispute. Failing such designation by the parties, the arbitral tribunal shall apply the law, which it determines to be appropriate. 2. The arbitral tribunal shall decide as amiable compositeur or ex aequo et bono (without law) if the parties have expressly authorized it to do so. 3. The arbitral tribunal shall decide in accordance with the terms of the contract and shall take into account any usage of trade applicable to the transaction.
Article 42: Allocation of Costs	The arbitral tribunal may apportion costs between the parties if it determines that apportionment is reasonable.

Numerous countries have adopted the UNCITRAL Model Arbitration rules as their national arbitration laws.[12]

Arbitration and the Principle of Equitable Decision-Making[13]

In reaching decisions, arbitral tribunals use both hard (mandatory) and soft (voluntary) law. Applicable national laws and international sales law (CISG) are forms of hard law. The area of soft law includes the practices, usage, and customs of international merchants. In the area of international private law, a comparative analysis of national contract law regimes can uncover basic, core general principles common to most legal systems, such as freedom of contract and the principle of good faith.

One advantage of arbitration is that arbitral tribunals are not restricted by formal rules of civil procedure or restrictive rules of evidence.[14] As such, commercial arbitrators often seek solutions from commercial practice and trade usage. In addition, they feel less restrictive in using other types of soft law in fabricating fair and reasonable awards. For example, soft law has played an important role in regulating financial institutions and their relationships.

In recent times there has been a renewed interest by scholars, lending institutions, and regulators in Islamic financial law. It has been studied and utilized as an alternative source for resolving financial disputes.[15] The notion of customary practice is strong in the Islamic legal system: *urf* (Arabic for custom), and public interest are sources for determining or interpreting *Shari'a* law.[16] Islamic financial law is a form of customary law and the Islamic dispute resolution system has a good amount of commonality with arbitration. The major difference between international arbitration and *Shari'a* law includes that the parties are not free to select their governing law through a choice of law clause. Muslims are obligated to apply *Shari'a* law to resolve all their disputes. Also, judicial review is necessary to ensure that the award is consistent with the principles of Islamic law.[17] In the end, it is plausible to state that in the area of financial arbitration, the acceptance and the interpretation of arbitration agreements have been notably influenced by *Shari'a* law, as it is the primary source of law and public policy of many countries in the Islamic world. The growth in business relations between international companies and the Islamic world highlights the importance of understanding *Shari'a* law in international arbitration.

The voluntary use of Islamic financial law is a recent example of how commercial contract law disputes are especially conducive and open to the application of soft law. Due to contract law's private nature, arbitrators and courts look to the parties' characteristics (diamond merchants, cotton exporters, energy dealers, and so forth); the totality of the circumstances surrounding the formation of a contract, including the trade usage found in a given trade; and in general business customs to render decisions. Indeed, contract law—whether Chinese contract law, CISG, American Uniform Commercial Code (UCC), or the German Civil Code (BGB)—acts much like soft laws since contracting parties are able to derogate from the default rules of these supposedly hard laws. Lisa Spagnolo argues that the CISG, although a mandatory law, may also be applied as soft law.[18] As such, arbitrators should focus on party intent, good faith, and trade usage in interpreting CISG rules. In other instances, domestic laws, such as the English Sale of Goods Act and the Swiss Civil Code, have been used as neutral "soft" laws in international business disputes. While most legal systems recognize a strict hierarchy of sources of law where the lower sources of the hierarchy are prohibited from conflicting with higher sources, arbitral panels may view sources of law in a less hierarchical way. In commercial contract law, customary law, including business customs, trade usage, and commercial practice may be given more weight than the hard law rules.

Soft law comes in many different forms, from general, abstract principles to the minutiae of highly technical trade usage. In the EU, the European Court of Justice has observed general principles found in EU Member States in interpreting EU law. One of the oldest types of soft law is the *lex mercatoria* (merchant law),[19] which has been many centuries in development. There have been three eras of the *lex mercatoria*. It first appeared in the "Roman *ius gentium*, as the formally autonomous source of law regulating the economic relations between Roman citizens and foreigners."[20] Soft law "reappeared in the 11th century under the guise of the *lex mercatoria*," which developed as a body of merchant customs and practices.[21] High points include the development of international financial instruments and principles of trade by the Italian city-states of Venice, Florence, and Genoa. Soon thereafter, saw the development of English merchant law and the use of ad hoc merchant tribunals in Europe to settle business disputes, prior to the establishment of functioning court systems. "The *lex mercatoria* was self-enforced by the very merchant class that generated it, through private merchant arbitration, guild courts, market courts, and fair courts consisting of merchants or guild members. An efficient system of merchant consular courts originated in Italy around 1150 and spread all over Europe."[22] Subsequently, merchant customs and practices were incorporated into the hard law, such as the common law, used by established court systems. It is easy to make the analogy between these merchant courts and modern commercial arbitration, as well as the analogy between the law merchant and modern soft law.

Toward the last part of the twentieth century, as a truly global marketplace developed, there has been a development of a new *lex mercatoria* where the global business community creates substantive rules (business usage, customs, and practices) and controls the adjudication of disputes and the application of the substantive rules through private international commercial arbitration. The new *lex mercatoria* is different from earlier versions in that it is more cosmopolitan, more diverse, and created by a wide variety of entities, both private and public:

> *Soft law displays a peculiar mixture of spontaneous and organized processes; the "new lex mercatoria" blurs the distinction between private and public law, as well as developing by the relations between intergovernmental agencies and organizations (UNCITRAL, UNIDROIT, IMO) and private, highly organized, bodies (ICC, ILA).*[23]

The flexible use of different sources of law—hard and soft—by arbitrators is aided and protected by the narrow grounds for appealing an arbitration award. In 2013, the High Court of Australia was asked to overturn an arbitration award "due to an error of law on the face of the award." The court noted that: "Neither Article 28 of the Model Law [UNCITRAL Model Law on International Commercial Arbitration as adopted as the law of Australia] nor an implied term of an arbitration agreement requires an arbitral award to be correct in law."[24] The court reasoned that the primary directive of the Model Law, as well as the New York Convention, is to enforce foreign arbitral awards and not to review such awards for errors in the application of law. Furthermore, the *Guide to the UNCITRAL Model Law on International Commercial Arbitration* notes that, under Article 28, an arbitral panel is not required to apply the law chosen by the parties in a manner that a competent court would have applied the law. Simply put, an arbitral tribunal may need to apply the parties' designated law, but it does not need to apply it correctly. The Model Law narrowly limits the reasons for judicial intervention or nonenforcement of arbitral awards. Article 36(1) lists the grounds for vacating an arbitral award as bias and partiality of the arbitrators, the unfairness of the process, and when enforcement of the award "would be contrary to public policy" of the enforcing court.

Custom Arbitration Clause

Since an arbitration clause is negotiated by the parties, it provides a high degree of flexibility including the selection of an arbitration association, arbitration rules, location of the arbitration, language of the arbitration, and the qualifications of the arbitrators. A vague, simple arbitration clause is often not worth the paper it's printed on, since issues it does not deal with will likely need to be resolved by an arbitral panel or court. This is unfortunate since, depending on the complexity of the issues in dispute, the parties can control the costs and duration of the arbitration through a customized arbitration clause. Model arbitration and mediation clauses can help parties begin to draft contract terms that meet their needs. However, while model arbitration clauses offer a number of specific options, they are not exhaustive and do not include all possible provisions that may need to be considered or may be desirable in particular contracts. Below are examples of model arbitration and mediation clauses.

> Model Arbitration Clause for International Contracts
>
> Any dispute, controversy, or claim arising out, relating to, or in connection with, this contract, or the breach, termination or validity of the contract shall be settled through arbitration. The arbitration shall be conducted in accordance with the Rules of Arbitration of the Court of Arbitration of Madrid in effect at the time of the arbitration. The seat of the arbitration shall be Madrid, Spain and shall be conducted in the Spanish language. Three arbitrators, who shall be selected in accordance with the above arbitration rules, shall conduct the arbitration. The arbitral award shall be in writing and shall be final and binding. The award may include the allocation of costs, including reasonable attorney's fees and disbursements. The award may be entered and enforced in any court having jurisdiction over the parties or their assets.

This clause makes clear that *all* issues and disputes pertaining to the contract are to be arbitrated, and it provides a complete set of rules and procedures in referencing the Madrid rules of arbitration. The *entry of judgment* language ("may be entered in any court") is essential to show intent that any arbitration award is to be final and binding. Model clauses are sufficient in most cases, but parties still need to negotiate choice of law, discovery rules, and the power of arbitrators to order interim relief. In practice, it is best for the parties to negotiate a custom clause. The additional time spent negotiating and drafting the clause will be well spent given the costs of international dispute resolution. Figure 5.3 *Focus on Transactions*: "Issues in Drafting a Custom Arbitration Clause" lists a number of issues that should be addressed in negotiating a custom arbitration clause.

- **Governing Law:** Given the diversity of national legal systems, all international contracts should have a clearly written choice of law clause. The choice of law clause can direct the arbitrator to make based upon international customary law (*lex mercatoria*) or be empowered to grant any remedy that fairness or equity dictates.
- **Escrow Provision:** Given the cost of enforcing judgments and arbitral awards in the international setting, the parties may want to ensure payment by requiring the establishment of an escrow fund. The fund may be established with the arbitration association, a law firm, or an independent escrow agent such as a commercial bank.
- **Venue of Arbitration:** A specific city should be named as the place of arbitration. The selection of the city of arbitration rests upon a number of factors, including location within a country that is a signatory to the New York Convention and the language of the proceeding.

Figure 5.3 Focus on Transactions: Issues in Drafting a Custom Arbitration Clause.

- **Selection of Arbitrators:** There are two types of selection processes—party-appointed and association-appointed. The parties, especially when only one arbitrator is being used, may delegate the selection to the arbitration association. For a three-person arbitration panel, each party commonly selects one arbitrator from a list provided by the association. The party-selected arbitrators select the third arbitrator jointly.
- **Qualifications of Arbitrators:** The parties may state the requirements of the arbitrators to be appointed. In a complicated transaction, such as an intellectual property transfer, the parties may list different qualifications for each arbitrator.
- **Discovery:** Most arbitration rules minimize the amount of discovery of evidence. Depending on the complexity of the claims and sensitivity of the information, the parties may want to provide for discovery. The contract should specify as to what type of discovery is permitted. The clause should limit the time available for discovery in order to avoid the dangers of creating a litigation-type of arbitration. Another option is to have the issue be determined under the 2010 International Bar Association's Rules on Taking Evidence in International Arbitration. The IBA Rules blend both the civil and common law approaches to the taking of evidence.
- **Remedies:** The parties may elect to restrict the type and amount of damages to be awarded through arbitration. For example, the clause may exclude the awarding of punitive or consequential damages.
- **Reasoned Awards:** Most arbitration rules do not require the arbitrators to give reasons for their decision, but a reasoned award offers future guidance for the parties. Therefore, the arbitration clause should require an itemized or reasoned award; it should state that the "award shall specify all findings of fact and conclusions of law."

Figure 5.3 (Continued)

Additional matters to be considered for inclusion in the arbitration clause include (1) consolidation of claims and claims of other parties; (2) time limitations; and (3) allocation of costs. Most arbitration rules provide that the arbitrators, once selected, may order interim relief. Arbitration associations have revised their rules to provide an arbitration procedure that will allow a party to obtain *emergency measures* and relief. As noted above, in the past, if a party to an arbitration agreement needed interim relief, such as an injunction to prevent someone from infringing on its IP rights or a cease and desist order to prevent property subject to the arbitration from being sold, it would have to go to a court to get such orders. The trend, however, is to have the arbitration association provide emergency arbitrators to grant such relief.

If there are more than two parties to the contract, or if the parties are entering into several related contracts, they may wish to consider including a consolidation clause that any arbitrations among them or with respect to the related contracts will be consolidated into a single proceeding. Most national laws regulate specific time limits within which claims must be initiated (limitation period or statute of limitations). The parties may wish to consider whether a specific time limit should be placed on the period of time to commence an arbitration and on the length of the arbitration proceeding.

The best approach in drafting a custom arbitration clause is to start with a standard clause and then customize it based upon a checklist of common issues with straightforward and simple answers to each issue on the checklist. Table 5.3 provides an example of a simple checklist.

Table 5.3 Arbitration Clause Checklist with Suggested Answers.

Issue	*Answer*
How many arbitrators should be required?	Three.
What should be the characteristics of the arbitrators?	Characteristics should vary depending on the type of contract and subject of a contract. The goal is to select a blend of arbitrators, with different areas of expertise related to the subject of the dispute. For example, in a complicated IPR dispute, the panel may include a lawyer who is a specialist in IPR law, an accountant expert in calculating damages and royalties, and a businessperson with experience in IPR licensing.
What is the language of the arbitration?	Common Language or secondary language, most commonly English or Spanish.
Should the arbitration panel be required to give a reasoned opinion?	The award should state the arbitrators' findings of fact and the reasons for their decision.
What is the location of the arbitration?	Subject to negotiations.
Should there be a period for discovery of evidence?	Depends on the complexity of the arbitration and the amount of money in dispute (no more than four months).
What discovery rules should be used?	Subject to negotiations. Options include the International Bar Association's Rules for Taking Evidence.
Should a time (duration) of the arbitration be fixed?	If a speedy arbitration is appropriate, then the Fast-Track Procedure provided under Article 38 of the ICC Rules should be considered.

(Continued)

Table 5.3 (Continued)

Issue	*Answer*
Should the parties give the arbitrators the power to grant "interim relief," such as orders not to destroy evidence or injunctions not to sell the goods in dispute?	The alternative is to have to go for a court order, which is likely to be more costly and take more time. Arbitration rules have been amended to allow the appointment of an "Emergency Arbitrator" for the purpose of issuing such orders.
Should the arbitrators be given the power as to what issues they have jurisdiction to hear (scope of the arbitration)?	Unless there are specific issues, such as tort claims, that the parties want to "carve out" of the arbitration clause to be decided by a court, it is best to have the arbitrators determine scope due to the cost of litigating over the issue in court. Arbitration rules and national laws differ on whether the arbitrators or the courts have the power to determine the scope of the arbitration.
Should the amount of damages be limited?	Sometimes the parties will negotiate high–low amounts of damages to be awarded.

ICC Rules of Optional Conciliation and Mediation Rules

Conciliation and mediation are informal ADR procedures used to resolve business disputes prior to proceeding the more costly processes of arbitration or litigation. The basic difference between mediation and conciliation is the role played by the third party. In mediation, the mediator acts as a facilitator who helps the parties negotiate a settlement. Conversely, in conciliation, the conciliator takes a more interventionist approach by offering solutions to the parties in the hope of settling their disputes.

The ICC Rules of Optional Conciliation simplify the process of beginning conciliation. The parties simply apply for conciliation, along with a $500 application fee. The Secretary General of the ICC appoints a single conciliator. The conciliator then sets a time period for the parties to present their arguments. The conciliator may or may not make settlement recommendations and, unlike in arbitration, may meet individually with either party. The ICC Schedule of Conciliation and Arbitration Costs fixes administrative expenses for conciliation at one-quarter of the amount of arbitration.

Concerns for confidentiality are emphasized in the rules' general mandate that the "confidential nature of the conciliation process shall be respected by every person." Use of the following conciliation-generated information in a subsequent arbitration or court proceeding is specifically prohibited: (1) views expressed or suggested by any party with regard to a settlement; (2) proposals enunciated by the conciliator; and (3) the fact that one of the parties was agreeable to the conciliator's recommendations.

An alternative method is found in mediation rules. The model mediation clause below provides a flexible procedure aimed at achieving a negotiated settlement with the help of a neutral facilitator.

Model Mediation Clause for International Contracts

If a dispute, controversy, or claim arises out of or relates to this contract, or the breach, termination, or validity thereof, and if either party decides that the dispute cannot be settled through direct negotiations, the parties agree to endeavor to settle the dispute in an amicable manner by mediation pursuant to JAMS International Mediation Rules. If this mediation does not result in a settlement, then the dispute shall be resolved by arbitration pursuant to the arbitration clause in this contract.

JAMS International's slogan is that "JAMS doesn't just resolve disputes—we solve problems."[25]

It is highly recommended that contracting parties consider the use of a **med-arb clause** or multistep clause that allows for various methods of alternative dispute resolutions (mediation/conciliation, mini-trials, arbitration) to be utilized in most contract disputes. Conciliation or mediation as a required precursor to arbitration is generally advantageous to both parties. First, mediation has been shown to be highly successful in resolving disputes promptly and preserving the long-term solidarity of the contractual relationship. Second, if mediation is unsuccessful, the parties will have a better understanding of the issues in dispute, which is likely to lead to a more efficient arbitration. Mediation may be more appealing if the clause states that the arbitrators may include mediation costs in their arbitration award. The downside of mediation is minimal, since either party retains the power to end the mediation at any time in order to proceed to arbitration.

Conciliation makes especial sense in an international business dispute because of the increased chance that misunderstandings are due to cultural and language differences. Unfortunately, international mediation or conciliation is an underutilized dispute resolution device. Therefore, it is recommended that the arbitration clause state expressly that the parties have agreed to submit voluntarily to conciliation or mediation before they proceed with a formal arbitration.

Legality of Arbitration and Forum Selection Clauses

A well-written arbitration clause will answer not only the question of how a contract dispute is to be resolved, but also where the dispute is to be resolved. In the latter sense, an arbitration clause acts as a forum selection clause. The U.S. Supreme Court in the *Bremen v. Zapata Off-Shore Co.*[26] case held that a forum selection clause should be voided only in unusual cases. The court determined that forum selection clauses are to be enforced fully unless a party meets "the heavy burden of showing that its enforcement would be unreasonable, unfair, or unjust." The court reasoned that the security and predictability of international contracts and contract dispute resolution must be ensured. "The elimination of uncertainties by agreeing in advance on a forum acceptable to both parties is an indispensable element in international trade and contracting." However, some national courts have voided forum selection clauses as usurping the court's jurisdiction. The *Tennessee Imports, Inc.* case below explores the issues of the arbitrability of specific issues and the enforceability of arbitration clauses.

Tennessee Imports, Inc. v. Pier Paulo Filippi and Prix Italia S.R.L.

745 F. Supp. 1314 (Mid D. Tenn. 1990)

Judge. Plaintiff, Tennessee Imports, Inc., brought this action for breach of contract and tortious interference with contract against defendant Prix Italia an Italian corporation. The contract provided that "should any dispute arise between the contractual parties or in connection with the contract, then both parties agree to the competence of the Arbitration Court of the Chamber of Commerce in Venice, Italy." Tennessee Imports argued that enforcement of this provision would deny it effective relief. Furthermore, it claimed that the tortious interference claim is not within the scope of the forum selection clause. The defendants responded as follows:

(1) the Arbitration Court is a well-recognized and competent arbitral body; and (2) the contract was the result of "arms-length negotiations by experienced and sophisticated business entities."

Federal Arbitration Act

Since the forum selection clause at issue is also an arbitration clause, it is subject to U.S. Federal Arbitration Act, enacted in 1924 "to ensure judicial enforcement of privately made agreements to arbitrate." The Act sets up "a presumption in favor of arbitration," and requires that courts "rigorously enforce agreements to arbitrate." In the field of international commerce, this presumption in favor of arbitration was strengthened by adoption of the New York Convention (Convention). The U.S. applies the Convention, on the basis of reciprocity. Italy is also a member of the Convention.

The Convention allows only a limited inquiry by the courts in determining the enforceability of arbitration clauses found in international commercial agreements. In making this determination, the Court must first address three questions: (1) Is there an agreement in writing to arbitrate the subject of the dispute? (2) Does the agreement provide for arbitration in the territory of a signatory country to the Convention? (3) Does the agreement arise out of a legal relationship, whether contractual or not, which is commercial in nature? In the case of *narrow arbitration clauses*, the court will determine if issues fall within the scope of an arbitration clause before referring them to arbitration. In the case of *broad arbitration clauses*, arbitrability of issues will be left to the arbitrators to determine (whether an issue falls within the scope of a clause). Most standard clauses ("any and all related claims") are considered to be broad in scope.

Enforceability of the Arbitration Clause

The sales contract contains an express agreement to arbitrate and provides for arbitration in Italy. Thus, if the disputes between these parties fall within the scope of their arbitration agreement, this Court must enforce that agreement. Tennessee Imports cannot escape arbitration merely by characterizing its claims as sounding in tort (delict). Courts have consistently held that broad arbitration clauses encompass contract-based tort claims.

Tennessee Imports argues that Prix used its superior economic power to obtain the arbitration clause and, as such, it is unconscionable. The arbitration clause in this case was not hidden in the small print boilerplate of a standard form contract. Tennessee Imports appears to have had ample opportunity to examine the contract before executing it. Having made its choice, Tennessee Imports must now abide by it. The parties are hereby REFERRED to arbitration.

Case Highlights

- Arbitration clauses that state the place for arbitration also serve as forum selection clauses
- In a case involving a "narrow" arbitration clause, the court will determine if issues fall within the scope of an arbitration clause before referring them to arbitration
- In case of "broad" arbitration clauses, the arbitrators will generally determine the arbitrability of an issue
- Courts may issue a preliminary injunction if it deems preliminary injunctive relief necessary to ensure that the arbitration process remains a meaningful one
- Courts are not receptive to attacks on the enforceability of an arbitration clause on the ground of unconscionability, especially when both parties are merchants.

Challenging an Arbitration Award: Judicial Control of Arbitral Awards

Arbitration awards are considered to be "final and binding." Rarely will a court overturn an arbitration award based upon the merits of the case. The fact that the arbitrators misinterpreted the evidence or made the "wrong" decision is not grounds to appeal an arbitration award. However, there are grounds based upon the process or procedure of the arbitration that can lead to a judicial review and reversal (vacating) of arbitration awards. A challenge to the award can be based on the claim that the arbitrators were not independent or impartial. IBA Guidelines on Conflicts of Interest in International Arbitration adopts both a subjective and objective test for impartiality/independence. The subjective test requires an arbitrator to voluntarily withdraw if she has any doubt as to her impartiality. The objective test looks at the facts surrounding the arbitration to see if there is an appearance of impropriety. The test is whether the circumstances involving the arbitrator and the dispute raise "justifiable doubts" as to the independence of the arbitrator. Note that there need not be an actual conflict of interest, but only the appearance of potential conflict.[27]

Other grounds, besides arbitrator neutrality, for challenging an arbitration award include: (1) the arbitration tribunal or panel had no jurisdiction over the dispute or a particular issue in the dispute. Also, the New York Convention recognizes the **public policy exception.** Simply stated, a court may refuse to enforce a foreign arbitration award if to do so would violate public policy of the court's country. Unfortunately, the public policy exception has caused quite a bit of confusion. The notion of public policy varies widely across countries.[28] For example, the *EU Directive on Unfair Contract Terms in Consumer Contracts* voids arbitration clauses in consumer contracts when: (1) the arbitration panel failed to give fair notice or an opportunity to be heard to one of the parties; (2) the arbitration panel did not allow the admission of credible and important evidence; (3) the arbitration agreement was not valid; (4) the arbitration panel did not follow the instructions provided in the arbitration clause; and (5) the subject matter of the dispute was not within the scope of the arbitration clause. These challenges should be made before the beginning of the arbitration and not after its conclusion.[1] Many courts will reject such a challenge after the issuance of the award.

Rise of New Commercial Courts

The more enlightened legal systems, such as Germany, recognized the need for special commercial courts to fairly judge commercial contract disputes. This old idea has had a recent renaissance as more countries have created commercial courts, which may act as a feasible alternative to arbitration. One reason given to explain the current trend in the creation of national commercial courts is that specialization of the judiciary is needed due to the increased specialization of the law itself and the growth of complex legal relations.[29]

Long-standing commercial courts in Germany and the UK have been joined by new commercial courts in Australia, Belgium, Croatia, Dubai, France, the Netherlands, Serbia, Singapore, and Qatar.[30] These specialized courts adopt some of the features of arbitration, such as expert decision-making. Some of the non-English courts allow for proceedings to be conducted in English. For example, the Dutch Commercial Court, established in 2018, allows proceedings to be conducted in Dutch or English. Other courts permit foreign or international judges to sit with domestic judges on the court, giving the court the aura of neutrality associated with arbitration. A particular advantage for the new commercial courts in EU countries is that as members of the EU, they benefit from the effects of automatic recognition and enforcement of judicial decisions afforded to all EU Member States.[31]

Chapter Summary

1. International litigation is more costly than purely domestic litigation. Important issues in international litigation include determining the court with legal jurisdiction, proper service of process, ability to get discovery of evidence, and the enforceability of judgments. If more than one court has legal jurisdiction over a case, then the proper court may be decided under the *forum non conveniens* doctrine.

1 See DiMatteo, Larry A., Marta Infantino and Nathalie Potin, *Judicial Control over Arbitration Awards: Scope, Vacation, and Public Policy* (Cambridge University Press 2021).

2. Techniques for ensuring the proper service of the summons and complaint are through dual service or through the Hague Service Convention.
3. There are a number of defenses or immunities from litigation, found in statutory laws or judicially created doctrines, barring lawsuits against a country and its representatives, such as foreign sovereign immunity and diplomatic immunities.
4. The American Alien Tort Claims Act allows foreign parties to bring lawsuits against American parties in American courts for certain tort claims, such as human rights violations. Claimants also may sue for foreign acts of torture and extrajudicial killings under the Torture Victim Protection Act.
5. The country's law that a court applies to a case will be determined either by a choice of law clause found in the contract or by the use of judicial conflict of laws (private international law) rules. Conflict of laws rules determine the applicable law if there is no choice of law clause or the court voids the choice of law as a matter of public policy.
6. Arbitration is the most common and preferred means of international dispute resolution. One of the reasons for this is that arbitration awards are easier to enforce than judicial judgments due to the Convention on the Recognition and Enforcement of Foreign Arbitral Awards, popularly known as the New York Convention.
7. International commercial arbitrations are generally conducted under arbitration rules published by one of the world's highly recognized arbitration associations, such as the International Chamber of Commerce (ICC), American Arbitration Association (AAA), London Court of International Arbitration, China International Economic and Trade Arbitration Commission (CIETAC), and so forth.
8. International arbitrators are primarily tasked to render fair and equitable decisions. As such, arbitrators are more willing to use trade usage and business customs, also known as the *lex mercatoria*, in making their decisions. Arbitration awards are final and can only be appealed for a limited number of reasons, such as arbitrator misconduct.
9. The arbitration clause is one of the most important clauses in an international contract and should be custom drafted to deal with such issues as the requirement of a reasoned award, applicable law, language of the arbitration, the amount of discovery permitted, qualifications of the arbitrators, and provisions for emergency measures.

Key Terms

Act of State
Alien Tort Claims Act (ATCA)
American Arbitration Association (AAA)
Brussels Convention
Choice of Law Clause
Conflict of Law Rules
Discovery
Doctrine of *Renvoi*
Doctrine of Sovereign Immunity
Dual Service
Forum Non Conveniens Doctrine
Hague Convention on International Jurisdiction and

Foreign Judgments in Civil and Commercial Matters
Hague Evidence Convention
Hague Service Convention
Inter-American Convention on the Extraterritorial Validity of Foreign Judgments
International Chamber of Commerce (ICC)
Lugano Convention
Med-Arb Clause
New York Convention
Personal Jurisdiction Rule of Reciprocity
Service of Process

Chapter Problems

1. Abraham Lincoln once gave this advice relating to litigation: "Persuade your neighbors to compromise whenever they can. Point out to them how the nominal winner is often the real loser—in fees, expenses, and waste of time. As a peacemaker, the lawyer has a superior opportunity of being a good man." The Roman philosopher Cicero once admonished that "the litigious spirit is more often found with ignorance than with knowledge of law." Do you agree with this view of litigation? What would you recommend for improving the dispute resolution system?
2. Several securities investors who were customers of a broker signed a standard agreement that included a clause requiring the arbitration of any controversies relating to their accounts. When the investments turned sour, the investors sued the broker and the broker's principal. The defendant moved that the claims be submitted to arbitration, under the agreement. Should the plaintiffs be forced to arbitrate their securities law claims? Does the public policy of full enforcement of the securities laws prevail over the public policy favoring arbitration? *Rodriguez de Quijas v. Shearson/American Express, Inc.*, 490 U.S. 477 (1989).
3. Your son has been killed in a car accident in a foreign country. You believe a U.S. agency is withholding information that may provide insight into the cause of the accident. You file a motion to compel the agency to comply with your subpoena requesting certain documents. Will the court compel the agency to comply with the subpoena? Does the notion of sovereign immunity enter into the court's determination? *In re Application of Mohamed al Fayed*, 92 F. Supp. 2d 137 (D.D.C., 2000).
4. Pursuant to a request by a foreign court, a legal alien resident of the U.S. is asked to testify about his activities during World War II and his immigration to the U.S. Can he be compelled to testify against himself? Does the Fifth Amendment's privilege against self-incrimination extend to the fear of being prosecuted by a foreign nation? *United States v. Balsys*, 118 S. Ct. 2218 (1998).
5. A seller from Country A and a purchaser of services from Country B enter into a contract for servicing of heavy machinery at the purchaser's factory. The service contract included an exculpatory clause that relieved the seller of all liability relating to his work. Country A's law generally enforces such clauses, while Country B's law often voids such clauses. The choice of law clause in the contract provided that Country A's law would apply to the

contract. Soon after the seller serviced the machinery, it malfunctioned, injuring two workers and causing substantial property damage to the purchaser's factory. The purchaser party brought suit in Country B. The seller sought a dismissal, citing the exculpatory clause. What factors will the court in Country B look at in determining the validity of the choice of law clause as it relates to the issues of this case?

Internet Exercises

1. Review the model arbitration and mediation clauses published by the International Chamber of Commerce at http://www.iccwbo.org/index_court. asp.
2. Review the index of the 35 international conventions sponsored by the Hague Conference on Private International Law at http://www.hcch.net/e/conventions/index.html.

Other Internet Sources

International Bar Association: http://www.ibanet.org.
Foreign Sovereign Immunities Act: http://www.state.gov/documents/ organization/153980.pdf.
Hague Evidence Convention: http://www.hcch.net/e/conventions/index.html.
ICC International Court of Arbitration: http://www.iccwbo.org/index_court.asp (ICC rules and model clauses).
American Society of International Law: http://www.asil.org (Click on "Topics" and click on "Transnational Litigation, Arbitration, and Dispute Resolution.")
American Arbitration Association: http://www.adr.org.

Notes

1 Service of process involves the delivery of a summons and complaint to the defendant. The summons provides notice to the defendant of where and when it needs to appear in court. A complaint consists of a statement of facts, the claims or causes of action against the defendant, and the remedies or damages being sought by the plaintiff.
2 See Curtis Bradley, "Supreme Court Holds that Alien Tort Statute Does Not Apply to Conduct in Foreign Countries," 17 *ASIL Insights* (April 18, 2013).
3 Ibid.
4 See Louise Ellen Teitz, "Another Hague Judgments Convention? Bucking the Past to Provide for the Future," 30 *Duke Journal of Comparative and International Law* 491 (2019).
5 § 187: Law of the State Chosen by the Parties.
6 Willis Reese, "Conflict of Laws and the Restatement Second," 28 *Law & Contemporary Problems* 679 (1963).

7 Shahla F. Ali, "Approaching the Arbitration Table: Comparing the Advantages of Arbitration as seen by Practitioners in East Asia and the West," 28 *Review of Litigation* 735, 741–742 (2009).
8 Ibid. at 759.
9 Steven C. Nelson, "Alternatives to Litigation of International Disputes," 23 *International Lawyer* 187, 199 (1989).
10 Andrew M. Pardieck, "Virtuous Ways and Beautiful Customs: The Role of Alternative Dispute Resolution in Japan," 11 *Temple International & Comparative Law Journal* 31, 33, 37–42, 44–45, 55 (1997).
11 Courts are still essential for the enforcement of arbitral award and may vacate such awards. See L. DiMatteo, M. Infantino and N. Potin, *Judicial Control over Arbitral Awards* (Cambridge University Press 2021).
12 Adopting countries include Australia, Austria, Canada, Chile, Croatia, Denmark, Egypt, Estonia, Germany, Greece, Hong Kong (China), Hungary, India, Ireland, Japan, Mexico, Nigeria, Norway, the Philippines, Poland, Russia, Singapore, South Korea, Spain, Thailand, Turkey, Ukraine, and Venezuela.
13 Larry A. DiMatteo, "Soft Law and the Principle of Fair and Equitable Decision Making in International Contract Arbitration," 1 *Chinese Journal of Comparative Law* 1 (Oxford University Press 2013) (material in this section is taken from this article).
14 Ibid.
15 Ahmad Alkhamees, "International Arbitration and Shari'a Law: Context, Scope, and Intersections," 28 *Journal of International Arbitration* 255, 261 (2011).
16 Charles Trumbull, "Islamic Arbitration: A New Path for Interpreting Islamic Legal Contracts," 59 *Vanderbilt Law Review* 609 (2006).
17 See Alkhamees above.
18 Lisa Spagnolo, "CISG as Soft Law and Choice of Law" in *International Sales Law: A Global Challenge* (ed. Larry A. DiMatteo, Cambridge University Press: New York 2013).
19 Harold J. Berman and Colin Kaufman, "The Law of International Commercial Transactions (Lex Mercatoria)," 19 *Harvard International Law Journal* 221 (1978).
20 Anna Di Robilant, "Genealogies of Soft Law" 54 *The American Journal of Comparative Law* 499, 518–519 (2006).
21 Ibid. at 519.
22 Ibid. at 520.
23 Ibid. at 524.
24 *TCL* Air *Conditioner (Zhongshan) Co. Ltd. v. The Judges of the Federal Court of Australia* [2013] HCA 5 (March 13, 2013).
25 See JAMS International at https://www.jamsadr.com/about.
26 407 U.S. 1 (1971).
27 Margaret L. Moses, *International Commercial Arbitration* 137 (2nd ed. 2012).
28 For a comparative analysis of the public policy exception and other issues, such as arbitrator bias and misconduct, see Larry A. DiMatteo, Marta Infantino and Nathalie Potin (eds), *Judicial Control over Arbitral Awards: Scope, Vacation and Public Policy* (Cambridge University Press 2020).
29 Heike Gramckow and Barry Walsh, *Developing Specialized Court Services—International Experiences and Lessons Learned*, The World Bank, 2013, available at: http://documents.worldbank.org/curated/en/688441468335989050/pdf /819 *460WP0Devel00Box379851B00PUBLIC0.pdf*, 22.3.2018.

30 See, e.g., F. Tiba, "The Emergence of Hybrid International Commercial Courts and the Future of Cross-Border Dispute Resolution in Asia," 14 *Loyola University Chicago International Law Review* 31 (2016).

31 Ioana Knoll Tudor, "Specialized Chambers for International Commercial Disputes: Paris in the Spotlight," Kluwer Arbitration Blog, 2018, available at: http://arbitrationblog.kluwerarbitration.com/2018/02/14/specialised-chambers-international-commercial-disputes-paris-spotlight/, 25.7.2019.

Chapter 6

International and National Trade Regulation

This chapter is the first of two covering international and governmental regulation of international business transactions or trade. The modern world free trade system evolved under the **General Agreement on Tariffs and Trade** (**GATT**). The postwar success of GATT led to the establishment of the **World Trade Organization** (**WTO**). The primary purpose of the WTO is to remove barriers to international trade. This chapter will review the WTO and the agreements it has been empowered to enforce. International trade has also been affected by the development of strong regional trading blocs. The **European Union** (**EU**) and the 2020 US–Mexico–Canada Agreement (USMCA)[1] are two examples of regional trade integration.

> **Free Trade Era:** The modern free trade era began in the late 1940s with the U.S. and UK push for a world trade organization to prevent the protectionism (high tariffs and quota restrictions) that existed before and during the Great Depression. GATT was established in 1948, and over a 60-year period it succeeded in cutting average tariffs in the developed world from 40 percent to 4 percent.

In this chapter we will examine the relationship between national trade regulation and the world trading system by focusing on national import and export regulations.

DOI: 10.4324/9781003469230-7

WTO and the World Trading System

The WTO has 164 member countries (see Figure 6.1: "WTO Member Countries") that make up 96.7 percent of world GDP. The economic theory that underlies the WTO system is the **theory of comparative advantage** espoused by economist David Ricardo in the early nineteenth century in *On the Principles of Political Economy and Taxation* in 1817. Ricardo's theory was an international version of Adam Smith's idea of the "specialization of labor" as espoused in his 1776 book, *An Inquiry into the Nature and Causes of the Wealth of Nations* (Image 6.1).

Put simply, economic growth can be obtained by allowing people to do the things they are best at doing and then trading or buying goods and services that are more efficiently produced by other countries. This is the rationale behind the

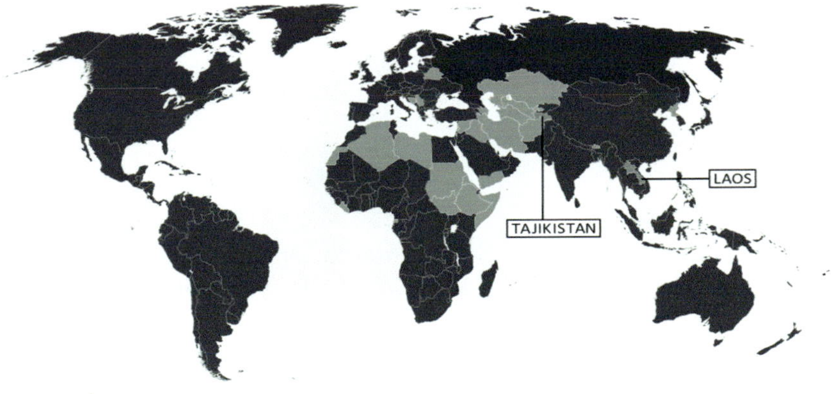

Figure 6.1 WTO Member Countries.
Source: Wikimedia Commons.

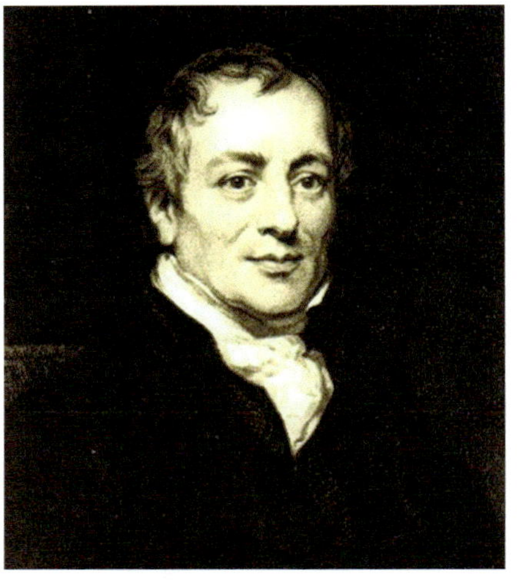

Image 6.1 David Ricardo (1772–1823).

widely accepted view that free trade or the removal of artificial obstacles (tariffs and quotas) to trade between nations will lead to overall economic growth.

The map in Figure 6.1 shows 159 of the 166 member countries of the WTO. Tajikistan and Laos joined in 2013. Since then, Yemen joined in 2014, Kazakhstan and the Seychelles in 2015, and Afghanistan in 2016. The two largest economies that remain nonmembers are Iran and Algeria.

GATT System

Before the establishment of the WTO, the multilateral trading system was known as GATT. The initial aim of GATT was to expand free trade through the reduction of tariffs (duties)[2] worldwide. High tariff rates were one of the major factors that led to the length of the Great Depression. There have been seven *rounds* (trade negotiations) of GATT since its creation in 1948, culminating with the **Uruguay Round** in 1994, which established the WTO as a permanent international organization. The economic benefits of eliminating tariffs are shown in Figure 6.2: "Theory of Free Trade."

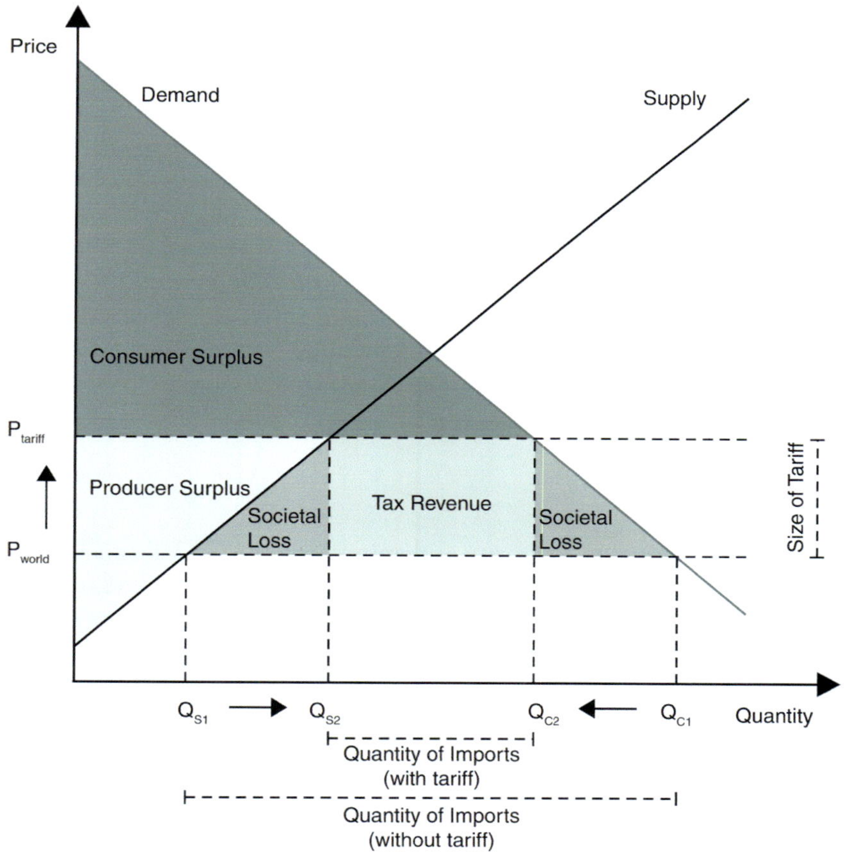

Figure 6.2 Theory of Free Trade.
(Disadvantage of Tariffs).

Figure 6.2 shows the effect of placing a tariff on an imported good. Before the assessment of the tariff, the price of the good in the market is *P-World*. The price rises due to the tariff to *P-Tariff*. The higher price causes domestic production to rise from *QS1* to *QS2*, thereby reducing demand from *QC1* to *QC2*. In this scenario, consumers are worse off because the consumer surplus area becomes smaller, while the producer surplus becomes larger and then gains additional tax revenues. However, the loss to consumers is greater than gains of producers and increased government revenues. The net societal loss is shown by the two triangles. Thus, in a world of tariffs, the reduction of tariffs results in a net gain for society.[3]

The Uruguay Round not only established the WTO, but also included a package of agreements expanding into nontariff areas such as illegal government subsidies of domestic industries, obstacles to sales of services, and infringement of intellectual property rights. Trade barriers include not only tariffs, but also quantitative restrictions, import licensing, and customs barriers; standards, testing, labeling, and certification; government procurement, export subsidies, service barriers, lack of intellectual property protection, and investment barriers. The package of WTO Agreements covers all these types of trade barriers and include the **General Agreement on Trade in Services (GATS)**, **Agreement on Trade-Related Aspects of Intellectual Property Rights (TRIPS)**, and General Agreement on Government Procurement, which was revised in 2012.

Despite the liberalization of the world trading system through GATT and the WTO, major areas of dispute remain. The conclusion of the *Doha Round* (2001) was delayed due to a division between "North" (developed) and "South" (less developed) countries. However, an agreement was reached, known as the **Bali Package** in 2013. The Agreement focuses on reducing import tariffs and agricultural subsidies, with the goal of making it easier for developing countries to trade in global markets. The Bali agreement also focused on reforming customs bureaucracies and formalities to facilitate trade.[4]

WTO Principles

The WTO is the governing authority and enforcer of the GATT and WTO agreements. The WTO international trade regime is based on three fundamental principles: (1) most-favored-nation principle, (2) national treatment principle, and (3) the principle of transparency. All three aim to advance the notion of non-discrimination by which countries are mandated not to discriminate among different foreign trading partners or between domestic goods and imported goods. See Figure 6.3 *Doing Business Internationally*: "Menu of WTO Principles." The **most-favored-nation principle** has helped to reduce tariff rates internationally. This is because when two countries negotiate a lower tariff rate between themselves, they must also provide the lower rate to all other WTO countries. If a country grants benefits to a trading partner through a bilateral agreement, then it must also grant those benefits to all other members of the WTO. Thus, when a country lowers a trade barrier or opens up a domestic market it has to do so for all

Nondiscrimination

A country should not discriminate between its trading partners and it should not discriminate between its own and foreign products, services, or nationals.

Open Access

Lowering trade barriers is one of the most obvious ways of encouraging trade; barriers include customs duties (tariffs) and measures such as import bans or quotas that restrict quantities selectively.

Predictable and Transparent

Foreign companies, investors, and governments should be confident that trade barriers should not be raised arbitrarily.

More Competitive

Discouraging "unfair" practices, such as export subsidies and dumping products at below cost to gain market share distorts the free market.

More Beneficial for Least Developed Countries (LDCs)

LDCs should be given more time to adjust, greater flexibility, and special privileges.

Protection of the Environment

The WTO's agreements permit members to take measures to protect not only the environment but also public health, animal health and plant health. However, these measures must be applied in the same way to both national and foreign businesses. In other words, members must not use environmental protection measures as a means of disguising protectionist policies. Critics of the WTO have argued that the WTO has failed to sufficiently address the last two principles: "more beneficial for least developed countries" and "protection of the environment."

Figure 6.3 Doing Business Internationally: Menu of WTO Principles.

its trading partners. The exception to this rule are **free trade agreements** (**FTAs**), which allow two or more countries to form a free trade area, such as USMCA or a customs union, such as the EU, that allows the area or union to be treated as a single country for purposes of complying with the most-favored-nation principle. Thus, the charging of lower (preferential) tariffs to countries within an FTA does not violate WTO rules. There are currently over 300 FTAs in the world.

The **national treatment principle** prohibits the discrimination between imported goods and domestically produced goods. For example, imported goods cannot be subjected to direct or indirect taxes or charges in excess of those charged on domestic products. The national treatment principle applies once goods, intellectual property rights, or services enter a foreign market, although they can be treated differently at the time of importation. Therefore, charging customs duties on imported goods is not a violation of the national treatment principle. However, import requirements that are disguised trade barriers would be subject to attack as a violation of the national treatment principle. For example, requiring foreign goods to satisfy higher standards or to pass more rigorous testing or inspections than domestic goods would be illegal. The *Warren Corp. v. EPA* case that follows illustrates the fact that international obligations as required under GATT may conflict with domestic requirements.

George E. Warren Corp. v. Environmental Protection Agency

164 F.3d 676 (D.C. Cir. 1998)

A rule promulgated by the Environmental Protection Agency (EPA) regulates emissions from conventional gasoline for motor vehicles and changes the way importers and foreign refiners of conventional gasoline sold in the U.S. had been treated under the prior rule. The EPA sets standards for individual baselines under which domestic refiners, foreign refiners, and importers are all treated differently. However, domestic dealers were able to provide the baselines for their products but importing companies could not. The World Trade Organization (WTO) held the rule violated the antidiscrimination norm of GATT. The U.S. Trade Representative advised the WTO that the U.S. intended to comply with its decision. The EPA proposed to adopt the optional baseline approach, allowing foreign refiners either to accept the statutory baseline or to petition the EPA for permission to establish an individual baseline.

A number of U.S. companies challenged the legality of that rule since it did not include domestic refiners. There is a fundamental distinction between EPA's ability to monitor and enforce regulatory requirements that would apply against domestic as opposed to foreign refiners. Simply put, domestic refiners are subject to the full panoply of EPA's regulatory jurisdiction and compliance monitoring, while not all foreign refiners may be subject to EPA's regulatory jurisdiction with equivalent certainty. The petitions for review are DENIED.

Case Highlights

- WTO's national treatment principle requires that individuals and firms of foreign countries are given the same competitive opportunities, including market access, as are available to domestic parties
- International agreements prevail over conflicting national statutory mandates
- Federal regulatory agencies may weigh different factors (such as international commitments) when rendering a decision or applying a regulation to a situation with international ramifications as opposed to a purely domestic one.

The **principle of transparency** requires WTO countries to make their import and customs laws accessible to importing parties. Furthermore, import regulations should be stable and clear so that importers will not be confused as to the requirements for importation. The WTO agreements require governments to fully disclose import policies and practices publicly. Disguised barriers to trade, such as unsubstantiated quality and health restrictions, often violate both the national treatment and transparency principles.

Consequences of Trade Wars

A trade war is when a nation imposes tariffs or quotas on imports and foreign countries retaliate.[5] Trade wars are a form of trade protectionism in which at least one of the countries wants to force the other to make trade concessions, such as reduce tariffs, increase market access, and increase protection of intellectual property. Its self-interested purpose is to protect domestic industries and create jobs, since increased tariffs give a competitive advantage to domestic producers. But in the long run, a trade war costs jobs by disrupting global supply chains that domestic industries depend on and reduces exports as the other country raises its tariffs, resulting in a decrease in economic growth and an increase in the costs of goods to the consumer.

> Historical examples are abundant on how **protectionist tariffs** hurt the global economy. The most powerful example is that an increase in tariff rates was one of the major factors leading to the Great Depression. The 1930 U.S. Smoot-Hawley Tariff Law (increasing tariffs by an average of over 40 percent) aimed at protecting American farmers. It led to a trade war that worsened the Great Depression. The trade war reduced international trade by 65 percent. In essence, it turned a great recession into a Great Depression.

The stated purpose of the Trump trade wars was to reduce the U.S. $621 billion balance of trade deficit and create American jobs. He initiated three trade wars, including a global tariff on steel, a tariff on European autos, and tariffs on numerous Chinese imports. Subsequently, American farmers suffered from retaliatory tariffs imposed by China and Europe. An unintended consequence of the trade wars has been to motivate other countries to enter into free trade agreements (excluding the U.S.), such as the revision of EU–Mexico agreement and the establishment of a new EU–Japan agreement. The increase in steel tariffs raised costs to American industries dependent on imported metals such as the aerospace industry. In addition, the U.S. is the world's largest steel importer, thanks to users like automakers.15 Steel importers employ 6.5 million workers compared to 147,000 workers in the U.S. steel industry. Costs from the steel tariffs on the automobile industry (which employs over 6 million workers) outweighed any benefits to domestic steel industries (only about 150,000 workers).

The interdependency of countries exporting and importing is due to the rapid rise of global supply chains. For example, about half of American imports from

China are used by U.S. manufacturers to make other products. Thus, increasing tariffs raise the costs to American manufacturers forcing them either to raise prices or discharge workers.

The Trump trade wars also damaged the standing of the WTO. Eight countries filed complaints with the World Trade Organization (Canada, India, Mexico, the EU, Norway, Switzerland, China, and Russia). Unfortunately, the WTO's Dispute Resolution Understanding (DSU) is slow-moving and the claims failed to deter Trump. The largest and most robust trade war was the one between the U.S. and China.

Another reason Trump gave for the trade war was to curtail forced technology transfers to Chinese companies. China requires foreign companies who want to sell products in China to share their trade secrets. Trump began raising tariffs on select Chinese imports and continued to expand the list of products covered by new tariffs.

China retaliated by raising tariffs on some U.S. exports and canceled all U.S. soybean import contracts. Eventually, China agreed to increase its purchases of U.S. exports and reduce the trade deficit. In sum, trade wars slow global economic growth, increase unemployment, increase consumer prices, and in the long-term the protection of domestic industries as the need for innovation is reduced due to the decrease in competition. Trade wars beyond the short-term hurt rather than help domestic economies. This was the conclusion reached by David Ricardo 200 years ago in his theory of international trade that predicted economic growth through the specialization of labor across countries, which became the core rationale for international free trade.

WTO Agreements

The 1980s and 1990s witnessed a tremendous liberalization of international trade law. The breadth of trade liberalization was evident in the breadth of the 1994 WTO Agreements. A number of the Agreements, mostly of a technical nature, benefit international exporters and importers: Agreement on the Application of Sanitary and Phytosanitary Measures; Agreement on Technical Barriers to Trade; Customs Valuation Code; Agreement on Preshipment Inspection; Agreement on Rules of Origin; Agreement on Import Licensing Procedures; and Agreement on Government Procurement.

The Agreement on the Application of Sanitary and Phytosanitary Measures (SPS) and the Agreement on Technical Barriers to Trade (TBT) will be discussed later in this chapter. Other parts of the WTO Agreements will be discussed elsewhere: General Agreement on Trade in Services (GATS) in Chapter 14; Agreement on Trade-Related Aspects of Intellectual Property Rights (TRIPS) in Chapter 15; and Agreement on Trade-Related Investment Measures (TRIMs) in Chapter 16.

WTO and the Importation of "Illegal" Goods

Countries are allowed to retaliate against countries that violate WTO principles. These punitive barriers are generally enacted in response to the giving of illegal **subsidies** to companies by a foreign government or when an exporter is accused of **dumping** goods on a foreign market. A subsidy is when a government grants a domestic industry some benefit not granted to a foreign industry. Dumping is when a foreign company exports and sells goods at below market prices. Dumping can be proved by evidence that the goods are sold below cost or at a price that is lower than the price the goods are sold at in the exporter's home country. Before enacting any countervailing measures (tariffs), a country must seek WTO permission through the WTO DSU process. The respective cases of both countries are presented to an ad hoc WTO panel, which then renders a decision, providing a specific remedy, generally a tariff increase for an illegal subsidy or a **countervailing duty** in dumping cases.

Sanitary and Phytosanitary Measures Agreement

The **Agreement on the Application of Sanitary and Phytosanitary Measures (SPS)** sets out the basic rules for food safety, as well as animal and plant health standards. Sanitary (human and animal health) and phytosanitary (plant health) measures are defined as any measures needed to: (1) protect human or animal life from risks arising from additives, contaminants, toxins, or disease-causing organisms in their food; (2) protect human life from plant- or animal-carried diseases; (3) protect animal or plant life from pests, diseases, or disease-causing organisms; or (4) prevent or limit other damage to a country from the entry, establishment, or spread of pests. The SPS Agreement allows countries to set their own standards but requires that they must be based on science. The basic aim of the SPS Agreement is to maintain the sovereign right of any government to provide the level of health protection it deems appropriate. Countries maintain measures to ensure that food is safe for consumers, and to prevent the spread of pests or diseases among animals and plants. These SPS measures can take many forms, such as requiring products to come from a disease-free area, inspection of products, specific treatment or processing of products, setting of allowable maximum levels of pesticide use, or permitted use of only certain additives in food.

Fear of Protectionism

Sanitary and phytosanitary measures, by their very nature, restrict trade. However, governments are sometimes pressured to go beyond what is needed for health protection and to use SPS restrictions to shield domestic producers from economic competition. SPS restrictions, which are not actually required for health reasons, can be a very effective protectionist device due to their technical complexity. The best defense to claims that a country's SPS standards are disguised barriers to trade is for member countries to use international standards and guidelines where they exist.

Justification for SPS Measures

Measures to ensure food safety and to protect the health of animals and plants should be based as far as possible on the analysis and assessment of objective and accurate scientific data. In the *United States v. India* and *United States v. European Union* cases that follow, the WTO found national SPS standards to be in noncompliance with the risk assessment and scientific basis requirements of the SPS Agreement. The *United States v. India* WTO case shows how national safety measures can affect trade, especially when they act as disguised restrictions.

United States v. India

WTO Decision on Imports of Poultry and Other Agricultural Products (October 14, 2014)

On March 6, 2012, the U.S. requested consultations with India with respect to the prohibitions by India on the importation of various agricultural products because of concerns related to Avian Influenza (AI). The U.S. claims that the measures are inconsistent with provisions of the SPS Agreement. On March 15, 2012, Colombia requested to join the consultations. On May 11, 2012, the U.S. requested the establishment of a panel.

Panel Findings

This dispute concerns India's import prohibition affecting certain agricultural products from countries reporting Notifiable Avian Influenza (NAI) to the World Organisation for Animal Health (OIE). This import prohibition is maintained through India's Avian Influenza (AI) measures. The U.S. complained that India's AI measures amounted to an import prohibition that was not based on the relevant international standard (OIE Terrestrial Code) or on a scientific risk assessment.

As with the majority of SPS cases, the Panel decided to seek advice of experts and international organizations. The Panel consulted with the OIE on the interpretation of the OIE Terrestrial Code and with three individual experts on AI surveillance regimes with particular respect to India's domestic measures and its disease situation.

The Panel found that: In respect of the U.S.'s claims pursuant to the SPS Agreement, the Panel found as a preliminary matter that India's AI measures are SPS measures within the meaning of the SPS Agreement. The Panel further found that:

- India's AI measures are inconsistent with the SPS Agreement because they are not "based on" the relevant international standard (OIE Terrestrial Code);
- India's AI measures are inconsistent with the SPS Agreement because they are not based on a risk assessment;
- India's AI measures are inconsistent with the SPS Agreement because they arbitrarily and unjustifiably discriminated between Members where identical or similar conditions prevail and are applied in a manner which constitutes a disguised restriction on international trade;
- India's AI measures are inconsistent with the SPS Agreement because they are significantly more trade-restrictive than required to achieve India's appropriate level of protection;
- India acted inconsistently with the SPS Agreement because it failed to comply with a number of notification and publication requirements;
- India filed an appeal challenging the findings of the Panel.

Findings of the Appellate Body

Finding 1: The Appellate Body (AB) agreed with the Panel that India's AI measures were not based on: (1) a risk assessment; (2) evidence that its measures were the minimum needed to protect human, animal, or plant life or health; and (3) scientific principles. However, the AB found that the Panel's failure to consider India's presumption that its restrictions were based on international standards and had a scientific basis was in error.

Finding 2: The AB found that the Panel did not err in finding that the U.S. had identified alternative measures that would achieve India's appropriate level of protection. The AB upholds the Panel's findings that India's AI measures were inconsistent and were significantly more trade-restrictive than required to achieve India's appropriate level of protection.

Finding 3: The AB upholds the Panel's finding that India's AI measures are inconsistent with the prohibition against arbitrary or unjustifiable discrimination.

Case Highlights

- A country's product, health, and safety standards should not be used as disguised trade barriers
- National regulatory agencies need to balance potential health, safety, and environmental concerns with the nation's obligations under the WTO Agreements
- WTO's SPS Agreement requires that health, environmental, and safety standards are based on scientific evidence, that they are made transparent to foreign importers, and that they not be any broader than necessary.

Alternative Measures and Risk Assessment

If an acceptable level of risk can be achieved in alternative ways (such as treatment, quarantine, or increased inspection) that are not as trade restrictive, then the importing country should adopt the less restrictive standards to meet their health objective. Furthermore, if another country can show that the measures it applies provide the same level of health protection, these should be accepted as equivalent. The SPS Agreement requires that SPS measures, and the reasons for them, be made transparent to importers. Countries must establish SPS measures on the basis of an appropriate assessment of the actual risks involved, and, if requested, make known what factors they took into consideration, the assessment procedures they used, and the level of risk they determined to be acceptable. Governments are also required to notify other countries of any new or changed SPS requirements which affect trade, and to set up offices (Enquiry Points) to respond to requests for more information on new or existing measures.

Genetically Modified Food Case

The U.S. exports large quantities of genetically modified food products to the EU. The EU's position is that it has not adopted any general position either in favor of or against GMOs. The EU asserts it recognizes the potential benefits of genetically modified organisms (GMOs), but the long-term health consequences are unknown. The EU as a whole and individual EU countries have implemented special measures based on the *precautionary principle* (see discussion of the principle below) before approving import and marketing of GMOs within the EU. The *United States v. European Union* case below is a composite of three WTO dispute settlement proceedings brought by the U.S. against the EU.

United States v. European Union

Genetically Modified Organisms in Foods Case (DS 291, 292, and 293)

The EU placed a five-year moratorium on the importation of foods with genetically modified organisms (GMOs). More specifically, the prohibition related to crops engineered through biotechnology or genetically modified crops. U.S., Argentina, and Canada filed a complaint with the WTO. The claim argued that the moratorium was an illegal obstacle to trade under the WTO Agreements. The U.S. asserted that a number of EU Member States maintain national marketing and import bans on biotech products even though those products had already been approved by the EU for import.[6]

According to the U.S., the measures are inconsistent with the EU's obligations under the WTO's SPS Agreement; Agriculture Agreement; and the TBT (Technical Barriers to Trade) Agreement. Australia, Argentina, Brazil, Canada, Chile, Colombia, India, Mexico, New Zealand, and Peru joined with the U.S. in the consultations.

Panel and Appellate Body Proceedings

The panel found that the EU applied a general *de facto* moratorium on the approval of biotech products and found that the moratorium violated the SPS Agreement. The panel held that SPS's *risk assessment* and *sufficient scientific evidence* requirements were not satisfied. The EU moratorium was a procedural decision and not a substantive one and, therefore, there was no required risk assessment performed or finding of sufficient scientific evidence. The Panel found that the general moratorium led to undue delay in the completion of the EU approval procedure for the importation of the products.

Subsequently, the U.S. and the EU notified the DSB that they had agreed that a reasonable period of time for the EU to implement the recommendations and rulings of the DSB would be 12 months.

Case Highlights

- If substantial differences exist over health or safety standards between countries, the WTO DSU process (see below) may take a half dozen years

to conclude an acceptable resolution. Two reasons for such a drawn-out process are demonstrated in the GMO cases: First, the complexity of the health issues and the supporting or non-supporting scientific evidence; second, losing countries may not fully comply with the WTO ruling, which leads to further negotiations and proceedings to obtain approval from the WTO to implement retaliatory sanctions against the noncomplying party
- In order to justify the EU's general moratorium against the importation of GMO products, the SPS Agreement mandates that two requirements must be met: Unbiased risk assessment and a finding of sufficient scientific evidence to support the imposition of the standard. The WTO found that the EU did not perform the required risk assessment to determine if scientific evidence existed to support its health standard
- The WTO also ruled that the health standards directed at specific products were not supported by sufficient scientific evidence
- The WTO SPS Agreement does not adopt the precautionary principle found in environmental law (see below).

Precautionary Principle

The basic message of the *precautionary principle* is that, on some occasions, measures against a possible hazard should be taken even if the available scientific evidence is not enough to conclude the existence of the hazard. The precautionary principle states that when scientific evidence can neither prove nor disprove that an activity or substance is environmentally damaging, the activity should not progress, and the substance should not be released into the environment. The principle assigns the burden of proof to the potentially polluting industries or countries.

Agreement on Technical Barriers to Trade (TBT)

The SPS and TBT Agreements both target illicit national standards and policies that unduly restrict international trade. As defined in the WTO's TBT Agreement, a standard is a technical specification contained in a document that specifies the characteristics of a product such as levels of quality, performance, safety, or dimensions. Standards may include terminology, symbols, testing, packaging, marking, and labeling requirements. The SPS Agreement focuses on health and safety standards applied to the importation of foodstuffs, while the TBT Agreement is much broader in scope in that it prohibits technical standards relating to any type of product that acts as a disguised trade barrier. The TBT Agreement requires countries to use international standards wherever possible and provide notification of all relevant changes to the "enquiry point" established in their countries.

TBT measures could cover any subject, from car safety to energy-saving devices, to the shape of food cartons. TBT measures include pharmaceutical restrictions or the labeling of cigarettes. Most food labeling requirements, nutrition claims and concerns, quality and packaging regulations are covered by the

TBT Agreement. Some packaging and labeling requirements, if directly related to the safety of the food, are also subject to the SPS Agreement.

Other WTO Agreements

Other agreements are also directly related to national import requirements. The **Customs Valuation Code** attempts to standardize country challenges to the valuations placed on goods being imported for purposes of assessing duties and tariffs. It places the burden of proof on the importer to provide additional evidence of valuation. The **Agreement on Preshipment Inspection** pertains to an importing country's right to preshipment inspections. The **Agreement on Import Licensing Procedures** is based upon the principle that application procedures should be made as simple as possible.

Quantitative Restrictions

A quantitative trade restriction relates to the limitation or prevention of certain amounts of a good from being imported into a country. The importing country may want to reduce the amount of a good that can be imported in order to protect domestic businesses (**quota**), to prevent goods from entering the country due to health and safety concerns (**moratorium**), and a complete prohibition on the importation of all goods from a certain country for political reasons (**embargo**).

The WTO requires the general elimination of quantitative restrictions—except in defined circumstances. Members' notifications on quantitative restrictions are compiled in a WTO database, which is accessible to the public. Exceptions to the prohibition of quantitative restrictions include: (1) temporary export prohibitions or restrictions to prevent or relieve *critical shortages of foodstuffs* or other products essential to the exporting party; (2) import and export prohibitions or restrictions necessary for the application of *standards or regulations* for the classification, grading, or marketing of commodities; and (3) import restrictions on any *agricultural or fisheries products* necessary for the enforcement of governmental measures.

Governments use import restrictions to protect public health or safety, such as the EU's moratorium on GMO products and U.S. prohibited imports of European livestock because "foot and mouth disease" had infected large numbers of cattle in Europe. The other major purpose of quantitative restrictions is to serve political objectives. The restrictions have been used as punitive sanctions against countries accused of human rights violations, acts of aggression, and for national security reasons.

Cuban Embargo and the WTO's National Security Exception

Embargoes of all trade with a foreign country are rare and often short-lived. The most controversial one is the U.S.'s 60-year embargo of Cuba. The *Helms-Burton Act* (Cuban Liberty and Democratic Solidarity Act) extended the

American embargo to include not only U.S. firms but also overseas firms owned or controlled by "U.S. persons." Helms-Burton also subjected foreign companies doing business with Cuba to litigation in the U.S. The Act resulted in serious foreign relations problems. European, Canadian, and Mexican officials charged the U.S. with unlawfully exercising its jurisdiction extraterritorially, in that it was threatening to punish lawful activity—trade, investment, and tourism carried out by residents of their countries.[7]

The WTO Agreements provide a "national security exception." The exception provides a defense for measures that would otherwise be inconsistent with WTO obligations. The rationale behind the exception is that national security is important to all nations, and for an international organization to disregard the importance of this subject and to override national concerns and policies would lead powerful trading nations to ignore or disregard WTO rules.

WTO Dispute Settlement System

The ***Dispute Settlement Understanding*** (**DSU**) came into force with the establishment of the WTO in 1995.[8] Under the DSU, member countries of the WTO agreed that claims for violating trade rules would no longer be subject to unilateral national actions. Instead, disputes would be settled under the *DSU.* Member countries may file complaints charging another country or countries of violating WTO rules. The DSU established the **Dispute Settlement System** (**DSS**). The DSS of the WTO is a cornerstone of the international trading system. An abstaining country could be faced with WTO-sanctioned retaliatory measures and threatened with expulsion from the WTO.

The DSU established the **Dispute Settlement Body** (**DSB**) as the sole authority for appointing panels of experts to decide cases. Before taking any formal action, the disputing countries must consult with each other in an attempt to settle the dispute. Upon the failure of consultation, the complaining country can request that a panel be established to hear the dispute. **WTO panels** are like tribunals, usually consisting of three, sometimes five, experts. The activities of the panel are confidential. Before the hearing, each side prepares its case in writing. At the first hearing, both parties present their cases. At a second hearing, both parties submit written rebuttals and present oral arguments. The panel may also consult experts or appoint an advisory group of experts to prepare a report.

The panel prepares a first draft report and submits it to both parties for comments. It then submits an interim report consisting of its findings and conclusions, allowing either party one week in order to request a review. If a review is requested, the panel has two weeks to hold additional meetings with the parties. The panel then submits a *final report*, which becomes the ruling of the DSB (unless rejected by a unanimous vote of the DSB). The losing party, then must prepare and submit a proposal to implement the ruling. In cases where the losing party fails to implement the ruling within a reasonable period of time, the parties must negotiate compensation pending a full implementation. If the parties do not agree on compensation, then the DSB will authorize measures of retaliation for the winning country.

> **Dispute Settlement Acronyms**
>
> Dispute Settlement Understanding: DSU
> Dispute Settlement System: DSS
> Dispute Settlement Body: DSB
> Appellate Body: AB
> The DSU established the DSS, which includes a three-tier system: Dispute Resolution Panels to AB to DSB (issues measures of retaliation in cases of noncompliance).

The diagram of the dispute resolution procedure created by the DSU is shown in Figure 6.4. The process begins at the bottom of the diagram with consultations between the disputing parties. At the top of the chart is the case where, despite a ruling by the Appellate Body, the losing country fails to comply, which leads to the final step where the DSB authorizes retaliatory sanctions against the noncomplying party.

WTO panels normally consist of three persons of appropriate background and experience from countries not party to the dispute. The Secretariat maintains a list of experts satisfying the criteria for particular types of disputes. The concept of appellate review is an important feature of the DSU. An Appellate Body is composed of seven members, three of whom will serve on any one case. An appeal will be limited to issues of WTO law covered in the panel report and legal interpretations developed by the panel. Further provisions set out rules for compensation or the **suspension** of concessions in the event of non-implementation. Disagreements over the proposed level of suspension may be referred to arbitration.[9] The next section provides an illustration of the WTO DSS at work in the famous U.S.–EU Bananas Dispute.

"Bananas Dispute"

A WTO Dispute Resolution Panel held that the EU had illegally placed restrictions on the importation of bananas into EU countries. The EU objected to the amount of the penalty granted, which included the *suspension* of certain preferred tariff rates as not being equivalent to the level of ***nullification*** or ***impairment*** of benefits suffered by the other countries. The level of suspension was submitted for arbitration. Pursuant to the DSU, the level of suspension is to be determined by the following principles: (1) the complaining party should first seek suspension of benefits in the *same sector* as that in which the impairment or nullification was found; (2) if this is not practical, then it should seek suspension or concessions in other sectors under the same agreement; and (3) if that is not practical, then it should seek a suspension under another covered agreement.[10] The basic rationale of these principles is to ensure that suspensions or concessions across different sectors remain the exception and not the rule in order to prevent an escalation of animosities and a broader trade war.

The panel decision held that the EU import regime pertaining to bananas violated WTO principles. The revised import regime instituted by the EU in

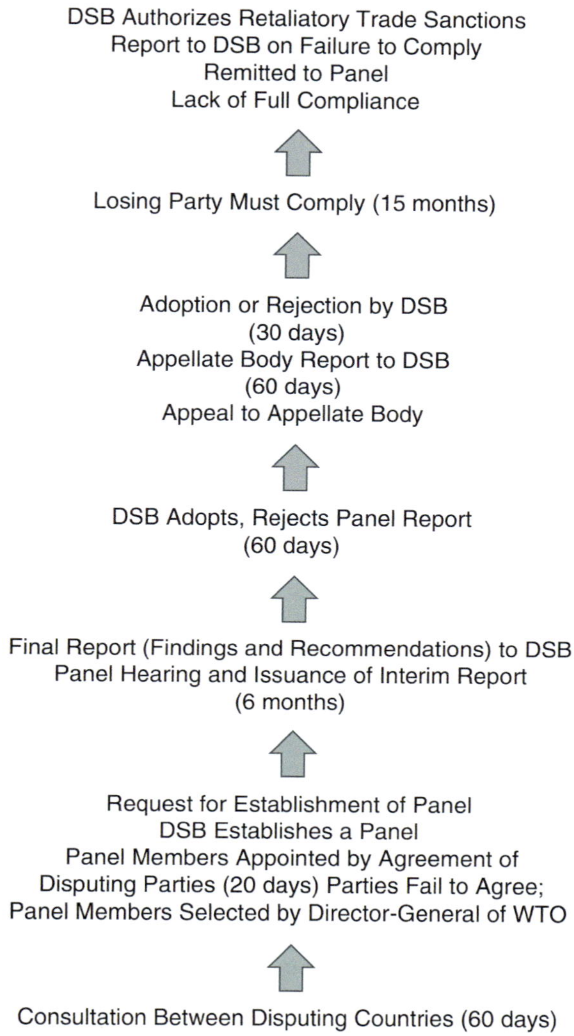

Figure 6.4 WTO Dispute Settlement System.

response to the decision continued to place tariff quotas on bananas imported from the Caribbean and South America. This violated the national treatment principle. The arbitration panel held that the revised banana import regime of the EU continued to violate the national treatment principle.

Anti-Dumping

Dumping is considered an unfair trade practice when it disrupts markets and injures producers of competitive products in the importing country. The WTO permits the imposition of special anti-dumping duties on goods equal to the difference between their export price and their "normal value." An anti-dumping duty is a special duty imposed to offset the price effect of dumping (importing) goods below their normal value and which is determined to be materially harmful to domestic producers. The WTO system of enforcement allows for unilateral retaliation at the national level for illegal dumping and subsidies.

The WTO Anti-dumping Agreement authorizes importing countries to impose extra tariffs on imports found to be dumped causing material injury or posing a threat to the domestic industry producing a like product. Dumping or price discrimination is the selling of exported goods below normal value. A product's "normal value" is the comparable price for sales within the exporting country or the cost of production plus overhead and profit. Injury due to goods being imported at "less than fair value" can be proven showing one of the following: (1) sales lost to imports sold at "less than fair value"; (2) suppression of export prices through underselling; (3) lost profits; (4) reduced employment or capacity utilization; (5) declining sales; (6) growth of imports; (7) reduced product development abilities; or (8) magnitude of the dumping margin.[11] Anti-dumping duties can be as high as 400 percent of the value of the goods being imported and can be assessed for periods of up to 20 years.

Anti-Dumping and the Zeroing Case

The EU launched WTO disputes against the U.S. for the use of a methodology called **zeroing** in the calculation of anti-dumping duty rates. The WTO Appellate Body has consistently condemned the practice of zeroing as unfair. Anti-dumping authorities calculate the margin of dumping for a product by computing the difference between normal value and the import price for each model or type of a particular product and aggregate the results to determine the amount of the anti-dumping duty. Zeroing is the practice when the authority omits the cases where the export price was *higher* than normal value. By doing so, it inflates dumping margins and the duties imposed on the exporter. See Figure 6.5 "Consequences of Zeroing."

The consequences of zeroing are best demonstrated through an example. Suppose three shipments of the same product are imported into the U.S. during a DOC review period. At the time of export: (1) when the first shipment arrived, the product sold at $1,000 in its home country (country of export) with the import price (U.S.) set at $900; (2) when the second shipment arrived, the home price was $1000 and the import price was $1,100; and (3) when the third shipment arrived, the home price was $1000 and the import price was $1,000. The difference between the home price and the import price is recognized as dumping. The first shipment, taken alone, generates a $100 ($1,000–$900 = $100) anti-dumping duty, but the three shipments taken together would generate no anti-dumping duty ($100 + –$100 + 0 = 0). Under WTO rules, there would be no duties owed to the U.S. because during the review period (three shipments) the *average* home market price ($1,000) was the same as the average import price ($1,000).

Figure 6.5 Consequences of Zeroing.

When applying zeroing, the U.S. compares the price of the product in its home market with the price of the product on the U.S. market, but disregards, by setting at zero, all transactions in which the price of the product on the home market is smaller than the price on the U.S. market. Thus, the second shipment is registered as a 0 and not as a –100. The U.S. authorities would then recognize a dumping margin of $100 ($100 + 0 + 0). It would then apply an anti-dumping duty at a rate of 3.33 percent. The anti-dumping duty rate is the percentage of the dumping margin ($100) to the total value of the goods imported ($3000). Other countries deem this to be unfair since it captures foreign exporters that make a strong effort not to dump their products. For example, 19 times out of 20, an exporter exports goods at or above the home market prices and, yet, is made to pay an anti-dumping duty on all 20 shipments (19 zeros for above market pricing + the anti-dumping margin of the one case of underpricing). This is the case in the majority of anti-dumping cases.

Figure 6.5 (Continued).

Illegal Subsidies

Illegal subsidies are government payments or other financially quantifiable benefits provided to domestic producers or exporters contingent on the export of their goods and services. Countervailing duties are imposed against illegally subsidized imported goods or against the exporting country to offset the amount of government subsidies, which cause material injury to a domestic industry in the country of import. Illegal government subsidies, given to an exporter by its home country, result in the lowering of import pricing, which gives the exporter a competitive advantage over domestically produced products. The WTO's **Code on Subsidies and Countervailing Duties** allows an importing country to impose countervailing duties when it can prove that a foreign subsidy would cause injury to a domestic industry. Figure 6.6 *Comparative Law*: "United States Found in Violation of WTO Agreement on Subsidies" discusses a WTO case in which tax credits provided to exporters by the U.S. Foreign Sales Corporation tax regime were held to be illegal export subsidies.

WTO Authorized Unilateral Actions

The WTO Agreements allow countries to take unilateral actions in some situations when their national laws on trade are violated. An example is Section 301 of the U.S. **Tariff Act of 1974**.

Section 301 of the Tariff Act of 1974

The Office of the **U.S. Trade Representative** (**USTR**) is authorized by statute to retaliate against activities of other countries that are deemed to violate U.S. rights under international trade agreements. USTR retaliation is popularly referred to

A panel created by the DSB issued its final report concluding that the U.S. Foreign Sales Corporation (FSC) tax regime creates illegal export subsidies. The FSC provides tax credits for exporting goods in order to promote U.S. exports in a manner compatible with the agreements negotiated between the U.S. and its trading partners. The EU filed a complaint against the United States. Specifically, the EU complaint alleged that the FSC regime violates the export subsidy prohibitions of the WTO Agreement on Subsidies and Countervailing Measures. After consultations between the EU and the U.S. failed to resolve their differences, the EU requested that the WTO's DSB form a panel to rule on the issue. The panel concluded that the U.S. FSC regime created illegal export subsidies and should be abolished. In reaching that conclusion, the WTO panel found that the FSC regime "clearly confers a benefit, in as much as that American exporters need not pay certain taxes."

Figure 6.6 Comparative Law: United States Found in Violation of WTO Agreement on Subsidies.

as Section 301 sanctions.[12] Section 301 provides a means to counter a broad range of unfair foreign trade practices, including discriminatory rules of origin, discriminatory government procurement, licensing systems, quotas, exchange controls, restrictive business practices, discriminatory bilateral agreements, taxes that discriminate against U.S. products, and discriminatory product standards. See Figure 6.6 on how a U.S. practice was deemed to be an illegal subsidy.

The interested company seeking to invoke Section 301 must provide detailed information on both the foreign trade practice complained of and its impact on domestic commerce. If the allegations are found to be true, the USTR may retaliate by suspending trade agreement concessions, imposing duties or other import restrictions, imposing fees or restrictions on services, restricting service sector authorizations, or by procuring compensatory benefits for the U.S. Before such sanctions can be levied, the USTR is required to enter bilateral negotiations with the offending country. If the dispute remains unresolved, the USTR is authorized to impose *unilateral* trade restrictions equal to the amount of harm to commerce. The *Delverde USA v. United States* case explores the meaning of an illegal foreign subsidy and the assessment of a countervailing duty.

The EU challenged the unilateral nature of Section 301 as a violation of the WTO Agreements. It alleged that the speed of retaliation under Section 301 violated the WTO DSU. The WTO DSB upheld a WTO panel's report that the rights exercised by the U.S. under Section 301 did not violate the DSU. The practice of the USTR to consult with the foreign government in order to resolve the dispute before authorizing sanctions satisfied the requirements of the WTO. For a review of the use of Section 301, see Figure 6.7 *Doing Business Internationally*: "Applying Section 301."

Actionable practices under Section 301 are acts or policies engaged in by trading partners that violate a trade agreement, or are found to be unjustifiable, unreasonable, or discriminatory, and burden or restrict U.S. commerce:

(1) *Trade Agreement Violations*: Where a country violates the terms of a bilateral or multilateral agreement, Section 301 can be invoked to impose sanctions against imports of that country.
(2) *Unjustifiable, Unreasonable, and Discriminatory Practices*: An act, policy, or practice is regarded as "unjustifiable" if it denies most-favored-nation treatment to domestic exports or national treatment to national business interests, if it fails to protect intellectual property rights, or if it denies businesses the right of establishment in a foreign country. The term "unreasonable" refers to acts, policies, or practices that are "unfair and inequitable," If imported products, services, or investments are less favorably treated than those products supplied by domestic or other countries' products, then this constitutes "discriminatory practices." Other types of unfair trade practices found actionable include: (1) *Discriminatory Government Procurement Practices* and *Discriminatory Quotas, Tariffs, and Licensing Schemes*.
(3) *Burdens or Restricts Domestic Commerce*: The term refers to the transnational flow of goods and a foreign practice "burdens or restricts" commerce if it causes immediate harm to domestic markets or forecloses future market opportunities.
(4) *Retaliation and Settlement* under Section 301 provides that, before any trade sanctions may be imposed, the USTR must consult with the government of the country charged with an offending practice with a view toward a negotiated settlement of the dispute. Section 301 has gained increased importance as a means of enforcing the results of binding dispute settlements issued by the WTO.

Figure 6.7 Doing Business Internationally: Applying Section 301.

Criticism of the WTO: Protecting the Environment

For most WTO members, environmental issues have been at best ancillary to core international trade issues and disputes.[13] Critics have cited a number of WTO rulings that appear to place free trade issues above environmental concerns. One decision held that parts of U.S. environmental law were inconsistent with WTO rules, which exempts certain kinds of domestic legislation from the WTO's overall ban on discriminatory trade restrictions. The sacrifice of national environmental standards to free trade has been criticized by many environmentalists and labor activists.

National Import and Export Regulation

Countries' export and import regulations directly impact an exporter or importer's ability to undertake profitable international trade transactions. National regulation may bar an exporter's ability to honor a contract if he is precluded from exporting his goods. Also, the cost of importing can be dramatically changed in the event that the duties assigned to a transaction differ from what was expected by the importer. This chapter addresses the relationship between customs regulations and private business transactions.

In importing, the assessment of duties and marking requirements are crucial determinations. A miscalculation of duty owed to the government of import could convert an otherwise profitable import transaction into a loss. In addition to duties, penalties for violating the customs laws can be substantial. Failure to conform to a country's marking or country-of-origin requirements can result in the goods being barred from importation. Also to be studied are laws and regulations relating to the legal exporting of goods.

Import Requirements and Duties

In order to import goods into a foreign country, the importer must satisfy a number of requirements. The three basic types of laws that regulate the importation of goods include: (1) assessment of duties; (2) marking requirements; and (3) standards requirements. Fortunately, there is general agreement among most countries on how to classify goods and assess import duties. The fundamental factors used to determine the customs duties are classification of the type of goods, valuation, and country of origin.

The classification of the type of good being imported is determined by the application of the **harmonized tariff schedule** (**HTS**). The **World Customs Organization** (**WCO**) publishes the HTS, which is used by WTO member countries. Some countries publish their own version of the HTS. The HTS classification number determines the duty rate to be applied to imported goods.

The **country of origin** determination is used to determine if the goods are subject to a WTO's most-favored-nation rate and other more favorable rates provided in Free Trade Agreements, or a rate provided by the **generalized system of preferences** (**GSP**). The GSP is a framework under which developed countries give preferential tariff treatment to manufactured goods imported from developing countries.

HTS classification consists of a series of numbers that identify categories of goods beginning with broad categories. As numbers are added, the description becomes increasingly more specific. The HTS uses the following groupings: section, chapter, heading, and subheading. Twenty-two sections broadly cover products from different industries; 99 chapters of group products by industry ranging from agricultural and component products to finished products. Each grouping is represented by a series of numbers. The first six digits of a tariff classification, uniform for all countries using the WCO system, represent the chapter and heading levels. The first two digits refer to the chapter, and the next four to the heading and subheadings.

World Customs Organization makes changes and publishes the HTS. However, each country must then adopt the changes to conform its HTS to the WCO's HTS. WCO member countries are responsible for 98 percent of all international trade.

The HTS is divided into 22 sections and 99 chapters. The 22 sections divide imports into the following categories:

Section 1: Live Animals, Animal Products
Section 2: Vegetable Products
Section 3: Animal or Vegetable Oils, Fats
Section 4: Prepared Foodstuffs, Alcohol
Section 5: Mineral Products
Section 6: Chemicals Products
Section 7: Plastics and Rubber
Section 8: Hides, Skins, Furs, Handbags
Section 9: Wood, Cork, Straw, Baskets
Section 10: Pulp and Paper Products
Section 11: Textile and Textile Products
Section 12: Footwear, Umbrellas, Whips
Section 13: Stone, Plaster, Cement, Ceramic
Section 14: Pearls, Precious Metals, Jewels
Section 15: Base Metals
Section 16: Machinery, Appliances
Section 17: Vehicles, Boats, Aircraft
Section 18: Watches, Other Instruments
Section 19: Arms and Ammunition
Section 20: Manufactured Articles
Section 21: Works of Art
Section 22: Special Classifications

The HTS is nearly 4,000 pages in length, which demonstrates the high degree of specificity that is expected in classifying imported goods. It is the responsibility of the importer to select the proper classification number subject to the review of national customs authorities (**Customs**). Given the variety of classification choices, importers are often tempted to select a classification number with the lowest tariff rate. However, the HTS provides rules of interpretation, found below in Figure 6.8 *Focus on Transactions*: "Clothing not Knitted or Crocheted," which provides an example of how the HTS classification system is applied to determine the appropriate classification for a type of clothing fabric. The rules of interpretation must be followed in selecting the classification of the goods to be imported. Failure to do so often leads to a delay in the importation and the assessment of penalties.

This excerpt from the HTS found in Table 6.1 illustrates the complexity of important decisions made to determine classification number of a product and the consequences of that selection (tariff rate). The HTS has seven columns.

The HTS classification system is detailed and complex. For examples, Section 11 on Textiles (excerpt from Chapter 11 in Table 5.1) contains 14 chapters or general product classifications: Silk; Wool and Animal Hair; Cotton Silk; Vegetable Fibers and Paper Yarn; Man-Made Filaments; Man-Made Fibers; Wadding and Ropes; Carpets; Woven Fabrics, Lace, and Tapestries; Laminated and Industrial Textiles; Knitted or Crocheted Fabrics; Clothing (Knitted or Crocheted); Clothing (not Knitted or Crocheted); and Other Textile Articles and Rags. Within the general product classifications are 414 headings and subheadings in the schedule for Chapter 61, including one entitled "Clothing (not Knitted or Crocheted)." The first page of that Chapter is provided below.

Figure 6.8 Focus on Transactions: Clothing not Knitted or Crocheted.

Table 6.1 HTS, Section 11, Chapter 61, page 1 of 73 (http://hts.usitc.gov).

Heading Subheading	*Stat Suffix*	*Article Description*	*Unit or Qty*	*General Duty Rate*	*1 Special Duty Rate*	*2*
6101		Men's or boys' overcoats, carcoats, capes, cloaks, anoraks (including ski-jackets), windbreakers and similar articles			Free (0%): (AU, BH, CA, CL, IL, JO, KR, MA, MX, OM, P, PA, PE, SG)[14]	50%
6101.20.00		Of cotton		15.9%		
	10	Men's (334)	doz./kg			
	20	Boy's (334)	doz./kg			
6101.30		Of manmade fibers				
6101.30.10	00	Containing 25 percent or more by weight of leather (634)	doz./kg	5.6%	Free: (AU, BH, CA, CL, IL, JO, KR, MA, MX, OM, PA, PE, SG)	35%
		Other:				
6101.30.15	00	Containing 23 percent or more by weight of wool or fine animal hair (434)	doz./kg	38 cents/ kg + 10%	Free: Same as above	77 cents/ kg + 54.5%
6101.30.20		Other			Free: Same as above	72%
	10	Men's (634)	doz./kg			
	20	Boys' (634)	doz./kg			
6101.90		Of other textile materials:				
6101.90.05	00	Of wool or fine animal hair (434)	doz./kg	61 cents/ kg +16%	Free: Same as above, except OM 18.5 cents/ kg + 4.8%	77 cents/ kg + 54.5%
6101.90.10	00	Containing 70 percent or more by weight of silk or silk waste (734)	doz./kg	0.9%	Free: Same as above	45%
6101.90.90		Other		5.7%	Free: Same as above	45%
	10	Subject to cotton restraints (334)	doz./kg			

(Continued)

Table 6.1 (Continued)

Heading Subheading	*Stat Suffix*	*Article Description*	*Unit or Qty*	*General Duty Rate*	*1 Special Duty Rate*	*2*
	20	Subject to wool restraints (434)	doz./kg			
	30	Subject to man-made fiber restraints (634)	doz./kg			
	60	Other (834)	doz./kg			

Column 1 provides the heading and subheading for the goods being classified. The different numbered headings essentially make up the HTS classification number. Column 3 provides a description of the goods. The first description given is at the "heading level." This heading provides a "general description" of the goods covered. Its description states: "Men's or boys' overcoats, carcoats, capes, cloaks, anoraks (including ski-jackets), windbreakers and similar articles." The importer begins by finding the heading that best describes the goods being imported. The importer then scrolls down the HTS viewing all the subheadings that differentiate goods covered by the heading. Goods are differentiated based upon whether the garment is made for "men" or "boys" and by the type of material used to make the garment (cotton, man-made fibers, other textile materials, such as wool). Column 2 "Stat Suffix" provides access to all the rulings relating to the specific heading or subheadings, such as sample rulings issued by Customs. If there is no relevant ruling, then the importer can either determine a reasonable classification or ask Customs for a ruling on the importer's question or selection of a classification (see Figure 6.9). Seeking a ruling is the correct course of action if the importer is unsure of a reasonable classification and a misclassification could result in higher duties being assessed.

August 26, 1999
CLA-2-62: RR: NC: WA: 357 E85138
CATEGORY: Classification
TARIFF NO.: 6202.91.1000
Ms. Jeannine Smith, Sammie Bauer, Inc.
RE: The tariff classification of a woman's padded sleeveless jacket from China
Dear Ms. Smith:
In your letter dated August 2, 1999, you requested a classification ruling.
The sample submitted, style number 23904122, is a woman's hip-length reversible padded sleeveless jacket. One side of the garment is constructed of a knit 100% polyester fleece fabric that is quilted in a diamond pattern to a nonwoven batting fill. The other side is constructed of a woven plaid 85% wool/15% nylon fabric.

Figure 6.9 Sample Letter (HTS Classification) (Issued by CBP).

The garment will be imported under item number 008-0272 in regular sizes, under item number 008-0273 in petite sizes and under item number 008-0274 in tall sizes. The garment features a V-neck style collar and oversized armholes. The garment has a full front opening that is secured by a left-over-right two-button closure on the knit fabric side and by a right-over-left two-button closure on the woven fabric side. The woven fabric side of the garment has two front patch pockets at the waist. The garment is bound at the edges by piping composed of a knit polyester fleece fabric. Although this garment has a left-over-right button closure on the knit fabric side, the cutting specifications that you submitted for the garment clearly indicate that it is designed for a woman.

Figure 6.9 (Continued).

Column 4 provides the amount or number of items being imported. Since the product is clothing, the amount being imported is measured by a number of items (dozens) or weight of the items (kilograms). Column 5 is the *general duty rate*, the rate given to all WTO members based on the most-favored-nation principle. Column 6 is the lower or preferential rates provided by the GSP or free trade agreements. In looking at the 6101 part of Chapter 61, depending on the item and the country of export, the tariff could be as little as 0 percent. This information is found in the column entitled "Special Duty Rate." Elsewhere in the HTS the non–most-favored-nation rates reach as high as 100 percent (column 7). The non-WTO rates show the major benefits obtained through WTO membership.

General and Additional Rules of Interpretation

The **HTS Rules of Interpretation** for selecting the proper classification of a product consist of *general rules* and *additional rules*. The brevity of the rules of interpretation belies the complexity of the classification determination. The rules of interpretation are followed by 937 pages of "notes" that provide definitions for interpreting the chapters of the HTS. The General Rules of Interpretation are summarized in Figure 6.10 "General Rules of Interpretation."

Mutatis mutandis: Latin for "the necessary changes having been made." In the above case, it means that when determining the appropriate subheadings, the same rules used to determine headings shall be used to determine the appropriate subheading, but only between subheadings under the same heading, but not in trying to compare subheadings under different headings.

The rules of interpretation recognize that there is often no exact fit between the good being imported and a HTS tariff classification. When more than one tariff selection is possible, the additional rules are the means by which the importer and Customs make the final selection. The primary rule of interpretation is the **rule of specificity**. It requires the use of a heading and subheading that provides a

Rule 1 The chosen HTS classification must have the essential character of the complete or finished article. The classification should state that the article is complete or finished, or alternatively as unassembled or disassembled.
Rule 3 When goods are, *prima facie*, classifiable under two or more headings, classification shall be selected as follows:

(a) When two or more headings apply to mixed or composite goods, those headings are to be regarded as equally specific in relation to those goods;
(b) Mixtures and composite goods consisting of different materials or made up of different components, shall be classified based on the material or component, which gives them their *essential character*;
(c) When goods cannot be classified by reference to 3(a) or 3(b), they shall be classified under the heading which occurs last in numerical order.

Rule 4 Goods that cannot be classified in accordance with the above rules shall be classified under the heading appropriate to the goods to which they are most akin.
Rule 6 For legal purposes, the classification of goods in the subheadings of a heading shall be determined according to the terms of those subheadings and *mutatis mutandis* (although there are differences, the items are of the same class), to the above rules, on the understanding that only subheadings at the same level are comparable.
Additional Rule of Interpretation: *principal use* of the good: "Tariff classification is determined by the use of the goods at the date of importation."

Figure 6.10 General Rules of Interpretation.

more specific description of the good over one that gives a more general description. If neither description is considered more specific, then the heading for the material, component, or function (principal use of the good) that provides the **essential character** of the good is to be used.

Over time, as more headings are added to the HTS, the rule of specificity and the essential character rule may result in a change of classification for a specific product. A change of classification may result in a different duty rate being applied, so it is important for importers to keep up to date on changes or additions to the HTS. The need for additions to tariff classifications is especially apparent in the area of technology products.

The general rule-making authority of Customs to clarify parts of the HTS that are unclear as to particular goods or services was recognized by the U.S. Supreme Court in *United States v. Haggar Apparel Co.* The *Haggar* case also discusses Section 9802 of the HTS, which provides a special exemption from tariff duties for items temporarily exported for assembly and then returned.

The *United States v. Haggar* case introduced Section 9802, which allows importers to deduct the value of assembly from duty assessment. This exemption is given for "articles assembled abroad in whole or in part of fabricated components that are products of the importing country." It also extends the exemption to any advancement in value or improvement in condition that is a result of "operations incidental to the assembly process such as cleaning, lubricating, and painting."

United States v. Haggar Apparel Company

526 U.S. 380 (1999)

Justice Kennedy. This case concerns regulations relating to the customs classification of certain imported goods issued by the Customs Service.

Respondent Haggar Apparel Co. designs, manufactures, and markets apparel for men. This matter arises from a refund proceeding for duties imposed on men's trousers (pants) shipped by Haggar to this country from an assembly plant it controlled in Mexico. The fabric had been cut in the U.S. and then shipped to Mexico, along with the thread, buttons, and zippers necessary to complete the garments. There trousers were sewn and reshipped to the U.S. If this case involved mere assembly without other steps, the imported garments would have been eligible for the duty exemption, which Haggar is claiming.

Haggar in the Government's view added one other step at the Mexican plant: permapressing. Permapressing is designed to maintain a garment's crease in the desired place and to avoid other creases or wrinkles that detract from the trousers' proper appearance. Customs claimed that permapressing was an added process in addition to assembly and denied a duty exemption. Haggar claimed the permapressing was simply part of the assembly process or an "operation incidental to the assembly process."

Customs is responsible for the proper classification of imported goods under the tariff schedules (HTS). The statutes authorizing customs classification regulations are consistent with the usual rule that regulations of an administering agency warrant judicial deference. If the agency's statutory interpretation fills a gap or defines a term in a way that is reasonable, we give that judgment controlling weight.

Case Highlights

- Permapressing clothes are not assembled under Section 9802 or an "operation incidental to the assembly process"
- Merely because a process, operation, or treatment fails to produce a substantial transformation does not automatically result in it being able to obtain a duty exemption under Section 9802

This exemption has resulted in the creation of a corridor of assembly plants, popularly known as *maquiladoras*, along the U.S.–Mexico border. ***Maquiladora*** or "in-bond" industry allows foreign importers to ship components into Mexico duty-free for assembly and reexport. The key issue of contention between Customs and importers is the definition of "fabrication."

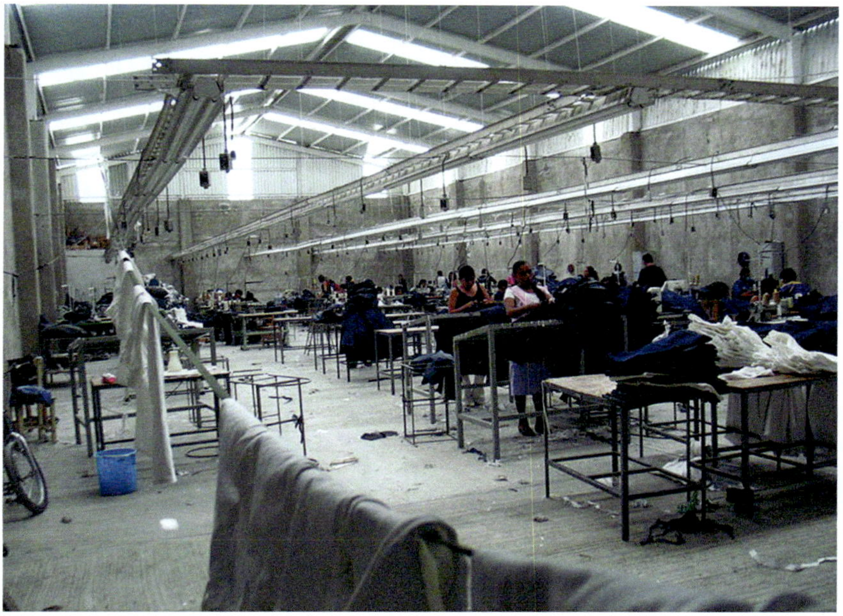

Image 6.2 *Maquiladora* Factory.

The term *maquiladora* in the Spanish language refers to the practice of millers charging a maquila or "miller's portion" for processing another person's grain.

Maquiladora (or *maquila*) is a manufacturing operation in a free trade zone (FTZ), where companies import material and equipment on a duty- and tariff-free basis for assembly, processing, or manufacturing. The assembled, processed, or manufactured products are then usually exported back to the country of origin. The difference between mere assembly (resulting in lower or no tariffs) and fabrication is discussed in the *Samsonite* case.

Samsonite Corp. v. United States

889 F.2d 1074 (Fed. Cir. 1989)

Judge. This case involves the denial by Customs of a deduction from assessed duties of the cost of an item that had been manufactured domestically, including a component imported from Mexico. The component consisted of metal strips used by Samsonite to assemble luggage. The strips were sent by Samsonite to Mexico where the strips were bent by machine into a squared-sided form and riveted on the open ends, thereby became the bottom plates of completed frame assemblies. Customs classified the imported merchandise as luggage under Item 706.62 of the HTS and assessed a 20 percent *ad valorem* duty on its value less the cost or value of certain components of the luggage that had been manufactured in the U.S. Customs denied a deduction from the value of the luggage for the cost of the steel strips.

The court held that the steel strips "were not exported in condition ready for assembly." It found that the "bending process" to which the strips were subjected "did more than 'adjust' the article." To obtain a deduction for fabricated articles assembled abroad, the components:

(1) must have been exported to Mexico "in condition ready for assembly without further fabrication"; (2) must not have lost their physical identity in the articles by change in form, shape, or otherwise; and (3) must not have been advanced in value or improved in condition "except by being assembled" except "by operations incidental to the assembly process such as cleaning, lubricating, and painting." The bending and shaping of the strips constituted "fabrication" and not mere assembly and operations incidental to the assembly process.

Case Highlights

- In order to obtain the duty exemption for offshore assembly found in Section 9802, the exported items must be ready for assembly without further fabrication
- The ethical issues related to the *Maquiladora* industry are discussed in Figure 6.11's "Focus on Ethics."

Buy Domestic Goods Laws

Some national laws restrict government procurement of foreign-made goods. They are found at different levels of government. An example is the 1983 Pennsylvania Buy American Act, which requires government agencies to buy steel only from American companies. The *National Foreign Trade Council v. Baker* case stated that such a law does not violate the WTO's "national treatment principle" because they "do not single out a particular foreign country for particular treatment." This is an illogical proposition since even though it applies to all countries' steel exports, there are only a few countries that export steel into the U.S. in substantial amounts. To think that the act doesn't discriminate against those countries is absurd. The WTO's Agreement on Government Procurement does not bar the use of Buy American Acts. However, the sweep of the Buy American laws is greatly diminished for two reasons. First, the Acts provide a number of exceptions that allow for the purchase of foreign products: (a) if the domestic product is more expensive than an identical foreign-sourced product by a certain percentage; (b) if the product is not available domestically in sufficient quantity or quality; or (c) if doing so is in the public interest.

Cheap Mexican labor is attractive to foreign manufacturers to stay competitive with other major export countries, but the treatment of the workers in these plants along the northern Mexican border raises grave ethical issues. Poverty is a key factor that motivates people to work in maquiladoras despite unsafe and unsanitary working conditions. However, the wage set by the Mexican government is barely enough to help sustain a family. The majority of *maquiladora* employees are young women. Along with the abuse of cheap labor, environmental policies are not strictly enforced. Streams and rivers in the border region have been ecologically devastated as a consequence of the *maquila* industry. These facts raise a number of important questions: (1) How should the economic benefits of attracting foreign investments be balanced against the marginal improvements of the workers' quality of life? (2) Is the argument that the jobs created by the *maquiladora* industry are better than no jobs at all the ultimate winning argument? (3) Does corporate social responsibility require the payment of a "living wage?" (4) Who is ultimately responsible for cleaning up the resulting environmental disaster?

Figure 6.11 Focus on Ethics: Ethics Issues of *Maquiladora* Industry.

Assessment of Duties

An import duty is a tax imposed on imports by Customs after the HTS rate is determined. Duties are generally based on the value of the goods (***ad valorem* duties**); other factors include weight or quantity (**specific duties**), or a combination (compound duties). *Ad valorem* literally means "according to value" and refers to any charge, duty, or tax that is applied as a percentage of value. The assessment of import tariffs or duties is a product of three variables: (1) classification of the goods being imported; (2) valuation of the goods; and (3) the country of origin. Figure 6.12 *Focus on Transactions*: "Dutiable Status of Goods" outlines the factors involved in applying these three elements in determining the amount of duties to be assessed on imported goods.

Dutiable Status is the CBP determination of the amount of duty (tax) owed by the importer. The above three columns summarize the factors used in calculating the duty owed. Column 1 (Classification) and Column 3 (Country of Origin) determine the rate (%). Column 2 (Valuation) determines the value of the imported goods. The value of the goods is then multiplied by the rate to determine duty owed. See Figure 6.12 Focus on Transactions: "Dutiable Status of Goods."

CLASSIFICATION+	*VALUATION+* **Transaction Value**	*COUNTRY OF ORIGIN*
Harmonized Tariff Schedule Common/Commercial Meaning Rule of Relative Specificity Essential Character Principle Principle Use Rule Latest Entry Rule Doctrine of the Entireties Chief Weight Rule (Textiles)	Price paid Packing Costs Commissions (by buyer) Value of "Assists" Royalties/Fees (by buyer) Proceeds of Resale (accruing to seller)	**"Rules-of-Origin" Rules of Interpretation:** Grown, mined, produced, manufactured "Substantial Transformation Test" • new article • value added • process versus assembly • producer to consumer good

Figure 6.12 Focus on Transactions: Dutiable Status of Goods.

Transaction Value

The WTO's *Valuation Code* provides the basic method for determining the value of goods for customs purposes. The Valuation Code uses the concept of **transaction value** as the basis for determining the value of imported goods. It states that such valuation is to be determined on a *commercially realistic basis*. A good's transaction value is the price that would be paid in a sale between two unrelated parties in the ordinary course of business or the costs of the goods to the importer. Conflicts arise over what items of costs should be included in the transaction value. The items most contested include commissions paid by the importer,[15] royalties or fees paid by the importer after importation,[16] the value of *assists*[17] (material, equipment, or services provided to the exporter by the importer), and proceeds of resales paid to the original seller.

Four alternative valuation methods are used when an arm's length transaction (transaction between affiliated parties) is not present. The most preferred method is to use the transaction value of identical goods. This is the price charged by the same manufacturer or importer to an unrelated customer. The second valuation method looks at the transaction value of similar types of goods. This would be the price charged for nearly identical goods sold by the same manufacturer. The third valuation method is the use of the **deductive value** of the goods. The deductive value is the price at which the goods are ultimately sold to the end user or ultimate purchaser in the country of importation. The importer is allowed to *deduct* a number of costs from that price, including international freight, duties, and certain commissions. For example, foreign inland freight costs can be deducted but only if they are separately invoiced. Although selling commissions are included in determining dutiable value, commissions paid by the buyer are not dutiable. Therefore, by proving that any middleman is acting as the buyer's purchasing agent, the buyer's commission can be excluded from the valuation.

In order to reduce the transaction value and hence the amount of tariff duties, a sophisticated importer will attempt to *unbundle* the import transaction into dutiable and nondutiable parts. If goods are purchased on credit that requires the payment of interest, the importer should separate the credit part of the sale from the sale of goods. Another example of unbundling is when an import contract provides for an inspection of goods at the port of shipment. If the seller obtains and pays for an inspection certificate, those costs are included in the transaction value, but inspection services paid for by the buyer are not part of the transaction value.

The final, least-preferred alternative method is the **computed value** of the goods. This value is fabricated by adding the manufacturer's actual labor and material costs, along with an estimate of its general expenses and profits. The importer is allowed to deduct certain types of expenses before duties are assessed, such as: (1) profits and expenses incurred in the country of importation; (2) costs of legal services, travel expenses, and accounting costs.

Customs Valuation in the EU

The EU approach to customs valuation is similar to that found in the EU Council Regulation 2913/92 established the EU's *Customs Code*, which bases the valuation of imported goods on the notion of transaction value or the "price actually paid" (Article 28). Article 29 provides that transaction value must be adjusted upward for any proceeds of subsequent sales that are remitted by the buyer to the exporter, directly or indirectly. Customs value includes the costs of packing, commission and brokerage, and royalty and license fees (Article 32). Items that are not included in the customs valuation include freight charges, charges incurred subsequent to import, and finance charges (Article 33). EU tariff system is fully harmonized. **TARIC** or Integrated Tariff of the European Communities is designed to show the various rules applying to specific products when imported into the EU. This includes the provisions of the HTS, but also additional provisions specified in EU law, such as tariff suspensions, tariff quotas, and tariff preferences.

Drawback of Customs Duties

Drawback is a form of tax relief in which a lawfully collected customs duty is refunded or remitted wholly or in part because of the particular use made of the commodity on which the duty was collected. Companies that import materials or components that they process or assemble for reexport may obtain drawback refunds of duties paid on the imported merchandise. This practice encourages exports by permitting exporters to compete in foreign markets without the handicap of including in their sales prices the duties paid on imported components. Also, if products or materials of foreign origin imported for domestic consumption are exported or are destroyed within three years of the date of importation, then duties paid on the imported merchandise are refundable as a drawback.

Foreign Trade Zones

To encourage and facilitate international trade, countries all over the world have established **free trade zones** (**FTZ**) or **export-processing zones** (**EPZ**), which include special economic zones, bonded warehouses, free ports, and customs zones. FTZs are an important tool of international trade. FTZs provide the advantages of entering within an area of the country without formally passing through customs. This allows for the delay in paying tariffs until the goods are formally entered into the country. The goods or materials may be processed or assembled within the FTZ and then either imported into the country or exported out of the FTZ to another country.

FTZs have evolved from initial assembly and simple processing activities to encompass high-tech and science parks, finance zones, logistics centers, and even tourist resorts. They now include not only general-type zones but also single-industry zones or commodity zones. The zones are restricted-access areas, in or adjacent to a Customs port of entry. Although located within the country, they are not considered inside the country for purposes of paying tariffs. For import and reexport activities, no customs duties, federal excise (export) taxes, or state or local *ad valorem* taxes are charged on foreign goods moved into FTZs. These facilities are available for storage, repacking, inspection, exhibition, assembly, manufacturing, and other processing.

A customs-bonded warehouse is a building or other secured area in which goods may be stored without payment of duties. A bonded warehouse is more limited in scope than the FTZ. An importer may consider storing finished products in a bonded warehouse for a period of time if the importer expects duty rates to decrease or if a quota or other restrictions on importation are expected to be repealed, but manufacturing is not permitted unless the goods are subsequently exported. When goods enter a bonded warehouse, both the importer and the warehouse proprietor incur financial and legal liability under a bond.

> **Import Quotas:** There are two types of quotas: (1) a physical or "absolute quota," and (2) a "tariff rate quota." The former type limits the quantity of certain goods that may enter a country during a specific period. The latter type permits a specified quantity of imported merchandise to be entered at a reduced tariff rate during the quota period; however, quantities entered in excess of the quota limit during that period are subject to a higher tariff rate.

Prior to any manipulation or manufacture, which would change its tariff classification, an importer may apply to the Port Director to have imported merchandise in the zone given **privileged foreign status**. The merchandise is classified and appraised, and duties and taxes are determined as of the date the application is filed. When such merchandise is entered into the country, either in its original state or after manipulation or manufacture, the applicable duties and taxes would be paid based on the rate established when privileged foreign status was granted. This would be beneficial if the importer fears that the tariff rate might be increased in the future.

Section 337 of Tariff Act of 1930

Longstanding laws, found in many countries, allow for unilateral action against "unfair practices" related to the importation of goods. For example, Section 337 of the U.S. Tariff Act seeks to prevent infringement on intellectual property rights and harm to domestic industry. If found to be in violation, goods may be denied entry into the country. It may also issue a cease and desist order targeted at future violations and levy civil penalties (fines). Customs also has the power to seize and destroy targeted goods.

Country of Origin

The creation of global supply chains and the global manufacture of goods present problems in determining the country of origin for a good. The country of origin of a good is used to determine the applicable tariff rate and whether any quantitative restrictions are relevant. For example, a product of a less developed country is often given a reduced tariff rate under the GSP. Also, lower tariffs and restrictions are available for goods produced within free trade areas.

Unfortunately, country of origin determinations can be complicated and uncertain for a number of reasons. First, country of origin rules generally come from national import laws and countries have used different criteria and have varied in their interpretations. Second, the rise of the global marketplace for goods, services, and raw materials has resulted in products being manufactured in different stages in different countries with component parts coming from all over the world.

Country of origin rules are also used to conform to import laws pertaining to the labeling of products ("Made in China" or "Made in France") manufactured, produced, assembled, or made from materials from different countries. A number of methods have been developed to make this determination. **Substantial transformation** is considered the primary test in country of origin determinations. Under this approach, the country of origin is the last country in which a good or product was substantially transformed. A substantial transformation occurs when a product is changed into a new or different product, for example, when a good has changed from a producer good to a consumer good.

Another definition of a substantial transformation is where a good is "manufactured into a new and different article, having a distinctive name, character, or use from that of the original article."[18] Factors often utilized in applying this test include whether the good went through a tariff classification change, the amount of value added because of the transformation, and the complexity of the processing operation. The **value-added test** is based upon the use of percentages, either of the value added or percentage of component parts coming from imported materials, to determine the country of origin. The EU uses this method as part of a multistep approach depending on the type of product being imported. In general, nonregional materials or components need to be sufficiently transformed in order to result in a tariff classification change.

A number of problems are associated with the value-added method. First, it penalizes least-developed countries because of their low costs of labor and raw materials. Second, multinational enterprises may manipulate transfer pricing among their affiliated companies to reduce the value of imported materials in order to avoid tariff duties or to ensure a certain country of origin designation.

> **Transfer Pricing** is the setting of the price for goods and services sold between controlled or related legal entities within an enterprise. In principle, a transfer price should match either what the seller would charge an independent arm's length customer or would pay an arm's length supplier. Companies often misuse transfer pricing to lower profits in a division of an enterprise that is located in a country that levies high taxes and to raise profits in a country that has low taxes. Transfer pricing is a major illegal tool for corporate tax avoidance.

The **specified processes test** expressly lists the types of processes or operations that are considered to confer country of origin status. However, this test has not been used comprehensively. Instead, it has been used in a piecemeal fashion to target certain products. For example, EU Commission Regulation 288/99 grants origin status to an integrated circuit wherever it undergoes diffusion. An example of a negative version of the test is EU Regulation 2071/89, which holds that the location of the assembly of an optical system does not provide a presumption that that location is the country of origin for imported photocopiers. The final method of origin determination is the **change in tariff classification** approach. This test bases country of origin status upon any change in a product that results in a change in its tariff classification.

The WTO adopted the Origin Agreement in order to harmonize the different national rules and establish the **Technical Committee on Rules of Origin** to interpret the rules. The Origin Agreement requires all WTO countries to publish their nation's origin rules and applications of their rules. It also requires members to give a binding assessment to anyone who requests an advanced determination of origin. The next section explores the application of country of origin rules to national marking requirements.

Country of Origin Marking Requirements

National **marking requirements** require that imported goods be marked in a conspicuous place in such manner to show the name of ultimate purchaser. The ultimate purchaser is the last person in the country of import who receives the article in the form in which it was imported. Figure 6.13 provides some of the technical aspects to the marking of goods. National laws provide severe punishment including fines and imprisonment for anyone destroying, removing, or altering a required mark.

Countries' requirements for packaging and labeling products vary from country to country. The box shows the basic requirements for Canada.

Canada's Consumer Packaging and Labelling Act

Three Mandatory Statements on Labels
Product Identity Declaration (Product's generic name or function)
Product Net Quantity (Metric system)
Dealer's Name and Place of Business
Other Requirements
Statements must be written in English and French
Quebec Law: English text cannot be larger than French text

- *Legibility*: The marking must be legible. This means it must be of an adequate size, and clear enough, to be read easily by a person of normal vision.
- *Conspicuousness*: The marking should be located in a conspicuous place. It must be where it can be seen with a casual handling of the article. Markings cannot be covered or concealed by subsequent attachments or additions.
- *Permanency*: The article should be marked as indelibly and permanently as the nature of the product will permit so that it remains until the article reaches the ultimate purchaser.
- *Abbreviations and Spellings*: Abbreviations that unmistakably indicate the name of a country (Luxemb. for Luxembourg) and variant spellings (Italie for Italy) are acceptable. However, EU. is not an acceptable abbreviation since it does not indicate an individual country of origin.
- *Forms of Marking*: The best form of marking are ones that become a part of the article, such as branding, stenciling, stamping, printing, and molding or embossing.
- *Special Marking Requirements*: There are also product-specific marking requirements. For example, Chapter 91 of the HTS sets forth special marking requirements for watches and clocks. Under normal marking requirements, the watch's country of origin must appear conspicuously and legibly on the dial face. In addition, watches must be marked on one of the bridges or top plates with the name of the country of manufacture, name of the manufacturer, and the number of jewels, if any, serving a mechanical purpose. Watch cases shall be marked on the inside or outside of the back to show the name of the country of manufacture, and the name of the manufacturer or purchaser.
- *No Marking Required*: Articles produced more than 20 years prior to their importation need not specify their country of origin.

Figure 6.13 Technical Requirements of Marking.

Markings and Free Trade Agreements

FTAs often include marking requirements relating to trading within the free trade area. For example, the U.S., Canada, and Mexico are members of the 2020 USMCA, which offers lower tariffs for items produced in those three countries. There is a specific USMCA Certificate of Origin for items produced in those three countries. USMCA provides a formula to determine whether a good was produced in a USMCA country, in order to take advantage of lower tariff rates. USMCA defines something made in Canada, Mexico or the U.S. as something on average which is 60 percent of transaction value or 55 percent using the net cost method if the labor and component parts were supplied by a USMCA country (regional value). Specific products, like automobiles, require higher percentages of regional materials, labor, and services. The regional content requirement for automobiles is 60%, increasing to 64% in 2024, and 74% in 2027.

National Import and Export Restrictions, Requirements, and Standards

The main existing barriers to trade are those involving Technical Barriers to Trade (TBT) and national health and safety standards.

Standards Requirements

The existence of non-harmonized standards for similar products or technologies in different countries or regions can contribute to so-called "technical barriers to trade." Standards are technical specifications or other precise criteria to be used as rules, guidelines, or definitions of characteristics, to ensure that materials, products, processes, and services are fit for their intended purposes. Country-specific standards are not always transparent and, in the past, may have acted as barriers to trade.

In more recent times, there have been regional efforts to harmonize product standards. In the EU, standards harmonization has allowed for the free movement of goods within the Union. Voluntary standards have been developed that allow a company to affix an **ecolabel** to its products. An ecolabel is a voluntary mark awarded by the EU to producers that show their products are significantly less harmful to the environment than similar products. The EU's **CE mark** is an "umbrella" label that warrants that the good bearing the mark meets all relevant EU Directives relating to that type of product, including quality and safety requirements.

The International Labour Organization (ILO) has been active in developing international labor standards. The ILO was established in 1919 and became a specialized agency of the United Nations in 1946. It seeks to promote social justice in areas such as employment, pay, health, working conditions, and freedom of association among workers.

Export Regulations

The different licenses available for exporting goods are: (1) **validated license**, authorizing a specific export and (2) **general license**, authorizing exports, without application by the exporter. The term general license is a misnomer because it does not result in a license being issued by the government. The **general license** is a grant of authority to all exporters and is sufficient for most of the goods being exported. No application for exportation or government approval is needed when exporting under a general license, just a filing of a declaration.

Validated licenses require written approval from a designated government authority. Exporters of some types of goods (those involving encryption, armaments) or goods to be exported to certain countries (where exporting in general or exporting of certain goods are prohibited) must obtain a validated license. Some countries require exporters to place the intended place of destination on commercial invoices and bills of lading for most export sales. These statements alert foreign buyers of goods and documents that diversion to another country is prohibited. An example of a destination control statement follows: "These commodities, technology, or software were exported from France in accordance with export regulations, and diversion to other than the list country is prohibited under French law."

In order to expedite the application process to obtain a validated license, the exporter should obtain an "International Import Certificate" or a **Statement by Ultimate Consignee and Purchaser** (Figure 6.14). The former is issued by the government of importation and certifies that the goods will be disposed of in the designated country. The Statement by Ultimate Consignee and Purchaser is an assurance from the purchaser that the goods will not be resold or disposed of contrary to the requirements of the export license.

A freight forwarder or customs broker may assist the exporter in preparing documentation, including the Statement by Ultimate Consignee and Purchaser form. For more information on exporting, see Figure 6.15 *Focus on Transactions*: "Helpful Hints for Exporters."

The severity of punishment for failing to obtain the appropriate export license is demonstrated in the hypothetical case of *United States v. Shetterly.*

United States v. Donald Shetterly

971 F.2d 67 (7th Cir. 1992)

Judge. After a jury trial, Donald Shetterly was convicted of attempting to export a controlled microwave amplifier to Belarus without an export license and was sentenced to 41 months' imprisonment. He now appeals his conviction and sentence. Mr. Shetterly sent electronic equipment, including microwave amplifiers and computer software, to a person in Belarus. The importer requested Shetterly to purchase an amplifier from Berkshire Technologies, Inc., a California company. Berkshire informed Shetterly that the amplifier was on the Department of Commerce's Commodity Control List (CCL) and required a validated license to export.

One of the purposes of the CCL is to protect national security. A validated license requires the exporter to file a license application before exporting commodities that cannot be exported under a general license. Mr. Shetterly argues that the technology involved was already available abroad. American law states that anyone who "knowingly violates or conspires to or attempts to violate any provision of the export regulations commits a crime." Mr. Shetterly contends that an exportation or attempted exportation of a controlled commodity without a license becomes a crime only if the exporter knows that a license is required. The government was only required to prove beyond a reasonable doubt that Mr. Shetterly knowingly exported or attempted to export a controlled commodity, without obtaining the appropriate export license.

Mr. Shetterly also alleges the district court erred in failing to consider the degree to which the violation threatened U.S. security interests, the volume of commerce involved, the extent of planning or sophistication, and whether there were multiple occurrences in determining a sentence. The fact that subsequently a validated license was no longer required to export the Berkshire amplifier out of the country is immaterial.

Case Highlights

- Export licenses are required for exporting certain commodities
- A general license requires merely that the commodity meets certain standards—no license application is required, and no license document is issued
- A good that is on a Commodity Control List requires a validated license
- Knowingly exporting or attempting to export a controlled commodity without a license is a crime.

Free Trade Agreements

This chapter will review four types of methods or agreements used to increase the free flow of goods, services, and investments between countries. These trade and investment enhancing agreements are reviewed in order of their bindingness and scope: (1) **free trade agreements** (**FTAs**); (2) **bilateral investment treaties** (**BITs**); (3) **cooperation agreements**; and (4) **free or foreign trade zones** (**FTZs**). FTZs were covered earlier. After the World Trade Organization's (WTO) Agreements, these country to country or countries agreements are the most important means of facilitating international trade. While the WTO is worldwide in scope, FTAs entail a smaller group of countries.

The FTA creates competitive advantages (lower tariffs, removal of quantitative restrictions) among the countries of the FTA that are not extended to countries outside of the FTA. This would normally violate the WTO's most-favored-nation and national treatment principles, which require one WTO member country to treat all other WTO countries in the same manner. However, Article XXIV of the WTO Agreement provides an exception for FTAs that meet certain requirements. Article XXIV states:

FORM **BIS-711**
FORM APPROVED UNDER OMB
CONTROL NO. 0694-0021, 0694-0093

U.S. DEPARTMENT OF COMMERCE
BUREAU OF INDUSTRY AND SECURITY
Information furnished herewith is subject to the provisions of Section 12(c) of the Export Administration Act of 1979, as amended, 50 U.S.C. app 2411(c) and its unauthorized disclosure is prohibited by law.

DATE RECEIVED
(Leave Blank)

STATEMENT BY ULTIMATE CONSIGNEE AND PURCHASER

1. ULTIMATE CONSIGNEE	CITY	
ADDRESS LINE 1	COUNTRY	
ADDRESS LINE 2	POSTAL CODE	TELEPHONE OR FAX

2. DISPOSITION OR USE OF ITEMS BY ULTIMATE CONSIGNEE NAMED IN BLOCK 1
We certify that the items: *(left mouse click in the appropriate box below)*

A. ☐ Will be used by us (as capital equipment) in the form in which received in a manufacturing process in the country named in Block 1 and will not be reexported or incorporated into an end product.

B. ☐ Will be processed or incorporated by us into the following product (s) ______
to be manufactured in the country named in Block 1 for distribution in ______

C. ☐ Will be resold by us in the form in which received in the country named in Block 1 for use or consumption therein.
The specific end-use by my customer will be ______

D. ☐ Will be reexported by us in the form in which received to ______

E. ☐ Other (describe fully) ______

NOTE: If BOX (D) is checked, acceptance of this form by the Bureau of Industry and Security as a supporting document for license applications shall not be construed as an authorization to reexport the items to which the form applies unless specific approval has been obtained from the Bureau of Industry and Security for such export.

3. NATURE OF BUSINESS OF ULTIMATE CONSIGNEE NAMED IN BLOCK 1
A. The nature of our usual business is ______

B. Our business relationship with the U.S. exporter is ______

and we have had this business relationship for ____ year(s).

4. ADDITIONAL INFORMATION

5. ASSISTANCE IN PREPARING STATEMENT

STATEMENT OF ULTIMATE CONSIGNEE AND PURCHASER
We certify that all of the facts contained in this statement are true and correct to the best of our knowledge and we do not know of any additional facts which are inconsistent with the above statement. We shall promptly send a supplemental statement to the U.S. Exporter, disclosing any change of facts or intentions set forth in this statement which occurs after the statement has been prepared and forwarded, except as specifically authorized by the U.S. Export Administration Regulations (15 CFR parts 730-774), or by prior written approval of the Bureau of Industry and Security, we will not reexport, resell, or otherwise dispose of any items approved on a license supported by this statement (1) to any country not approved for export as brought to our attention by means of a bill of lading, commercial invoice, or any other means, or(2) to any person if we know that it will result directly or indirectly, in disposition of the items contrary to the representations made in this statement or contrary to Export Administration Regulations.

6. SIGNATURE OF OFFICIAL OF ULTIMATE CONSIGNEE	**7.** NAME OF PURCHASER	
NAME OF OFFICIAL	SIGNATURE OF PURCHASER	
TITLE OF OFFICIAL	NAME OF OFFICIAL	
DATE *(mmmm,dd,yyyy)*	TITLE OF OFFICIAL	
CERTIFICATION FOR USE OF U.S. EXPORTER - We certify that no corrections, additions, or alterations were made on this form by us after the form was signed by the (ultimate consignee)(purchaser).	DATE *(mmmm,dd,yyyy)*	
8. NAME OF EXPORTER	SIGNATURE OF PERSON AUTHORIZED TO CERTIFY FOR EXPORTER	
NAME OF PERSON SIGNING THIS DOCUMENT	TITLE OF PERSON SIGNING THIS DOCUMENT	DATE *(mmmm,dd,yyyy)*

We acknowledge that the making of any false statements or concealment of any material fact in connection with this statement may result in imprisonment or fine, or both and denial, in whole or in part, of participation in U.S. exports and reexports.

Public reporting burden for this collection of information is estimated to average 15 minutes per response plus one minute for recordkeeping, including the time for reviewing instruments, searching existing data sources, gathering and maintaining the data needed, and completing and reviewing the collection of information. Send comments regarding this burden estimate or any other aspect of this collection of information, including suggestions for reducing this burden, to the Director of Administration, Room 3889, Bureau of Industry and Security, U.S. Department of Commerce, Washington, DC 20230, and to the Office of Management and Budget Paperwork Reduction Project (0694-0021, 0694-0093), Washington, D.C. 20503. Notwithstanding any other provision of law, no person is obligated to respond to nor shall a person be subject to a penalty for failure to comply with a collection of information subject to the Paperwork Reduction Act unless that collection of information displays a currently valid OMB Control Number.

Figure 6.14 Statement by Ultimate Consignee and Purchaser.

The contracting parties of the WTO recognize the desirability of increasing freedom of trade by the development, through voluntary agreements, of closer integration between the economies of the countries party to such agreements. They also recognize that the purpose of a customs union or of a free-trade area should be to facilitate trade between the constituent territories and not to raise barriers to the trade with other WTO members.

1 Determine if a validated export license is required.
2 Fully describe commodities or technical data on export shipping documents.
3 Use the applicable destination control statement on commercial invoices, airway bills, and bills of lading.
4 Avoid shipments after the expiration date on the validated export license.
5 Enter the applicable validated export license number or general license symbol on the export declaration.
6 Make certain the export documents clearly identify the exporter, intermediate consignee, and ultimate consignee (purchaser).
7 Designate an appropriate person to monitor export transactions to ensure compliance with export regulations.

Exportation of certain specific goods may also require approval from a number of other government agencies.

Figure 6.15 Focus on Transactions: Helpful Hints for Exporters.

WTO and FTAs: Technically, FTAs violate the rules of the WTO in that they allow certain countries to offer lower tariff rates to each other without offering the same rates to all other WTO members. This violates a core principle of the WTO—the "most-favored-nation" principle that mandates the lower tariff rates between two WTO countries must be provided to all other WTO members. The most-favored-nation principle has been a major force in lowering worldwide tariff rates over the last half-century. The WTO Agreement provides exceptions for establishing a free trade area (NAFTA) or an external common customs union (EU), under Article XXIV of the General Agreement on Tariffs and Trade (GATT) and Article V of the General Agreement on Trade in Services (GATS).

In essence, Article XXIV treats the FTA as a singular country: "Each such customs territory shall, exclusively for the purposes of the territorial application of the WTO Agreement, be treated as though it were a contracting party." By being recognized as a single entity for WTO purposes, FTAs cannot be accused of violating the most-favored-nation or national treatment principles. The new generation of FTAs have expanded their scope, beyond trade in goods and services, and the protection of foreign investment. Many FTAs include provisions on environmental protection, labor and employment rights, and the protection of intellectual property rights. The trend over the past few decades has seen a proliferation in FTAs.

BITs have been a longstanding method whereby two countries provide assurances to one another's citizens, companies, and investors doing business in each other's country. BITs consist of legally binding obligations, with a pre-agreed DSU process in the event a country breaches the treaty.

Cooperation Agreements (formerly known as Friendship Agreements) are opening statements of cooperation between two countries that do not have a tradition of trade between them. These agreements are less detailed in nature than BITs. They are preliminary in nature and serve to establish the basis for freer trade and cooperation that hopefully will lead to a broader and more binding BIT.

Benefits of Free Trade Agreements

The objectives of FTAs include the expansion and diversification of trade; elimination of barriers to trade in goods and services; increased investment opportunities; and advancement of effective environmental protection, labor rights, and the enforcement of intellectual property rights. These objectives are accomplished through the implementation of the core principles of national treatment, most-favored-nation treatment, and transparency promoted by the WTO.

Any company looking to export its products or services should check to see if its country has negotiated favorable treatment for its citizens and companies through an FTA. Accessing FTA benefits for your product may require more record keeping, but it can also give your product a competitive advantage versus products from other countries. Some types of opportunities frequently found in FTAs include: (1) the ability to bid on government procurement contracts in an FTA partner country; (2) the ability for an investor to receive prompt, adequate, and effective compensation if its investment in the FTA partner country is expropriated (taken) by the government; (3) the ability for service suppliers to supply their services in FTA partner countries; (4) protection and enforcement of intellectual property rights; and (5) the ability for exporters to participate in the development of product standards in FTA partner countries.

United States–Mexico–Canada Agreement (USMCA)

In 2020, Canada, Mexico, and the U.S. entered into a new FTA (replacing the North American Free Trade Agreement or NAFTA). Canada and Mexico are America's two largest export markets; they buy more American goods and services than any other country in the world.

The objectives of the USMCA, as in most FTAs, are to promote the principles of national treatment, most-favored-nation treatment, and transparency, and more specifically, to: (1) eliminate barriers to trade, and facilitate the cross-border movement of goods and services; (2) promote conditions of fair competition; (3) increase investment opportunities; (4) provide adequate and effective protection and enforcement of intellectual property rights; and (5) create effective procedures for the resolution of disputes. See Figure 6.16 "USMCA Facts."

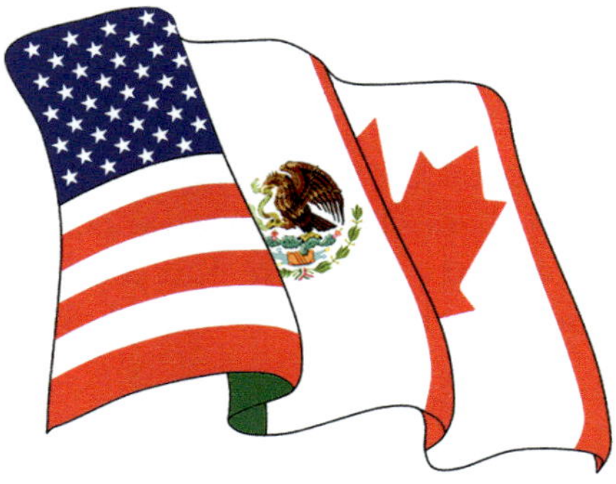

Image 6.3 United States–Mexico–Canada Agreement (USMCA).
Source: https://usmca.com.

The USMCA affirms existing rights and obligations with respect to each other under the *General Agreement on Tariffs and Trade*. Also, other international agreements are given priority over USMCA, including the Convention on International Trade in Endangered Species, Montreal Protocol on Substances that Deplete the Ozone Layer, and the Basel Convention on the Control of Transboundary Movements of Hazardous Wastes.

In order to obtain the benefits of the preferential tariff rates, goods must come from within the FTA. The **Rules of Origin** (**ROO**) describe how exported goods shipped to a country or a region may qualify for duty-free or reduced-duty benefits. In determining the country of origin, a number of tests or rules apply including substantial transformation, product-specific, and percentage-based formulas. Goods must be certified as **regional goods** in order to cross USMCA borders freely, which means the goods originated in a USMCA country or passed the test of **substantial transformation** (where a good or material is further processed), which usually results in a *tariff classification change* for the goods.

However, for some goods, such as certain textile products, the materials used to produce the goods must go through a **triple transformation** in order to obtain regional-goods status. Other products, like automobiles, electronics, and machinery, have to pass stringent *cost tests*. Depending on the type of good, somewhere between 55 and 60 percent of the good's costs must be regional in origin. In sum, ROO may require: (1) a change in tariff classification; (2) a regional value-content requirement; or (3) both a change in tariff classification and a regional value-content requirement. Each product type has its own specific ROOs. The criteria for determining entitlement for the lower USMCA tariffs based on the ROO include: (1) the good is "wholly obtained or produced entirely" in the territory of one or more of the USMCA countries; (2) the good is produced entirely in the territory, but not all of the materials used originated in a USMCA country, but the good goes through a tariff classification change in the USMCA country or satisfies the regional value-content requirement or a combination of both; and (3) the good is an originating agricultural good and

Positive

- The biggest changes made by USMCA include higher rules-of-origin requirements for the auto sector, marginally greater U.S. access to the Canadian dairy market, and a scale-back of the investor-state dispute settlement (ISDS) rules.
- Sections of USMCA are devoted to intellectual property. These provisions include ensuring data can be transferred cross-border, guaranteeing enforceable consumer protections in the digital marketplace, and continuing to provide strong patent protection for innovators.
- The USMCA labor chapter includes clear language that commits each country to implement policies that protect workers against wage and employment discrimination on the basis of sex, including with regard to pregnancy, sexual harassment, sexual orientation, gender identity, and caregiving responsibilities. It also provides for the inspection of factories in Mexico to determine if they comply with Mexico's new labor laws that allow workers to unionize.

Negatives

- The USMCA does not address climate change.
- The USMCA extends data and patent protections for pharmaceuticals (extends data protection for biologic drugs from eight years to 10 years). This represents a step backward because it further delays the entry of generic medicines and will keep drug prices higher.
- USMCA severely limits investor–state dispute settlement (ISDS). The rules of ISDS protect firms that invest abroad against unfair treatment by foreign governments in three major ways. First, they restrict direct and indirect expropriation. Direct expropriation means outright seizure of foreign firms' property without compensation; indirect expropriation refers to opaque taxes and regulations. Also, ISDS requires governments to provide "fair and equitable treatment" to foreign firms. ISDS rules are enforced by international arbitration, which enables foreign firms to challenge unfair treatment by governments and win money awards.

Figure 6.16 USMCA Facts.

is not subject to a quantitative restriction in the importing USMCA country because it is a "qualifying good."

Anti-Dumping and Countervailing Duty Determinations

As with the WTO Agreements in the exporting and importing of goods, the two major areas of disputes under USMCA involve the dumping of goods and **illegal government subsidies**, which allow domestic manufacturers and growers to export and sell their goods at below market prices. Dumping is the sale of goods in foreign markets at prices below those charged for *comparable sales* in the home market or that are *below the cost of production*. As discussed previously, **anti-dumping duties** are special levies or tariffs imposed on imported merchandise to protect an affected domestic industry from injury caused by the sale of dumped goods. Generally, illegal subsidies occur when imported goods benefit from foreign government financial assistance. Examples of subsidies include loans at preferential rates, grants, tax incentives, or the providing of goods or services by a government at prices below market levels. A **countervailing duty (CVD)** is a special duty imposed on imported merchandise to protect a domestic industry from injury caused by illegally subsidized imports being sold at below market prices. An injury is caused by dumped or subsidized imports resulting in lost sales, reduced prices, lost market share, decreased profits, and other such difficulties for the injured industry.

Disputes are resolved through independent **binational review panels** that make "final determinations" (rulings) in the areas of anti-dumping duties and countervailing duties. The two Binational Panel Decisions that follow focus on the two key elements needed to sustain a case of dumping: (1) differential between the "normal value" of goods and the dumping price; and (2) material injury requirement (the dumping of goods is causing or threatens harm to a domestic industry of the country of import). *National Gypsum* reviews issues that relate to the first element. In that case, the American exporter of gypsum board was accused of dumping goods onto the Canadian market. A key fact is that, over a three-year period, the American share of the Canadian gypsum market doubled in size.

Final Determination: Minster of National Revenue Regarding Gypsum Board Originating From USA

National Gypsum submits that the Final Determination was in error of law in respect of its selection of the period of investigation (POI) for the examination of exports of gypsum board to Canada. Complainant also argues that Revenue Canada erred in not including certain interest expenses in the calculation of the "costs of production" of certain U.S. exporters such as National Gypsum for the purposes of determining the **normal value** of like goods. In selecting the POI, the objective is to select a period which accurately reflects the exporter's price levels to Canada and in the country of export. The issue is whether a two-month period is reasonable. It was argued that Canada did not capture a representative picture of pricing and did not obtain the data necessary to provide a reasonable estimate of the margin of dumping.

It is our view that Canada concluded that there were no significant trends or seasonal factors affecting imports. Our own review of the data and the material concerning the industry indicates that it was subject to seasonal trends typical of the construction industry, with larger sales at higher prices in the summer months. The Panel finds that it was unreasonable for Revenue Canada to maintain the two-month POI throughout its investigation.

"The normal value of the goods shall be determined, as the aggregate of the *cost of production* of the goods; including, an amount for administrative, selling and all other costs; and an amount for profits." The interest expenses at issue are simply part of each exporter's general costs of doing business (financing) and thus must be accounted for in the calculation of normal value on a **constructed-value basis**. For whatever reason and however incurred, the interest expenses in question became part of the actual costs of the corporation and are "attributable" to the goods it produces. This means simply that all costs of a corporation, paid or accruing as payables, must be spread in some reasonable manner over the products being exported

Case Highlights

- Following a substantive complaint, the first step in the DSU process is determining the "period of investigation." This will be the period of time that the government agency will review the import transactions subject to the complaint. The government agency conducting this investigation has discretion in setting the POI
- The next step is to determine the "normal value" or price of the goods to be compared to the actual price charged for the exported goods
- The common ways for determining the price include the price charged in the exporter's domestic market or by calculating the "costs of production" including reasonable overhead expenses and profits
- The third step requires the government agency to determine if the dumping or illegal subsidy "has caused, is causing or is likely to cause *material injury*" to domestic industries or businesses
- In determining normal value, "all costs" of doing business must be factored into the calculation. The Binational Review Panel held that Canada had failed to factor in a *pro rata* share of the interest costs paid by the exporting company on its general business loans.

Another case dealt with the issue of the harm caused to a country's domestic industry due to the illegal dumping of imported goods. The *Hot-Rolled Carbon Steel* case deals with the requirement of showing "injury to a domestic industry" in the case of illegal dumping.

Review Panel: Certain Hot-Rolled Carbon Steel Originating in Mexico

The Panel held that certain Hot-Rolled Carbon Steel Plate originating in or exported from Mexico, People's Republic of China, Republic of South Africa, and the Russian Federation did not cause injury to a domestic industry but were threatening to cause injury. The importance of the issue is the **cumulative effect** of the alleged dumping from the different countries. Thus, the primary issue is whether the Mexican imports should have been the subject of a separate analysis. The law allows for accumulation where: (1) margin of dumping from each of the countries in question is not insignificant; (2) the volume of the goods from each of those countries is not negligible; and (3) an assessment of dumping margins on a cumulative basis is appropriate considering the conditions of competition between the dumped goods and the same goods in the country of importation.

The Tribunal weighed additional factors for determining whether there is a causal relationship between the dumping of any goods and the threat of injury. These factors include the following: (1) the volumes and the prices of undumped goods; (2) contraction in demand; (3) changes in patterns of consumption; (4) trade restrictive practices of and competition between foreign and domestic producers; (5) developments in technology; and (6) expert performance and productivity of the domestic industry. The Tribunal must determine whether there is a causal relationship between the dumping of the goods and the threat of material injury.

Finally, the Tribunal notes that in finding of a threat of material injury to the domestic industry requires that the "circumstances in which the dumping or subsidizing of [the subject] goods would cause injury [must be] clearly foreseen and imminent."

Case Highlights

- In order to win a dumping-of-goods claim, it must be proven that the alleged dumping caused or threatened to cause injury to a domestic industry in the importing country. Alternatively stated, there has to be a causal connection between the price of the imported goods and a material injury caused to a domestic industry
- Dumping charges may be brought against more than one country (in this case, China, Mexico, South Africa, and Russia), and the cumulative impact of the imports from all the countries may be used in making the "injury to domestic industry" determination.

Central America–Dominican Republic FTA (CAFTA–DR)

The areas of coverage of CAFTA-DR include an expanded menu common in modern FTAs: (1) National Treatment and Market Access for Goods; (2) Rules of Origin (ROO); (3) Sanitary and Phytosanitary Measures (SPS); (4) Technical Barriers to Trade (TBT); (5) Government Procurement; (6) Foreign Direct Investment (FDI); (7) Trade in Services; (8) Financial Services; (9) Telecommunications and Electronic Commerce; (10) Intellectual Property Rights (IPR); (11) Labor Rights; (12) Environment Protection; (13) Anti-Corruption; (14) Economic Sustainability; and (15) Dispute Settlement. Figure 6.17 provides excerpts from the "preamble" of the CAFTA–DR, which highlights the goals and purposes of the agreement. It illustrates the core areas and principles found in FTAs, including: expanding market access for trade in goods and services, improved transparency of customs regulations, protection of intellectual property, improvement of workers' rights, and the need to promote environmental protection and sustainable development. Importantly, CAFTA–DR FTA recognizes the differences in the member countries' levels of development and the size of their economies (see italicized phrases in the Preamble).

STRENGTHEN the special bonds of friendship and cooperation among their nations and promote regional economic integration; CONTRIBUTE to the harmonious development and expansion of world trade; CREATE an expanded market for their goods and services while recognizing the *differences in their levels of development and the size of their economies*; ESTABLISH clear and mutually advantageous rules governing their trade; ENSURE a predictable commercial

Figure 6.17 Preamble: Central America–Dominican Republic FTA (CAFTA–DR).

framework for business planning and investment; SEEK to facilitate regional trade by promoting efficient and transparent customs procedures; ENHANCE the competitiveness of the countries' firms in global markets; FOSTER creativity and innovation, and promote trade in goods and services that are the subject of intellectual property rights; PROMOTE transparency and eliminate bribery and corruption in international trade and investment; PROTECT, enhance, and enforce basic workers' rights; CREATE new employment opportunities and improve working conditions and living standards; IMPLEMENT this Agreement in a manner consistent with environmental protection and promote sustainable development; PRESERVE their *flexibility to safeguard the public welfare*; and CONTRIBUTE to hemispheric integration.

Figure 6.17 (Continued).

Trans-Pacific Partnership (TPP)

The TPP is a free trade agreement among Pacific Rim countries (see Image 6.4). The text consists of 30 chapters, covering tariffs on goods and services, intellectual property (IP) rights, e-commerce rules, labor and environmental standards, dispute resolution mechanisms, and many other aspects of global trade. The TPP covers 40 percent of world trade and its purpose is to create a fully integrated economic area and establish consistent rules for global investment. President Obama saw it as a means to counteract Chinese economic power in the region. However, President Trump withdrew the U.S. from the final round of TPP negotiations. The remaining 11 countries (TPP-11) continued to negotiate and finalized an agreement called the Comprehensive and Progressive Agreement for Trans-Pacific Partnership (CPTPP), which entered into force for those countries on December 30, 2018. The 11 countries form a trading bloc representing 495 million consumers and 13.5% of global GDP.

The CPTPP has been labeled as a "next-generation" trade agreement. On e-commerce, the CPTPP largely prohibits data localization and prohibits customs duties on electronic transmissions. It facilitates regionalized supply chains and liberalizes trade in services beyond the participating countries' WTO commitments. It also calls for domestic adoption of internationally agreed-upon labor laws and environmental commitments. Some of the important provisions of the CPTPP include:

- Elimination of tariffs across a broad range of sectors. Most tariff lines became duty-free when the Agreement entered into force. Tariffs on other goods will be eliminated gradually over "phase-out" periods, which vary by country;
- Export-Import restrictions (other than tariffs) can only be applied in cases of supply, conservation of natural resources where domestic consumption or production is also restrained, and restrictions imposed in conjunction with domestic price stabilization schemes;
- Prohibition on agricultural export subsidies;

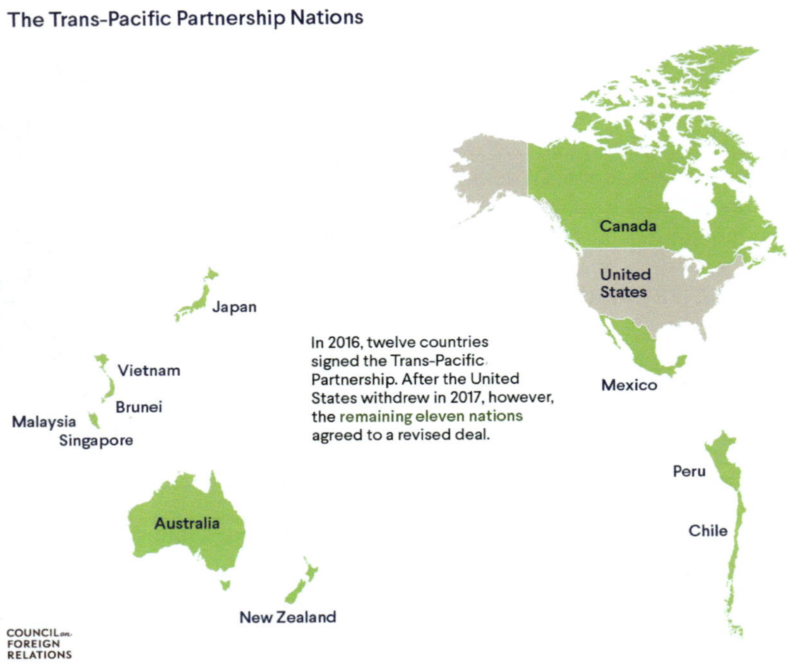

Image 6.4 The Trans-Pacific Partnership Nations (Australia, Brunei, Canada, Chile, Malaysia, Mexico, New Zealand, Peru, Singapore, Vietnam). Note: United Kingdom has become a signatory and the People's Republic of China has applied for membership.

Source: https://commons.wikimedia.org/wiki/File:CPTPP_Trade_Agreement_Map.svg.

- Rules of Origin: (1) wholly obtained, such as goods that are grown, raised, caught, or extracted within a member country, (2) from nonoriginating materials that undergo production that satisfies the applicable **product-specific rule of origin** (**PSRO**);
- The PSRO requires that: (1) one that requires a change to the tariff classification of the good, but that excludes the use of certain nonoriginating materials; and (2) allows for the use of the excluded nonoriginating materials, provided that a **regional value content** (**RVC**) requirement is fulfilled;
- An example of a product-specific rule is motor vehicles must have a 45% regional value content and motor vehicle parts ranges from 35% to 45%;
- Requires each party to provide advance rulings on tariff classification, the origin of a good, as well as the application of customs valuation criteria within 150 days of receiving the request and the necessary information;
- Countries use trade remedies to protect their industries from unfair, trade-distorting practices of other trading partners and from surges in imports that cause harm to domestic producers;

- There are three main types of trade remedies: (1) **Safeguard measures** (temporary duties applied in response to sudden increases of imports in a specific sector), (2) **Anti-dumping duties**: (imposed when exporters sell goods to importers at a lower price than the domestic price, or at unprofitable prices), and (3) **Countervailing duties** (imposed to protect domestic producers from subsidy-aided foreign exports);
- Established a Committee on SPS Measures to facilitate information-sharing and exchange and cooperation among parties; and resolving issues at an early stage;
- TBT chapter encourages the use of internationally accepted standards and provides national treatment for conformity national assessment bodies;
- Chapter on state-owned enterprises (SOEs) and designated monopolies chapter establishes rules to promote fair competition and prevent market distortion by governments;
- Each CPTPP party must establish a user-friendly website targeted at small and medium-sized enterprises (SMEs) and establishes a SME Committee;
- Detailed standards for intellectual property of any trade agreement, as well as protections against intellectual property theft against corporations operating abroad;
- CPTPP commits parties to a number of international IP treaties, such as the Patent Cooperation Treaty, and the WIPO "Internet treaties" dealing with copyright and related rights in the digital environment.

State-owned enterprises (**SOEs**) are commercial entities that are owned or controlled through ownership interests by governments. Some SOEs deliver public services, but many others operate in competition with private companies and are motivated by profit. SOEs may receive various forms of commercial advantage from government, such as regulatory or financial preferences. These advantages can have trade-distorting effects and can give these entities an unfair advantage when they compete with private companies.

In response to the CPTPP, China is pushing for a separate trade agreement (Regional Comprehensive Economic Partnership or RCEP), which would include 16 Asia-Pacific countries[19] but exclude the U.S. It has also launched its Belt and Road Initiative, which seeks to develop trade and energy infrastructure throughout South and Central Asia.

Bilateral Investment Treaties (BITS)

BITs aim to: (1) protect investment abroad in countries where investor rights are not already protected through existing agreements (such as FTAs); (2) encourage the adoption of market-oriented policies that treat foreign private investment in an open, transparent, and nondiscriminatory way; and (3) support the development of international legal standards consistent with these objectives.

BITs provide six core benefits. First, they require that investors and their "covered investments" (investments of an individual or company of one of the BIT countries in the territory of the other country) be treated as favorably as the host country treats its own investors and the investments from any third-party country. The BIT requires that investors receive the better of national treatment or most-favored-nation treatment for the entire duration of the investment (from establishment or acquisition, through management, operation, and expansion, to disposition or liquidation). Second, BITs establish clear limits on the **expropriation** of investments and provide for payment of prompt, adequate, and effective compensation when expropriation takes place. Third, BITs provide for the transferability of investment-related funds (repatriation) into and out of a host country. Fourth, BITs restrict the imposition of **performance requirements**, such as local content rules (require a percentage of the materials used in producing goods in the foreign country to be from that country) or export quotas, as a condition for the establishment, acquisition, expansion, management, conduct, or operation of an investment. Fifth, BITs give investors the right to submit an investment dispute against the host government to international arbitration. Countries negotiate BITs on the basis of a model agreement. The model BIT and its core provisions will be examined in the Estonia–U.S. Bilateral Investment Treaty.

Estonia–U.S. Bilateral Investment Treaty

The Estonia–U.S. Bilateral Investment Treaty focuses on one type of international business—foreign direct investment (FDI). The objectives of the Treaty are to protect investments in each other's country by requiring foreign investments to receive national treatment and most-favored-nation treatment. Performance requirements may not be imposed upon or enforced against investments. Expropriation can occur only in accordance with international law standards; that is, the expropriation must be for a public purpose; be applied in a nondiscriminatory manner; in accordance with due process of law; and upon payment of prompt, adequate, and effective compensation. The unrestricted transfer, in a freely usable currency, of funds related to an investment is guaranteed. Investments can be made either directly or indirectly through one or more subsidiaries, including companies controlled in other countries. "Fair and equitable" treatment is guaranteed to investing companies. It also prohibits a country from impairing, through arbitrary or discriminatory means, the management, operation, maintenance, use, enjoyment, acquisition, expansion, or disposal of a foreign investment. Neither country may impose additional requirements such as those conditioning investment on the export of goods produced or the need to purchase local goods or services (content or performance requirements).

The Treaty incorporates the international law standards for expropriation and compensation. These rights also apply to direct or indirect state measures "tantamount to expropriation or nationalization," and thus apply to *creeping expropriation* (changes in government regulations or taxes) that result in a substantial deprivation of the benefit of an investment without the formal taking of title to the investment. Compensation must be equivalent to the fair market value of the expropriated investment, be paid without delay, and include interest at a commercially reasonable rate from the date of expropriation.

The countries agree to permit "fund transfers related to an investment to be made freely and without delay into and out of its territories." Transfers are to be made in "freely usable currencies." Freely usable is a standard of the International Monetary Fund (IMF); at present, there are six freely usable currencies: the U.S. dollar, Japanese yen, European euro, Swiss franc, Chinese yuan, and British pound sterling.

In the area of dispute resolution, the investor may consent to submission of the dispute for binding arbitration to either ICSID (if the host country is a member) or ad hoc arbitration using the UNCITRAL Arbitration Rules. It also provides that at any arbitration other under the guidance of the ICSID rules arbitration shall take place in a country that is a party to the United Nations Convention on the Recognition and Enforcement of Foreign Arbitral Awards (New York Convention). BITs allow for **sectoral** (industry) **exceptions** to national and most-favored-nation treatment. Exceptions may include air transportation, ocean and coastal shipping, banking, insurance, securities and other financial services, government grants, government insurance and loan programs, energy and power production, customhouse brokers, ownership of real property, ownership and operation of broadcast or common carrier radio and television stations, use of land and natural resources, mining on the public domain, and maritime and maritime-related services. Some of these exceptions relate to the **requirement of reciprocity**. Reciprocity provisions deny both national and most-favored-nation treatment in these areas to countries that do not provide access to foreign companies to their respective markets.

Cooperation Agreements

Cooperation Agreements are called by different names. The two most common names are Trade and Investment Framework Agreements (TIFAs) and Trade and Investment Cooperation Agreements (TICAs), which provide principles for dialogue on trade and investment issues between countries. These agreements all serve as a forum for governments to meet and discuss issues of mutual interest with the objective of improving cooperation and enhancing opportunities for trade and investment. The **Trade Councils** set up by these agreements consult on a wide range of issues related to trade and investment. Topics for consultation and possible further cooperation include market access issues, labor rights, environment, protection and enforcement of intellectual property rights, and capacity building, if the Agreement is between a developed country and a lesser developed country. See Figure 6.18 *Comparative Law*: "Cooperation Agreements," which provides excerpts from the EU–Georgia Partnership and Cooperation Agreement.

- Figure 6.18 below on Cooperation Agreements restates many of the requirements needed to join the EU including "respect for democracy, principles of international law, and human rights."
- It directs Georgia to conform to the major international conventions and principles as it transitions to a potential member of the EU. It notes the importance of the United Nations Charter, as well as the New York Convention on the enforcement of arbitration awards.
- In the area of trade, it commits the EU and Georgia to the application of the most-favored-nation principle, compliance with WTO rules, and encourages Georgia to bring its intellectual property protections, environmental regulations, and consumer protection laws up to international (European) standards.

DESIROUS of encouraging the process of regional cooperation in the areas covered by this Agreement with neighboring countries in order to promote the prosperity and stability of the region;

CONSIDERING the commitment of the Parties to liberalize trade, in conformity with World Trade Organization (WTO) rules, THE PARTIES HAVE AGREED AS FOLLOWS:

Article 2: Respect for democracy, principles of international law, and human rights as defined in particular in the United Nations Charter, the Helsinki Final Act, and the Charter of Paris for a New Europe, as well as the principles of market economy.

Article 9: The Parties shall accord to one another most-favored-nation treatment in all areas in respect of customs duties and charges applied to imports and exports, including the method of collecting such duties and charges; provisions relating to customs clearance, transit, warehouses and transhipment; taxes and other internal charges of any kind applied directly or indirectly to imported goods; methods of payment and the transfer of such payments; and the rules relating to the sale, purchase, transport, distribution, and use of goods on the domestic market.

Article 42: Pursuant to the provisions of this Article, Georgia shall continue to improve the protection of intellectual, industrial, and commercial property rights in order to provide for a level of protection similar to that existing in the European Union, including effective means of enforcing such rights.

Article 57: Cooperation shall aim at combating the deterioration of the environment and in particular the effective monitoring of pollution levels and assessment of the environment; combating local, regional, and transboundary air and water pollution; safety of industrial plants; classification and safe handling of chemicals; and global climate change.

Article 66: The Parties will enter into close cooperation aimed at achieving compatibility between their systems of consumer protection.

Article 89: Within the limits of their respective powers and competencies, the Parties shall encourage the adoption of arbitration for the settlement of disputes in any arbitration center that is a signatory to the Convention on Recognition and Enforcement of Foreign Arbitral Awards (New York Convention).

Figure 6.18 Comparative Law: Cooperation Agreements.

The **Asia-Pacific Economic Cooperation** (APEC)[20] is a regional economic forum established in 1989 to leverage the growing interdependence of the Asia-Pacific region. APEC's purpose is to increase negotiations between all member nations concerning common trade issues. It ensures that goods, services, investment, and people move easily across borders. Members facilitate this trade through faster customs procedures at borders; more favorable business climates behind the border; and aligning regulations and standards across the region. APEC economies comprise 44 percent of world trade and 54 percent of global GDP.

Chapter Summary

1. The free trade era began with the establishment of GATT in 1948 with the goal of reducing worldwide tariff rates. With the establishment of the WTO and the DSB in 1994, the free trade agenda expanded to reducing nontariff barriers to trade. The package of agreements known as the 1994 WTO Agreements covers most areas of nontariff trade barriers.
2. The three foundational principles of WTO are: (1) most-favored-nation principle; (2) national treatment principle; and (3) transparency principle. The most-favored-nation principle requires WTO members to offer its lowest tariff rates to members of the WTO. The application of this principle is the method by which tariff rates have been lowered. The national treatment principle applies once goods have been imported into a country. Once foreign goods pass through customs, they are to be treated the same as goods produced in the country of import. The principle of transparency requires countries to provide clear and accessible customs regulations so that they are not used as disguised barriers to trade.
3. The WTO Agreements established the WTO and was packaged with a list of side agreements dealing with most aspects of international trade including infringement of intellectual property rights, trade in services, foreign direct investment, and government procurement. In order to be a member of the WTO a country must not only accept the central WTO agreement but also must accept all of the side agreements.
4. Quantitative barriers to trade include quotas, moratoriums, and embargoes.
5. Two of the major violations of WTO rules are the dumping (selling price below normal value) of goods on foreign markets and illegal government subsidies of national producers and exporters.
6. Countries have the right to establish their own health, safety, environmental, and technical barriers. However, the Agreement on the Application of Sanitary and Phytosanitary Measures (SPS) and the Agreement on Technical Barriers to Trade (TBT) provide rules to prevent standards from being used as disguised trade barriers.
7. The WTO Dispute Settlement System provides an orderly process for resolving trade disputes. The system requires the disputing countries to consult in the hope of reaching a negotiated settlement. If a settlement is not voluntarily reached, then an expert panel reviews the arguments and evidence and

issues a report, which is then reviewed by the Dispute Resolution Body for approval. A party may appeal the ruling to the Appellate Body. The losing party can often delay implementation of the ruling but will eventually comply to avoid or minimize retaliatory sanctions. The process, although drawn out at times, has prevented trade wars between disputing countries.

8. Countries may take unilateral actions under WTO rules for unfair trade practices. Such unilateral measures are authorized under Section 301 (retaliation for breaches of trade agreements and unjustifiable, unreasonable, or discriminatory acts against American businesses).
9. The WTO trading system has been criticized for ignoring environmental, human rights, and antipoverty concerns.
10. Three basic types of laws regulate the importation of goods: (1) assessment of duties; (2) marking requirements; and (3) standards requirements.
11. The harmonized tariff schedule (HTS), published by the World Customs Organization, provides the product descriptions and accompanying tariff rates that are used by most trading countries.
12. Tariff rates below those offered under the WTO are available through free trade areas, such as USMCA, customs unions, such as the EU, and through the generalized system of preferences (GSP), which is targeted to helping less developed countries.
13. Importers are responsible for determining the proper classification in the HTS that best describes the good being imported.
14. The import duties owed by the importer are determined using three variables: (1) classification of the goods (HTS), (2) the country of origin, and (3) the value of the goods. The first two variables are used to determine the tariff rate, which is then applied against the value of the goods to determine the amount of the duty.
15. Drawback is a form of tax relief in which a lawfully collected customs duty is refunded or remitted wholly or in part because of the particular use made of the commodity on which the duty was collected.
16. Tariff duties and fees may be voided, at least temporarily, by the use of free trade zones and bonded warehouses.
17. Determining and verifying country of origin is an important part of the importation process, as well as satisfying highly technical "marking" requirements.
18. Only certain sensitive products or products being exported to certain countries need to obtain government approval before exportation.
19. Free trade agreements (FTAs) are exceptions to the WTO's most-favored-nation and national treatment principles in that two or more countries may enter into an FTA to provide lower tariff rates to each other than the normal WTO rates.
20. Bilateral investment treaties (BITs) are binding agreements between two countries that provide assurances to one another's citizens, companies, and investors doing business in each other's country. They primarily protect foreign investment from expropriation or creeping expropriation and allow private companies to bring a claim against the host country through international arbitration.

21. Rules of Origin (ROO) are a key component of FTAs in that they determine which products are "regional goods" that benefit from the preferential rates provided by the FTA. Products are USMCA or regional goods if they originated in a USMCA country (grown or produced) or are made of materials from other countries that have been "substantially transformed" in a USMCA country and/or meet certain content requirements.
22. In order to prove a case of the dumping of goods, the complainant and investigating authority must prove that the goods were priced below the market price of products and the selling of the goods caused, was causing, or threatened to cause material injury to a domestic industry.
23. FTAs between countries at different levels of development, such as the Central America–Dominican Republic FTA (CAFTA–DR FTA) and Trans-Pacific Partnership (TPP), need to contain capacity building obligations, to assist the least-developed countries of the FTA to meet their obligations.

Key Terms

Ad Valorem Duties
Agreement on Customs Valuation
Agreement on Import Licensing Procedures
Agreement on Preshipment Inspection
Agreement on the Application of Sanitary and Phytosanitary Measures (SPS)
Agreement on Technical Barriers to Trade (TBT)
Agreement on Trade-Related Aspects of Intellectual Property Rights (TRIPS)
Anti-Dumping Duties
Asia-Pacific Economic Cooperation (APEC)
Bali Package
Bilateral Investment Treaties (BITs)
Binding Commitments
Bonded Warehouse
Capacity Building
Cease and Desist Order
CE Mark
Central America–Dominican Republic FTA (CAFTA–DR)
Change in Tariff
Classification Test
Computed Value
Constructed-Value Basis
Cooperation Agreement
Countervailing Duties
Country of Origin Rules
Cumulative Effect
Customs Valuation Code
Deductive Value
Dispute Settlement Body (DSB)
Dispute Settlement System (DSS)
Domestic Status
Drawback (Tariffs)
Dumping
Ecolabel
Embargoes
Essential Character
European Union (EU)
Final Determination
Free Trade Agreements (FTAs)
Free Trade Zone (FTZ)
General Agreement on Tariffs and Trade (GATT)
General Agreement on Trade in Services (GATS)
General License
Generalized System of Preferences (GSP)
Harmonized Tariff Schedule (HTS)
Illegal Subsidies
Impairment
Marking Requirement

Material Injury
Most-Favored-Nation Principle
Nontariff Barriers (NTBs)
National Treatment Principle
Normal Value
North American Free Trade Agreement (NAFTA)
Nullification
Principle of Transparency
Privileged Foreign Status
Quota (Quantitative Restrictions)
Reciprocity, Requirement of
Regional or Qualified Goods
Rules of Origin (ROO)
Rule of Specificity
Safeguards
Sanitary and Phytosanitary Measures (SPS)
Specified Processes Test
Subsidies
Substantial Transformation
Sunset Reviews
Suspension
TARIC
Tariff Act of 1930
Tariff Act of 1974
Theory of Comparative Advantage
Transatlantic Trade and Investment Partnership (T-TIP)
Trans-Pacific Partnership (TPP)
Transaction Value
Transfer Pricing
Triple Transformation
Ultimate Purchaser
Uruguay Round
Validated License
Value-Added Test
World Customs Organization (WCO)
World Trade Organization (WTO)
WTO Dispute Settlement
WTO Panels
Zeroing

Chapter Problems

1. How can the free trade mandate of the World Trade Organization (WTO) be reconciled with the concerns of labor, environmental, and consumer groups? What is meant by the word *free* in the term *free trade?* Does free mean no restrictions on the flow of labor, capital, goods, services, and technology? Should free trade be limited by other concerns such as local disruption? Should local cultural concerns be a limitation on the nonregulation of trade? How can the WTO dispute resolution and enforcement process be reconciled with a country's assertion of national sovereignty over its national laws and regulations?
2. The Agreement on the Application of Sanitary and Phytosanitary Measures (SPS) and the Agreement on Technical Barriers to Trade (TBT) related to national standards may act as disguised barriers to trade. What are the differences in coverage between the SPS and TBT? Can the SPS and TBT both apply to the importation of a product?
3. The United Nations Conference on Trade and Development (UNCTAD) asserts that the 48 poorest nations of the world, including 33 in Africa, are failing to benefit from globalization and freer trade. In fact, there is evidence that poverty is worsening in many of these countries. What can be done to improve the effect of free trade on these impoverished countries? Should the WTO take a greater role in obtaining preferential tariff treatment for goods exported from these countries? How can developed countries continue to justify protection of domestic industries such as agriculture and textiles through the granting of subsidies?

4. How can one reconcile restrictive immigration policies with the notion of free trade? Why should goods, services, and capital be allowed to move freely and not persons? How do the restrictive immigration laws sanctioned under USMCA compare with the EU's "Four Freedoms" of goods, services, capital, and persons and the EU's movement toward EU passports and citizenship? How does one reconcile U.S. interests in "border control" with its own liberal democratic principles? How does one reconcile the call to "regain control of our borders" with the government's policy not to harass employers of illegal aliens in industries where their labor is needed? What are the ethical arguments against proposals to prohibit undocumented immigrants from receiving emergency medical care or public schooling? One argument can be found in the U.S. Constitution, where no distinction is made between legal and illegal immigrants in the admonition that "all [persons] are endowed by their Creator with inalienable rights." How has the EU's free movement of people been impacted by refugees fleeing starvation and violence in Africa? How does Brexit impact the free flow of people between the UK, including Northern Ireland, and the EU?
5. One can argue that regional trade areas like the EU work like "mini-GATTS." In such systems it is inevitable that national concerns and sovereignty will conflict with the free trade dictates of the union. National subsidies traditionally given to domestic agricultural industries are one instance. France has a longstanding policy of granting aid to olive growers. Can France continue to give such aid under the auspices of the EU? If so, does it need the permission of the EU?
6. Ralph Nader and Lori Wallach had this to say about the World Trade Organization: "The binding provisions that define the WTO's functions and scope do not incorporate any environmental, health, labor, or human rights considerations. There is nothing in the institutional principles of the WTO to inject any procedural safeguards of openness, participation, or accountability. The WTO 'DSU process' is the mechanism that enforces WTO control over member countries. WTO panel members are selected from qualifications that produce panelists with a uniformly pro-trade perspective. The new rules favor the largest, most developed nations. The WTO requires all members to agree to be bound by all WTO accords. The rule forces many countries, usually small ones, to accept trade in areas that might be undesirable in the long run. WTO rules are now enforceable as regards all existing federal, state, and local laws. In effect, countries have voluntarily sacrificed their own sovereignty. The WTO's rules and powerful enforcement mechanism promote downward harmonization of wages, environmental, worker, and health standards. Some international trade is useful, while other global trading favors corporate advantages over those of workers, consumers, and the environment. Concentrating power in international organizations, as trade pacts do, tends to remove critical decisions from citizen control."[21] Do you agree with Nader and Wallach's assessment of the dangers of the WTO? Do you think the dangers outweigh the benefits? What role should governments play in balancing the promotion of free trade through organizations like the WTO and the concerns addressed in the quote above?

7. The CBP determined that the aluminum ingots that were shipped to the U.S. from Canada were not of Canadian origin. The ingots contained less than 1 percent materials from countries other than Canada. The CBP imposed a tariff of 0.19 percent on aluminum ingots imported from Canada. The Court of International Trade ruled in favor of the CBP, finding that the aluminum underwent "substantial transformation" because a foreign-origin substance (grain refiner) was mixed with the aluminum to make the ingots less likely to crack and therefore worked a substantial transformation. Alcan protested that the tariff should be the 0.038 percent that would apply under USMCA if the ingots had not undergone "substantial transformation" with goods that originated from outside of Canada. Do you think that the Court's decision was correct? *Alcan Aluminum Corp. v. U.S.*, 165 F.3d 898 (Fed. Cir. 1999) (case involves the NAFTA, the predecessor agreement to the USMCA).
8. Import documentation requirements and other regulations imposed by foreign governments vary from country to country. It is vital that exporters be aware of the regulations that apply to their own operations and transactions. Many governments, for instance, require consular invoices, certificates of inspection, health certification, and various other documents. Select a country and research its basic documentary requirements for the importation of goods.
9. What are the differences between free trade agreements and bilateral investment treaties?
10. What are free trade zones, and what benefits do they provide to manufacturers or suppliers and the host country?
11. What are the differences between USMCA and the common market of the EU?
12. Match the items on the right column with the appropriate items on the left column (answers below).

i.	Rules of Origin	a.	Host Country Laws
ii.	Regional Goods	b.	Government Procurement of $100,000
iii.	Foreign Trade Zone	c.	ECCN
iv.	ICSID	d.	Binational Review Panels
v.	Creeping Expropriation	e.	Bilateral Investment Treaties
vi.	Technical Barriers to Trade	f.	Substantial Transformation
vii.	Export Control Classification	g.	Investor-Country Arbitration Association
viii.	USMCA Disputes	h.	Customs and Border Protection (CBP)
ix.	KORUS FTA	i.	"Behind-the-Border" Barriers
x.	Foreign Direct Investment	j.	Goods from FTA Countries

Internet Exercises

1. Review recent developments in the area of trade law by reviewing the following websites: http://www.jus.uio.no/lm/international.economic.law/ itl.html and http://www.ita.doc.gov (U.S. International Trade Administration).
2. Read the overview of the WTO at http://www.wto.org.
3. Review recent WTO decisions that highlight the intersection between trade and environmental issues. See, for example, http://www.worldtradelaw.net.
4. You are an importer of outboard motorboats from South Korea. Search the harmonized tariff schedule (HTS) at https://hts.usitc.gov to determine the duty rate you will be required to pay.
5. You have completed an export contract and need to ship goods from Miami, Florida to Buenos Aires, Argentina. Determine which shipping lines are available for such a shipment and research the documentation needed for such a shipment. See the following websites: http://www.mgn.com ("Maritime Global Net") and http://www.tradeport.org. (TradePort is a comprehensive site on international shipping and trade.)

Other Internet Sources

World Trade Organization: http://www.wto.org.
WTO documents: http://www.worldtradelaw.net.
Text of WTO codes and agreements: http://www.wto.org/english/docs_e/docs_e.htm.
U.S. Harmonized Tariff Schedule: http://www.usitc.gov.
World Customs Organization: http://www.wcoomd.org.
EU Ecolabel: http://ec.europa.eu/environment/ecolabel/.
CE Mark: http://www.cemarking.net.

[Answers to Problem 12: i (f), ii (j), iii (h), iv (g), v (a), vi (i), vii (c), viii (d), ix (b), x (e).]

Notes

1 Replaced the 1989 North American Free Trade Agreement (NAFTA).
2 The words "tariff" and "duty" will be used interchangeably throughout this chapter.
3 See Alan C. Stockman, *Introduction to Economics* (2nd ed. Dryden Press 1999); N. Gregory Mankiw, *Macroeconomics* (10th ed. Worth Publishers 2019).
4 "Historical Trade Package Sealed at WTO Bali Meeting," *Global Times* (Xinhua Publisher, December 7, 2013).
5 Kimberly Amadeo, "Trade Wars and Their Effect on the Economy," *The Balance* (Dec. 7, 2019), https://www.thebalance.com/trade-wars-definition-how-it-affects -you-4159973.
6 See Debra Strauss, "Feast or Famine: The Impact of the WTO Decision Favoring the U.S. Biotechnology Industry in the EU Ban of Genetically Modified Foods," 45 *American Business Law Journal* 775 (2008).

7 John H. Jackson, "Helms-Burton, the U.S. and the WTO," 2 *ASIL Insights* (March 3, 1997).
8 See Michael J. Trebilcock, *International Trade Law* (Elgar 2015).
9 Source: World Trade Organization.
10 In the area of services, the WTO has developed a "Services Sectoral Classification List" that identifies service sectors.
11 19 U.S.C. § 1677.
12 See Section 301 at 19 U.SC. §§ 2411–19 (1994).
13 Stephen L. Kass and Jean M. McCarroll, "Having It All: Trade, Development, Environmental, and Human Rights," *New York Law Journal* (May 5, 2000).
14 These initials are country codes, for example, BH refers to Bahrain, CL to Colombia, and SG to Singapore.
15 19 U.S.C.A. § 1401a (b)(1)(B). See *Monarch Luggage Co. v. U.S.*, 715 F. Supp. 1115 (1989).
16 19 U.S.C.A. § 1401a (b)(1)(D).
17 19 U.S.C.A. §§ 1401a (b)(1)(C0 7 1401a (h)(1). See *Texas Apparel Co. v. U.S.*, 698 F. Supp. 932 (Ct. of Int'l Trade 1988).
18 *Anheuser-Busch v. United States*, 207 U.S. 556 (1908).
19 Brunei, Cambodia, Indonesia, Laos, Malaysia, Myanmar, Philippines, Singapore, Thailand, Vietnam, Australia, India, Japan, South Korea, and New Zealand.
20 APEX comprises countries that border the Pacific Ocean: Australia, Brunei, Canada, Chile, China, Hong Kong, Indonesia, Japan, South Korea, Malaysia, Mexico, New Zealand, Papua New Guinea, Peru, Philippines, Russia, Singapore, Taiwan, Thailand, U.S., and Vietnam.
21 Ralph Nader and Lori Wallach, "GATT, NAFTA, and the Subversion of the Democratic Process" at http://www3.uakron.edu/worldciv/pascher/nader.html.

Part II

Comparative and International Law

Chapter 7

European Union and People's Republic of China

European Union

The EU consists of 27 countries with a combined population of over 500 million. Croatia was the last country to be admitted into the EU in 2013. The UK became the first country to leave the EU in 2020. See Figure 7.1 "Map of the European Union." Despite the great disparity of wealth across the EU, as a single entity it has become a major economic power.

The Treaty of Rome established the "**Four Freedoms**," which continue to guide the EU to the present: (a) free movement of goods; (b) free movement of persons; (c) free movement of services; and (d) free movement of capital. Along with the "Four Freedoms," the general principles of the EU include: (1) fundamental human rights; (2) subsidiarity; (3) proportionality; (4) legitimate expectations; (5) nondiscrimination; and (6) legality and legal certainty. The first three principles will be discussed in depth later in this chapter. For an introduction to these principles, see Figure 7.2 "Summary of EU Principles." The *principle of legitimate expectations* prohibits the adoption of retroactive or *ex post facto* laws. The **principle of nondiscrimination** refers to the preservation of civil rights. Article 13 of the Treaty of Amsterdam empowers the **EU Council** to take appropriate action to combat discrimination based on sex, racial or ethnic origin, religion or belief, disability, age, or *sexual orientation*. Council Directive 76/207, the Equal Treatment Directive, mandates EU Member States to implement into their national laws the principle of equal treatment of men and women in employment.

The **European Court of Justice** (**ECJ**) recognized the *principle of legality and legal certainty* in the case of *Leden van de Ministerraad*.[1] It examined whether a European arrest warrant violated the principle of legality. The Court states

DOI: 10.4324/9781003469230-9

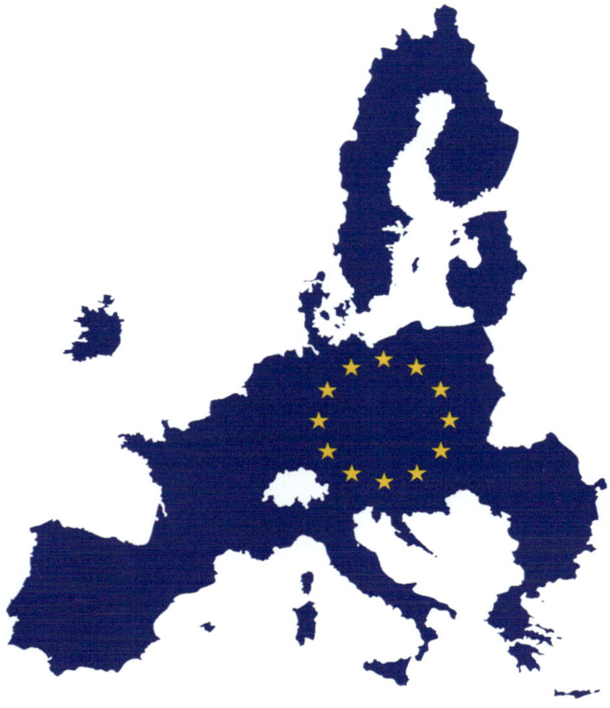

Figure 7.1 Map of the European Union.
Source: Hayden120, Wikimedia Commons.

that: "this principle implies that legislation must define clearly offences and the penalties." That condition is met when individuals are able to determine which types of acts or conduct make them criminally liable. The Court rejected challenges to the European arrest warrant based on legality.

In *Jungbunzlauer v. Commission*,[2] a company was fined for a violation of **competition (antitrust) law.** The **EU Commission** has the power to impose fines of up to 10 percent of a company's preceding year's gross revenues for a violation of competition law. The company argued that the law violated the

Four Freedoms The goal of the EU is to ensure the free movement of persons, goods, services, and capital.	*Legitimate Expectations* A new law cannot punish past conduct. The law prohibits the adoption of retroactive laws.
Subsidiarity EU shall act only if and insofar as the objectives of the proposed action cannot be sufficiently achieved by the member States.	*Non-discrimination* Member states shall not arbitrarily discriminate against individuals on the basis of characteristics that are not relevant to their abilities.
Proportionality The EU law may not exceed what is necessary to achieve the legitimate objectives of the EU.	*Legality and Legal Certainty* Laws must be clear, transparent, and subject to interpretation by a reasonable person with the help of legal counsel.

Figure 7.2 Summary of EU Principles.

principle of legality because it did not adequately specify the penalties for violations of competition law. The Court ruled that the principle of legality is a corollary of the general principle of legal certainty, which required that civil and criminal penalties be sufficiently precise. However, it ruled against the company and found the law to be adequately precise. The standard is whether a person "with the assistance of counsel" would be able to understand the law and its consequences.

Evolution of the EU

The establishment of the EU is the culmination of a lengthy historical process started at the end of World War II. The EU was constructed through a series of Treaties beginning with the 1952 **Treaty of Paris**, which created the European Coal and Steel Community (ECSC). The next major step was the creation of the common market with the establishment of the European Economic Community (EEC) by the **Treaty of Rome** (renamed the Treaty on the Functioning of the European Union or TFEU) in 1957. The 1992 **Maastricht Treaty** (officially "Treaty on European Union" or TEU) began the process of transforming the economic union into a political union with the creation of the European Community (EC). The 1997 Treaty of Amsterdam adopted the **Schengen Agreement**, which abolished physical borders between EU countries. Three non-EU countries also signed the Schengen Agreement—Iceland, Norway, and Switzerland. The **Lisbon Treaty** of 2009 created a political union (government) known as the European Union.

Germany and France have been the driving force behind the idea of the EU, with the third major power, the UK, being a reluctant partner, leaving the EU in 2020 in what is called **Brexit**. There are 27 members of the EU from Western, Central, and Eastern Europe.[3] Candidate countries on the "road" to membership include Albania, Iceland, Montenegro, Serbia, Former Yugoslav Republic of Macedonia, and Turkey. Applications have been submitted for membership by Albania and Serbia. To become a member a country must respect democracy, have a functioning market economy, a civil servant system, and agree to accept all of the laws of the EU (***acquis communautaire***).

> ***Acquis Communautaire*** (*acquis* meaning "that which has been agreed upon"; *communautaire* meaning "community"): The *acquis* refers to all the rights and obligation of the members of the EU. It refers to the entire body of law generated by the EU or relating to the EU (Treaties, Directives, Regulations, Policies, and Decisions of the EU Court of Justice). Before entering the EU, a candidate country must agree to make the *acquis* a part of its national law.

Norway is not a member of the EU; neither are Iceland or Switzerland, but these countries have entered, along with Liechtenstein, into free trade agreements (FTAs) with the EU. The UK will in some form join this group of affiliated countries.

Treaty of Lisbon

The Treaty of Lisbon is the EU's most important foundational document, creating a full-fledged political union with its own independent government structure. The Treaty of Lisbon established the Council President as the leader of the EU and made the EU lawmaking process more efficient by doing away with unanimous voting in most areas of EU governance. At the same time, the Treaty of Lisbon recognized the importance of the sovereignty of individual member countries by establishing a consultation mechanism between the EU lawmaking institutions and national parliaments. Proposed new laws now have to be submitted to national parliaments for review and the national parliaments have the right to raise objections to EU draft legislation.

The Treaty also made the **Charter of Fundamental Rights** part of EU law. The major "Articles" of the treaty include:

> *Article 2, EU Values*: The EU is founded on the values of respect for human dignity, freedom, democracy, equality, the rule of law and respect for human rights, including the rights of persons belonging to minorities. These values are common to the Member States in a society in which pluralism, nondiscrimination, tolerance, justice, solidarity, and equality between women and men prevail.
>
> *Article 3, Free Movement of Persons*: The EU shall offer its citizens an area of freedom, security, and justice without internal frontiers, in which the free movement of persons is ensured in conjunction with appropriate measures with respect to external border controls, asylum, immigration, and the prevention and combating of crime.
>
> *Article 5, EU Enumerated Powers (Competencies)*: Under the principle of conferral, the EU shall act only within the limits of the competencies conferred upon it by the Member States. Competencies not conferred upon the EU in the Treaties remain with the Member States.

These three articles reaffirm three crucial tenets of the EU. Article 2 essentially reiterates the rights provided under the Charter of Fundamental Rights as core constitutional values of the EU. It is similar to the function played by the American Bill of Rights.

Four Freedoms

The "Four Freedoms," noted above, are the **free movement of goods, free movement of persons, free movement of services**, and **free movement of capital.** The free movement of goods within the EU is of critical importance to foreign exporters since it creates a single market after the point of entry. A foreign exporter only needs to import and clear customs in one of the 27 EU countries. After the initial importation, the goods can be freely distributed throughout the EU.

Free Movement of Goods

Article 90 of the TEU states: "No Member State shall impose, directly or indirectly, on the products of other EU Member States any internal taxation in excess of that imposed directly or indirectly on similar domestic products." There is a prohibition on customs duties on imports and exports between Member States,[4] as well as a prohibition against quantitative restrictions (quotas) on imports and exports between Member States.[5]

In the *Cassis de Dijon* case,[6] an importer of liqueur from France to Germany challenged a German law that prohibited importation of certain alcoholic drinks if they did *not* have a high enough alcohol content. The importer argued that the minimum level of alcohol requirement violated the guarantee of free movement of goods. The Germans claimed that drinks with a low alcoholic content encouraged people to drink more and become alcoholics. [*Can you believe this argument?*] The Court rejected the German argument based on proportionality criteria.[7] In other words, discouraging alcoholism is a legitimate goal, so the first requirement of proportionality is met. However, the means chosen did not rationally advance that legitimate goal. Instead, the rule was a *disguised* protection favoring German manufacturers of liqueurs, who made their liqueurs with stronger alcohol content.

There can only be discrimination if imported goods are discriminated against in relationship to similar domestic goods. The question is how do national customs officials and courts determine if goods are similar? Factors used in making the similarity determination include if the goods fall within the same tax category, how the goods were manufactured, substances used in their manufacture, and whether consumers would regard the goods as substitutes.

Quantitative Restrictions and Measures Equivalent to Quantitative Restrictions (MEQRs)

Article 28 of the Treaty of Rome provides that: "Quantitative restrictions on imports and all measures having equivalent effect shall be prohibited between Member States." Equivalent effect means that the restriction does not expressly limit the amount of goods being imported, as in a quota system, but the restriction has the equivalent effect of a quota in illegally limiting the amount of goods being imported. The ECJ has broadly defined what constitutes a **measure equivalent to a quantitative restriction** (**MEQR**) and includes commercial rules and regulations that seemingly have nothing to do with imported goods, including opening hours for stores.

Exceptions to Quantitative Restrictions and MEQRs

Article 30 of the Treaty of Rome allows EU Member States to restrict imports for the following reasons: (1) public morality; (2) public policy or public security; (3) protection of health and life of humans, animals, or plants; (4) protection of national treasures possessing artistic, historic, or archaeological value; and (5) protection of industrial or commercial property. The ECJ has narrowly construed these exceptions for fear that they could be used as disguised trade barriers.

Public Morality

In *Quietlynn Limited v. Southend Borough Council*,[8] the defendants were convicted for importing obscene material into the UK in violation of its customs laws. The ECJ concluded that ordinarily there would be no problem with such laws against violations of public morality. The issue was whether the restrictions served that purpose in a nondiscriminatory manner. The Court reasoned that: "If such materials could be freely manufactured or sold domestically, then the quantitative restriction contained in the customs law was not a means of protecting morality, but rather an arbitrary discrimination or a disguised restriction on trade between Member States." The Court held that even though such materials were available domestically, they were not legally available. Therefore, the quantitative restriction on such imports was justified under the **public morality clause**.

Public Policy and Public Security

In the past, certain types of products have been considered necessary for national defense. In *Campus Oil v. Minister for Industry and Energy*,[9] an Irish law mandated that importers of oil had to purchase a proportion of their oil requirements from a refinery located in Ireland. Ireland argued that national security required that the country have at least one oil refinery. The ECJ agreed that this requirement served the purpose of national security.

Protection of Health and Life of Humans, Animals, and Plants

In the area of health and safety inspection requirements for imported goods, the ECJ has shown a particular disdain for dual inspection requirements that require inspections in the exporting country and again when the goods are imported. The UK, in *Commission v. United Kingdom*,[10] placed a ban on poultry, meat, and eggs from other EU Member States in order to prevent the spread of a disease affecting poultry. The ECJ found that the UK ban violated EU law, noting that importation was allowed, but only if the exporting countries instituted stronger protective measures against the disease than those required of UK farmers.

In the areas of government charges imposed to inspect goods or the costs of obtaining the required inspection, the ECJ has held that if the inspection is deemed necessary for health or safety reasons, then charges related to the inspection are permitted. This is only in the case when the inspection is imposed on an importer as part of a general scheme of regulation that applies equally to domestic producers and is therefore not equivalent to customs duty.

Free Movement of Persons (Citizens and Workers)

Article 39 of the Treaty prohibits both direct and indirect discrimination on grounds of nationality in the context of foreign workers. Treaty Article 39(2) states that the free movement of workers "shall entail the abolition of any discrimination based on nationality between workers of the Member states as regards employment, remuneration and other conditions of work and employment." Article 7(2) of Regulation 1612/68 provides that an EU worker shall enjoy the same "social and tax advantages" as national workers.

There are exceptions to the freedom of movement based on grounds of "public policy, public security or public health." In *Adoui and Cornuaille v. Belgian State*,[11] two French nationals were denied residence permits by Belgium on grounds of public policy, since the women were alleged to be working as prostitutes. The ECJ ruled against Belgium since prostitution was legal in Belgium. Therefore, the women's conduct, even if true, could not be regarded as sufficiently serious to justify deportation. However, the freedom to immigrate to other countries has been destructive to some countries, such as Bulgaria, which lost about 20 percent of its population after entering the EU, and has caused ethnic and racial strife, anti-immigrant sentiment, and increasing xenophobia, in countries such as Denmark, Poland, and Romania.

Freedom of Establishment

Article 43 of the Treaty of Rome prohibits restrictions on the freedom of establishment by EU nationals. This includes the right to establish agencies, branches, or subsidiaries in other countries of the EU. Article 43 defines the freedom of establishment to include "the right to take up and pursue activities as self-employed persons."

In the area of professional qualifications, the ECJ held that the Paris Bar Association was not justified in denying admission to a Belgian lawyer because he did not hold a French law degree, since a French university recognized his Belgian law degree as being equivalent to a French law degree. The case did not hold that simply because someone is a lawyer in one country that the lawyer can automatically practice law in other EU countries. The ECJ more narrowly held that holding a specific national law degree was not by itself a reason to deny admission to practice law in another country. For example, in the above case, the Belgian lawyer had passed the required French bar exam for admission to the profession of *avocat* (lawyer) in France.

The ECJ went a step further in the *Vlassopoulou v. Ministerium für Justiz, Bundes* case[12] by holding that even if a foreign lawyer has not passed a country's bar examination, the national authorities were obliged to perform an *assessment of equivalence* ("comparison between the specialized knowledge and abilities certified by those diplomas and the knowledge and qualifications required by the national rules"). In that case, a Greek lawyer had practiced with a law firm in Germany for a number of years but had not passed the German bar exam.

The **principle of mutual recognition** is established by Article 47 of the Treaty, which calls for the adoption of directives for the "mutual recognition of diplomas, certificates and other evidence of formal qualifications." However, EU countries have been slow in recognizing foreign qualifications. Countries are most likely delaying such recognition to protect their citizens that practice in those areas.

Freedom of Services

Treaty rules on the freedom of establishment and services were part of the goal of creating the Common Market. Under the Treaty, the right to establishment and the right to provide services are conditional on the adoption of directives. Nonetheless, the ECJ ruled that both Article 43 (freedom of establishment) and Articles 49 and 50 (freedom of services) have a direct effect on national laws.

The Treaty expressly prohibited discrimination against foreign nationals or companies exercising their rights to establish a business or to provide services. The ECJ declared that the rules on establishment and services apply to non-discriminatory obstacles to free movement. The 2009 EU Services Directive[13] provides additional rules to facilitate the permanent establishment of businesses throughout the EU, as well as cross-border services to allow people and companies to provide their services in other EU countries, without establishing a permanent office or presence. The Directive covers a wide range of services including business, construction, education, real estate, regulated professions (law, medicine, accounting, engineering, and so forth), and retail services. However, the Directive does not apply to financial, electronic communication, transport, healthcare, or social services.

Free Movement of Capital

The free movement of capital is essential to the functioning of a **common market** since it leads to more integrated, open, and efficient financial markets and services. Under a common market system, people are free to open bank accounts, buy shares in nondomestic companies, and purchase foreign real estate. Companies from one country should be able to invest in and manage companies in other EU countries. Directive 88/361/EEC requires the removal of all restrictions of capital movements within the EU. The Maastricht Treaty provides that all restrictions on capital movements and payments are prohibited whether between member countries or between a member country and a non-EU country. Unlike the Directive, the Treaty provision has direct effect in all EU countries.

What Are Capital Movements?

(1) Movement of money from an investor in one country to a financial institution in another country
(2) Foreign Direct Investment (investing in or acquiring a foreign company)
(3) Real estate investments
(4) Securities investments (shares, bonds, trust instruments)
(5) Loans and credits

There are some exceptions to the free movement of capital both within the EU and with third party countries. These are primarily linked to taxation, supervision, public policy, money laundering, and financial sanctions imposed under the Common Foreign and Security Policy, such as was done against Russia due to its invasion of Ukraine.

EU Institutions

There are four major institutions that make up the EU government: Council, Commission, Parliament, and EU Court of Justice (ECJ). See Figure 7.3 "EU Institutions" and Figure 7.4 "EU Government and Political System."

Council of the EU

The **Council of the EU** has five main roles: (1) passing laws in conjunction with the Parliament; (2) setting EU economic policy; (3) implementing security and foreign relations policy; (4) coordinating police and judicial matters; and (5) passing a budget with the Parliament. The Council is headed by a rotating President who serves for six months with a representative of each member country taking its turn. When the heads (presidents or prime ministers) of each country meet, the group is referred to as the **European Council**, which is the highest political body in the EU.

The members of the EU Parliament are directly elected by the people and represent their individual constituencies. The Commission's focus and loyalty is to the EU as a whole. A few areas, such as defense and taxation, still require unanimous votes. An example is the sanctions placed against Russia for its invasion and annexation of Crimea in 2014 and its intervention in support of rebels in eastern Ukraine.

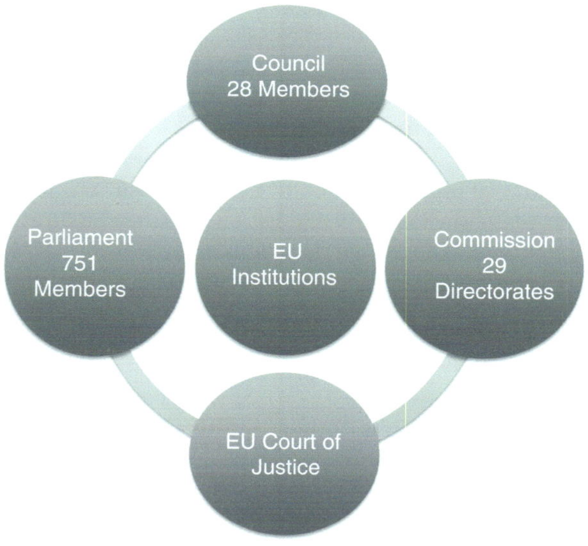

Figure 7.3 EU Institutions.

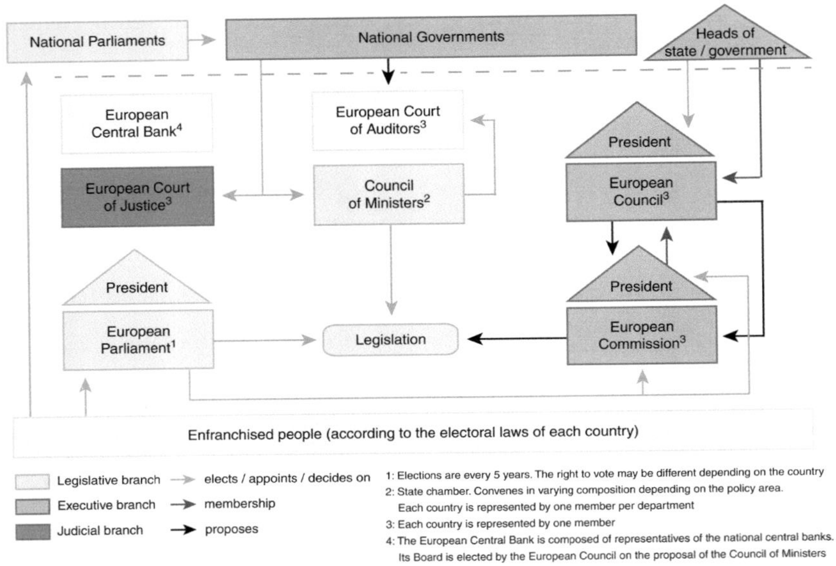

Figure 7.4 EU Government and Political System.

Source: 111Alleskönner, WikiCommons.

Which Council?

Council of the European Union

It is one of the three main EU institutions, along with the Commission and the Parliament. It is made up of government ministers from each of the member countries. It has permanent headquarters in Brussels.

The European Council

It is the highest political body of the EU made up of the heads of each of the countries. It meets only four times a year.

Council of Europe

It is an international organization of 47 European countries that is NOT a part of the EU. It was established in 1949 and has headquarters in Strasbourg (France). Its objective is to foster common and democratic principles for all of Europe.

EU Commission

The EU Commission is headed by 27 commissioners, one each appointed by a member country. The Commission is composed of departments called **Directorates-General (DGs)**, which are responsible for different areas of government. For example, Directorate IV is assigned the area of monitoring competition (antitrust) law. Thus, if a foreign company wants to merge or acquire a company located in the EU, it will have to obtain the approval of this Directorate if the combined market share of the two companies is above a certain percentage.

Other important DGs for foreign companies doing business in the EU include Trade; Taxation and Customs Union; Mobility and Transport; Health and Consumers; Environment; and Employment, Social Affairs, and Inclusion.

EU Parliament

The Parliament is the only directly elected institution of the EU. There are 751 Members of the European Parliament (MEPs) who are elected for terms of five years. The Parliament acts as a co-legislator with the Council through a process called co-decision. The Parliament also has the power to approve the budget. Under co-decision, EU measures have to be agreed to by both the Council of Ministers and by the Parliament. For most laws to pass, a double majority or qualified majority voting (55 percent of the Member States comprising and 65 percent of the population) of the Council and the Parliament is required.

European Court of Justice

The Court of Justice or *Cour de Justice de l'Union Européenne* (ECJ) is charged with the interpretation and application of the EU's treaties and the laws made under those treaties by the EU's institutions. The ECJ is the highest judicial authority in the EU. Its jurisdiction includes examining the legality of EU laws and measures, and its interpretations of EU law are final. The Treaty of Lisbon established a lower court called the General Court (previously known as the Court of First Instance), whose decisions are appealable to the ECJ. It should be noted that the **European Court of Human Rights** (**ECtHR**) is not an EU court. It is an international court established by the Council of Europe's **European Convention on Human Rights** (**ECHR**).

Jurisdiction of the European Court of Justice

The ECJ's areas of jurisdiction include: (1) cases brought by EU institutions against Member States not complying with or implementing EU law; (2) cases brought by Member States or individuals against EU institutions for overstepping their enumerated powers (competencies); (3) cases brought by individuals against a Member State for not properly implementing EU law; (4) cases brought by one Member State against another Member State; (5) cases appealed from the General Court; and (6) referrals from national courts for an opinion on the meaning of EU law.

Under the last category of jurisdiction, the ECJ issues rulings and opinions on the meaning of EU law in cases referred to it from courts or tribunals of member countries.[14] The national court to which it is addressed is bound by the interpretation given. The Court's judgment also binds other national courts before which a problem of the same nature is raised. The rationale for this procedure is to ensure the uniform application of EU law by avoiding divergent national court interpretations. In the *Costa v. ENEL* case, the ECJ reaffirmed the *principle of supremacy* of EU law and the right of national courts to seek opinions of the ECJ on EU law.

Costa v. ENEL

ECLI:EU:C:1964:66

Judgment of the European Court of Justice

Mr. Costa was an Italian citizen who had owned shares in an electricity company and opposed the nationalization of the electricity industry in Italy. He argued that the nationalization of the electricity industry violated the Treaty of Rome. The Italian court, the *Giudice Conciliatore of Milan*, referred the case to the ECJ. The ECJ held that the EU legal system is an integral part of the legal systems of the EU Member States and which their courts are bound to apply. Therefore, the questions put by *Giudice Conciliatore of Milan* are admissible insofar as they relate in this case to the interpretation of EU law.

Case Highlights

- The **principle of supremacy** holds that when a national law conflicts with an EU law the EU law controls. A subsequent national law that conflicts with EU law is *void ab initio* (from the very beginning)
- National courts have the right to seek an opinion of the ECJ on matters of EU law.

European Central Bank

The **European Central Bank** (ECB) was founded in 1988 and is located in Frankfurt, Germany. It is the central bank for the euro and is responsible for the monetary policy of the Eurozone. Its main responsibility is to maintain financial and price stability in countries that use the euro as their national currency. The ECB is "owned" by the central banks of all the EU member countries. The ECB is independent of the other institutions of the EU. Prior to the 2008 financial and sovereign debt crises, the ECB rarely interceded in a meaningful way to impact the monetary policies of EU Member States. The debt crises, beginning in 2010, required the EU and the IMF to bail out Cyprus, Greece, Ireland, and Portugal. In 2014, Ireland and Portugal exited their bailout programs successfully, but the crisis continued to get worse in Greece, forcing the ECB to exercise its powers to save the euro.

Sovereign Debt Crisis refers to the situation when a country can no longer make required debt payments on loans and government bonds. In such cases, the International Monetary Fund (IMF), along with the ECB in the case of the Eurozone, lend money to the potentially defaulting country in exchange for structural reforms aimed at cutting the country's debt in the hope of increasing the country's ability to pay its debts in the future.

EU Lawmaking Process

The EU is a government of enumerated powers known as the **principle of conferral.** The EU has no power to legislate in areas outside of its "competencies." EU Treaties describe three types of EU **competencies:** (1) *exclusive competence,* including legislating in areas related to the regulation of the customs union; competition rules necessary for the internal market; monetary policy in the Eurozone; fisheries; and common commercial policy; (2) *shared competence* recognizes that in some areas the EU and its member countries share power, such as in the areas of the internal market; social policy (mostly with employment rights); economic, social, and territorial cohesion; agriculture; environment; consumer protection; transport; trans-European networks; energy; security and justice; and public health; (3) *supporting competence* is where the national countries have the primary power with the EU acting in a supporting or coordinating role. This area includes the protection and improvement of human health, industry, culture, tourism, education, youth, sport, vocational training, civil protection (natural disasters), and administrative cooperation between national authorities.

In areas that do not fall within the EU's *exclusive* areas of competency, two principles control the extent of the EU's lawmaking powers—the **principle of subsidiarity** and the **principle of proportionality.** Under the principle of subsidiarity, the EU shall act only if the objectives of the proposed action cannot be sufficiently achieved by the Member States, either at the regional or local level, by reason of the scale or effects of the proposed action make it better achieved at the EU level. At the same time, under the principle of proportionality, when the EU acts (legislates), it shall not exceed the scope of its competency. Under the principle of proportionality, action of the EU may not exceed what is necessary to achieve its objectives. Unanimity applies within the Council in certain areas, such as EU security and foreign policy. The Council may act alone, without consulting Parliament, in setting the EU's common external tariff or in the negotiation of free trade agreements.

Sources of EU Law

Community law can be divided into two parts—primary and secondary law. The primary law is the fundamental law of the EU (treaties). Secondary sources of law consist of types of legislation enacted by EU institutions. The three types of laws are: (1) regulations; (2) directives; and (3) decisions, recommendations, and opinions.

A **regulation** has general application and is legally binding and directly applicable in all Member States (**direct effect**). Since regulations have direct effect, they become the law of each member country and, therefore, do not need national implementing legislation as do directives. A **directive** is legally binding but gives the Member States flexibility as to how the prescribed results are to be achieved. A directive leaves to member countries the choice of form and methods of implementation. The EU Commission may bring an enforcement action against a Member State if it believes the state has not properly implemented the directive.

A *decision* is legally binding, but only on those to whom it is addressed. It is often employed in the area of competition law. If the Commission suspects that a violation of competition law has occurred, it may investigate and issue a decision finding a company or individual has violated the law. *Recommendations* and *opinions* have no binding force. They may set out important EU policy positions.

EU Law and Direct Effect

EU Treaty Articles and Regulations have a direct effect[15] in each of the EU Member States. The major case in this area is *Van Gend en Loos*. The issue in the case was whether private parties could bring a lawsuit in a national court to enforce EU treaty provisions.

Van Gend en Loos

ECLI:EU:C:1963

The claimant asserted that the Netherlands had increased the import duty on a good from another EU Member State in violation of EU law, which forbids increasing national duties.[16] The Dutch argued that there was no increase of tariff rates but that the goods had simply been reclassified. The issue was whether an individual could invoke a Treaty provision in a national court. The ECJ concluded that since Treaty provisions had direct effect, private citizens had the right to sue. The Court concluded that individuals could invoke Treaty provisions in national courts.

Case Highlights

- The ECJ is the highest authority in interpreting EU law
- EU Treaties have direct effect (immediately becomes a part of national law)
- Private parties have the standing to litigate violations of EU law in national courts.

The doctrine of direct effect and the *Van Gend en Loos* interpretation are an important part of EU law.[17] In effect, the ECJ treats all EU Treaties as constitutional in nature.

The next foundational case involved the awarding of damages against a county for not implementing EU directives. The *Francovich* case addressed this issue.

Francovich and Bonifaci v. Italy

ECLI:EU:C:1991:428

The EU adopted Directive 80/987, the purpose of which was to protect individuals who worked for companies that became insolvent. It did this by requiring EU Member States to set up compensation funds for the benefit of employees. The Commission brought an enforcement action against Italy, and the Court ruled that Italy violated its obligations under EU law by failing to implement the Directive.

The Court concluded that Directive 80/987 lacked direct effect either because it was not sufficiently precise or because it required further implementing measures in the form of setting up the fund from which individuals were to be compensated. Therefore, the parties could not rely upon the Directive in filing suit against Italy. The Court went on further to consider whether a Member State could, nonetheless, be made to pay damages for failure to implement a directive. The Court reasoned that a Member State could be liable in damages for failure to implement a directive based on "the general scheme and basic principles of the Treaty." Three conditions must be satisfied to extend such liability. First, the Directive must confer rights on individuals; second, determine the rights by reference to the Directive; and third, there must be a causal relationship between the failure to implement the Directive and the damages suffered. The Court held that the claimants met all three of the conditions for liability.

Case Highlights

- According to the conditions laid down in *Van Gend en Loos*, EU directives do not have direct effect in that they do not immediately become the law of member countries
- *Francovich* lays down three conditions for holding a member country liable to private parties for failing to implement an EU directive
- By allowing parties to sue when a directive is not implemented (or not implemented properly), the Court in *Francovich* minimized the fact that directives do not have direct effect.

EU Charter of Fundamental Rights

The Charter of Fundamental Rights became EU law in 2009 under the Maastricht Treaty. The Charter is broad in scope, containing some 54 articles divided into seven titles. The first six titles deal with substantive rights under the headings: dignity, freedoms, equality, solidarity, citizens' rights, and justice, while the last title deals with the interpretation and application of the Charter. The Charter expands the traditional notion of human rights to include a wide array of fundamental rights including guarantying the right to life; prohibition of death penalty, eugenic practices, and human cloning; protection of personal data; right to education; rights of the child; rights of the elderly; right of access to placement services; protection in the event of unjustified dismissal; fair and just working conditions; environmental protection; and right to good administration.

EU Citizenship: Any person who holds the nationality of a member country is automatically an EU citizen. EU citizenship is additional to and does not replace national citizenship. EU citizens are free to move and reside within the EU, run as a candidate for the EU Parliament, and receive equal access to EU civil servant jobs.

Importing Goods into the EU

As noted earlier, the most beneficial aspect of the EU to exporters from foreign countries is the uniformity of the entry process and freedom to move goods within the EU. The process of importing goods begins with the filing of an *Entry Declaration Form*. Once the form is reviewed and entry accepted, payment of tariff duties and value-added taxes (VAT) are calculated and paid. The tariff and VAT owed are determined using the EU **Customs Procedure Code** (**CPC**). The rate is a percentage (*ad valorem*) that is multiplied against the value of the goods to determine the amount of duty owed. Figure 7.5 "Importing to Europe" provides a simplified checklist of required steps needed to successfully export goods to Europe.

The imported goods must comply with all applicable quality, technical, and safety standards. The EU has made compliance with different national standards much easier. In the area of quality, the EU developed the **CE mark** (*Conformité Europiénne*). The CE mark harmonizes quality standards throughout the EU and was created under EU Directives 94/25/EC and 2003/44/EC. If the product has been CE mark certified, then the issue of quality is satisfied. The EU has authorized private companies, called "notified bodies," to provide the verifications. CE certification requires the manufacturer to submit to periodic audits of its production process and the checking of random samples of their products in order to maintain CE certification.

Eurozone

The euro (€) is the official currency of 19 out of 27 EU member countries. These countries are collectively known as the Eurozone.[18] A number of non-EU countries also use the euro as their national currencies, including Andorra, Kosovo, Montenegro, Monaco, San Marino, and Vatican City. The euro symbol was inspired by the Greek letter epsilon or E, a reference to the cradle of European civilization and the letter "ε" for Europe. The two parallel lines running through the symbol represent "stability." See Image 7.1 of the euro symbol.

1
Check Statistics

Due Diligence the amount of similar products are already being exporting to the EU from other countries

2
Click on Resources

Product Codes

Chamber of Commerce & Customs Offices in Each EU Country

3
Use Custom Code to Categorize your Product

Open Search Box

Browse Classification Box or type keyword
Define Product, Exporting and Importing Countries

4
Check Requirements (health, safety & technical standards)

Check for Required Payment of Internal Taxes (VAT or Excise Taxes)

5
Check Customs Duties

Standard Rate for Imported Product

Or

Preferential Rate due to Trade Agreement
Check for Quota Restrictions or Antidumping Duties

6
Check "Rules of Origin"

Obtain Certificate of Origin (Minimum input or processing requirements)

Figure 7.5 Importing to Europe.
Source: http://exporthelp.europa.eu.

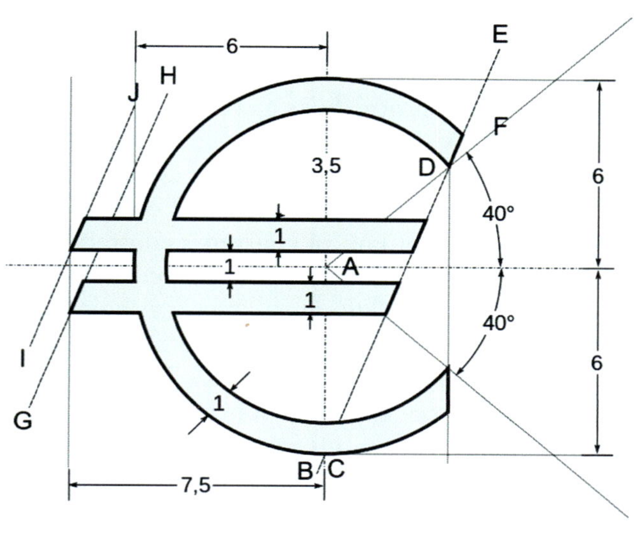

Image 7.1 Euro Symbol.

EU *Acquis Communautaire*

The EU *acquis communautaire* simply refers to the complete body of EU law (currently about 110,000 documents). The term is also used to refer to bodies of law broken down by specific subject areas, such as the Consumer Law *acquis*. This brief summary will focus on EU law relating to business or private law areas. EU law is published in the Official Journal of the European Union. Examples of EU law are found in other chapters of this book. This section summarizes some of the ones directly impacting consumers and the sale of goods.

Database Protection

The EU was one of the first to recognize the value of databases and to provide database protection. Directive 96/9/EC 11 on the legal protection of databases provides a *sui generis* right of protection for 15 years from the date of completion. It defines database as a collection of independent works, data, or other materials arranged in a systematic or methodical way and individually accessible by electronic or other means. In order to obtain database protection, the creator of the database must show that there has been qualitatively or quantitatively a *substantial investment* in either obtaining, verifying, or presenting the contents to prevent extraction or reutilization of the whole or of a substantial part, evaluated qualitatively or quantitatively, of the contents of that database. Few countries provide such an intellectual property-like protection, including the U.S.

Consumer Law

The body of consumer law includes 90 directives and a number of regulations. A majority of current EU directives define the consumer as a "natural person who is acting for the purposes which are outside his trade, business and profession." Council Regulation (EC) No. 44/2001 on jurisdiction and the recognition and enforcement of judgments in civil and commercial matters (Brussels I) states that: "A consumer may bring proceedings against the other party to a contract either in the courts of the Member State in which that party is domiciled or in the courts for the place where the consumer is domiciled." Regulation (EC) No. 593/2008 on the law applicable to contractual obligations (Rome I) states that: "In an absence of choice of law, in consumer contracts, the contract shall be governed by the law of the country where the consumer has his habitual residence." If there is a choice of law clause, "such a choice may not, however, have the result of depriving the consumer of the protection afforded to him or her by provisions that cannot be derogated from." The Rome II Regulation (EC No. 694/2007) addresses choice of law in noncontractual matters, such as tort (delict), unjust enrichment, *negotiorum gestio* (acting as an agent without permission), and *culpa contrahendo* (pre-contractual liability).

One of the early interventions into private law by the EU was the creation of a consumer contract law. This took the form of standard form and standard terms regulation embodied in Directive 93/13/EEC on unfair terms in consumer contracts. The Unfair Contract Terms Directive protects consumers against unfair standard contract terms imposed by traders. It mandates that: (1) "Standard contract terms have to be drafted in plain intelligible language and ambiguities are to be interpreted in favour of consumers." (2) "Contract terms are unfair and, therefore, not binding on consumers if, contrary to the requirements of good faith, they cause significant imbalance in the parties' rights and obligations to the detriment of the consumer." (3) It recognizes a presumption of unfairness for contract terms that were not individually negotiated. A term shall always be regarded as not individually negotiated where it has been drafted in advance and the consumer has therefore not been able to influence the substance of the term, particularly in the context of a pre-formulated standard contract. (4) The Directive provides a nonexhaustive list of terms considered being unfair, including limiting legal liability for personal injury; limiting the legal rights of the consumer against the seller in the event of total or partial nonperformance or inadequate performance; authorizing the seller or supplier to dissolve the contract on a discretionary basis where the same facility is not granted to the consumer; enabling the seller or supplier to terminate a contract of indeterminate duration without reasonable notice; automatically extending a contract of fixed duration where the consumer does not indicate otherwise; enabling the seller or supplier to alter the terms of the contract unilaterally; and excluding or hindering the consumer's right to take legal action or exercise any other legal remedy, particularly by requiring the consumer to take disputes exclusively to arbitration. The Directive has been amended by Directive (EU) 2019/2161 requiring Member States to provide for effective penalties in case of violations of the Directive by May 2022.

EU Consumer Rights Directive (CRD)

The core consumer protection law is EU Directive 2011/83/EU (CRD). Highlights of the CRD are listed below as provided in EU Guidance notes.

- CRD shall apply under the conditions and to the extent set out in its provisions, to any contract concluded between a trader and a consumer.
- Precontract **information disclosures** require traders prior to the conclusion of consumer contracts, to "provide the consumer with the following information in a clear and comprehensible manner, if that information is not already apparent from the context" including: "main characteristics of the goods or services; identity of the trader; total price of the goods or services; arrangements for payment, delivery, performance, the time by which the trader undertakes to deliver the goods or to perform the service, and the trader's complaint handling policy; reminder of the existence of a legal guarantee of conformity for goods, the existence and the conditions of after-sales services and commercial guarantees; duration of the contract and conditions for terminating the contract; functionality, including applicable technical protection measures, of digital content; and relevant interoperability of digital content with hardware and software that the trader is aware of or can reasonably be expected to have been aware." (Article 5)

- Information requirements for **distance** and **off-premises contracts**, including information about the functionality and interoperability of digital content. It regulates the **right of withdrawal** (length of the withdrawal period, procedure, and effects of the withdrawal), including a standard withdrawal form that must be provided by traders and may be used by consumers to notify the withdrawal from the contract. The CRD also requires disclosure of "the existence and the conditions of after-sale customer assistance, after-sales services and commercial guarantees; existence of relevant codes of conduct; and the possibility of having recourse to an out-of-court complaint and redress mechanism, to which the trader is subject, and the methods for having access to it." (Article 6)
- The consumer shall have a period of 14 days to withdraw from a distance or off-premises contract, without giving any reason, and without incurring any costs. (Article 14); Article 16 provides a list of exceptions to the consumer's right of withdrawal, such as when the goods were made according to the consumer's specifications or clearly personalized; where the consumer has specifically requested a visit from the trader for the purpose of carrying out urgent repairs or maintenance; the supply of digital content which is not supplied on a tangible medium if the performance; supply of sealed audio or sealed video recordings or sealed computer software which were unsealed after delivery; and contracts concluded at a public auction.
- It provides rules on delivery and passing of risk applicable to contracts for the sale of goods as well as certain rules applicable to all types of consumer contracts including rules regarding the fees for the use of certain means of payment (e.g., credit or debit cards); rules regarding the charges for calling telephone hotlines operated by traders; and a prohibition to use pre-ticked boxes on websites for charging extra payments in addition to the remuneration for the trader's main contractual obligation.

The CRD is one of the foundations of EU consumer laws, which through the CRD and other laws provide consumers with the rights to truthful advertising; to have faulty goods repaired or replaced; to contracts without unfair clauses; to return most goods purchased online within 14 days; to access goods and services on the same terms as local customers; and to free assistance from European Consumer Centres.

General Data Protection Regulation 2015 (GDPR)

The **General Data Protection Regulation 2015** or GDPR[19] is a set of rules designed to give EU citizens more control over their personal data. It entered into force on May 28, 2018. EU data protection rules apply to the European Economic Area (EEA), which includes all EU countries and non-EU countries, including Iceland, Liechtenstein, and Norway. The GDPR applies to any organization operating within the EU, as well as any organization outside of the EU which offer goods or services to customers or businesses in the EU. That ultimately means that almost every major corporation in the world needs a GDPR compliance strategy. When personal data is transferred outside the EEA, special safeguards are foreseen to ensure that the protection travels with the data. The reform of EU data protection legislation provides mechanisms that allow for the transfer of data to third countries, including adequacy decisions, standard contractual clauses, binding corporate rules, certification mechanisms, and codes of conduct.

The core of the GDPR is the recognition of a list of rights owed to individuals (data subjects) by entities that process personal data. These entities are divided into data controllers (data collectors)[20] and data processors.[21] The rights include:

- *Right to Notice of Use and Rights.* The controller shall, at the time when personal data are obtained, provide the data subject with the following further information necessary to ensure fair and transparent processing: period for which the personal data will be stored; right to request from the controller access to and rectification (correction) or erasure of personal data; the right to withdraw consent at any time; right to lodge a complaint with a supervisory authority; and the existence of automated decision-making, including profiling.
- *Right to Access.* The controller shall take appropriate measures to provide information relating to processing to the data subject in a concise, transparent, intelligible, and easily accessible form, using clear and plain language and that information shall be provided in writing, or by other means, including, where appropriate, by electronic means to the data subject.
- *Right to Rectification.* The data subject shall have the right to obtain from the controller without undue delay the rectification of inaccurate personal data concerning him or her.
- *Right to Erasure ("to be forgotten").* The controller is obligated to erase personal data when: (a) personal data are no longer necessary in relation to the purposes for which they were collected; (b) the data subject withdraws consent; (c) personal data have been unlawfully processed.
- *Right to Restrict Processing.* Where processing has been restricted such personal data shall, with the exception of storage, only be processed with the data subject's consent.
- *Right to Data Portability.* The data subjects shall have the right to receive their personal data, which they had provided to a controller, in a structured, commonly used, and machine-readable format and have the right to transmit those data to another controller.
- *Right to Object.* Where personal data are processed for direct marketing purposes, the data subjects shall have the right to object to the use of their personal data for such marketing, which includes profiling to the extent that it is related to such direct marketing.

The GDPR, in sum, requires the consent of subjects for data processing, anonymity of individuals whose data is being collected to protect privacy, data breach notifications, safely handling the transfer of data across borders, and requires companies to appoint a data protection officer to oversee GDPR compliance.

GDPR Compliance

Companies that use data for any reason must take steps to ensure they are GDPR compliant. Organizations that have at least 250 employees or conduct higher-risk data processing are required to keep an up-to-date and detailed list of their processing activities and be prepared to show that list to regulators upon request. The best way to demonstrate GDPR compliance is by using data protection impact assessment organizations (IAOs). Article 25 (Data Process Design) requires that "the controller shall, both at the time of the determination of the means for processing and at the time of the processing itself, implement appropriate technical and organisational measures designed to implement data-protection principles, such as data minimization, in an effective manner and to integrate the necessary safeguards into the processing of data subjects." This is an example where new technologies, such as artificial intelligence, can be used to ensure regulatory compliance. In essence, technological design can be used to police itself through monitoring and automatically issuing required notifications.

GDPR compliance can be ensured by conducting a **Data Protection Impact Assessment (DPIA)**. A DPIA is an audit of an organization's own processes and procedures that measures how these processes affect or might compromise the privacy of the individuals whose data it stores, collects, or processes. A **data protection officer (DPO)** is needed for regular and systematic monitoring of data subjects on a large scale. In order to avoid unexpected penalties, when in doubt companies should obtain consent from data subjects. In an audit, companies need to be able to prove that they received approval from customers to use their information.

Brexit and Consumer Protection

It is difficult to speculate as to the future of the consumer protection *acquis* in a post-Brexit world. The most positive approach, economically speaking, would be that the UK remains in the EEA, meaning that the UK remains legally obliged to adhere to EU consumer law. The consumer law *acquis* developed as part of the progress toward a truly internal or common market in which consumer law would largely be harmonized throughout the EU. Beyond the goal of harmonization, the consumer *acquis* has substantially improved consumer protection law. It has reduced instances of misleading advertising and unfair trade practices, and most importantly it granted the Competition and Markets Authority with additional powers of enforcement. But whether the UK will continue to defer to that Authority or follow the rulings of the CJEU is doubtful in the current political environment. Unless the UK expressly repeals the EU-required consumer protections, those protections remain the domestic law of the country. In other words, from a formal point of view, EU law is demoted to the status of foreign law. Disharmony in consumer and other areas of law between the UK and the EU is inevitable since there will be a lack of coordination that a political union provides. The UK will likely repeal or modify some of its EU related legal infrastructure and the EU will continue to evolve its brand of consumer law as interpreted by the CJEU. However, if the UK remains in the EEA, then such divergence would be minimized. The common law is an unruly thing since

British courts will no longer view themselves bound by EU law or recognize the precedential value of European court decisions.

UK courts are likely to narrowly construe consumer law obligations as they adhere to freedom of contract rationales. The role that the Charter of Fundamental Rights, which plays an important part in the evolution of EU case law, will have in the UK is uncertain.[22] The UK may have to develop its own product standards, which would not be in the interest of UK exporters. The result will be a decrease in the harmonization of regulations and standards between the UK and the EU. The removal of automatic mutual recognition in product standards would create a barrier to trade. The hope is that the UK and the EU will negotiate a trade agreement that would avoid this problem.

EU Competition Law

Articles 81 and 82 of the Treaty of Rome (Articles 101 and 102 of the TFEU) established the core parameters of EU competition (antitrust) law. Article 81 of the Treaty prohibits monopolies, abuse of dominant positions (large market share), and anticompetitive collusion between competitors. A major debate in EU competition law is how the government and courts should balance the pro- and anticompetitive effects of an agreement.

Regulation 17/62 shifted from the need to obtain prior authorization, under which agreements had to be notified to the EU Commission (Directorate Competition or DG COMP) in order to obtain approval, to a directly applicable exemption system. The exemption system categorizes different types of agreements (franchising, mergers and acquisitions below a certain market share, and so forth) as being exempt from the competition law. These exempt categories of agreements are called **block exemptions**. In areas where there is no applicable block exemption, the parties must receive formal approval from the EU Commission. The various block exemptions currently in force include:

- *Franchising*: Regulation 2790/1999 (vertical distribution, purchasing, and franchising agreements);
- *Licensing*: Regulation 240/96 (technology transfer agreements);
- *Auto Dealerships*: Regulation 1400/2002 (vertical agreements and concerted practices in the motor vehicle sector);
- *Specialization*: Regulation 2658/2000 (specialization agreements); and
- *Research & Development*: Regulation 2659/2000 (research and development agreements).

Brexit and the Future of the EU

The history of the EU has been one movement from the development of a common market to one of a political union with a trans-European government. It has also been a story of expansion from the six original countries to 28, with more countries seeking entry. Unfortunately, the second decade of the

21st century has witnessed a populist backlash against international free trade and globalism, with anti-immigrant, anti-EU movements gaining strength in Hungary, Poland, and numerous other EU countries, as well as in the U.S. The first true break in the EU came with the 2020 withdrawal agreement between the UK and EU, popularly called Brexit.

The two issues that are now being confronted are the negotiation of a reconstituted trade relationship between the UK and the EU and whether this shock to European unity will lead to further departures from the EU. Such departures will come at great economic costs, especially to the weaker national economies, and reduce the role of the EU as an economic superpower. At this time, the focus is on the reality of Brexit. A side issue is what effect Brexit will have on the unity of the UK. Figure 7.6 shows the vote margins across the UK in favor and against Brexit in the 2016 referendum.

It shows that substantial majorities in Scotland (62% opposed Brexit) and Northern Ireland (55.8% opposed Brexit) were against leaving the EU. Brexit poses a major problem for Northern Ireland because of the uncertainty as to the status of its border with the Republic of Ireland, where a hard border would cause a good deal of hardship. Time will tell whether the disunity over Brexit will lead to a dissolution of the UK as currently constituted.

The major issue will be the negotiation of a trade deal to ensure the tariff- and quota-free flow of goods between the EU and the UK. But the EU is likely to agree to such a free trade deal if the UK continues to maintain EU standards on quality, safety, health, and environmental matters. If the UK lowers its standards or does not comply with EU standards, then it will have a competitive

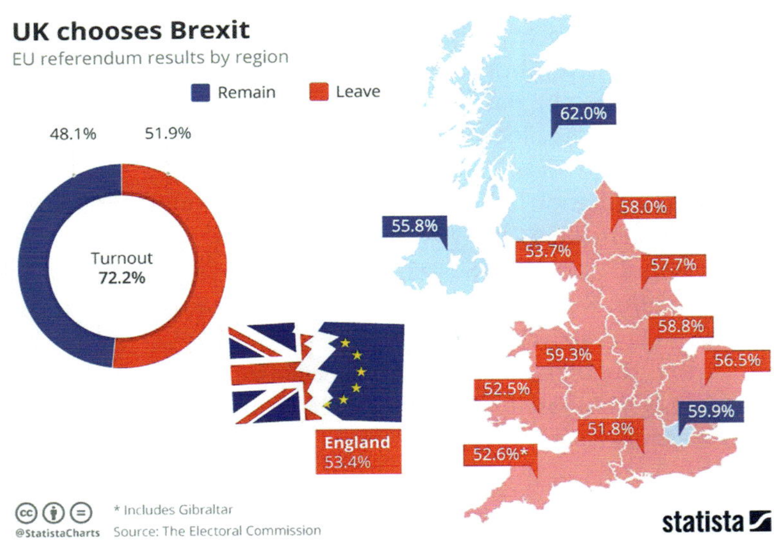

Figure 7.6 Brexit Vote in England and Wales, Northern Ireland, and Scotland.

Source: https://www.statista.com/chart/5100/uk-chooses-brexit/.

advantage over EU companies that are required to comply, in essence allowing the UK to "dump" goods into the EU market. If the economic consequences are significant, especially if the UK economy suffers, then populist movements will be cautious about threats of leaving the EU.

People's Republic of China

The rest of this chapter is devoted to the rise of China as a world economic power. It begins with a brief discussion of what has been called the BRIC countries. It illustrates two major factors relating to economic growth. First, the interdependency of national economies and capital markets make all countries susceptible to the dictates of the world economy. Second, government policies and decision-making can cause self-inflicted harm, even in periods of global economic growth.

BRIC Countries

Beginning in the 1980s, a number of national economies moved from impoverished or lesser-developed status to being relabeled as emerging economies. Four of these economies became known as the **BRIC countries**—Brazil, Russia, India, and China—due to their tremendous growth rates. However, since 2010 the strength of these economies has varied widely.[23] Brazil's growth rate (GDP) hit 7.53% in 2010, but fell to –3.55% in 2015, and leveled off at 1% beginning in 2018.

India's economic growth has varied widely: 11% in 2010, 4.5% in 2013, and 9% in 2016. Unfortunately, there has been a significant drop from 7.7% in 2018 to 4.5% in 2020. Russia's growth rate was 4.40% in 2010. Subsequently, there has been a sharp contraction in the Russian economy due to a number of mostly self-inflicted negative decisions (invasion of Ukraine leading to Western economic sanctions and failure to diversify an oil-gas export economy) and external events (drastic drop in oil prices). In 2015, the year following the invasion of Ukraine, Russian gross domestic product (GDP) decreased to 2.31%. By 2018, the Russian GDP growth rate improved to 2.25%. Projected GDP growth in Russia is a sluggish 1%.[24] In sum, Brazil and Russia have suffered substantial economic and political setbacks, while India continues to underperform despite its population of more than 1.3 billion people. In 2020, the worldwide coronavirus pandemic dramatically resulted in negative GDP growth. For example, GDP in the U.S. contracted 5% in the first quarter of 2020 and was –9.5% in the second quarter. Drastic drops in GDP occurred worldwide in the second quarter of 2020 including, France –14%; EU as a whole –12%; Russia –8.5%; Brazil –9.4%; and India projected –11%.

In 2010, China's growth rate stood at 10.64% but has gradually declined to 6.60% in 2018. China is viewed as an economic miracle with growth rates increasing from 3.89% in 1989, reaching 11% to 14% from 1992 to 1995, and exceeded 8% each year from 1996 to 2013. However, with the increase of manufacturing in lower-cost countries (Indonesia, Malaysia, Vietnam), China's export-based economy has begun to falter, and the continued negative effect on the economy by inefficient state-owned enterprises (SOEs), which make up about one-third of the economy, has slowed its growth. On the positive side, China now sells more goods internally with the development of a robust consumer market and has invested heavily in the creation of a technology sector. Nonetheless, growth rates are expected to slow to about 5–6% by the early 2020s. After decades of growth, China is now the world's third largest economy, next to the U.S. and the EU.

Economies vary in their capacities and weaknesses, and there is no guarantee that other countries will be as successful as China. The progression to higher levels of economic development inevitably include various setbacks and take various lengths of time to achieve. Russia is a case study. A major factor in its demise was its invasion of Ukraine in violation of international law, which led to Western sanctions, along with a dramatic drop in oil prices. More common reasons for a country's struggle to advance economically include: (1) high rates of corruption; (2) failure to restructure its economy to be more open and reduce waste and inefficiency in its regulatory and government structures; and (3) failure to diversify its economy. Russia is a prime example of the latter phenomenon. The country remains largely dependent on revenues generated by its oil and gas sector.

People's Republic of China

China has come a long way economically in a short period of time. China was a closed, planned economy with little inward foreign investment and a restricted international trade sector. Beginning in the 1980s, China began to open to foreign investors. It enacted a variety of Western-style laws in the process of transitioning to a market economy. China was admitted to the World Trade Organization (WTO) in 2001. WTO membership recognized how far China had come in creating a modern legal system, as well as a body of free market-oriented substantive laws. The size of its industrial and manufacturing sector now rivals that of the U.S. See Image 7.2 for "Map of China."

China's tremendous GDP growth since the 1980s has shown its ability to develop a market economy and robust international trade sector within a non-democratic political regime. However, in order to develop a more mature, developed economy it will have to continue opening up to the outside world by loosening restrictions on its financial markets and refrain from manipulating the value of its currency (*yuan*). It will also have to transition from low-wage, cheap-goods manufacturing to a more innovation-driven economy, which it is currently attempting to do.

China has been able to sustain such growth despite regularly ranking low in surveys of economic freedom.[25] Some of the reasons for this ranking include: (1) China's weak judicial system, which is vulnerable to political influence; (2) power and wealth is concentrated in **state-owned enterprises (SOEs)** and local

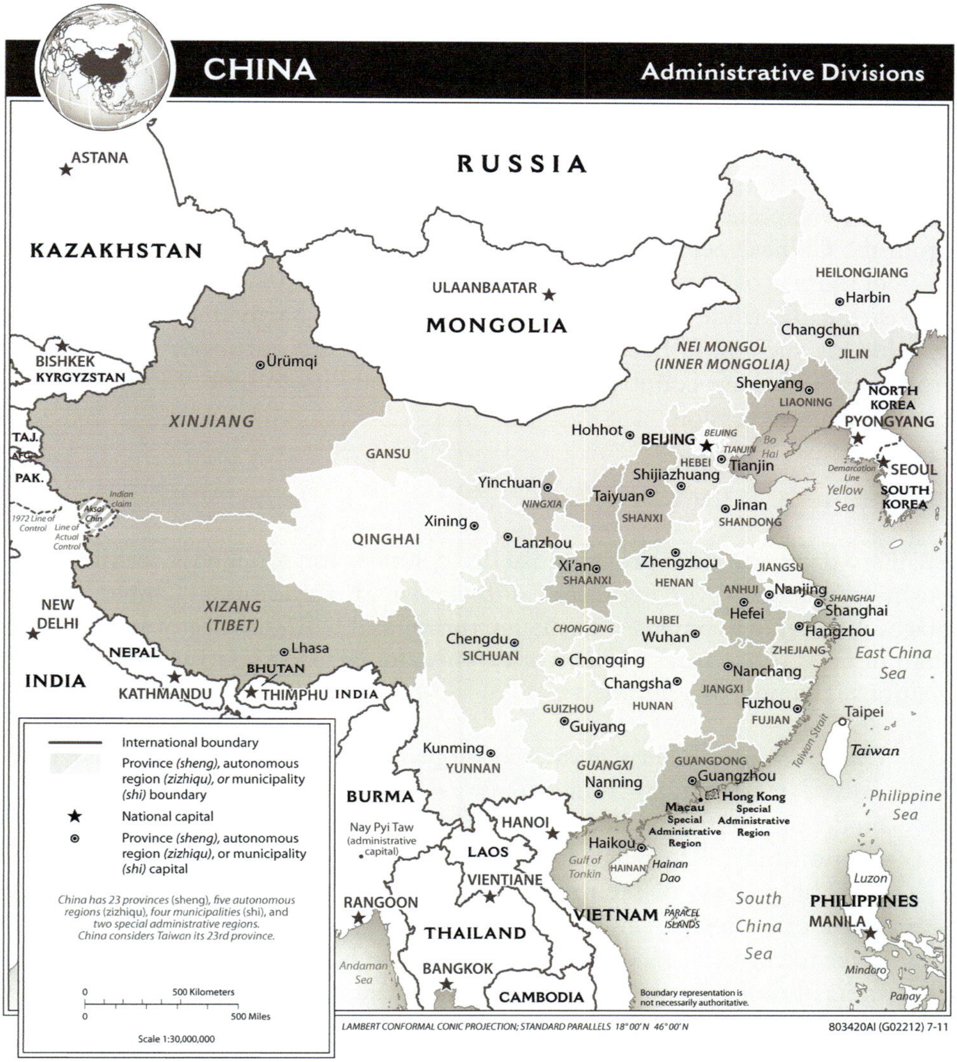

Image 7.2 Map of China.

governments—SOEs regularly lose money but benefit from greater access to capital and lower financing costs, while small and medium-sized companies suffer from the lack of access to credit; (3) lack of labor mobility; (4) high levels of corruption in government and in the judicial system; and (5) high levels of bureaucratic obstacles to obtain necessary licenses and permits (regulatory inefficiency).

The Chinese economy has also suffered due to an ongoing trade war with the U.S. beginning in 2018, along with the breakout of the coronavirus in 2020. The rationale for the Trump trade war with China is that China illegally subsidizes its export industries, manipulates the value of the yuan, does not have open access to some of its industries, and fails to protect foreign intellectual property rights, as well as engaging in espionage to steal trade secrets (may result in civil and criminal liability), resulting in a large negative balance of trade for the U.S. ($420 billion in 2018). Most of these rationales are based on fact, but at the cost of ignoring the free trade system as represented by the World Trade Organization (WTO). The marginalization of the WTO will have long-term consequences if countries weaponize obstacles to free trade to gain economic or political ends. From the Chinese perspective, the trade war is a disguised attempt by the U.S. to stem the rise of China as an economic and military power.

Historically, trade wars have caused much more harm than any perceived benefits, as such wars between such large economies harm not only bilateral trade between those countries but also has the ability to send the entire global economy into recession.

Language and Culture

Business decisions may prove unusually complex for foreigners seeking to do business in China. Evolving from Confucianism, the traditional Chinese culture places much more emphasis on the nurturing and maintenance of relationships than in most other areas of the world. This emphasis on relationships and connections is known as ***guanxi***:

> *Guanxi* and Western models of approaching a transaction need to be viewed in tandem: a strong enough relationship gains entry to the Western model of negotiation and hopefully to an eventual contract and continued relationships. The bigger the risk, the stronger the *guanxi* will need to be. The process of securing a contract in China is rarely the free market auction paradigm Westerners expect. For example, the parties may determine the terms of a business contract; however, all the local implications of doing business (like dealing with suppliers) will be determined by *guanxi*.[26]

At times, Chinese business persons may not seem serious in the negotiating of contracts, but this appearance of antipathy is due to cultural differences. Chinese companies and government agencies are extremely hierarchical with minimal delegation of decision-making powers from senior to junior officers. Under this system, rank is of primary importance. This causes problems when Western companies send junior officers (middle management) with the power to negotiate contracts. In return, the government agency or company sends junior officers lacking the authority to make a contract. The result, from the Western perspective, is that the Chinese parties are unnecessarily delaying the negotiations or not negotiating in good faith when, in fact, the junior officers need to present contract proposals to senior officers who feel free to neglect what was agreed upon during the negotiations. Therefore, it is important that the Western company send a high-ranking officer, depending on the size and importance of the deal. For the same reason, it is important to verify the authority of the party on the other side of the negotiations. When dealing with government officials, it is vital to find out which government officials have the power of approval and try to engage them in the negotiations as soon as is feasible.

Chinese Government

In 1992, a new **Constitution** or **Basic Law** was enacted, which provides the current structure of government, judicial system, and individual rights. It has three substantive parts that provide the general principles of government, the basic structure of government, and the fundamental rights and *duties* of citizens. The notion of the duties of citizens demonstrates the difference between a democratic constitution and a socialist constitution. In democracies, the constitution is seen as the supreme authority. In China, the Communist Party is the supreme authority and not the Constitution. As such the PRC's Constitution is more a statement of policies. The fact that it is not fundamental law in the way of the U.S. Constitution is shown by the fact that the 1992 Constitution is the fourth constitution enacted since 1949. The common division of authority between executive, legislative, and judicial branches characterizes the Chinese governmental structure. However, the allocation of power and independence of the three branches does not resemble the separation of powers created in constitutional democracies.

Executive Branch

The most powerful positions in the Chinese government are the President and Vice President, who are elected by the **National People's Congress** (**NPC**).

The **State Council** is the highest organ of government. Ministers head the numerous ministries or commissions of government. The State Council and its ministries are equivalent to the executive and legislative agencies. The ministries adopt regulations, rules, and orders, as well as prepare proposals to submit to the NPC, such as plans for economic development, foreign affairs, and approval of international treaties and agreements.

Legislative Branch

People's congresses exist at all levels—national, regional, and local. The most powerful is the NPC. They make up the basic units of political power in China. Deputies to the town and local congresses are directly elected. The deputies at the lower level elect deputies at the county level. The NPC's **Standing Committee** is the highest level of legislative power. The NPC is responsible for creating and supervising all administrative and judicial units of the government. The legislative powers of the NPC include electing the President, amending the Constitution, enacting basic laws, and electing the President of the Supreme People's Court. The NPC meets only once a year for two weeks. When not in session, the Standing Committee exercises all the above listed powers of the NPC.

Judicial Branch

The judicial system consists of the **Supreme People's Court.** Article 129 of the Constitution describes the courts as "state organs for legal supervision," which means that the courts are accountable to the Standing Committee. Below the Supreme People's Court are 31 Higher People's Courts and 376 Intermediate People's Courts at the provincial level; below these courts are some 3,000 Basic People's Courts at the county level, which are further subdivided into town and village courts called People's Tribunals. Litigants are generally limited to one appeal on matters of law. However, parties can forsake an appeal and instead ask for a second trial—after the decision at the trial level the case may be reviewed *de novo* (on matters of facts and law) by a higher court. After the second trial there is no right to appeal, even as to matters of law.

Chinese Legal System

The modern Chinese legal system is a relatively new creation. The People's Republic of China was created in 1949 as a communist state with a planned economy. The government owned all property, or the property was held in some form of communal ownership. The center of the industrial economy was the SOE system. Due to the inefficiencies of such a system, China failed to take advantage of its enormous economic potential. All social reforms and economic progress came to an end with the purge known as the Cultural Revolution, beginning in 1966 and ending with the death of **Mao Zedong** in 1976.

Modern China was essentially constructed beginning with the ascendency of **Deng Xiaoping** to power in 1978. Deng immediately began to install economic reforms leading to the market economy of today. He also revived the legal system which had all but ceased to function in order to support the economic rule of law. Despite this rapid improvement, the government remains firmly in control of such important areas as banking, electricity, steel production, oil and gas exploration, telecommunications, and transport systems. It is in these markets that foreign investment and competition have been prohibited. It is in these areas that SOEs dominate and it is clear that further reforms (privatization) are needed.

Chinese Constitution

The Constitution of the PRC guarantees the basic rights of citizens including the right to vote, freedom of speech, press, assembly, association, and religion, as well as a right to personal dignity. In 2014, the Constitution was amended to expressly guarantee human rights and recognize private ownership, but ownership of real estate was limited to a fixed period of time.

In preparation for its entry into the WTO in 2001, there was a rapid passage of all sorts of laws to conform to the requirements of the different WTO Agreements. Included in the massive creation of laws and regulations was an effort to improve its legal system. As a civil law system, decisions of higher courts have no mandatory precedential value—each case stands alone and does not bind other courts. However, in practice, the lower courts follow the interpretations and decisions of the Supreme People's Courts. See Figure 7.7 for the structure of the "Chinese Court System."

Organization and Responsibilities of People's Courts

The **Law on the Organization of People's Courts** divides local courts into three levels. First-hearing (trial) cases under their jurisdiction include those involving national security, criminal cases that may involve life imprisonment or the death penalty, criminal cases committed by foreigners, or cases involving Chinese citizens violating the lawful rights and interests of foreigners. According to the Law on Civil Procedure, civil cases heard by Intermediate Courts are major foreign-related cases, cases of major implications within their jurisdictions, and cases that Intermediate Courts are ordered to hear by the Supreme People's Court. Intermediate Courts are authorized to hear the following cases: verification of patent rights, customs cases, and suits against administrative actions taken by governments of the provinces. Their jurisdiction also includes trial cases transferred by lower courts and they also have the power to examine decisions of the lower courts at their discretion.

Higher Courts' responsibilities include: (1) criminal, civil, and administrative cases of major proportions and complications under their jurisdiction, as provided for by the law; (2) first-hearing (trial) cases transferred by lower courts;

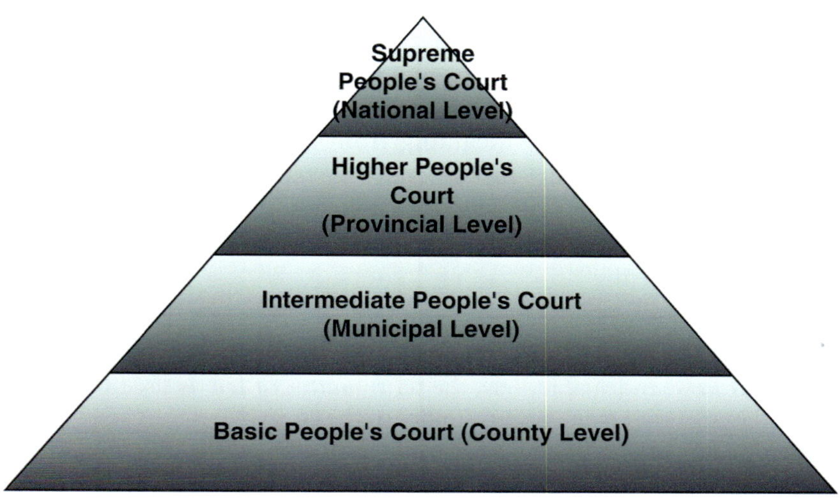

Figure 7.7 Chinese Court System.

(3) cases appealing or protesting the verdicts and decisions made by lower courts;
(4) cases appealing the verdicts and rulings made by the Maritime Court.

Maritime Courts are special courts set up to hear maritime or shipping cases. In May 1989, the Supreme People's Court decided on the Scope of Cases to Be Handled by Maritime Courts. That decision specified that Maritime Courts handle maritime or commercial cases between Chinese citizens, between Chinese citizens and foreign citizens, and between foreign citizens, involving maritime torts and disputes, damage claims involving the collision of vessels, and claims involving vessels discharging or leaking hazardous materials. It also hears commercial disputes involving shipping contracts, cases involving seaman labor contracts, cases involving maritime insurance, and cases involving applications filed with Chinese Maritime Courts by litigants for recognition and the enforcement of arbitration awards.

The Supreme People's Court, located in Beijing, supervises the lower and specialized courts. It also functions to harmonize Chinese law by issuing *judicial interpretations* on how to apply the law and by publishing *guiding cases*, often by using hypothetical cases.

The **Standing Committee of the People's Congress** at the lower levels of government have the power to approve appointments and to remove judges. Article 12 of the Law on the Organization of People's Courts, as noted above, establishes a two-trial system, with the decision of the second or higher court being the final judgment. This means a case is closed after going through two levels of trial. Because of the two-court trial system, there is no further right to appeal. In order to compensate for the lack of a right to a further appeal, the **System for Judicial Supervision**, also known as the *re-examination system* was created. This system refers to a special arrangement for a higher court to re-examine judgments and rulings that have already taken effect. It actually represents a remedy to the system where the decision of second instance (trial) is final. This judicial supervision procedure can only be initiated by presidents of courts, superior courts, and the Supreme People's Court on grounds that the lower court judgment or ruling contained errors in the establishment of facts or application of laws.

Some cases are referred directly from a trial court to a higher court. In such cases, the ruling of the higher court is final with no right to appeal. Such referrals can be done at any level, including from a higher court to the Supreme People's Court. In sum, the Chinese court system functions differently than the appellate court systems found in other countries. As is clear from the above discussion, no matter the level the Chinese courts often act both as trial courts and as courts of appeal.

Matter of Law: In legal actions, the term *matter of law* is used to define a particular area that is the responsibility of the court. Matter of law is distinguished from *matter of fact*. All questions concerning the determination of fact are for the jury, though a judge may determine the facts if a jury trial is waived or is not permitted under the law. Judges rule on all matters of law, including pre-trial motions, trial objections to the introduction of particular evidence or testimony, proposed jury instructions, and post-trial motions.

Due to the lack of a proper appeals process and the newness of China's law codes, the Supreme People's Court has needed to innovate to provide guidance to lower courts in the application of new Western-style laws. For about two decades, the Court has issued **Interpretative Decisions** explaining how the lower courts should deal with issues of how laws should be interpreted and applied (many of these Interpretative Decisions have been translated into English). The Supreme People's Court's interpretations are not mandatory in nature but are viewed as persuasive sources of law. For example, Chinese Contract Law is unclear regarding whether a party may escape liability for a breach of contract due to hardship. The Supreme People's Court issued an interpretation that recognized that an excuse for breach of contract due to hardship, caused by a change of circumstances, was implicitly found in contract law. A more recent innovation has been the publication of **Guiding Cases.** Under this new case guidance system, a "case guidance office coordinates research on guiding cases." The "guiding cases" are ones that satisfy any of the following requirements: (a) issues of wide interest to society; (b) when the enacted law is not specific enough; (c) cases that are considered to be common or typical; or (d) complicated cases or new types of cases.

Role of Lawyers

Article 1 of the **Lawyers Law** states that the mission of lawyers is to maintain the lawful rights and interests of the parties to a suit and maintain proper implementation of law. Chinese lawyers play an independent role in lawsuits. They do not represent the courts, nor do they solely represent the interests of their clients; they are independent. Lawyers practice in the name of their law firms. The Lawyers Law provides for three forms of law firms: state-funded, cooperative, and partnership. Article 23 states that lawyers should undertake business through their law firm, which should sign a written contract with their clients, charge them fees in compliance with state regulations, and record the fees into their books.

Lawyers have gained in importance since the conversion from a communist to a market economy, and the subsequent passage of numerous substantive laws, have provided persons and companies rights that they did not previously possess. There has been a cultural shift from viewing litigation as dishonorable to it being a way of protecting a person's rights. Also, legal education and the professionalism of judges has improved.

Arbitration Law and Arbitration Panels

Arbitration committees are formed with members from government departments and chambers of commerce. The **Arbitration Law of the People's Republic of China,** promulgated on August 31, 1994, unified arbitration practices across the country and harmonized China's arbitration system with internationally accepted principles and practices. The **China Arbitration Association** is a self-disciplinary organization of arbitrators. It supervises arbitration committees and their members. Arbitrators must meet the following qualifications: (1) eight full years in the arbitration field, eight full years in the legal profession, or eight full years as a judge; (2) specialized in legal research and teaching and holding a senior professional title; and (3) familiar with legal knowledge, specializing in economic and trade activities.

Arbitration is a preferred means of dispute resolution for foreigners for a number of reasons. First, the judicial expertise of the lower courts in the Chinese court system is uneven, especially when applying the Western-style laws. Second, the courts can be slow and inefficient. Third, arbitration is party-controlled. The parties can negotiate a custom arbitration clause to alleviate the concerns of the foreign party, including selecting the language of the arbitration. Fourth, China has developed some outstanding arbitration venues and continues to develop a more expansive arbitration system. The major international arbitration institution in China is the **China International Economic and Trade Arbitration Commission** (CIETAC).

CIETAC has offices in Beijing, Shenzhen, Shanghai, Chongqing, and Hong Kong, among many other cities. It has a worldwide reputation and is one of the fastest growing arbitration venues in the world—in 1985 it heard 35 arbitration disputes and has continued to grow, hearing 3,333 cases in 2019. It amended its rules ("2015 Rules") to make them closer to international standards and practices. The new rules, as is the international trend, provide for the appointment of **emergency arbitrators** able to grant interim relief, such as injunctions. In 2014, a Chinese court, for the first time, upheld the validity of **hybrid arbitration clauses.** In that case, the arbitration clause called for CIETAC arbitration, but under the UNCITRAL Model Arbitration Rules. These improvements and its pool of expert arbitrators make CIETAC an appealing venue for Western parties seeking to avoid the Chinese court system.

Chinese Substantive Law

After a brief review of Chinese legal history, the following substantive law areas, most closely related to doing business in China, will be reviewed: company and commercial, property, contract, intellectual property, investment, joint venture, franchise, and administrative law. China has a long history relating to the development of a general civil code but has not adopted one in the modern era (post-1930s) until now.

History of Chinese Law

Traditional Chinese law was heavily based upon cultural practices in which formal law played a relatively minor role. The parties themselves, guided by cultural norms and customs, generally settled their own disputes. Confucianism was an important influence on the Chinese view of the role of law in society.

Confucius lived from 551–479 BC. The *Analects of Confucius* is a compilation of his sayings and ideas. He stressed personal and governmental morality, correctness of social relationships, justice, and sincerity. His work became the basis for Chinese tradition and thought. He is also credited with stating an early version of the *Golden Rule*: "Do not do to others what you do not want done to yourself."

Confucius preached the idea that society should be self-regulating through the advancement of education, persuasion, and virtue, and not by the force of law. Thus, the guiding force for social and economic relationships was the *li* (moral values). In contrast, beginning with the *Qin* Dynasty (221–206 BC), the importance of clear, formal legal rules or *fa* became more valued. But Confucianism remained the state ideology into the twentieth century.

A legal code writing tradition began with the *Qin* and *Han* Dynasties. However, these early legal codes were largely limited to criminal law. The more comprehensive and meaningful code was the **Tang Code** of the seventh century AD. Code writing culminated with the 1740 **Great Qing Code**, which consisted of 436 statutes. These indigenous dynastic codes set the basis for the categorization of China as a civil law system. This continues to the present, as China committed to enacting a comprehensive civil code by 2020. The new Chinese Civil Code became effective on January 1, 2021.

Chinese law has been influenced by other legal systems, including the common law. However, in the end, Chinese leaders selected a civil law system, as opposed to a common law system, because it was a better fit given the civil law's reliance on general principles or general clauses, which can be found in the code-like precepts of Confucius; therefore, the individuality of the common law is not a good fit for Chinese society.[27] German law has had the greatest influence on the development of Chinese commercial and business laws.

On March 15, 2015, the Twelfth National People's Congress promulgated the first part of China's first comprehensive General Civil Code, entitled **General Rules of the Civil Law of the People's Republic of China** (**General Rules**). The law went into effect on October 1, 2017. This initial part consists of 206 articles and will play a crucial role in interpreting the rest of the Code.

The General Rules include conflicting principles and articles due to the remaining influence of Chinese customary law and socialist principles. The importance of freedom of contract is found in a number of the general principles. Article 3 espouses that personal and property rights "are protected by the law; no organisation or individual may infringe upon such rights and interests." The notions of individual free will and private autonomy are found in the phrase "equal status," used in a number of the general principles. Freedom of contract and its basis in mutual consent is made clear in Article 5's phrase, stating that "civil activities shall follow the principles of voluntariness" and that engaging in civil activities, such as entering or terminating a contract, would be recognized "according to the parties' intentions."

The remaining principles place constraints on the absoluteness of freedom of contract. They can be viewed both from the perspectives of Confucian-socialist values and Western legal norms. Communitarian and fairness norms are found in all legal systems—the differences are a matter of degree rather than kind. Article 6 requires contracting parties to "follow the principles of fairness in reasonably determining the rights and obligations of all parties concerned," while Article 7 recognizes that each party "shall follow the principles of good faith, adhere to honesty and keep their commitments."

The customary nature of Chinese law is evidenced in Article 8's requirement that civil activities shall not "go against the public order and good customs." Article 10 again notes that when the rule of law fails to resolve a dispute, then "usual practice may be followed, but the public order and good customs shall not be infringed upon." Finally, a new principle is introduced in the General Rules, not found in the 1999 Chinese Contract Law. Article 9 states that it is the duty of all legal persons to conduct business in a way that protects the environment. The communal harm caused by China's rapid industrialization is now recognized as a core concern of Chinese society.

The importance of status and reputation embedded in Confucian values is also recognized in the areas of remedies for breach of contract. General Rules Article 179 requires the breaching party to "eliminate the impact or restore the reputation" of the non-breaching party through the unique remedy of "apology"—a proper apology or a restoration of reputation being recognized as an independent remedy than that of mere payment of damages. The socialist history of China is seen in the General Rules Article 185, which allows the Communist Party to guard its legitimacy by claiming civil liability against any person who infringes on the "reputation and honour of heroic martyrs and public interests are damaged." It is through such provisions that the Communist Party acts as the gatekeeper to the past.

As noted at the beginning of this section, Confucianism's worldview is that each person has a certain role to play in the creation of a harmonious society and that personal relationships, or *guanxi*, remain a key feature of Chinese society. Guanxi suggests that relationships include mutual obligation, reciprocity, and goodwill. This type of view sees contracts as minor reflections of a contractual relationship—instead of seeing breach of contract as triggering a legal right, it sees breach as triggering a moral right to adjust the contract: "Once *guanxi* is established between two people, each can ask a favor of the other with the expectation that the debt incurred will be repaid sometime in the future." Thus, Westerners negotiating contracts in China should be aware of how constructs like *guanxi* impact the Chinese view of the lesser role of formal contracts compared to the importance of maintaining the relationship and the normalcy of requests for subsequent changes to the contract.

Company and Corporation Law

There are many more approvals needed in order to form a company in China, and it takes at least a month. The **Company Law of the People's Republic of**

China was based largely on the company laws of Taiwan, France, Germany, and Japan. The **New Company Law** is particularly important because it relates to foreign investment in China (establishment of businesses and manufacturing plants). Chinese foreign investment law requires that operations by foreign investors be conducted through a **Chinese Limited Liability Company.**[28] In doing business with Chinese companies, it is important for the foreign investor to verify that the company has legal ownership of property that it seeks to purchase. This is shown in the ongoing dispute in *Apple v. Proview*. A seemingly IP law issue became an issue of corporate law in a dispute over the ownership of the "iPad" trademark. Proview Shenzhen registered a trademark in China for something called IPAD long before Apple began producing its famous iPad. Apple had the choice of bringing a lawsuit to force the assignment of the trademark or to negotiate for the voluntary assignment of the trademark. It chose the latter approach and negotiated an assignment agreement with UK Proview (parent company) and its Taiwan subsidiary (Taiwan Proview). To Apple's surprise, the trademark was held by a Chinese subsidiary of Proview. The issue was whether the trademark assignment agreement was binding on Proview's subsidiary. Article 3 of the **Chinese Corporate Law** states that "a company is a *legal person*, which has independent property of a legal person and enjoys the property rights of a legal person."

The independence of a company from related or affiliated entities is referred to as **personality confusion**. In such cases, the Chinese court will weigh the following factors related to the affiliated companies: (1) asset confusion, such as combined funding and mixed financial management; (2) business confusion, such as the overlap of business scope or business crossings; (3) labor and personnel confusion, such as joint legal representative, senior management, or the bilateral employment of the employees; and (4) confusion of the place of business.

Under the current case, the China mainland subsidiary and the Taiwanese subsidiary are financially, operationally, managerially, and geographically separate entities. Moreover, there are no controlling shareholders common between the two companies. Therefore, there was little personality confusion between the two companies, and therefore Apple was not likely to win its lawsuit, forcing Apple to bring a lawsuit for trademark infringement. Eventually, the dispute was settled through mediation. Even though this was a clear case of trademark infringement, Apple agreed to pay $60 million to Proview Shenzhen for the assignment. This was a small cost given the size of the Chinese market for iPads. The case demonstrates the importance of being familiar with Chinese business law and to perform due diligence to determine the true owner of a particular right.

Another facet of the Chinese market system is the decentralized nature of government regulation where despite nationwide laws, the application and enforcement of those laws vary widely throughout China. Local governments are given substantial power to regulate businesses "in the light of the specific local conditions and actual needs." The local communist party exerts undue influence over state regulatory agencies and often intercede to protect SOEs at the expense of foreign-owned companies.

Property Rights Law of 2007

The real property law has separate provisions for immovable property (land and buildings) and movable property (goods or materials). All land is technically owned by the State or by a collective. Collectives are found mostly in the rural areas. Article 8 of the **Land Administration Law** states that the land in the urban areas is owned by the State, while "land in rural and suburban areas is owned by *peasant collectives*." For example, a village may control the surrounding farmland as a collective. In urban areas, private entities petition the government for a **right to use** the land. A development company first obtains a right to use land to construct an apartment or condominium building. Upon completion, buyers of the individual units obtain a right to use the unit for a period of time. For the owner of a home or apartment, the right to use (ownership) is a maximum of 70 years.

The law also allows for the renewal of the right to use but is silent as to whether the renewal would be for another 70 years or less. It is also silent as to whether the "owner" would have to pay a fee for the renewal. The right of use for commercial property (manufacturing plants, stores, warehouses, and so forth) is 50 years. The right to use land for farming, owned by a peasant collective, is a period of 30 years. However, land contracted out for 30 years may be reclaimed and reallocated upon a two-thirds vote of the village assembly, subject to the approval of the town government and the agriculture department of the county government. The hope is that the new civil code will provide greater clarification.

Thus, despite the recognition of private property, the spirit behind the law is that such property should be used to advance social interests. Individuals can privately own residential houses and apartments, although not the land on which the buildings are situated. Real estate may be transferred through sale, gift, or other legal means. Private parties do not own *fee simple title* (common law's complete and total ownership). Instead, they "buy" real estate based upon long-term leases. The new civil code is expected to extend land use rights of residential properties automatically after the 70-year right of use expires.

When real estate is transferred, the land-use rights and home ownership are transferred simultaneously. Restrictions that may apply to the transfer of real estate include prohibiting transfer when the land-use rights are reclaimed by the state in accordance with the law, when the property has not been properly registered, or when certificates of ownership have not been obtained. Both urban land-use rights and home ownership are subject to registration. The registration is performed through local authorities at or above the county level; certificates are issued to confirm land rights and ownership.

Foreign businesspeople in China must understand the history and extent of private property rights in China. The number of required administrative approvals to obtain property can be frustrating for a Westerner anxious to do business in China. A **New Property Law** went into effect in 2017. Article 3 of the law shows the confusing nature of property law in China since it blends the concept of communal ownership (socialism) with the private property rights found in a market economy:

> In the primary stage of socialism, the State upholds the basic economic system under which public ownership is dominant and allows the economic sectors of diverse forms of ownership to develop side by side. The State consolidates and develops the public sectors of the economy, and encourages, supports and guides the development of the non-public sectors of the economy. The State maintains a socialist market economy and guarantees the equal status and the right to development of all the mainstays of the market.

In the case of apartment-condominium buildings, Article 76 of the Property Law requires only a majority vote of the unit owners for most matters involving the management of the building. However, in two cases a supermajority is required—raising or using funds for the maintenance of the building and renovation of the building. In those cases, supermajority votes are required (two-thirds) of the ownership of the square meters of the individual units and two-thirds or more of the total number of unit owners.

In place of the recording of a deed, it is important to register a **Certificate of the Right to Use** in the **Real Property Registry**. If a property is sold to more than one person, the first one to register is deemed to be the owner. The land registry is conclusive evidence of ownership. In fact, any contract affecting real property should also be registered immediately. For example, a contract to lease some office space should be recorded in the Real Property Registry.

Chinese Contract Law

Formal contracts and contract rules serve the primary functions that they do elsewhere in the world. They provide a framework for economic relationships, a blueprint of the parties' obligations, and allow parties to plan for the future. The difference is between the formal view of written contracts as static instruments and the sanctity of contractual rights (Western view), versus the Eastern view that formal contracts are starting points meant to be flexible and subject to adjustment. Thus, where a Western party sees a Chinese request to renegotiate terms in the contract as an act of bad faith, the Chinese party sees it as a natural phenomenon of cooperation and mutual interests embedded in the business relationship.[29] There is evidence, however, that the introduction of formal contract law has begun to loosen the grip of cultural norms on contractual relationships. The rise of commercial and contract litigation in Chinese courts demonstrates that business and ordinary persons now see the law and litigation as a means of protecting their interests.

China's transformation into a market economy and ascendancy into a global economic power increases the importance of the study of its Chinese private law (contract, torts, and property). The twin pillars of a market economy are private property and contracts (the ability to transfer private property). The evolution of Chinese contract law provides an opportunity to study the influences of foreign laws and the formal **transplantation** of foreign and international law into a different cultural and legal tradition. Legal transplantation (so named by

Scottish-American legal scholar Alan Watson in his 1974 book entitled *Legal Transplants*) means the moving of a legal rule, a law, or an entire system of law from one country to another. Transplantation is also referred to as the *reception* of foreign law. The most dramatic example was Europe's reception of Roman law. China's development of a private contract law, beginning in the mid-1980s, has been characterized by the breadth of the foreign law influences involved in that development. However, the variety of sources used by the drafters of the 1999 **Chinese Contract Law** (**CCL**) has had unintended consequences. The CCL possesses a number of "gaps" and inconsistencies because of the variety of influences and partial transplantations used in its drafting.

China has gone through a series of receptions and legal transplantations from foreign and international private laws in transitioning to a market economy. In order to facilitate trade, it adopted the Foreign Economic Contract Law of 1985 (FECL) to assure foreign parties that a modern contract law would apply to their transactions. It adopted the Technology Contract Law in 1987. In 1988, China became an original signatory to the United Nations Convention on Contracts for the International Sale of Goods (CISG). The adoption of the CISG showed that China had the foresight of seeing the benefits of a uniform international sales law to an emerging economy. In 1999, China elected to harmonize its domestic and foreign contract laws through the adoption of the CCL.

It was inevitable that problems would appear in adopting foreign law due to a number of factors: (1) problem of translating foreign legal concepts, principles, and rules from one language to another; (2) problem of introducing a new foreign legal regime into an existing legal and cultural tradition; and (3) introducing a foreign text into a country without an existing body of jurisprudence or expertise to apply the new law properly and consistently.

The more successful of the receptions was China's adoption of the CISG. One reason for this is the wealth of international case law and commentaries that Chinese legal bodies have been able to use in applying the CISG's provisions. Currently, there is no hard evidence of whether or not the Chinese courts have adeptly applied the CISG in a consistent way. However, there is strong evidence that Chinese arbitral bodies have successfully done so. China's premier international arbitral body, the CIETAC, has issued awards that have generally been well-reasoned and of high quality, showing its ability to understand and properly apply the CISG in an unbiased manner.

Chinese private law reflects the influence of European civil laws, especially German law, and to some extent they have been influenced by the common law. The problem of legal transplants is that the text of the law is easily movable from one country to the next, but legal tradition, legal reasoning, and legal theory are not so easily transplanted. Professor Shiyuan Han has made such a case in the area of pre-contractual liability. China adopted the civil law doctrine of ***culpa in contrahendo*** or bad faith negotiations. The important point that Han makes is that the ability of the Chinese courts to understand and apply such a concept depends on what he calls "theory reception." A law of pre-contractual liability is more than a set of fixed rules; it is based upon a broad theory of good faith. The use of multiple sources in drafting the CCL and subsequently in the drafting of the Chinese Civil Code of 2021 (CISG, UNIDROIT Principles of International Commercial Contracts, German BGB, and American Uniform Commercial Code) has resulted in less than a clear and comprehensive contract law. This has caused substantial confusion in the Chinese courts in applying its rules in a uniform manner.

Chinese courts, much like arbitral panels, balance the interests of the parties, as well as society and the State, to render fair and equitable decisions. Thus, Chinese courts avoid the strict enforcement of contract rights and contract law rules. Second, such a view of contracts requires a broad contextual approach to contract interpretation including considering the background relationship of the parties, the circumstances relating to the formation and performance of the contract, and customary practices in a trade or business. Judges bring a three-fold framework in the interpretation of law and contracts: *heqing* (feelings, relationship, and circumstances), *heli* (reason), and *hefa* (legal rules).[30] This leads to inconsistent application of seemingly clear and fixed rules. An example is the Chinese courts' overuse of the implied duty of good faith.

Duty of Good Faith in Chinese Law

The concept of good faith and fairness is found throughout Chinese contract law. The most recent provisions are found in the 2017 General Principles of Civil Law, which provides "General Rules" for the rest of the new Civil Code, which was adopted on May 28, 2020 and became effective on January 1, 2021. Some of the principles found in the General Rules dealing with the interpretation of contract include:

1. The contracting parties "shall follow the principles of good faith, adhere to honesty and keep their commitments." (Article 7)
2. When interpreting a contract the interpreter shall view it "in light of the words and expressions used in the interpretation of contract, the related terms in the contract, the purpose of the contract, the usage of transaction and the *principle of good faith*; the use of the words, in combination with the relevant terms, the nature and purpose of the conduct, the habits and the *principle of good faith* shall not be restricted by the used words and sentences, the relevant clauses, the nature and purpose of the conduct, the habits and the *principle of good faith* shall be considered in combination to determine the genuine meaning of [the contract]." (Article 142)
3. Article 6 states that the parties "shall follow the principles of fairness in determining reasonably the rights and obligations of all parties concerned."
4. Articles 39 and 40 provide standard terms regulation that requires the terms to "comply with the principle of fairness when Regulation determining the rights and duties of the parties, shall, in a reasonable manner, draw the attention of the other party to the terms which exclude or limit his liability and term is void if it increases the liability of the other party or deprives the other party of a major right." Under Article 6, non-negotiated terms provided by one party to another must meet a threshold of reasonableness and fairness to be enforceable.

Current Chinese law, as noted above, also recognizes good faith in the negotiation of contract and in post-contract obligations. A party that negotiates in bad faith under the pretext of concluding a contract; intentionally concealing a material fact; and in negotiating preliminary agreements is liable in damages.[31,32] Unfortunately, Chinese courts have used the good faith and fairness principles to avoid the application of the more precise rules of contract law, which may provide a clear answer to a dispute or as a tool to force the parties into mediation.

Improvements in Chinese Courts

The divergence between formal law and its erratic application in the court system, through the use of good faith and other malleable cultural norms, may be diminishing. The improvement in legal reasoning skills in the judiciary, which the Supreme People's Court aids by offering legal education and guidance through the issuance of "Interpretations" and Guiding Opinions, has led to the judiciary delivering more consistent and objective decisions. With these new skill sets, courts will likely move away from extralegal sources of law (cultural norms or customary law) and issue decisions based on the "rule of law."

However, the lack of an independent court system hampers the impact that the judiciary's improved knowledge of China's Western-style laws and legal reasoning skills will have on the overall legal system. There have been some moves in the direction of greater independence, but for the time being, the continued professionalization of the judiciary is the most likely area of improvement. At the same time, it is important to realize that a more independent and objective judiciary is unlikely to change the Chinese concept of the rule of law, which does not assume the eventual creation of a liberal democracy.

Intellectual Property Law

China and the U.S. reached several important agreements covering intellectual property rights through the **U.S.–China Joint Commission on Commerce and Trade (JCCT)**. The State Administration for Industry and Commerce (SAIC) is the authority in charge of enforcement against online counterfeiting. More recently, China authorized the creation of special courts to hear Intellectual Property Rights (IPR) claims, with judges having specialized training in IPR law (trademark, copyright, and patent rights).

Nonetheless, China has become famous for producing counterfeit goods in violation of IPR. The common way of dealing with this problem is to punish the offending country with trade sanctions through the WTO or unilaterally through U.S. trade law, as is shown by the Trump trade war with China. Due to the size of the Chinese consumer market, foreign companies have been willing to continue to do business there despite inadequate IPR protections. IPR owners have had to take innovative methods to reduce the infringement on their rights. One method has been the creation of **Brand Protection Units** that work with local police authorities to raid the operations of counterfeiters. Figure 7.8 gives

1 Register your IP rights with Chinese authorities and secure management control.
2 Assign responsibilities for internal IPR security.
3 Use direct sales and design outsourcing.
4 Audit licensing and distribution contracts, and manufacturing partners.
5 Install tracing and labeling control systems.
6 Explore uniform pricing.
7 Police inventory.
8 Educate consumers.
9 Make allies with local officials and domestic companies (such as retailers).
10 Avoid lawsuits by dealing directly with counterfeiters.

Figure 7.8 Ten Strategies for Fighting IPR Infringement in China.

a few other "real world" examples of proactive non-sanction-based methods of combating illegal counterfeiting.

Another problem in China has been bad faith trademark filings ("trademark squatting"), where the authorities have taken a tolerant approach. However, the problem of trademark squatting has also attracted substantial attention from the Supreme People's Court. The Supreme People's Court has called for the full use of current laws in order to curb bad faith trademark filings. In order to better protect IPR, the new Civil Code provides for, in its section on torts, the assessment of punitive damages for the infringement of intellectual property rights (IPRs).

Chinese Cyber Security Law of 2017

As a contrast to the EU's General Data Protection Regulation (GDPR), which seeks to protect individual rights and rein in the actions of large corporations, China's Cybersecurity Law (CL) provides an alternative vision about how countries can choose to protect personal data. Article 9 of the CL states that "network operators must obey social norms and commercial ethics, be honest and credible, perform obligations to protect network security, accept supervision from the government and public, and bear social responsibility." The vagueness of this provision, as well as undefined concepts of national security and public interest contained within the Law, increases the government's grounds to obtain data and reduces a foreign company's ability to contest a government demand for data access. Furthermore, domestic competitors can request spot checks on foreign firms.

China's Law emphasizes the accessibility of data to government authorities. Network operators are required to cooperate with Chinese crime and security investigators by providing complete access to data. Companies have been asked to provide source codes, encryption, or other crucial information for review by the government, increasing the risk that this information is given to local competitors, or kept and used by the government itself. The key aspects of the new cyber security regulations are briefly overviewed below.

1. *Data localization*. The new law stipulates that the personal data of Chinese citizens should be kept within the territory of China. Before data operators can transfer the data outside the country, they must undergo a security assessment and get approval from the National Cyberspace Administration and State Council.

2. *Handling of personal data*. The CL, like the GDPR, states that the collection, usage, and storage of personal and sensitive data can be done only in specified cases. Individuals have the right to access, modify, and delete their personal data if such data is handled in an improper or erroneous manner.
3. *Requirements for network operators*. The definition of a network operator is broadly defined to include most Chinese businesses that operate IT networks. The law obliges network operators to obtain users' consent for data collection and processing and publish privacy notices.
4. *Network security requirements*. Businesses are obliged to employ network security safeguards, such as preparing and implementing contingency plans for mitigating network security incidents, reporting possible security risks, and assisting Chinese authorities in investigating and combating cybercrimes.
5. *Term for security maintenance*. Chinese businesses selling network-related services and products are required to provide maintenance of their products and services for the length of the contract.
6. *Prior certification*. Cyber security-related products and services have to be certified in advance and meet safety inspection requirements. The certification process is conducted by the Chinese government.
7. *Personal liability and identity registration*. Individuals have to provide their personal information when purchasing certain types of products and services online (domain names and social network accounts). This requirement aims to assist the Chinese government in *halting the spread of rumors and filtering fake information in the cyberspace*.
8. *Legal liability*. Entities failing to comply with the law will be "blacklisted" by the Chinese government and face monetary penalties. Serious infringements may result in the suspension of business activities.

On the positive side, the law focuses on protecting personal information and individual privacy by standardizing the collection and usage of personal information. As such, companies will now be required to introduce security measures to protect sensitive data. In some cases, firms will need to undergo a security review before moving data out of China. The law unfortunately does not clearly define "sensitive data." The government will be tempted to broadly construe the term so that it can gain access to greater amounts of personal information.

Investment Law

In the area of investor protections, China has been willing to provide protections to foreign investors through bilateral investment treaties (BITs). Historically, BITs were aimed at protecting investments from developed countries in developing countries. The first BIT was signed in 1959 between Germany and Pakistan. Subsequently, BITs combined substantive investment protection with binding investor-country arbitration at the **International Centre for Settlement of Investment Disputes** (ICSID).

More recent investment agreements with Germany, ASEAN, New Zealand, Chile, and Canada show China is updating its investment protection standards. The Chinese model BIT is closely aligned with the texts developed by the British and Germans. Along with actively pursuing BITs in the 1980s and 1990s, China became a party to the **Multilateral Investment Guarantee Agency Convention (MIGA)** and signed the **ICSID (Investor-Country Arbitration) Convention.**

BITs with developed countries primarily served the purpose to build economic infrastructure through inbound investment, especially to secure acquisition or control of technology and other advanced skills. Conversely, China has entered into BITs with developing countries, especially in Southeast Asia and Africa in order to strengthen diplomatic alliances, and to obtain access to natural resources. This second use of BITs reflects the growth of the Chinese economy and the importance of investor protections to outward investments by the Chinese. The trend in other countries has been to diminish the need for BITs. For example, Brazil refuses to negotiate new BITs, South Africa is attempting to terminate existing BITs, and India has frozen current BIT negotiations pending approval of a new model BIT.[33]

Joint Venturing in China

A joint venture is a business arrangement in which the participants create either a contractual relationship or establish a new business entity. The joint venturers share investment and operation expenses, management responsibilities, and profits and losses. The Chinese government encourages foreign investors to use this form of company in order to obtain advanced technology. In return, foreign investors obtain low labor costs, low production costs, and access to the Chinese market. After a joint venture is registered, the entity is considered a Chinese legal entity and must abide by Chinese law.

However, unlike most countries, this strategy is not simply a matter of two companies negotiating and entering into a joint venture agreement. The joint venture must obtain the approval of various agencies of the Chinese government. The controlling law is the **Foreign Equity Joint Venture Enterprise Law.** A foreign party must obtain the approval of the **Ministry of Commerce** as well as the need to obtain approval of provincial and municipal governments where the joint venture is to be located.

The approval process includes the submission, in the Chinese language, of an application; feasibility study; the joint venture agreement and the articles of association; and a list of the officers of the joint venture. The government agencies must approve or disapprove the joint venture within three months, or they can prolong the process by asking for amendments to the documents. The most common ground for withholding approval is the "unfairness of the joint venture agreement." The Chinese authorities require more Chinese-friendly terms. Upon receiving a **Certificate of Approval**, the joint venture then has one month to register with government authorities and obtain a business license.

Joint ventures often include the licensing or transfer of technology, which must receive separate approval from the government authorities. This review is intrusive in that it may require changes in the licensing agreement to make it more favorable to the licensee. Article 43 states that the agreement must meet the following criteria: royalty fees must be fair and reasonable; there can be no restrictions on the export of goods using the technology; the duration of license is not to exceed ten years; after the expiration of the license, the Chinese parties may continue to use the technology; and any improvements made to the technology shall be shared between the parties. Thus, many of the pro-licensor clauses used in intellectual property licenses would not be enforceable under Chinese law. For excerpts of the Law on Chinese–Foreign Joint Ventures, see Figure 7.9. Figure 7.10 provides "Tips on Managing Chinese Joint Ventures."

Franchise Law of China

In February 2005, the Chinese Ministry of Commerce and the State Council enacted the first comprehensive regulations on franchising. Unfortunately, it failed to clearly define the franchisor's disclosure requirements.[34] The 2007 **Law**

Article 1: China permits foreign companies to join with Chinese companies to establish joint ventures in accordance with the *principle of equality and mutual benefit* and subject to approval by the Chinese government.
Article 2: China shall not *nationalize* or take over joint ventures.
Article 3: The joint venture agreement, contract, and articles of association signed by the parties to the venture must be submitted to the competent Chinese authorities for *examination and approval*.
Article 4: A joint venture shall take the form of a *limited liability company*. The proportion of the investment contributed by the foreign joint venture partner should generally not be less than *25 percent* of the registered capital of a joint venture.
Article 5: The technology and the equipment that serve as the investment of the foreign partner in a joint venture must be *advanced technology*.
Article 6: The chairman of the *Board of Directors* shall be a party from one side of the venture and vice-chairman a party from the other party.
Article 7: Joint ventures shall provide necessary conditions for the activities of the *trade unions* within the enterprises.
Article 8: A foreign partner in a joint venture that reinvests in China its share of the net profit may apply for refund of a part of the *income taxes* already paid.
Article 9: A joint venture shall open a *foreign exchange account* with a bank approved by the state foreign exchange administration.
Article 10: In its purchase of required raw and processed materials, a joint venture may make the purchases from the Chinese market or the international market according to the principle of being fair and rational. A joint venture is encouraged to market its products outside China.
Article 13: If the parties to a joint venture with a prescribed *duration* or contract period agree to extend the period, they must obtain approval from the relevant government authorities.

Figure 7.9 Law on Chinese–Foreign Joint Ventures.

Seeking Alternatives: Because of the risks, joint ventures should not be entered unless necessary. If a partner is not needed, a better alternative is the Wholly Foreign-Owned Enterprise (WFOE).
Long-Term Consequences: Joint venture partners are often potential competitors. A long-term risk that needs to be guarded is the sharing of confidential information with the joint partner. It is also prudent to enter into a noncompetition agreement with the Chinese partner.
Due Diligence: It is important to investigate potential joint venture partners in regard to reputation, bribery, and any history of regulatory noncompliance.
Technology Transfer: As a practical matter, technology should be segmented and distinguished so that the complete core technology is not exposed. If possible, the critical core technology should be embodied incomponents or materials produced elsewhere and supplied to the joint venture by the foreign party. All trademarks including company and brand names, should be registered with Chinese authorities before beginning negotiations with any Chinese companies.
Exit Strategy: Chinese law does not allow a party to a joint venture to unilaterally terminate the agreement. Therefore, the joint venture agreements should provide a list of events, such as failure to meet certain sales levels or management deadlock that would automatically create a right to terminate the joint venture. The agreement should also make it clear that termination of the joint venture also terminates provisions in the technology transfer and licensing contracts.

Figure 7.10 Tips on Managing Chinese Joint Ventures.

on Franchise Regulations, Article 22(8) provides that the franchisor must provide enough information in order for a prospective franchisee to "evaluate" the "operational results or status." The word "evaluation" imposes an "enhanced disclosure duty on franchisors, because franchisors are required not only to disclose the numerical data about the sales of the existing franchisees in China, but also to provide a prediction as to the potential sales of the (proposed) franchise."[35] The State Council also adopted the **Regulations on the Administration of Commercial Franchise**, which complete the process of recognizing franchising as a legal structure and business model in China. The law requires that the franchisor must make specific disclosures to provide franchisees, by providing operational handbooks, with long-term guidance, technical support, training, and other services. It also includes substantial penalty provisions for noncompliance. The new Regulations also provide franchisors greater freedom of contract to insert stronger protective clauses in the franchise agreement. It allows the parties to decide on the length of the franchisee's right of rescission (termination). The new Regulations allow the parties to allocate product liability. Under the previous law, the franchisor and franchisee were *jointly and severally liable*. It also expressly allows a clause that requires the franchisor's consent to the assignment of the franchise and for a change of location. It can now be said that China has a modern franchise law that makes it easier for foreign franchisors to enter the Chinese market.

Administrative Law

Administrative law relates to government regulations and the government's enforcement of those regulations. If a company or person believes it has been improperly fined, denied government permits or approvals, or has been subject to an illegal enforcement action, it may want to contest those decisions.[36] Oftentimes, the basis for the dispute is a government agency's interpretation of a law. In China, the law provides that a party may pursue administrative relief or proceed directly to litigation. If a claimant pursues administrative relief, or what is called *administrative reconsideration*, it may be precluded from pursuing a remedy in the court system.

One problem that Chinese administrative law presents is its obsoleteness. The basic **Administrative Litigation Law (ALL)** was enacted in 1989. It was revised in 2014 in order to provide private parties with greater abilities to challenge official state actions. Unfortunately, numerous shortcomings remain from the 1989 law. One scholar offers this reason: "It shows the lack of consensus among political elites to improve legislation used to pursue a higher level of protection of citizens' rights and supervision of government institutions to ensure their functioning within the framework of legal constraint."[37] In order to contest a government or agency decision in court, a claimant is confronted with a number of problems: (1) difficulty in getting a court to accept the complaint; (2) difficulty in receiving a decision from the court within a reasonable period of time; and (3) difficulty in enforcing the judgments of the court.[38] Because of the lack of statutory amendments, administrative law is mostly found in the judicial interpretations of the Supreme People's Court, such as the **Explanations on Several Issues Concerning the Implementation of Administrative Litigation Law**. The **Administrative Reconsideration Law (ARL)** allows a party to appeal the decision of a government official or government body to a higher level of the administrative agency. In practice, most claimants proceed immediately to the courts. However, there are a number of exceptions to the right to litigate in which a party must first pursue administrative reconsideration before being allowed to file a judicial claim. This includes disputes over the ownership of natural resources, tax disputes, competition (antitrust) actions, and trademark disputes (validity of trademark). Also, administrative reconsideration decisions are final (no right to appeal to a court) when issued by the State Council.

Another obstacle to obtaining a judicial resolution in challenging administrative actions is the overuse of mediation (*tiao je*) or reconciliation (*he jie*). This is an issue that applies to all forms of litigation but is especially problematic in administrative litigation. The Supreme People's Court's **Opinion on the Positive Roles of Litigant Mediation in Constructing Socialist Harmonious Society** encourages mediation throughout the litigation process. The problem is that the courts, especially in administrative litigation, are hesitant to rule against government authorities and use mediation to avoid deciding, and to prolong the litigation process. In this regard, mediation is used as a coercive device (either settle or wait a long time for a decision). Chinese lawyers have created a set of terms that prove the point: *yi ya cu tiao* (mediation by coercion); *yi pan ya tiao* (a veiled threat that the court's decision will be worse than a mediated outcome); and *yi you ya tiao* (delaying of a decision in order to coerce mediation).

In sum, the ALL and ARL have advanced China's evolution into a modern legal system. The image of the government official as being above the law—"officials are dignitaries and citizens are humble"—has been diminished and replaced with the principle that citizens have the right to sue their government.[39] However, obtaining a remedy against the government is difficult because of a lack of judicial independence, especially in administrative law matters where administrative agencies are considered more powerful than the courts.

Rise of Specialized Courts

The Chinese government has recognized the low quality of its lower courts and has responded through the establishment of specialized courts. China's bankruptcy law was enforced by local courts until the development of specialized bankruptcy courts between 2007 and 2017. Even though the 2007 reform aligned Chinese bankruptcy law with those in the U.S. and Europe, timely resolution of state-owned firms in financial distress remains a problem due to the influence of local governments.

Two international commercial courts were established in June 2018, respectively located in Shenzhen and Xi'an. International commercial courts mainly hear first-instance international commercial cases where the amount in controversy exceeds RMB 300 million. The Supreme People's Court (SPC) is also responsible for formulating judicial interpretations. Judicial interpretations are a set of rules formulated to harmonize the courts' understanding of specific legal provisions and to unify trial standards. In practice, they have equal effect to the law. Cases from northern China, certain special types of cases, such as intellectual property, maritime disputes, and foreign-related commercial disputes are handled by the SPC.

There are two IP-related divisions in Beijing: the SPC's "Intellectual Property Division" (Third Civil Division) and the SPC's "Intellectual Property Tribunal" established in 2019. Their names are very similar, but their functions are different. Before 2019, all kinds of intellectual property cases were handled by the Third Civil Division. After 2019, second instance appeals with strong technical features, such as invention, patents, and technical secrets are subject to jurisdiction of the newly established Intellectual Property Tribunal.

Other specialized courts in China mainly include intellectual property courts, Internet courts, financial courts, and maritime courts. These courts include the Intellectual Property Courts in Beijing, Shanghai, and Guangzhou; the Internet Courts located in Beijing, Guangzhou, and Hangzhou; the Financial Court in Shanghai; and the Maritime Courts located in Shanghai, Guangzhou, Tianjin, Dalian, Ningbo, Xiamen, Qingdao, Wuhan, Beihai, Haikou, and Nanjing.

Summary: Law in Books Versus Law in Action

Given the role of the Communist Party as the government behind the government, a divergence remains between the meaning of substantive law and its functional use, as well as uncertainty in its application. The independence and quality of the Chinese courts still remain an issue and until that issue is resolved the legal system will remain less than fully functional.[40] Despite the cultivation of a free market system, communism, as represented by the Communist Party, continues to influence Chinese culture with its emphasis on the common good and the importance of maintaining relationships and obedience to superiors in the governmental and societal hierarchy.

The outsized power of Chinese local governments is a major challenge for the maintenance of the rule of law and certainty in application of the law, as they often interpret the law to advance local needs and protect local corruption at the expense of enforcing national law and regulations. Despite the rhetoric of the rule of law and equality before the law, the reality is that courts are not viewed as superior to state agencies: "In the bureaucratic hierarchy, courts are only parallel to, rather than superior to, other units of the Chinese bureaucracy. When courts seek to enforce judgments, agencies whose actions are required to assist the courts sometimes refuse to cooperate."[41,42] This is due to the fact that local judges are hired and paid by the local government and Communist Party apparatus. The Communist Party as shadow government is discussed in the next section.

Communist Party

Even though foreigners doing business in China obtain approvals and licenses from the government, it is important to realize that the real power in China resides in the **Communist Party** (**Party**). The structure of the Party is a mirror image of the structure of the Chinese government. At the national level, power resides in the NPC and **Central Committee.** The **Standing Committee** is made up of four or five members and is the source of ultimate power; however, its power has been consolidated in the current **President**. At the provincial level there are provincial committees of the Party, and so forth, through the levels of municipal, county, and village governments.

The Party is a political and not a governmental agency. However, the Party controls every facet of government and society. Membership in the Party is needed to advance in government, academia, business, and many other professions. The NPC meets once every five years. The Central Committee organizes an annual plenary session generally consisting of a few thousand delegates chosen by the Committee. See Figure 7.11 on the "Communist Party Structure."

As noted above, the Party is a hierarchical system of concentrated power duplicated at the provincial and local levels of the country. The system extends to the level of local organizations (***danwei***) in the factories, and workers in companies, farms, townships, and villages, as well as school and neighborhood

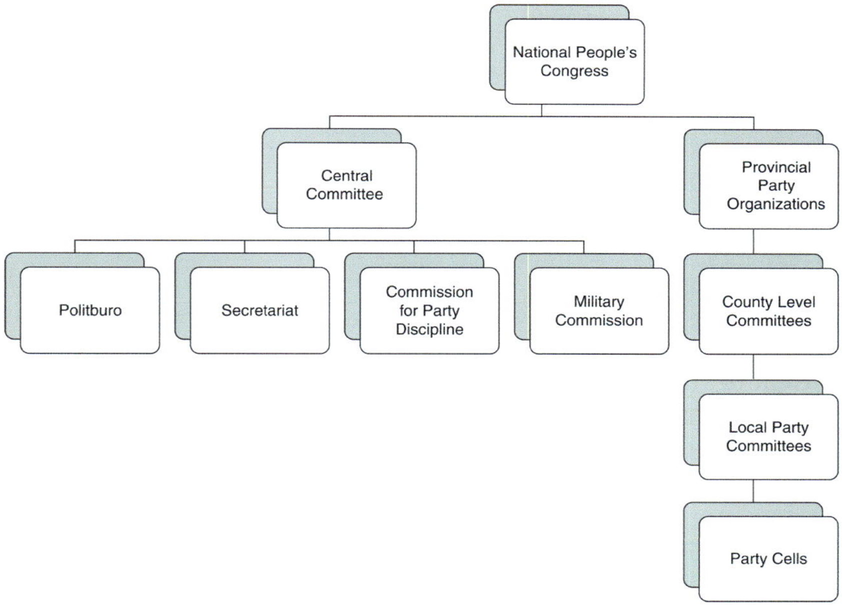

Figure 7.11 Communist Party Structure.

organizations. Any such organization must have at least three members from the Party on their leadership authority. Each of the *danwei* must have a primary Party committee, which then answers to a larger Party committee (*danwei* with more than 100 Party members). The purpose of these committees is to act as a conduit between the people and the Party by promoting Party ideology, recruiting new members to the Party, and to monitor the day-to-day activities of the people. The Party controls the government by creating lists of Party members used to fill government positions. This is known as the **nomenklatura** system in which the Organization Department of the Central Committee of the Communist Party of China acts as a human resource department to fill government positions with Party members.

Hong Kong's Common Law Tradition

The legal tradition in Hong Kong installed during the 99 years of British rule is the common law, as opposed to the civil-customary law system of Mainland China. Hong Kong also has its own legal currency (Hong Kong dollar), customs jurisdiction, and does not require a visa for visits of 90 days or less.

Given its history of treating the rule of law, especially procedural law, as a core principle, administrative litigation is much more robust as compared to the Mainland. Also, due to its common law tradition, administrative litigation comes under the broader common law term of **judicial review**. After Hong Kong's separation from the UK, Article 81 of the Basic Law established a new higher court called the **Court of Final Appeal** (CFA), creating a four-tier court system, with the CFA on top of the hierarchy, followed by the Court of Appeal, the Court of First Instance, and the District Court. It is a hybrid system in that the Court of First Instance and the District Court are both trial courts; however, the Court of First Instance can hear appeals from the District Court. Also, depending on the nature of the case, appeals from the District Court can go directly to the Court of Appeal. It is important to note that since Hong Kong has its own Basic Law (Constitution), the PSC in Beijing has no authority to review the decisions of the Hong Kong CFA.

Under British rule, the courts were open to hear personal claims of individuals against Hong Kong government agencies. These rights were exercised freely and often. Thus, even though the people of Hong Kong were not given political rights (right to vote), they were given personal rights. The tradition of common law judicial review was recognized in Article 35 of the Basic Law: This is a more meaningful right than is found in Mainland China because of Hong Kong's tradition of an independent judiciary.

Losing Independence

However, Mainland China has exerted more and more pressure and control over the Hong Kong government. In 2014, students protested in the streets; these protests became known as the **Occupy Central Movement**. The key issue, among a number of complaints, was the overall tone of a "White Paper" issued by China's State Council essentially redefining the meaning of "one country, two systems." The White Paper emphasized "one country," giving total control over the Hong Kong government to the Mainland government. Specifically, it reneged on a promise to allow open elections for Mayor to all candidates in 2017. "Hongkongers"[43] view the current mayor as a representative of the Communist Party and not representative of the interests of Hong Kong. The White Paper discussed above mentioned for the first time that judges needed to be "patriots" as well as administrators, which threatens the core principle of an independent judiciary in Hong Kong.[44]

What began in early 2019 as peaceful marches against a bill to allow the extradition of defendants to Mainland China exploded by mid-year into a direct challenge to Beijing's grip on Hong Kong that carried into 2020. The spread of a new coronavirus from China has diminished major protests, but activists say dissatisfaction with the government's response to the pandemic will further fuel their movement. The seriousness and violence of the recent protests have resulted in dramatic decreases in tourism and retail sales, as well as capital flight to safer places, such as Singapore. The future of Hong Kong's independence and status as a world financial center is uncertain.

The uniqueness of Hong Kong as a part of China has been based upon its system of a freely elected government, recognition of personal freedoms (that have built up since the withdrawal of UK rule in 1997), and an independent judiciary. This uniqueness has allowed Hong Kong to become a major tourist location and an international financial center. Unfortunately, recent developments have greatly diminished Hong Kong's uniqueness. On June 30, 2020, China imposed a Security Law on Hong Kong in violation of the 1997 Joint Declaration with the UK, which some critics have called "the end of Hong Kong." The new law is broadly worded, stating it is illegal to voice an opinion or take actions that threaten secession (breaking away from the Mainland); subversion (undermining the power or authority of the central government); terrorism (using violence or intimidation against people); and collusion (with foreign or external forces). The law effectively ends the rights to freedom of speech and peaceful assembly (protests). Its other draconian measures include a maximum sentence of life in prison; establishment of a Mainland security office in Hong Kong, government right to wire-tap and put under surveillance anyone they suspect of anti-government activities and the ability to bring prosecutions to the Mainland. The result has been to dampen the protest movement, with many protest organizers fleeing to other countries. Western countries have condemned the security law and Chinese encroachment into Hong Kong, but no meaningful coordinated response has so far been established. Sadly, this development is likely a *fait accompli* (irreversible) since the Chinese government will withstand any economic sanctions in order to maintain its dominance of Hong Kong. The next concern is whether China will aggressively pursue a unification of Taiwan by an armed invasion.

Chapter Summary

European Union

1. The EU is founded on a series of Treaties beginning with the Treaty of Paris in 1953 and the Treaty of Rome that established the European Economic Community (EEC). Other Treaties changed the EEC to a broader European Community (EC). The EC was transformed into the EU with the enactment of the Maastricht Treaty, officially known as the "Treaty on European Union" or TEU. The TEU established the EU as a separate governmental political entity. The 2009 implementation of the Treaty of Lisbon made the EU a fully functioning democratic government.
2. The seven EU institutions are the Council of the EU (Council), the European Council, the European Parliament, the Commission, the European Court of Justice, the European Central Bank, and the Court of Auditors.
3. The four freedoms embedded in EU law are the free movements of persons, goods, services, and capital.
4. EU law prohibits countries from indirect discrimination against imported goods in favor of domestic goods. Disguised or unintentional restrictions on trade are referred to as measures equivalent to a quantitative restriction (MEQR).
5. The two lawmaking bodies are the Council and the European Parliament. Most laws are passed under the "ordinary legislative procedure," which requires a majority vote of the European Parliament and a "qualified majority vote" (QMV), also known as double majority, voting in the Council.

6. EU lawmaking is limited by the principles of subsidiarity and proportionality. The principle of subsidiarity holds that the EU may only act (make laws) where action of individual countries would be insufficient. The principle of proportionality holds that the content and form of EU law shall not exceed what is necessary to achieve the objectives of the Treaties.
7. The two major types of laws enacted by the Council and the European Parliament are regulations and directives. Regulations have a direct effect, meaning that upon enactment they immediately become part of the national laws of the EU Member States. Directives do not have a direct effect, but only become part of national law through a further legislative action at the national level. Because of the need for subsequent legislation, the implementation of the principles and rules of directives may vary across EU countries.
8. The European Court of Justice (ECJ) is the supreme court of the EU that hears claims brought by: (a) EU institutions against a member country for violations of EU law or failure to implement EU law (directive), (b) a member country against the EU for overstepping its powers (competencies) under EU treaties, (c) a member country against another member country for violating EU law (disguised restrictions on imports), (d) individual EU citizens or nationals against a member country for failing to obey EU law or for damages caused by a country's failure to implement EU law, and (e) referrals from national courts requesting an interpretation of EU law.
9. The Charter of Fundamental Rights provides a litany of rights based upon six tenets: dignity, freedom, equality, solidarity, citizens' rights, and justice.
10. The EU General Data Privacy Regulation (GDPR) provides a substantial body of rights to individuals over their personal information or data. The GDPR places substantial obligations on data controllers and processors, inside and outside of the EU, to be GDPR compliant.
11. The EU Unfair Contract Terms Directive and the EU Consumer Rights Act 2015 are cornerstones of EU consumer contract law.

People's Republic of China

1. In China's transformation from a socialist planned economy to a market (capitalist) economy, it passed many Western-style commercial laws including investment, joint venture, property, contract, and intellectual property laws. Most importantly, China recognized private property rights and the freedom to transfer property. It was one of the original signatories to the United Nations Convention on Contracts for the International Sale of Goods (CISG). China's retooling of substantive laws was recognized by its entry into the World Trade Organization (WTO).
2. China's major competitive advantages include the world's largest consumer market; willingness to adopt and constantly modernize its business laws and regulations to attract foreign investment; and cultural norms, such as a strong work ethic, the importance of saving, and the importance of

community (*guanxi*) that includes respect for others and the obligation to take care of the elderly.

3. China's political-governmental system can be described as parallel systems in which the Communist Party acts as a shadow government and is the true holder of power. The Communist Party structure mimics the government structure and the organization of society. The smallest societal organization or "cell," such as local charities, must include members of the Communist Party.
4. Hong Kong demonstrates the diversity of the Chinese legal system with Mainland China's system based on civil and customary law, Hong Kong's system based upon English common law, and Macau's Portuguese civil law. Hong Kong has a long tradition of viewing the courts as having the power of judicial review over government decisions. In comparison, administrative litigation on the Mainland is inefficient as courts are reluctant to overturn decisions of state agencies.
5. A foreign company considering an equity joint venture is restricted by numerous requirements in the Chinese Joint Venture Law. These requirements include the need to obtain an examination and approval of the joint venture agreement by government agencies, according to the *principle of equality and mutual benefit*; organize the joint venture as a Chinese limited liability company; the need to provide advanced technology; and the need to maintain a foreign exchange account.
6. Chinese contract law is a product of legal transplantation and reception of various foreign legal systems. The basic contract law (Chinese Contract Law) is based upon the Convention on Contracts for the International Sale of Goods, UNIDROIT Principles of International Commercial Contracts, German law, and some influences from the common law and the American Uniform Commercial Code.
7. The Chinese administrative law system includes the Administrative Reconsideration Law and the Administrative Litigation Law. The person or company challenging a decision or failure to act of a government agency has the choice of appealing to a higher level of the government (reconsideration) or to directly file a claim in the court system (litigation).

Key Terms: China

Administrative Litigation Law (ALL)
Administrative Reconsideration Law (ARL)
Arbitration Law of the People's Republic of China
Basic Law (Constitution)
Basic Law of the Hong Kong Special Administrative Region
BRIC Countries
Certificate of Approval
Certificate of the Right to Use
China Arbitration Association
China International Economic and Trade Arbitration Commission (CIETAC)
Chinese Contract Law (CCL)
Closer Economic Partnership Arrangement (CEPA)

Communist Party
Company Law of the People's Republic of China
Concrete Administrative Action
Confucius; Confucianism
Corruption Perception Index
Court of Final Appeal (CFA)
Culpa in Contrahendo
Danwei
Emergency Arbitrators
General Rules of the Civil Law of the People's Republic of China
Guanxi
Guiding Cases
Hybrid Arbitration Clause
ICSID (Investor-Country Arbitration) Convention
International Centre for Settlement of Investment Disputes (ICSID)
Interpretative Decisions
Law on Franchise Regulations
Law on the Organization of People's Courts
Lawyers Law
Ministry of Foreign Trade and Economic Cooperation (MOFTEC)
Multilateral Investment Guarantee Agency Convention (MIGA)
National People's Congress
Nomenklatura System
Occupy Central Movement
One Country, Two Systems
Opinion on Positive Roles of Litigant Mediation
Real Property Registry
Regulations on the Administration of Commercial Franchise
Right to Use Shadow Banking
Sino-Foreign Equity Joint Venture Enterprise Law (EJV)
Special Administrative Region (SAR)
Standing Committee
State Council
State-Owned Enterprise (SOE)
Supreme People's Court
Transplantation

Chapter Problems

1. Match the terms on the left with the ones on the right (answer key is below).

i. Direct Effect	a. Principle of Legitimate Expectation
ii. Equal Treatment Directive	b. MEQRs
iii. Maastricht Treaty	c. European Convention on Human Rights
iv. Indirect Discrimination	d. Principle of Mutual Recognition
v. Competition Law	e. Department of EU Commission
vi. CE Mark	f. Ordinary Legislative Procedure
vii. EU Commission	g. Treaty on European Union (TEU)
viii. Double Majority Voting	h. EU is Government of Limited Powers
ix. Directorate	i. Regulation
x. Principle of Conferral	j. Issues Binding "Decisions"
xi. Council of Europe	k. Quality Standard
xii. No Retroactive Laws	l. Block Exemptions

2. Why would EU lawmakers choose the directive form of law over the regulation form of law? What difference does it make to EU nationals and companies?
3. The Schengen Agreement was meant to erase the national borders between countries to allow the unrestricted movement of persons. Immigration from crises in Africa, Syria, and internal migration from poorer to richer countries

of the EU has led some countries to question the benefits of being a Schengen country. How can the EU balance the fundamental policy of free movement of persons with the concerns of EU Member States in controlling their borders?

4. Bulgaria is one of the poorer countries within the EU and does not seem to have benefited as much as other countries from its integration into the EU. Poland has developed a strong market economy and has been recognized as a "developed country." Compare the experiences of Poland and Bulgaria in joining the EU. What have been the problems in Bulgaria that have prevented it from substantially improving its standard of living?
5. Corruption has been a major problem in some of the newer members of the EU (Bulgaria) and in Eastern Europe (Serbia, Ukraine). What is the relationship between corruption and economic prosperity? Why have some EU countries been able to control corruption and others have failed? What has the EU done to assist anticorruption efforts in Bulgaria?
6. What is the difference between international business transactions (exporting or importing of goods, services, or intellectual property) and "doing business" in a country? What are the benefits of establishing a business in China? What are the risks of doing business in China? How can a business minimize the risks of doing business in China?
7. What are the differences between the legal systems of Mainland China and Hong Kong? What is the role of law in society? What are the differences between the "rule of law" in Hong Kong as compared to Mainland China?
8. What are the benefits of establishing a business in Hong Kong and not in Mainland China? What is the strategic value of placing your business in Hong Kong?
9. *Ethics Question*: How should a company respond to China's discrimination of certain minority groups and human rights violations? How does your company deal with the prevalence of corruption in government agencies? See Chapter 2.
10. Does China have adequate laws for protecting intellectual property rights? Why is the counterfeiting and piracy of goods protected by patent and trademark law so common in China? What can your company do to protect its rights? What provisions should be incorporated into your licensing contracts?

[Answers to Problem 1: i(i); ii(d); iii(g); iv(b); v(l); vi(k); vii(j); viii(f); ix(e); x(h); xi(c); xii(a).]

Internet Exercises

1. Review the EU Charter of Fundamental Rights (EUCFR) (available at http://www.europarl.europa.eu/charter/pdf/text_en.pdf). What human rights does the EUCFR recognize that are not found in other human rights documents, such as United Nations Universal Declaration of Human Rights (https://www.un.org/en/universal-declaration-human-rights)?

2. Review the Europa website (official website of the EU) at http://europa.eu. Pretend you are deciding on whether to establish an office in Italy, Hungary, or the Czech Republic. Go to the website, click on "countries" under the category "How the EU Works," and do some preliminary research. What are some of the benefits and risks of doing business in those three countries? Next, review and compare the information provided in the U.S. Commercial Country Guides (www.export.gov) for those three countries at www.export.gov/Italy (click on "Country Commercial Guide"); http://www.export.gov/hungary; (click "Doing Business in Hungary"); and http://www.export.gov/czechrepublic (click on "Market Research on Czech Republic") and then click under "Country Commercial Guide."
3. Use the website http://www.lawinfochina.com to research one of China's provinces for the purpose of doing business. Select a rural province and compare its environment and laws for doing business with doing business in Beijing or Shanghai.
4. Go to the Transparency International website at www.transparency.org. Research the rates of corruption and the criteria used for the rankings and compare the BRIC countries (Brazil, Russia, India, and China) with Japan, the Republic of Korea (South Korea), Taiwan, Singapore, and Malaysia.

Other Internet Sources

Delegation of the EU to the U.S.: http://www.euintheus.org.
European Union News: http://wn.com/european_union.
European Central Bank: www.ecb.europa.eu.
European Central Bank, Ecosystem: http://www.ecb.europa.eu/euro/html/index. en.html.
Go to export.gov/china for current articles on China, along with trade and industry news.
Chinese Government site entitled "Invest in China": http://www.fdi.gov.cn/pub/FDI_EN/default.htm (click on "English").
American Chamber of Commerce in China: http://www.amchamchina.org.
Exporting to China: http://www.e-to-china.com.

Notes

1 ECLI:EU:C:2007:261.
2 ECLI:EU:T:2006:270.
3 Austria, Belgium, Bulgaria, Croatia, Cyprus, the Czech Republic, Denmark, Estonia, Finland, France, Germany, Greece, Hungary, Ireland, Italy, Latvia, Lithuania, Luxembourg, Malta, the Netherlands, Poland, Portugal, Romania, Slovakia, Slovenia, Spain, Sweden.
4 TEU, Article 25.
5 TEU, Articles 28 and 30.
6 ECLI:EU:C:1979:42.

7 Bruce Carolan, *EU Law for Students in Ireland* (Gill & Macmillan Ltd 2009) 128–29.
8 ECLI:EU:C:1990:184.
9 ECLI:EU:C:1984:256.
10 ECLI:EU:C:1982:261.
11 ECLI:EU:C:1982:183.
12 ECLI:EU:C:1990:426.
13 Directive 2006/123 effective December 28, 2009.
14 Carolan, *EU Law for Students in Ireland* (much of the material in this section was influenced by Professor Carolan's excellent analysis of EU law).
15 Ibid. at 80–82.
16 Note this case occurred prior to the removal of all tariffs between countries of the EU.
17 Carolan, *EU Law for Students in Ireland* 84 (2009).
18 Countries that retain their own national currencies are Bulgaria (lev or BGN), Croatia (kuna or HRK), the Czech Republic (koruna or CZK), Denmark (krone or DKK), Hungary (forint or HUF), Poland (złoty or PLN), Romania (leu or RON), and Sweden (krona or SEK).
19 See https://gdpr-info.eu.
20 Controller means the natural or legal person, public authority, agency, or other body which, alone or jointly with others, determines the purposes and means of the processing of personal data.
21 Processor means a natural or legal person, public authority, agency, or other body which processes personal data on behalf of the controller.
22 It should be noted that the UK and Poland are not formally bound by the Charter even after it became EU law.
23 The following rates do not account for the severe effects on the global economy of the coronavirus.
24 This projection does not account for the drastic drop in oil prices in 2020, reaching as low as $3 per barrel.
25 See http://www.heritage.org/index/country/china.
26 Lawrence J. Trautman, "An American Entrepreneur in China: Potholes and Roadblocks on the Silk Road to Prosperity," 12 *Wake Forest Journal of Business & Intellectual Property Law* 425, 431–433 (2012).
27 Larry A. DiMatteo, "'Rule of Law' in China: The Confrontation of Formal Law and Cultural Norms," 51 *Cornell International Law Journal* 391 (2018).
28 See Steven M. Dickinson, "Introduction to the New Company Law of the People's Republic of China," 16 *Pacific Rim Law & Policy Journal Association* 1 (2007).
29 Patricia Pattison and Daniel Herron, "The Mountains Are High and the Emperor Is Far Away: Sanctity of Contract Law in China," 40 *American Business Law Journal* 459, 488 (2003).
30 Marina Timoteo, "Vague Notions in Chinese Contract Law: The Case of Heli," 18 *European Review of Private Law* 939, 942 (2010).
31 CCL Art. 42; Interpretation of the Supreme People's Court on Issues Concerning the Application of Law in the Trial of Cases of Disputes over Sales and Purchase Contracts (Mar. 31, 2012).
32 Taken from Robert Bird, "Defending Intellectual Property Rights in the BRIC Economies," 42 *American Business Law Journal* 317, 355–357 (2006).

33 Source: UNCTAD, World Investment Report 2015 at http://unctad.org.en/Pages/ DIAE/World%20Investment%20Report/Annex-Tables.aspx and see also Giuseppe Matteo Vaccaro-Incisa, "The Evolution of China's Policy and Treaty Practice in International Investment Law," 4 *Official Law Journal Bocconi School of Law* 89 (2014). Also available at http://papers.ssrn.com/sol3/papers.cfm?abstract_id=2635199.

34 The information for this section was taken from Michele Lee, "Franchising in China: Legal Challenges when First Entering the Chinese Market," 19 *American University International Law Review* 949 (2004).

35 Ibid.

36 Concrete administrative actions, subject to challenge, include: the assessment of administrative penalties, fines, revocation of business licenses or permits; orders suspending business operations; seizure or freezing of property; infringement on the management of a business; refusal to reply to an application or request for a permit or license; and infringement on property rights.

37 Ibid. at 18.

38 Yuwen Li and Yun Ma, "The Hurdle Is High: The Administrative Litigation System in the People's Republic of China" in *Administrative Litigation Systems in Greater China and Europe* (ed. Yuwen Li, Ashgate, 2014), 15.

39 Ibid. at 40.

40 Stanley Lubman, "Looking for Law in China," 20 *Columbia Journal of Asian Law* 1, 29 (2006).

41 Ibid. at 29.

42 See https://www.transparency.org/cpi2019.

43 This term was recognized in the 2014 edition of the *Oxford English Dictionary*.

44 Carol Jones, *Lost in China? Law, Culture, and Identity in Post-1997 Hong Kong* (Cambridge University Press, 2015) 8.

Chapter 8

Comparative Legal Systems

How people view the role of law in society is shaped by the society's cultural and legal traditions. Within a given legal tradition, rules of law and their applications by courts are understandable and coherent. However, in the area of international business transactions, there is often a "clash of traditions" that may lead to misunderstandings and disputes. Furthermore, even in cases where a foreign party is correct on the legal issues and this correctness is confirmed by a foreign court, the remedies given (such as specific performance, injunction, and damages) may be far below the level given in the foreign party's own legal system. Thus, an astute businessperson and international transactional lawyer should be aware of the differences in legal traditions and legal systems where they plan on doing business.

The uncertainty of applicable law in international business transactions is resolved by **private international law** or **conflict of laws**; the rules courts use to determine the applicable law to related disputes. Conflict of law rules are complex and can result in unexpected results. The application of foreign law and resolving disputes in foreign courts are minimized through the use of **choice of law** and **forum selection clauses**. The problem with such clauses is that they are not foolproof, since a foreign court may simply disregard their application on public policy grounds (forum court finds a foreign legal rule to be against the public policy of the court's national law). The safest way to avoid the application of a foreign law is through an **arbitration clause**. But, even in cases of arbitration, foreign legal traditions and influences play a role since the arbitrators are products of one or more legal traditions and foreign legal systems. In addition, arbitrators often do not feel constrained by the need to apply a specific national law. Unlike courts, arbitration tribunals are willing to look at a variety of sources (different national laws, international soft laws, *lex mercatoria*) in rendering fair and equitable awards.[1]

DOI: 10.4324/9781003469230-10

Knowledge of the legal system of the foreign party will allow for the negotiations of contract terms that will be enforceable in the foreign court system. Also, culture plays a major role in how contracts are negotiated. Negotiation styles between businesspersons from Western and Eastern cultures often lead to misunderstandings. The Western businessperson is anxious to negotiate in earnest (hard bargaining) in the hope of concluding a contract as expeditiously as possible. The Eastern businessperson, especially in Japan and China, will take affront to this "rush to contract" by using a more prolonged "courtship" in order to first build a relationship and trust between the parties. The businessperson from a common law (English-speaking) legal system should be aware that the civil law legal system recognizes pre-contractual liability for negotiating in bad faith. There is no such type of liability in the common law.

There can also be differences in style between parties of the same legal tradition. For example, Americans generally prefer long, detailed contracts that painstakingly describe contractual rights and duties. German businesspersons, much like the Japanese, prefer shorter contracts limiting the detailed provisions to technical aspects of the product or service being sold. In the case of the Japanese and German businesspersons, the rationale for entering shorter, less detailed contracts comes from different aspects of their legal and cultural traditions.

The Japanese and Chinese cultures have shaped their view of the role of law in society. The importance of law and contracts is somewhat diminished by customary law, which includes deference to status, relationships, and communal harmony. In the German legal tradition, the principle of good faith plays a dominant role in German contract law. No matter how detailed a contract, the court views it through the prism of good faith. Through this perspective the strict enforcement of contractual rights may be deemed as an act of bad faith. In comparison, the common law strictly enforces contracts under the principle of freedom of contract.

The first part of this chapter will provide general background on the different terms used in describing legal systems and the comparative approach to understanding law. The second part will briefly review some of the main legal traditions found in the world, including common, civil, Asian, and Islamic legal systems, as well as the phenomenon of mixed legal systems. The two most dominant legal traditions—**civil law** and **common law traditions**—will be a major focus of the review. In studying the Asian legal tradition, the chapter will focus on the Chinese and Japanese legal traditions. It only briefly discusses the **Hindu legal tradition** found in India. The reason is that India, over the past 100 years or so, adopted the common law tradition due to it being colonized by the English and its continued membership in the **British Commonwealth of Nations**. The other tradition not covered is the Jewish or **Talmudic legal tradition**. Again, this is due to the fact that Israeli secular law is primarily of the civil law tradition with influences from the common law. The Hindu and Talmudic traditions remain important because they continue to influence the common and civil law. **Mixed jurisdictions** include a handful of countries or entities that combine more than one legal tradition. This group includes Louisiana, Quebec, Scotland, and South Africa, which are blends of the civil and common law traditions. The mixed jurisdictions have been heavily studied because they allow for a unique understanding of comparative law.

The third part examines the problems relating to the **transformation of law** in countries of the former Soviet Union and in China's transition from a socialist planned economy to a market economy. The final part of the chapter will examine the emergence of transnational private law (contract, sales, and property laws) that transcends legal traditions and national laws. At the same time, it will discuss the convergence of legal traditions instigated by the free trade era and globalization.

Legal Traditions and Legal Systems

A **legal system** is the body of rules that regulates a given country. A **legal family**, such as the Franco or Napoleonic and Germanic versions of the civil law, is a group of national legal systems that are part of the same legal tradition. A legal tradition is a product of the historical evolution of ways of looking at law and its role in society. Each legal tradition has distinctive characteristics on how law is formulated, applied, and interpreted.

National legal systems are grouped into or aligned with recognized legal traditions and legal families. However, the fact that a country's legal system is a part of a given legal tradition doesn't mean that countries within a given legal tradition have identical laws. Much of the difference between legal traditions is related to methods of legal thinking and judicial reasoning. See Image 8.3 for a "Map of the Legal Systems of the World."

Some of the differences between national legal systems are obvious, and others are subtler. For example, the civil law tradition, which evolved out of **Roman law**, is divided into two families of law—the **Franco-Roman** and the **Germanic legal families**. Image 8.4 shows the former Roman Empire as it split between the Western and Eastern halves. After the barbarian invasions destroyed the Western Empire with the fall of Rome in 476, the Eastern Empire, known as Byzantium, continued to flourish. Its capital city was Constantinople (modern-day Istanbul), and the Empire continued in existence in some form until 1453. Byzantium's importance to law is its production of the **Justinian Code** or ***Corpus Juris Civilis*** ("Body of Civil Law") in 529–534 CE (see Images 8.1 and 8.2). The *Corpus Juris Civilis* organized Roman law into a coherent document. It was later introduced in Western Europe and became the foundation for modern-day civil law. The common law evolved in England and is the law of the British Commonwealth countries and the U.S.[2] Despite the overwhelming similarity in legal concepts and principles in the common law countries, they have evolved differently in important ways since the various countries gained their independence.

> *Corpus Juris Civilis*: It consists of the *Code* (*Codex*), which is a compilation, by selection and extraction, of imperial enactments; the *Digest* or *Pandects*, which is an encyclopedia composed of mostly brief extracts from the writings of Roman jurists; and the *Institutes*, which acts as a student textbook.

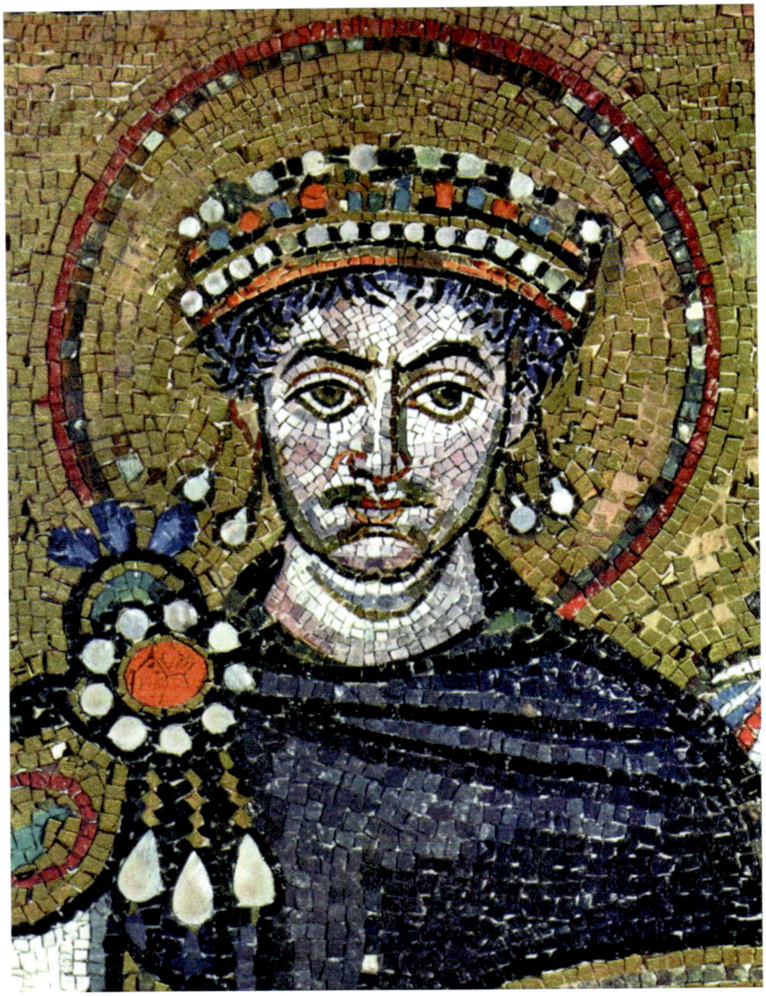

Image 8.1 Portrait of Justinian I (482–565 CE).

Comparative Contract Law

Comparative contract law research has been undertaken for a number of reasons. First, it has been used as a teaching device to educate students on different legal systems—typically focusing on the differences between the civil and common law systems. A deep literature can be found in the comparative analysis of civil law systems, especially between the Germanic and Franco legal traditions.[3] Second, comparative contract law has been used as a source in the drafting of international law instruments. The most important example of this is the drafting of the United Nations **Convention on Contracts for the International Sale of Goods (CISG)**. The CISG drew heavily from common and civil law systems. Interestingly, the CISG has not only provided a degree of supranational harmonization, but it has been used as a comparative law instrument in the reformation

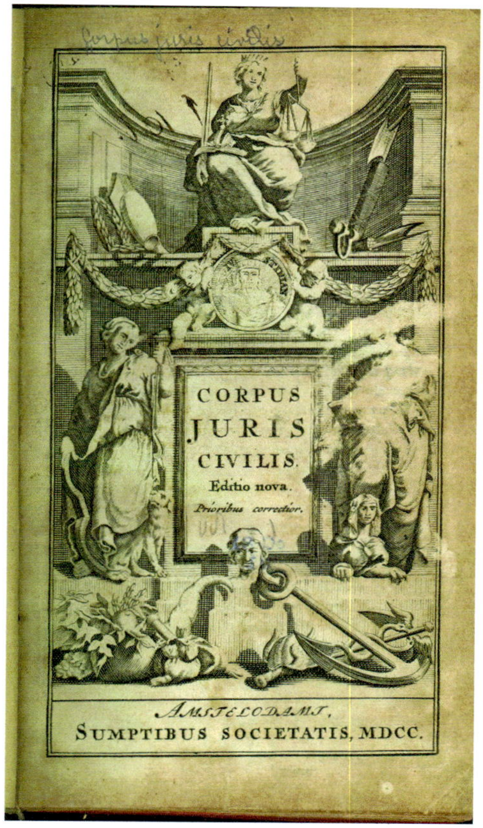

Image 8.2 *Corpus Juris Civilis.*

or modernization of national laws. The CISG has influenced the modernization of contract and sales law in China, Germany, the Netherlands, and to a lesser extent in the revisions of the French, Japanese, and Spanish Civil Codes.

Third, foreign laws that are considered more advanced or have developed a new body of rules are often borrowed from other countries. These borrowings vary from various degrees of influences to **legal transplantations**—the taking of legal rules and codes from one legal system and transplanting them into another national legal system.[4] One interesting example is the country of Vietnam, which has been influenced by a variety of legal systems: "The country has absorbed an abundance of imported legal traditions. In successive historical periods—Chinese, French colonial, socialist, and Western commercial—legal ideas have created a layered legal architecture, the new overlaying the old."[5] The most recent examples can be seen in the transplantation or reception of Western commercial laws by former Soviet-bloc countries and China as they transitioned from planned socialist to market economies.

The virtue of comparative law is that it can be used as a method to better understand the evolution of law. Comparative law is also a powerful tool for reforming law as it provides options used in other systems. Alan Watson

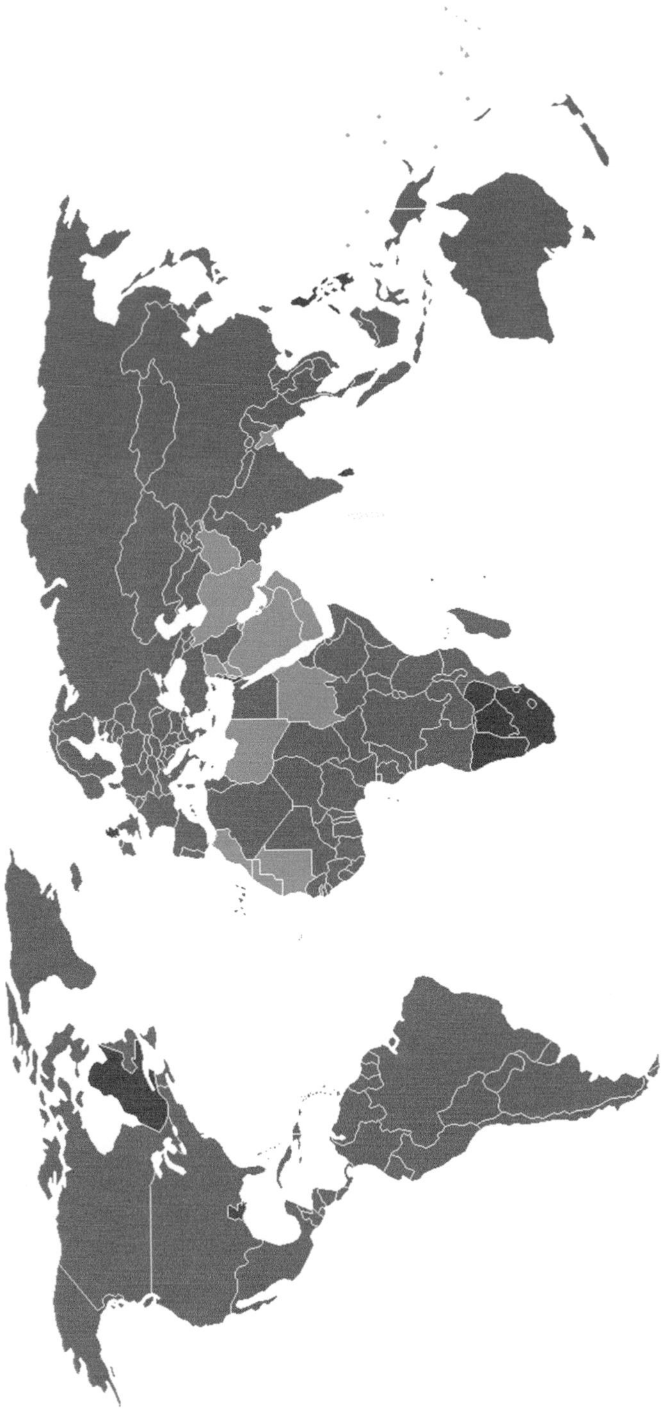

Image 8.3 Map of the Legal Systems of the World.

Darkest Gray: Mixed Jurisdictions (civil-common law); Dark Gray: Civil Law; Medium Gray: Common Law; Light Gray: Islamic Law.

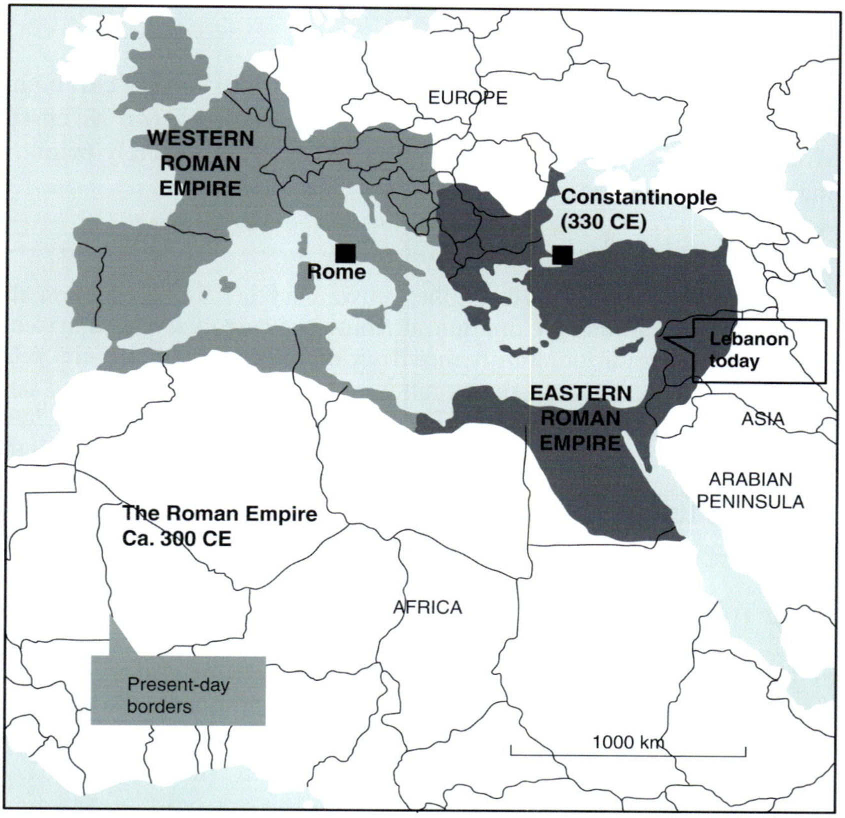

Image 8.4 Western and Eastern Roman Empire.
(Division Roman after the Death of Theodosius I in 395 CE.)

notes that legal transplantations are subject to interpretation by the courts of the receiving country. This disconnection between text and context means the rules "may equally operate to different effect in the two societies, even though they are expressed in apparently similar terms."[6] This is especially the case when introducing Western, highly formalized law into a country with non-Western cultural and legal traditions. In China's case, cultural tradition is heavily based upon the social and status-based influences of **Confucianism**[7] in which formalized private law has historically played a far lesser role and where cultural norms play a greater role in business relationships, and resort to the courts as a means of dispute resolution is disfavored.

There are two traditional approaches used in comparative law studies—the **common core** and the **better rules** approaches. The first approach, championed by Continental European Scholars, such as Rodolfo Sacco in Italy and Rudolf Schlesinger at Cornell University in the 1950s and 1960s, analyzed the commonalities among different legal systems. The second approach analyzes the differences among legal systems and assesses which of their different rules are the "better" ones. The aim of comparative law research is to identify better solutions in foreign legal systems and then to recommend their incorporation into domestic law.

Major Legal Traditions

It is important to note that the role of law and courts in society can be heavily influenced by broader historical and societal practices, known as **customary law**. Mongolia is one of the few remaining legal systems that rely primarily on customary law.

Customary Law: As the term implies, customary law is based upon the customs of a community. Common attributes of customary legal systems include an oral tradition, an organized set of rules regulating social relations, and that members of the community approve of the rules and customs. Customary law is the basis of or has influenced the present-day laws in approximately 40 countries, mostly in Africa, but some in the Pacific Islands, Europe, and the Near East. Customary law is also referred to as "indigenous law" or "folk law."

Civil Law Tradition

The civil law tradition emanated out of continental Europe and spread throughout the world during the era of empire and colonialism involving France, Netherlands, Portugal, Spain, and Germany. It is the legal tradition found throughout Europe (except for the UK and Ireland), most of Africa, South America, and Asia. See Figure 8.1 on the "Evolution of Civil Law Systems" and Figure 8.2 on "Civil and Common Law Concepts and Milestones."

The civil law is a code-based legal system, while the common law is based upon judge-made or case law, especially in the areas of private law—contracts, property, and torts. The civil law traces its origins to Roman law. The modern continental European legal systems are far more advanced and comprehensive than the Roman legal system, but Roman law is still taught in many European law schools. However, Roman law was not directly adopted into the legal systems of Europe. After the collapse of the Roman Empire in the eastern part of Europe, Roman law was no longer used except in a few parts of Italy. Instead,

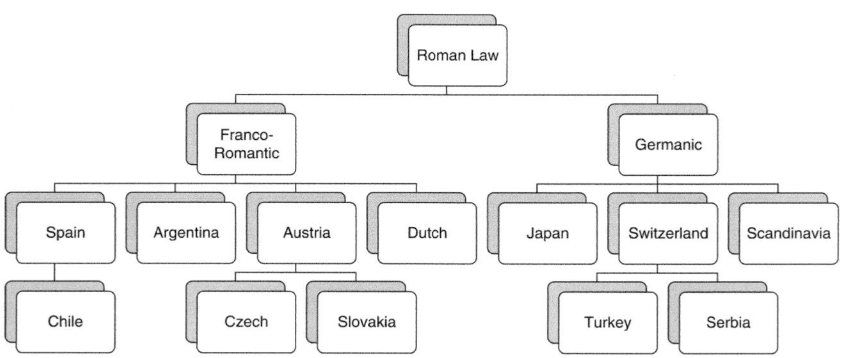

Figure 8.1 Evolution of Civil Law Systems.

post-Roman law was based upon local customary, folk, or tribal law. These "native" laws, such as the law of Germanic tribes, were mainly unwritten. It also served to support the feudal system of land ownership, which bound most of the people (serfs) to the land.

Roman law was "rediscovered" in the eleventh century.[8] The rediscovery of Roman law was at least partially a reaction to the expansion of Arabic law throughout much of the Mediterranean Sea. Part of the legal void was filled by the expansion of Catholicism and the use of canon or church law. Canon law did not replace Roman law but worked alongside of it to replace local, customary law.

The creation of the nation-state and the separation of church and state required a grander and more rational system of law. Inspired by nationalism and using Roman law as a guiding force, French law emerged in the sixteenth century, culminating later in the codification of a Civil Code under Napoléon in 1804. It was the "world's first national, systematic and rational codification of law."[9] About a century later a more advanced code developed in Germany with the enactment of the German Civil Code (**Bürgerliches Gesetzbuch**) of 1900. The German Civil Code was seen as a highly rational law that continued in service until its replacement by a revised code in 2002.

The three most important features of the civil law system that distinguishes it from the common law include: (1) the dominant source of law are codes, usually consisting of a grand Civil Code, along with more specific codes, such as commercial law codes; (2) judge-controlled investigative form of procedure; (3) rejection of judicial cases or court decisions as a form of lawmaking; and (4) the importance of legal academics to the lawmaking process in the enactment of new statutes or in the interpretation of statutes. Under the civil law tradition judges are empowered to establish or find the facts. This approach, known as the inquisitorial or investigative style of civil or criminal procedure, places the judge as an active investigator in uncovering the facts of a dispute or prosecution. In contrast, in the common law, the judge is detached from the fact-finding process, leaving to lawyers for each side of the case to present the facts, often through witness testimony. This system is referred to as the adversarial system of civil or criminal procedure.

The **Napoleonic Code** or ***Code Napoléon***, and officially the *Code civil des Français*, was established under Napoleon I (Napoléon Bonaparte) in 1804. The code forbade privileges based on birth, allowed freedom of religion, and specified that government appointments be based upon merit. The categories of the Napoleonic Code were not drawn from earlier French laws, but instead from Justinian's sixth-century codification of Roman law, the *Corpus Juris Civilis*, and, within it, the *Institutes*, which divides the law into persons, things, and actions; likewise, the Napoleonic Code is divided into the laws of persons, property, and acquisition of property (contracts).

The French Civil Code has influenced the development of the laws of Argentina, Austria, Belgium, Bolivia, Chile, Colombia, Costa Rica, Croatia, the Czech Republic, Democratic Republic of the Congo, Dominican Republic, Ecuador, Haiti, Lithuania, the Netherlands, Slovakia, Spain, and Vietnam.

The German Civil Code has influenced the development of the laws of Denmark, Estonia, Finland, Greece, Japan, Mongolia, Norway, Serbia, Slovenia, Sweden, Switzerland, Taiwan, and Turkey. The Scandinavian countries are a unique civil law system with German and purely Scandinavian influences and are sometimes categorized as the Scandinavian legal system. German law has also had a strong influence on the development of modern Chinese law, as well as traditional customary law and Russian law. Other mixed but primarily civil law systems include Portuguese civil law, which was influenced by the Napoleonic Code and the German Civil Code. Macau, a special administrative region of China, is based on the Portuguese Civil Code. There are also a number of unusual transplantations of foreign laws. For example, Romanian law is based upon the Civil Code of Quebec. The law of Turkey is based upon Swiss law. Before discussing the common law tradition, Figure 8.2 provides explanations of key civil and common law concepts and historical milestones.

Blackstone Commentaries—Sir William Blackstone wrote the *Commentaries on the Laws of England*, four volumes entitled Rights of Persons, Rights of Things, Private Wrongs, and Public Wrongs. It was a very influential treatise, published in 1765 1770, that impacted the development of English and American law.

Bracton Commentaries Henry de Bracton (1210 1260) wrote *On the Laws and Customs of England*, setting out coherently the law of the royal courts through his use of categories drawn from Roman law.

Canon Law the body of laws that govern the Catholic Church and its members, deriving from the decrees and rules (canons) made by the pope and ecclesiastical councils.

Civil Law the system of law that emerged in continental Europe beginning in the Middle Ages and is based on codified law drawn from national legislation and custom, as well as ancient Roman law.

Code the collection of laws of a country or laws related to a particular subject.

Codification the process of compiling and systematizing laws into a code.

Common Law the system of law that emerged in England beginning in the Middle Ages and is based on case law and precedent rather than codified law.

Corpus Juris Civilis meaning bod y of civil laws, the name given to the compilation of Roman law ordered by the Byzantine emperor Justinian I in 529 CE.

Digest or Pandects part of the *Corpus Juris Civilis* consisting of compendium or digest of juristic writings on Roman law totaling 50 books.

English Law traces back to the year 1189, which had no comprehensive codification of the law and has developed mainly through judicial precedents. It is the basis of the law of the 53 countries of the Commonwealth of Nations (including Australia, Bangladesh, Canada, India, Malaysia, Pakistan, Singapore, Tanzania, and Uganda) and the United States. In modern times, it has been grouped with American law and referred to as Anglo-American law.

Equity in English common law tradition, a body of legal principles that emerged to supplement the common law when the strict rules of its application would limit or prevent a just outcome.

French Law the French Civil Code or *Code Napoléon*, based on principles of Roman law and customary law, was adopted in 1804. It served as a model law for Brazil, Egypt, Lebanon, Louisiana (U.S.), Quebec (Canada), Romania, and Spain. The Civil Code was revised in 2016.

German Law modern German law began with the work of legal scholars known as the Pandectists who revived the formalities of Roman law as in the *Corpus Juris Civilis*; with the unification of Germany in 1871, a major process of legal standardization ensued, beginning with criminal law and procedural law and culminating in the Bürgerliches Gesetzbuch (Book of Civil Law or

Figure 8.2 Comparative Law: Civil and Common Law Concepts and Milestones.

BGB), which was adopted in 1900 and revised in 2002. The BGB served as a model law for the countries of Brazil (also influenced by French law), China, Estonia, Greece, Italy (also influenced by French law), Japan, Latvia, the Netherlands, Portugal (also influenced by French law), South Korea, Thailand, Switzerland, and Ukraine.

Institutes of Justinian part of *Corpus Juris Civilis* intended to be used in the training of lawyers (textbook).

Justinian Code part of the *Corpus Juris Civilis* that codifies Roman law (written early in the sixth century CE).

Precedent a judicial decision in a court case that may serve as an authoritative example in future similar cases.

Writ a formal written order from a judicial or administrative authority that directs a form of legal action. Originally, writs were royal orders from the court of the English king.

Yearbooks collections of common law court cases and judicial opinions organized by year beginning in the mid-thirteenth century to 1535, when officially printed and bound editions called *Reports* began to be published.

Figure 8.2 (Continued)

Common Law Tradition

The common law countries are the English-speaking countries of the British Empire and subsequently were part of the British Commonwealth of Nations. The U.S. was an exception, having separated from England by way of a revolution in 1783. Upon its independence, the U.S. adopted the English common law as the law of the new American states. The American Revolution separated the U.S. from England much earlier than the other common law countries, and, therefore, U.S. common law has diverged from English law in important ways. Thus, the two most influential common law systems are the English and American, which are popularly referred to as **Anglo-American law**. The other common law countries include Australia, Bahamas, Bangladesh, Canada (except for the Province of Quebec), Cyprus, Hong Kong, India, Ireland, Israel (civil law and Halakha influences), Jamaica, Malaysia, Myanmar, New Zealand, Nigeria, Pakistan (with Islamic law influences), Singapore (with Islamic or *Shari'a* law), and Uganda. See Table 8.1 for a "Comparison of Civil and Common Law Systems."

It is interesting to note that the Roman Empire controlled most of England for four centuries ending in 410 CE. However, Roman law had no lasting effect on the development of law directly related to the Roman conquest. After the collapse of the Roman Empire, there was no uniform system of law; instead, law was found in customary law and practices mostly at the local level. The common law tradition evolved in England after the Norman Conquest of 1066

Table 8.1 Comparison of Civil and Common Law Systems.

Characteristics	*Civil Law*	*Common Law*
Other Names	Continental, Romano-Germanic	English, Anglo-American, judge-made
Legal System	Originated in Europe; its core principles are found in statutory code, which is the main source of law	Originated in England; its core principles are found in case law or judge-made law
Sources of Law	Codes and statutes	Judge-made; legislation (statutes)
Role of Judges	Acts as an investigator whose decisions only affect the parties to the case	Makes ruling; decisions set precedents that must be followed by lower courts in future cases (stare decisis)
Qualifications of Judges	Career Judges (trained in law school to be judges)	Lawyers (appointed or elected)
Countries	Continental European countries, most African and South American countries, as well as Russia, China, and Japan	Former members of the British Commonwealth (English-speaking countries), such as Canada, India, and Australia, and the U.S.
Role of Legal Scholarship	Secondary Source of Law	Major Source of Law in some countries, such as Germany
Legal Reasoning	Inductive (from facts)	Deductive (from principles of law)
Role of Juries	Only in criminal cases	Only in criminal cases; except for U.S. (Constitution provides right to civil jury)
Role of Lawyers	Inquisitional System (judge asks questions)	Adversarial (lawyers ask questions)
Judicial Review of Statutes	No	Yes

by the French. William the Conqueror became king after winning the Battle of Hastings in 1066.

See Image 8.5 for a sketch of the "Battle of Hastings." William the Conqueror centralized the political system, which allowed for the development of a court system and a "national" law, which was spoken in Anglo-Norman French.[10] The Norman Conquest laid the groundwork for the common law in the early twelfth century.

Landmark events in the development of English law include: (1) the **Doomsday Book** (1086), which catalogued land ownership in England, allowing the king to collect taxes more effectively; (2) the **Magna Carta** (1215), signed by King John, that recognized limitations on the king's power; and (3) the **Statute of**

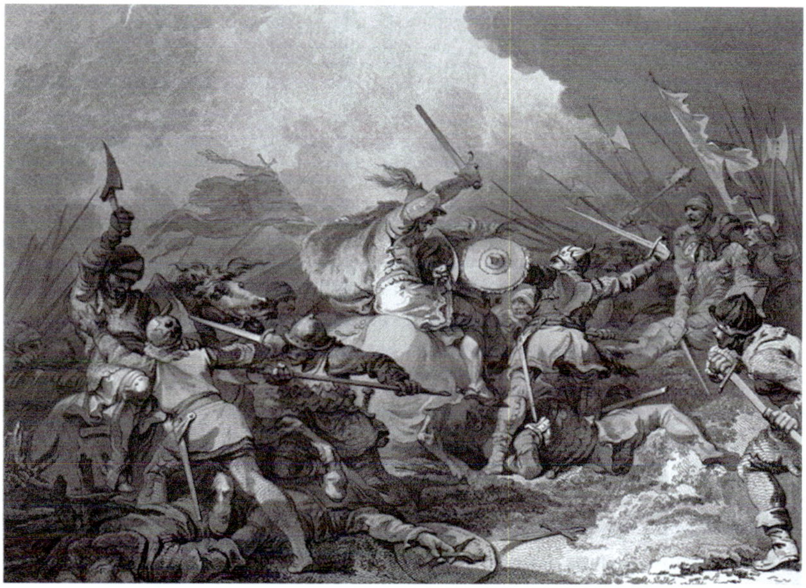

Image 8.5 Battle of Hastings.

Westminster (1285), which recognized the *writ system* and the ability to appeal from the local courts to the royal courts. A writ is an order from a court to proceed with an action. It is the predecessor to what we now know as causes of action (breach of contract, negligence, trespass, and so forth). However, the writs were narrow, and a party could not pursue a legal action in many cases since there was no applicable writ. For example, there was no writ for a breach of contract until the *writ of assumpsit*, which was an action in tort (harm to person or property), was extended to breach of contract in *Slade's Case* in 1602. The action of *assumpsit* was technically a type of trespass due to deceit. The court in *Slade's Case* used a fiction in reasoning that there was an inherent promise in a contract to pay the money, and that failing to pay is a type of deceit. The result was assumpsit became the basis for the cause of action for breach of contract.

The rise of equity courts (in the fifteenth century) created a dual court system—the royal or law courts, which applied the common law and the courts of equity, which initially applied canon law, before developing their own general principles of justice and equity. This proved to be an inefficient system since the two courts provided different remedies. The law courts primarily awarded money damages (legal remedy), and the equity courts issued equitable remedies, such as injunctions (orders to stop doing something) and specific performance (an order to do something). So, if someone is infringing on another's copyright, the party would first have to go to an equity court to obtain an injunction to stop the infringement. The party would then have to start a second action in a law court to collect damages for the harm inflicted by the infringement. This system was adopted in the American colonies and surprisingly persisted into the late nineteenth century, when a single set of civil procedure rules was adopted establishing a unified court system. Many of the equitable principles developed in the equity courts are now found in the "law" (principles of good faith, unconscionability or unfairness, promissory estoppel, and so forth).

Remnants of the old equity system remain to the present. For example, the U.S. state of Delaware maintains a dual court system. It still has a Court of Chancery that continues to exist since the American Revolution. The jurisdiction of the court is simply to hear and determine all matters and causes in equity. Its primary power is its ability to issue injunctions. The Court of Chancery has played an important role in the development of American corporation law.

> **Writ:** The word "writ" is still in use in the U.S. legal system and means to petition a court for an order, such as *writ of mandamus* (court order to force the government to do something it is required to do, such as issue a permit), *writ of habeas corpus* (ordering the government to bring a prisoner or detainee to court and to explain the reasons for his or her detention), and the *writ of certiorari* (petition to the Supreme Court to hear a case on appeal).

The core characteristic of the common law system, implicit in the idea of judge-made law, is the **law of precedent** or ***stare decisis*** ("let the decision stand"), which requires lower courts to follow the rulings (of law) handed down by higher courts. See Figure 8.3, case study on "Legal Reasoning in the Common Law."[11] Thus, when an issue comes before a lower court and the issue was previously decided by a higher court in the same court system, the lower court must apply the decision of the upper court. Interestingly, the common law is found at the state level in the U.S. due to the U.S. Supreme Court's decision in the 1938 case of *Erie Railroad Company v. Tompkins*. In that decision, popularly known as the ***Erie* doctrine**, the Court held that a Federal court could not create Federal common law in cases involving parties from two different states (diversity jurisdiction). Therefore, in the private law areas (contract, tort, real property) there are 53 American common laws (50 states, Puerto Rico, U.S. Virgin Islands, and Washington, D.C.).

Canadian Legal System

Canada came into existence through the British North American Act of 1867, which created a confederation of states governed by the constitution (Magna Carta) of the UK. Despite subsequently passing a "new" constitution, the Constitution of 1867 remains in effect. The 1867 Constitution divides law-making power between the federal and provincial governments and makes the

Common law legal reasoning is the process by which a court makes a decision. In that decision the courts enunciate in great detail the reasons for their decision.

Justification by Authority (law of precedent): In the common law, the law of precedent or ***stare decisis*** ("let the decision stand") often leads a court to a finding based on prior authority (case law). In such cases, the legal mandate is to follow the rulings of higher courts. Hence, the justification is from authority and not one of substance. Justifications of substance (justice, fairness, and logic) would have already been espoused in the prior decision of the upper court. The common law system, whether in England, the British Commonwealth, or the United States, has stayed true to the role of courts as the institution entrusted with the interpretation, application, and, at times, the creation of the law.

Judge-Made Law and the Appellate Process: The idea of judge-made private law remains the bedrock of common law systems. Coherency in such a system is ensured through the appellate court process. The appellate courts are entrusted to "unify" the law if there are conflicting rulings, decisions, or interpretations in lower courts (within the scope of their appellate jurisdictions).

Distinguishing Cases: Change is also part of the system, which means higher courts may overturn their own precedents. This process is generally done gradually, often by a process of distinguishing the previous precedent from the facts of current cases. Over time, this distinguishing or creating exceptions reduces the original precedent or rule to insignificance, at which point the court will formally overturn the precedent. So, for example, the U.S. Supreme Court in a 7 to 1 vote in *Plessy v. Ferguson*[12] held that the principle of "separate but equal" was constitutional, leading the way to black and white-only public schools (segregation). It overturned that decision in a 9 to 0 vote in *Brown v. Topeka Board of Education*,[13] holding that separate but equal was unconstitutional (leading to the integration of American schools and universities).

Ratio Decidendi and Dicta: A lower court only has to follow the reasons and findings of the superior court that were necessary in rendering its decision. The *stare decisis* part of a decision is called the ***ratio decidendi*** or the reason for the decision. At times, judges provide additional support or justification for their decisions or speculate on issues not necessary to decide the particular case being heard. This portion of the decision is referred to as *obiter dictum* or ***dicta*** and has no precedential value.

Well-Reasoned Decisions and "Avoiding" Precedent: This idea of the force of a precedent refers back to the idea that no two cases are ever identical. If confronted with a poorly justified precedent, a court may seek to distinguish the precedent from the case before the court, resulting in the narrowing of the scope of the precedent. Alternatively stated, a court may elect not to extend the precedent to similar, but not identical fact situations. This is one reason why courts in the common law system expend so much time in providing well-reasoned decisions so that future courts will have the justifications of the precedent readily available for future use. This also explains the evolution of nonbinding *dicta* as a way of a court supporting its recognition and application of a legal rule, as well as providing guidance for extensions of the rule (precedent) by future courts.

Figure 8.3 Case Study: Legal Reasoning in the Common Law.

law passed by the Canadian Parliament the supreme law of the country.[14] The Constitution Act of 1982 effected Canada's full legislative independence from the UK. The 1867 Constitution remains in effect.

Canada has 13 provinces and territories. Early in its development it was established that each province has the right to determine its own law subject to limitations provided in the *Constitution* (1982) and the *Charter of Rights and Freedoms*.[15] As a result, the English-speaking areas adopted English common law and Quebec adopted the French Civil Code. The provinces and territories, except for Quebec, follow the doctrine of *stare decisis*; the lower provincial courts must follow the decisions of the higher level courts (Court of Appeal). Interestingly, the different provinces adopted the English common law at different times, meaning the case law developed differently, creating unique bodies of case law in the different provinces. Just like the U.S., the common law provinces adopted the English dual court system involving the royal or common law courts and the **Courts of Chancery** or equity courts, and just like the U.S., the two court systems were merged in the late nineteenth century.

The 1867 Constitution allows the provinces to establish their own court systems; therefore, there are some variations across the court system. The Canadian court system is illustrated in Figure 8.4.

A few distinguishing characteristics of the Canadian court system will be mentioned here. First, the provincial courts hear both civil and criminal matters. Second, depending on the province, some small claims courts have jurisdiction over disputes involving up to $50,000. Third, not shown in Figure 8.4, some provinces have created their own specialized courts. For example, Ontario has established specialized courts for drug-related matters, domestic violence, and mental health cases. The Canadian Supreme Court is located in the national capital of Ottawa. It hears appeals from Provincial Courts of Appeal including those from Quebec. Finally, the Supreme Court may take "references" submitted by the Prime Minister. For example, the court was referred the issue of the legality of same-sex marriage, which eventually led to its legalization in all the provinces.

Civil Law Versus Common Law

Civil law is primarily contrasted against common law. The original difference is that, historically, common law was developed by custom, beginning before there were any written laws and continuing to be applied by courts after there were written laws. Civil law developed out of the Roman law of Justinian's *Corpus Juris Civilis* that uses general legal principles. In later times, civil law

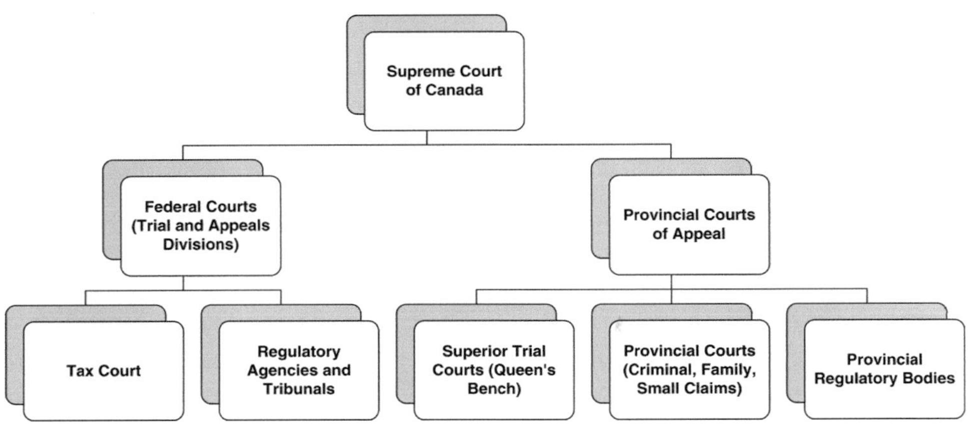

Figure 8.4 Canadian Court System.

became codified beginning in the second half of the eighteenth century, but the long-lasting civil codes came after the French Revolution, with the French Civil Code (*Napoleonic Code*) in 1804, Austrian Civil Code (*Allgemeines bürgerliches Gesetzbuch* or ABGB) in 1811, Dutch Civil Code (*Burgerlijk Wetboek* or BW) in 1838, 1889 Civil Code of Quebec in 1866, Spain (*Código Civil*) in 1889, and the German Civil Code (*Bürgerliches Gesetzbuch* or BGB) in 1900. The two most influential civil codes have been the French and German civil codes, which have influenced the drafting of civil codes in other countries.

The difference between civil law and common law is not so much that civil law is primarily based on statutory law, but in the legal reasoning and methodological approaches to the application of codes and statutes. In civil law countries, legislation is seen as the primary source of law. Courts base their decisions by directly referring to the codes and statutes. Courts thus have to reason extensively on the basis of general principles of the code, or by drawing analogies from statutory provisions. By contrast, in the common law system, cases are the primary source of law, while statutes are intrusions into the common law and are interpreted narrowly. It should be noted that statutes in the common law are embedded in a common law system. The importance of this fact is that courts rely heavily on other court decisions interpreting the relevant statute, rather than relying directly on the statute itself. In the civil law, each court directly interprets the code or statute without citing other court decisions.

There are considerable differences between the legal methodologies of various civil law countries and the common law countries. For example, common law judicial opinions are much longer and contain elaborate reasoning, whereas legal opinions in civil law countries are usually short and formal in nature. This is in principle true in France, where judges cite only legislation, but not prior case law. By contrast, court opinions in German-speaking countries can be long and normally discuss academic writing extensively, along with referring to other case decisions. Civil law judges are usually trained and promoted separately from lawyers, whereas common law judges are usually selected from accomplished and respected lawyers. Also, as seen in the German system, the influence of academic writing by law professors tends to be much greater than in other civil law countries.

Chinese Legal Tradition

The history of China is primarily a history of imperial dynasties. The Qing dynasty was the last, ending in 1912, followed by the Nationalist government (*Kuomintang*) led by Sun Yat-sen and later by Chiang Kai-Shek, before the Communist Revolution, led by Mao Zedong, in 1949. The current legal system and laws have evolved in only recent times after the Cultural Revolution (1966–1976) and the death of Mao in 1976. It was not until the move to a market economy, led by **Deng Xiaoping**, in the 1980s that we begin to see a modern legal system.[16]

President Deng Xiaoping instituted an ambitious program of economic and legal reforms to transition China from a planned economy to a market economy. Despite the success of these reforms and the resulting explosion of the Chinese economy based upon the exportation of goods, a number of legal orders remain from the prior system—agricultural collectives and **state-owned enterprises** (**SOEs**). Real property law remains underdeveloped, as village collectives own most rural areas, and individual home ownership is restricted to a 70-year lease. SOEs continue to dominate major parts of the economy.

Confucianism

The Chinese legal tradition traces its origins to about the sixth century BC. The tradition centers on the key issue of what is the role of law in society. To answer this question requires a review of the social and political policies dating back to the Qin (221–206 BC or BCE) and Han dynasties (206 BCE and 220 AD or CE). The two major schools of thought that make up the Chinese legal tradition are Confucianism and legalism.[17] Confucianism stressed the roles of education, cooperation, and living by moral examples in society. Law and the legal system were only, at best, a method of last resort. Instead of acting based upon legal obligations, legal obligations were subservient to moral obligations and maintaining the harmony of relationships within the community. Society was regulated by moral and societal values (*li*). The major sanction in such a view of society is shame or a loss of reputation. Confucianism also stressed respect for a person's position or role in society.

In contrast, legalism, which coexisted with Confucianism, stressed the use of law and a strong government as needed to properly regulate society. Legalism was more egalitarian in nature in that it believed in the creation of detailed legal rules (*fa*) to be applied to everyone regardless of their position in the social order. The influence of Confucianism did not deter the development of formal law. As early as the Qin dynasty, criminal law codes were enacted and developed. The most influential code was the ***Tang* Code** developed in the eighth and ninth centuries. The most comprehensive code was the ***Qing* Code** of 1740, which created a legal system, but, again, one primarily focused on criminal law. In the area of private relations and private transactions, Confucianism remained the dominant force. Thus, commercial and civil law remained largely underdeveloped. This was due to numerous factors, such as the lack of commercial codes, the agrarian focus of the economy, and the lack of a strong, independent merchant class able to develop informal merchant law, unlike the development of the law merchant (customary business law) in medieval Europe. As a result, the development of a robust law profession and the establishment of law schools were considered unnecessary. As a philosophy, Confucianism remained the dominant state ideology until the fall of the Qing dynasty in 1912. It continues to play an important role in modern

China, shaping the importance of relationships over contracts, respect for others, and the role of law in society.

Chinese Civil Code 2021: On January 1, 2021, the new Chinese Civil Code (CCC) replaced the Chinese Contract Law of 1999 (CCL). The contract provisions of the CCC mimic those of the CCL. One major change was the insertion of an express "hardship provision" that was missing in the CCL. Unfortunately, again the CCC failed to recognize the seller's "right to cure" defective goods, which was also missing in the CCL.

It was not until the modern era, beginning in 1978, that China enacted Western-style civil and commercial laws. The business laws enacted are most closely related to the civil law systems of Europe. In contract law, the two major events were China's adoption of the United Nations Convention on Contracts for the International Sale of Goods (CISG) in 1988 and the enactment of the uniform **Chinese Contract Law (CCL)** in 1999. The CISG is a Western-style law primarily negotiated between civil and common law representatives. The CCL is based upon the CISG, UNIDROIT Principles of International Commercial Contracts, as well as German law influences, and to a lesser extent by English common law. Thus, the CCL is understandable to any lawyer of the Western legal tradition. In 2015, the Chinese government announced that work would proceed with a general Civil Code along the lines of the civil law tradition. The **Chinese Civil Code** states its objectives as creating a "supreme document" codifying all private laws; the grounds of all civil responsibility; establishing a clear set of civil judicial standards; and to protect the rights of citizens by ensuring the fair operation of the civil justice system.

Islamic Legal Tradition

Many Muslim countries have adopted *Shari'a* or **Sharia law**. Examples include Saudi Arabia, Afghanistan, Iran, United Arab Emirates (UAE), Oman, Sudan, Malaysia, Pakistan, and Yemen. These countries have Western-style commercial laws, but *Sharia* (religious) law is considered to be the foundational and superior law. There are four sources of Islamic law including: (1) ***Quran*** (holy book) and Hadith (sayings of the Prophet); (2) ***Sunna*** (social and legal customs and practices); (3) ***Ijma*** (consensus of Islamic scholars); and (4) analogical reasoning. The *Quran* is mostly a guide for personal conduct—norms and guidelines that Muslims are to live by and the proper worship of Allah. The *Sunna* helps fill in the gaps in the *Quran*, but like the *Quran*, is mostly personal in nature. Both the *Quran* and *Sunna* are recordings of the words of the Prophet Muhammad. The interpretations of the *Quran* and *Sunna* by a consensus of scholars often leads to confusion since there is no uniform system of how scholars come together and issue interpretations; so, different groups of scholars may issue different interpretations. The use of analogical reasoning is most like the Western legal systems. For example, analogical reasoning is a common form of legal reasoning in the civil and common laws.

Religious Legal Systems stem from the sacred texts of religious traditions. The main types of religious law are *Sharia* in Islam, Halakha in Judaism, and canon law in Christianity.

The **Islamic legal tradition** traces its origins to the era of the Prophet Muhammad in the early seventh century CE. The *Sharia* law ("the path") is the basis of the Islamic legal system, derived from the *Quran* and *Hadith*. The *Quran* means "the recitation" and is the central religious text of Islam. Muslims believe that God verbally revealed the *Quran* to Muhammad through the angel Gabriel from 609 to 632 CE. The *Hadith* means "account" or "report." The *Hadith* literature is based on spoken reports that were in circulation in society after the death of Muhammad. Islamic scholars then compiled these *Hadiths* together in collections. The *Hadith* collections are different for the *Sunni* and *Shi'a* branches of Islam. The secondary sources of Islamic law are principles established by Islamic scholars based upon their interpretations of the *Quran* and *Hadith*. These legal rules are called *Ijma* (consensus). Last in importance is the *Qiyas*: when an issue is novel in that a rule cannot be found in the *Quran*, *Hadith*, or *Ijma*, the judge uses "analogical reasoning" to apply an accepted legal principle to the dispute. Judicial decisions are held in high regard but need not be followed in the way of *stare decisis* in the common law system.

Sunni Islam is the largest branch of Islam, accounting for about 88 percent of all Muslims. *Sunni* Muslims make up a majority of the populations of the countries of Albania, Bangladesh, Indonesia, Malaysia, and North Africa, including Egypt, Pakistan, Saudi Arabia, and Turkey, among others. The majority of *Shi'a* countries include Iran and Iraq (also has large minorities of Sunni and Kurds). A third branch, the *Ibadi*, is the majority religion in Oman. Despite the importance of the canonical texts noted above, Islamic law is not a religious law in the generally accepted sense. The confusion lies in the fact that most of the sacred law, such as the *Quran*, stems from the fact that very little of it deals with the subjects covered by most other legal systems. Therefore, most of the law in the areas of commerce and business come from man-made law and not religious law: "The first, *Ibadiit* (ritual), deals with purely religious matters. The second *Muamalat* (transactions) deals with the subjects, which comprise the content of other legal systems."[18] The *Quran* contains very few legal provisions (only 190 of the 6,237 verses contain legal provisions), and those provisions deal with family and inheritance law. Thus, the legal rules (*fiqh*) found in the *Muamalat* are man-made and are not part of religious law. *Muamalat* is a set of rules related to worldly matters such as business and commerce transactions, finances, and lending matters. Since the charging of interest on a loan and payment of interest on money deposits are illegal under the Islamic legal system, Islam financial rules have been widely studied and used.

Most Muslim countries have adopted modern commercial codes and laws. France colonized much of North Africa and the Middle East in the early nineteenth century. Thus, those areas were introduced to the **French Civil Code** (**Code Napoléon**) of 1804. A majority of Muslim countries in those areas have modern commercial codes based upon the civil law tradition. For example, Egypt adopted a civil and commercial code based upon the French Civil Code. It was updated in 1948 to include Islamic principles and decisions of the Egyptian courts. Again, a new Egyptian commercial code, based heavily on the CISG, was adopted in 1999.

> **Analogical Reasoning:** This method of reasoning is used when there is no authority, principle, or rule that directly addresses an issue. In the common law system, the judge would look to prior cases (precedent) with similar fact patterns to extend, adjust, or create a rule to fix the gap in the law. In the civil law system, if there is a gap (*lacuna*) in a code or statute, the judge looks to other code provisions to derive a rule by analogy to fill in the gap.

Sharia law provides fundamental principles, which apply if there is no specific legislation on a topic or issue. It is also used or cited in the interpretation of statutes. Alongside *Sharia* law are modern statutes, which are applied and interpreted in ways similar to other modern legal systems; however, the courts may still cite *Sharia* law in supporting a particular interpretation of a statute. There is also a great amount of variation in the influence or role *Sharia* law plays in a given national legal system. In Saudi Arabia, *Sharia* law touches all aspects of society including the business realm, while Turkey has officially purged Islamic law from its legal system. Before leaving the subject of Islamic law, it is important to point out that this review is simplistic in every way given the complexity and numerous sources of Islamic law. More detail of the sources of Islamic law is provided in Figure 8.5. The summation of all the interpretations taken from the sources listed in Figure 8.5 makes up the body of *Fiqh*, *Furu*, and *Fatwa* (laws and rules).

Islamic Contract Law

The *Quran* refers to commercial transaction in only a few instances. Islamic scholars have not fashioned a general theory of contracts. Instead, they created rules for particular types of contracts; the most important set of rules is for sales contracts (*bay*), which served as a model for gift (*hiba*), hire (*ija 'ra*) (employment or services contracts), and the loan (*a 'riya*). Even though *Sharia* principles may be used to interpret the code or the contract, most issues in contract law are answered by the modern commercial codes.

Islamic Banking and Financial Law

Islamic banking is consistent with the principles of *Sharia* law. *Al Wadi'ah* means lodge, leave, or deposit. In Islamic banking, *wadi'ah* refers to a safekeeping instrument that allows a person to keep the wealth or assets belonging to oneself with another person. In fact, it was practiced before Islam came into existence. Under an Islamic scheme of savings, customers are assured of interest-free safekeeping services. If the bank cannot charge interest and the depositor

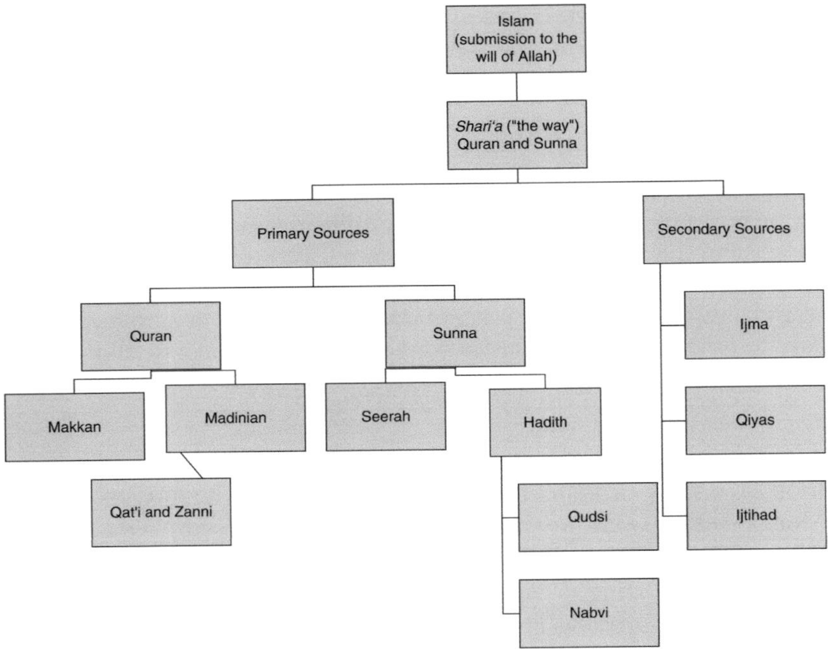

Figure 8.5 Summary of Islamic Law.

cannot receive interest, does that mean the bank gets free use of the depositor's money? The banks may offer their customers a ***hiba*** or gift based on the earnings of the bank through the investments using their customers' money.

The *Quran* prohibits the charging of ***riba*** or interest on the lending of money. The prohibition of *riba* (usury) is based on a broader prohibition against making unearned profits. Thus, charging an above-market price in the sale of goods would violate the prohibition of *riba*. However, if the above-market price is shown not to be a product of fraud or monopolistic practices, then the premium price could be considered a gift from the buyer to the seller. Unlike the common law, gift promises are binding contracts.

Ways have been developed in lending and financial transactions to avoid violating the prohibition of *riba*. First, the bank can take an ownership stake in the project that it is lending money to support and hope to earn profits if the venture proves successful. Second, some Muslim countries allow for the payment of interest on delayed payments. Eventually, Islamic rules (*Fiqh al-Muamalat*) have been developed to allow financial transactions that would not violate the *riba* prohibition. For example, instead of lending money for a person or company to buy property, the bank would buy the property directly and then resell the property at a profit to the other party and allow the other party to pay through installments. For a brief summary of the characteristics of the civil, common, Islamic, and socialist legal systems, see Table 8.2 on "Comparison of Four Legal Systems."

Table 8.2 Comparison of Four Legal Systems.

Characteristics	*Civil Law*	*Common Law*	*Islamic Law*	*Socialist Law*
Other Names	Continental; Romano-Germanic	Anglo-American; judge-made law	Religious Law; Shari'a	Socialistic
Sources of Law	Codes and Statutes	Cases and Statutes	Religious Documents and Religious case law	Statutes
Role of Judges	Dominate Trial; research and find evidence; asks questions directly of the witnesses	Neutral, Impartial Referees; Lawyers present evidence and ask questions of the witnesses	Judges play Secondary Role	Judge Dominates the Trial
Judicial Independence	High	High	Varies from Country to Country	Low
Role of Judicial Branch (Courts)	Share Power with Other Parts of Government	Courts have Separate and Equal Power with Other Branches of Government	Historically, Courts are Subordinate to Shari'a law; Modern, Subordinate to Executive Branch	Courts Inferior to Legislative Branch
Countries	All EU states (except the UK and Ireland), All of Continental Latin America (except Guyana and Belize), Quebec, All of East Asia (except Hong Kong), Congo, Azerbaijan, Kuwait, Iraq, Russia, Turkey, Egypt, Madagascar, Lebanon, Switzerland, Indonesia, Vietnam, Thailand	Australia, UK (except Scotland), India (except Goa), Nigeria, Ireland, Singapore, Hong Kong, USA (except Louisiana), Canada (except Quebec), New Zealand, Pakistan, Malaysia, Bangladesh	Many Muslim countries have adopted parts of Shari'a Law. Examples include Saudi Arabia, Afghanistan, Iran, UAE, Oman, Sudan, Malaysia, Pakistan, and Yemen	No Longer in Existence, but still influences the application of law in China, Russia, and some former Soviet-bloc Countries
Use of Juries	Only in Criminal Trials	Trial Level	Allowed by Maliki School of Sunni Islam (countries of Northern Africa)	Sometimes at the Lowest Level of Court System

Hindu Legal System

Hindu law is one of the world's oldest legal traditions. But Hinduism is more than the formal written law of the Western legal tradition; it is captured by the more elusive term of ***dharma***, which describes things like what is considered appropriate behavior, duties, rights, laws, conduct, virtues, and the right way of living. *Dharma* has multiple meanings and is used in Hindu law, philosophy, religion, and Buddhism. The notion of *Dharma* (duty or propriety) is found in India's ancient legal texts. In Hindu philosophy, justice, social harmony, and happiness require that people live per dharma. The *Dharmaśāstra* is a compilation of a large volume of Hindu treatises called ***Shastra*** or *Śāstra* meaning "rules." They are important within the Hindu tradition—first, as a source of religious law describing the life of an ideal householder and, second, as a symbol of the summation of Hindu knowledge about religion, law, and ethics.

As we saw with the Chinese transplantation and reception of Western-style laws, so too was Hindu law pushed aside beginning with the period of English colonialism in the seventeenth century. But also, as in China where Confucianism continues to play a role in the social and cultural values held by the Chinese people, the values that underlie Hindu law continue to play a role in modern-day India. The English installed the case law system so, just as we sometimes refer to Anglo-American law, we can speak of Anglo-Hindu law. The role of Hindu tribunals and customs-based law, as well as the arrival of common law legislation, diluted the influence of traditional Hindu law. In the nineteenth century, statutes, as well as a criminal law and civil procedure, replaced Hindu contract and property laws. Upon independence in 1949, India retained most of English law but recast it into a **Hindu Code**. More importantly, much of India remains rural; where the old law traditions remain strong, often formal law is ignored as the caste system is still entrenched in daily life.

Mixed Jurisdictions

Two of the more important mixed law systems are Scotland and South Africa. Each entity combines features of the civil and common law systems. South Africa still shows strong features of the civil law, due to its earlier colonization by the Dutch, despite being a member of the British Commonwealth. Scots law has a basis derived from Roman law, and combines features of civil law, dating back to the *Corpus Juris Civilis*, common law, and customary or local law from the High Middle Ages (900–1300). Scotland has been part of the UK since its 1707 union with England and has increasingly followed the common law.

Scotland

Scotland is part of the United Kingdom of England, Wales, and Northern Ireland. However, Scotland has retained its own legal identity—its own Parliament, legal profession, and court system. Nonetheless, Scottish cases are appealable to the highest English courts. Roman law influenced early Scottish law with the establishment of Scottish law schools in the fifteenth century and the study of canon law. The ***Regiam Majestatem*** (early fourteenth century), shown in Image 8.6, is the earliest surviving work on Scottish law. It consists of a comprehensive digest of early Scottish law in four books, treating (1) civil actions and jurisdictions, (2) judgments and executions, (3) contracts, and (4) crimes. But the influence of Roman law on Scottish law is often overstated, with English common law being the major influence on Scottish law since the unification of England and Scotland in the eighteenth century.

The remnants of Roman law produced a rather chaotic body or system of law. This was largely elevated by the "institutional writers" led by Viscount Stair, whose treatise, ***The Institutions of the Law of Scotland***, was published in 1681. Stair's work organized the different sources of Scottish law (customary, feudal, and Roman or canon law) into a coherent system of law.[19] However, beginning in the nineteenth century, the overloaded Scottish court system shifted from

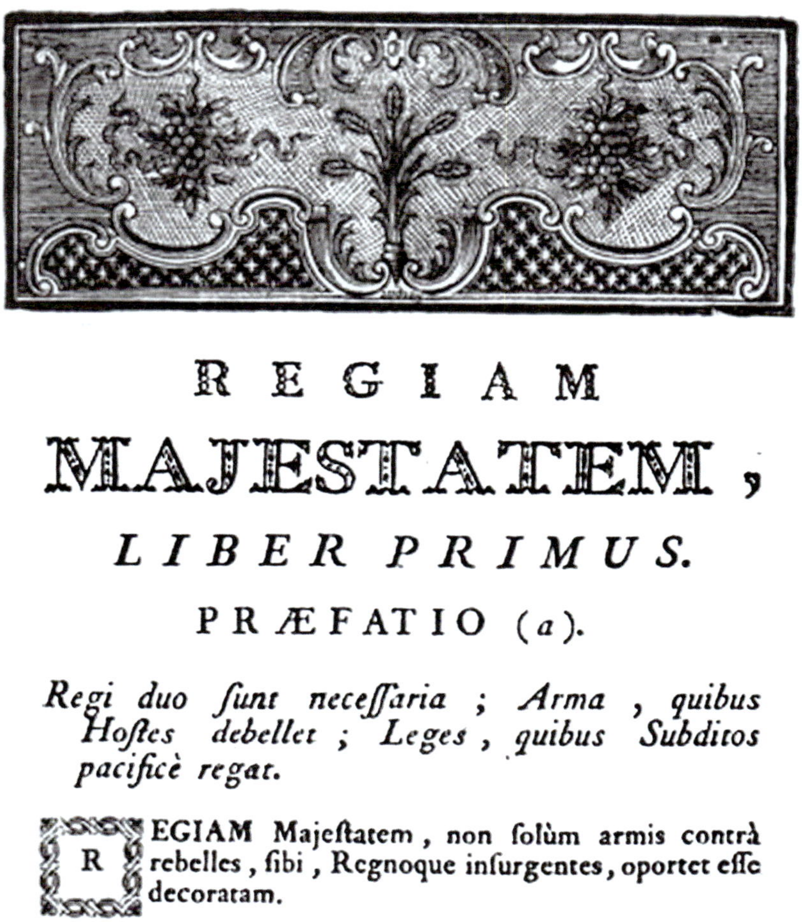

REGIAM

MAJESTATEM,

LIBER PRIMUS.

PRÆFATIO (*a*).

Regi duo ſunt neceſſaria; Arma, quibus Hoſtes debellet; Leges, quibus Subditos pacificè regat.

REGIAM Majeſtatem, non ſolùm armis contrà rebelles, ſibi, Regnoque inſurgentes, oportet eſſe decoratam.

Image 8.6 *Regiam Majestatem.*

dealing with each case as unique and moved toward the common law's rule of precedent, looking more to case law than to Roman law or the works of the institutional writers. In modern times, reforms to English and Scottish law have been coordinated by **Law Commissions**. The Law Commission Act of 1965 established two commissions, the English Law Commission and the Scottish Law Commission. Because of the remaining differences between the English and Scottish laws, the two commissions act in consultation with each other in drafting law and in revising existing laws.

South Africa

South Africa is considered an emerging economy or newly industrialized country with a population of about 50 million people. It was subject to both British and Dutch colonialism. Thus, Afrikaans (Dutch derivative) and English are two of its major languages; however, there are 11 official languages. The Constitution is the supreme law in the country. The primary sources of South African law are Dutch-Roman commercial law, as well as English common law. The Dutch brought Dutch-Roman law, but this was before the enactment of the French Napoleonic Code, so the Dutch introduced a relatively undeveloped civil law when the British colonized South Africa in the nineteenth century, resulting in a hybrid legal system similar to Scottish law.

South African contract law is primarily based upon Old Dutch law with a fair amount of influence from English common law.[20] This amounted to confusion as to what was required to create an enforceable contract. The common law requires that a contract must be supported by reciprocal *consideration* (exchange of value), while consideration is not required under the civil law. Under the civil law all "serious" agreements are enforceable with or without consideration. Instead, the civil law requires *causa*, which vaguely means there is a recognized purpose or reason for the contract. The *causa* makes an agreement serious and, thus, an enforceable contract. In 1874, Chief Justice Lord Henry de Villiers provided an innovative solution by asserting that *causa* meant that the purpose of the agreement was an exchange of values (consideration).[21] In 1919, the confusion was resolved when the court in *Conradie v. Rossouw*[22] held that common law's doctrine of consideration was not part of South African law. A contract is enforceable as long as the parties show proper *causa*. Unfortunately, the meaning of *causa* still remains a vague, but flexible, doctrine.

Transnational Law

A great many of international business disputes are resolved through arbitration. Reputable arbitration associations have been established throughout the world including in Cairo, China (Center for International Economic Trade and Commerce), London (International Court of Trade), Moscow, Paris (**International Chamber of Commerce**), Stockholm, and the U.S. (American Arbitration Association). Unlike courts that must follow mandatory national laws, arbitration tribunals often use international sources of law, such as business customs, usage, commercial practice, as well as international model laws (UNIDROIT Principles of International Commercial Contracts, Principles of European Contract Law, and the European Common Frame of Reference). Arbitrators see their role not so much as the application of law but as rendering "fair and equitable" decisions. As such, they use numerous sources of laws that together have been called transnational law or the new *lex mercatoria*.

An autonomous new *lex mercatoria* or transnational commercial law is a separate category of legal system beyond the traditional dichotomy of domestic or national laws and public international law (treaties, free trade agreements, WTO rules). The make-up of the *lex mercatoria* includes: (1) general principles of law, derived from a comparative analysis of the common core of domestic legal systems; (2) the usages and customs of the international business community as expressed in standard form contracts, model clauses, and trade manuals (industry standards); and (3) decisions of international commercial arbitration panels. Many of its rules are found in lists of principles, rules and standards, codes of conduct, or best practices of trade associations and nongovernmental organizations.[23] Its enforcement rests predominantly on social sanctions such as reputation and exclusion from the business community.

The **privatization of lawmaking** is seen in the nonlegislative codifications of general principles of law, as well as private codifications of trade usage and commercial custom promulgated by nonstate actors. The most important examples of the former are the **UNIDROIT Principles of International Commercial Contracts** (**PICC**). Prominent examples for the latter are the International Commercial Chamber's **INCOTERMS** (trade terms) and the **Uniform Customs and Practice for Documentary Credits** (**UCP**), both drafted and continuously revised by the ICC. For a review of INCOTERMS, see Chapter 12 on "Documentary Transactions," and for a discussion of the UCP, see Chapter 13 on "International Trade Finance." As these instruments aspire to express uniform rules for international commerce not attached to any specific state legal system, they form part of a transnational commercial law.

Lex Mercatoria and Arbitration

As noted above, the growing importance of transnational rules in international contracts is related to the importance of international commercial arbitration as the premier means of dispute resolution in international business transactions. Parties negotiating international contracts will often feel the need to submit their agreement to neutral rules, which do not favor either of the parties. A traditional compromise solution, which is frequently used in international trade, consists in submitting the contract to the law of a third country, choosing well-respected commercial laws such as English or Swiss law. This solution is certainly more balanced than the choice of the law of the country of one of the two parties, since it gives neither of them the advantage of having recourse to their own laws.

Since it is rare that parties have a working knowledge of the law of another country (and because they will typically not have time to verify whether the contract fully complies with such law), businesspeople and their legal advisors have become increasingly interested in transnational rules. These rules allow them to create an alternative neutral legal framework for their international contracts. The theory of ***lex mercatoria*** is an alternative response to the demand to have international contracts governed by national law. According to this theory, international contracts can be ruled by an "anational" system of principles and rules generally accepted in international commerce. These rules can be found in the industry-specific contract practices, clauses commonly used in international commercial contracts, and in the general principles of international business law. Arbitration practice has evolved the principle that arbitrators have the right to apply general principles of the *lex mercatoria* instead of national laws.

Article 21(1) of the ICC arbitration rules states the following:

> *Applicable rules of law*: The parties shall be free to agree upon the rules of law to be applied by the arbitral tribunal to the merits of the dispute. In the absence of any such agreement, the arbitral tribunal shall apply the rules of law, which it determines to be appropriate.

Arbitration decisions have recognized that when the contract in dispute selects a country's law as the law of the case (choice of law clause), the *lex mercatoria* may still be used even when it conflicts with the chosen law. An International Arbitration Court at the Chamber of Commerce and Industry of the Russian Federation decided a case concerning a contract between a Russian and a German company. It held that possible disputes should be decided in conformity with the *lex mercatoria* despite the existence of a clause choosing German and Russian law. In an arbitral award on December 22, 2004, the Tribunal of International Commercial Arbitration at the Ukrainian Chamber of Commerce and Trade, concerning a sales contract, applied the CISG, the *lex mercatoria*, and the UNIDROIT Principles in deciding the case. This application of multiple sources of hard law (CISG) and soft law (*lex mercatoria*; UNIDROIT Principles) is common in international arbitration.

Soft versus Hard Law: Soft law refers to rules that are neither strictly binding in nature nor completely lacking legal significance. In the context of international law, soft law refers to guidelines, policy declarations, or codes of conduct, which set standards of conduct. However, they are not directly enforceable. Hard law refers to binding laws. In the context of international business law, hard law includes national laws, as well as treaties and other international agreements.

Despite arbitration panels' greater flexibility in using hard and soft laws, they will feel bound to follow a country's law chosen by the parties. However, sometimes the parties fail to insert a choice of law clause in their contract, leaving the arbitrators with a decision to use a hard law (national law) or soft law. Here are the common approaches to this issue used in arbitration:

1. Arbitral panels or tribunals will not apply *lex mercatoria* if the parties have expressly chosen a domestic (national) law.
2. There is nevertheless some space for supplementing inadequate domestic laws through the referencing of general principles, such as the UNIDROIT Principles and trade usages, but only to the extent this is admissible under the applicable domestic law.
3. If the parties have chosen a domestic law as the applicable law together with transnational rules, arbitrators have greater discretion (as compared to courts) when deciding on possible conflicts between the transnational rules and the applicable law.
4. In some cases, arbitrators may apply the *lex mercatoria* instead of a domestic law when the parties have made no choice of the applicable law.

In the last case (no choice of law clause), arbitration panels will commonly determine which country's law is closest to the case and apply that law. However, in the famous case of this kind, the *Norsolor* case,[24] the arbitrators applied the *lex mercatoria* in a dispute regarding the termination of a contract between a French seller and a Turkish agent. The agent claimed damages for the goodwill developed on behalf of the seller during the contract. However, the right to receive such damages was recognized by French law but not by Turkish law. The arbitrators decided that selecting one of the two national laws through conflict of law rules was not an adequate solution and decided as follows:

> Faced with the difficulty of choosing a national law the application of which is sufficiently compelling, the Tribunal considered that it was appropriate, given the international nature of the agreement, to leave aside any compelling reference to a specific legislation, be it Turkish or French, and to apply the international *lex mercatoria*.

In the context of the *lex mercatoria* the tribunal applied the **principle of good faith** and awarded damages to the agent. In several other cases, the arbitrators applied *lex mercatoria* or general principles of law when it appeared that neither party wanted to apply the other party's law or when the parties expressed the desire to have the dispute decided on the basis of nonstate rules by stating that disputes shall be decided, for instance, through reference to international law or "according to the laws of natural justice."

Another interesting example is the *Arthur Andersen* case,[25] where the arbitration clause provided, with respect to the applicable law, the following:

> The arbitrator shall decide in accordance with the terms of this Agreement and of the Articles and Bylaws of Andersen S.C. In interpreting the provisions of this Agreement, the arbitrator shall not be bound to apply the substantive law of any jurisdiction but shall be guided by the policies and considerations set forth in the Preamble of this Agreement and the Articles and Bylaws of Andersen, S.C., considering *general principles of equity*.

The sole arbitrator decided to apply the general principles of law and the general principles of equity commonly accepted by the legal systems of most countries.

He concluded that the UNIDROIT Principles was "a reliable source of international commercial law in international arbitration."

Chapter Summary

1. National law is a product of a given legal tradition, which shapes how the role of law is viewed by society, as well as the reach and scope of law. Legal traditions not only determine substantive law, but also the ways that legal claims are processed by the legal system, role of lawyers, role of judges, role of juries, and types of remedies and damages available. These concerns are of central importance in international transactions, especially when the contracting parties are from different legal traditions. Businesspersons try to reduce the risks of the application of foreign laws through the insertion of choice of law, forum selection, and arbitration clauses in their contracts.
2. The typology of comparative law breaks down the laws of the world into legal traditions, legal families, and national legal systems. *Legal traditions* are bodies of law that have a unique history and are often a product of cultural norms. Most national laws are categorized as being within a handful of legal traditions. The legal traditions covered in this chapter are civil, common, Islamic, Hindu, Chinese, and the law of mixed jurisdictions (Scotland and South Africa). The laws of the UK (excluding Scotland), U.S., and Australia are of the common law tradition. The laws of France, Germany, and Turkey are of the civil law tradition. *Legal families* are the grouping of different countries within the same legal tradition. The civil law tradition is divided into countries of the Franco-Romanic or Napoleonic and Germanic legal families. The French and German Civil Codes have heavily influenced the civil laws of other countries. *National legal systems* include the study of countries' legal systems that are part of the same legal tradition or legal family. Two countries that are part of the same tradition or family may still have substantial differences. The UK and the U.S. are both common law countries but have been independent national systems for over 240 years. As such, despite a great deal of commonality, the two laws have evolved in different ways. France and Germany are both part of the civil law tradition, but their civil codes are often compared because of their numerous differences. French and Spanish laws are part of the Franco legal family, but also display significant differences.
3. Comparative law examines the differences between legal systems. It also analyzes the influences that one or more legal systems have had on other legal systems through the processes of reception and legal transplantation. Examples of such transborder influences and borrowing are China and Vietnam. Modern-day Chinese contract law is a product of influences from international sales law (CISG), international "soft law" (UNIDROIT Principles), German law, socialistic law, as well as common law. Vietnamese law is a product of Chinese, French colonial, socialist, and Western laws.
4. The world's two major legal traditions are the civil and common laws. The civil law evolved in continental Europe out of Roman law, as espoused in the *Corpus Juris Civilis* (Justinian Code). The common law evolved from

the High Middle Ages as the customary law of England. The major difference between the two is the source of their laws—civil law is code or statute based, while common law is based on judge-made decisions through the law of precedent (*stare decisis*). The traditions also differ regarding the role of judges, juries, and lawyers; the types of legal reasoning used; and the role of legal scholarship in judicial decision-making.

5. Islamic law is based on religious law known as *Shari'a* law. Technically, *Shari'a* law impacts all facets of life, but it is mostly dedicated to how people of faith should live their lives and focuses on morality, religious practices, and conduct. One example of the impact of the *Shari'a* on international law is the increasing influence of Islamic finance or banking law in which charging interest (*riba*) is considered a violation of Islamic law. Most of the Islamic law countries have Western-style civil and commercial codes to govern business practices.
6. With the advent of the free trade area and the proliferation of international trade, there has been a development of transnational law and the *lex mercatoria* that transcends national legal systems. Transnational law is a blend of hard law (mandatory) and soft law (nonmandatory business customs and general principles). The CISG is an example of hard transnational law and has been adopted by nearly 100 countries. Soft law in the form of business practices or trade usage is exemplified by manuals issued by the International Chamber of Commerce in Paris in the areas of trade terms (INCOTERMS 2020) and rules relating to letters of credit (UCP). The fact that arbitration is the preferred means of dispute resolution in international business has been a major force in developing transnational law.

Key Terms

Analogical Reasoning Anglo-American Law Arbitration Clause
Better Rules (comparative law)
British Commonwealth of Nations
Bürgerliches Gesetzbuch (BGB) (German Civil Code)
Chinese Civil Code
Chinese Contract Law (CCL)
Choice of Law Clause
Civil Law Tradition
Common Core
Common Law Tradition
Conflict of Laws
Confucianism
Convention on Contracts for the International Sale of Goods (CISG)
Corpus Juris Civilis (Justinian Code)
Courts of Chancery
Customary Law
Dharma Dicta
Erie Doctrine
Forum Selection Clause
Franco Legal Family
French Civil Code
Germanic Legal Family
Guanxi
Hindu Code
Ijma
INCOTERMS
Institutions of the Law of Scotland
International Chamber of Commerce
Islamic Banking
Islamic Legal Tradition
Law Commissions (English and Scottish)
Legal Family
Legal System
Legal Transplantation

Lex Mercatoria
Magna Carta
Mixed Jurisdiction
Napoleonic Code (*Code Napoléon*)
Qing Code
Quran
Principle of Good Faith
Privatization of Lawmaking
Ratio Decidendi
Regiam Majestatem
Riba
Roman Law
Shari'a Law
Shastra
Stare Decisis (precedent)
State-Owned Enterprises (SOEs)
Statute of Westminster
Sunna
Talmudic Legal Tradition
Tang Code
Transnational Law
UNIDROIT
Principles of International Commercial Contracts (PICC)
Uniform Customs and Practices for Documentary Credits (UCP)

Chapter Problems

1. What are the major legal traditions in the world, and what are their distinctive characteristics?
2. How do a country's cultural values and practices affect its legal tradition? How does a country's culture impact the role of law in society? How does culture impact on private parties' use of the courts and legal system? Most importantly, how do cultural values and the view of the role of law (especially the role of contracts) determine how you should engage a possible business partner in another country?
3. What roles does Confucianism play in modern-day China? How does its influence affect the negotiation and drafting of contracts?
4. How is the common law different from the civil law? Statutes have proliferated in both common and civil law countries, so how can it be said that the common law is judge-made law? What is the difference between the role of statutes in the common versus the civil law?
5. Connect the items on the left with the terms that are most clearly related on the right (answers on the next page):

i. Legal Tradition	a. social and legal customs and practices
ii. Legal Family	b. specific performance and injunction remedies
iii. Legal System	c. Chinese criminal code
iv. *Corpus Juris Civilis*	d. Codification of Roman law
v. Writs	e. Canadian law
vi. Sunna	f. French Civil Code
vii. "Face-saving"	g. Germanic-Roman law
viii. Courts of Equity	h. Civil law
ix. *Qing* Code	i. Old English law
x. Napoleonic Code	j. Asian cultural value

Internet Exercises

1. Review the following sources to gain a better understanding of Roman law: https://www.law.berkeley.edu/library/robbins/RomanLegalTradition.html (Roman Legal Tradition and the Compilation of Justinian); http://romanlegaltradition.org (Roman Legal Tradition). See also Franz Wieacker, "The Importance of Roman Law to Western Civilization and Western Legal Thought," 4 *Boston College International and Comparative Law Review* 257 (1981) (available at http://lawdigitalcommons.bc.edu/cgi/viewcontent.cgi?article=1585&context=iclr).
2. Make a list of countries that you are unsure have what type of legal system and go to: "Listing of Legal Systems" in the CIA World Factbook at https:// www.cia.gov/library/publications/the-world-factbook/fields/2100.html#136.
3. Examine the troubling use of English words and legal concepts in laws of non-English countries. See Silvia Ferreri and L. DiMatteo, "Terminology Matters: Dangers of Superficial Transplantation," 37 *Boston University International Law Journal* 35 (2019) at https://scholarship.law.ufl.edu/cgi/viewcontent.cgi?article=1879&context=facultypub.

Other Internet Sources

CIA Maps: Page-sized base maps are in the public domain. Accordingly, they may be copied freely without permission of the Central Intelligence Agency (CIA): https://www.cia.gov/library/publications/resources/cia-maps-publications.

World Legal Systems: http://www.juriglobe.ca/eng/index.php (University of Ottawa).

[Answers to Problem 5: i (h); ii (g); iii (e); iv (d); v (i); vi (a); vii (j); viii (b); ix (c); x (f).]

Notes

1 See Larry A. DiMatteo, "Principle of Fair and Equitable Decision-Making in International Contract Arbitration and Its Affinity to International Soft Law," 1 *Chinese Journal of Comparative Law* 1 (2013).

2 The U.S. is not a member of the 53 members of the British Commonwealth, mostly all of which had been colonized as part of the British Empire. The U.S. is the only former colony country that obtained independence through revolution.

3 See, e.g., H. Patrick Glenn, *Legal Traditions of the World* (2nd ed. Oxford University Press 2004) 125–169.

4 Mathias Siems, *Comparative Law* (2nd ed. Cambridge University Press 2018) 191–220 (Chapter 8: "Legal Transplants").

5 John Gillespie, *Transplanting Commercial Law Reform* (Ashgate 2006).

6 Alan Watson, *Legal Transplants: An Approach to Comparative Law* 20 (University of Georgia Press 1974).

7 See Patricia Pattison and Daniel Herron, "The Mountains Are High and the Emperor Is Far Away: Sanctity of Contract in China," 40 *American Business Law Journal* 459 (2003).

8 Glenn, *Legal Traditions of the World* (2004) 131.

9 Ibid. at 134–135.

10 This is why "Legal English," which is now taught throughout the world, is derived mostly from French, along with Latin.

11 For a critical review of common law legal reasoning see L. DiMatteo, "When Penalties Are not Penalties?—A Study of Judicial Reasoning," 88 *George Washington University Law Review* 1846 (2017).

12 163 U.S. 537 (1896).

13 347 U.S. 483 (1954).

14 See Richard Yates, *Legal Fundamentals for Canadian Business* (4th ed. Pearson Canada 2016); John A. Willes and John H. Willes, *Contemporary Canadian Business Law* (11th ed. McGraw-Hill 2015).

15 The Charter is found in Part I of the Constitution Act, 1982. It guarantees the civil rights and liberties of every citizen in Canada, such as freedom of expression, of religion, and of mobility. Part II addresses the rights of Aboriginal peoples.

16 The Chinese legal system and the role of the Chinese Communist Party are discussed in Chapter 7.

17 Daniel Chow, *The Legal System of the People's Republic of China* (3rd ed. West Academic Publishing 2015).

18 Gamal Moursi Badr, "Islamic Law: Its Relation to Other Legal Systems," 26 *American Journal of Comparative Law* 187 (1978).

19 Robin White, Ian Willock and Hector MacQueen, *The Scottish Legal System* (5th ed. Bloomsbury 2013).

20 See D. Hutchinson and C. J. Pretorius, *The Law of Contract in South Africa* (6th ed. Kluwer Law International 2019).

21 *Alexander v. Perry* (1874) 4 Buch 59.

22 1919 AD 279.

23 G.P. Calliess, "Lex Mercatoria," 52 *ZenTra Working Papers in Transnational Studies* (April 2015).

24 ICC arbitral award 3131/1979, *Pabalk Tikaret Limited Sirketi v. Norsolor S.A*, in Sigvard Jarvin and Yves Derains, *ICC Awards 1974–1985* (ICC Publishing 1990), p. 122.

25 *Andersen Consulting v. Arthur Andersen Business*, ICC International Court of Arbitration, Case No. 9797, available at http://www.unilex.info/case.cfm?id=668.

Chapter 9

Comparative and International Contract Law

Knowledge of substantive law rules and principles is imperative in drafting a good contract. At the international level, the general principles of contract law are less specific and are applied sporadically by national courts. It may be necessary to know the law of the country of your foreign contracting party in order to avoid misunderstandings. Cultural and language differences, however, may prevent a contract from ever being formed. In order to increase the likelihood of success when negotiating with a foreign party, knowledge of the other party's culture and negotiating style is important.

Business behavior differs among cultures. Some cultures focus on the importance of developing a contractual and social relationship and not on the importance of a specific deal. Many cultures view a formal, detailed contract as unnecessary and hindering the development of a strong contractual relationship where the parties mutually work through problems: "For many Asian cultures the contract does not represent finality but is a starting point of a relationship."[1] It is assumed that the contract will be renegotiated if conditions change. In contrast, Western businesspersons view a contract as something that should be strictly enforced by the courts. This chapter will review some of the cultural nuances in negotiating a contract in an international setting with a focus on Japan. It will then shift focus to the differences in substantive contract law at the national and international levels with an emphasis on the area of precontractual liability.

Negotiating an International Contract

International contract negotiation is a very difficult and complicated affair; the nuances of language and culture make it risky for the unsophisticated importer or exporter. The added time invested to negotiate an international contract

DOI: 10.4324/9781003469230-11

carefully will provide significant dividends in the long term. First, an agreement that successfully overcomes language, cultural, and legal differences will better reflect basic understandings and minimize misunderstandings. Second, the trust developed during the negotiation stage often sets the foundation for a long-term international business relationship.

Misunderstandings in negotiation of a contract are often due to differences in the meaning assigned to similar words. In high-context cultures (Japan, Latin America, and Arabic cultures), meaning is much more constructed from the way the words are used (context) than the meaning of the actual words used. In high-context cultures there is greater reliance on nonverbal cues, silence is respected, attention to detail is not highly valued, and words are not always given their literal meanings.

The differences in negotiating styles are attributable to different cultural views of the role of law. In Chinese and Japanese cultures, shame and bad reputation are considered serious sanctions. In Western cultures, litigation is more quickly resorted to, while litigation is disfavored in China and Japan. At times, in these countries, litigation may not be pursued even in meritorious cases if the party views litigation as having a negative effect on its reputation. For the Japanese, contracts are win–win scenarios rather than zero-sum (win–lose) scenarios. The zero-sum scenario views the role of contract negotiations as obtaining the most one-sided contract possible. Win–win scenarios view contract negotiations as maximizing benefits for both parties. See Table 9.1 "Negotiating Styles and Cultural Traits."

Table 9.1 Negotiating Styles and Cultural Traits.

Countries	*Relationship vs. Contract Focused*	*More or Less Detail Oriented*	*Direct vs. Indirect Bargaining*	*Win–Lose vs. Win–Win*	*Cultural Traits*
Arabic	Relational	Less	Indirect	Win–Lose	Role of women in negotiations is restricted; influence of religious law
Brazil	Contract	Less	Both	Win–Lose	Not reluctant to reject proposals
China	Relational	Less	Indirect	Win–Win	More approvals needed leads to longer negotiations; transaction should benefit the State
Japan	Relational	Less	Indirect	Win–Win	Consensus-building within company to approve contract; formality and courtesy important
Russia	Relational	Medium	Direct	Win–Lose	Not as trusting of the rule of law; do not question authority

The descriptions in Table 9.1 are highly generalized and can vary from company to company and from country to country. For example, the Japanese have learned the Western view of the importance of the written contract. Therefore, the length and detail of a contract will be different between two Japanese companies and a Japanese and a Western company.

Cultural awareness at the minimum includes the appropriate way to greet another party, common courtesies expected in social interactions, business ethics, decision-making practices, formalities, and proper business attire, and, unfortunately, in some countries there may be gender issues. First, greetings in some countries may be oriented to "bowing" instead of handshaking. Second, in some cultures, a dinner begins with a toast (alcohol) and during the dinner a party may go around the table to toast with individuals directly; this is a sign of respect and to refuse would be a breach of etiquette. Third, some cultures have the practice of gift giving, which may be considered illegal or unethical in other cultures. Fourth, in some cultures the person you are negotiating with may not be the person who makes the decisions; in some cultures, decision-making is done through consensus building. Fifth, it may be best to keep a formal, more respectful approach when first meeting a person; it is best to let the other person decide when a more informal relationship is in order. Sixth, in some cultures what one may consider to be an informal event may still require formal attire. The most problematic cultural trait is signs of racial and gender bias. Do not assume that the biases of the negotiating party reflect or define the views of the country or its people.

The substantive laws and commercial means of doing business are amazingly similar among the world's different legal systems, but the differences in contract customs are profound. Even though the importance of a written contract is universally recognized in principle, executing a long, detailed contract may be frowned upon in some countries: "In many cultures, if one is required to write down the agreement, it will destroy the trust and render the agreement invalid."[2] Cultural differences have practical importance in the negotiation and formation of a contract. The Confucian influence of harmony (*wa*) permeates contracting in Japan and China. Thus, a style of hard bargaining is likely to meet with failure. It is important to state a position firmly and at the same time not to disturb the *wa* or harmony of the negotiation.

Wa is reflected in the approach to negotiation as the process of developing a trusting business relationship and not the simple formation of a contract. Any disputes should be dealt with through acts of conciliation. All questions are to be answered through a process of *reconcilement*, which is a process where parties negotiate adjustments to the contract in order to restore the harmony in their relationship. The contract provides a basic framework that allows for modification and flexibility. As a result, contract provisions are written not to be rigid, but to be flexible and changeable. In case of changed circumstances parties are expected to renegotiate in good faith, and there is an implied understanding that clauses are to be applied leniently in the area of performance.

It is important to understand the authority of the other negotiating party and her place in the chain of command. A longer negotiation period may be due not to the other party's reluctance or gamesmanship but to her lack of authority to complete a deal on her own. For example, in some Eastern cultures business decisions are based upon reaching a consensus within a company.

A number of criteria must be satisfied in order for cross-cultural contract negotiations to conclude successfully. First, the negotiations should lead to a written contract that is enforceable in the countries of both parties. Second, the contract should reflect a full understanding of rights and duties of the parties for the purpose of developing a strong business relationship. Third, dispute resolution should be addressed in the contract. Because of the cost, inconvenience, and uncertainty of transnational litigation, the contract should outline cost-effective and relationship-preserving means of dispute resolution. Some countries, such as China and Japan, have long emphasized conciliation or mediation as the preferred means of dispute resolution. Special attention should be devoted to the issue of "changed circumstances," since various legal and business cultures deal with this issue differently. Common law countries emphasize the strict enforcement of contractual rights regardless of circumstances. In contrast, some civil law countries will not strictly enforce a contract if there has been a change in circumstances. Therefore, the contract should deal with the issues of renegotiation and modification of the contract in the event of such changes.

Principles of International Contract Law

Despite the differences in how foreign laws deal with the negotiation, interpretation, and enforcement of contracts, there are tremendous similarities among the different legal systems in how the law supports commercial transactions. Most differences are a matter of style and not substance. Along with the similarities among legal systems in commercial law, a trend has been evidenced toward developing a unified body of international business law. This trend can be seen at work on a number of levels. First, the growth of **customary international law** (standardized trade usage, business customs, and general principles) is seen with the almost universal adoption of the International Chamber of Commerce's standards in the area of trade terms (**INCOTERMS**) and letters of credit (Uniform Customs and Practices for Documentary Credits or **UCP**). Second, the increased publication and citation of international commercial arbitration decisions are evidence of the development of an international commercial jurisprudence not tied directly to national laws. Finally, there have been important developments in the enactment of international treaties and conventions unifying international private law. The clearest example was the ratification of the United Nations Convention on Contracts for the International Sale of Goods (**CISG**) on January 1, 1988. The CISG will be covered in detail in Chapter 11. For examples of international private law conventions, see Figure 9.1 *Comparative Law*: "International Commercial Law Conventions."

When drafting an international contract there are at least three possible sources of law, including the national laws of each of the parties and international contract law or the ***lex mercatoria***. The *lex mercatoria* or "law of merchants" refers to business customs or trade usage developed by businesspersons throughout the world.

- United Nations Convention on Contracts for the International Sale of Goods, ratified January 1, 1988
- United Nations Convention on the Limitation Period of the International Sale of Goods, ratified January 1, 1988
- UNCITRAL (United Nations Commission on International Trade Law) Independent Guarantees and Stand-by Letters of Credit
- United Nations Convention on Carriage of Goods by Sea (Hamburg Rules, ratified 1992)
- United Nations Convention on Multimodal Transport
- UNIDROIT (International Institute for the Unification of Private Law, or Rome Institute) Convention on International Financial Leasing
- UNIDROIT Convention on International Factoring
- UNIDROIT Principles of International Commercial Contracts
- United Nations Convention on the Recognition and Enforcement of Foreign Arbitral Awards (New York Convention)
- UNCITRAL Model Law on International Commercial Arbitration

Figure 9.1 Comparative Law: International Commercial Law Conventions.

Danish professor Ole Lando listed the following seven sources[3] of the *lex mercatoria* that can be used in the interpretation of contracts:

- *Public International Law*: There are provisions in the Vienna Convention on Treaties that can be applied to private international contracts.
- *Uniform Laws*: The Hague Rules (codified as COGSA) and the Convention on Contracts for the International Sale of Goods (CISG) are examples of successful attempts at uniform international laws.
- *General Principles of Contract Law*: The best example of a general principle of contract law found in most national legal systems is *pacta sunt servanda* or what is referred to in the common law as *sanctity of contract*.
- *Rules of International Organizations*: Courts may look to nonbinding rules published by such international organizations as the United Nations, the Organisation for European Co-operation and Development (OECD), and the International Institute for the Unification of Private Law (UNIDROIT).
- *Custom and Usage*: The clearest examples of custom and usage or *customary international law* that has reached a level of almost universal acceptance are the standards and rules published by the International Chamber of Commerce in the area of trade terms (INCOTERMS) and letters of credit (Uniform Customs and Practices for Documentary Credits or UCP).
- *Standard Form Contracts*: Once again, the ICC is a good source for standard form contracts and standard clauses. For example, the ICC publishes standard or model forms of Distribution and Agency Agreements. They also publish a manual to be used in the drafting of *force majeure* and hardship clauses.
- *Arbitral Decisions*: Although not widely reported, arbitral decisions provide an outstanding resource for principles.

A lawyer may attempt to reduce her need to know a foreign law by using a choice of law clause. However, she must become knowledgeable about the mandatory or immutable rules and regulations found in the foreign law. The contract drafter should also be aware of generally recognized international contract principles. These principles are brought to bear by courts and arbitration panels

- Exclusion of trade usage (Articles 1.8, 4.3(f))
- Four corners clause (integration or merger clause) (Articles 2.17 and 2.18)
- Time of performance, early performance, late performance (Articles 6.1.1, 6.1.5, and 7.1.5)
- Order of performance (Article 6.1.4)
- Place of performance, place of payment (Article 6.1.6)
- Form of payment (Articles 6.1.7 and 6.1.8)
- Currency of payment (Article 6.1.9)
- Transportation costs, other expenses (Article 6.1.11)
- Government approvals (Articles 6.1.13–6.1.17)
- Hardship clause (Articles 6.2.1–6.2.3)
- *Force majeure* clause (Article 7.1.7)
- Termination clause, notice provisions (Articles 7.3.1 and 7.3.2)
- Forum selection and arbitration clauses (Article 7.3.5(3))
- Limitation of liability clause (Article 7.1.6)
- Interest on delinquent payments (Article 7.4.9)
- Damages, liquidated damages clause (Articles 7.4.1–7.4.4 and 7.4.13)

Figure 9.2 Focus on Transactions: Checklist of Important International Contract Clauses.

in the interpretation of contracts. The general principle is that contracts should be enforced according to their terms under the doctrine of ***pacta sunt servanda***. However, *pacta sunt servanda* is qualified by the concept of ***abus de droit***—the rule that unfair or unconscionable contracts and clauses should not be enforced.

The general duty of good faith is another generally accepted principle of contract law. The civil law concept *culpa in contrahendo* requires that the parties negotiate in good faith. In German law, the good faith principle plays a key role in issues relating to the performance and interpretation of contracts. In contrast, the UK and India still reject a general implied duty of good faith, while other common law countries including Australia, Canada, and the U.S. have recognized the concept of good faith in the area of performance and enforcement of contracts. The notion of good faith should guide a businessperson's response to all communications from a foreign party. Failure to respond to a letter or request is often regarded as evidence of assent to its terms, for example, under the civil law notion of ***nachfrist* notice** (time extension), in which a party makes a request for additional time to perform. In the event that the receiving party fails to respond or fails to give a commercially viable reason for a denial of the request, then the extension is automatically granted. There is no counterpart to this notion in the common law.

An astute lawyer should develop checklists of important clauses to be negotiated into international contracts. Figure 9.2 *Focus on Transactions*: "Checklist of Important International Contract Clauses" is an example of a checklist prepared by the **International Chamber of Commerce** (ICC)[4] using the **UNIDROIT Principles of International Commercial Contracts** (PICC). The material in parentheses refers to the relevant articles of the *UNIDROIT Principles*. The next section examines the process of contract interpretation that is pivotal to the resolution of contract disputes.

Contract Interpretation

The major approach to contract interpretation is the *objective theory of contract* (interpretation of the meaning of the objective manifestations of intent is known as the **reasonable person standard**). The common law embraces this approach, while the civil law first applies the *subjective theory of contract* (agreement-in-fact or actual intent), but then turns to the objective theory if the subjective meaning cannot be determined. An important part of contract law pertains to the rules or standards used by courts in the interpretation of contracts. In the objective theory of contract, the standard of review is the meaning attached to the contract by a reasonable person (reasonable person standard). Put simply, it is not what a party or parties to a contract think a contract clause means; it is what a reasonable third person interprets it to mean. Thus, it is not what a party knows that is important; it is what a party has a *reason to know* or *should know*. What a party *should know* is unconcerned with actual knowledge.[5]

The determination of the objective intent of a party is based on what they had reason to know or should have known. The judge or arbitrator determines this intent through the **totality of the circumstances analysis.**[6] This analysis considers all the circumstances of the contract, including the contract itself, prior dealings between the parties, how the parties performed the contract, subsequent modifications to the contract, and relevant business customs and trade usage. *Should know* is more a judicial reflection regarding what is reasonable given the characteristics of the parties and the circumstances. The focus on what a party should have known is based on a reasonable interpretation working in a particular business or industry (energy dealers, cotton dealers, precious metals dealers, and so forth).[7]

Contract interpretation has also been affected by statutory law. The **English Unfair Contract Terms Act of 1977** (as well as the EU Directive on Unfair Terms in Consumer Contracts) adopts a presumption of unreasonableness for indemnity or exculpatory clauses that "by reference to any contract term a party is made to indemnify another party in respect of liability for negligence or breach of contract."[8] For international sales contracts it voids any choice of law clause whose purpose is the avoidance of the Unfair Contract Terms Act. This statute is an example of how mandatory rules pre-empt a court's search for the contractual intent of the parties. The intent of the parties regarding such a clause becomes irrelevant because the clause is invalidated by statute.

Customary law, by way of examining current custom and trade usage, has often been the vehicle by which the common law fabricated the reasonable person in interpreting contracts. Justice Turley in the 1842 case *Jacob v. State* noted that: "Common law sources are to be found in the usage, habits, manners, and customs of people. The common law of a country will be modified, and extended by analogy, *construction, and custom*, so as to embrace new relations, springing up from time to time, from a change of society."[9] The courts use the reasonable person standard to discourage unconscionable practices and encourage the development of judicially approved standards of reasonableness.

Liquidated Damages and Penalty Clauses

Liquidated damages clauses stipulate the damages that will be payable upon a breach of the contract, technically eliminating the need for a court action or arbitral proceeding. These clauses, also known as penalty clauses, are not uniformly enforced under all national legal systems. The common law system requires courts to void liquidated damages clauses that act as penalties (a penalty is an amount of damages above what would be collectable from a court; something above compensatory damages). This voiding of penalties is a minority approach under most national laws. The French Civil Code deals directly with the issue of liquidated damages or penalty clauses. As a general rule, penalties are enforceable, but Article 1231-5 allows the courts to provide alternative relief if the stipulated amount is *manifestly excessive*. It expressly grants courts the authority to reduce or increase the penalty if it is deemed to be manifestly excessive or low. In Japan, there is a strong presumption that penalty clauses are enforceable. Article 420(3) of the Japanese Civil Code states that: "a penalty clause is presumed to be a determination in advance of the amount of compensation due for damages." Article 420(1) of the Japanese Civil Code precludes a court from reforming (adjusting) the contract amount.

The laws of Denmark, Sweden, Finland, and Norway allow either the voiding or reformation (adjustment) of a penalty clause deemed unreasonable. The Russian Civil Code provides that "the debtor must pay the penalty established for the breach regardless of whether or not the creditor has suffered damages as a result of the breach" and, in Article 190, allows a court to reduce the amount of the penalty or liquidated damages if it is "extraordinarily large in comparison with the creditor's actual losses." In contrast, Anglo-American common law simply mandates the voiding of all penalty clauses. Although, there has been recent evidence that the common law is becoming more liberal and enforcing some penalty clauses. In 2015, the UK Supreme Court upheld the enforceability of penalties in commercial and consumer contracts in the combined cases of *Cavendish Square v. Makdessi* and *Parking Eye v. Barry*.[10] The Court reasoned that the penal character of a clause is a question of construction, to which evidence of the commercial background is relevant. In sum, there may be a reasonable justification for a penalty other than to punish the breaching party.

In order to provide some uniformity between the common law and civil law, the Council of Europe adopted *Resolution (78)3 on Penal Clauses in Civil Law*. See Figure 9.3 *Comparative Law*: "Penalty Clauses in Europe and the United States." It adopts the civil law approach that the "sum stipulated may be reduced by the court when it is manifestly excessive." In its Explanatory Memorandum, the Committee on Legal Cooperation explained that some penal clauses are "*stricto sensu* (arbitrarily set) whose main purpose is to act as a threat to induce the promisor to perform" while others are "a genuine pre-assessment of damages or liquidated damages." However, unlike in the common law, the clauses that are *stricto sensu* are not invalid *per se* under the civil law. In short, it is acceptable under the civil law for a liquidated damages clause to serve as not only a means for just compensation, but also an incentive to induce performance.

It should be noted that a businessperson from a common law country should be aware that penalties are enforced in most countries and are recognized by international arbitrators.

Doctrine of *Arrhes* and Inspection Rights

French law allows for the use of deposits as a way of fixing damages unrelated to actual damages. If the deposit holder cancels the contract, then that party must refund twice the amount of the deposit. The rules embodied in the doctrine of *arrhes* can be understood as the use of deposits as liquidated damages.

Council of Europe Resolution (78) 3 (On Penal Clauses in Civil Law)

Considering that the aim of the Council of Europe is to achieve greater unity between its members, in particular the adoption of common rules in the field of law, and considering that it is necessary to provide judicial control over penal clauses in civil law in appropriate cases where the penalty is manifestly excessive.

Article 2

The promisee may not obtain concurrently performance of the principal obligation, as specified in the contract, and payment of the sum stipulated in the penal clause unless the sum was stipulated for delayed performance.

Article 7

The court may reduce the sum stipulated when it is determined to be manifestly excessive.

Explanatory Memorandum

The legal systems of member states have devised various means to enable courts to exercise a certain control over penal clauses, although the circumstances under which this control can be exercised differ considerably from one state to another. It is one of the essential aims of the present resolution to contribute towards a *harmonisation* of the laws of the member states.

It is left to each legal system to determine under what precise circumstances the sum concerned is manifestly excessive. It is suggested that in a given case the courts may have regard to a number of factors such as:

i Comparing the damage pre-estimated by the parties at the time of contracting and the damage actually suffered by the promisee.

ii The legitimate interests of the parties including the promisee's non-pecuniary interests.

iii The category of contract and the circumstances under which it was concluded, in particular the relative social and economic position of the parties, or the fact that the contract was a standard form contract.

iv The reason for the failure to perform, in particular the good or bad faith of the promisor.

Law of Liquidated Damages in the United States

UCC Section 2-718: Liquidation or Limitation of Damages

Damages for breach may be liquidated in the agreement but only at an amount, which is reasonable in the light of the anticipated or actual harm caused by the breach, the difficulties of proof of loss, and the inconvenience of obtaining an adequate remedy. A term fixing unreasonably large liquidated damages is void as a penalty.

Restatement (Second) of Contracts Section 356, Comment b.

Factor 1: The amount fixed is reasonable to the extent that it approximates the actual loss caused by the breach. Furthermore, the amount affixed is reasonable to the extent that it approximates the loss anticipated at the time of the making of the contract.

Factor 2: If the difficulty of proof is great, considerable latitude is allowed in the approximation of anticipated or actual harm.

Figure 9.3 Comparative Law: Penalty Clauses in Europe and the United States.

Furthermore, the potentially penal nature of retaining the entire deposit or doubling the amount refunded is disregarded under this doctrine. A uniquely French rule requires that "with regard to wine, oil, and other things, which it is customary to taste before buying, there is no sale so long as the buyer has not yet tasted and approved them." This would be contrary to the general rules of distant selling or documentary transactions (see Chapter 12).

Execution in Counterpart: Some countries do not recognize the ability of the parties to sign two different copies of their agreement—one signs one copy and the other signs another copy; they then exchange the forms, but no one form has both signatures—as adequate to form a contract. In the sale of goods there is often an exchange of forms with only one signature on each, but they are different forms, such as a price quotation (seller), purchasing order (buyer), or a confirmation (seller or buyer). This exchange of forms is considered sufficient to form a sale of goods contract.

National Contract Laws

This section will review the **French Civil Code**, **Russian Civil Code**, and the **Chinese Contract Law** (CCL). It will also review the **Principles of European Contract Law** (PECL), which is viewed as a model law that has been influential in the revision of national contract laws.

French Civil Code

On October 1, 2016, the revised French Civil Code entered into force replacing the iconic Napoleonic Code of 1804. The new Code modernized and substantially changed French contract law. The rationales given for the revision were that it had become obsolete, had lost international influence, and was unfriendly to international business. The provisions discussed below highlight the convergence of law, as the new provisions drew from the Convention on Contracts for the International Sale of Goods (CISG), the UNIDROIT Principles of International Commercial Contracts (PICC), and the Principles of European Contract Law (PECL).

From a comparative law perspective, the Code drops the civil law notion of *causa* (cause) (objective cause related to the goal of the contract; subjective cause required that the parties entered into the contract for legitimate reasons) as a requirement for an enforceable contract. Article 1128 only requires consent, capacity to contract, and legal subject matter.

Precontractual Obligations

Article 1104 extends the duty of good faith in the performance of a contract to include the negotiation of the contract. It also expands the duty to disclose material information in the negotiation of a contract. Article 1112-1 provides that if one party to the contract negotiations is aware of information which would be determinative for the consent of the other party, it must inform such other party if it is clear that the other party is unaware of the information or relies on the first party to provide all significant information.

Offer-Acceptance Rules

Article 1115 provides that contractual offers may be retracted if they have not yet reached the offeree. However, Article 1116 states that if an offer is received (but not yet accepted) the offer remains open (irrevocable) for the period for acceptance stated in the offer or, if no such period is fixed, then the offer remains open for a reasonable period (see CISG, Article 16(2)). Article 1119 states that if the general conditions (standard terms) in the offer and acceptance are in conflict ("battle of the forms" scenario), then neither of the conflicting conditions are effective (they cancel each other out). This is popularly known as the "*knock-out rule.*"

Abuse of Bargaining Power and Standard Terms

One of the general principles listed as a rationale for revising the French Civil Code was to address the problem of unfair terms where one party takes advantage of a weaker party. Article 1110 introduces a statutory definition of a standard form contract (*contrat d'adhésion*) for the first time. A standard form contract is one where the "general conditions, removed from negotiations, are determined in advance by one of the parties." Article 1171 introduces the notion of contractual imbalance in standard form agreements imposed by one party on another, contractual clauses (other than those dealing with the principal object of the contract or with the price of the service provided) which create a significant imbalance (*déséquilibre significatif*) between the rights and obligations of the parties to the contract can be deleted by the judge at the request of the party suffering from the significant imbalance in the contract. Article 1143 provides that violence (duress or threat) exists when a party, abusing the state of dependency in which its co-contracting party finds itself, obtains from the co-contracting party a concession or term the co-contracting party would not have otherwise agreed to in the absence of such constraint, and coercing party benefits from a manifestly excessive advantage.

Interpretation of Contracts

French law has historically required courts to interpret contracts based upon the actual subjective intention (agreement-in-fact) of the parties rather than merely interpreting the objective meaning of the words of the contract as is done in the common law (reasonable person standard). Article 1188 now states that if the mutual intention of the parties cannot be determined, the contract is to be interpreted according to a reasonable person placed in the same situation. In the area of standard form agreements, Article 1190 adopts the common law's *contra proferentem* rule that ambiguous terms are to be interpreted against the party who drafted the contract (see CISG, Article 8(2)).

Hardship and Force Majeure

Article 1195 provides that if a change in circumstances which could not have been predicted at the time the contract was entered into renders performance of the contract excessively onerous for a contractual party who had not assumed such risk, such party may request that the other party renegotiate the contract. If the other party refuses to renegotiate or in the event that the renegotiation is not successful, the requesting party may request a court to adapt (adjust) the contract. The judge may revise the contract or terminate it.

Force majeure is defined by Article 1218: (1) as the occurrence of an event which is beyond the control of the obligor; (2) which could not have been reasonably foreseen at the time of the entry into the contract; and (3) the effects of which cannot be avoided by appropriate measures and prevents performance of its obligation. If the effects are temporary, the performance of the obligation is suspended unless the delay resulting therefrom justifies termination of the contract. The provisions on hardship and force majeure, as well as the new rules relating to adhesion contracts and standard terms give substantial powers to the courts to intervene into contracts.[11]

Remedies

Article 1217 sets out several different remedies for contractual nonperformance:

> *Refusal.* Refusal of the performing party to perform its own obligations or suspension of such performance is allowed when it is manifestly clear that the other party will not perform on the date performance if the consequences of such nonperformance are sufficiently serious for the otherwise performing party (common law's "anticipatory repudiation").
>
> *Specific performance* (*exécution forcée*) shall be granted after serving formal notice on the nonperforming party to perform and unless such performance is impossible or if there exists manifest disproportion between the cost of performing and the value of performance to the obligee (promisee).
>
> *Accept imperfect performance* and request a reduction in price.
>
> *Termination of the contract*, where the contract specifies those obligations the nonperformance of which will trigger the termination of the contract (*clause résolutoire*). If the contract does not contain a *clause résolutoire*, the obligee may terminate the contract if there is a sufficiently serious case of nonperformance by simple notification but at its risk.
>
> *Damages* can always be claimed, either alone or in conjunction with the other remedies.

This is a much more flexible remedial regime than under the old Code and gives courts more power to provide a just remedy.

Collateral Obligations

It is important to realize that national differences in the requirements of and restrictions on contracting are often found throughout a country's regulatory network. These noncontract law regulations impact directly on contract issues. For example, Article 433 of the **German Civil Code** indicates that a producer or supplier of goods in an ongoing relationship, such as a distribution agreement, has a "*collateral obligation* to have replacement parts ready for delivery even if there is no special agreement." In contrast, in the common law, issues of after-sales service and replacement parts supply are left to the private agreement of the contracting parties.

Law in Action

Another area of concern for the international entrepreneur is the difference between "law in books" and "law in action." A number of countries have enacted modern Westernized commercial codes, but uniformity in their interpretation and application is lacking. An example is the law of many Islamic countries where there is a direct interrelationship between religious and secular codes. The main body of law, the ***Sharia*** law comprises religious, social, and legal mandates. The main body of this source of law was completed by the early tenth century, at least as practiced by the majority Sunni sect. Beginning with the Ottoman Empire in the nineteenth century, however, "the *Sharia* lost its exclusivity as the governing law of contracts to a combination of sacred and secular laws."[12]

The secular laws have included a modern codification of contract and commercial law with which a Western businessperson would be quite comfortable. For example, Saudi Arabia has enacted a set of regulations, including ones governing commercial law, negotiable instruments, and corporate law. The problem for an outside businessperson is that the principles of the *Sharia* still take precedence over these secular statutes. Most of the judges in the secular court system have religious training, and their decisions are reviewed by a Commercial Board to ensure conformity with *Sharia* law. The application and intrusion of religious principles into commercial law disputes is sporadic, but it is important to note that a party may seek to overcome a decision based on the commercial codes by resorting to *Sharia* principles.

Chinese Contract Law

On 1 January 2021, China adopted the Chinese Civil Code (CCC), which is aligned with the civil law tradition, but also has similarities to the common law tradition. The obligations area of the CCC maintained most of the provisions of the 1999 Chinese Contract Law (CCL). There are some differences, mostly for the better, such as expressly adopting a hardship provision, previously recognized by the Supreme People's Court. The most obvious difference is seen in its general principles where remnants of the former socialist system persist. It accepts the core principle of freedom of contract that the parties may make any agreement that does not violate the law. However, the other general principles place limits on such freedom, such as "neither party may impose its will on the other party" and the "parties should take each other's reasonable interests into account" when performing the contract. Article 5 states that "the parties shall abide by the principle of fairness in prescribing their rights and obligations." Such a principle has no counterpart in the common law.

The duty of good faith in the performance of contract is found in American contract law but has been rejected in English law. The CCC's version of good faith is similar to that found in German law. In German law, good faith is a core principle, which influences all areas of contracts, such as precontract negotiations, performance, and contract interpretation. Unlike the common law, the CCC obligates parties to negotiate in good faith. The CCC provides that a party is not acting in good faith if they: (1) entered into negotiations with no real intention of reaching an agreement; (2) take unfair advantage of the other party's dependence, economic distress, or weakness; and (3) negotiate an unconscionable (overly one-sided) bargain.

Anticipatory Repudiation (Breach)

The CCC adopts the concept of anticipatory repudiation (breach), which allows a party to anticipate a future breach in order to immediately terminate the contract and sue for damages. Article 527 states: "The party who is to perform the obligation first may suspend his performance if he has definite evidence that the other party's (1) business operation has significantly deteriorated; (2) has removed assets or surreptitiously withdrawn funds in order to evade his obligations; (3) has lost his commercial goodwill; and (4) has lost or may lose the ability to perform his obligation. If a party suspends his performance without definite evidence, he shall be liable for breach of contract."

Initially, the party declaring an anticipatory repudiation may only suspend the contract and not terminate the contract pending the other party's response. The party first must give the other party a notice of repudiation in a timely manner. Article 528 allows the other party to provide evidence (assurance) that it will perform on time. Performance shall be resumed if the other party provides "appropriate security."

Liquidated Damages and Deposits

Article 585 recognizes the enforceability of liquidated damages (pre-agreed damages) but "if the agreed liquidated damages are lower than the loss incurred, the parties may apply to the people's court or arbitral institution for an increase; if the agreed liquidated damages are *excessively higher* than the loss incurred, the parties may apply to the people's court or arbitral institution for an appropriate reduction." Despite using the common law term of liquidated damages, Article 585 adopts the civil law rule that penalties (an amount above actual damages) are enforceable unless the amount is manifestly excessive. The common law rejects the enforceability of penalty clauses.[13]

Interestingly, the CCC also adopts the "deposit rule" found in the French doctrine of *arrhes*. Articles 586 and 587 of the CCC recognize a party's option to deliver a deposit as security relating to a contract. As with the doctrine of *arrhes*, if the party that gives the deposit fails to perform, the party holding the deposit is allowed to keep it. If the party holding the deposit fails to perform, then "he shall return double the amount of the deposit." However, in the case where the contract provides for a deposit and liquidated damages, Articles 588 and 589 state that "where the parties have stipulated both liquidated damages and deposit and a party breaches the contract, the other party may choose to apply the liquidated damages clause or the deposit clause," but not both.

Standard Terms

The CCC also regulates **standard terms**. Standard terms are defined as "terms which are formulated in advance for repeated use by a party and which are not negotiated with the other party when concluding the contract." Article 496 provides the party supplying standard terms "shall comply with the principle of fairness when determining the rights and duties of the parties, shall, in a reasonable manner, draw the attention of the other party to the terms which exclude or limit his liability, and shall, upon the other party's request, explain such terms." Thus, standard terms that are overly one-sided or would "surprise" the other party if he knew of their existence and meaning are unenforceable. The CCC expressly voids exemption (disclaimer) clauses that limit a party's liability for personal injury or liability for property loss caused by the party acting either intentionally or as a result of gross negligence.

Sales Contracts

Article 619 requires the seller of goods to properly package the goods for shipment. If there is no agreement on the manner of packaging or if the agreement is unclear, the customary manner of packaging shall be applied; if there is no such customary manner (trade usage), the manner of packaging that is adequate to protect the subject matter shall be adopted. An important issue in sale of goods involves long-term supply contracts. The key issue being if a party fails to deliver an installment or make a payment, or the seller delivers an installment of defective goods, does the nonbreaching party have the right to terminate the entire contract (including future installments)? Article 166 deals with this issue by providing the following rules: (1) if the seller fails to deliver one of the installments or delivers defective goods, the buyer may terminate the contract in respect of that one installment; (2) if the seller fails to deliver one of the installments or fails to deliver it in conformity with the agreement, thereby making it impossible for all the future installments to accomplish the purpose of the contract, the buyer may terminate the contract in respect of that installment and all future installments; and (3) where the buyer terminates the contract in respect of one of the installments, if that installment and other installments are interdependent, he may terminate the contract in respect of all the delivered and undelivered installments.

Principles of European Contract Law

The **Principles of European Contract Law (PECL)** aim to provide a Community-wide infrastructure of contract law. Article 1.101 states that the PECL may apply when the parties select them as their choice of law and when the contract is to be governed by general principles of law or the *lex mercatoria*. The PECL, like the CISG, serves as a fairly written compromise choice of law. The CISG is a better choice in a sale of goods transaction, while the PECL applies to all types of contracts.

Precontractual Liability and Breach of Confidentiality

The PECL recognizes **precontractual liability** and the duty of good faith negotiations. Failure to negotiate in good faith is grounds for contractual liability. Thus, terminating a negotiation without giving a viable reason is not appropriate. A party can be held liable for losses caused to the other party.[14] Article 2.302, **Breach of Confidentiality**, recognizes a duty not to disclose confidential information obtained in the course of negotiations. Also, statements made during the negotiations may provide separate grounds for liability under Article 6.101 ("Statements Giving Rise to Contractual Obligation"). It states that if a professional supplier gives information about the quality or uses of services or goods when marketing or advertising or otherwise before a contract is concluded then the "statement is to be treated as giving rise to a contractual obligation." This precontractual line of obligation further extends to agents of the supplier. It is imperative that the exporter-supplier review its advertisements, promotional brochures, and practices of foreign sales representatives in order to avoid such liability.

Merger and Modification Clauses

A review of the PECL demonstrates a large amount of similarity with the common law of contracts. It also shows significant differences. The following review outlines some of the differences and notes comparable provisions in the CISG. The PECL adopt the CISG's approach to formalities. Article 2.101 is almost identical to Article 11 of the CISG: "A contract need not be concluded or evidenced in writing nor is it subject to any other requirement as to form. The contract may be proved by any means, including witnesses." The PECL goes farther than the CISG in rejecting provisions that reduce the admissibility of evidence in a contract dispute. Written modification and merger clauses may not be enforceable under Articles 2.105 and 2.106, which state that **written modification clauses** (clause requires a written instrument to change the contract) only provide a presumption. The other party may still introduce extrinsic evidence from outside the written contract in order to rebut the presumption. The articles further state that: "a party may by its statements or conduct be precluded from asserting such a clause."[15] This idea can be found in the common law principles of *waiver* (failure to enforce a term within a reasonable time) and *estoppel* (party communicates to other party that a writing is not required).

A **merger clause** (prohibits the use of extrinsic evidence to contradict a term in the contract) found in a standard form or in the general conditions section of a contract may be ignored. The standard merger clause states that the document into which it is incorporated is a final integration of the parties' agreement and supersedes all other statements, writings, or correspondences. A merger clause that is *individually negotiated* will be enforced, otherwise the clause establishes only a presumption. However, even when fully negotiated a merger clause can be voided in the case of ambiguity in the contract or on grounds of waiver.

> PECL Article 2.209(3): "General conditions of contract are terms which have been formulated in advance for an indefinite number of contracts of a certain nature, and which have not been individually negotiated between the parties."

Contract Formation: Offer-Acceptance Rules

A number of rules in the area of **offer** should be noted. First, the exporter should be aware that a circular, advertisement, or proposal, considered by him as an invitation to offer may be construed as a standing offer under the PECL. Article 2.201 states that "a proposal to supply goods or services at stated prices made by a professional supplier in a public advertisement or a catalogue, or by a display of goods, is *presumed* to be an offer to sell or supply at that price until the stock of goods, or the supplier's capacity to supply the service, is exhausted." Second, the **firm offer rule** (irrevocable offer) is expanded to further restrict offeror from revoking the offer. An offer may not be revoked if it indicates that it is irrevocable or fixes a time for acceptance. More importantly, under the PECL any offer may be recognized as a firm offer if it is "reasonable for the offeree to rely on the offer being irrevocable and the offeree has acted in reliance on the offer." Thus, the offer need not give any assurance that it will remain open.

In the area of **acceptance**, not surprisingly, the common law's dispatch or mailbox rule is rejected for the civil law's receipt rule. Under the PECL, a contract is concluded when the acceptance reaches the offeror.[16] It would seem that the receipt rule for acceptance would provide the offeror with an additional period to revoke the offer. But like under Article 18 of the CISG, the right to revoke an offer is frozen when the acceptance is dispatched[17] even though the acceptance is not effective until receipt. However, in the event that the acceptance does not reach the offeror within a reasonable time, then the revocation is unfrozen and prevents the formation of a contract. In the case where a revocation has not already been sent, a late acceptance due to problems of transmission gives the offeror the option to reject the acceptance if he informs the offeree, "without delay," that the offer has lapsed.[18]

The **battle of forms** scenario[19] commonly found in international sale of goods transactions is dealt with in Article 2.208 titled "Modified Acceptance" and Article 2.209 titled "Conflicting General Conditions." The offeree's form that gives a definite assent to the offer creates a contract unless it possesses additional or different terms that materially alter the offer. Article 2.208 recognizes that the parties can include contract language to control the battle of forms scenario. The offeror may incorporate a clause in its offer to the effect that it "expressly limits acceptance to the terms of the offer."

The offeree may condition its acceptance upon the offeror's assent to its additional terms. Article 2.208 requires that the offeror must expressly agree to the additional terms in order for the conditional acceptance to effectuate a contract. The offeree can obtain an agreement to the additional terms when he requires the offeror to sign and return the conditional acceptance. A conditional acceptance will be treated as a rejection if the offeror's assent to the additional or different terms "does not reach the offeree within a reasonable time." Article 2.209 provides that the fine print terms in offer and acceptance forms will generally be considered as "general conditions" and only the general conditions (standard terms) that are "common in substance" become a part of the contract. Thus, conflicting general conditions would not become a part of the contract.

Defenses to Breach of Contract

In the area of **genuineness of assent**, the PECL recognize many of the same contract voiding events found in the common law. The terminology in parentheses is the common law equivalent to the invalidating rule found in the PECL. A party has the right to void a contract due to one party's mistake as to facts or law (unilateral mistake),[20] mutual mistake,[21] fraud,[22] threats (duress),[23] unfair advantage (undue influence),[24] and unfair terms (unconscionability).[25] In the area of mutual mistake, the court is directed not to void the contract but rather to adjust (reform) the contract. It states that where both parties made the same mistake, the court may at the request of either party bring the contract into accordance with what might reasonably have been agreed had the mistake not occurred.

The notion of **economic duress** is not placed under the threats (duress) umbrella but within the notion of unfair advantage (undue influence). A party may avoid a contract if at the time of contracting "it was dependent on or had a relationship of trust with the other party, was in *economic distress* or had urgent needs, was improvident, ignorant, inexperienced, or lacking bargaining skills." In contrast, the notion that the party had "no reasonable alternative" is found in the article on threats. The article on fraud recognizes a substantial duty to disclose information. The general duty of good faith and fair dealing is also applied to require a duty to disclose under certain circumstances. Factors to be considered in determining the need for disclosure include whether one of the parties had "special expertise," the cost of obtaining the information, whether the other party could reasonably have acquired the information on its own, and whether the information would have been material to the decision-maker.

The PECL adopt the civil law notion of *nachfrist* notice. The nonperforming party may obtain an extension of the time of performance by giving notice to the other party. Generally, the extension must be given unless the nonbreaching party gives a commercially viable reason for not granting the extension. After the expiration of the extension, the nonbreaching party may terminate the contract even for minor breaches. There is no such provision for requesting or granting additional time in the common law.

Exemption from Liability

In the area of contractual excuse for breach, the PECL recognize the notion of **an impediment** as a ground to excuse a breaching party for his nonperformance. The test of impediment is similar to that found in the common law excuse doctrines (impossibility and frustration of purpose). The impediment must not have been "reasonably expected" and must be beyond the control of the nonperforming party.[26] The nonperforming party must give prompt notice of the impediment or be liable for damages resulting from the nonreceipt of prompt notice. In the event that the impediment is perceived to be temporary in nature, the nonperforming party is not excused from the contract but is granted a temporary suspension of performance.

Agency Rules

A unique feature of the PECL is its coverage of the **agency** relationship. Since the agency relationship is common in international transactions, as in the hiring of a foreign sales representative or distributor, the section on agency law is appropriate for review. Its coverage of the agency contract is limited to the relationship between third parties and the principal or agent. It does not govern the relationship between the principal and agent. The rules on agency are divided into those governing **direct representation** and those governing **indirect representation.** Direct representation is when the agent acts in the name of the principal. In contrast, indirect representation is when a third party is unaware that the agent is acting on behalf of a principal.

UNIDROIT Principles of International Commercial Contracts

UNIDROIT is a specialized agency of the United Nations that promotes the unification of law. Its Principles of International Commercial Contracts (PICC) primarily differs from the CISG (see Chapter 10) in three ways. First, it is not for adoption as a domestic law of international contracts. It is intended merely to provide neutral principles acceptable for guidance for lawyers and businesspersons from different legal systems. Second, it provides a set of general principles applicable to all types of contracts. In contrast, the CISG applies only to the commercial sale of goods and supplies a number of specific rules for that type of transaction. Third, the PICC covers contract negotiations, while the CISG deals merely with the mechanics of offer and acceptance.

Those drafting an international contract of any type may want to review the PICC. A number of features of the PICC should be noted. The first group of features involves the formation of contracts: (1) there is no writing requirement. The PICC simply states that a contract "may be proved by any means, including witnesses."[27] Representations made during the negotiation stage may be entered into evidence, even if they conflict with the written contract; (2) international trade usage is recognized. The parties are "bound by a usage that is widely known and regularly observed in international trade"; (3) Article 2.16 recognizes a duty of confidentiality for information obtained during the course of negotiations; and (4) Article 2.20, titled "Surprising Terms,"[28] provides a means for a party to void fine print terms in a standard form contract. It provides that terms that a party "could not reasonably have expected" will not be enforced. A conspicuous and clearly written but unusual term is enforceable, however.

The PICC expressly covers precontractual liability for conduct during the negotiation phase. Along with the potential of liability for bad faith negotiation, the PICC acknowledges the fine line between negotiation and contract in three ways: First, a contract does not require an agreement on all details of the transaction. Second, sometimes negotiations are not actually finished when one of the parties starts to perform. For instance, the legal departments of the two companies may still be discussing the contract terms when the sales department of the seller already has sent the goods. In such a situation, the shipment of the

Tip 1: Even if not legally required to, put the contract in writing! **Tip 2:** Negotiate a choice of law clause. **Tip 3:** Custom-design a forum selection or arbitration clause. **Tip 4:** Negotiate a specific *force majeure* clause. **Tip 5:** Expressly allocate the risk of currency exchange rate fluctuations. **Tip 6:** In long-term or multiple installments contracts, negotiate a detailed price escalation clause.	**Tip 7:** Assure payment and performance through third-party devices such as confirmed letters of credit, standby letters of credit, performance bonds, and bank guarantees. **Tip 8:** Seek the expert advice of international lawyers, foreign legal counsel, international bankers, freight forwarders, customs brokers, insurance brokers, and governmental agencies.

Figure 9.4 Focus on Transactions: Practical Tips for International Contracting.

goods can be considered as acceptance of the offer (unilateral contract). Third, sometimes parties to a contract intentionally leave **open terms**—terms to be agreed on in future negotiations.

The PICC is indicative of how most civil law legal systems affix liability in the negotiation stage. Parties are generally required to act in good faith during the negotiation phase. For example, a termination of lengthy negotiations without a justified reason will be considered bad faith and subject the party to a suit for damages or expenses. Damages may include claims for expenses related to the negotiations, including travel, research, and consulting costs. It may also support a claim for indirect damages such as lost profits from other potential deals that the innocent party did not pursue in order to negotiate with the terminating party (opportunity costs).

In the area of performance, the PICC includes a section on **hardship**. Hardship is defined as "where the occurrence of events fundamentally alters the equilibrium of the contract."[29] In order for a party to claim a hardship, it must show that the event causing the hardship could not reasonably have been taken into account at the time of contracting, that the event was beyond its control, and that the party did not assume the risks of the event occurring. Hardship allows the party to "request negotiations." In the event that the parties do not agree to an adjustment or settlement, the court is instructed to either terminate the contract or adjust the contract to restore its equilibrium[30] (Article 6.2.3). Figure 9.4 *Focus on Transactions*: "Practical Tips for International Contracting" provides practical advice for international contracting.

Precontractual Liability

Under common law, a negotiating party owes no duty of good faith to the other party during the negotiation of a contract. A party may terminate negotiations in bad faith and not be liable for the other party's expenses, with one major exception. The doctrine of **promissory estoppel** extends contractual liability to protect someone who reasonably relied upon the belief that the parties would conclude a final agreement. Section 90 of the American *Restatement (Second) of Contracts* allows a court to give a remedy if a person makes a promise, the other party reasonably relies upon, and an injustice would be done if the court fails to provide a remedy. A cause of action for promissory estoppel is not found in English common law, where it can only be used as a defense to a claim.

The court, in *Nimrod Marketing v. Texas Energy Corp.*, held that a purchasing agent who expended money in reliance on obtaining a contract from a client could sue for damages when the client elected to use another purchasing agent. The client had sent a letter to the agent that stated: "Acting pursuant to your responsibilities as our purchasing agent, it is our hope to begin construction of the housing shortly upon obtaining a contract with the foreign government." The court ruled that based upon the doctrine of promissory estoppel, the agent had reasonably relied upon the assurance in the letter.

Nimrod Marketing Ltd. v. Texas Energy Investment Corp.

769 F.2d 1076 (5th Cir. 1985)

Texas Energy was negotiating a contract with a foreign government to build low-cost housing, and Nimrod Marketing (Overseas) Ltd. (Nimrod) was Texas Energy's purchasing agent for supplies and materials. After Nimrod started acquiring materials, Texas Energy withdrew from its contract with the foreign government. Nimrod brought a claim under the theory of promissory estoppel. The lower court awarded damages. The court held Texas Energy liable for damages, since they had knowledge of the special circumstances producing damages upon its breach of the (noncontractual or nonbinding) agreement.

Circuit Judge. Nimrod and its president, Tom Anderson-Slight sued Texas Energy for cancelation charges and expenses resulting from a breach of a purchasing agent agreement. The district court found liability based on the doctrine of promissory estoppel and awarded damages. Texas Energy was negotiating with the Nigerian government (joint venture with Nigerian investors) to build low-cost housing for Russian steelworkers in Nigeria. In furthering the venture, Texas Energy and the Nigerians formed a partnership named Advanced Technology Ltd. (ATL).

The partners were immediately confronted with the complex task of getting building materials, equipment, and supplies into Nigeria and arranging for payment with Nigerian funds. William Houston, construction superintendent for Texas Energy, himself seated on an airplane next to Tom Anderson-Slight, president of Nimrod. Nimrod, an experienced international trading company, had numerous dealings in West Africa. Upon learning of Texas Energy's need for help in the purchasing and shipping of goods to Nigeria, Anderson-Slight told Houston of his company's interest in acting as Texas Energy's purchasing agent for the Nigerian project. Thereafter, Texas Energy and Nimrod managers met in London to discuss the project in depth. Texas Energy provided a list of needed supplies including equipment, construction material, food, and living quarters. Nimrod provided price quotes for the items on the list.

Anderson-Slight met senior officials of Texas Energy to explain the documentation necessary for shipments to Nigeria. During the visit, purchase orders were issued by ATL. Items were color-coded to reflect priority in shipment. The initial purchase orders covered items color-coded green, indicating to be shipped immediately. During this visit, Anderson-Slight was given two "comfort letters" (comfort letters are nonbinding promises or assurances), appointing Nimrod as purchasing agent for the Nigerian project for Texas Energy and ATL.

Promissory Estoppel

Acting pursuant to the comfort letters, purchase orders, and verbal authorizations, Nimrod began acquiring equipment and materials from its suppliers. Nimrod also incurred expenses for trips to Nigeria. Several weeks later, Texas Energy informed Nimrod that because of a disagreement over financing with their Nigerian partners they were withdrawing from the project. Nimrod filed suit seeking damages for expenses and charges incurred in canceling the contracts with its suppliers, grounding their claims on promissory estoppel.

The trial court rendered judgment in favor of Nimrod on a finding that they had relied on the "comfort letters" to their detriment and awarded damages for cancelation charges and out-of-pocket expenses. In computing the cancelation charges, the trial court applied the monetary exchange rate for British pounds sterling into U.S. dollars applicable on the date of the notification from Texas Energy. There was a large fluctuation in the exchange rate from $1.90 per pound sterling at the time of notification to $1.4045 per pound sterling at the date of judgment.

Recovery of Cancelation Charges

Texas Energy argues that the court erred in allowing recovery for cancelation charges. Under well-settled Texas law, losses resulting from collateral contracts are recoverable in an action for breach of contract if the breaching party "had knowledge of the special circumstances producing such damages." Texas Energy was aware that Nimrod began placing orders for supplies, equipment, and material pursuant to the comfort letters and purchase orders. They clearly had knowledge of the special circumstances producing damages upon their breach of the purchasing agent relationship.

Rate of Exchange

Texas Energy and ATL contend that the district court erred in its calculation of damages in dollars. They maintain that the court should have converted the amounts due to the three suppliers as of the date of judgment, not the date of the breach. We agree that the trial judge erred in this respect. Recovery under the theory of promissory estoppel is limited to "the amount necessary to compensate that party for a loss already suffered." AFFIRMED.

Case Highlights

- Promissory estoppel, a creation of the common law, allows recovery of out-of-pocket expenses (reliance damages), but not for lost profits, which would be the remedy for a breach of contract (expectation damages) (since there is no formal contract to enforce)

- Section 90 of the American Restatement of Contracts provides three requirements, which must be proved in order to collect under promissory estoppel: (1) an assurance or promise; (2) the other party's reasonable reliance on that assurance (incurs expenses); and (3) an injustice would be done unless the court provides some sort of remedy (reliance damages). All three of these requirements exist in the *Nimrod* case: (1) Texas Energy made assurances to Nimrod that it would use Nimrod to procure materials for its Nigerian project; (2) Nimrod moved quickly, based on the assurance, to prepare for delivering the supplies (prepared engineering drawings, purchased cargo space on ships, ordered materials from its suppliers), especially since Texas Energy was "confronted with the complex task of getting building materials, equipment, and supplies into Nigeria" in order to complete the project on time; and (3) it would be unjust to have Nimrod bear the costs it incurred on behalf of Texas Energy
- The party causing the harm should not benefit from the good faith of others such as the willingness of Nimrod's suppliers to delay demand of cancelation charges related to Nimrod's orders until the conclusion of the litigation
- Promissory estoppel focus is not on the person giving the promise, but on the actions or expectations of the party receiving the promise. Promissory estoppel is based not on promise theory (as in breach of contract; breach of promise), but is based on reliance theory, which is why it is called "detrimental reliance" in Section 90 of the Restatement
- Preliminary agreements or comfort letters generally are not sufficient to form a contract, but they may be the basis for a promissory estoppel claim
- In order to succeed on a promissory estoppel claim, the plaintiff must show that it reasonably relied on the defendant's promise or assurance to its detriment
- The damages awarded in promissory estoppel are limited to the out-of-pocket or reliance damages of the relying party. A party may not recover lost profits under promissory estoppel
- In calculating damages, an important factor for the court is deciding the applicable currency and exchange rates, as well as the appropriate time when the conversion is to be made.

The *Nimrod* case examined the use of promissory estoppel to collect damages due to a promise or assurance of a future contract between business parties. Promissory estoppel is used when no formal contract is formed.

The importance of the line between negotiations and contract was more recently explored in *Novecon Ltd. v. Bulgarian-American Enterprise Fund.*[31] A Federal Court held that no contract was formed when one party responded to a letter from a second party by stating that it agreed to the terms of the second party's proposal. The case involved Novecon, a company that develops business projects in Bulgaria. Novecon proposed a joint venture for a construction project in Sofia on land owned by Batsov, which was to get a share of the project for contributing its land. A construction loan was to come from Bulgarian-American

Enterprise Fund (BAEF). There were four letters between Novecon and BAEF concerning who would have what responsibility for the project. BAEF's last letter said that there were unresolved issues with Batsov that had to be settled before the matter could be finalized. Novecon replied that it accepted the terms of the offer, and that it understood that BAEF would resolve matters with Batsov.

Negotiations between BAEF and Batsov did not go well, and BAEF withdrew from the project. Novecon sued for breach of contract. The court dismissed the case, reasoning that "for an enforceable contract to exist there must be both (1) agreement as to all material terms and (2) intention of the parties to be bound." The court held that the parties "will not be bound to a preliminary agreement unless the evidence presented clearly indicates that they intended to be bound at that point."

Examining the legal system of Germany allows us to compare how other countries deal with the potential liability of precontractual correspondences and instruments. German law is less dependent than the common law upon the literal designation of writings or instruments as legal or nonlegal. German courts look to the purpose of a letter or a writing to determine if it creates an enforceable contractual obligation. One might argue that even informal business letters, seemingly not binding on the surface, are more likely to have legal consequences under this purpose-oriented approach to enforceability. The presumption is that most businesspersons would not spend time negotiating and drafting letters and documents unless they believed them to be legally binding.

Culpa in Contrahendo

Unlike in the U.S., the idea of precontractual liability is accepted in most of the world's national legal systems. In the civil law, one form of precontractual liability, ***culpa in contrahendo***, which straddles contract and tort laws, recognizes liability premised on an implied duty of the parties to act in good faith during the negotiations of a contract. In contrast, the common law mandates good faith only during the performance and enforcement of contracts (except for the UK and India who entirely reject the good faith principle). Good faith under the civil law system means more than not breaking off negotiations in bad faith. Numerous duties are assigned to the negotiating parties. Under Dutch law, there are duties to disclose essential information, to investigate in order to obtain necessary information, and to refrain from negotiating with third parties. A Dutch court in *Plas v. Valburg, Hoge Road*[32] divided precontract negotiations into three different stages.[33]

Plas v. Valburg, Hoge Road

18-6 Nederlandse Jurisprudentie 723 (1983)

A construction firm, Plas, submitted a tender or bid to build a municipal swimming pool in the Town of Valburg. Its proposal was considered to be the best one by the Mayor and the municipal councilors agreed to the plan. The proposal was within the budget made available for the project. However, the City Council rejected the recommended bid in favor of an alternative tender at a lower price. Plas sued for expenses and damages. The court held that there are three steps in most contract negotiations that result in the creation of numerous rights and duties. During the initial stage of negotiations either party is free to break off negotiations without any liability to the other party. The next stage or "continuing stage" of negotiations allows either party to break off negotiations, but the breaking off party remains obligated to compensate the other party for at least some of its expenses (common law's reliance damages). These types of damages are grounded upon Dutch tort law. In short, the breaking off of negotiations is deemed to be a tortious act.

During the third and final stage of negotiations, the parties are not free to break off negotiations. To do so would be considered within the doctrine of *culpa in contrahendo* or an infringement of the rules of good faith negotiation. This stage is entered into when the parties mutually and reasonably expect that a contract of some kind would result from the negotiations. The breaking off party is obligated to pay for the expectancy damages of the other party. These damages include any expenses incurred and the profits that would have been made by that party.

Decision. The parties had not entered into the third or final stage of negotiations. Therefore, it is inappropriate to award Plas damages for lost profits. The negotiations had entered into the second or continuing stage and, therefore, Plas may recover the expenses incurred in preparing its bid proposal.

Case Highlights

- The preliminary or initial stage of negotiations result in no legal liability
- Bad faith termination during the second or continuing stage of negotiations results in a claim for out-of-pocket expenses or what are referred to as reliance damages
- The parties are prohibited from terminating negotiations during the third or final stage of negotiations without being liable for full contract damages, known as expectancy damages.

Expenses include costs that can be connected directly to the negotiations, including travel, estimating expenses, and possibly damages that result from the fact that the prejudiced party was not able to conclude a contract with a third party during the negotiations. Under German law, to find a party liable for breaking off negotiations it would have to be shown that the party breaking off negotiations: (1) indicated to the other party that the negotiations would lead to a conclusion of a contract; and (2) failed to give a commercially reasonable explanation for the termination of negotiations. German law also allows for liability for bad faith negotiation even when a contract is concluded; in short, when one of the parties' reasonable expectations are not satisfied. This type of liability includes cases involving the nondisclosure of essential information. In the common law, recovery would be based on an action for intentional misrepresentation or fraud.

The case of *Grifoni v. Euratom* shows that negotiations do not automatically lead to precontractual liability.

Grifoni v. Euratom

ECLI:EU:C:1990:134

In the context of a tendering procedure for the performance of certain tin plating and iron work to be carried out at the Euratom Research Center, the applicant, following Euratom's invitation to tender, submitted an offer, which was accepted by Euratom. A precontractual agreement was concluded governing the future relations between the parties including the following clause: "the successful tenderer has the sole responsibility to ensure that safety rules are obeyed." Soon thereafter, the applicant climbed onto the roof of the Research Center in order to take measurements. The applicant fell from a height of 4.5 meters and suffered serious injuries.

Opinion. The accident occurred when the contract was not yet in force. It follows that contractual liability is precluded. However, it remains to be considered whether it is possible to find in Section 1337 of the Italian Civil Code, a precontractual liability or *culpa in contrahendo.* As a matter of general legal theory, for precontractual liability to exist there must be some practical relationship with the subject matter of the future contract—a relationship against which the traditional obligation of good faith is measured. In the present case, the relationship between the event in question and the contract is merely chronological inasmuch as the event occurred prior to the entry into force of the contract. Consequently, it appears that in the present case neither contractual nor precontractual liabilities were established.

Case Highlights

- The incurring of damages during the negotiation of a contract does not automatically lead to precontractual liability
- The precontractual agreement shielded the owner from any liability relating to accidents and was enforceable against a claim for personal injuries.

It is important for businesspersons to understand the potential for precontractual liability in international business dealings. First, there is no true counterpart to such liability in the common law system. Thus, what are considered *mere negotiations* in the common law can lead to unexpected legal liability in international business negotiations. Second, the effect of damages granted for a bad faith termination of negotiations can be catastrophic. Under the doctrine of *culpa in contrahendo*, a court has the authority to grant full contract damages, including lost profits.

One of the most common and important contracts that an exporter or manufacturer enters is with a foreign distributor for its products. This contract and relationship are vital to the successful marketing, sales, and distribution of products into a foreign market. The hypothetical case below deals with the negotiation of an exclusive distributorship agreement.

Case A v. B: *Culpa in Contrahendo* and Joint Liability

A party to negotiations with a view to entering an exclusive distributorship agreement, without valid reason, breaks off negotiations just as the deal was about to be completed, is liable for damages. This is especially the case where the party knowingly allows the other party to incur considerable expense in order to be ready to perform its side of the contract and where both parties had clearly expressed their intention to enter into a permanent relationship. The correspondence between the parties showed that there was consensus on the essential elements of the agreement.

In such a scenario, a German court would likely find for the plaintiff on the tort claim of *culpa in contrahendo*. The reason for the break off negotiations was because the defendant was induced by its parent company to terminate the negotiations. In such a case, the parent company would be held to be jointly liable along with its subsidiary. The plaintiff claims the following damages: (1) advertising expenses incurred in the promotion of defendant's products; (2) investments related to carrying out the expected contract; and (3) loss of opportunity. We find that the advertising expenses were reasonable and necessary because the products in question were unknown in Belgium and Luxembourg.

The plaintiff claims that it purchased a building, along with office equipment and a new computer system, in order to service the new distributorship agreement. It seeks to recover three years of the depreciation value (term of the distributorship) of these investments. Claims for damages are restricted by two principles. First, the damages must be assessed *in concreto* (certain, not speculative). Second, the victim is obligated to do everything to minimize damages (duty to mitigate). The facts indicate that the plaintiff had acquired other distributorship contracts that are also serviced by the new investments. We hold that the expenses in question do not appear to constitute injury having a necessary causal connection with the defendant's fault.

Finally, the plaintiff also claims the loss of profits anticipated from the distributorship for three years. The plaintiff estimates that its minimum lost profit amounts to 15 percent of the planned sales quota for the three years. We believe that 8 percent is more realistic because the plaintiff agreed to bear a number of expenses. JUDGMENT for the plaintiff.

Case Highlights

- Elements that favor an award in *culpa in contrahendo* include the suddenness of the termination, the finality of the negotiations, and knowingly allowing the other party to incur expenses
- The nonterminating party is entitled to expenses and investments incurred in preparing to perform the contract, along with damages related to lost opportunity or lost profits
- The nonterminating party's claims for damages are limited to losses that are provable with certainty and by its duty to mitigate.

Precontractual Instruments

Another issue in the area of precontractual liability is whether preliminary agreements are enforceable, either in contract or promissory estoppel.[34] If parties do not intend to be bound by an agreement until it is in writing and signed, then there is no contract until that event occurs. However, an informal agreement can be binding even though the parties contemplate entering into a final formal written contract. A court will weigh a number of factors to determine whether the parties intended to be bound before entering into a formal written contract, including whether there has been a partial performance, whether there were still outstanding issues, and the complexity of the transaction.

Precontractual instruments are found in most areas of trade and finance; examples include letters of intent, letters of support, and letters of assurance. For want of a better term, they will be referred to as **comfort instruments.**[35] Comfort instruments are generally given to encourage another party to enter into a contractual obligation. They may be made in conjunction with the direct negotiations between the parties or by a third party to the negotiations. For example, a parent company may send a letter of assurance or support "encouraging" a bank to lend money to its subsidiary. The issue becomes whether such informal letters can lead to contractual liability.

The typical comfort instrument tries to offer a guaranty-type of assurance without the resultant guaranty-type of liability. In the 1923 English case of *Rose & Frank Co. v. Crompton*,[36] the Court expressly recognized the doctrinal inconsistencies in the language of such letter. It weighed the assurance language with the disclaimer language (no liability), ultimately deciding that the disclaimer language was the more dominant. It determined that the operative phrase in the letter was that it was a *contract of honor* and not a basis for contractual liability. The line between contract and noncontract remains ambiguous.

Internationally, courts have been more likely to enforce such instruments. The civil law system, for instance, seems to place less weight on the semantic labeling of instruments, which allows for greater flexibility in affixing contractual liability than is found in the common law. For example, French jurisprudence renders a contrary presumption, finding that comfort instruments possess an implied intent to be binding ***obligations de faire*** (contracts). The presumption is grounded in the belief that parties generally do not intend to create meaningless contractual-type documentation.

Tortious Interference With Contract

Texaco v. Pennzoil illustrates that simply knowing the black-letter rules of contract may not be enough to avoid liability. In that case, Getty and Pennzoil reached an "agreement in principle" and held a news conference announcing the tentative agreement. Before the parties entered a formal agreement, Getty entered into a formal contract to sell to Texaco. Despite the fact that the sale of Getty Oil to Pennzoil was never finalized, Texaco was held liable for tortious interference of contract for its successful attempt to buy Getty. A jury awarded

Pennzoil $7.53 billion in compensatory damages and an additional $3 billion in punitive damages. Texaco subsequently filed for bankruptcy protection before settling out of court with Pennzoil. Pennzoil and Getty had entered into a "memorandum of agreement" but a final, formal agreement was never signed. Furthermore, industry custom indicated that the term *agreement* is different than the term *contract*. Thus, such memorandums are generally considered preliminary and conditional on the signing of a formal contract. Nonetheless, the jury found there was a contractual "meeting of the minds" and that, but for the interference by Texaco, the parties would have signed a formal contract.

Consumer Contracts

Contracts are categorized into two types: (1) business-to-business (B2B) or commercial contracts; and (2) business-to-consumer (B2C) or consumer contracts. In many legal systems, most notably in the EU, a separate body of contract law has been formed that can be labeled as **consumer contract law**. These specialized bodies of consumer contract laws are important to exporters and importers of goods in which the ultimate purchaser is a consumer. In contrast, American common law does not distinguish between consumer and commercial contracts.

EU Consumer Law *Acquis*

The EU has long created special rules to protect consumers in contracts with merchants. They have passed numerous laws in this area, most notably the Directive on Unfair Terms in Consumer Contracts. Subsequently, it has increasingly viewed consumer contracts differently than commercial contracts through the passage of more and more laws that seek to protect consumers. This body of law is referred to as the consumer law *acquis*. The UK enacted the Consumer Rights Act of 2015, which consolidates previous **consumer protection laws**. It also gives consumers a number of new rights and remedies, including provisions for alternative dispute resolution (ADR).

> *Acquis* or *acquis communautaire* is the accumulated legislation, legal acts, and court decisions which constitute a body of EU law. *Acquis* is defined in French as "that which has been acquired or obtained," and *communautaire* as "of the community." Thus, laws dealing with consumers make up the consumer law *acquis*. All of EU law would simply be the EU *acquis*.

Most common law countries have enacted European-style consumer contract law relating to "unfair terms," see Figure 9.5 *Comparative Law*: "New Zealand Fair Trading Act: Unfair Terms in Consumer Contracts."

Most of modern business is transacted using standard forms and within these forms are "boilerplate" or fine print terms, which consumers fail to read or

The 2013 Fair Trading Act, in New Zealand, bans unfair terms in consumer contracts. The regulations relating to this Act form part of the "Consumer NZ" "Play Fair" campaign to increase awareness of the new law and related consumer issues. The Act applies to standard-form consumer contracts.

What makes a term "unfair"? The Act defines an unfair term as one that would "would cause a significant imbalance between the rights of the company and the consumer, is not reasonably necessary to protect the legitimate interests of the company, or would cause detriment to the consumer if it were to be applied or relied on." The Act contains a list of terms that courts are likely to regard as unfair. For example:

- terms that would allow a company to unilaterally vary the terms of the contract;
- terms that would allow a company to unilaterally renew or terminate the contract;
- terms that would penalize consumers for breaching or terminating the contract;
- terms that would allow a company to vary the price without giving consumers the right to terminate the contract; and
- terms that allow a company to vary the characteristics of the goods or services to be supplied.

Even though the New Zealand Act is a consumer protection device, only the New Zealand Commerce Commission can enforce it (no private standing to sue by consumers).

Figure 9.5 Comparative Law: New Zealand Fair Trading Act: Unfair Terms in Consumer Contracts.

even if they are read the consumer may fail to understand them. The above laws seek to prevent companies from abusing their power by inserting abusive terms in consumer contracts. However, some countries, like the U.S., do not regulate standard terms under the rationale of freedom of contract. The only tool that American courts have to void enforcing abusive terms is the **doctrine of unconscionability.** The doctrine of unconscionability allows courts to void or change contract terms that are unusually harsh and that "shock the conscience," meaning they are so grossly unfair (substantive unconscionability) and are the result of one-sided bargaining power (procedural unconscionability). The Consumer Law Acquis continues to grow with the enactment of the General Directive on Privacy Rights (GDPR) and the Artificial Intelligence Act of 2024 (AI Act) (see Chapter 19), as well as updating of the Products Liability Directive.

Consumer Contract Law in the U.S.

In the U.S., the idea of a separate consumer contract law has been rejected. However, in the sale of goods, there is what is known as the merchant–consumer distinction found in Article 2 of the Uniform Commercial Code (UCC). Karl Llewellyn, the drafter of Article 2 ("Sale of Goods"), wanted to have separate rules for business transactions and consumer transactions, as well as having business sales disputes decided by specialized "merchant courts." The drafting committee rejected both those ideas. However, Llewellyn was able to write some sales law rules that reflected the power discrepancies often found in B2C transactions. In some areas, Article 2 provides added protections for consumers, and in other cases, it provides rules that only pertain to merchants. A merchant is defined in Section 2-104(1) as "a person who deals in goods of the kind or otherwise by his occupation holds himself out as having knowledge or skill peculiar to the practices or goods involved in the transaction or to whom such knowledge or skill may be attributed by his employment of an agent or broker or other intermediary who by his occupation holds himself out as having such knowledge or skill." Therefore, in some situations a person may be acting as a merchant, and in other situations, the person would be considered as a consumer. For example, an owner of a marina may be considered as being a merchant in the buying and selling of boats but would be a consumer for purposes of buying computer equipment for its office.

Chapter Summary

1. In negotiating with a foreign party, it is important to research the foreign country's cultural and negotiating norms. Some countries, like Japan and China, have different approaches to contract negotiations in that they take additional time to build up a relationship before undertaking the hard bargaining of negotiating the contract. It is also important to realize that decision-making may be done through consensus and that the person you are negotiating with may not have the power to agree to contract terms.
2. There are numerous sources of international contract law, but the applicable law will usually be the law of the country of one of the parties or a neutral country's law. Courts and especially arbitration tribunals often recognize customary international law (business usage and customs, as well as generally recognized principles) that can pre-empt the application of the legal rules of the applicable national law. The customs and usage of business or industries are referred to as the *lex mercatoria*. Two general principles of international law include *pacta sunt servanda* or the parties should honor their contracts, and courts should strictly enforce contracts, and the principle of *abus de droit*—unfair or unconscionable contracts, and clauses should not be enforced.
3. Sources of international contract law are also found in international legal instruments, such as the Convention on Contracts for the International Sale of Goods (CISG), the UNIDROIT Principles of International Commercial Contracts (PICC), and publications of the International Chamber of Commerce (ICC), such as *INCOTERMS* 2020 (see Chapter 12) and the *UCP 600* (see Chapter 13).
4. There are some stark differences between different legal systems. For example, the civil law enforces penalty clauses, while such clauses are

unenforceable under the common law; the French Civil Code recognizes the doctrine of *arrhes* that relates to the retaining and refunding of deposits, while the common law has no such doctrine.

5. Formalities required to form a contract vary among legal systems. Also, different systems vary as to the enforceability of standard terms and standard form contracts or contracts of adhesion. The U.S. and the UK generally enforce such terms, while such terms are highly regulated under German law and by EU law when one of the parties is a consumer.
6. Chinese Contract Law is interesting to study because it is a blend of rules taken from the civil law (mostly German law) and common law, as well as international instruments, such as the CISG and the PICC.
7. The Principles of European Contract Law (PECL) provides a comprehensive set of contract law rules. The PECL is not a mandatory law but can be used by countries reforming their national laws and can be used in drafting contracts.
8. The PICC is a well-established model law that can be used for all types of contracts, as compared to the CISG, which only covers sale of goods transactions.
9. A major difference between the civil and common laws is in the area of precontractual liability. The civil law recognizes the duty to negotiate in good faith; the common law does not. The civil law recognizes the tort of *culpa in contrahendo* (bad faith negotiations), which allows a party to sue for damages against a party breaking off negotiations. If the negotiations were long-term and the parties had agreed on the material terms, then a party may sue for full contract damages (lost profits) against the party breaking off negotiations. The closest the common law gets to precontractual liability is the doctrine of promissory estoppel, where a party may sue for out of pocket expenses (reliance damages) if it had reasonably relied on the promise or assurance of another party and an injustice would be done unless the court provides some remedy.
10. Precontractual instruments, such as letters of intent or comfort letters, are generally not enforceable, although they are more likely to lead to liability in some civil law countries.
11. Consumer contracts are treated differently in the EU, where there is a separate consumer contract law, while the American Uniform Commercial Code applies equally to commercial and consumer sales transactions.

Key Terms

Abus de Droit
Acquis or Acquis Communautaire
Battle of Forms
Breach of Confidentiality
Chinese Contract Law (CCL)
Comfort Instruments
Consumer Contract Law
Consumer Law Acquis
Contract of Adhesion
Convention on Contracts for the International Sale of Goods (CISG)
Council of Europe

Culpa in Contrahendo
Customary International Law
Direct Representation
Doctrine of *Arrhes*
Doctrine of Unconscionability
English Unfair Contract Terms Act of 1977
EU Directive on Unfair Terms
French Civil Code
Genuineness of Assent
German Civil Code
Hardship
Impediment
Implied Warranty for a Particular Purpose
Implied Warranty of Merchantability
INCOTERMS
Indirect Representation
International Chamber of Commerce (ICC)
International Institute for the Unification of Private Law (UNIDROIT)
Lex Mercatoria
Liquidated Damage Clause (penalty)
Merger Clause
Nachfrist Notice
Obligations de Faire
Open Terms
Pacta Sunt Servanda
Precontractual Liability
Price Reduction (Remedy)
Principles of European Contract Law (PECL)
Promissory Estoppel
Restatement (Second) of Contracts
Russian Civil Code
Sharia Law
Specific Performance
Standard Terms
Statute of Frauds
Totality of the Circumstances Analysis
UNIDROIT Principles of International Commercial Contracts (PICC)
Uniform Commercial Code (UCC)
Wa (harmony)
Written Modification Clause

Chapter Problems

1. Justice Cardozo noted a profound change in the law of contracts and the reduced role of formality as a requirement for contractual liability in the following quote: "The law has outgrown its primitive stage of formalism when the precise word was the sovereign talisman, and every slip was fatal. It takes a broader view today. A promise may be lacking, and yet the whole writing may be *instinct with an obligation*, imperfectly expressed." *Wood v. Duff-Gordon*, 222 N.Y. 88 (1917). If this is true, what are the consequences for precontractual liability? Do contracts have to be very detailed in order to be enforceable?
2. Two firms work together to prepare a complex bid for a buyer. One firm (Company A) dropped the other (Company B) before getting the bid. After working for some time on specifications, negotiating with the buyer, and being chosen as a final candidate for the job, Company A told Company B that it was disappointed with Company B's behavior and obtained the contract on its own, with minor modifications from the joint proposal submitted previously. Company B sued Company A for breach after Company A subcontracted the work to another firm. Since there was no formal subcontract, what theory of recovery can Company B allege? What types of damages, if

any, may Company B claim? *TACS Corp. v. Trans World Communications, Inc.*, 155 F.3d 659 (3rd Cir. 1998).

3. Review the *Bojangles*, *Plas*, *Grifoni*, and *SA Pasquasy* cases on preliminary agreements and *culpa in contrahendo* and answer the following questions. What could the party being sued have done differently to avoid liability? Would your answer be different under U.S. law as compared to civil law?

Internet Exercises

1. Review Schedule 2 ("Consumer contract terms which may be regarded as unfair") of the Consumer Rights Act of 2015 to see which terms are considered unfair and enforceable when placed in consumer contracts. You can find Schedule 2 at http://www.legislation.gov.uk/ukpga/2015/15/schedule /2/ enacted. Are exculpatory clauses (limits liability of merchants for harm caused by merchant's negligence) enforceable under the 2015 Act?
2. Review the European Commission's home page for Consumer Affairs at http://europa.eu/pol/cons/index_en.htm. What types of consumer protection initiatives has the EU undertaken? What areas in the subject index would be a concern for an international businessperson?
3. Read the "overview" of the Council of Europe, along with the different subject areas within the organization, and associated links: www.coe.int/en /web/portal/home.

Other Internet Sources

International Trade Administration—Information on foreign culture and customs: http://trade.gov.

For links to **modern *lex mercatoria***: www.jus.uio.no/lm.

UNIDROIT—menu of sponsored conventions: www.unidroit.org.

UK Department of Trade and Industry—**English unfair terms in consumer contracts regulations**: www.gov.uk (search "unfair terms").

Council of Europe: www.coe.int.

Principles of European Contract Law: www.jus.uio.no/lm/eu.contract.principles. parts.1.to.3.2002 or www.ufsia.ac.be/~estorme/PECL2en.html.

Notes

1 Claude Cellich, "Review of *Cross-Cultural Business Negotiations* by Donald W. Hendon, Rebecca A. Hendon, and Paula Herbig," 10 *Journal of International Consumer Marketing* 120 (1998).

2 Magoroh Maruyama, "Contracts in Cultures," 10 *Human Systems Management* 33 (1991).

3 Ole Lando, "The *Lex Mercatoria* in International Commercial Arbitration," 34 *International and Comparative Law Quarterly* 747 (1985).

4 International Chamber of Commerce, *The UNIDROIT Principles for International Commercial Contracts: A New Lex Mercatoria?* (ICC Publishing 1995).
5 Restatement (Second) of Contracts at § 19, Comment *b*.
6 See Larry A. DiMatteo, "The Counterpoise of Contracts: The Reasonable Person Standard and the Subjectivity of Judgment," 48 *South Carolina Law Review* 293, 318 (1997).
7 Restatement (Second) of Contracts at § 221, Comment *b*.
8 Unfair Contract Terms Act § 4(1) (1977).
9 22 Tenn. 493, 514–515 (1842).
10 [2015] UKSC 67. See L. DiMatteo, "An Examination of Judicial Reasoning—When a Penalty Is not a Penalty," 85 *George Washington Law Review* (2017).
11 S. Rowan, "The New French Law of Contract," 66 *International & Comparative Law* Quarterly 805 (2017).
12 Nabil Saleh, "The Law Governing Contracts in Arabia," 38 *International and Comparative Law Quarterly* 761, 763 (1989).
13 See UCC § 2-718.
14 Principles of European Contract Law (PECL) at Article 2.301 (Negotiations Contrary to Good Faith).
15 See PECL at Article 4.110(2)(b) (Unfair Terms Not Individually Negotiated).
16 PECL at Article 2.205 (Time of Conclusion of the Contract).
17 PECL at Article 2.202 (Revocation of an Offer).
18 PECL at Article 2.207(2) (Late Acceptance).
19 Compare American Uniform Commercial Code (UCC) §2-207 to CISG Article 19.
20 PECL at Article 4.103 (Mistake as to Facts or Law).
21 PECL at Article 4.105(3) (Adaptation of Contract).
22 PECL at Article 4.107 (Fraud).
23 PECL at Article 4.108 (Threats).
24 PECL at Article 4.109 (Excessive Benefit or Unfair Advantage).
25 PECL at Article 4.110 (Unfair Terms which have not been Individually Negotiated).
26 PECL at Article 8.108 (Excuse Due to an Impediment). Compare UCC § 2-615 (Impracticability) and CISG Article 74.
27 PICC Article 1.2. Compare UCC §§ 2-201 and 2-202.
28 The concept of surprising terms is found in the German Civil Code (BGB).
29 PICC Article 6.2.2. Compare UCC § 2-615.
30 The idea of contract equilibrium is a key principle in German law.
31 1999 WL 683006 (DC Cir.).
32 729 S.W.2d 768 (Tex. Ct. App. 1987).
33 See Michael Tegethoff, "*Culpa in Contrahendo* in German and Dutch Law—A Comparison of Precontractual Liability," 5 *Maastricht Journal of European and Comparative Law* 341, 347 (1998).
34 The three-stage approach in *Plas v. Valburg* is used here only for illustrative purposes; Dutch law actually uses a broader reasonableness standard.
35 See generally Larry A. DiMatteo and Rene Sacasas, "Credit and Value Comfort Instruments," 47 *Baylor Law Review* 357 (1995).
36 [1924] All E.R. 245, 255 (Ct. App. 1923).

Chapter 10

International Sales Law

The success of **international customary law** (trade usage, business customs, soft law principles) provided a strong foundation for an international convention on sales law. Examples of the expansion of international customary law in commercial transactions include the universal acceptance of the International Chamber of Commerce's INCOTERMS (glossary of trade terms) and its regulations relating to international letters of credit (Uniform Customs and Practices for Documentary Credits or UCP). The major area lacking uniformity was the law covering the underlying transaction—the sales contract. The **United Nations Convention on Contracts for the International Sale of Goods** (**CISG**), effective January 1, 1988, is the most successful attempt to fill in this gap.

This chapter will review the CISG in detail as a way to review the major issues of international sales law. The CISG borrows from the common and civil laws, as such it contains concepts and rules not found in one or the other system. These differences are most likely to result in unexpected legal liability for businesspersons not familiar with these "foreign" concepts. See the Appendix to read the actual provisions of the CISG.

International Sales Law

Lex mercatoria or law of merchants refers to a system of rules of law created by international merchants, independent of any national legal system, for the purpose of governing international business transactions. The adoption in 1980 of the CISG marked a milestone in the development of the new *lex mercatoria*. Adopting countries now have two sale of goods laws, domestic and international laws. The CISG, however, is an optional law and the parties may *opt out* of it through a choice of law clause in their contracts. At the current rate

DOI: 10.4324/9781003469230-12

of adoption, there will be more than 100 countries that will have adopted the CISG. The list of the contracting states includes most of the world's major trading countries including Australia, Brazil, China, Canada, France, Germany, Italy, Mexico, Russia, Spain, the Nordic countries, and the U.S. Countries that have not adopted the CISG include India and the UK.

The CISG covers most substantive issues of sales law. The CISG is divided into four parts: **General Provisions** (Articles 1–13), **Contract Formation** (Articles 14–24), **Rights and Obligations** (Articles 25–88), and **Ratification** (Articles 89–101). There are, however, areas not covered under the CISG, including products liability, the legality of contracts, the capacity of the parties to contract, and whether the nonbreaching party is entitled to specific performance. These substantive areas would still need to be decided under a national law of contract.

Scope of the CISG

Article 1 of the CISG provides the two core principles upon which CISG jurisdiction is determined: internationality (countries of the contracting parties) and the type of transaction (sale of goods). The first principle is divided into two types of jurisdiction—one where the two parties are from different CISG countries (Article 1(1)(a)) and the other where only one of the parties is from a CISG country (Article 1(1)(b)). Under the second type, the CISG applies when a court or arbitral tribunal uses its conflict of law rules to determine the law of the dispute. If the conflict of law rules directs the court or tribunal to the party whose country has ratified the CISG, then the CISG becomes the law of the dispute.[1]

In determining the country of a party for CISG jurisdiction purposes, the courts must decide the party's **place of business** that is most closely connected to the particular transaction. Article 10 states that: "the place of business is that which has the closest relationship to the contract and its performance." Therefore, the CISG applies when two parties are incorporated in the same country but the deal was negotiated by one of the companies' foreign offices.

The second principle relates to the definition of the sale of goods covered under the CISG. The CISG does not apply to: (1) consumer sales (goods purchased for personal, family, or household use); goods sold by auction; sales of ships, vessels, or aircraft; sales by execution of law (lien foreclosure); or the sale of electricity; (2) goods that were produced where a preponderant part of the "seller's" obligations is to provide services or labor, or when the "buyer" supplies a substantial amount of the materials used in producing the good.

Choice of Law and Conflict of Law

A **choice of law clause** used to avoid application of the CISG must be carefully drafted. For example, two parties from different countries (U.S. and France) may intend the domestic sales law (civil or commercial code) to be the law of the transaction. To that end, the parties negotiate the following choice of law clause: "the law of the State of New York shall apply to all disputes." Prior to the adoption of the CISG, the law of New York would be the state's version of the American Uniform Commercial Code, but now it would be the CISG as federal law preempts the application of state law. If the parties intended to choose the UCC or the French Civil Code they would need to draft a clear choice of law clause by making the choice explicit: the applicable law is the "Uniform Commercial Code of the State of New York" (or the "French Civil Code").

Another ground for the use of the CISG in a dispute is based in customary international law. An arbitral panel or a court may use the CISG as evidence of trade usage in place of applying the law of an individual country. This happened in *International Chamber of Commerce Arbitration Case No. 5713 of 1989.* In that case, the contract did not contain a choice of law clause. The arbitrators selected the applicable law by applying conflict of law rules. However, the tribunal disregarded the domestic law's shorter statute of limitations period in favor of the two-year period provided in the CISG. In short, the arbitral tribunal used the CISG as evidence of international trade usage to avoid what it deemed to be an unfair domestic law. The use of the CISG as evidence of customary international law makes sense since it possesses a universal appeal that many arbitrators will find appealing in their search for a *lex mercatoria*-type of justification for their awards. The terse, clear, and nonlegal language of the CISG makes it easy to apply as a soft law.[2]

Commercial Sale of Goods

The CISG covers only transactions for the sale of goods. Thus, sales of services and transfers of intellectual property rights would not come under the jurisdiction of the CISG. There are many transactions, however, that include more than one subject matter. For example, the sale of computer software is often a **mixed sale** involving the sale of a tangible item, like a flash drive, along with a service or technical assistance agreement, and a license pertaining to intellectual property rights. Article 3 provides a two-part test to distinguish a service contract from a sale of goods. First, a contract is not for the sale of goods if the buyer provides a substantial part of the materials used in the production of the goods. This would be considered a contract for labor or assembly services. Second, a preponderant part of the contract is for the supply of labor or services.

In *Micro Data Systems, Inc. v. Dharma Systems*,[3] the court held that labor can be considered as a component part of a good when determining the applicability of the sales law to a mixed sale transaction. In that case, the buyer agreed to pay $125,000 for software and $125,000 for services necessary to adapt the system to the buyer's needs. The court ruled that the "services" were not services to be rendered directly to the buyer, but merely the labor for producing modified software.

According to Article 3's second test a software sale will be considered within the scope of the CISG only if a preponderant part of the transaction is for tangible goods. If, for example, a company contracts for software to computerize its inventory the court may look to the allocation of the price within the contract among the different components. Thus, if the contract provided for $20,000 worth of database software and $15,000 worth of support services, the contract would be considered predominantly one for the sale of goods and covered by the CISG.

One suggested resolution for the intangibility of technology and software is to treat such items as **virtual goods.**[4] Virtual goods could be treated like conventional goods for purposes of the CISG. The CISG expressly uses the term "sales" when defining its coverage. Its definition of goods is based primarily upon the concept of *movability*. Software clearly satisfies the requirement of movability. However, items sold by way of licenses are considered not to be sale of goods. Nonetheless, software licensing agreements often have the characteristics of sale of goods transactions. If the copy being licensed is one for perpetual use for which the licensee (buyer) pays a one-time licensing fee, then the software is essentially being sold even though the "license" retains title in the name of the licensor. The general opinion is the CISG is likely to cover sales of "off the shelf" software (standard or fungible), but customized software is not covered.

Parol Evidence Rule and CISG

Some countries require that a sales contract be in a written form. Also, in the common law, a final written agreement is protected from being contradicted by other types of evidence (extrinsic to the contract) through the **parol evidence rule**. This rule is also found in the American Uniform Commercial Code (UCC). The parol evidence rule protects the sanctity of the written contract intended to be the final agreement or integration of the parties' negotiations. The rule prevents admitting into evidence any prior or contemporaneous oral statements or writings that contradict the contract. In contrast, the CISG applies the view of many civil law countries that a written contract is not required in order to enforce an agreement and that the written contract is only a part of the evidence used in the interpretation of contracts.

There is a major exception to the UCC's writing requirement (statute of frauds) known as the **written confirmation rule**, which is also recognized in other legal systems, such as Germany. It states that a writing sent by one of the parties confirming the conclusion of a contract is sufficient to satisfy the writing requirement and that the confirmation is strong evidence of the terms of the contract. So, for example, if two parties reach an oral agreement in person, by e-mail, or by telephone, one of the parties may send a written (electronic) confirmation of the agreement. If the other party fails to object to the terms of the confirmation in a timely manner, then the confirmation is deemed to bind the parties to a contract on the terms of the confirmation. Under the UCC, the notice of objection to the terms of the confirmation must be given within ten days of the receipt.[5]

The parol evidence rule seeks to preserve the integrity of written contracts, intended to be the final agreement (integration) by refusing to allow previous oral and written communications from *contradicting* the written form. However, such final written agreements may be *explained* or *supplemented* by extrinsic evidence such as, prior dealings, trade usage, or course of performance information. **Prior dealings** include prior contracts and performances between the parties that establish a common basis of understanding for interpreting subsequent contracts.

Trade usage refers to the customs and practices regularly observed in a given trade or business. Usages of trade provide the background meaning of words and terms developed by merchants in that trade. A person in a trade or business is presumed to know the usages and meanings used in that trade or business. **Course of performance** is premised on the fact that the parties' conduct in performing the contract is a good indication of what they believe to be its meaning.[6]

The CISG in its Article 11 states that a "contract need not be evidenced by writing." Also, a contract and its terms may be proven "by *any* means," including witness testimony. Therefore, prior oral statements regarding anything, including quality and performance, are potentially enforceable. Also, oral assurances given to persuade another party to enter into a contract may be used to prove intent or support a claim for misrepresentation. In sum, the potential for liability for representations made during the negotiation stage is greater in the CISG than under the common law.

Articles 12 allows contracting states to opt out of Article 11's no writing requirement. Some countries, mostly the former countries of the Soviet Union and socialist law countries, have opted out in favor of domestic laws that require a written document. These countries include Russia, Ukraine, Belarus, Estonia, Hungary, Argentina, and Chile. China at first opted out of the "no writing requirement," but subsequently withdrew its declaration of opting-out (oral agreements are fully enforceable). It is important for the businessperson to research when formalities are required (written instrument, notary, registration) in a given country, despite the existence of Article 11. The importance of the parol evidence rule to contract disputes is discussed in *MCC-Marble Ceramic Center v. Ceramica Nuova D'Agostino*. The court is asked to determine if the common law's parol evidence rule is applicable to the CISG.

MCC-Marble Ceramic Center v. Ceramica Nuova D'Agostino

144 F.3d 1384 (11th Cir. 1998)

"MCC" is a Florida corporation engaged in the retail sales of imported tiles. "D'Agostino" is an Italian manufacturer of tiles. At a trade show they orally agreed on a sale of tiles. The agreed terms were placed on D'Agostino's standard order forms. The executed forms were printed in Italian. MCC brought suit claiming a breach of the requirements contract when D'Agostino failed to satisfy a number of orders. D'Agostino responded that it was under no legal obligation to fill the orders because MCC had defaulted on payment for previous shipments. MCC responded that the earlier shipments of tiles were of a lower quality than contracted for and that it was entitled to reduce payment in proportion to the defects. D'Agostino replied that Clause 4 on the reverse side of the order form required that all complaints for defects must be made in writing not later than ten days after receipt of the tiles. MCC argued that the parties never intended the terms and conditions printed on the reverse of the order form to apply to their agreement.

Judge. Article 8 of the CISG provides: "For purposes of this Convention statements made by and other conduct of a party are to be interpreted according to his intent where the other party knew or should have been aware of what that intent was. Due consideration is to be given to *all* relevant circumstances of the case including negotiations." The plain language of the CISG requires an inquiry into a party's subjective intent as long as the other party was aware of that intent. MCC argues that it did not intend to be bound by the terms on the manufacturer's form since they were in Italian. We find it nothing short of astounding that an individual, purportedly experienced in commercial matters, would sign a contract in a foreign language and expect not to be bound simply because he could not comprehend its terms. The general proposition is that standard terms will bind parties who sign contracts regardless of whether they have read them or understand them.

The issue here is whether the parol evidence rule applies to the CISG. It is important whether the testimony of MCC's subjective intent and D'Agostino's awareness of that intent will be admitted to contradict the terms of the written contract. The parol evidence rule, contrary to its title, is a substantive rule of law, not a rule of evidence. The Uniform Commercial Code includes a version of the parol evidence rule that states that "a writing intended by the parties as a final expression of their agreement may not be contradicted by evidence of any prior agreement or contemporaneous oral agreement." The CISG contains no express statement on the role of parol evidence. However, Article 8(3) of the CISG expressly directs the courts to give "due consideration to all relevant circumstances of the case including the negotiations." It is a clear instruction to admit and consider parol evidence regarding the negotiations to the extent they reveal the parties' subjective intent.

Another court appears to have arrived at a contrary conclusion. In *Beijing Metals & Minerals Import/Export Corp. v. American Bus. Ctr., Inc.*, the court held that the parol evidence rule would apply regardless of whether Texas law or the CISG governed the dispute. We find the Beijing opinion not particularly persuasive on this point.

Our reading of Article 8(3) as a rejection of the parol evidence rule is in accordance with the weight of academic authority. Furthermore, a wide number of other States that are parties to the CISG have rejected the rule in their domestic jurisdictions. One of the primary factors motivating the negotiation and adoption of the CISG was to provide parties to international contracts for the sale of goods with some degree of certainty as to the principles of law that would govern potential disputes. Courts applying the CISG cannot upset the parties' reliance on the CISG by substituting familiar principles of domestic law such as the parol evidence rule when the CISG requires a different result. To the extent parties wish to avoid parol evidence problems they can do so by including a **merger clause** in their agreement that extinguishes any and all prior agreements and understandings not expressed in the writing.

Article 8 requires a court to consider any "practices which the parties have established between themselves, usage, and any subsequent conduct of the parties" in interpreting contracts. Whether the parties intended to adhere to the ten-day limit for complaints of defects, as stated on the reverse of the contract, will have an impact on whether MCC was bound to adhere to the limit in order to preserve its warranty claims. The CISG precludes the application of the parol evidence rule, which would otherwise bar the consideration of evidence concerning a prior or contemporaneously negotiated oral agreement (subjective intent).

Case Highlights

- The CISG encourages a "totality of the circumstances" analysis in the interpretation of contracts, which includes a review of the written terms of a contract in the context of the negotiation of the contract, including oral representation, prior dealings, subsequent performance, and trade usage
- Since the CISG has been adopted in numerous countries, any previous foreign decisions on a particular issue should be reviewed in order to obtain uniform interpretations of the CISG
- The CISG provides a price reduction in its Article 50 as a remedy for the delivery of nonconforming goods
- The two-year period found in Article 39 of the CISG is the outside limit for giving a notice of defect. However, a party must give notice within a reasonable time, which will normally mean within days of finding the defect. In addition, the parties can agree to a shorter notice period
- Under American common law, fine print or standard terms are automatically recognized as part of the contract (including in consumer contracts); terms found in other documents can be included through "incorporation by reference" (terms do not have to appear in the contract but are referred to in the contract).

CISG and the American Uniform Commercial Code

This section will focus on the substantive provisions of the CISG. For purposes of illustration, its provisions will be compared to relevant provisions in the American UCC's Article 2 (sale of goods) (see Table 10.1 *Comparative Law*: "Comparison of CISG and UCC"). This comparison will show that despite the great deal of commonality between the CISG and domestic sales laws, fundamental differences are also present. It is important that the CISG be understood and applied effectively by exporters and importers. It not only places some unique responsibilities on sellers and buyers of goods, but it also provides a number of rights and remedies not found in domestic sales laws, such as the UCC or the German BGB.

Contract Formation: Offer-Acceptance Rules

Articles 14–24 of the CISG is a blend of civil and common law rules. All legal systems recognize the formation of a contract when an **offer** and **acceptance** are exchanged (exchange of promises or bilateral contract). The offeror is the party making an offer to contract. The offeree is the party that receives an offer and is empowered to create a binding contract through an acceptance of the offer. The key issue is determining the exact time of formation. This

Table 10.1 *Comparative Law*: Comparison of CISG and UCC.

Description of Topic	*CISG Article*	*UCC Section*
Writing Requirement	11, 13, and 14	2-201
Parol Evidence Rule	8 and 9	2-202
Contract Formation	14, 19–21, and 23	2-204
Obligation of Good Faith	Implied	1-202
Revocability of Offer (Firm Offer Rule)	16	2-205
Time of Acceptance	18	2-206
Battle of Forms	14 and 19	2-207
Fixing Price Term	14, 55, and 56	2-305
Place of Delivery	57	2-308
Time of Delivery	33, 47, 48, and 63	2-309
Place of Payment/Time for Payment	57	2-310
Avoidance (Termination) & Manner of Rejection	81 and 86	2-602
Right to Reject Goods	25 and 49	2-601
Warranty of Title	41 and 42	2-312
Express and Implied Warranties	35	2-313 to 2-316
Duty and Right to Inspection	38	2-513
Nonconformity; Nondelivery	36, 49, and 51	2-601
Notice of Nonconformity	39	2-607(3)(a)
Fundamental Breach; Notice	25 and 49	2-608
Anticipatory Breach (Repudiation)	71–73	2-609 and 610
Price Reduction Remedy	50	None
Nachfrist Notice	47, 48, and 63	None
Excuse or Exemption from Liability	79	2-615
Notice of Excuse	27	2-616

determination is important in order to decide the effectiveness of attempted **revocations** of offers by **offerors** and **rejections** (subsequent to the sending of an acceptance) by **offerees**. Sometimes a contract is formed when the offeror invites the offeree to accept by the commencing of performance (unilateral contract). Commencement of performance may not be sufficient, however. Most legal systems require the offeree to notify the offeror within a reasonable time that performance has commenced.[7]

The common law rule known as the dispatch or **mailbox rule** holds that a contract is formed upon the sending of the acceptance by placing it into a reasonable means of transmission. Other legal systems of the world, and the CISG, determine the conclusion of a contract when the acceptance or notice of the

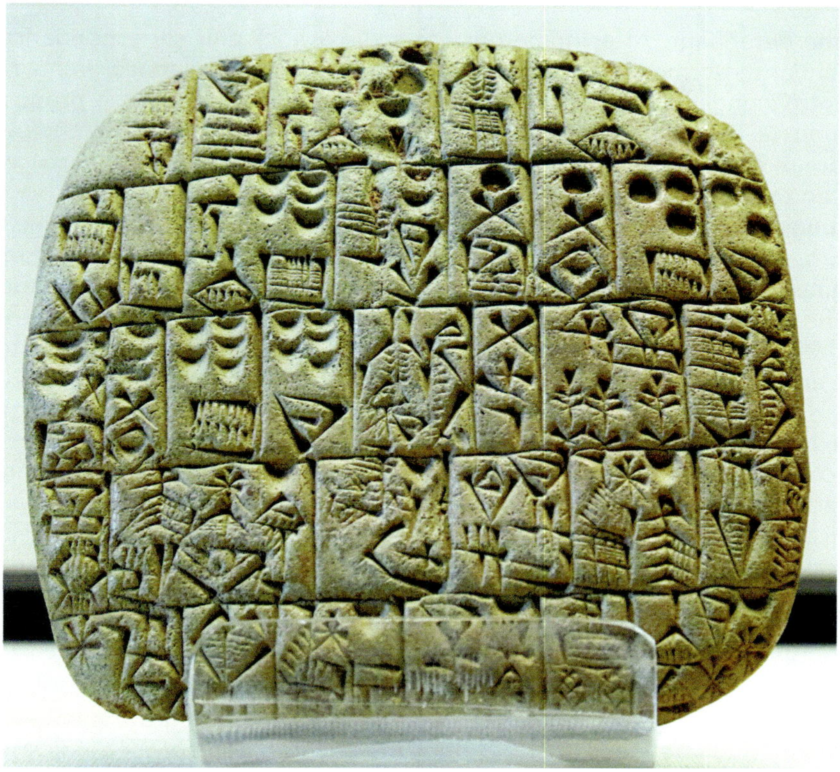

Image 10.1 Ancient Sales Contract (Louvre).
Source: Stone Sales Contract, Wikimedia Commons.

acceptance is received by the original offeror. Article 1326 of the Italian Civil Code states that an acceptance must be communicated to the offeror within the term that is deemed reasonable according to the nature of the business or trade customs.

Many international commercial transactions involve long-term negotiations, along with numerous exchanges of correspondences and documents. It is often the difficult task of a court or arbitral tribunal to analyze the numerous exchanges to determine if and when a contract was formed. The following Hungarian court decision, *Pratt & Whitney Corp. v. Malev Hungarian Airlines*, was one of the first to apply these rules.

Pratt & Whitney Corp. v. Malev Hungarian Airlines

Metropolitan Court of Budapest, 13 Bp. P.O.B. 16 (1991)

Malev Airlines (defendant) entered into negotiations with Pratt & Whitney (plaintiff) to supply it with jet engines to be installed on jumbo jets that defendant was purchasing from Boeing Aircraft and Airbus of France. After in-depth negotiations, Pratt & Whitney sent a detailed written proposal to the defendant. After numerous other discussions and correspondences, defendant informed plaintiff in a letter that it no longer planned on buying plaintiff's engines. The issues for the court included whether the proposal without a fixed price or quantity was an offer, whether the defendant's response was an acceptance, and whether the sale of aircraft parts was within the coverage of the CISG.

Hungarian Court. Article 2 of the CISG excludes from coverage the sale of "ships, vessels, hovercraft, or aircraft." Does this exclusion include aircraft engines and parts? Such component parts are covered as contracts relating to the production of goods as defined in Article 3 of the CISG. The defendant argues that plaintiff's proposal was of a general informative character, not an offer, but only a letter of intent. Furthermore, there were further discussions regarding the equipment after receiving the proposal and the merchandise was not properly defined in that proposal.

According to Article 14 of the CISG, a proposal to be an offer need only be addressed to one or more definite persons, be adequately specific, and indicate the offeror's intention to bind itself in case of an acceptance. A proposal is adequately defined if it indicates the goods and fixes the quantity and price expressly or contains provisions for their determination. We hold that the proposal leaves no doubt about its subject, that it indicates unambiguously the goods subject to the sale. That it leaves to the buyer the exact engine to be purchased along with the quantity of the order is not critical. The number of engines will be decided based upon the number of airplanes the defendant decides to buy in the future. The proper indication of the goods is not affected by the condition that according to the proposal the buyer could choose from among the enumerated engines. Plaintiff's proposal was a legal offer under the CISG. The next issue was whether defendant's response was an acceptance under Article 18 of the CISG. It is noted that the offer contained the language that the defendant's "acceptance of this proposal is conditional upon the approvals of the governments of Hungary and the United States." This condition does not prevent the formation of a contract. Article 23 of the CISG states that a contract becomes valid when the offeror receives a notification of acceptance. The defendant's first response (despite later changing its mind) established a valid agreement. The court finds the defendant in breach of contract under the CISG.

Case Highlights

- Although ships, vessels, and aircraft are excluded from the CISG, a sale of parts for such items is covered by the CISG
- An offer is sufficient even if it allows the offeree to fix the quantity term at a later date
- A conditional acceptance does not prevent the formation of a contract.

General Conditions or Standard Terms

Most international export transactions make use of standard forms to expedite the negotiation and conclusion of contracts. These forms, such as *pro forma* invoices, commercial invoices, price quotations, purchase orders, and written confirmations act as the offers and acceptances in the contract formation process. The chronological order of the communications will determine, for example, if a purchase order acts as an offer or as an acceptance.

Most exporters and importers will review the front page of the other party's form. Few will take the time to read and understand the "Terms and Conditions" on the reverse. Not reading the fine print or *boilerplate terms* is dangerous because the terms on the reverse side of each party's respective forms are often in conflict or contain terms that the other party would not have agreed to if it was aware of them at the time of formation. For example, the "Terms and Conditions" in Figure 10.1 *Focus on Transactions*: "Pro Forma Invoice" absolve the seller of any responsibility for the goods when they are delivered to a third party such as a freight forwarder or common carrier (paragraphs 1, 2, 3). This term may conflict with the trade term on the face of the form.

As noted earlier, not all contracts are formed through the exchange of promises: "I offer to sell" followed by an "I accept" (bilateral contracts). Contracts may also be formed by a promise followed by conduct or performance (unilateral contracts). An offer may invite an acceptance by performance and not require a return promise of acceptance. For example, the offer may state "send goods immediately." In such a case, the sending of the goods is the acceptance. The *Golden Valley Grape Juice* case that follows discusses an interesting example of acceptance by conduct—the attachment of one contract to another contract. The case involved Party A sending a contract (offer) to Party B; Party B then attached that contract to an offer he made to Party C (resell the goods to be received from Party A). The question for the court was whether the attachment of Party A's contract to the Party C contract was an act of Party B accepting Party A's offer to sell. The common law, allows the court to imply one contract into the other through incorporation by reference. The *Golden Valley* case also discusses the issue of how to incorporate standard terms into a contract and the issue of the enforceability of forum selection clauses.

Terms and Conditions

1. *Services by Third Parties*: Unless the Seller carries, stores, or otherwise physically handles the shipment, and the loss, damage, or delay occurs during such activity, the Seller assumes no liability as a carrier, but undertakes only to use reasonable care in the selection of carriers.
2. *Liability Limitations of Third Parties*: Seller is authorized to select all necessary third parties as required to transport the goods, all of whom shall be considered as the agents of the Purchaser. The Seller shall not be liable for any loss, damage, expense, or delay to the goods for any reason whatsoever when the goods are in the possession of third parties.
3. *Choosing Routes or Agents*: Unless specified by the Customer in writing, the Company has complete freedom in choosing the means and route for delivery of the goods.

Figure 10.1 Focus on Transactions: Pro Forma Invoice.

4. *Quotations Not Binding*: Quotations as to fees, rates of duty, freight charges, insurance premiums, or other charges are for informational purposes only and are subject to change without notice unless the Company in writing specifically undertakes the transportation of the shipment at the specified rate.
5. *Limitation of $50 per Shipment*: The Customer agrees that the Company shall in no event be liable for any loss, expense, or delay to the goods resulting from the negligence or fault of the Company for any amount in excess of $50 per shipment.
6. *Presenting Claims*: In no event shall the Company be liable for any act or omission or default unless the claim is presented to it at its office within 60 days from the date of exportation of the goods in a written statement to which sworn proof of claim shall be attached.
7. *General Lien on Any Property*: Seller shall have a general lien on any and all property of the Purchaser in its possession or en route, for all claims for charges, expenses or advances incurred by the Seller in connection with any shipments to the Purchaser, and if such claims remain unsatisfied for a period of 30 days, the Seller may sell at public auction or private sale, and apply the net proceeds of the sale to the payment of the amount due to the Seller.
8. *No Responsibility for Governmental Requirements*: It is the responsibility of the Purchaser to know and inform the Seller of the marking requirements of the country of importation, and all other safety and health regulations, and all other requirements of law or official regulations. The Seller shall not be responsible for action taken by any government agency against the shipment.
9. *Construction of Terms and Venue*: The foregoing terms and conditions shall be construed according to the German Civil Code (BGB). No legal proceeding against the Seller may be instituted by Purchaser, its assigns or subrogee, except in the City of Bremen, Germany.
10. *Costs of Collection*: Purchaser shall pay all costs, charges, and expenses including attorney s fees, reasonably incurred or paid by Seller because of the failure of the Purchaser to perform and comply with the terms and conditions of this agreement.

Figure 10.1 (Continued)

Golden Valley Grape Juice and Wine, LLC v. Centrisys Corporation

2010 U.S. Dist. LEXIS (E. Dist. Cal. 2010)

This dispute arises from a contract between plaintiff Golden Valley Grape Juice and Wine, LLC (Golden Valley) of California and defendant Centrisys Corporation (Centrisys) of Wisconsin. Golden Valley purchased a centrifuge from Centrisys. Separator Technology Solutions Pty Ltd. (STS), an Australian business entity, manufactured the centrifuge and sold it under a separate agreement with Centrisys. The centrifuge proved to be defective. Golden Valley filed this action against Centrisys. Centrisys then filed a third-party complaint against STS. STS's offer was contained in a sales quote to Centrisys. The sales quote identified the goods, the quantity of goods, and the price to constitute as a sufficient offer under CISG Article 14. The offer sent to Centrisys included an attachment containing *General Conditions*. In the General Conditions was a forum selection clause that said any dispute would be heard in Victoria, Australia. After receiving the sales quote, Centrisys then incorporated the STS quote into its presentation to Golden Valley.

Centrisys argues that the mere receipt of the General Conditions is not an acceptance of the conditions. Centrisys argues that it did not affirmatively agree to the General Conditions. Pursuant to the CISG, acceptance does not require a signature or formalistic adoption of the offered terms. Pursuant to Article 18(3), "the offeree may indicate assent by performing an act, such as one relating to the dispatch of the goods or payment of the price, without notice to the offeror, the acceptance is effective at the moment the act is performed."

The Court held that Centrisys' action of including STS's price quote in its bid to Golden Valley constituted an acceptance of STS's General Conditions even though enforcement of the forum selection clause meant that Centrisys would have to bring a second lawsuit instead of combining the two claims in one lawsuit (*Golden Valley v. Centrisys* in the U.S. and *Centrisys v. STS* in Australia). A forum selection clause is presumptively valid; the party seeking to avoid a forum selection clause bears a "heavy burden" to establish a ground upon which the clause is unenforceable. Forum selection clauses should be honored "absent some compelling and countervailing reason." Motion to dismiss for change of venue by Third Party Defendants is GRANTED.

Case Highlights

- Contracts may be formed by acceptance through a promise ("I accept") or by the conduct of the party receiving the offer. In this case the act of including the offer in a subsequent contract with another party was an acceptance that bound the contract
- In acceptance by conduct, the offeror must have allowed for acceptance by conduct or performance instead of a statement of acceptance
- The CISG does not provide a rule for the incorporation of general conditions (standard terms) into a contract. The Court held that the attachment of general conditions to an e-mail was sufficient to make them part of the contract
- The U.S. Supreme Court held that forum selection clauses should be enforced unless there is a strong public policy reason against their enforcement.

Paragraph 4 in Figure 10.1 makes the seller's quotations as to freight and insurance *nonbinding*. Paragraph 5 limits the seller's liability for its own negligent acts to $50 per shipment. Paragraph 6 requires the buyer to notify seller of any defects in the goods within 60 days of the date of exportation or lose its right to sue for breach of warranty. Paragraph 7 allows the seller to retain a lien on the goods for "all charges or expenses incurred by the Seller in connection with the shipment to the Purchaser." Paragraph 8 absolves the seller from any governmental requirements pertaining to the shipment of the goods including marking and health regulations. Paragraph 9 mandates that any dispute must be settled in a court near the seller and using the law of the seller's place of business. Paragraph 10 passes the costs of any litigation brought by the seller, including attorneys' fees, to the purchaser. The one-sided nature of these terms will become important in a subsequent contract dispute. A court, especially in civil law countries, may void some or all of these clauses if they are deemed not a part of the contract, unreasonable, or are considered "surprise terms" (re-allocating liability commonly assumed by one party to the other party). The common law is more likely to strictly enforce these terms as part of the contract unless they are deemed unconscionable (overly one-sided). However, the application of the unconscionability principle is generally reserved for consumer and not commercial contracts.

Battle of Forms

Exchanging forms with conflicting or varying terms is referred to as the **battle of the forms**. Article 19 of the CISG resolves the conflict of terms in the exchange of forms differently than Article 2-207 of the American UCC. For example, a seller responds to a purchase order ("offer") with a confirming invoice ("acceptance"). The confirming invoice, however, includes **additional terms** that limit the purchaser's ability to make a claim for breach of warranty by providing a short notice period. What is the legal effect of the additional notice requirement? If construed as a nonmaterial modification, the CISG and the UCC would acknowledge the contract formation, incorporating the additional term. Article 19(3) of the CISG, however, broadly defines *material* to include "among other things, price, payment, quality and quantity of the goods, place and time of delivery, *extent of one party's liability to the other*, or relating to the settlement of disputes." In essence, the CISG adopts the old common law's **mirror image rule** in which the acceptance must be a mirror image of the offer. Thus, under the CISG the additional term converts the attempted acceptance into a counteroffer, resulting in a finding of no contract. In contrast, the UCC does not define "material" and the case law has interpreted this to mean that there are no material terms, and only requires evidence that the parties intended to enter a contract to find an enforceable contract.

The impact of the CISG's adoption of the mirror image rule may be profound. The use of standard forms in the formation of modern sales contracts is a universal practice. Invariably, any time seller's and buyer's forms are exchanged there will be conflicting terms in the fine print that neither party is likely to read. Under the CISG's broad materiality standard, the contracts are technically unenforceable.

A German court recognized the reality of standard form contracting and ignored the broad materiality definition in Article 19(3). It held that a restrictive notice provision pertaining to claims of defects was not a material term. The notice of nonconformity (defect) term would seem to come within the purview of Article 19(3) as a term relating to the "extent of one party's liability to the other party." The German court, nonetheless, held otherwise. One way to avoid a battle of the forms scenario is to use a single or model contract form that both parties sign. The battle of the forms' scenario is illustrated in *Filanto, S.p.A. v. Chilewich International Corp.* In that case, one of the parties attempted in its offer to incorporate another document by reference. A belated acceptance attempted to delete the reference in order to avoid an arbitration clause. The issues for the court were whether a contract had been formed and, if so, under whose terms.

Filanto, S.p.A. v. Chilewich International Corp.

789 F. Supp. 1229 (S.D.N.Y. 1992)

An Italian footwear manufacturer brought action against a New York export–import firm, alleging breach of contract. This case is a striking example of how a lawsuit involving a relatively straightforward international commercial transaction can raise an array of complex questions. Defendant Chilewich signed a contract with a Russian buyer for a long-term supply of footwear. This "Russian contract" contained an arbitration clause: "All disputes are to be settled by the Arbitration Tribunal of the Chamber of Commerce in Moscow, Russia."

Chilewich then entered into negotiations with Filanto, an Italian manufacturer, to supply the shoes needed for the Russian contract. After a negotiation meeting, Chilewich sent Filanto a letter, dated July 27, 1989, that stated: "Attached please find our contract to cover the purchases from you. Same is governed by the conditions which are enumerated in the standard contract in effect with the Russian buyers, copy of which is also enclosed." Subsequently, Chilewich procured a letter of credit to the benefit of Filanto as required under the contract. Soon thereafter, Filanto began to perform on the contract.

On September 2, 1989, Chilewich received a letter from Filanto that included the following statement: "Returning back the enclosed contracts signed for acceptance, so we do not misunderstand, regarding the Russian contract, we have to respect only the following points: Packing and marking, way of shipment, and delivery." After its Russian buyer rejected an earlier shipment of shoes, Chilewich never purchased a subsequent order. It is Chilewich's failure to do so that forms the basis of this lawsuit. Chilewich commenced an arbitration action in Moscow. Filanto moved to enjoin the arbitration, or alternatively, for an order directing that arbitration be held in New York rather than Moscow because of unsettled political conditions in Russia.

Chief Judge. The facts indicate that when Filanto thought it was desirable to do so, it recognized that it was bound by the *incorporation by reference* of portions of the Russian contract. The Convention on the Recognition and Enforcement of Foreign Arbitral Awards (New York Convention) requires courts to recognize "any agreement in writing under which the parties undertake to submit to arbitration." The term "agreement in writing" is defined as "an arbitral clause in a contract or an arbitration agreement, signed by the parties or contained in an exchange of letters or telegrams." The threshold question is whether these parties actually agreed to arbitrate their disputes. The applicable law is the CISG. The parties offer varying interpretations of the numerous letters and documents exchanged between them. There simply is no satisfactory explanation as to why Filanto failed to object to the incorporation by reference of the Russian contract in a timely fashion. Chilewich had in the meantime commenced its performance under the Agreement by furnishing a letter of credit to Filanto. An offeree who, knowing that the offeror has commenced performance and fails to notify the offeror of its objection to the terms of the contract within a reasonable time will be deemed to have assented to those terms. The August 7, 1990, acceptance, noting its objection to the arbitration clause, to Chilewich's March 13, 1990 Memorandum

Agreement was untimely due to Filanto's awareness of Chilewich's commencement of performance. Furthermore, Filanto's June 21, 1991, letter refers to the "Master Purchase Contract" (Russian contract). This letter comes within CISG Article 8(3) that states "in determining the intent of a party due consideration is to be given to any *subsequent conduct* of the parties."

Heeding the presumption in favor of arbitration, which is even stronger in the context of international commercial transactions, the Court holds that Filanto is bound by the terms of the March 13 Memorandum Agreement and must arbitrate its dispute in Moscow.

Case Highlights

- The New York Convention requires courts to enforce reasonable arbitration clauses
- The ability of one party to add or delete contract terms in the battle of the forms scenario is lost if the party delays its response (rejection) beyond a reasonable time or after the other party begins performance
- A court will take into consideration the conduct of the parties following the formation of the contract (course of performance) when interpreting a contract.

Contract Interpretation

The common law and the CISG take different approaches to the interpretation of contracts. Contract interpretation involves: (1) determining what makes up the contract (oral statements, written agreement, multiple written instruments); (2) determining the meaning of the contract; and (3) determining what types of evidence (written contract, prior dealings or practices between the parties, how the parties subsequently interpreted the contract in performing on the contract, and/or business customs and trade usage) should be considered in attaching meaning to the contract.

The common law uses the **objective theory of contract**, where the focus is not on the parties' actual subjective intent, but on the meaning a neutral (fictitious) third party (**reasonable person standard**) would attach to the parties' words and conduct (objective manifestations). The meaning of a contract is not based on what a party thought the meaning was, but on what his actions and words would be interpreted to mean under the contract. The strongest evidence of objective meaning is the written contract. Therefore, under the common law if a written contract is deemed to be the final agreement (integration), then other types of extrinsic evidence that would show the parties' actual intent cannot be used to contradict the written contract (parol evidence rule). In civil law, the court's first order approach is to find the subjective meaning of the contract (parties' actual intent). Under this approach evidence outside of the written contract is important to determine actual intent. Often subjective meaning cannot be determined. The civil law then shifts to a second order approach—the reasonable person standard. The CISG has no parol evidence rule, so all types of evidence, even oral statements that contradict the written contract, are admissible evidence. Furthermore, the CISG follows the civil law approach and instructs the courts to determine the parties' actual subjective intent. The reasonable person standard (objective intent) is only to be used if the evidence is unclear as to what the parties actually intended. The *Tee Vee Toons* case that follows explores the practical applications of the subjective and objective theories of contract interpretation, and how they determine the types of evidence a court will consider in deciding a case.

Tee Vee Toons v. Gerhard Schubert GmbH

00 Civ 5189 (RCC) (S.D.N.Y. 2006)

In the early part of the 1990s, Tee Vee Toons (TVT) record company invented and patented a biodegradable-cardboard "flip-top" packaging called the "Biobox," which was designed to provide a secure, environmentally friendly way to package audio and video cassettes. TVT and Schubert entered into a written contract for Schubert to build a Biobox-production system. Shortly thereafter, problems started accumulating. First, Schubert experienced delays that set the project back two years and when the Biobox-production system (Schubert System) was finally finished and delivered the system malfunctioned frequently. TVT commenced this action, asserting various contracts and tort claims and claiming that they suffered millions of dollars in damages, including money paid to Schubert for the system and repairs, money spent on other technicians and equipment to try to fix or replace components, money spent to set up its production facility, money that will have to be spent to replace the facility, money spent on administration of the Biobox project, and lost profits.

Unlike American contract law, the CISG contains no statute of frauds; therefore, oral statements between the parties may be used to prove a contract and the terms of the contract. The CISG "allows all relevant information into evidence even if it contradicts the written documentation." CISG Article 8 explains how such oral evidence should be interpreted:

1. For the purposes of the CISG, statements made by and other conduct of a party are to be interpreted according to his intent where the other party knew or could not have been unaware what that intent was.
2. If the preceding paragraph is not applicable, statements made by and other conduct of a party are to be interpreted according to the understanding that a reasonable person of the same kind as the other party and under the same circumstances.
3. In determining the intent of a party or the understanding of a reasonable person, due consideration should be given to all relevant circumstances of the case including the negotiations, any practices which the parties have established between themselves, usages, and any subsequent conduct of the parties.

CISG Article 8(1) "requires a court to consider ... evidence of the parties' subjective intent" and Article 8(3) requires "consideration of parol evidence regarding the negotiations to the extent they reveal the parties' subjective intent." TVT asserts its contract claims under Articles 35 and 36 of the CISG, alleging the Schubert System "was not fit for the ordinary purpose of an automatic erecting, loading, and closing system for a flip-top cassette carton, and it was not fit for the particular purpose, namely, the rapid and reliable production of Biobox packaging cartons." Schubert argues, however, that provisions in the Terms and Conditions attached to the Price Quotation effectively disclaimed the Article 35 warranties. TVT counters that: "there was an oral understanding between TVT and Schubert's agent that the onerous 'boilerplate language' of the Terms and Conditions would *not* apply." The matter is made more complex because one of the provisions in the Terms and Conditions section is a merger clause, which extinguishes all prior oral agreements. The question is whether the merger clause, under the principles of the CISG, voids a prior oral agreement.

There exists a genuine issue of material fact as to whether Schubert and TVT shared the intent to be bound by the "Terms and Conditions." The CISG Advisory Council has noted that "extrinsic evidence [such as the oral dealings] should be excluded, if the parties actually did or intend the Merger Clause to have this effect." This suggests that if either party had a contrary intent, the Merger Clause between them would have no effect. Dismissal is inappropriate on TVT's Article 35(2)(a)–(b) claim because there is a genuine issue of material fact regarding the parties' intent to incorporate the Terms and Conditions, and Merger Clause therein. The lower court is required to determine the subjective intent of the parties.

Case Highlights

- Unlike American sales law, the CISG contains no statute of frauds (written form requirement) or parol evidence rule (written contracts cannot be contradicted by other types of evidence); therefore, oral statements between the parties may be used to prove a contract and the terms of the contract
- CISG Article 8 adopts both the subjective (actual intent) and objective (manifestations of intent) approaches to contract interpretation. Contracts are to be interpreted based upon evidence of the parties' actual subjective intent. If this is inconclusive, contracts are to be interpreted using the reasonable person standard (objective intent)
- In this case, the written contract's **standard terms** included a *disclaimer of implied warranties* found in CISG Article 35 (implied warranty of merchantability for ordinary purpose and implied warranty for a particular purpose), however, the buyer argued that the disclaimer of warranties was not part of the contract because the parties had orally agreed that the standard terms did not apply
- The common law's parol evidence rule would bar the use of the evidence of oral statements that contradict the written contract, while the CISG has no such rule and the evidence of an oral agreement is admissible. A merger clause is a contract term that restates the parol evidence rule by prohibiting the consideration of extrinsic evidence (oral representations)

- If the court determines the parties had subjectively agreed that standard terms would not apply despite the objective fact that they were included in the contract, then the disclaimer in the standard terms is unenforceable and the buyer would be able to bring claims of breach of implied warranties (CISG Article 35). If the court finds that the standard terms did apply under the reasonable person standard, then the disclaimer would be effective, and the merger clause would prevent the buyer from presenting evidence of the oral agreement. The second issue addressed by the court was whether the parties subjectively intended the merger to prevent the admission of extrinsic evidence that shows true intent.

A famous case of contract interpretation involved the judicial attempt to define the word "chicken." The *Frigaliment Importing v. B.N.S. International Sales Corp.* case illustrates how a court attempts to define terms in a contract through a reading of the contract and its use of evidence of prior dealings, course of performance, and trade usage. It also discusses a number of important legal concepts including the **four-corners analysis**, the **totality of the circumstances**, and the **reasonable person standard**.

Frigaliment Importing v. B.N.S. International Sales Corp.

190 F. Supp. 116 (S.D.N.Y. 1960)

Action by buyer of chicken against seller for breach of warranty. The seller (New York) entered into a contract to sell to plaintiff (Swiss): "US fresh Frozen Chicken, Grade A, Government Inspected, 2½ to 3 lbs." When the initial shipment arrived in Switzerland, the plaintiff found that the birds were not young chickens suitable for broiling and frying but stewing chickens or "fowl." The issue is, what is a chicken? (See Image 10.2: "What Is a Chicken?")

Friendly, Circuit Judge. Plaintiff says "chicken" means a young chicken, suitable for broiling and frying. Defendant says "chicken" means any bird of the genus that meets contract specifications on weight and quality, including "stewing chickens." Assuming that both parties were acting in good faith, the case illustrates Oliver Wendell Holmes Jr's remark "that the making of a contract depends not on the agreement of two minds in one intention, but on the agreement of two sets of external signs—not on the parties' having *meant* the same thing but on having *said* the same thing." Since the word "chicken" standing alone is ambiguous, I turn first to see whether the contract itself offers any aid to its interpretation.

Plaintiff's first contention hinges on an exchange of correspondence, which preceded the formal contract. After testing the market price, plaintiff accepted, and sent defendant a confirmation. These and subsequent communications were predominantly in German, although they used the English word "chicken." Defendant's agent testified that when asked by plaintiff's agent what kind of chicken was wanted, he received the answer "any kind of chickens." Defendant argues that if plaintiff was sincere in thinking it was entitled to young chickens, plaintiff would not have allowed the second shipment.

Plaintiff's next contention is that there was a definite trade usage that "chicken" meant "young chickens"; however, there was no proof offered of the alleged usage; it is quite plain that defendant's belief was to the contrary. One witness stated that a careful businessman protected himself by using the words "stewing" or "fowl" when he wished older birds. An employee of a company that publishes a daily market report on the poultry trade gave his view that the trade meaning of "chicken" was "broilers and fryers." Defendant provided a witness that said that in the trade, "chicken" would encompass various classifications of chicken. Defendant also provided a regulation of the Department of Agriculture that defined "chickens" as various classes including "*broiler or fryer*, roaster, capon, stag, hen or *stewing* chicken or *fowl*."

When all the evidence is reviewed, it is clear defendant believed it could comply with the contracts by delivering stewing chickens; it is equally plain that plaintiff's own subjective intent was to obtain broilers and fryers. Because plaintiff has not met its burden of showing that "chicken" was used in the narrower sense, judgment is entered dismissing the complaint.

Case Highlights

- Four-corners analysis requires a court or arbitral panel to find the answer to the issue in dispute within the contract
- In a *totality of the circumstances analysis* the court or arbitrator looks outside of the contract to interpret its meaning
- Under the *reasonable person standard*, the contract is interpreted from the perspective of a reasonable person in that particular trade or business.

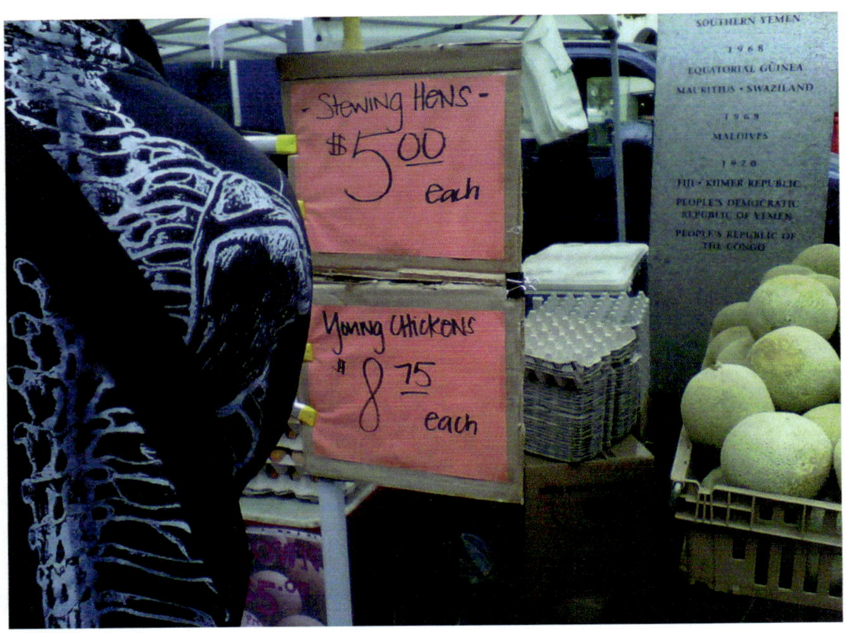

Image 10.2 What Is a Chicken?

The *Frigaliment* case illustrates the hierarchy of tools that courts use in interpreting contracts. The first level is studying the language of the contract to determine its meaning. This is sometimes referred to as a four-corners analysis or the **plain meaning rule**. If the language is unclear, the court proceeds to the next level of analysis by analyzing the relationship and actions of the contracting parties. First, it will look at evidence of "course of performance" in which the court reviews the post-formation conduct of the parties to determine what the parties believed that the contract meant. If the meaning is still unclear, the court will study any prior contracts or dealings between the parties to infer a previously established meaning. The final level of analysis is to infer a meaning from trade usage or business custom. In *Frigaliment* none of these levels of analysis provided a clear meaning for the word *chicken*. The result was the plaintiff lost because of its failure to meet its burden of proof regarding the meaning of the word.

The totality of the circumstances analyzes all levels of evidence. Lord Wilberforce in *Reardon Smith Line, Ltd.*[8] defined the totality of the circumstances analysis as the need in "commercial contracts for the court to know the commercial purpose of the contract. This presupposes knowledge of the genesis of the transaction, background, context, and the market in which the parties were operating." The background and context include oral negotiations, prior dealings, trade usage, and custom. The common law has long used the reasonable person standard as an aid in interpreting contracts. The reasonable person reflects the totality of the circumstances analysis because it is often constructed using the trade usage, customs, and practices of businesspersons in a particular trade or business.

Karl Llewellyn, in writing UCC Article 2 (Sale of Goods), devised two roles for the reasonable person standard in the area of standard form contracts: (1) to interpret the meaning of the terms expressly negotiated by the parties; and (2) to determine what non-negotiated terms are to be expelled due to unreasonableness. The reasonable person standard is also used to determine what reasonable terms are to be inferred to fill in gaps in the contract. For purposes of determining reasonableness, the reasonable person standard looks to the terms generally found in contracts of a given type (licensing, energy contracts, franchise contract, and so forth).[9]

Duty to Inspect and Proper Notice

A purchaser of goods may reject delivered goods if it gives timely and effective notice of a nonconformity. The buyer has three duties under the CISG. First, Article 38(1) requires the buyer to inspect the goods "within as short a period as is practicable." Second, the buyer must inform the seller of the nonconformity "within a reasonable time after it has discovered or ought to have discovered the nonconformity." Any claim for nonconformity is time barred if not reported within two years of delivery to the buyer. Third, the notice to the seller must specify the nature of the nonconformity.

A German court dealt with the notion of due diligence in the inspection of goods. Following customer complaints about measurements, sewing quality, and color fading of shoes, a German retailer canceled a second order with an Italian manufacturer. The goods were shipped, nonetheless. The retailer inspected a selected sample of the shoes and failed to detect any nonconformity. Following additional customer complaints, the retailer attempted to reject the second order due to nonconformity. The court found in favor of the seller, holding that the expiration of 16 days rendered the buyer's notice as untimely.[10] In recent years, the German courts have loosened the requirement for giving notice "within a reasonable time" to what is sometimes called the "golden month." It also determined that the buyer failed in performing a reasonable inspection. Because the buyer was aware of nonconformities stemming from the first order, it should have performed a more detailed inspection of the shoes in the second order. The court presumed that such an inspection would have uncovered the nonconformity at an earlier date.

In another case, pursuant to an installment contract a German clothing retailer gave notice of nonconformity to an Italian seller of fashion goods after delivery of two shipments. The notice stated that the goods failed to conform because of "poor workmanship and improper fit." The German court held the notice ineffective due to its lack of specificity. One reason for the specificity requirement is that it may allow the seller to "cure" the defects. Also, a buyer who merely rejects without stating details of why is deemed to be acting in bad faith.

Nachfrist *Notice*

A concept foreign to Anglo-American contract law is the civil law notion of ***nachfrist* notice**, which is incorporated into the CISG's Articles 47–49 and 63. The underlying premise behind this concept is that a delay in performance does not in itself constitute a material breach of the contract. The notion allows a buyer or seller to fix an additional time for performance beyond that which is specified in the contract. The additional time must be of a reasonable duration. The reasonableness of the time extension will depend on the nature, extent, and consequences of the delay, along with the importance to the buyer of prompt delivery.

The buyer may give *nachfrist* notice to the seller that it will accept delivery beyond the time prescribed, and the seller may request a *nachfrist* extension.

The nonbreaching party is then enjoined from taking legal action during the *nachfrist* period and must accept any proper tender of performance during that period. The recipient of such a request is obligated to respond to the request. Failure to do so results in the automatic granting of the additional time. The failure of the breaching party to perform during the extension allows the other party to declare an immediate voiding of the contract. See Figure 10.2 *Comparative Law*: "A *Nachfrist* Case Study."

A business unaware of the practice of *nachfrist* notice will be subject to unintended liabilities. It may mistake a *nachfrist* notice as a meaningless, nonlegal request for more time. Failure to respond in a proper way will result in an unintentional grant of additional time for performance. This likely will be compounded

A contract between an Italian clothing manufacturer and a German retailer provided for the sale of "autumn goods, to be delivered July, August, September, plus or minus." The first delivery of the goods was made on September 26. The retailer rejected the delivery of the goods as untimely. The court rejected the buyer's argument that the term "autumn goods" envisioned delivery of three equal shipments for the months of July, August, and September.

What could the German importer have done differently to avoid such a misunderstanding? First, it should have defined the delivery of "autumn goods" more carefully in the contract. Second, as suggested by the German court, they could have made use of *nachfrist* notice as provided in the CISG. The purchaser could have sent notice pursuant to Article 47 of the CISG. Article 47 states that the "buyer may fix an additional period of time of reasonable length for performance by the seller." Such notice of the granting of an additional time to perform is normally given in conjunction with a fixed and known delivery date. The German court held that "the buyer did not effectively void the contract by refusing acceptance of the goods *without fixing an additional period* in the previous cases of nondelivery."

The use of *nachfrist* notice in this situation would have been evidence that the parties had indeed intended multiple delivery dates in July, August, and September. The decision holds out the possibility that *nachfrist* notice may be used to fix an unspecified delivery date. At the minimum, it would have placed a burden upon the exporter to respond to the request for delivery. The failure of the exporter to respond would have allowed the German importer to declare the contract as voided and to seek substituted goods elsewhere (Article 49).

Figure 10.2 Comparative Law: A *Nachfrist* Case Study.

by it rejecting delivery of goods during the *nachfrist* period as untimely. The result would be it will be liable for breach of contract and not the party delivering after the delivery date fixed in the contract. The existence of an express "time of the essence" clause, fixing the delivery date as a material and absolute, is unlikely to provide a party protection from the use of *nachfrist* notice.

Businesses need to realize that the receipt of seemingly meaningless communications may have legal consequences.

Seller's Right to Cure

The CISG provides the seller a broad **right to cure** (repair or replace) defective goods. Article 48 of the CISG allows the seller to cure after the contract date for delivery unless such late delivery would cause the buyer "unreasonable inconvenience or uncertainty." The buyer retains the right to sue for damages and expenses caused by the delay or by the initial delivery of nonconforming goods. In some countries, the right to cure ends on the delivery date specified in the contract. In such a case, the right to cure is only relevant when the seller delivers the goods early (before the delivery date).

Anticipatory Breach and Adequate Assurance

Anticipatory breach is a concept of Anglo-American legal derivation. The civil law does not recognize the right of a party to avoid or suspend their contract obligation in anticipation of a breach by the other party (German law has something similar known as the "defense of security"), where contract avoidance is permitted only at the time of breach or by way of a court order. Article 71 of the CISG allows a party to suspend its performance if it becomes clear that the other party will not perform. It gives two broad grounds for anticipatory breach: First, the other party has become seriously deficient in its ability to perform or its creditworthiness has faltered. Second, the other party's lack of preparation or insufficiency of its performance to date has called into question its ability or willingness to perform under the contract. When one party anticipates a breach by the other party and suspends performance, it must give immediate notice of the suspension.

The suspending party must lift its suspension in the event that the other party provides **adequate assurance** that it will perform as contracted. Examples of adequate assurance, depending on the type of good, include providing paid receipts for materials or a bank guarantee. Failure to give such adequate assurance within a reasonable time results in a repudiation (termination) of the contract.

Damages

The damage provisions in the CISG are found in Articles 74 to 77. Article 74 provides the general measure of damages. It adopts the common law rule that damages should be limited to those that were foreseeable at the time of contract formation, popularly known as the rules of *Hadley v. Baxendale*.[11] The damages that can be collected are restricted in three ways. First, only foreseeable **damages** related to the breach may be sued upon. Article 74 states that "damages may not exceed the loss which the party in breach foresaw or ought to have foreseen at the time of the conclusion of the contract." Second, damages will be limited to those that are provable with some degree of certainty. Therefore, purely speculative damages are not collectable.

Third, Article 77 provides that even if the loss was foreseeable and its amount is certain, the nonbreaching party will be limited in its recovery in the event it failed to mitigate damages. Article 77 provides that if a party "fails to take such measures to mitigate the loss, the party in breach may claim a reduction in damages in the amount by which the loss should have been mitigated." For example, if a buyer has a source for substituted goods, it must make efforts to obtain the substituted goods. In the case of a fundamental breach, Article 75 allows the nonbreaching party to avoid the contract. It also authorizes the nonbreaching party to obtain substituted goods. The nonbreaching party may then sue the breaching party for the difference between the contract price (of the voided contract) and the price of the substituted goods. If the nonbreaching party elects not to procure substituted goods, Article 76 allows it to recover the difference between the contract price and the market price at the time of avoidance (termination).

The *Delchi Carrier, S.p.A. v. Rotorex Corp.* case that follows examines the different types of damages that are available in a typical breach of contract case. The case involves the delivery of defective goods. The goods involved in the transaction were component parts used by the buyer in the production of air conditioning units. The court assesses the damages that the buyer may collect when the delivery of defective goods results in a production slowdown at its plant. The court also decides on the types of out-of-pocket expenses the buyer can collect against the seller.

Delchi Carrier, S.p.A. v. Rotorex Corp.

71 F.3d 1024 (2d Cir. 1995)

The case involved a warranty dispute between a seller of compressors ("Rotorex") and a purchaser ("Delchi"). The trial court determined that the compressors failed to conform to the specifications provided in the contract or the sample provided by Rotorex to Delchi. After Rotorex failed to cure the defects, Delchi brought suit for breach of contract and recovery of damages, including consequential damages for lost profits. The lost profits were allegedly due to the lost volume caused by the closing of the assembly line for four days until the compressors were repaired. They also sued for incidental damages such as the cost to repair the compressors, the cost of storage, and the costs of expediting substitute goods.

Circuit Judge. The governing law of this case is the CISG. Article 74 allows for Delchi to collect monetary damages that are equal to its loss, including lost profits. Those damages are limited, however, to damages *foreseeable* at the time of the formation of the contract. Its first claim of damages is the cost of repairing the nonconforming compressors. These damages are recoverable because it was a foreseeable result of Rotorex's breach. Pursuant to Article 77 of the CISG, Delchi attempted to mitigate its losses by expediting a shipment of previously ordered Sanyo compressors. The expedited shipment cannot be considered as *cover* (purchase of substituted goods) under Article 75, because they were previously ordered. Nonetheless, Delchi's actions in expediting the shipment were commercially reasonable and reasonably foreseeable. Therefore, Delchi is entitled to recover the additional cost of air shipment. Delchi is also entitled to the incidental costs of handling and storage of the rejected compressors.

The CISG permits recovery of lost profits resulting from a diminished volume of sales. In conformity to the common law, to recover lost profits under the CISG, a party must provide sufficient evidence to estimate the amount of damages with *reasonable certainty*. Delchi proved with sufficient certainty (existing customer contracts that were terminated) a lost profit of 546,377.62 lire. However, Delchi did not prove with sufficient certainty lost sales from "anticipated (future) profits" (due to lost customers and negative reputation effects). Delchi's claim of 4,000 additional lost sales is supported only by speculative testimony of sales agents. Delchi is entitled to compensatory damages for those expenses incurred in repairing nonconforming goods, expediting substitute goods, storage of rejected goods, and reasonably certain lost profits. Lost profits do not include profits that arise from anticipated sales that cannot be determined by reasonable certainty.

Case Highlights

- Article 74 of the CISG allows a party to collect any foreseeable damages incurred due to a breach of contract
- Article 77 of the CISG requires the plaintiff to mitigate its damages. Expenses incurred, such as expediting shipment of substitute goods, are recoverable against the breaching party
- The plaintiff may also collect incidental damages, such as costs incurred in repairing, storing, and protecting the defective goods
- A plaintiff may collect lost profits caused by delivery of defective goods, but only those profits that can be proven with reasonable certainty
- In sum, under the CISG and the UCC, damages are restricted by three principles: (1) they must have been foreseeable at the time that contract was signed; (2) they were not caused by the plaintiff's failure to mitigate; and (3) they must be proven with reasonable certainty and are not merely speculative.

The CISG does not allow for recovery for breach of warranty that results in injury to persons or property. Article 5 of the CISG states that it does not cover claims resulting from the "liability of the seller for death or personal injury caused by the goods to any person." Therefore, **products liability** remains to be determined under national laws. For example, American law[12] allows for the recovery of consequential damages stemming from the seller's breach due to "injury to person or property proximately resulting from any breach of warranty."

Warranty Provisions

The warranties that are of concern to most seller-exporters are implied warranties that a court may use to hold the seller liable for nonconforming goods. Article 35 of the CISG recognizes two implied warranties—**implied warranty of merchantability** and **implied warranty for a particular purpose.** Other countries have similar warranties, but use different terminology, such as "satisfactory quality." See Figure 10.3 *Comparative Law*: "UCC Section 2-314(2)." A sale of fungible commodities is normally governed by the implied warranty of merchantability. Section 2-314 states it is implied that for the goods to be merchantable they must be "fit for the ordinary purposes for which such goods are used." For example, a 20,000 BTU air-conditioning unit should produce 20,000 BTU of air conditioning. However, if the buyer relies on the seller's expertise to provide sufficient air conditioning equipment and the seller recommends a 20,000 BTU unit, the unit must be sufficient to cool the space discussed. If the unit produces 20,000 BTU but fails to sufficiently cool the room or building, then it breaches the implied warranty for a particular purpose. Article 35 of the CISG states that the goods are to conform to "any purpose expressly or impliedly made known to the seller" at the time of the formation of the contract.

Goods to be *merchantable* must:

(a) pass without objection in the trade under the contract description;
(b) in the case of fungible goods, are of fair average quality within the description;
(c) are fit for the ordinary purposes for which such goods are used;
(d) run, within the variations permitted by the agreement, of even kind, quality, and quantity within each unit and among all units involved;
(e) are adequately contained, packaged, and labeled as the agreement may require; and
(f) conform to the promises or affirmations of fact made on the container or label if any.

Comment 2: Goods delivered under an agreement made by a merchant in a given line of trade must be of a quality comparable to generally acceptable goods in that line of trade under the description of the goods used in the agreement.

The CISG specifically makes it a breach of warranty if the seller fails to adequately package goods for shipment, whether or not the type of packaging is described in the contract.

Figure 10.3 Comparative Law: UCC Section 2-314(2).

The *T.J. Stevenson* case that follows discusses the warranty of merchantability and the importance of giving notice when receiving defective or nonconforming goods. Failure to give timely notice will result in the buyer losing its right to remedies, including the right to reject the defective goods and to sue for damages.

T.J. Stevenson & Co. v. Bags of Flour

629 F.2d 338 (5th Cir. 1980)

This action stems from insect infestation of wheat flour, which had been shipped on an ocean carrier. The carrier claimed a lien on the cargo for freight, detention, and expenses, and also sought recovery of damages from the miller-seller and the consignee or buyer (Bolivia). The miller filed counterclaims against Bolivia and the carrier and Bolivia counterclaimed for breach of warranty. The Republic of Bolivia had entered into a contract for the purchase of 26,618 metric tons of flour from Seller. The contract contained the following delivery term: "Delivery of goods by SELLER to the carrier at point of shipment shall constitute delivery to BUYER." Upon satisfactory delivery, the price was payable by irrevocable letter of credit. The contract also contained an express warranty of merchantability: "Seller warrants that the product sold shall be of merchantable quality." The warranty clause contained the following notice requirements: "BUYER hereby waives any claim based on the quality of the goods unless, within twenty days of the arrival of goods at destination, BUYER sends SELLER a notice specifying the nature of the complaint."

Circuit Judge. With this decision we hopefully end an amphibious imbroglio (very confusing situation) and commercial law practitioner's nightmare. Without pause to reflect on the complications that simple insects—confused flour beetles or otherwise—can create in the lives of men and Courts, we proceed to explain our decision. One issue permeates this case: What was the source of the flour infestation? The District Judge rightly concluded that infestation began either on the rail cars or at the mill supplying the flour.

The Warranty

The lower court judge rightly held that the flour failed to meet the warranty provision of the contract due to the substantial degree of infestation. American law defines merchantable as goods that "are fit for the ordinary purposes for which such goods are used" (must be of a quality comparable to that generally acceptable in that line of trade). Furthermore, "merchantable goods must be *honestly resalable in the normal course of business because they are what they purport to be.*" We have often recognized that no food is completely pure. Here the question is: How much live infestation renders consumer-destined flour unfit for the ordinary purposes for which it is used? Trade usage and course of dealing point to but one conclusion: Although flour may be "fit for human consumption" in the sense that it can be eaten without causing sickness, it is nonetheless not of merchantable quality.

Risk of Loss

The next question is determining if the risk of infestation was on the seller or the buyer. The infestation in this case began before the flour reached the port warehouse. The real issue is which party is responsible for the further infestation of the flour in the warehouses or on the ship. The delivery (trade) term in the contract read as follows: "F.A.S. MOBILE, ALABAMA for export." Under the FAS term, risk of loss passes to the buyer when the goods are duly delivered to the carrier. However, since the flour failed to conform to the contract the buyer had the right of rejection since the risk of their loss remains on the seller until cure or acceptance. Since it was materially nonconforming at the time it arrived in Mobile, Bolivia could have rejected the flour at that time. We therefore conclude the risk of loss of the infested flour remained on the seller.

Breach of Warranty and Fundamental Breach

In order for Bolivia to win on its warranty claim, it must satisfy the relevant notice requirements. The buyer must give notice of nonconformity (CISG Article 39) within a reasonable time after it discovers or should have discovered the nonconformity or lose its right to claim a remedy. Furthermore, the contract added the contractual requirement that notice must be in writing "within twenty days after arrival of the goods." The seller contends that it never received adequate notice of the defects. However, the facts show that the parties were in "continuous communication" from the time that Bolivia telexed its bank that no further payments would be permitted under the "irrevocable" letter of credit. From this view of the parties' conduct, one may infer that seller was aware of the buyer's dissatisfaction. Its awareness operated as a waiver of the specific notice provisions of the contract. The seller's responses to the buyer's complaints established a course of performance in which the formal notice requirement in the contract should be disregarded. Defendant (seller) was liable for breach of warranty.

Case Highlights

- Under the UCC any defect is grounds for rejection (perfect tender rule). The CISG gives a right of rejection only if there is a fundamental breach
- The court disregarded the specific notice requirements of the contract by imputing actual notice from the actions and correspondence between the parties after the goods were delivered
- FAS stands for Free Alongside Ship. Under this term, the risk of loss to the goods is transferred to the buyer when the goods are delivered to the port of shipment and ready for loading onto the ship. However, the court found that since the goods were defective upon delivery to the ship the risk of loss never passed to the buyer
- If nonconforming goods can be resold for another purpose, then a court, under the CISG, is likely to find that a breach did not constitute a fundamental breach. In such a case, the buyer has no right to reject the goods. Instead, the buyer may make use of the price reduction remedy provided for in Article 50 of the CISG. Under this remedy, the buyer can unilaterally reduce the price of the goods by the difference in value between the goods in their defective condition and the value of conforming goods (this remedy is found in the civil law, but not in the common law).

It is common for parties to enter into long-term supply contracts that entail multiple shipments or installments of goods. A key issue is whether a shipment or installment of nonconforming goods allow the buyer to terminate the contract for fundamental breach or does the buyer only have the right to reject the single installment? Single or limited deliveries of nonconforming goods are generally not grounds to terminate a long-term supply contract. Factors that would allow a termination include continuous deliveries of nonconforming goods, the consequences of receiving nonconforming goods, such as a shutting down of a manufacturing plant, or when the installments are of different goods to be assembled in the future.

Disclaimer of Warranty

Often a seller will attempt to disclaim all warranties or will want to limit its liability through a **limited express warranty. Disclaimers** should be drafted with clear and conspicuous language (easily noticeable when reviewing the contract). Language such as the "Purchaser Takes as Is" is considered clear disclaimer language. However, the CISG provides no formal requirements for disclaimers. Any form of disclaimer is technically enforceable under the CISG. Figure 10.4 *Focus on Transactions*: "Limited Liability and Disclaimer in Software Contracts"[13] illustrates the type of disclaimer language used by merchants.

LICENSE: The User shall have a nontransferable license to modify and use the product for functions performed in User's business. The product includes both hardware and firmware[14] that is proprietary to the seller who retains said rights. RESALE OR OTHER TRANSFER OF THE PRODUCT BY THE FIRST PURCHASER IS A VIOLATION OF THE TERMS OF THIS AGREEMENT. ANY AND ALL WARRANTIES ARE TERMINATED UPON SUCH A TRANSFER. Upon termination of the license, the User shall destroy all copies of and copies of and modifications to the Firmware.

LIMITED WARRANTY & DISCLAIMER: THE PRODUCT IS PROVIDED TO THE ORIGINAL USER A S IS, WITHOUT WARRANTY OF ANY KIND, EITHER EXPRESSED OR IMPLIED, INCLUDING, BUT NOT LIMITED TO THE IMPLIED WARRANTIES OF MERCHANTABILITY OR FITNESS FOR A PARTICULAR PURPOSE.

LIMITATION OF REMEDIES: Seller's entire liability and User's exclusive remedy shall be the repair and replacement including materials and labor for a period of one year unless the product has been abused, misused, or modified. IN NO EVENT WILL SELLER BE LIABLE TO THE USER FOR ANY DAMAGES, INCLUDING ANY LOST PROFITS, INCIDENTAL OR CONSEQUENTIAL DAMAGES ARISING OUT OF THE USE OR INABILITY TO USE THE PRODUCT.

THE USER FURTHER AGREES THAT THIS DOCUMENT IS THE COMPLETE AND EXCLUSIVE STATEMENT OF THE AGREEMENT BETWEEN THE USER AND THE SELLER, WHICH SUPERSEDES ANY PROPOSAL OR PRIOR AGREEMENT, ORAL OR WRITTEN.

Figure 10.4 Focus on Transactions: Limited Liability and Disclaimer in Software Contracts.

In Figure 10.4, some of the language is printed in capital letters. This capitalization is meant to satisfy the law in some countries that require disclaimers of implied warranties to be conspicuously stated so as to alert the buyer. There is no conspicuousness requirement in the CISG. Therefore, a disclaimer may be placed within the fine print terms. The final sentence of the disclaimer is an example of a merger clause. It is meant to bar the buyer from claiming that the seller through oral representations or other documents gave a different warranty.

Contractual Excuses

All legal systems provide relief for someone who despite good faith intentions is unable to perform. Although in technical breach of the contract, the court will excuse or exempt the breaching party from claims for damages. The common law fabricated the **doctrine of impossibility** and the **doctrine of frustration.** The former requires the contracting party to be objectively prevented from performing and generally entails the destruction of the subject matter of the contract. Under the doctrine of frustration, the performance may still be objectively possible but the reason for the performance has ceased. For example, a hotel charges five times its normal rate for the final weekend of the Wimbledon tennis championship. Because of the threat of a major storm, Wimbledon is postponed. The purpose for renting a room at the exorbitant rate has been frustrated. The booking renter will be relieved of its obligations to pay for the room and receive a refund for the advanced payment. The availability of contractual excuses in the civil law countries vary. In Belgium and France, *pacta sunt servanda* or sanctity of contract generally prevails over requests for an excuse. If the contract does not provide an excuse through a *force majeure* clause, then the contract will be enforced without any modification to its terms, unless impossibility of performance is due to an Act of God, government intervention, or a port strike. In England, the doctrine of frustration remains the premier excuse doctrine. The parties are relieved of their contractual obligations as of the date of frustration; the courts do not have the authority to modify or reform the contract. In Germany, if the "basis of the transaction" has evaporated, then the courts are free to excuse a party or to reform (adjust) the contract in accordance with the changed circumstances.

Article 79 of the CISG allows for an excuse if nonperformance is due to an **impediment** that is beyond the control of the breaching party and was not foreseeable at the time of contract formation. However, the excuse is not permanent; performance is suspended for the duration of the impediment. The person attempting to exercise an Article 79 impediment must give prompt notice of the impediment to the other party. Failure to do so exposes the party to damages resulting from not giving notice.

All the excuse doctrines revolve around all or some of the following parameters: lack of foreseeability, undue hardship, and being beyond the party's control. Most excuse doctrines require that the changed circumstances were **objectively unforeseeable** at the time of contract formation. If they were foreseeable, then the losses resulting from the breach will be considered as an allocated risk to be borne by the party assigned the risk, expressly or implicitly in the contract. For example, if the buyer agrees to pay in the seller's currency, then the buyer has impliedly agreed to assume the risk of currency fluctuations. If the buyer voids the contract due to a dramatic decline in its currency vis-à-vis the seller's currency it will be liable for full contract damages. **Undue hardship** generally means more than a mere loss. The fact that the contract becomes unprofitable for one of the parties is insufficient; the loss must be near catastrophic. Beyond control means the event is a type of *force majeure* (superior force) that it was impossible for the party to avoid or overcome. The UNIDROIT Principles summarize these factors: (1) an event or hardship that *fundamentally alters* the contractual equilibrium due to a change in costs or values; (2) the event could not *reasonably* have been considered at the time of the conclusion of the contract; and (3) the event was *beyond the control* of the breaching party. International Chamber of Commerce *Arbitration Case No. 6281* involves a seller's attempt to claim frustration due to an increase in the market price of steel.

Force Majeure Clause

The ***force majeure*** clause lists the type of events that allow the parties an excuse out of the contract. *Force majeure* events may include wars, blockades, strikes, governmental interference or approval, fire, transportation problems, and others.

The parties are free to recognize any event as one to be given *force majeure* effect. A *force majeure* clause should be custom drafted to consider the type of industry, as well as the countries and type of carriage (transport) involved. A *force majeure* clause allows a party to terminate its obligations under a contract due to the occurrence of something described in the clause. Like commercial hardship, a *force majeure* clause excuses nonperformance when circumstances beyond the control of the parties prevent performance. ICC Case No. 6281 discusses whether a fluctuation in the market price of a product can be grounds for a defense of hardship.

International Chamber of Commerce

Case No. 6281 of 26 August 1989

The parties entered into a contract for the sale of 80,000 metric tons of steel bars at a price of $190 per ton with delivery. The contract provided the buyer with an option to purchase an additional 80,000 metric tons. Subsequently, the buyer informed seller that it would exercise the option. The seller requested $215 per ton for the additional delivery. In response, the buyer purchased 80,000 tons from another supplier at a price of $216 and brought suit against seller for the difference between the original contract price of $190 and the price spent for the substituted goods.

Paris, France. Article 133 of the Yugoslav Law on Obligations allowed for a rescission (termination) of a contract due to "changed circumstances." The seller argued that it should be released from the contract due to changed circumstances, namely the increase in the market price of steel. The arbitrator determined that world market prices of products, such as steel, often fluctuate, and therefore the price increase was foreseeable. Also, the amount of harm caused by a cost or price fluctuation must exceed a reasonable entrepreneurial risk. An increase in market prices from $190 to $215 amounts to slightly less than 13.16%, well within the customary margin.

The buyer's purchase from another supplier, however, cannot be interpreted as a substitute purchase because he had failed to inform the seller of his intention to do so. Buyer's damage is limited to the difference between the $190 and $215 and not the $216 replacement price.

Seller shall reimburse the buyer in the amount of $2,000,000 (80,000 × $25).

Case Highlights

- Most price or cost increases will not be considered the type of unforeseeable event that provides a party an excuse for breaching a contract
- Losses due to cost increases, market price changes, or currency fluctuations are considered allocated risks and are to be borne by the party that is allocated the risk in the contract
- The nonbreaching party may have to accept a price increase under the duty to mitigate damages (such as in this case, where the market (substituted) price was greater than the price increase sought by the seller). It would then be able to recoup the price increase by suing for damages.

Hardship Principle: In the civil law, a second type of excuse is recognized where performance is still possible but can only be performed by one of the parties incurring an undue burden due to a change in circumstances, generally involving an unexpected and dramatic increase in the costs of materials. The fact that a contract has become more onerous (more costly or less profitable) on one of the parties is insufficient for a hardship claim; the burden must be excessively onerous. The performance is still possible but to require performance would severely affect the equilibrium of the contract (value being exchanged has dramatically changed to the benefit of one of the parties). In such cases, the parties have a legal duty to negotiate an adjustment; if they fail to reach an agreement the party claiming hardship may petition a court or arbitral tribunal for an adjustment or termination of the contract. The excuse of hardship is found in the civil law, but not in the common law. However, American law for the sale of goods recognizes hardship under the doctrine of impracticability. In fact, this is an empty principle since courts rarely use it in commercial transactions. If the parties want to require a contract adjustment in common law countries, they can simply insert a hardship clause into their contracts. Finally, just as in *force majeure* or impossibility, the hardship must not have been foreseeable at the time of the conclusion of the contract; if it was foreseeable then its occurrence will be deemed to be an allocated risk preventing a claim for hardship.

The *force majeure* clause that excuses a breaching party from liability for nonperformance is common under most national legal systems. *Force majeure* refers to "extraordinary events" that make it impossible for one of the parties to perform.[15] Under most national laws, to qualify as a *force majeure* event four criteria need to be satisfied: (1) the event must be external to the transaction and the parties; (2) it must render the performance radically different from that originally contemplated; (3) it must have been unforeseeable (objectively); and (4) its occurrence must be beyond the control of the party to prevent.

The case of *Bende & Sons, Inc. v. Crown Recreation, Inc.*[16] illustrates that the concept of foreseeability can be irrationally expanded by courts ("all things are foreseeable in hindsight"). In that case, a seller of combat boots sought an excuse for nonperformance due to the derailment of the train transporting the boots. The seller sought the excuse of hardship (commercial impracticability). Section 2-615 of the UCC provides for an excuse for nonperformance when performance is "made impracticable by the occurrence of a contingency the nonoccurrence of which was a basic assumption (reasonable expectations of contractual equilibrium) on which the contract was made." The court rejected the defense, holding that the derailment was an allocated risk because "common sense dictates that they could easily have foreseen such an occurrence!" This broad view of foreseeability is more often found in common law and even more so under Chinese law, where natural disasters (a widely recognized *force majeure* event), have been held to be foreseeable.

In *Phillips Puerto Rico Core, Inc. v. Tradax Petroleum*[17] liability rested upon the interpretation of a standard *force majeure* clause in relationship to the trade term in the contract. The clause in question read as follows:

> *FORCE MAJEURE*: In the event of any strike, fire or other event falling within the term Force Majeure preventing or delaying shipment or delivery of the goods by the seller then the contract period of shipment or delivery shall be extended by 30 days on request made within seven days of its occurrence. Should shipment or delivery of the goods continue to be prevented beyond 30 days, the unaffected (non-breaching) party may cancel the unfulfilled balance of the contract. Should the contract thus be cancelled and/or performance be prevented during any extension to the shipment or delivery period neither party shall have any claim against the other.

The case involved a Cost and Freight (C&F) contract for goods to be shipped from Algeria to Puerto Rico. The U.S. Coast Guard unexpectedly detained the ship while in transit. The purchaser brought suit against the seller for breach of contract, and the seller claimed an excuse under the *force majeure* clause. The court held that the defense was not necessary because under the C&F term the risk of loss had already passed to the purchaser at the port of shipment.

The *force majeure* clause should be a highly negotiated, customized provision dealing with the particulars of the specific parties, industry, and type of contract. Unfortunately, most contracts utilize vaguely worded standard *force majeure* or exemption clauses like the one above. The International Chamber of Commerce has created a slightly more elaborate standard *force majeure* clause:[18,19]

> A party is not liable for a failure to perform if he can prove that: (1) the failure was due to an impediment beyond his control, (2) he could not have reasonably foreseen the impediment at the time of contract formation, and (3) he could not have reasonably avoided or overcome its effects.
>
> An impediment includes but is not limited to: War, hostilities, and acts of piracy; Natural disasters; Explosions, fires, and destruction of machinery; Boycotts, strikes, lockouts, and work stoppages which occur in the enterprise of the party seeking relief; and Acts of authority (government).
>
> A party seeking relief pursuant to this clause shall give notice as soon as practicable. Failure to give timely notice makes the party liable in damages for losses that could otherwise have been avoided. Notice shall also be given when the impediment ceases.
>
> The relief granted under this clause is a postponement of the time for performance for such period as may be reasonable. The nonbreaching party may also suspend his own performance. Either party may terminate the contract in the event that the impediment persists for a period of [...] days. Upon the termination of the contract, each party may retain whatever he has received, but must account to the other party for any unjust enrichment.

The concept of *force majeure* is incorporated in Article 79 of the CISG. Article 79 refers to a *force majeure* event as an impediment. *Impediment* does not mean inconvenient, or more costly, or difficult to perform. Regarding the impediments enumerated above, work stoppages or strikes at a supplier or subcontractor are generally not sufficient causes. This presumption may be overcome if, for example, the contract specifies the use of the particular supplier or subcontractor. Impediments may vary over time; see Figure 10.5 "Case Study: Coronavirus."

Limitation Period

Another important contract law issue is the statute of limitations or limitation period that will be applied to any future claims of the parties. It is always advisable for the parties to agree upon a reasonable limitation period. The United Nations sponsored **Convention on the Limitation Period in the International Sale of Goods** provides uniform rules governing the period of time within which a party may bring a claim related to the sales contract. The Convention prescribes a four-year limitation period for most claims. The four-year limitation

The coronavirus (COVID-19) pandemic resulted in worldwide business shutdowns, disruptions in the supply chain, and labour stoppages. The virus initially centered in China before developing into a global threat and being declared an international public health emergency by the World Health Organization. It raises the question of what effect does such an event have on the enforceability and liability for breach of contract? Do nonperforming parties have legitimate defenses related to *force majeure* clauses, or the legal defences of impossibility or *force majeure*, frustration, and hardship? The answers to these questions are not as simple as one would expect due to the variation in national laws. English law requires specific contractual provisions and for affected parties to prove that their ability to perform the contract has been made impossible by the outbreak, while the China Council for the Promotion of International Trade issued more than 4,000 *force majeure* certificates on March 3, 2020 alone.

The central issue is whether the pandemic is a *force majeure* event. The standard *force majeure* clause often repeats the same occurrences as found in the *force majeure* doctrine. Two categories of *force majeure* related to the pandemic may apply act of government and Act of God. Is a virus conceivably an Act of God akin to a natural disaster? Governments have intervened to mitigate the harm of the pandemic through travel restrictions and stay at home orders. But this alone does not seem to be sufficient if the goods can still be shipped or delivered. Also, does the pandemic, if recognized as a defense, result in the termination or suspension of the contract? Maybe termination is appropriate in one-off transactions, while suspension may be in order for long-term supply contracts. Also, a breaching party would lose any such defenses if it failed to give proper notice. The fact that the pandemic was a central news event and commonly known does not waive the specific notice requirements found in contracts or contract law.

All of the doctrines require that any event must be unforeseeable at the time of contracting. Is a pandemic a foreseeable event or, if theoretically foreseeable, was it such an extraordinary event to warrant an excuse from contract liability? A stronger case may be made under Article 79 of the CISG, which states that the event is something that the party could not have reasonably taken into account at the time of the conclusion of the contract. The commonsense answer is that a pandemic of this intensity is not something that a party would have taken account of, but this is unlikely to be the case in the future. One of the results of the terrorists attack on the United States on 9/11 was a severe

Figure 10.5 Case Study: Coronavirus.

depression in the airline industry. Some of the airlines defaulted on their loans and claimed the defense of impossibility. The defense was rejected because it was not a *force majeure* event compared to the destruction of airplanes.[20] An associated issue is whether the pandemic is a covered event in business interruption insurance. Often these policies have a pathogen exclusion so an insured company would have had to purchase an endorsement to specifically get coverage. However, a strong argument can be made that government actions in response to the pandemic that causes business interruption should be covered. There are other clauses or types of contracts that have been made uncertain by the pandemic. For example, employees who contract the virus are likely to sue their employers under tort law. Acquisition and merger contracts include Material Adverse Change (MAC) clauses Does a pandemic constitute a MAC?

In sum, the COVID-19 pandemic will result in much litigation involving commercial contracts and changes in the law going forward. Legal cases will need to determine if the excuse doctrines are applicable; is a pandemic an Act of God?; Was it foreseeable? If so, does it result in suspension or termination? *Force majeure* clauses will be rewritten to include pandemics, but what severity of a virus and its infectiousness rises to the level of excuse under such a clause? The COVID-19 pandemic provides a good example of the limitations of the hardship doctrine (since both parties are likely to have claims of hardship) and of the difficulty in drafting *force majeure* clauses.

Since the *force majeure* clause generally does not recognize changes in circumstances that result in mere hardship, the parties may expand the clause to include events that mak performance not impossible but unduly costly. Such a clause is referred to as a **hardship clause**. Hardship as noted above, can be defined as an, occurrence that fundamentally alters the contractual equilibrium by placing an excessive burden on one of the parties. The parties are to consult in good faith in the hope of amicably revising the contract. If no agreement is reached, the burdened party may seek relief in court or in arbitration.

Figure 10.5 (Continued)

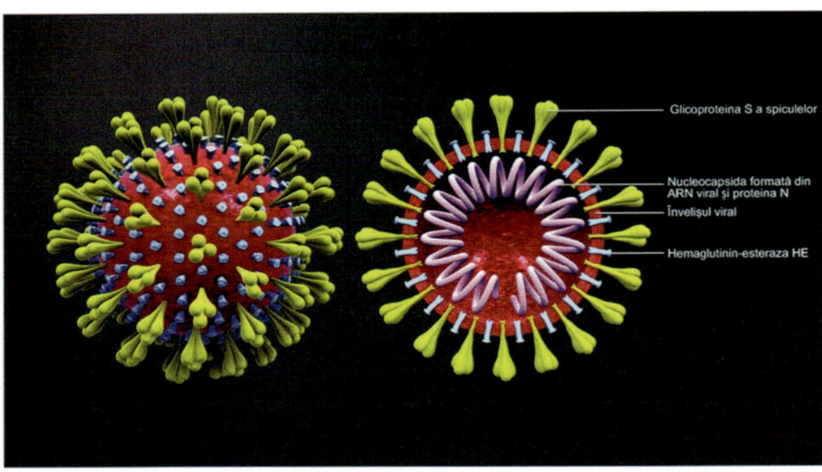

Image 10.3 Coronavirus (Covid-19).

Source: Wikimedia Commons, author: https://www.scientificanimations.com.

period can be shortened through the adoption of restrictive notice provisions. Sellers often require that notice of a nonconformity or defect be done promptly.

The Convention outlines when the period is to be tolled or suspended. A tolling of the limitation period is granted when there is a submission to arbitrate the claim. Article 14 states that when the parties submit a claim to arbitration, "the limitation period shall cease to run." The Convention does place an outer limit for the tolling of the limitation period: Article 23 states that "notwithstanding the provisions of this Convention, a limitation period shall in any event expire no later than ten years from the date on which it commenced."

Associated limitation periods vary greatly from country to country and from cause of action to cause of action. Two common statutes of limitation periods are provided for breach of warranty and products liability claims. EU law provides for an extended ten-year statute of limitation for products liability claims. In comparison, the limitation period for warranty claims is two years starting from the date of delivery of the goods.

Chapter Summary

1. The Convention on Contracts for the International Sale of Goods (CISG) has been the most successful attempt at the unification of international sales law. However, it is limited in scope, leaving numerous areas of contract law to be decided under domestic or national sales laws. Areas such as validity of contracts, specific performance, and products liability are not covered by the CISG.
2. The CISG makes it easy to form contracts because of a lack of formality requirements. For example, a written contract is not required; oral contracts are fully enforceable. Also, the CISG has an open evidence regime where the existence of a formal written contract does not prevent other evidence, including witness testimony from being used to determine the "actual" meaning of the contract.
3. The CISG adopted the subjective theory of contract (actual party intent) as the principal rule of contract interpretation, but also adopts the objective theory of contract (reasonable person standard) if the evidence does not support a finding of subjective intent.
4. The CISG adopts offer-acceptance rules similar to those found in the common law except for the CISG's rejection of the common law's mailbox (dispatch) rule in favor of the civil law's receipt rule. Under the CISG, a contract is formed when the acceptance is received by the offeror.
5. In contract interpretation, the courts or arbitral tribunals will often look at a number of sources to ascribe meaning to the contract. If the contract is clearly written, many courts will not look any further in deciding the contract dispute. If the contract is ambiguous or is missing a term, courts will look to prior dealings between the contracting parties, as well as evidence taken from the subsequent performance of the contract (course of performance). Finally, if the meaning of the contract is unclear, courts will look to business customs and trade usage to clarify the ambiguity or to fill in a gap in the contract.

6. Under the CISG, the buyer of goods has a duty to inspect the goods promptly after their delivery and to give immediate notice of any nonconformity (defects) in the goods to the seller. If the buyer delays in performing these duties it will lose the right to sue for damages due to the defects in the goods. Upon receiving the notice of nonconformity, the seller will have a reasonable time to "cure" the defects (repair or replace the defective goods). The delivery of defective goods does not give the buyer the right to reject the goods unless the defects are considered to be a fundamental breach of the contract.
7. The CISG has two concepts not found in the common law of contracts—*nachfrist* notice and the price reduction remedy. *Nachfrist* notice allows either party to request a time extension for performing past the deadline set in the contract. The seller may request additional time to deliver the goods and the buyer may request additional time to make payment. The party receiving a reasonable *nachfrist* request must give the additional time unless it has a commercially viable reason for denying the request. Failure to perform before the expiration of the *nachfrist* period of time is deemed to be a fundamental breach, which allows the nonbreaching party to avoid (terminate) the contract and sue for damages.
8. CISG warranty law states (unless disclaimed) that goods must satisfy the implied warranties of merchantable quality and for a particular purpose. The difference between the two warranties is the first one relates to a guarantee that the goods will serve their ordinary purpose (a toaster should be able to toast bread), while in the second one the buyer relies on the judgment and skills of the seller to provide a product that will serve the buyer's particular purpose (a toaster that also acts as an oven).
9. The CISG provides that the nonbreaching party may collect all "foreseeable" damages caused by the breach of contract including expenses incurred, lost profits, incidental expenses, and foreseeable consequential damages. The nonbreaching party has a duty to avoid or mitigate damages if it is reasonable to do so. If a party fails to mitigate, then the damages that could have been avoided, although caused by the breach, are not collectable.
10. Excuse is the concept that a party should be relieved of liability for breaching a contract if the breach was caused by an unforeseeable event, such as an Act of God (natural disasters). The common law recognizes the excuses of impossibility *force majeure* and frustration of purpose. Article 79 provides an excuse known as "impediment." The factors usually applied in a court for finding an excuse include: (1) the event that caused the breach was not "foreseeable" at the time of contract formation; (2) avoiding or preventing the event from occurring was beyond the control of the breaching party; and (3) it would be unreasonable to expect the breaching party to overcome the impediment (undue burden).

Key Terms

Adequate Assurance
Anticipatory Breach
Battle of the Forms
Bilateral Contract

Boilerplate (Standard) Terms
Choice of Law Clause
Conflict of Law Rules
Consequential Damages
Contract Formation
Convention on the Limitation Period in the International Sale of Goods
Course of Performance
Disclaimer
Doctrine of Frustration
Doctrine of Impossibility
Doctrine of Impracticability
Force Majeure
Four Corners Analysis
Hardship Clause
Impediment
Implied Warranty for a Particular Purpose
Implied Warranty of Merchantability
International Customary Law
Jurisdiction
Lex Mercatoria
Limited Express Warranty
Mailbox Rule
Merger Clause
Mirror Image Rule
Mixed Sale
Nachfrist Notice
Objective Theory of Contract
Offeree
Offeror
Parol Evidence Rule
Plain Meaning Rule
Prior Dealings
Products Liability
Ratification
Reasonable Person Standard
Revocation
Right to Cure
Software Sales
Specially Manufactured Goods
Standard Terms
Statute of Frauds
Totality of the Circumstances
Trade Usage
Undue Hardship
Uniform Commercial Code (UCC)
Unilateral Contract
Written Confirmation Rule

Chapter Problems

1. Compare the UCC's treatment of anticipatory repudiation and adequate assurance in 2-609 and 2-610 with the CISG's treatment in Articles 71–73. Can you find any significant differences?
2. In many transactions involving technology transfer, the contract provides for the sale of both goods and services. Does the CISG apply to such contracts?
3. How do courts determine which national laws apply in a given case?
4. An exception that the offeror is the master of the offer (power to revoke offer) is the firm offer rule, which provides that "an offer given by a *merchant* in a *signed writing* which gives *assurance* that it will be held open is not revocable, but in no event may such period of irrevocability exceed three months" (UCC Section 2-205). The CISG's firm offer rule is found in Article 16. It provides that an offer cannot be revoked "if it indicates that it is irrevocable or if it was reasonable for the offeree to rely on the offer being irrevocable and the offeree has acted in reliance on the offer." Do you see any significant differences between these two versions of the firm offer rule? Which version is broader? Why?

5. Drafting Exercise:
   a. As a seller and exporter of goods you are negotiating a long-term (three-year) installment contract. Because of the length of the contract, an open price term (term to be fixed at a later time or periodically) needs to be negotiated. Write a clause that anticipates the risks involved into entering a long-term supply contract. What cost factors should be described in detail in order to allow for the proper adjustment of the price term? Also, how would one interrelate the open price term with a *force majeure* clause?
   b. You are negotiating a contract for the shipment of goods from the Dominican Republic to the Middle East. The risks and costs of the shipment will be yours to the point of destination. Draft a *force majeure* clause. What events would you want to be considered as *force majeure?* Should some occurrences provide for an excuse (termination) and others for suspension?
   c. In a "battle of the forms" situation, the additional terms in the acceptance often become a part of the contract. Assuming that you are the offeror, draft language for your offer would preclude those additional terms from entering the contract. Assuming that you are the offeree, draft a clause for your acceptance that would make it clear that there is no contract unless it is on the terms of the acceptance (counteroffer).
6. A business manager corresponds with numerous contacts in the international business world. She sends letters and faxes to agents, customers, suppliers, distributors, lenders, and many others. Most businesspersons have been educated to believe that they would expose their companies to liability if and only if they enter into a formal written contract. The formal written contract is a product of the company's lawyers. They are also aware that under the American common law's statute of frauds they are not liable for oral promises. They further (incorrectly) rationalize that the statute of frauds requires a fully negotiated, written agreement signed by both parties. Therefore, they often say or write things aimed at encouraging another party to take some action. They say things and write letters under the assumption that they would not be held liable until they enter a formal agreement. How have these assumptions changed with the enactment of the CISG? Can businesspersons be held liable for promises or assurances made in simple business letters? How can a manager avoid such unintended liability?
7. The EU has a directive pertaining to warranties in consumer transactions. Compare the selected provisions of Directive 99/44/EC with the warranty provisions found in the UCC (Sections 2-312 to 2-316) and CISG (Articles 35–44). Note that the European word for "warranty" is "guarantee."

Internet Exercises

1. Review how Islamic Law deals with commercial transactions. See http://www.oxfordislamicstudies.com/article/opr/t236/e0156 and http://www.islamic-finance.com/item13_f.htm.

2. Select a country and research its sales law using the Cornell Law School Legal Information Institute at http://www.law.cornell.edu. Click on "Get the Law" at the top; then click "Law by Jurisdiction" on the drop-down menu and then click on "World Law" on the second drop-down menu.

Other Internet Sources

Case and arbitral law on the CISG: http://www.cisg.law.pace.edu.

Cornell Legal Information Institute—U.S. conflict of law rules: http://www .law. cornell.edu/topics/conflicts.html.

United Nations Commission on International Trade Law (UNCITRAL) (foreign case law on CISG or CLOUT): http://www.uncitral.org/uncitral/en/case _law. html.

UNIDROIT (International Institute for the Unification of Private Law): http:// www.unidroit.org.

Notes

1 However, a few countries, like the U.S., opted out of Article 1(1)(b) jurisdiction, meaning their courts only apply when both parties are from CISG countries.

2 See Larry A. DiMatteo, "The CISG as Source of International Customary Law," American Arbitration Association, *Dispute Resolution Journal* 75 (1998).

3 148 F.3d 649 (7th Cir. 1998).

4 See Marcus Larson, "Applying Uniform Sales Law to International Software Transactions," 5 *Tulane Journal of International and Comparative Law* 445 (1997).

5 UCC §2-201.

6 UCC §2-208 of the UCC states that "any course of performance accepted or acquiesced in without objection shall be relevant to determine the meaning of the agreement."

7 UCC §2-206(2) ("where the beginning of a requested performance is a reasonable mode of acceptance an offeror who is not notified of acceptance within a reasonable time may treat the offer as having lapsed before acceptance.")

8 *Reardon Smith Line, Ltd. v. Yngvar Hansen-Tangen* [1976] 1 W.L.R. 989, 996 (Eng. H.L.)

9 See generally Larry A. DiMatteo, "The Counterpoise of Contracts: The Reasonable Person Standard and the Subjectivity of Judgment," 48 *South Carolina Law Review* 293, 338–341 (1997).

10 General Court of Stuttgart, 3 KFh 97/89, CLOUT Case No. 4 (Case Law on UNCITRAL Text). (CLOUT is a reporting service accessible through the United Nations document services.)

11 156 Eng. Rep. 145 (1854).

12 UCC Section 2-715.

13 Source: American Bar Association.

14 Firmware is a specific class of computer software that provides the low-level control (operating system) for a device's specific hardware.

15 Theo Rauh, "Legal Consequences of *Force Majeure* under German, Swiss, English, and United States' Law," 25 *Denver Journal of International Law and Policy* 151 (1996).
16 548 F. Supp. 1018 (E.D. Louisiana 1982).
17 782 F.2d 314 (1985).
18 ICC Publication No. 421, "*Force Majeure* and Hardship," (1985).
19 *U.S. Bancorp v. Ameriquest Holdings*, 2004 Westlaw 2801601 (Dist. Minn. 2004).

Part III

International Business Transactions

Chapter 11

Transport of Goods

In transporting goods throughout the world, a number of different types of **common carriers** are utilized. Common carriers are companies that contract with the public for transportation of goods or persons and include commercial airlines, overnight courier services, and international shipping by sea. Each type of common carrier or carriage contract is governed by its own **unimodal transport convention** or by a **multimodal transport convention**. The most important international transport conventions are listed in Table 11.1 *Doing Business Internationally*: "International Transport Conventions," which also shows the limited liability provided to the common carriers.

Since international transport of goods involves numerous modes of shipment, issues of risk of loss and liability can become complicated. The leg of transport (land, rail, ocean) in which the loss-inducing event occurs determines the convention to be applied. Determining liability is further complicated by the existence of different legal regimes for a given mode of transport (transborder shipments). There are also alternative conventions or rules that may apply. For example, in ocean carriage there are three alternative legal regimes—the **Hague, Hague-Visby**, and **Hamburg Rules**.

Most international transport of goods necessarily includes ocean carriage, and despite the increased use of multimodal transport documents, the **ocean bill of lading** remains the paramount title document. The Hague and the Hague-Visby Rules[1] have been enacted into national laws under the title **Carriage of Goods by Sea Act (COGSA)**. The Hague Rules and COGSA will be used interchangeably in this chapter. After reviewing the Hague Rules and the related topic of marine insurance, there will be a brief analysis of the CIM (trucking) and CMR (shipment by rail) Conventions. But, first we will discuss the premier air carriage convention—the **Warsaw Convention**.

DOI: 10.4324/9781003469230-14

Table 11.1 *Doing Business Internationally:* International Transport Conventions.

Name	*Type of Transport*	*Description*
Warsaw Convention	Air	Liability Caps: $75,000 per person; $400 per luggage ($1,400 within U.S.)
Montreal Accord	Air	Unlimited Liability if Harm Due to Gross Negligence
Hague Rules	Ocean	$500 per package limitation
Hague-Visby Rules	Ocean	$1,000 per package limitation
Hamburg Rules	Ocean	
International Convention Concerning the Carriage of Goods by Rail (CIM Convention)	Railway	17 units of account per kilogram Wastage in transit: carrier not liable for 2 percent reduction of liquids or moist goods and 1 percent waste in dry goods items
Convention on the Contract for the International Carriage of Goods by Road (CMR)	Truck	25 gold francs per kilogram of gross weight short
UNCTAD/ICC Rules for Multimodal Transport Documents 1991	Multimodal	8.33 SDR per kilogram

Air Waybill and the Warsaw Convention

As a contract of carriage, the **air waybill** incorporates by reference the Warsaw Convention, which has been ratified by over 150 countries. Like the Hague Rules, the Warsaw Convention limits liability for the common carrier. The standard terms and conditions of the air waybill generally state that the liability limitation is "17 SDRs or approximately $20 per kilogram." The Warsaw Convention shares numerous similarities with the Hague Rules. For example, it allows for the extension of coverage to other parties involved in the carriage through a *Himalaya clause*. It states that: "any exclusion or limitation of liability applicable to the carrier shall apply to the benefit of the carrier's agents, servants, and representatives and any person whose aircraft is used by carrier for carriage."

Sea Waybill: There are different types of waybills: air waybill, inland waybill, and the sea waybill. The inland waybill can also include rail waybill. The waybill is not a document of title as is the ocean bill of lading. They are also not negotiable (transferable) as is the negotiable (order) ocean bill of lading. Waybills act as contracts between the shipper and the common carrier and serve as proof of delivery of the goods to the common carrier. The sea waybill shows that the goods are "on board" the ship, but since it is not a title document, it need not be presented to the common carrier in order to take delivery of the goods. This often allows the buyer to obtain the goods sooner since it is not waiting for delivery of an ocean bill of lading.

The air carrier is also protected from most claims of *material deviation*. The Convention states that "carriers may substitute alternative carriers or may without notice and with due regard to the interests of the shipper substitute other means of transportation. Carrier is authorized to select the routing or to change or deviate from the routing shown on the face of the air waybill." In the area of notice of damage, the consignee or person entitled to take delivery must promptly inspect the goods. It then must send a written complaint "of visible damage to the goods, immediately after discovery of the damage and at the latest within 14 days from receipt of the goods." The Convention provides for a two-year statute of limitation for the filing of claims.

International Ocean Carriage Conventions

Liability of common carriers is fixed by a combination of international conventions and national laws. National laws define issues of title and negotiability, while the international conventions impose the minimum duties of the carriers and provide limits to carrier liability. This was not always the case. Carriers, at one time, were able to shield themselves from liability by incorporating broad limitation of liability or **exculpatory clauses**. After many disputes with shippers, a compromise on issues of liability, known as the Hague Rules, was adopted in 1924. The Hague Rules established a number of carrier responsibilities such as the requirement to undertake due diligence in providing a seaworthy ship, to not deviate materially from the carriage contract, and to provide shippers with the opportunity to declare a higher value for their goods. In return, the shipping companies are provided a limitation of liability to cap their potential liabilities, along with a number of exemptions from liability.

There are three international conventions that regulate the liability of common carriers in the international transport of goods by sea: the Hague Rules, Hague-Visby Rules, and Hamburg Rules. The Hague-Visby rules updated the Hague Rules, but some countries, including the U.S., have failed to ratify the update. The liability of the carrier and associated companies is directly affected depending on which version is applied. Under the Hague-Visby Rules, the limit of liability is significantly increased. The Hamburg Rules are more pro-shipper than the Hague or Hague-Visby Rules. However, under the Hamburg Rules carrier liability protections are automatically extended to the servants or third-party contractors of the carriers.

The *Prima U.S., Inc. v. Panalpina, Inc. M/V Addiriyah* case introduces the different third parties involved in the international shipment of goods, including common carriers, stevedores, freight forwarders, non-vessel operating common carriers, and the custom brokers.

Prima U.S., Inc. v. Panalpina, Inc.

223 F.3d 126 (2d Cir. 2000)

Circuit Judge. Westinghouse contracted with Panalpina, a "freight forwarder," for the transportation and shipment of an electric transformer from the manufacturer in Italy to the ultimate consignee, 3M Corporation in Iowa. Panalpina, as freight forwarder, was to oversee all of the transportation for the transformer, both on land and over sea. As is the industry custom, Panalpina did not issue a bill of lading for the shipment. Pursuant to the standard terms listed on the reverse side of the contract, Panalpina undertook to exercise "reasonable care" in the selection of common carriers to carry, store, or otherwise handle the goods. The standard terms also limited Panalpina's liability for losses to $50 per shipment, and disclaimed liability for all consequential or special damages in excess of this amount. These were the same terms utilized in the prior ten-year course of dealing involving more than 1,000 transactions between Westinghouse and Panalpina. Panalpina arranged for the transformer to be picked up at a factory in Italy and brought to the Port of Genoa.

In Genoa, Panalpina hired Toscano, a customs broker, to coordinate the movement of the transformer through the Port of Genoa. Because the transformer was oversized, it had to be secured to a 40-foot "flat-rack" container for ocean shipment. Panalpina hired CSM, a local stevedore, to load the transformer onto the appropriate container, and to lash it securely for loading aboard the *M/V Addiriyah*.

During the ocean voyage, the *Addiriyah* encountered heavy seas and the transformer, which CSM had negligently lashed to its flat-rack, broke loose, crushing a laser-cutting machine owned by Prima. Prima filed a complaint for damages against Westinghouse and Panalpina. Westinghouse brought a third-party action for indemnification against Panalpina. Panalpina asserted that it acted only as a freight forwarder, not a carrier, and is not obligated to the shipper or other parties for damages.

The job of a "non-vessel operating common carrier" (NVOCC) is to consolidate cargo from numerous shippers into larger groups for shipment by an ocean carrier. An NVOCC issues a bill of lading to each shipper. If anything happens to the goods during the voyage the NVOCC is liable to the shipper because of the bill of lading that it issued. A freight forwarder, on the other hand, simply facilitates the movement of cargo to the ocean vessel. The freight forwarder secures cargo space on a ship, gives advice on governmental licensing requirements, selects the proper port of exit, and arranges to have the cargo reach the seaboard in time to meet the designated vessel.

Unlike a carrier, a freight forwarder does not issue a bill of lading and is therefore not liable to a shipper. Of course, a party that calls itself a freight forwarder might in fact be performing the functions of a carrier, in which case function would govern over form. But the burden of demonstrating any deviation from what freight forwarders normally do in the maritime context is on the party who would show such deviation or that the forwarder negligently selected parties to carry out the shipment. Therefore, Panalpina is not obligated to indemnify Westinghouse.

Case Highlights

- The "non-vessel operating common carrier" (NVOCC) consolidates cargo from numerous shippers into larger groups for shipment by an ocean carrier
- Unlike a carrier, a freight forwarder does not issue a bill of lading and is not liable for damage to the goods while in the possession of a carrier
- The freight forwarder is liable if it negligently selects a third party, such as a common carrier or customs broker, who proves to be incompetent.

Hamburg Rules

The Hamburg Rules (1978 UN Convention on Carriage of Goods by Sea) provide an alternative to the long-established Hague Rules (1924) and Hague-Visby Rules (1968). The impetus for the creation of the Hamburg Rules came from the developing world, who saw the Hague Rules as favoring the developed countries.

This dissatisfaction was based in part upon the perception that the overall allocation of responsibilities and risks achieved by the Hague Rules was inequitable since they heavily favored carriers at the expense of shippers. The Hamburg Rules should not be disregarded since they have been adopted in 34 countries, including many from Africa. The Hamburg Rules are the result of a movement to establish a modern and uniform international legal regime to govern the carriage of goods by sea.

The Hamburg Rules cover loss or damage occurring while the goods are in the custody of the carrier prior to loading and after discharge, while the Hague

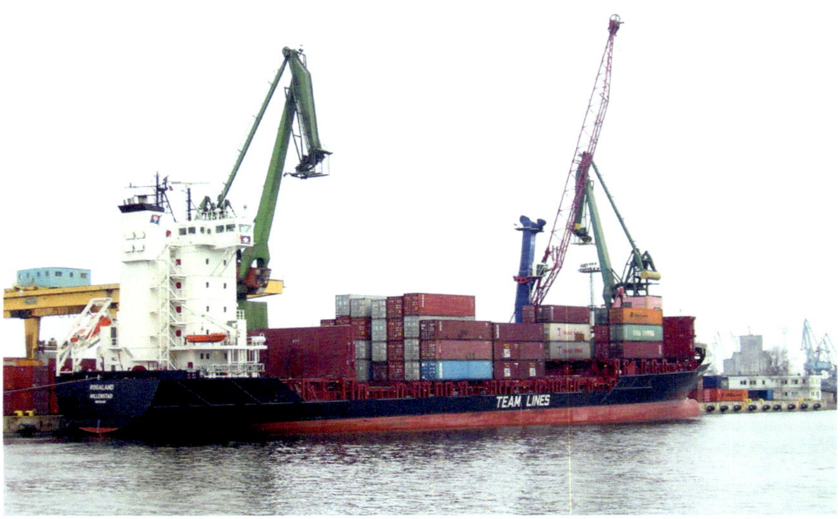

Image 11.1 Loading of a Cargo Ship.

Source: Stan Shebs at Wikimedia Commons.

Rules only cover the period from the time the goods are loaded onto the ship to the time they are unloaded. The Hamburg Rules are superior on this point since, in modern shipping practice, carriers often take and retain custody of goods in port before and after the actual sea carriage. It has been estimated that most loss and damage to goods occur while the goods are in port.

While the Hague Rules provide that the carrier is liable for loss or damage resulting from his failure to exercise due diligence to make the ship seaworthy, to properly man, equip, and supply the ship, and to make its storage areas fit and safe for the carriage of goods, a long list of exemptions relieve the carrier from such liability. The most significant of these exemptions frees the carrier from liability if the loss or damage arises from faulty navigation or management of the ship, the so-called "nautical fault" exception. The original justification for the nautical fault exception was the inability of the shipowner to communicate with and exercise effective control over its vessel during long voyages at sea. However, subsequent developments in communications and the reduction of voyage times have rendered the justification obsolete. The Hamburg Rules effect a more balanced and equitable allocation of risks and responsibilities between carriers and shippers. Liability is based on the principle of presumed fault or neglect. The carrier may escape liability only if it proves that its servants or agents took all measures that could reasonably be required to avoid the occurrence. The liability of the carrier under the Hamburg Rules corresponds with the liability imposed upon carriers under international conventions for transport, such as road and rail. The Hague Rules do not cover goods carried on deck by agreement of the parties, permitting the carrier to disclaim all liability for such cargo. However, developments in transport and packaging techniques, in particular containerization, have made it possible for cargo to be safely carried on deck. It is common for containers to be stored on the deck of modern container ships. The Hamburg Rules expressly permit the carrier to carry goods on deck when such carriage is in accordance with the usage of the particular trade. Therefore, the carrier is liable on the basis of presumed fault or neglect for loss in respect of goods carried on deck. Historically, sea voyages were subject to innumerable uncontrollable hazards, which frequently resulted in delays and deviations. Because of this unpredictability, the Hague Rules do not cover the liability of the carrier for delay in delivery. However, this is no longer the case due to modern shipping technology. Thus, the Hamburg Rules govern the liability of the carrier for delay in delivery in the same manner as liability for loss of or damage to the goods.

Limitation of Liability

The liability of the common carrier is limited to an amount equivalent to 835 units of account per package or other shipping unit or 2.5 units of account per kilogram of gross weight of the goods lost or damaged, whichever is the higher. The units of account is the **Special Drawing Right** (**SDR**) as defined by the **International Monetary Fund** (**IMF**). The SDR is calculated daily based on the exchange values of five currencies.[2]

IMF's Special Drawing Right: The SDR is a claim on freely usable currencies of IMF members. The SDR is valued on a basket of currencies, however, the amount or weight of each currency that makes up the basket varies as follows: the euro (30.93%), Japanese yen (8.33%), British pound sterling (8.09%), Chinese yuan (10.92%), and U.S. dollar (41.73%).[3] The basket of currencies expanded to include the Chinese renminbi (RMB) or yuan as the fifth currency, effective October 1, 2016.

Issuance and Contents of the Bill of Lading

When the carrier takes the goods in his charge, the carrier must, on demand of the shipper, issue a bill of lading. It is customary for the master of the ship to sign the bill of lading on behalf of the carrier. The bill of lading must include certain details, such as:

a. General statement of the nature of the goods, marks necessary for identification, any dangerous character of the goods, the number of packages or pieces, and the weight of the goods or their quantity as furnished by the shipper;
b. Apparent condition of the goods;
c. Name of the shipper;
d. Port of loading and the date on which the goods were taken over by the carrier;
e. Port of destination;
f. Number of originals of the bill of lading;
g. Place of issuance of the bill of lading;
h. Signature of the carrier or a person acting on its behalf;
i. Statement, if applicable, that the goods shall or may be carried on deck;
j. Any increased limit or limits of liability where agreed upon.

If the goods are delivered to the port, but not yet loaded on the ship, the common carrier is obligated to issue a **received for shipment bill of lading**. After the goods have been loaded on board, the carrier issues to the shipper an **on-board bill of lading** which, in addition to the above particulars, must state that the goods are on board a named ship, and the date of loading.

Carriage of Goods by Sea Act (COGSA)

The Carriage of Goods by Sea Act or COGSA[4] in most countries is a codification of the Hague, Hague-Visby, or Hamburg Rules. For example, in the U.S., COGSA is modeled after the Hague Rules and in the UK it is modeled on the Hague-Visby Rules. COGSA applies only to shipments evidenced by a bill of lading issued by a common carrier or a charter party. A **charter party** is when a shipper leases the entire ship from the ship's owner. COGSA would apply if the charter party then enters into carriage contracts with third parties and issues bills of lading in conjunction with these contracts. Unless the bill of lading

Duration: This insurance attaches from the time the goods leave the warehouse or place of storage at the place named herein for the commencement of the transit and terminates either:

1 On delivery to the Consignee's or other final warehouse or place of storage at the destination named herein,
2 On delivery to any warehouse, whether prior to or at the destination named herein, which the assured elects to use either for:
   i Storage in the ordinary course of transit, or
   ii Allocation or distribution, or
3 On the expiration of 60 days after the completion of discharge overside of the goods from the oversea vessel at the final port of discharge, whichever shall occur first. This insurance shall remain in force during delay beyond the control of the assured, any deviation, forced discharge, reshipment or transhipment arising from the exercise of a liberty granted to shipowners under the contract of affreightment (carriage).

Figure 11.1 Focus on Transactions: Warehouse to Warehouse Clause.

Source: Institute of London Underwriters, Clause A.

extends the period of coverage, COGSA does not cover the time when the goods are in the possession of the common carrier before loading and after discharge (unloading). However, bills of lading generally incorporate a **marine extension** or **warehouse to warehouse clause** to extend the period of coverage. See Figure 11.1 *Focus on Transactions*: "Warehouse to Warehouse Clause."

Specialized companies, such as stevedore companies, are used by the common carrier to move the goods at the port and load and offload the goods. COGSA protection is extended to these third-party companies through the use of a **Himalaya clause**. General language is sufficient to extend COGSA defenses to stevedores. The following provision is an example of a typical Himalaya clause:

> *No servant or agent of the Carrier (including every independent contractor from time to time employed by the Carrier) shall in any circumstances whatsoever be under any liability whatsoever to the Merchant (shipper). Every right, exemption, defense and immunity of whatsoever nature applicable to the Carrier shall also be available and shall extend to protect every such servant or agent of the Carrier.*[5]

Most companies working in conjunction with the common carrier are extended the same COGSA protections. For example, marine terminal operators have been extended protection under a general Himalaya clause.[6]

The primary objective of COGSA is to limit the liability of the common carrier while at the same time ensuring a claim for damages by shippers. COGSA limits the liability of the common carrier to $500 (Hague Rules) or $1,000 (Hague-Visby Rules) per package. It also provides 17 exemptions that fully exempt the common carrier from liability for damage or loss to the goods.

Carrier Liability

The primary grounds for common carrier liability are found in a single paragraph in the Hague Rules, which states:

> *Neither the carrier nor the ship shall in any event be or become liable for any loss or damage to or in connection with the transportation of goods*

> *in an amount exceeding $500 per package, or in case of goods not shipped in packages, per customary freight unit (2), or the equivalent of that sum in other currency, unless the nature and value of such goods have been declared by the shipper before shipment and inserted in the bill of lading. This declaration, if embodied in the bill of lading, shall be prima facie evidence, but shall not be conclusive on the carrier. In no event shall the carrier be liable for more than the amount of damage actually sustained.*[7]

The carrier's liability under COGSA is determined in one of two ways. First, an amount per package multiplied by the number of packages listed or described in the bill of lading. It is important to note that the $500 or $1,000 per package amount is an upper limit. If the goods have a value of less than per package limit, then the carrier is liable only for the lesser amount. Second, an amount declared by the shipper on the bill of lading. Again, if the value of the goods is less than the amount declared the carrier is liable only for the true value.

Some types of goods are not "packaged" for shipment. COGSA provides an alternative in such cases known as the **customary freight unit** or **CFU** to determine the number of packages to determine amount of liability. Examples include measurements used for bulk goods, such as tons (coal), cubic yards (wheat), or barrels (oil). COGSA offers three sources for the determination of value: commodity exchange price, current market price, or "the normal value of goods of the same kind and quality."

The carrier is liable for an undeclared higher value if it failed to give the shipper "a *fair opportunity* to choose a higher liability by paying a corresponding greater charge."[8] Common carriers generally honor the duty to provide fair opportunity to declare a higher value by providing notice and a space to declare a higher value on the face of the bill of lading.

Carrier's Duties

COGSA lists a number of duties of the carrier that if not followed can leave the carrier unprotected by COGSA. If the losses relate to these recognized duties, then the **per package limitation** and **exemptions** are removed, and the common carrier becomes liable for the full amount of damages. These duties include performance of **due diligence** in providing a seaworthy ship, not committing a **material deviation**, and providing a **fair opportunity** for the shipper to declare a value above the per package limitation.

The carrier has a general duty to issue a bill of lading when receiving goods from the shipper. The bill must include basic information, including "leading marks" provided by the shipper for the identification of the goods; the number of packages or pieces, or the quantity, or weight as furnished by the shipper; and the apparent order or condition of the goods. Thus, the carrier becomes a guarantor of the information provided by the shipper and placed on the bill of lading.

If the goods delivered are not in the condition as stated on the bill of lading or there is a **shortage** as to quantity, then the shipper or the party receiving the goods meets its burden of proof by providing the bill of lading as evidence. The party making a claim must first give notice of loss either at the port of discharge or at the time of receiving the goods from the carrier. If the loss is not apparent at the time of receiving the goods, then notice must be given in writing within three days. Failure to give notice is *prima facie* evidence that the goods received were as indicated on the bill of lading. Upon the giving of the required notice, COGSA requires the claiming party to commence suit within one year of the delivery of the goods.

COGSA prohibits any attempts by the carrier to insert into its bill of lading more restrictive procedural requirements or attempts to further limit its duties and liabilities. The question has arisen whether an arbitration clause in the bill of lading is subject to challenge under this limitation. The U.S. Supreme Court has held that an arbitration clause in the bill of lading was not subject to attack under COGSA.[9] The Court referred to the **Federal Arbitration Act** (**FAA**)[10] for the general premise that arbitration is a favored means of dispute resolution (see Chapter 4). One exception is where a forum selection clause and a choice of law clause are used to deprive the shipper from pursuing its statutory remedies under COGSA. Also, a ***force majeure* clause** in the bill of lading is also recognized by the courts.

Seaworthiness

The common carrier must satisfy two general duties in order to gain the protections of COGSA. First, it must perform due diligence in preparing the ship. Second, the ship must be seaworthy at the time of departure. In the event that the ship becomes unseaworthy after it leaves the port of shipment, the common carrier remains protected under COGSA. A ship is considered seaworthy if it meets four requirements. First, the ship must be appropriate for the type of carriage. Factors in making this determination include the type of goods being transported

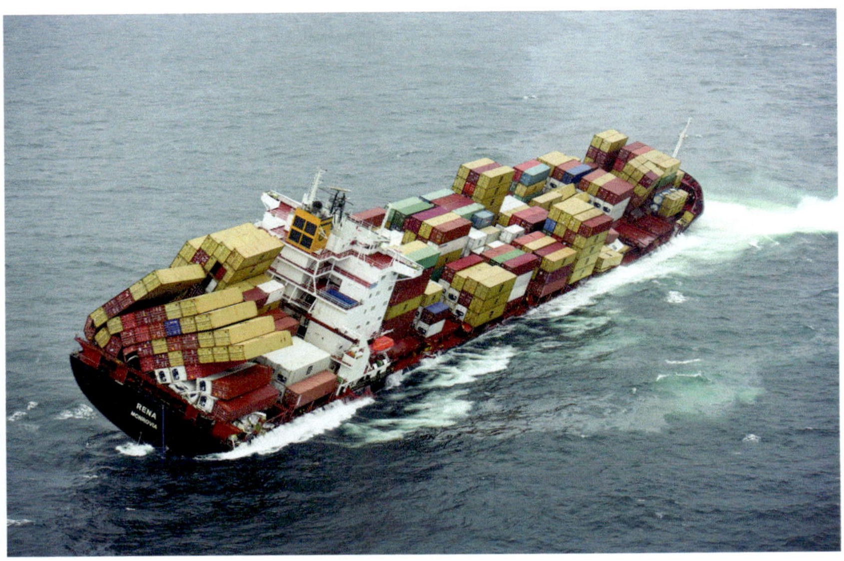

Image 11.2 Disaster at Sea.
Source: New Zealand Defence Force, Wikimedia Commons.

and the anticipated route of transit: a ship that is seaworthy for travel on a lake or river may be unseaworthy for ocean carriage; a ship may be seaworthy for the carriage of containers but unseaworthy for the shipment of bulk goods. Second, the ship must be properly equipped for the "reception, carriage, and preservation" of the goods. All mechanical devices such as fire suppression equipment and refrigeration units must be properly maintained and functioning.

Third, the common carrier must supply a competent crew, properly trained to operate the ship and its equipment. Fourth, the carrier must "properly load, handle, stow, and discharge the goods carried." Proper **stowage** varies according to the types of goods being transported. Goods that are susceptible to moving must be properly lashed or secured in the hull of the ship. The *Manifest Shipping* case focuses on two elements of seaworthiness—ship's equipment and competency of the crew.

Manifest Shipping v. Uni-Polaris Insurance Co.

1 Lloyd's L. R. 651 (Q.B. 1995)

Justice. *Star Sea* had an engine room and cargo holds protected from fire by a full flood carbon dioxide extinguishing system. It also had an electrically powered fire pump in the engine room and an additional emergency fire pump. The ship was inspected by the Belgian port authority and found to have a nonworking emergency fire pump. The emergency fire pump was improperly repaired. On the return trip to South America a fire started in the engine room. The shipowner filed a claim under its marine insurance policy for a total loss. The lower court held that, because the fire involved electrical cables, the fact that the emergency pipe was not working did not materially affect the spread of the fire.

However, the court analyzed whether the ship was unseaworthy due to the incompetence of the ship's master and crew. The master demonstrated an ignorance of the workings of the carbon dioxide fire suppression system. The master was unaware of the need to use the carbon dioxide system as soon as he knew of the fire. Instead, the system was not discharged until at least two and one-half hours after the fire had started. The issue was whether this was mere negligence or a level of incompetence that would render the ship unseaworthy. In fact, given the master's years of experience he possessed general competence. However, since he did not undergo fire training and demonstrated gross ignorance of its essentials, his conduct can only be characterized as incompetence. Therefore, the vessel was unseaworthy, and therefore the loss is not covered by the carrier protections afforded by COGSA.

Case Highlights

- Under COGSA, for a ship to be seaworthy its equipment must be in good working order and the crew must be competent in operating the equipment
- A non-operational fire suppression system will generally render a ship unseaworthy
- A ship's captain or master may possess general competence but still be judged incompetent regarding the operation of the ship's equipment.

Per Package Limitation

COGSA (Hague Rules) provides a liability limitation to the common carrier of $500 per package. An often litigated issue is what is considered a "package"? A common problem is the existence of a number of different "packages" for a court to choose in assessing damages. The different means of quantifying a shipment of goods may stem from how the goods are packaged or how they are described in the bill of lading. In *Sony Magnetic Products Inc. v. Merivienti*,[11] Sony packed a standard cargo container with video cassette tapes. Sony first placed the tapes into 1,320 cardboard cartons and then strapped the cartons onto 52 wooden pallets. The carrier issued Sony a bill of lading with the following description: "Description of Packages and Goods, 1 × 40 foot container STC [said to contain]: 1,320 Cartons." The bill of lading did not reserve space for designating the value of the cargo, but the attached export certificate showed a value of $424,765.44. The court found that each of the 1,320 cartons was a "package" for purposes of COGSA, capping liability at $660,000, and then awarded $424,765.44, the actual damages sustained by Sony as evidenced by the invoice value of the tapes. The court in *Vegas v. Compania Anonima Venezolana*[12] ruled that an ambiguity on a bill of lading, regarding the number of packages, should be resolved in favor of the shipper. Like the shipper in *Sony*, Vegas had consolidated cartons of goods onto pallets. Unlike the shipper in *Sony*, Vegas disclosed the number of cartons that had been consolidated onto pallets. The *Vegas* court resolved the ambiguity, a stated number of cartons and a lesser number of pallets, on the bill of lading in favor of the shipper, resulting in a larger number of packages.

Sony Magnetic Products Inc. v. Merivienti

863 F.2d 1537 (11th Cir. 1989)

Circuit Judge. Sony Magnetic Products contacted Page & Jones, a freight forwarder, to arrange for the transportation of a container of video cassette tapes from the U.S. to England. Page & Jones reserved space with Atlantic Cargo Services on board the *M/S Finnhawk*. Sony packed its cargo of video cassette tapes into a standard shipping container. As the *M/S Finnhawk*'s deck crane was lifting the container of tapes up to the vessel's cargo deck, the hydraulic motor of the crane exploded causing the container to drop to the concrete loading deck below.

The first issue on appeal is whether the lower court properly imposed liability on the common carrier under COGSA for the damage to the video cassette tapes. The shipper (Sony) establishes a *prima facie* case under COGSA by proving that the carrier received the cargo in good condition. A carrier can rebut a shipper's *prima facie* case by establishing either that it exercised due diligence to prevent the damage to the cargo by properly handling, stowing, and caring for it on a seaworthy ship or that it was not liable under a COGSA exemption. If the carrier is able to rebut the shipper's *prima facie* case, the burden then shifts back to the shipper to show that the carrier's negligence was the cause of the damages.

The common carrier attempted to establish that the accident was the result of a latent defect in the motor of the *M/S Finnhawk*'s crane, one of the enumerated exemptions. In addition, the crane was properly maintained and inspected. COGSA provides as follows:

> Neither the carrier nor the ship shall be responsible for loss or damage arising or resulting from—latent defects not discoverable by due diligence. A latent defect is one that is not discoverable upon reasonable inspection or by any known and customary test.

It is held that the common carrier had not sustained its burden of proving the loss was caused by a latent defect.

Case Highlights

- Oftentimes, the bill of lading is prepared by the freight forwarder, on behalf of the shipper, and submitted to the carrier for signature
- Presenting a clean bill of lading satisfies the shipper's initial burden of proving that it has delivered cargo in good condition to the carrier
- A carrier can rebut a shipper's *prima facie* case by establishing either that it exercised due diligence to prevent the damage to the cargo by properly handling, stowing, and caring for it in a seaworthy ship or that the harm resulted from one of the enumerated exemptions or causes
- The carrier has a heavy burden in proving that the loss was due to a "latent defect."

In *London Underwriters v. Sea-Land Service, Inc.*,[13] the court held that a yacht shipped in an on-deck cradle constituted a package. This would seem to be unfair since a yacht is more valuable than $1,000 (Hague-Visby Rules). But, in fact, it was a risk the shipper was willing to take by not inserting the true value into the bill of lading. A package is likely to be presumed if the cargo fits a plain, ordinary definition of "package." In short, if the cargo could not have been simply dumped in a hold, then it is likely to have been carried with some sort of packaging. Also, most courts will give great weight to the designation of the cargo as packages in the bill of lading. In this case, the description in the bill of lading simply stated: "3 yachts."

COGSA—An Exclusive Remedy

The purpose of COGSA was to achieve international uniformity and to balance the interests of carriers and shippers. The shipper needs only to provide a "clean" bill of lading to make a *prima facie* case for damages. From the carrier's perspective it provides the shipper an exclusive remedy and preempts other types of causes of action in contract or tort. Also, the person making the claim must be named on the bill of lading or had legally acquired the bill of lading. Shippers often use cargo consolidators, to combine different shippers' goods into a single container and reduce freight costs for each of the shippers. However, it is imperative that each shipper obtains a bill of lading for their goods in the container. Contracts (such as bills of lading) bind only named parties unless both parties to the contract express a mutual intent to benefit a third party.

Some bills of lading use the phrase "shipper, consignee, or owner of the goods" repeatedly in defining the conditions of the contract of carriage. One interpretation argues that the inclusion of the phrase "owner of the goods" in a bill of lading evinces a clear intent to benefit that class of persons. The court in *All Pacific Trading, Inc. v. Vessel M/V Hanjin Yosu*[14] considered a consolidated action brought by nine owners of damaged goods. Eight of the nine plaintiffs delivered their goods to different non-vessel operating common carriers (NVOCCs) who issued bills of lading to the shippers and then delivered the goods to the carrier, who in turn executed separate bills of lading to the NVOCCs. The court held that the owners had standing to sue the carrier since they were actual parties to the bills of lading because the bills stated that the carrier was obligated to the "owner of the goods."

COGSA Coverage

The Hague, Hague-Visby, and Hamburg Rules provide a relatively fair allocation of liability between the carrier and the shipper, however, there are some important differences. For example, the Hague Rules limit the liability of the carrier to the timeframe represented from "tackle to tackle" (loading and unloading) or from time of loading to time of discharge. This does not consider the time when the goods are in the control of the carrier before the loading and after the unloading of the cargo.

Warehouse to Warehouse and Tackle to Tackle Clauses

COGSA coverage covers the period from when goods pass over the imaginary line drawn upward from the rail of the ship during the loading and unloading of the goods. The tackle to tackle clause extends the coverage period from the time the process of loading is begun and when the goods are unloaded at the port of destination. Warehouse to warehouse clauses further expand coverage from the time the goods are entered into a warehouse prior to loading at the port of shipment until the goods exit the warehouse at the port of destination.

The Hamburg Rules extend the period of carrier responsibility to include when the goods are in the control of the carrier but not on the ship. Article 7 of the Hague Rules allows the parties to agree to extend the period of application to the period "prior to the loading, and subsequent to the discharge." This is generally done through the insertion of a warehouse to warehouse clause into the bill of lading. The *Mori Seiki USA v. M/V Alligator Triumph* case reviews the "tackle to tackle" coverage of the Hague Rules, the duty of the carrier to provide an opportunity to declare a higher value, and the use of a Himalaya clause to extend coverage to third parties.

Mori Seiki USA, Inc. v. M/V *Alligator Triumph*, Mitsui Lines

990 F.2d 444 (9th Cir. 1993)

Circuit Judge. Mori Seiki was the consignee of a precision lathe that was damaged while being transported from Japan to Texas. The lathe was damaged after it was unloaded from an ocean vessel at the Port of Los Angeles, but before it was released from the port. Mori Seiki filed suit seeking damages from the ocean carrier Mitsui (*M/V Alligator Triumph*), the seaport operator (Trans-Pacific Container), and the stevedore services firm, which unloaded and handled the lathe (Marine Terminals Corporation).

Applicability of COGSA After Discharge

By its own terms, the Hague Rules limit liability for cargo damage to $500 per package, if the damage occurs between the time cargo is loaded on to the ship and the time it is discharged from the ship. The bill of lading in this case stated that "with respect to loss or damage occurring during the period from the time when the Goods arrived at the sea terminal at the port of loading to the time when they left the sea terminal at the port of discharge the carrier shall be responsible for such loss or damage to the extent prescribed by the Hague Rules." The plain meaning of this language is that the liability limitation would extend to the period after the lathe was discharged from the ship, but before it was released from the sea terminal.

Extension of Liability Limitation Under the Himalaya Clause

Mitsui's bill of lading included a so-called "Himalaya clause," which is commonly used to extend a carrier's defenses and liability limitations to certain third parties performing services on its behalf. The court concluded that the seaport operator and the stevedore services company were covered by the Himalaya clause. Therefore, the Himalaya clause extended Mitsui's defenses and the $500 package liability limitation to Marine Terminals Corporation and Trans-Pacific Container.

Case Highlights

- The Hague covers only the ocean portion of the carriage unless contractually extended in the bill of lading
- The Himalaya clause is commonly inserted in the freight contract to extend a carrier's defenses and liability limitations (Hague Rules) to third parties performing services on its behalf, such as a stevedore company.

Carrier is defined more broadly by the Hamburg Rules. They define carrier as "any person by whom a contract of carriage of goods by sea has been concluded with a shipper." By not referring to "carrier," the Hamburg Rules apply to parties such as freight forwarders and terminal or non-vessel operating common carriers.

In addition, the Hamburg Rules provide specific rules for carriage above deck, while the Hague Rules exclude deck carriage from its application unless the parties incorporate a **clause paramount** in the bill of lading. The burden of proof is on the shipper under the Hague Rules to prove that any loss was due to the fault of the carrier. The burden is satisfied generally by the presentation of a *clean* bill of lading. In contrast, carrier fault is presumed under the Hamburg Rules. Article 5 of the Hamburg Rules states that "the carrier is liable for loss, damage, or delay that occurred while the goods were in its charge." It then expressly states that "as a rule, the burden of proof rests on the carrier."

A still unresolved issue is how best to deal with combined or **multimodal transport** contracts. The Hague Rules were enacted prior to the advent of **containerization.** Containerization allows a single container to be used in different modes of transit.[15] A container can be attached to a truck, placed on the bed of a railway car, and loaded onto a ship. The traditional approach was the recognition that the different unimodal conventions (rail, truck, ship) formed a network of liability. Each segment of the transport is governed by the convention applicable to that type of transportation. The proper convention to be applied would be determined based on where the damage occurred during the shipment. The International Chamber of Commerce's **Rules for Multimodal Transport Documents** simplify the multi-convention approach. It places a presumption in favor of the shipper: "If the stage cannot be established, the system of liability most favorable to the claimant of the relevant modes of transport is deemed to apply."[16]

Containerization posed a number of concerns as it relates to the application of COGSA. First, multimodal transport raises questions about the continued relevancy and importance of the traditional ocean bill of lading; newer multimodal transport documents have increasingly become popular. Second, can a container, filled with packages of goods, be itself considered a single package for purposes of calculating per package liability? The courts have held that multimodal containers are generally not to be considered as packages for the calculation of COGSA liability. The most specific (largest unit count) description of the goods stated in the bill of lading controls. In *Marcraft Clothes, Inc. v. M/V Kurobe Maru*[17] the bill of lading stated that the container was filled with 4,400 men's suits. The court held that each suit was a package for purposes of COGSA liability. In *All Pacific Trading v. Vessel M/V Hanjin Yosu*, the carrier inserted the following clause into the bill of lading: "Where the cargo has been packed into containers it is expressly agreed that the containers shown on the face of the bill of lading shall be considered the number of packages for the purpose of the application of the limitation of liability provided for herein." The carrier further argued that the container was the proper package because the rate agreement was determined based upon the number of containers and not by the number of packages within the containers. The court rejected the carrier's arguments that the containers were indeed the "packages." It focused upon the fact that elsewhere on the bill of lading there was a listing of the number of units in each container.[18] In order to avoid the classification of a container as a package, the shipper should provide a detailed description stating the number of packages within each container to be placed on the bill of lading.

Material Deviation

The next three sections will explore areas of carrier fault that result in the removal of a carrier's liability limitation under the per package rule. The three areas of unlimited liability are material deviation, failure to give fair opportunity to declare a higher value, and **misdelivery**. Material deviation claims can generally be divided into two groups—above-deck carriage of goods and a change in the expected route of the ship.

Above-deck carriage has historically been considered a material deviation, but this claim has severely diminished in modern times. The advent of containerization and more powerful ships have made above-deck carriage commonplace. Modern ships allow for larger cargo capacity by the stacking of containers below and above the deck lowering freight costs. The court in *DuPont de Nemours International v. Mormacvega*[19] recognized an implied exception to the Hague Rules that carriage on the deck of the ship is a material deviation. It held that it is not an unreasonable deviation from the carriage contract to carry the goods above deck if the ship is one designed for above-deck containerized carriage. Most bills of lading now reflect the practice of above-deck carriage by the incorporation of a clause paramount (shipper agreement to above-deck carriage). The provision below is an example of a clause paramount. The numbers in parentheses refer to the statements immediately before them and are explained in the paragraph that follows:

> *The bill of lading shall have effect subject to all the provisions of the Carriage of Goods by Sea Act (Hague Rules). The defenses and limitations of said Act shall apply to goods whether carried on or under the deck (1), to carriage of goods between ports (2), before the goods are loaded on and after they are discharged from the vessel, and throughout the entire time the goods are in the actual custody of Carrier (3), whether acting as carrier, bailee, or stevedore (4). Carrier shall be entitled to the full benefit of all rights and immunities under and all limitations and exemptions from liability contained in the Act. If any term of this bill of lading is repugnant to the Act or any other law compulsorily applicable, such term shall be void. This bill of lading shall be construed and the rights of the parties determined according to the laws of the (country) (5).*[20]

The above clause does more than simply extend COGSA to above-deck carriage: (1) It preempts the application of any other domestic law covering shipments between ports (2) It also extends COGSA's coverage beyond tackle to tackle to the entire period that the goods are in the possession of the carrier (3) Some courts have recognized this extension of COGSA even when the bill of lading fails to incorporate such a clause.[21] (4) It extends COGSA protection to all third parties involved with the transport of the goods by sea including stevedores (Himalaya Clause). (5) Finally, it has a choice of law clause as the law to be used to interpret the carriers' obligations and liabilities under the bill of lading.

The second ground for a claim of material deviation is an unreasonable route change. If the common carrier fails to follow a customary or reasonable shipping route, then it will be liable for damages resulting from late delivery. A defense to a material deviation in the route would be a change resulting from an emergency such as mechanical failure or governmental intervention.

Fair Opportunity

Courts examine bills of lading in deciding whether the common carrier has fulfilled its duty to give shippers a fair opportunity to declare a higher value. The *Travelers Indemnity Company v. Waterman Steamship Corp.* case explores the nuances of the carrier's duty to provide an opportunity to declare a higher value (in order to increase the liability of the carrier above the per package limitation).

Travelers Indemnity Company v. Waterman Steamship Corp.

26 F.3d 895 (9th Cir. 1994)

Circuit Judge. This action arose when a barge, carrying machinery and materials, operated by Waterman sank in the inner harbor of Alexandria, Egypt. Travelers Insurance sustained a loss of $1,174,876 and brought suit. The lower court found that the $500 per package or per customary freight unit (CFU) limitation on liability, set forth in COGSA (Hague Rules), controlled and found that 77 "packages" were damaged or lost. Specifically, COGSA provides that a carrier is liable for $500 per package or CFU unless shipper increases the carrier's liability by declaring on the bill of lading the value of the goods and paying a higher freight rate. The per package or per CFU limitation on liability only applies if the shipper is given a "fair opportunity" to declare a higher value.

The carrier must "bear an initial burden of producing *prima facie* evidence that demonstrates that it provided notice of a choice of liabilities and rates to the shipper." Normally, the carrier can meet this burden by showing the shipper the language contained in the Hague Rules. Travelers asserted Waterman was given prior to shipment the export declaration that reported the value of the total cargo to be $6,000,000. However, Waterman's bill of lading did not contain a designated space in which to declare a higher value.

The court held that the export declaration does not, in fact, constitute evidence that the shipper "would have opted for a higher liability had it been given a fair opportunity to do so." The party in this case was a sophisticated shipper of goods, was familiar with Waterman's shipping procedures, and its bill of lading.

Case Highlights

- A common carrier can take advantage of the $500 per package limitation only if it gives the shipper a "fair opportunity" to declare a higher value
- A common carrier will generally meet its burden to provide a fair opportunity to declare a higher value by placing a simple line on the bill of lading to insert the true value of the goods

- Designating a space on the front of the bill of lading to declare a higher value is not required by COGSA but has been recognized as a customary practice
- If a shipper declares a higher value the higher value inserted into the bill of lading is usually set at the **insured value**.

Insured Value: The combined value of the goods, inland and ocean freight charges, cost of packaging, freight forwarding and consular fees, and the cost of the insurance.

Misdelivery of Goods

Under COGSA, the carrier is obligated to deliver the goods to the holder, and only the holder, of the bill of lading (bill of lading is issued by the carrier and then is transmitted to the buyer or to someone assigned the bill while the goods are in transit). A cause of action accrues to the shipper in the event that delivery is made to someone not holding the bill of lading. The common carrier is liable for misdelivery, even after the goods are discharged from its ship, because the carrier remains a **bailee** of the goods until they are delivered to the holder of the bill of lading. The *law of bailment* places special duties of care on a party (bailee) who is entrusted with the goods of another party.

The special status of the common carrier under the law of bailment as represented in the Hague Rules is explored in *Allied Chemical International Corp. v. Companhia de Navegacao Lloyd Brasileiro*. In addition, the case illustrates that even though the bill of lading is the universally accepted document of title, national maritime customs and shipping practices need to be understood in order to protect against misdelivery.

Alternative arrangements are sometimes made for delivery to someone not holding a bill of lading. One common practice is when the common carrier agrees to release the goods to a consignee, not in possession of the bill of lading, upon the presentment of a bank guarantee. The bank guarantee absolves the carrier from any liability for misdelivery and allows for earlier delivery to the buyer prior to receipt of the bill of lading.

Allied Chemical International v. Companhia de Navegacao Lloyd Brasileiro

775 F.2d 476 (2d Cir. 1985)

Circuit Judge. Lloyd Brasileiro (Lloyd), an ocean carrier was found to be liable to Allied Chemical (Allied), a shipper, for the misdelivery of goods to the consignee (party listed on bill of lading to receive shipment), Banylsa. The carrier caused the goods to be delivered without requiring Banylsa to produce the original order bill of lading.

The sale contracts provided for sight drafts against documents (see Chapter 12) through Banco Bamerindus, a Brazilian bank. Lloyd's vessel arrived at the Port of Salvador and in accordance with local custom and trade usage, the carrier unloaded the goods at a warehouse under the control of the Administration of the Port of Salvador, an agency of the Brazilian government. Banylsa requested and received from Lloyd in accordance with Brazilian import regulations a "carta declaratoria," a letter declaring that the freight had been paid at the port of origin and that duties had been paid in Salvador. By virtue of the *carta declaratoria*, Banylsa was able to obtain possession of the goods from the government warehouse, although it had not paid for the goods and it was not in possession of the bill of lading. Allied made a demand on Lloyd for losses incurred as a result of the carrier's failure to request proper documentation before releasing the goods.

The documentary sale transaction enables a distant seller to protect himself from an insolvent or fraudulent foreign buyer by ensuring that the buyer can only take possession of the goods once it pays for and presents the bill of lading to the carrier. Most likely, the bill will be an order bill of lading, made to the order of or endorsed to the buyer. The carrier, the issuer of the bill of lading, is responsible for releasing the cargo only to the party who presents the original bill of lading. Delivery to the consignee named in the bill of lading does not suffice to discharge the carrier where the consignee does not hold the bill of lading. If the carrier delivers the goods to one other than the holder of the bill of lading, the carrier is liable for misdelivery.

When Lloyd discharged the cargo, it assumed the status of a bailee. A bailee is absolutely liable for misdelivering of the cargo. Therefore, under the Hague Rules and the law of bailment, Lloyd is liable for misdelivery.

Case Highlights

- The issuer of the bill of lading is responsible for releasing the cargo to the party who presents the original bill of lading
- A common carrier is considered as a *bailee* of the goods put in its charge. Therefore, it is liable in the law of bailment even after it discharges its obligations under the Hague Rules
- Despite the protections provided for under the Hague Rules, it is important to know the local customs and practices of the country of importation.

COGSA Exemptions

If the carrier fulfills its obligations as outlined previously, then its liability is limited to not more than $500 per package. In addition, it obtains the protection of **17 COGSA exemptions** (see Figure 11.2 *Comparative Law*: "17 COGSA Exemptions"). There are 16 enumerated exemptions and one "catch-all" exemption known as the **Q-clause exception.** The 16 enumerated exemptions include losses due to errors in navigation and management of the ship, fire, perils of the sea, acts of God, war, acts of public enemies, government seizure, quarantine restrictions, act or omission of the shipper, strikes, wastage due to inherent vice

Neither the carrier nor the ship shall be responsible for loss or damage arising or resulting from:

a act, neglect, or default of master or employees in the navigation or in the management of the ship;
b fire;
c perils of the sea;
d act of God (natural disasters);
e act of war;
f act of public enemies;
g arrest or restraint or seizure under legal process;
h quarantine restrictions;
i act or omission of the shipper or owner of the goods;
j strikes, lockouts, or stoppage of labor;
k riots and civil commotions;
l saving or attempting to save life or property at sea;
m wastage in bulk or weight or any other loss arising from inherent vice of the goods;
n insufficiency of packing;
o insufficiency of marks;
p latent defects not discoverable by due diligence;
q any other cause arising without actual fault or privity of the carrier, but the burden of proof shall be on the person claiming the benefit of this exception.

Figure 11.2 Comparative Law: 17 COGSA Exemptions.

(nature of the goods, such as steel products rusts while at sea), insufficiency of packing, and latent defects. Perils of the sea would include violent or catastrophic storms, but not normal storms at sea. Latent defects are those defects not discoverable by due diligence (inspection and testing).

The courts have narrowly interpreted most of the exemptions in order to allow shippers to collect on their claims. For example, the latent defect exception has not provided carriers much protection even when they perform due diligent inspections and testing. The "catch-all" exception or Q-clause grants the carrier a general exemption for any damages that arise from a cause that was not the "actual fault of the carrier." However, the Hague Rules state that the burden of proof is on the carrier to prove that its fault or negligence had not contributed to the loss. Courts have rarely granted an exemption from liability under the Q-clause.

Damage to goods attributable to one of these 17 causes, nonetheless, relieves the carrier of *all* liability. In contrast, the Hamburg Rules eliminates these exemptions and provides a presumption of carrier liability for loss except when occasioned by a fire. The Hague Rules provides a limitation period of one year for any claims of loss, while the Hamburg Rules provides a limitation period of two years. The Hague Rules provides for liability when goods are lost or damaged but makes no mention of liability for a delay in delivery. The Hamburg Rules designates "delay" as an equal ground for recovery. The *Lamb Head Shipping v. Jennings* case reviews the "perils of the sea" exemption as it relates to marine or hull insurance and how it interrelates to the carrier's duty of due diligence (to act competently).

Lamb Head Shipping v. Jennings

1 Lloyd's Law Report 624 (C.A. 1994)

The *Marel* sailed from Greece to Ghent with a load of Greek corn. While en route, it encountered adverse weather conditions, causing the ship to sink. The shipowner claimed under their marine hull insurance policy, contending that the vessel was lost due to *perils of the sea*, which was covered under the policy.

Justice. The burden of proving on the balance of probabilities that a vessel was lost by perils of the sea is on the shipowners. It is not sufficient for the owners merely to prove the incursion of seawater into the insured vessel. In fact, *Marel* was not overwhelmed by exceptionally bad weather. "Perils of the sea" does not include the ordinary action of wind and waves. The primary submission of the owners was that *Marel* was hit by a floating container. However, there was no evidence of a report of any container having been lost in the vicinity. The court also noted that, although the general condition of the vessel was good for her age, there had been various botched repairs. Therefore, the case is dismissed.

Case Highlights

- The shipowner has the burden to prove a loss due to a "peril of the sea" in making a claim under its marine insurance
- Perils of the sea do not include the ordinary action of wind and waves
- Failure to properly repair a ship opens the shipowner to a charge of a lack of due diligence in maintaining the seaworthiness of the vessel.

Freight Forwarders, Consolidators, and Multimodal Transport Operators

Shipment of goods internationally requires the use of essential third parties in the transport of goods, including **freight forwarders, multimodal transport operators** (**MTO**), and **marine insurance companies**. The freight forwarder serves three vital functions: (1) arranges for the shipment of goods with carriers (freight forwarder reserves space on a carrier through a **booking contract**); (2) acts as a freight consolidator (combines goods from a number of shippers); and (3) processes required documentation. In arranging for the shipment, the forwarder negotiates a freight rate with a carrier as an agent for the shipper. The negative repercussion of the role of the freight forwarder as agent is that it may bind the shipper to modifications made by the carrier to the standard carriage contract. The *Constructores Tecnicos v. Sea-Land Service, Inc.* case examines the ability of freight forwarders to bind shippers to material deviations.

Constructores Tecnicos v. Sea-Land Service, Inc.

945 F.2d 841 (5th Cir. 1991)

Circuit Judge. Constructores Tecnicos (Contec) of Honduras purchased a Ford LT 9000 Tandem Chassis diesel truck and various drilling accessories, including a portable drilling rig unit from JWS Equipment of Oklahoma. Contec contacted Golden Eagle Forwarding (Eagle), a freight forwarder, and requested that it arrange transportation from Oklahoma to Honduras. Eagle arranged transportation through Sea-Land Service (Sea-Land) and filled out a Sea-Land bill of lading, listing the cargo to be shipped but leaving the space for the freight rate blank. The bill of lading did not indicate whether the cargo was to be stowed on deck or below deck. Eagle then delivered the draft bill of lading to Sea-Land's office. The truck and equipment were loaded on the *M/V Vermillion Bay*, a vessel chartered by Sea-Land. The truck and some of the equipment were secured to a flat-rack, a form of open container, by chain lashings and stowed on deck.

The *M/V Vermillion Bay* encountered severe weather in the Gulf of Mexico on the fringes of Hurricane Gilbert. During the storm, nearby containers broke free of their lashings, causing severe damage to the truck. The ship changed course and docked at Port Everglades, Florida, where the truck was unloaded and deemed a total loss. Contec brought suit against Eagle, Sea-Land, and International Cargo and Surety Insurance Co.

Carrier loses the per package protection of COGSA if a deviation from the specifications contained in the contract of carriage (bill of lading) amounts to more than a reasonable deviation. The lower court held that a clean bill of lading entitles the shipper to below-deck stowage. The court cited a line of authority dating back to the late 19th century. The defendants argue that Contec had not dealt directly with the carrier, but rather through an intermediary freight forwarder who had the power to bind the shipper to on-deck shipment. The legal relationship of agency is the threshold question (agency relationship between shipper and freight forwarder). Control of the manner in which the forwarder performs his duties is the more important factor in deciding the agency question. The forwarder was free to select the carrier or line on which to ship the goods. If the shipper does not consent to on-deck stowage and cannot be deemed to have done so through a freight forwarder acting as its agent, the law's concern is with the shipper's expectations. Judgment awarding damages are granted in excess of the COGSA limitation of liability.

Case Highlights

- The freight forwarder acts as agent for the shipper in selecting a common carrier and booking cargo space
- The freight forwarder's knowledge of a common carrier's practices that would be deemed to be material deviations is not imputed to the shipper
- An express provision in the bill of lading or port custom may overcome the presumption in favor of below-deck stowage.

It has become a common practice for the forwarder to issue carrier-type documents such as the **forwarder's bill of lading** or receipt. In such cases, the forwarder assumes the liability of a carrier or a multimodal transport operator. Carrier liability, therefore, may extend not only to the actual carriers but also to *contractual* carriers. Freight forwarders also serve the important function of consolidating the shipments of a number of shippers to fill the available space being offered by carriers in order to reduce the freight costs to the individual shippers. Freight forwarders also aid in preparing necessary documentation needed for customs clearance. **Customs brokers** are also utilized to deal with customs authorities and to ensure compliance with customs regulations.[22]

MTOs, also known as combined transport operators, arrange for the shipment of goods using different modes of transport such as sea, rail, road, and air. They enter into separate contracts with the individual carriers. The major benefit to the shipper is that the MTO issues a single transport document for the entire transport and the shipper may make a claim for loss against the MTO no matter where the loss occurs during the transport. Because of the increased use of MTOs and freight forwarders as common carriers, the **through bill of lading** has become a commonly used document of title. The through bill of lading and the liabilities that emanate from it are explained in the *Mannesman Demag Corp.* case. The case also explains how containerization has transformed the shipping industry and its legal regimes. *Freight consolidators*, as noted above, are freight forwarders that also provide the service of freight consolidation (grouping different shipments from various shippers).

Mannesman Demag Corp. v. M/V Concert Express

225 F.3d 587 (5th Cir. 2000)

Circuit Judge. This case arises from damage sustained to an oxygen compressor owned by Mannesman while in transport from Germany to the U.S. Atlantic Shipping carried the goods from Bremerhaven to the Port of Baltimore, Maryland, aboard the *M/V Concert Express.* Trism Trucking was hired to transport the goods from Baltimore to Terre Haute, Indiana. While en route from Baltimore to Terre Haute, the goods were damaged when the truck's trailer overturned.

There was only one bill of lading for the entire transportation, issued by Atlantic. The bill is what is called a "through bill of lading." A through bill of lading is one by which an ocean carrier agrees to transport goods to their final destination including the use of railroad, truck, or air. The bill obligates the common carrier to transport the cargo "through" the port to its ultimate destination.

Until the advent of the containerization of cargo, the cargo owner typically would enter into shipment contracts with a new carrier each time the mode of transport changed. An inland carrier—a railroad, truck, or, in some cases, an inland barge operator—would carry the goods to a seaport under individual contracts of carriage. Different legal regimes arose to govern the parties' rights and liabilities, depending upon the mode of shipment. If the railroad did the damage, then the rules of liability governing railroads would apply. Maritime law would govern the liability of the steamship or ocean leg of the transport. Along came multimodal or intermodal shipping containers and everything changed. Now, the same steel cargo container can move freely between different modes of transport. Ocean carriers now offer "door to door" service. Rail carriers, truckers, or other transporters now contract, not with the owner of the goods, but as a subcontractor to the ocean line who offers complete transport packages.

By its terms, COGSA applies "tackle to tackle" only; it does not extend to losses that occur prior to loading or subsequent to discharge from a vessel. COGSA is at its core a maritime law; the Court is unwilling to rule that simply because private parties enter an intermodal agreement that federal maritime law is thus extended beyond its intended bounds. In this age of "containerized" cargoes subject to "multimodal" bills of lading, it is often difficult to locate precisely the points of legal delivery. Increasing efficiency and integration in cargo transport continues to blur the lines separating sea carrier responsibilities from those of others.

Case Highlights

- A through bill of lading is one by which an ocean carrier or MTO agrees to transport goods to their final destination. The intermodal or multimodal bills of lading do not necessarily prevent the application of the individual transport carriage conventions.

A Period of Responsibility Clause (such as a warehouse to warehouse clause) can be used to extend COGSA's application to the entire time the goods are within the carrier's custody. In many ways, the unimodal conventions are obsolete both in their content and in failing to provide for multimodal carriage contracts. Unfortunately, the United Nations Convention on International Multimodal Transport of Goods, signed in Geneva on May 24, 1980, has never entered into force.

Marine Insurance

Under international conventions, such as the Hague Rules and Warsaw Convention, a common carrier's liability is frequently limited. Buyers or sellers of goods protect themselves from such limitations by purchasing cargo insurance against losses due to damage or delay in transit. Exporters often obtain insurance on their own behalf, even if the terms of sale make the foreign buyer responsible for a loss.

Shipping goods across national boundaries—from one inland destination to a port of shipment, then to a port of destination and the inland point of destination—involves different types of insurance, including marine, war risk, comprehensive general liability, protection and indemnity, and excess insurance. This is further complicated by the fact that insurance providers will often distribute risk through **reinsurance**. Marine insurance is a contractual relationship between an underwriter and the insured (shipper), while reinsurance is a contract between different underwriters. As a general rule, the insurer may not reinsure on broader terms than are found in the underlying policy. Containerization has led to the creation of insurance policies that cover multiple modes of transportation.

In order to deal with these different issues of coverage, the transit insurance industry has produced a host of standard forms and clauses. Despite such standardization, variations are often negotiated by the parties. Marine insurance is a highly specialized industry that provides a variety of insurance policies, including hull, cargo, and liability policies. These policies protect ship and cargo owners from an assortment of risks, including damage to goods, damage to the ship, damage to others' property, and liability for injury and death. The most common property coverage is provided by **hull insurance**. The shipowner or charter party of a vessel obtains hull insurance. This protects the owner or charter party from losses due to damage to the vessel or its equipment (hull policies insure ships and cargo policies insure the goods being transported). War risk coverage is ordinarily excluded from the standard hull and cargo policies. The hull policy is a perils-only type of policy in that one may collect only for losses resulting from expressly listed causes but extended coverage is negotiable (such as an endorsement for war risk protection).

The two most popular extensions of coverage are through the **Inchmaree clause** and the **running down clause**. The Inchmaree or additional perils clause extends the list of covered perils to include losses due to negligence of the crew and damage arising from a latent defect which are exemptions under the Hague Rules. This clause is also commonly inserted in hull (shipowner) and cargo (shipper) insurance policies. The running down clause provides protection from liability for damages to another vessel caused by a collision with the insured ship. The best sources for hull insurance forms and clauses are Lloyd's of London and the American Institute's Hull Clauses.

Liability coverage is provided through **protection and indemnity insurance (P & I)**, offered through associations of shipping companies known as P & I clubs. P & I policies provide two broad categories of protection: third-party and contractual liability protection. Third-party liability coverage protects against damages caused to others due to marine collisions. Contractual liability coverage includes protection against passenger liability, liability for lost and damaged cargo, and the discharge of hazardous materials.

With the advent of container transport, the **through-transport policy** form of P & I insurance has become popular. A through-transport policy provides additional indemnification for third-party damage caused during inland transit. Another popular policy is **comprehensive general liability (CGL) coverage.**[23] CGL's most salient feature is its comprehensiveness. It also provides a broad duty on the part of the insurer to defend the carrier in related lawsuits or arbitrations. Thus, the insured is provided with the luxury of having legal services paid for by the insurance company even on claims where insurance coverage is unlikely.

Shippers commonly obtain umbrella or **excess insurance**. Insurance is often multi-layered due to the fact that the underlying insurance provider may be unwilling to provide the amount of coverage requested by the insured. The insured further limits its exposure by obtaining excess coverage for claims that exceed the amount of the underlying policies. The excess insurance policy incorporates one of a number of popular clauses that control when that coverage becomes available. An **escape clause** precludes any recovery if the type of claim is covered under an existing policy, even if that claim exceeds the amount of coverage provided by the underlying policy. An **excess clause** covers all claims outside the coverage of the underlying policy. The ***pro rata* clause** proportions the amount paid under the policy based upon the limits provided by other relevant policies.

Marine Cargo Insurance

Marine insurance policies are directed at one of two intended beneficiaries—the shipper and the common carrier. The most relevant policy for exporters and importers of goods is the **cargo policy**. The restrictions on coverage in cargo insurance revolve around three factors: (1) causes of loss that it protects against; (2) amount of coverage; and (3) duration of the coverage. The first factor relates to the selection of a perils policy versus an all risks policy. The second factor affects the decision to insure against total loss, known as free of particular average, or to insure against partial losses, known as *with* average. The third factor involves the incorporation of clauses in the marine insurance policy that would extend the coverage's duration to periods when the goods are on the shore or in a warehouse. These **extension clauses** include warehouse to warehouse, shore, and marine extension clauses.

> **Cargo Insurance Certificate:** A document indicating the type and amount of insurance coverage in force on a particular shipment. It includes the name of the insurance company and conditions of coverage. The original copy of the Cargo Insurance Certificate is required in the filing of a claim. Copies of documents necessary to support an insurance claim include the insurance policy or certificate, bill of lading, invoice, packing list, and a survey report (usually prepared by a claims agent).

As noted above, there are two general types of marine insurance policies: (1) **perils only policy**; and (2) **all risks policy**. Perils only policies pay only for losses due to expressly enumerated perils or causes listed in the policy (see Figure 11.3 *Focus on Transactions*: "Standard Perils Only Policy (ULA's Cargo B Clause)"). The burden is on the cargo owner to prove that the loss was due to one of the listed perils.[24] Under the perils only policy a loss caused by an

This insurance covers:

1 Loss or damage to the goods insured reasonably attributable to:

- a fire or explosion
- b vessel or craft being stranded, grounded, sunk, or capsized
- c overturning or derailment of land conveyance
- d collision or contact of vessel or craft with any external object other than water
- e discharge of cargo at a port of distress
- f earthquake, volcanic eruption, or lightning

2 Loss or damage caused by:

- g general average sacrifice
- h entry of sea, lake, or river water into vessel or place of storage
- i jettison or washing overboard

3 Total loss of any package lost overboard or dropped while being loaded on to or unloaded from vessel or craft.

Figure 11.3 Focus on Transactions: Standard Perils Only Policy (ULA's Cargo B Clause) (Risks Covered).

unforeseen event or occurrence would be borne by the owner of the goods. Broader coverage is available through the all risks policy. The all risks policy covers any losses except for those expressly exempted in the policy. The burden to prove that the loss was due to an excluded clause is placed upon the insurance company. Standard cargo policies, whether perils only or all risks, will not cover damages caused by war, revolution, riot, or strikes. These areas of loss are exempted by the **F.C. & S. clause** (free of capture and seizure) and the **S.R. & C.C. clause** (strikes and riots). The F.C. & S. clause has been interpreted to exclude any losses due to war or civil strife (rebellion and revolution). Coverage may be requested through an endorsement on the underlying policy or through a separate **war risk policy**. The decision to purchase additional coverage is likely to be based upon the expected route of transport and the types of goods being transported.

Marine insurance policies generally specify whether they cover less than total losses, known as **with average**, or whether they cover only total losses, **free of particular average** (**FPA**). The marine term for loss is the word *average*. The more comprehensive policy is one *with average*. This policy protects against partial as well as total losses. Most with average policies exclude coverage for losses of under 3 percent of the value of the goods. More recently, the Institute of London Underwriters opted to eliminate free of particular average from its standard clauses. Instead, it provides an alternative clause that allows the insurance company to narrow the list of specified risks that would be covered under the standard perils only policy.

Marine cargo insurance traditionally covers the period that the goods are on the ship. Due primarily to the importance of the bill of lading and the use of multimodal containers, the cargo policy is often made to cover risk of loss for periods of time before the loading and after the unloading of the goods. Extended periods of coverage are given by warehouse to warehouse or marine extension clauses (see Figure 11.1: "Warehouse to Warehouse Clause"). The marine extension or warehouse to warehouse clause extends the standard marine coverage to a period before the loading of the goods and a period between offloading and delivery to the consignee.

Shaver Transportation Co. offers an excellent review of some of the standard clauses found in most marine insurance policies. The clauses reviewed in *Shaver Transportation Co.* apply equally to perils only and all risk insurance policies. The clauses in the marine insurance policy that are referred to in the case have been excerpted and placed in Figure 11.4 *Focus on Transactions*: "Standard Marine Insurance Clauses." It is important to refer to these clauses when reading the case.

PERILS CLAUSE. Adventures and perils which Assurers[25] will bear are of the seas and inland waters, man of war, fires, enemies, pirates, rovers, assailing thieves, jettisons,[26] letters of mart,[27] reprisals, taking at sea, arrests, restraints and detainments of all kings, princes of people of a nation, condition or quality whatsoever, barratry of the master and mariners,[28] and all other perils, losses and misfortunes, that have or shall come to the detriment or damage to the goods and merchandise, or any part thereof.

FREE OF PARTICULAR AVERAGE CLAUSE (FPA). Other shipments covered are insured: Free of Particular Average unless caused by the vessel and/or interest insured being stranded, sunk, burst, on fire or in collision with another ship or vessel or with ice or with any substance other than water, but liable for jettison and/or washing overboard, irrespective of percentage (of loss).

WAREHOUSE TO WAREHOUSE CLAUSE. This insurance attaches from the time the goods leave the Warehouse and/or Store at the place named in the policy for transit and continues during the ordinary course of transit, including customary transhipment, until the goods are discharged overside from the overseas vessel at the final port. Thereafter, the insurance continues while the goods are in transit and/or awaiting transit until delivered to the final warehouse at the destination named in the policy for a period of 15 days (or 30 days if the destination to which the goods are insured is outside the limits of the port).

MARINE EXTENSION CLAUSE. This policy is extended to cover all shipments in accordance with the following clauses:

I Insurance attaches from the time the goods leave the warehouse at the place named in this policy and continues until the goods are delivered to the final warehouse.

II Insurance specially covers the goods during deviation, delay, forced discharge, reshipment, and transhipment.

III Insurance shall in no case be deemed to extend to cover loss, damage, or expense proximately caused by delay or inherent vice or nature of the subject matter insured.

SHORE COVERAGE CLAUSE. Including while on docks, wharves or elsewhere on shore and/or during land transportation, risks of collision, derailment, fire, lightning, sprinkler leakage, cyclones, hurricanes, earthquakes, floods, the rising of navigable waters, or any accident to the conveyance and/ or collapse and/or subsidence of docks and/or structures, and to pay loss or damage caused, even though the insurance be otherwise FPA.

LANDING AND WAREHOUSING CLAUSE. Notwithstanding any average warranty contained herein, Assurers agree to pay landing, warehousing, forwarding or other expenses and/or particular charges that are incurred, as well as any partial loss arising from transhipment. It will pay the insured value of any package, piece, or unit totally lost in loading, transhipment, and/or discharge.

Figure 11.4 Focus on Transactions: Standard Marine Insurance Clauses.

EXTRA-EXPENSES CLAUSE. Where, by reason of a peril insured against under this policy, extra expenses are incurred to destroy, dump, or otherwise dispose of the damaged goods, or where extra expenses are incurred in discharging from the vessel and/or craft and/or conveyance, such expenses will be recoverable in full in addition to the damage to the insured interest.

SUE AND LABOR CLAUSE. In case of any loss or misfortune, it shall be lawful and necessary to and for the Assured, his or their factors, servants and assigns, to sue, labor, and travel for, in, and about the defense, safeguard, and recovery of the said goods and merchandise, without prejudice to this insurance; nor shall the acts of the insured or insurers, in recovering, saving, and preserving the property insured, in case of disaster, be considered a waiver or an acceptance of abandonment; to the charges the Assurers will contribute according to the rate and quantity of the sum insured.

INCHMAREE CLAUSE. This insurance also covers any loss of or damage to the interest of insured, through the bursting of boilers, breakage of shafts or through any latent defect in the machinery, hull, or appurtenances, or from faults or errors in the navigation and/or management of the vessel by the Master, Mariners, Mates, Engineers, or Pilots; provided that this clause shall not be construed as covering loss arising out of delay, deterioration or loss of market.

NEGLIGENCE CLAUSE. Assured are not to be prejudiced by the presence of the negligence clause and/or latent defect clause in the bills of lading and/or charter party. The seaworthiness of the vessel and/or craft as between the Assured and Assurers is admitted, and the Assurers agree that in the event of unseaworthiness or wrongful act or misconduct of shipowner, charterer, their agents or servants, shall cause loss or damage to the cargo insured by sinking, stranding, fire, explosion, contact with seawater, or by any other cause of the nature of any of the risks assumed in the policy, the Assurers will (subject to the terms of average) pay to an innocent Assured the resulting loss.

Figure 11.4 (Continued)

Shaver Transportation Co. v. Travelers Indemnity Co.

481 F. Supp. 892 (D.C. Oregon 1979)

Judge. Shaver Transportation (Shaver), a barge company, contracted with Weyerhaeuser Company (Weyerhaeuser) to transport caustic soda from Weyerhaeuser's plant to a buyer of the soda, GATX. Following the terms of the agreement, Shaver arranged for marine cargo insurance with Travelers Insurance. Shaver decided on "Free from Particular Average" and "standard perils" policy supplemented with other cover clauses. Upon delivery to GATX, it was determined that the soda had been contaminated with tallow (beef fat). The parties agree that the contamination occurred as Shaver was loading the caustic soda into the barge. The barge had previously carried a load of tallow and Shaver had not thoroughly cleansed the barge's input lines. Travelers notified Shaver that the contamination did not represent a recoverable loss under the defendant's marine cargo policy. The issue in the case: Are the losses incurred by Shaver related to an insured event under the marine cargo insurance policy?

Recovery Under Perils of the Sea Clause and Free From Particular Average Clause

The Perils clause, which dates back several hundred years, defines the risks protected by the policy. In addition to a long list of "perils of the sea," the clause includes "all other perils, losses, and misfortunes that have or shall, come to the detriment or damage to the goods and merchandise." Shaver argues that the "forced" disposition of the caustic soda was like jettison (an enumerated peril). However, the contamination of the cargo occurred at the time of loading. Shaver cannot recover under the Perils clause of the policy.

Recovery Under Warehouse to Warehouse Clause; Marine Extension Clause; Shore Coverage Clause

These clauses do not define the nature of the risks covered by the policy but merely define where the coverage extends. To recover under either the Warehouse to Warehouse or the Marine Extension clause, Shaver must show that an insured peril existed, and the damage was proximately caused by that peril. The shore coverage clause provides coverage for enumerated risks occurring on shore. Shaver argues that contamination while loading is a shore accident. However, since the contamination occurred within the barge's intake lines, the incident arose "on board." Even if the clause were to apply, contamination of cargo is not within the enumerated risks covered by the shore coverage clause.

Recovery of Extraordinary Expenses Under Landing and Warehousing Clause; Extra Expenses Clause; Sue and Labor Clause

The losses suffered by Shaver were not caused by a peril covered by the policy. Recovery under these provisions is therefore precluded.

Recovery Under Inchmaree Clause

The purpose of the Inchmaree clause is to expand the coverage of the policy beyond the perils provision. It removes the exemption of liability of the vessel owner for fault or error in navigation or management of the ship. The shipowner retains liability for negligence in the care and custody of the cargo. If the act in question was a primary purpose of the ship, it is "in navigation or in management" of the ship. However, if the primary purpose is to affect the cargo, this is not "in navigation or in management." The contamination of the cargo was caused by fault in the care, custody, and control of the cargo and is not a covered peril.

Recovery Under Negligence Clause

The Negligence clause provides coverage against losses due to enumerated perils caused by the unseaworthiness of the vessel. "Seaworthiness" depends on such factors as the type of vessel, character of the voyage, reasonable weather, navigational conditions, and type of cargo. Shaver must demonstrate that the unseaworthiness of the barge caused a loss to cargo by one or more of the enumerated perils. Since contamination is not an enumerated peril, no recovery is possible under the Negligence clause. Shaver failed to use due diligence by not properly cleaning or inspecting the barge's input lines. Judgment shall be entered for Travelers Insurance.

Case Highlights

- Warehouse to warehouse and shore clauses do not define the nature of the risks covered by the policy but merely define where the coverage physically extends
- The Inchmaree clause allows a vessel owner to become exempt from liability for fault or error in navigation or management of the ship. In contrast, the shipowner retains liability for negligence in the care and custody of the cargo (stowage)
- A vessel is unseaworthy if it is not reasonably fit to carry the type of cargo undertaken to transport
- Since contamination is not an enumerated peril, no recovery is possible under the negligence clause.

Cargo insurance can be obtained for a single voyage or a fixed period of time. The most common form in exporting is the open or **general cover** form of insurance, which is not limited to a specific shipment but covers numerous shipments for a fixed period of time. The premium is calculated on the basis of the values declared by the shipper on the certificates issued for each shipment. A variant of the open cover policy is the **blanket policy** in which the shipper is not required to declare the individual values of each shipment. Instead, each shipment is covered up to the maximum amount of the policy.

The **Institute of London Underwriters** (**ILU**) is an association of marine insurance companies that publishes a manual of standard clauses. The sophisticated international exporter or importer should familiarize themselves with the standard forms and clauses published by the ILU, the **American Institute of Marine Underwriters** (**AIMU**), and Lloyd's of London. An example of such publications is the manual on Cargo Clauses published by the AIMU. In addition, the ILU and AIMU have drafted standard terms for particular trades.[29]

General Average

General average is a doctrine of maritime law that dates back 2,800 years. The doctrine provides that when a portion of a ship's cargo is sacrificed to save the rest of the cargo from a real and substantial peril, each owner of the goods saved contributes a pro rata amount to compensate for the loss to the owners of the sacrificed goods. Three types of events create a general average situation: (1) common danger to which ship, cargo, and crew are all exposed and which is imminent; (2) voluntary sacrifice of a part for the benefit of the whole; and (3) successful avoidance of the peril.[30]

Modern law has eased the "imminent" requirement by requiring only that a peril be real and substantial. Two classes of general average claims exist: sacrifices of part of a ship or cargo made to save the whole venture, and **extraordinary expenses** incurred by the shipowner for the joint benefit of the ship and its cargo. Thus, general average claims can be made by shipowners and cargo owners. The international convention that governs the calculation of general average losses is the **York-Antwerp Rules**. *Folger Coffee Company v. Olivebank* involves a claim for general average by a common carrier against cargo owners.

Folger Coffee Company v. *Olivebank*

201 F.3d 632 (5th Cir. 2000)

Judge. In this admiralty and maritime case, Folger Coffee Co. and its insurer, Gulf Insurance, seek to reverse the lower court's judgment that found (1) the vessel *M/V Olivebank* was entitled to use the general average on a salvage lien; and (2) Folger Coffee and Gulf Insurance owe their proportional share to the general average fund.

The *M/V Olivebank* left South Africa with cargo that included granite blocks, steel wire, and earth-moving equipment. During the voyage the vessel encountered severe weather and extremely rough seas that caused seawater to come over the deck. The vessel's emergency electrical system should have provided emergency lighting from batteries, followed by the automatic start-up of the emergency generator to provide electrical services for steering. The batteries failed and the emergency generator was ultimately started manually. It is undisputed that a skylight, or raised hatch, nine feet above deck and two levels above the electrical alternators, was open. It is also undisputed that outside deck-level vent covers were open and that these vents led to the alternator room. The captain of the vessel put out a Mayday and enlisted the help of a salvage tug. The tugs arrived in the late afternoon. The main engines were ultimately started prior to the arrival of the tug, and the vessel was able to sail to a port of refuge on its own power. The tug owner placed a salvage lien against the ship and cargo for its expenses.

The owners of the *M/V Olivebank* declared the general average, forcing the cargo owners to provide general average bonds and guarantees to cover its additional expenses (hiring the barge). Folger Coffee and Gulf Insurance maintain that the *M/V Olivebank* was not entitled to general average because the vessel was unseaworthy. The parties do not dispute that the bill of lading covering the cargo aboard the *M/V Olivebank* required general average contribution. Under the Hague Rules, once the owner of the vessel establishes that a general average act occurred, the cargo owners may avoid liability by establishing that the vessel was unseaworthy at the start of the voyage and that the unseaworthiness was the proximate cause of the general average event. The lower court found that the loss of power was caused by a combination of events and that the vessel was seaworthy when it left port and that the open skylight and the vent covers were not an issue of seaworthiness but were cases of neglect. The Hague Rules "exempts the carrier for liability from damage caused by 'act, neglect, or default of the master, mariner, pilot, or the workers on the carrier in the navigation or in the management of the ship.'" Lower Court Decision is AFFIRMED.

Case Highlights

- Under the Hague Rules, once the vessel establishes that a general average act occurred, the cargo owner might avoid liability only by establishing that the vessel was unseaworthy at the start of the voyage and that the unseaworthiness was the proximate cause of the general average event
- There is a fine line between actions that constitute errors in management for which the carrier is exempted and inaction that constitutes a lack of due diligence.

Transit by Road

International exporting-importing almost always includes ocean carriage. However, most companies are inland from ports so will also use other common carriers to transport goods to the port of shipment or from the port of destination to the buyer's place of business. The most common methods of inland transport are by truck, railway, or both. The main bodies of rules for trucking are found in the Convention on the Contract for the International Carriage of Goods by Road (CMR). Forty-five countries have ratified the CMR, including France, Germany, Hungary, Italy, Netherlands, Romania, Russia, Spain, Turkey, and UK. The CMR applies when the trucking route crosses over a border between two countries and one of the countries has adopted the CMR.

The primary document issued by the carrier is the **consignment note.** The International Road Transport Union publishes the standard consignment note.[31] The note is issued in triplicate (one for sender, one for consignee, one for carrier).[32] The contract of carriage is confirmed by the making out of a consignment note. The sender (seller or freight forwarder) is responsible for the accuracy of the information provided to the common carrier. On taking over the goods, the carrier checks, if inspection is possible, and must attest to the accuracy of the statements in the consignment note as to the number of packages, their marks, and the apparent condition of the goods and their packaging. The consignment note is *prima facie* evidence of the making of the contract of carriage, the conditions of the goods, and the receipt of the goods by the carrier.

The CMR provides the sender the right to stop the goods in transit, tranship to another location, or deliver the goods to someone other than the consignee. The carrier is liable for damages, loss of goods, and delay in delivery. The liability, unless a higher value is declared, is 8.33 SDRs per kilogram. The carrier is exempted from liability if the goods were defectively packaged, mishandled, loaded, stowed, or if the loss was due to the inherent nature of the goods (such as deterioration). The consignee is obligated to inspect the goods. The goods are presumed to be as described in the consignment note if the consignee fails to object to an apparent damage. If not apparent, then the consignee must give notice in seven days after the discovery of the damage within one-year of the date of delivery.

The typical method for calculating damages is the value of the goods fixed according to the commodity exchange price or, if there is no such price, according to the current market price or, if there is no commodity exchange price or current market price, by reference to the normal value of the goods of the same kind and quality, along with carriage charges, customs duties, and other charges incurred. A protocol to the CMR Convention recognizes the electronic consignment note—eCMR. Currently, the eCMR is available in Bulgaria, Czech Republic, Denmark, Estonia, France, Iran, Latvia, Lithuania, Luxembourg, Netherlands, Moldova, Russia, Slovakia, Slovenia, Spain, Switzerland, and Turkey.

Transit by Rail

The CIM Convention constitutes the legal basis for the conclusion of freight contracts in international transport by rail (railroads) using one standardized freight document (consignment note). CIM stands for Uniform Rules concerning the Contract of International Carriage of Goods by Rail and has been ratified by over 50 countries, mostly in Europe and the Middle East, including the EU.[33] The CIM applies when goods are transported between signatory countries. The CIM Rules also apply to carriage by inland waterway when the waterway portion is supplemental to the main carriage by rail.

The act of a shipper or intermediary of turning over goods to a railway is called a consignment. Article 28 of the CIM states: "The railway shall hand over the consignment note and deliver the goods to the consignee (receiver of goods) at the destination against a receipt and payment of the amounts chargeable to the consignee by the railway." The consignor (sender of goods) must provide the railway with a consignment note. Article 10 states: "Acceptance is established by the application to the consignment note of the stamp of the forwarding station, or accounting machine entry, showing the date of acceptance." There must be a separate consignment note for each single wagon or carload. The railway is liable for partial or total damages and for delayed delivery. The railway is provided a number of exemptions from liability, including, carriage in open wagons; inadequacy of packing; nature of certain goods which renders them inherently liable to total or partial loss or damage, especially through breakage, rust, interior and spontaneous decay or wastage, and the carriage of live animals. The CIM Rules follow the CMR with a number of differences. The differences mostly benefit the sender or consignor. The liability cap is higher than the CMR at 17 SDR per kilogram. Unlike the CMR, the consignee can also modify the transit while en route. The consignor should protect itself by negotiating a term preventing the consignee from changing the route. In cases of delayed delivery, under the CMR the carrier is liable for the cost of carriage, while under the CIM the carrier's liability can be as much as four times the cost of carriage. In cases of delayed delivery, a claim must be filed within 60 days. The major difference between the CIM and CMR is that the CIM gives the carrier the right of inspection. In cases where the goods are loaded by the consignor without inspection by the carrier, the consignment note is not evidence that the goods are in sound condition. If the consignor wants the verification of the carrier, it must pay the costs of the carrier's inspection. If the carrier loads the goods, then the goods are presumed to be in sound condition. In the event that the carriage contract does not allocate the responsibility, then the carrier is obligated to load and unload the goods. However, if the goods are being transported in a container the consignor is responsible for arranging the loading of the goods and the consignee is responsible for the unloading of the goods.

Transit by Inland Waterway

The Budapest Convention on the Carriage of Goods by Inland Waterway (CMNI) was adopted in 2000. The CMNI applies to transit on inland waterways, such as rivers, lakes, and canals, but can also apply where part of the transport is on a seaway. If the ocean transit is less than the inland waterway portion, and no bill of lading has been previously issued, then the CMNI applies. The CMNI is unique in a number of ways. First, the carrier is able to issue either a bill of lading or consignment note. Second, the CMNI places the point of passing of risk over to the carrier when the goods are placed onboard the vessel, meaning the carrier (vessel) is not responsible for the costs and risks of loading and unloading. Numerous countries with major transborder waterways—Bulgaria, Czech Republic, Germany, Luxembourg, Netherlands, Romania, and Switzerland—have adopted the Convention.

Chapter Summary

1. One of the most important parts of international sales is the transport of goods. Almost all shipment of goods sent across the world include the use of a cargo ship. How close to a port a company is located will depend on the types of common carriers used to transport the goods to the buyer. Commonly, multiple modes of transportation are used in the international transport of goods, including trucks, railroads, and ships.
2. Each of the different modes of transport is regulated by international carriage conventions. The purposes of carriage conventions include: (1) establishing the duties and responsibilities of the common carrier; (2) ensuring the shipper a certain level of damages in case of loss or damage to its goods; (3) limiting the liability of the common carrier; (4) providing a number of exemptions to the common carrier that would excuse it from any liability for loss due to one of the exemptions; and (5) requiring the common carrier to issue a document that shows ownership of the goods and the party to which the goods are to be delivered. In carriage by sea, the bill of lading is the key title document.

3. There are three major international ocean carrier conventions: Hague Rules, Hague-Visby Rules, and the Hamburg Rules. When a country adopts a carriage convention into law it is often retitled as the Carriage of Goods by Sea Act or COGSA. For example, the U.S. COGSA is an adoption of the Hague Rules, while the UK's COGSA is an adoption of the Hague-Visby Rules.
4. Under COGSA, the common carrier's liability is capped by a per package limitation. The shipper collects the actual value of the goods not to exceed $500 per package (Hague Rules). In cases of bulk transfers, the "package" would be a customary freight unit (CFU), such as a barrel of oil, a ton of coal, or cubic yard of corn. COGSA also provides 17 exemptions including "perils of the sea" and the "Q-clause exception" in which the common carrier is free from liability. The common carrier's protections may be extended to other parties, such as stevedores, through a Himalaya clause.
5. Common carriers have a number of duties, including providing a seaworthy ship, proper stowage of goods (secure placement of the goods in or above the deck of the ship), taking the contracted or customary sea route, and delivering the goods to the correct party (party holding the bill of lading). The carrier also has the duty to provide a fair opportunity for a shipper to declare a higher value (above the per package limit) for the goods. Providing a space on the bill of lading where the shipper can enter the actual value of the goods fulfills the fair opportunity obligation.
6. Shippers also use other third parties in the shipment process, including freight forwarders, freight consolidators, and customs brokers. In order to simplify the process of securing the different modes of transportation (truck, rail, and ocean carriage), along with the different bills of lading associated with each mode, multimodal transportation has become popular. In multimodal shipment, the shipper hires a single company to arrange all of the different legs of the shipment, and that company issues a single multimodal bill of lading.
7. The other major component of the shipping process is the procurement of suitable marine or cargo insurance. So, for example, if the common carrier were exempted due to the COSGA liability exemptions, the shipper would be able to make a claim under its insurance policy. There are many different types of marine insurance policies and clauses. The policy the shipper obtains or clauses the shipper negotiates will determine the types and amounts of losses the shipper is protected against. The most common policy is one "with average," which allows claims for partial loss or harm to the goods. There are two general types of marine insurance policies: (1) perils only policy and (2) all risks policy. The most common form of cargo insurance is the perils policy that pays only for losses due to expressly enumerated perils or causes.
8. Another important issue in obtaining marine insurance is the period of time in which the insurance is in effect. The most common form in exporting is the open or general cover form of insurance policy, which is not limited to a specific shipment, but covers numerous shipments for a fixed period of time

or until terminated by notice given by the shipper (insured) or the insurance company.

9. Under principles of maritime law, a shipper may be liable for damage caused to another shipper's goods under the doctrine of general average. The York-Antwerp Rules provide the means for *pro rata* assessment to all shippers with cargo on board a ship in which other shippers' goods were lost or damaged for the greater good of the ship and the remaining cargo. General average liability also occurs when the shipowner expends extraordinary expenses to ensure the safe transport of the goods. In such cases, the shippers are obligated to pay a *pro rata* share of the extraordinary expenses.
10. Other important international carriage conventions include the Convention on the Contract for the International Carriage of Goods by Road (CMR), Uniform Rules concerning the Contract of International Carriage of Goods by Rail (CIM), and Convention on the Carriage of Goods by Inland Waterway (CMNI).

Key Terms

Air Waybill
All Risks Policy
American Institute of Marine Underwriters (AIMU)
Bailment Blanket Policy
Booking Contract
Cargo Insurance Certificate
Cargo Policy
Carriage of Goods by Sea Act (COGSA)
Charter Party
CIM Convention
Clause Paramount
CMR Convention
COGSA (Hague) Exemptions
Comprehensive General Liability (CGL) Coverage
Common Carrier
Consignment Note
Containerization
COTIF
Customary Freight Unit (CFU)
Customs Brokers
Deck Cargo
Due Diligence
Excess Insurance
Extension Clause
Extraordinary Expenses
F.C. & S. Clause
Fair Opportunity
Force Majeure Clause
Forwarder's Bill of Lading
Free of Particular Average (FPA)
Freight Forwarder
General Average
General Cover
Hague Rules
Hague-Visby Rules
Hamburg Rules
Himalaya Clause
Hull Insurance
Inchmaree Clause
Institute of London Underwriters (ILU)
Insurance Services Office (ISO)
Insured Value
International Monetary Fund (IMF)
Marine Extension Clause
Material Deviation
Misdelivery
Multimodal Transport

Multimodal Transport Operator (MTO)
Ocean Bill of Lading
On-Board Bill of Lading
Per Package Limitation
Perils Only Policy
Pro Rata Clause
Protection and Indemnity (P & I) Policy
Q-Clause Exception
Reinsurance
Rules for Multimodal Transport Documents
Running Down Clause
S.R. & C.C. Clause
Seaworthiness
Special Drawing Rights (SDR)
Stowage
Through Bill of Lading
Through-Transport Policy
War Risk Policy
Warehouse to Warehouse Clause
Warsaw Convention
With Average
York-Antwerp Rules

Chapter Problems

1. What is the purpose of international carriage conventions? Why are they needed? Why are they important? In what ways do they favor the shipping companies or common carriers? What benefits do the international carriage conventions provide to the shippers?
2. What are the functions of freight forwarders and what is the relationship between freight forwarders and exporters?
3. A shipper obtains a marine (cargo) insurance policy for $25,000 on goods that had a real or market value of $8,000. If the goods are lost at sea, is the insurance company liable for $25,000, $8,000, or nothing?
4. An insured takes out a marine insurance policy on $50,000 worth of goods but fails to disclose his previous claims history. In fact, the insured had filed claims for loss on eight previous policies covering the transport of goods. Can the insurance company avoid making payment for loss to the insured goods?
5. A shipper obtains a cargo insurance policy on 400 sealed crates of "Grade A" industrial grinding wheels. In fact, the grinding wheels were contained in 400 burlap sacks and were of secondhand stock. Does such a variation in the description of the insured goods jeopardize the shipper's coverage?
6. Goods are jettisoned from a ship as a general average act. You file a claim against your marine insurance policy and receive full payment. Does the marine insurance company have a claim for general average against the shipowner and the other cargo owners?
7. During a time of hostilities, a shipowner hires a tug to tow the ship to lessen the danger from enemy submarines. Can the shipowner make a general average claim by arguing that the towing costs are extraordinary expenses incurred for the benefit of the ship and its cargo?
8. Plaintiff Tseng boarded an international flight from New York to Tel Aviv. Before being allowed to board, she was subjected to an intrusive security search. Tseng sued the airline in state court in New York for the torts of assault and false imprisonment. The Warsaw Convention does not address

such an injury. Will Tseng be allowed to continue her action under New York law? *El Al Israel Airlines, Ltd. v. Tseng*, 119 Sup. Ct. 662 (1999).

9. The plaintiffs are Dutch importers of commodities that include industrial leather gloves. Four shipments of gloves were made in 1982 and 1983. The insurance contract contained the following clause: "This insurance shall in no case be deemed to extend to cover loss, damage, or expense proximately caused by *inherent vice* or nature of the subject matter insured." The plaintiff claimed that the dropping of water from a source external to the goods damaged the gloves. The defendant asserted that the goods deteriorated as a result of their natural behavior. In short, the goods were damaged because the leather was not properly dried by the plaintiff. Is this a case of inherent vice? *Noten v. Harding*, 2 *Lloyd's Law Report* 283 (English Court of Appeal 1990).

Internet Exercises

1. Review the website of the International Maritime Bureau: www.iccwbo.org/ccs/menu_imb_bureau.asp. What types of services does this organization provide to international shippers?
2. Research the status of the BOLERO Project in the development of electronic documentation relating to the shipment of goods at www.bolero.net.
3. Your company has just entered into an export contract with a company in Chile. It is your job to arrange transport from the Port of Miami to Santiago, Chile. Check the shipping schedules to determine the best and fastest transit routes.

Other Internet Sources

Transportation Law Navigator—air and ocean transport: www.cargolaw.com.

English Carriage of Goods by Sea Act of 1971 (**Hague-Visby Rules**): www.jus.uio.no/lm/england.carriage.of.goods.by.sea.act.1971/doc.html.

Hamburg Rules: www.jus.uio.no/lm/un.sea.carriage.hamburg.rules.1978/doc.html.

ICC International Maritime Bureau: www.iccwbo.org/ccs/menu_imb_bureau.asp

Law of Freight Forwarding: www.unzco.com/basicguide/c10.html; and http://www.forwarderlaw.com.

Insurance Services Office: www.iso.com.

American Institute of Marine Underwriters: www.aimu.org.

Institute of London Underwriters: www.iua.co.uk.

Intergovernmental Organisation for International Carriage by Rail: http://otif.org/en ("Unified railway law to connect Europe, Asia and Africa").

Notes

1 The formal name of the Hague Rules is the Brussels Convention for the Unification of Certain Rules Relating to Bills of Lading.
2 For more details on the calculation, see IMF at http://www.imf.org/external/np/tre/sdr/sdrbasket.htm.
3 See International Monetary Fund at https://www.imf.org/en/About/Factsheets/Sheets/2016/08/01/14/51/Special-Drawing-Right-SDR.
4 46 U.S.C.A. § 1304.
5 *General Elec. Co. v. Inter-Ocean Shipping*, 862 F. Supp. 166, 169 (S.D. Tex. 1994).
6 See *Wemhoener Pressen v. Ceres Marine Terminals*, 5 F.3d 734 (4th Cir. 1993).
7 46 U.S.C. Appendix § 1304 (5).
8 *Cincinnati Milacron Ltd. v. M/V American Legend*, 784 F.2d 1161 (4th Cir. 1986).
9 *Vimar Seguros y Reaseguros v. M/V Sky Reefer*, 515 U.S. 528 (1995).
10 9 U.S.C.A. §§ 1, 2, 201 *et seq.*, 202.
11 An excerpt of this case is used in this chapter because it pertains to the enumerated exemption of "latent defect."
12 720 F.2d 629 (11th Cir. 1983).
13 881 F.2d at 761, 768 (9th Cir. 1989).
14 7 F.3d 1427 (9th Cir. 1993).
15 A *container* is a uniform, reusable metal box in which goods are shipped by vessel, truck, or rail. Standard lengths include 10, 20, 30, and 40 feet (40-foot containers generally hold about 40,000 pounds of cargo). See also, Laurence Alexander, "Containerization, the Per Package Limitation, and the Concept of 'Fair Opportunity,'" 11 *The Maritime Lawyer* 123 (1986).
16 Frank G.M. Smeele, "The Contract of Carriage" in *International Contracts: Aspects of Jurisdiction, Arbitration and Private International Law* 257 (ed. Marieele Koppenol-Laforce, 1996).
17 575 F. Supp. 239 (SDNY 1983).
18 See *Universal Leaf Tobacco Co. v. Companhia De Navegacao Maritima Netumar*, 993 F.2d 414 (4th Cir. 1993) (courts will not consider a container as a package if the bill of lading discloses the number of packages within the container).
19 493 F.2d 97 (2d Cir. 1974).
20 This clause was taken from *St. Paul Fire & Marine Ins. v. Sea-Land Service*, 745 F. Supp. 186, 188 (SDNY 1990).
21 See *Binladen BSB Landscaping v. M/V Nedlloyd Rotterdam*, 759 F.2d 1006 (2d Cir. 1985).
22 See Chapter 6, "International and National Trade Regulation."
23 Insurance Services Office (ISO), a private trade association, drafts this policy.
24 Additional coverage can be added through a war and riot risk clause and an Inchmaree clause.
25 Assured refers to the party insured by the policy. Assurer refers to the insurance company.
26 Cargo may be voluntarily sacrificed by jettison in the common good, giving rise to a general average loss.
27 Letters of mart or marque are government authorizations to commit piracy against a designated state or person.

28 Barratry is fraud or criminal conduct performed by the captain or the crew.
29 Hayden and Balick at 325.
30 See *Barnard v. Adams*, 51 U.S. 270 (1850).
31 See consignment note at http://www.iru.org/index/en_media.press.
32 The consignor is the seller or freight forwarder; the consignee is the buyer; and the common carrier is the transport company, such as a ship, truck, railway, or inland water operator.
33 The convention is sometimes also referred to as COTIF-CIM as the amendments to the initial 1890 convention over the years were brought together under the auspices of the Convention concerning

Chapter 12

Documentary Transactions

There are a number of methods of organizing an international sale of goods transaction. This chapter will focus on the **documentary collections transaction**, which is one of the common methods of mitigating the two main risks in international sales—the seller-exporter's risk of nonpayment for delivered goods and the buyer-importer's risk of not receiving goods for which it has paid. It does this by changing the sale of goods transaction to a sale of documents. In this way the buyer does not receive the documents to take control of the goods until making payment. In the same way, the seller does not give up the controlling documents without receiving payment. To accomplish this exchange while the goods are in transit, the use of trusted third parties is required. Commercial banks located near the seller and buyer act as "escrow agents," collecting the documents from the seller and exchanging them for payment provided by the buyer. The word seller will be used interchangeably with exporter and buyer will be used interchangeably with importer.

The remaining risk is the case where the buyer fails to show up to receive and pay for the documents. While the seller remains in control of the goods, it will have to incur expenses in finding a new buyer, retrieving the goods from a distant country, and, in the worst case, to write-off the entire value of the goods. In order to completely eliminate the seller's payment risk, the seller requires the buyer to provide a letter of credit from a commercial bank that guarantees payment to the seller. The letter of credit (issued by the buyer's bank) may also be guaranteed by the seller's bank in a **confirmed letter of credit**. Chapter 13 will explain the use of letters of credit in what is known as the **documentary credit transaction**.

DOI: 10.4324/9781003469230-15

Methods of Payment: Types of Sale Transactions

The method of payment agreed to by the two parties determines who will bear the burden of the risks of nonpayment (seller) and nondelivery (buyer). Figure 12.1 *Focus on Transactions*: "Methods of Payment Risk Scale" shows the different methods of payment on a risk scale from the perspective of the exporter–seller and importer–buyer. There are several basic methods of payment for products sold abroad. As with domestic sales, a major factor that determines the method of payment is the seller's level of trust in the buyer's ability and willingness to pay. The common methods of payment in international trade, ranked in order from the least secure for the exporter–seller are: (1) open account and consignment sales; (2) documentary collection; (3) documentary credit; and (4) cash in advance. Since getting paid in full and on time is of utmost concern to exporters, exporters carefully weigh these different methods of payment. For example, the buyer would much prefer an on-account or open account transaction in which it will not have to make payment until sometime after the delivery of the goods. In an open account transaction, the exporter simply bills the customer, who is expected to pay under agreed terms at a future date, such as net 30 or 60 days. Open account sales pose risks, such as the exporter needing to pursue collections abroad, which can be difficult and costly. In a foreign transaction, an open account should only be considered a satisfactory method of payment if the buyer is well established, has demonstrated a long and favorable payment record, has been thoroughly checked for creditworthiness, or there is a long history of dealings between the exporter and importer.

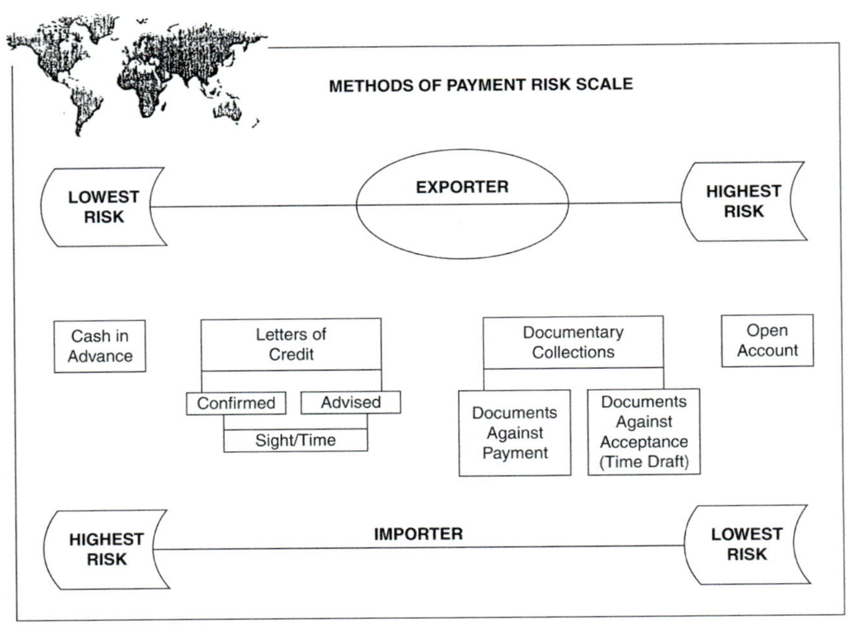

Figure 12.1 Focus on Transactions: Methods of Payment Risk Scale.

One variation of the on-account method is the **consignment of goods** transaction, which is a bit less risky for the seller. A consignment of goods is similar to the on-account transaction in that the seller waits to receive payment. The difference is that, in consignment sales, ownership (title) remains with the seller until the goods are sold to a third party. This method is most common when goods are shipped to a foreign distributor to be sold on behalf of the exporter. The exporter retains title to the goods until the distributor sells them. Once the goods are sold, payment is sent to the exporter. With this method, the exporter accepts a great deal of risk and loss of control over the goods. When this type of sale is contemplated, it is wise to consider some form of risk insurance.

The distributor-consignee acts as an intermediary between the seller–consignor and the buyer and is trusted to obtain payment from the ultimate buyer in exchange for the title from the seller. In both the on-account and consignment methods, the risk of nonpayment rests with the seller.

The most pro-seller method is the **cash in advance** transaction. In this case, the buyer pays in advance and then awaits delivery of the goods. This method places the risk of nondelivery with the buyer by paying for goods that may never be delivered. The seller is relieved of all collection problems and has immediate use of the money, especially if a wire transfer is required.

In order to eliminate the seller's payment risk and the buyer's delivery risk, the most commonly used methods in international trade are the documentary collections and documentary credit methods. Figure 12.1 shows that under the documentary collections and documentary letter-of-credit transactions, two types or times of payment are possible. If the seller wants to be paid immediately, then it would demand **Payment against Documents**, meaning that it will provide a **sight draft**, which requires the buyer to make payment when obtaining the documents. See Figure 12.2 *Focus on Transactions*: "Sight Draft." An alternative known as **Payment against Acceptance** is used when the seller allows the buyer additional time to make payment after receiving and accepting the

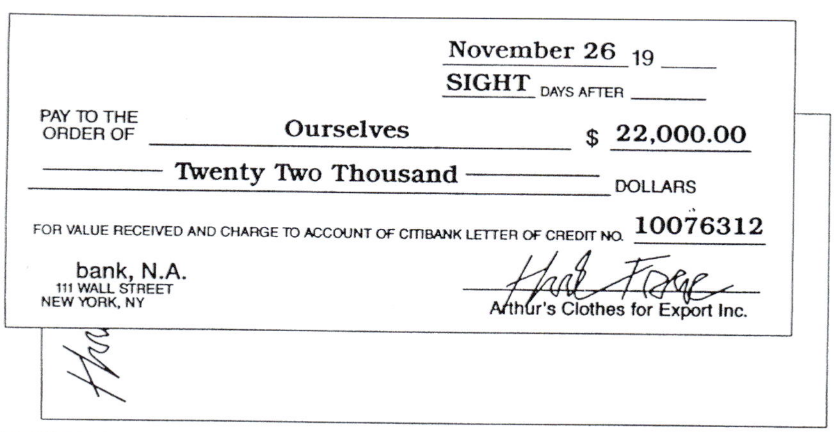

Figure 12.2 Focus on Transactions: Sight Draft.
Source: Wikimedia Commons.

documents (and receiving the goods). It does this by providing a **time draft** that states a time after the delivery in which the buyer must make payment. The sight draft in Figure 12.2 can easily be converted into a time draft by inserting a number of days in the blank: "SIGHT Days After."

The rest of this chapter examines the documentary sales transaction by focusing on the common documents in international sales transactions, including the key title document known as the **bill of lading**. It will also examine a key term found in all international sales contracts known as the trade term. Trade terms allocate the costs of freight, insurance, loading and unloading of the goods, customs clearance, and the payment of fees and tariffs at the country of importation, and most importantly the time when the **risk of loss** passes from the seller to the buyer. The terms used in almost all international contracts are those that are defined by the International Chamber of Commerce's manual entitled **Incoterms 2020**.

The two types of documentary transactions (collections and credit) lie between the two extremes of open account and cash in advance. Both methods involve the use of documents to ensure the passage of title to the goods to the buyer and payment to the seller while the goods are in transit. The difference is that the documentary credit transaction requires the buyer to obtain a letter of credit to guarantee payment to the seller. A documentary collections transaction is one in which the buyer is obligated to pay upon delivery of documents (not delivery of goods). The documentary credit transaction also requires payment upon delivery of documents, but that payment is further guaranteed by a commercial bank through the issuance of a letter of credit.

Open Account

An open account transaction is a sale where the goods are shipped and delivered before payment is due, which in international sales is typically within 30, 60, or 90 days after delivery. Buyers often ask exporters for open account terms since the extension of credit (time to pay after delivery) by the seller is common in domestic transactions, especially with repeat customers. The seller should only consider the open account method for known and trusted buyers. However, in a competitive marketplace, a seller that offers open account terms will have an advantage over its competitors who do not. The open account transaction is a form of seller financing in that the buyer often resells the goods and obtains payment before the time comes due for paying the seller. Ways of minimizing the risk of nonpayment under open account terms include export credit insurance and export factoring. Export factoring involves selling of open accounts (account receivables) to a factoring company who assumes the responsibility for collecting payments owed (to be discussed later in this chapter).

Cash in Advance

In the situation where the seller has superior bargaining power, especially in cases where its goods are in high demand and the buyer is a new customer, the seller will demand payment in advance before shipping the goods to the buyer. For international sales, wire transfers and credit cards are the most commonly used cash in advance payment options. However, escrow services via the Internet are another cash in advance option for small export transactions.

As noted in the open account, demanding cash in advance and not offering an open account makes a seller less competitive. Nonetheless, the seller should demand cash in advance in the following cases: (1) importer is a new customer or is not well established; (2) importer's creditworthiness is doubtful, unsatisfactory, or unverifiable; (3) political and commercial risks of the importer's home country are high; and (4) seller operates an Internet-based business where the acceptance of credit card payments is common. Credit card payment is a reasonable method for small consumer goods transactions, but in larger transactions a wire transfer is the most secure and least risky method of payment. Exporters should provide clear routing instructions to the importer when using this method, including the receiving bank's name and address, SWIFT (Society for Worldwide Interbank Financial Telecommunication) code, and bank account number.

In order to minimize the importers' delivery risk, escrow services can be used in a cash in advance transaction. In such a scenario, the importer sends payment through a trusted third party or escrow agent. After the escrow agent verifies payment, the exporter ships the goods. When the importer receives and accepts the goods, the funds are released by the escrow service to the exporter. International commercial banks are commonly used as escrow agents.

Documentary Collections

A documentary collection is a transaction whereby the exporter entrusts the collection of the payment for a sale to its bank (remitting bank), which sends the documents to the importer's bank (collecting bank) with instructions to release the documents to the buyer upon payment. Funds are received from the importer and remitted to the exporter through the banks. Documentary collections transactions involve using a **bank draft** that requires the importer to pay the face amount either at sight (Document against Payment) or on a specified date after receiving the documents (Document against Acceptance). Documentary collections are less expensive than transactions involving a letter of credit (documentary credit transaction). The term *draft* is used commonly in the U.S., while a **bill of exchange** is the term used in the UK and some other Commonwealth countries. The documentary collections transaction will be discussed below.

International Sales Contract

In international trade, the sales contract determines the characteristics of the export–import transaction. It is supported by other related contracts and trusted third parties, reflecting the complexity of the transaction. First, there is the carriage contract with a shipping company to transport the goods (generally by sea). Second, there is the contract for marine insurance. Third, the sale is usually financed by means of a banking transaction, often in the form of a letter of credit. A business contemplating exporting for the first time must educate itself on the different cost factors related to international sales transactions. Some of these additional expenses are related to the legal requirements found in the sales contract, such as the procurement of necessary documents, selecting the proper trade term (allocation of costs of shipping), and the need to obtain insurance. It is necessary to know these cost factors to determine the marketability of goods in a foreign market or the true costs of outsourcing (buying goods and materials from a foreign country). All additional expenses need to be incorporated into the contract price.

After the contract is formed, the seller contacts the freight forwarder to book shipment on a common carrier. The freight forwarder coordinates the movement of the goods, submits the export documentation to the Customs Service (sometimes with the aid of a Customs Broker), obtains the bill of lading from the carrier, and compiles other required documents.

Pricing Goods for Export

Before exporting to or entering a foreign market, an analysis of the factors that relate to the profitability of such an entry should be undertaken. Many new exporters calculate their export price by the **cost-plus method**. In the cost-plus method of calculation, the exporter starts with the domestic manufacturing cost and adds administration, research and development, overheads, freight forwarding, distributor margins, customs charges, and profit. The net effect of this pricing approach may be that the export price escalates into an uncompetitive range.

An alternative method of pricing for market entry is what is termed **marginal cost pricing**. This method considers the direct, out-of-pocket expenses of producing and selling products for export as a floor beneath which prices cannot be set without incurring a loss. For example, export products may have to be modified for the export market to accommodate different sizes, electrical systems, or labeling requirements. Changes of this nature increase costs. On the other hand, the export product may be a stripped-down version of the domestic product and therefore cost less to produce. Or, if additional products can be produced without increasing fixed costs, the incremental cost of producing additional products for export should be lower than the average production costs for the domestic market only.

In addition to production costs, overhead, and research and development, other costs should be allocated to domestic and export products in proportion to the benefit derived from those expenditures. Additional costs often associated with export sales include: (1) market research and credit checks; (2) business travel; (3) international postage and telephone rates; (4) translation costs; (5) commissions, training charges, and other costs involving foreign representatives;

(6) consultant and freight forwarding costs; and (7) product modification and special packaging.

After the price is determined, the exporter needs to determine if its goods are marketable in a foreign country. For most consumer goods, per capita income is a good gauge of a market's ability to pay. In lower per capita income markets, simplifying the product to reduce the selling price will increase marketability. The exporter must also keep in mind that currency valuations alter the affordability of goods. If the exporter's product or service is new to a particular foreign market, it may be able to set a higher price than is normally charged domestically. Only after it has estimated the cost, demand, and marketability versus competitors for its goods is the exporter–seller ready to prepare a *pro forma* invoice or price quotation and enter into an export contract.

Pro Forma *Invoice (Price Quotations)*

The prudent exporter realizes the importance of entering into a well-defined agreement. First, customs regulations and special documentary requirements make the international sale of goods transaction more complicated. Second, the exporting and importing transaction requires the use of various third parties, such as commercial banks, international common carriers, custom brokers, and freight forwarders. The form that describes the allocation of these costs between the seller and the buyer is the seller's ***pro forma*** invoice.

The *pro forma* invoice is an invoice provided by a seller prior to the shipment of goods, informing the buyer of the kinds and quantities of goods and their costs, as well as the time of shipment and specifies the sale and payment terms. It is generally the basis for the formation of the sales contract, along with the buyer's purchase order. Before preparing the *pro forma* invoice, the prudent exporter or importer should develop a checklist of important terms and documentary requirements it needs to incorporate into the contract. An example is provided in Figure 12.3 *Focus on Transactions*: "International Shipping

Commercial Invoice

- Will a commercial invoice suffice or is a customs or consular invoice required?
- Are all charges in accord with the original quotation?
- Are terms of delivery clear? Include a selection of a trade term from Incoterms 2020.
- Are terms of payment and currency of payment clearly stated?
- Are unit descriptions, measures, and prices stated in the same way on the documents?
- Is an export license required?

Figure 12.3 Focus on Transactions: International Shipping Checklist.

Packing List

- Are shipper and consignee clearly identified?
- Are all item descriptions and units of measure specifically described in the commercial invoice?
- Are package markings and numbers accurately applied?
- Does the packing list conform to the importing country's requirements?

Bill of Lading

- Are the consignee, shipper, and notify party clearly identified?
- Do descriptions, marks, and numbers match the commercial invoice and packing list?
- Are ocean bills of lading marked n oard?
- If freight charges are included on the commercial invoice, the bill of lading should be marked Prepaid
- Are any of the items classifiable as hazardous materials?

Certificate of Origin

- Is an origin certificate required by the destination country?

Miscellaneous Documents

- Preshipment inspection certificate?
- Insurance certificate?
- Phytosanitary inspection certificate?
- Weight certificate?

Figure 12.3 (Continued)

Checklist." Figure 12.4 *Focus on Transactions*: "Common Documents" provides a list of "Common Documents" used in international sales.

Since the foreign buyer may not be familiar with the product, the description of it in the *pro forma* invoice must be more detailed than it would be in a domestic quotation. The description should include: (1) buyer's name and address; (2) buyer's reference number and date of inquiry; (3) list of requested products and brief description; (4) price of each item (it is advisable to indicate whether items are new or used and to quote in domestic currency to reduce foreign-exchange risk); (5) gross and net shipping weight (in metric units where appropriate); (6) total cubic volume and

***Pro Forma* Invoice versus Commercial Invoice**: A *pro forma* invoice or "sample invoice" is created prior to the entering of a sales contract. It is often used as an offer that the buyer may accept to form a contract. The *pro forma* invoice is replicated in the final commercial invoice. The *pro forma* invoice can be used to obtain an import license or a foreign exchange permit. The commercial invoice is one of the required documents in a documentary transaction. It provides a detailed description of the goods, including prices, discounts, quantity, delivery, and payment terms. The commercial invoice is used by governments to determine the value of the goods for the purpose of the assessment of customs or import duties.

- *Certificate of Origin (COO)*: Signed statement required in certain nations attesting to the country origin of the export item. In free trade areas, a certificate of origin that certifies the export as regional goods is required to obtain lower import tariffs.
- *Certificate of Conformity*: Signed statement from a manufacturer attesting that a product meets certain technical standards.
- *Commercial Invoice*: Document prepared by the exporter or freight forwarder and required by the foreign buyer to prove ownership. In most cases, the commercial invoice is used to assess customs duties.
- *Consular Invoice*: Document required in some countries that describes the goods being shipped and is certified by the consular official of the foreign country stationed in the country of export.
- *Customs Declaration*: Document that describes the nature of the goods, value, consignee, and the ultimate destination required mostly for statistical purposes (such as determining countriess trade balances).
- *Customs Invoice*: Document used to clear goods through customs in the importing country by providing evidence of the value of goods. In some cases, the commercial invoice may be used for this purpose.
- *Packing List*: List that itemizes the exported material in each package and indicates the type of package, such as a box, crate, drum, or carton.
- *Inspection Certificate*: Document prepared by a third party to attest to the specifications of the goods shipped.
- *Insurance Certificate*: Document prepared by the exporter or freight forwarder that provides evidence that the goods are insured against loss or damage.
- *Pro Forma Invoice*: Invoice prepared by the exporter before shipping the goods, informing the buyer of the goods to be sent, their value, and other key specifications.
- *Export Declaration*: Government document or reporting requirement used to control exports and act as a source document for official export statistics.
- The *pro forma* invoice should not be confused with the commercial invoice. *Pro forma* invoices are not for payment purposes but are essentially price quotations in an invoice format. The invoice should be conspicuously marked "*pro forma* invoice." If a specific price is agreed upon or guaranteed by the exporter, the precise period during which the offer remains valid should be specified.

Figure 12.4 Focus on Transactions: Common Documents.

dimensions packed for export; (7) any trade discount; (8) delivery point; (9) terms of sale; (10) terms of payment: (11) insurance and shipping costs; (12) expiration period for quotation; (13) charges to be paid by buyer; (14) estimated shipping date from factory or port; and (15) estimated date of shipment arrival.

Documentary Collections Transaction

In order to alleviate the seller's risk of not being paid or the buyer's risk of not receiving the goods after making payment, most export contracts require a documentary transaction, which converts a sale of goods transaction to a sale of documents transaction. In a collections transaction, the buyer buys conforming documents from the seller while the goods are in transit. In this way, the seller is paid and the buyer receives title to the goods at the same time. Upon receiving the documents, the buyer is in a position to resell the goods to downstream buyers or to use the documents as collateral to obtain financing. In the event that the buyer refuses to pay for the documents, the seller still retains title and control of the goods. He can mitigate his losses by selling the goods to someone else through negotiation (transfer) of the documents.

One of the key documents in the documentary collections transaction is the **draft.** The banks use this instrument to effectuate payment to the seller upon the presentation of the documents to the buyer. A draft or bill of exchange is analogous to a check. A draft is a written, unconditional order for payment from the **drawer** (seller) to the **drawee** (buyer or buyer's bank). It directs the drawee to pay a specified sum of money, in a given currency, at a specific date to the payee (seller). Drafts that are paid when presented for payment are called sight drafts. *Sight* refers to the presentation of the required documents to the location stated in the contract, which is usually at the transmittal of the documents to the buyer's bank. Drafts that are payable at some time after presentation of the documents are called time drafts.

The documentary collections transaction allows the buyer to take possession either by making payment upon the presentation of the draft or by acceptance of the draft. The first type is called **Cash against Documents.** This type is the ordinary means of processing a documentary collections transaction. The Cash against Documents transaction uses a sight draft, which allows the exporter to retain title to the shipment until payment has been made. The sight draft is then processed through the banking system for immediate payment to the seller.

The second type of documentary collections transaction is referred to as **Cash against Acceptance.** In the Cash against Acceptance transaction, instructions are given by the seller to a bank indicating that the documents transferring title to the goods should be delivered to the buyer–drawee upon the buyer's acceptance of the attached time draft (and the other documents). The buyer's signature indicates its guarantee to pay the draft at some future time.

> **Document against Acceptance Collection:** A document against acceptance collection, which uses a time draft, is used when the exporter extends credit to the buyer. By signing and writing "accepted" on the draft, the buyer is formally obligated to pay within the stated time (under negotiable instrument law). When this is done, the time draft is then called a trade acceptance. A date draft differs slightly from a time draft in that it specifies a date on which payment is due, rather than a time period after acceptance of the draft.

The steps in the documentary collections transaction in chronological order are as follows: (1) entering into a sale contract; (2) exporter or importer hire carrier for transport of goods (depends on trade term); (3) obtain necessary insurance policies; (4) arrange inspection of goods prior to shipment; (5) prepare goods for shipment: packing, marking; (6) exporter delivers goods to common carrier and acquires bill of lading; (7) exporter obtains other shipping documents;

(8) exporter transmits shipping documents (delivery to a bank); (9) importer receives documents and payment is made; (10) goods are cleared through customs clearance in the country of delivery; and (11) final liquidation (payment) of customs duties and delivery to the importer.

Enlisting the services of commercial banks to transfer the documents is a common requirement of the standard international sales contract. The seller prepares the goods for shipment and obtains the necessary documents, such as the bill of lading. In order to diminish the risk of fraudulent documentation, a prudent buyer will negotiate inspection rights. Inspection of the goods takes place before the goods are loaded at the port of shipment. The inspection company issues an inspection certificate that the seller sends to the buyer, along with the other required documents.

The international sales contract almost always provides for transit of the goods by ocean carriage. The costs and risks of transit are allocated by the insertion of an Incoterm into the contract. Under the standard **CIF** term (Incoterms 2020) (Cost, Insurance, Freight), the seller obtains the services of a freight forwarding company and a common carrier to transport the goods to the buyer. The contract requires the seller to obtain a bill of lading from the common carrier to prove that the goods sent conform to the contract. The seller delivers the bill of lading, along with the other required documents to the bank for transmission to the buyer. Upon acceptance of the documents as conforming the bank sends payment to the seller. Upon receipt of the bill of lading and other documents the buyer is then able to take delivery of the goods for import.

The required documents are generally attached to a draft or bill of exchange. The seller writes the draft on the buyer's bank account and makes it payable to itself (seller). As noted above, the sight draft is paid immediately upon the presentation of the documents, while the time the time draft is paid within so many days of presentation of the documents. In that case, the buyer is required to sign and note "accepted" on the time draft before obtaining possession of the documents.

The bill of lading is a title document (see Figure 12.5 *Focus on Transactions*: "Bill of Lading") that allows the goods to be transferred while they are in transit to the port of destination. Without the bill of lading, or similar title document, the documentary transaction would not be possible. The bill of lading allows a sale of goods transaction to be converted to a sale of documents. Upon receiving the bill of lading, the buyer becomes the owner of the goods. Any dispute over the ownership of goods will be resolved in favor of the party in possession of the bill of lading and not the party in actual possession of the goods.

In order to obtain the bill of lading, the goods are delivered to the common carrier. The bill of lading is endorsed by the seller and sent via the seller's bank to the buyer's bank or to another intermediary along with a sight draft, invoices, and other supporting documents specified by the buyer in the sales contract, such as packing lists, consular invoices, and insurance certificates. The seller uses a local bank to transmit the documents through the banking system (which is made up of corresponding relations between banks) to the buyer's bank. The documents are presented to the buyer's bank along with a documentary collections letter or order, which includes a draft drawn on the buyer's account.

The buyer's bank notifies the buyer of the receipt of the documents and collects payment on the draft (sight draft) or notifies the seller of the buyer's acceptance of the draft (time draft). Following the payment or acceptance, the bill of lading and other documents are released to the buyer. The buyer transmits the shipping documents to its customs broker. The customs broker clears the goods through customs at the port of importation and arranges inland transport to the buyer's warehouse. Before the cargo can be released, the original ocean bill of lading must be properly endorsed by the buyer and surrendered to the carrier, since it is a document that is evidence of title.

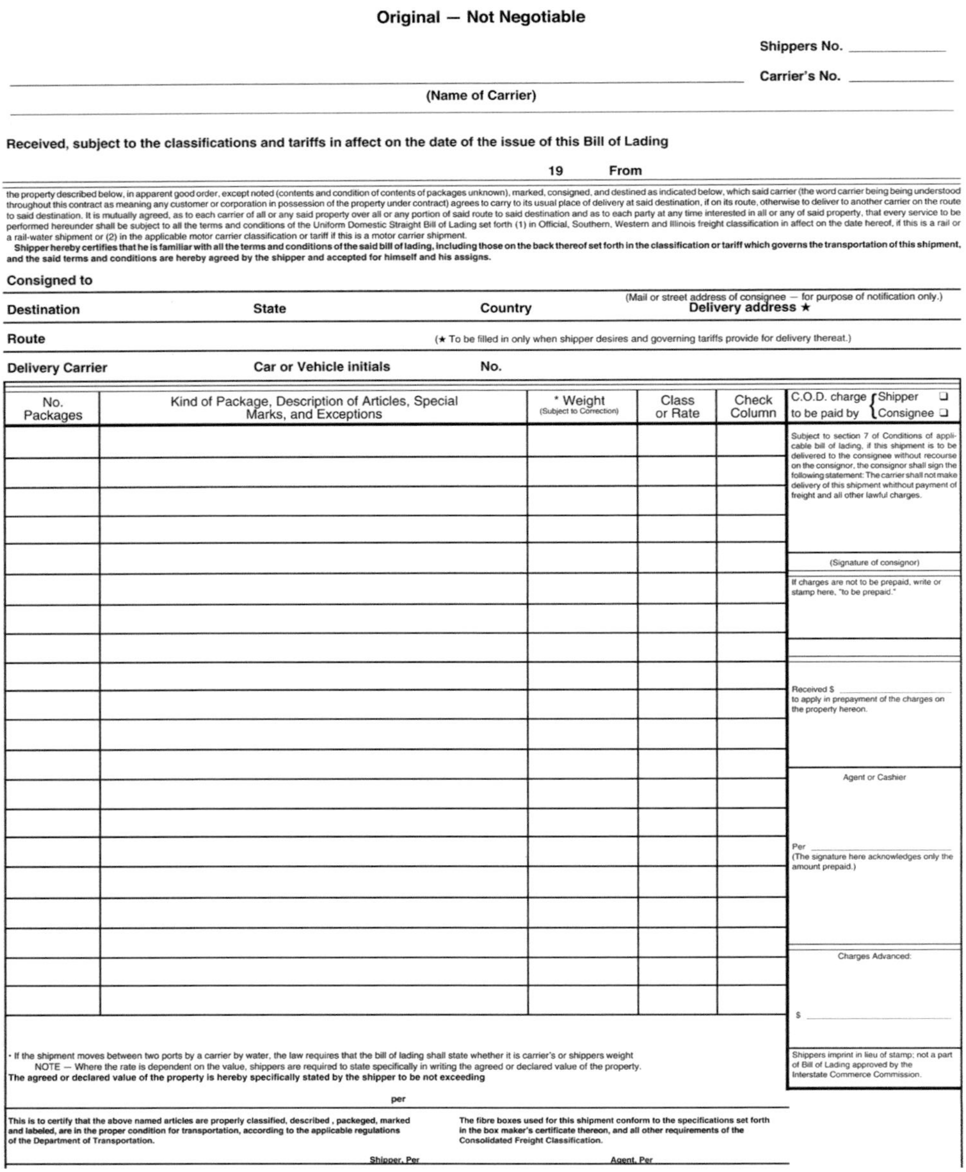

Original — Not Negotiable

Shippers No. ____________

Carrier's No. ____________

(Name of Carrier)

Received, subject to the classifications and tariffs in affect on the date of the issue of this Bill of Lading

19 From

the property described below, in apparent good order, except noted (contents and condition of contents of packages unknown), marked, consigned, and destined as indicated below, which said carrier (the word carrier being being understood throughout this contract as meaning any customer or corporation in possession of the property under contract) agrees to carry to its usual place of delivery at said destination, if on its route, otherwise to deliver to another carrier on the route to said destination. It is mutually agreed, as to each carrier of all or any said property over all or any portion of said route to said destination and as to each party at any time interested in all or any of said property, that every service to be performed hereunder shall be subject to all the terms and conditions of the Uniform Domestic Straight Bill of Lading set forth (1) in Official, Southern, Western and Illinois freight classification in affect on the date hereof, if this is a rail or a rail-water shipment or (2) in the applicable motor carrier classification or tariff if this is a motor carrier shipment.

Shipper hereby certifies that he is familiar with all the terms and conditions of the said bill of lading, including those on the back thereof set forth in the classification or tariff which governs the transportation of this shipment, and the said terms and conditions are hereby agreed by the shipper and accepted for himself and his assigns.

Consigned to

(Mail or street address of consignee — for purpose of notification only.)

Destination **State** **Country** **Delivery address ★**

Route (★ To be filled in only when shipper desires and governing tariffs provide for delivery thereat.)

Delivery Carrier **Car or Vehicle initials** **No.**

No. Packages	Kind of Package, Description of Articles, Special Marks, and Exceptions	* Weight (Subject to Correction)	Class or Rate	Check Column	C.O.D. charge to be paid by { Shipper ❑ Consignee ❑
					Subject to section 7 of Conditions of applicable bill of lading, if this shipment is to be delivered to the consignee without recourse on the consignor, the consignor shall sign the following statement: The carrier shall not make delivery of this shipment whithout payment of freight and all other lawful charges.
					(Signature of consignor)
					If charges are not to be prepaid, write or stamp here, "to be prepaid."
					Received $ ____________ to apply in prepayment of the charges on the property hereon.
					Agent or Cashier
					Per ____________ (The signature here acknowledges only the amount prepaid.)
					Charges Advanced: $ ____________
					Shippers imprint in lieu of stamp; not a part of Bill of Lading approved by the Interstate Commerce Commission.

• If the shipment moves between two ports by a carrier by water, the law requires that the bill of lading shall state whether it is carrier's or shippers weight

NOTE — Where the rate is dependent on the value, shippers are required to state specifically in writing the agreed or declared value of the property.

The agreed or declared value of the property is hereby specifically stated by the shipper to be not exceeding

per

This is to certify that the above named articles are properly classified, described , packeged, marked and labeled, are in the proper condition for transportation, according to the applicable regulations of the Department of Transportation.

The fibre boxes used for this shipment conform to the specifications set forth in the box maker's certificate thereon, and all other requirements of the Consolidated Freight Classification.

Shipper, Per **Agent, Per**

Figure 12.5 Focus on Transactions: Bill of Lading.

Source: Claudio Elias, Wikimedia Commons.

Documents in the Documentary Transaction

The following documents are commonly used in exporting; which of them are actually used in each case depends on the requirements of the importing countries, as well as the type of goods being transported. First, as in a domestic transaction, the **commercial invoice** is a bill for the goods prepared by the seller. A commercial invoice contains basic information about the transaction, including a description of the goods, the address of the buyer and seller, and the delivery and payment terms. Some governments use the commercial invoice to place a value on the goods in assessing customs duties.

Second, the bill of lading serves as a contract between the shipper of the goods and a common carrier. It is a receipt or evidence that the goods were received and placed in the control of the common carrier in good condition, and, most importantly, it is a document of title. A negotiable or order bill of lading can be bought, sold, or traded while goods are in transit. A straight bill of lading is nonnegotiable. The buyer needs the original bill of lading to take possession of the goods. See Figure 12.5 *Focus on Transactions*: "Bill of Lading." Note that the bill of lading in Figure 12.5 is mostly made up of blank space with the most important part being the area for inserting the description of the goods, kind of package, number of packages, weight when appropriate, and marking requirements. The exporter or its agent (freight forwarder) prepares the description for the bill of lading since the common carrier (shipping company) receives the goods in sealed steel containers. Under international carriage conventions, the common carrier is a guarantor of the description on the bill of lading even if it proves to be false or fraudulent.

Bearer Document: The negotiable bill of lading is considered a bearer document, similar to other financial instruments like bearer bonds. A holder of the instrument is paid or takes possession of goods immediately upon presentation of the document. This is why common carriers can only deliver the goods to a party holding the bill of lading, even though that party may not be the rightful owner. This is also the reason that the buyer should demand receipt of the "full set" of the bill of lading. Each copy of the bill of lading is a bearer document. If the bill of lading is made out or endorsed to a specific person or company, then only that person or company is entitled to receive delivery of the goods. A bill of lading that has a blank endorsement (consignee is not specified) is transformed into a bearer instrument.

Third, certain countries require a **consular invoice**, which is used to control and identify goods. The consular invoice is purchased from the local consulate of the country of import. Fourth, some countries require a signed statement as to the origin of the export item. Such **certificates of origin** are usually obtained through semi-official organizations such as a local chamber of commerce. In addition, free trade areas will have their own certificate of origin forms. In order to do so, the goods being imported must be coming from a country within the free trade area and meet minimum levels of regional content. It is likely that regional certificate of origins will no longer be required. For example, NAFTA required such a certificate but its replacement, 2020 USMCA, no longer requires a formal certification document. Certification of origin can be achieved using informal documentation, such as commercial invoices, and can be completed by the importer, exporter, or manufacturer. Certificates of origin may still be required by the buyer or by the country of importation.

Fifth, some buyers and countries may require a **certificate of inspection** attesting to the specifications of the goods shipped. Inspection certificates are often obtained from independent inspection and testing organizations. Sixth, if the seller provides insurance, then he must provide an **insurance certificate** or binder stating the type and amount of coverage. This insurance certificate is negotiable so that it can be transferred along with the bill of lading.

Seventh, countries of export generally require the filing of a **Shipper's Export Declaration**. The Declaration is used to control exports and compile trade statistics. It must be prepared and submitted to the Customs Service for export. Figure 12.6 *Comparative Law*: "Shipper's Export Declaration" is an example of such a form. It requires a **destination control statement** on shipping documents. Under this requirement, the commercial invoice and bill of lading for commercial shipments must display an **anti-diversion clause** notifying the carrier and all foreign parties that the products have been approved for export only to certain destinations and may not be diverted elsewhere. Most goods are exported under a general license, which merely requires a filing (no government approval necessary).

Eighth, a **packing slip** or list itemizing the material in each individual package being shipped is required. It gives the individual and gross weights and measurements for each package, along with the package markings. The packing list is attached to the outside of the package or container in a waterproof envelope marked "packing list enclosed." It allows the shipper or forwarding agent to determine the total shipment weight, volume, and where the cargo is being shipped. In addition, customs officials use the list to check the cargo. Some of the above documents were previously listed in Figure 12.4. A more detailed listing of the common documents used in the documentary transaction is found in Figure 12.7 *Doing Business Internationally*: "List of Export Documents."

The number of documents the exporter must obtain varies depending on the destination of the shipment and the type of goods. Because each country has different import regulations, the exporter must be careful to provide proper documentation. Exporters should seriously consider having a freight forwarder or customs broker handle the documentation.

Bill of Lading

The bill of lading, as noted above, is the traditional transport document and serves three functions: (1) carriage contract between the shipowner and the

U.S. DEPARTMENT OF COMM... – Economics and Statistics Administration – U.S. CENSUS BUR... BUREAU OF EXPORT ADMINISTRATION

FORM **7525-V** (7-18-2003) **SHIPPER'S EXPORT DECLARATION** OMB No. 0607-0152

1a. U.S. PRINCIPAL PARTY IN INTEREST (USPPI)(Complete name and address)
CONTINENTAL DUTY FREE INC.
P.O. BOX 52-4183
MIAMI, FL
ZIP CODE 33152

2. DATE OF EXPORTATION: FEB 07, 2008

3. TRANSPORTATION REFERENCE NO.: MIAELS028POR 007

b. USPPI'S EIN (IRS) OR ID NO.

c. PARTIES TO TRANSACTION: ☐ Related ☒ Non-related

4a. ULTIMATE CONSIGNEE *(Complete name and address)*
ERZULIA JOSEPH LUBIN
PORT DE PAIX, HAITI

b. INTERMEDIATE CONSIGNEE *(Complete name and address)*
SAME AS ABOVE

5a. FORWARDING AGENT *(Complete name and address)*
N/A

5b. FORWARDING AGENT'S EIN (IRS) NO.
N/A

6. POINT (STATE) OF ORIGIN OR FTZ NO.: FLORIDA

7. COUNTRY OF ULTIMATE DESTINATION: HAITI

8. LOADING PIER *(Vessel only)*: MIAMI RIVER

9. METHOD OF TRANSPORTATION *(Specify)*: VESSEL

14. CARRIER IDENTIFICATION CODE: LBRL

15. SHIPMENT REFERENCE NO.: MIAELS028POR 007

10. EXPORTING CARRIER: M/V EL SHADDAI

11. PORT OF EXPORT: MIAMI, FL

16. ENTRY NUMBER

17. HAZARDOUS MATERIALS: ☐ Yes ☒ No

12. PORT OF UNLOADING *(Vessel and air only)*: PORT DE PAIX

13. CONTAINERIZED *(Vessel only)*: ☐ Yes ☒ No

18. IN BOND CODE

19. ROUTED EXPORT TRANSACTION: ☐ Yes ☒ No

20. SCHEDULE B DESCRIPTION OF COMMODITIES *(Use columns 22–24)*

D/F or M (21)	SCHEDULE B NUMBER (22)	QUANTITY – SCHEDULE B UNIT(S) (23)	SHIPPING WEIGHT (Kilograms) (24)	VIN/PRODUCT NUMBER/ VEHICLE TITLE NUMBER (25)	VALUE (U.S. dollars, omit cents) (Selling price or cost if not sold) (26)
D	2401.20.5592 TABACCO	300 CASES	3402 K		$ 19,200

Figure 12.6 Comparative Law: Shipper's Export Declaration.

shipper (seller or buyer depending on trade term selected); (2) evidence of receipt that the goods were delivered to the carrier; and (3) document of title (see Figure 12.5 *Focus on Transactions*: "Bill of Lading"). Its function as a title document allows for the sale, transfer, and "collateralization" of the goods while in transit.

Lord Mustill, in discussing the third function of the bill of lading, stated that "it is a symbol of constructive possession of the goods which can transfer possession by endorsement and transfer; it is a transferable *key to the warehouse*."[1]

Although the bill of lading generally serves as a document of title, receipt, and carriage contract, other agreements may take its place. A freight or booking contract, may control the contractual relationship between the shipper and the common carrier. In *M & Z Trading Corp. v. Cargolift Ltd*,[2] the shipper argued that a prior freight agreement governed while the common carrier contended that its bill of lading constituted the contract. The terms of the prior agreement

Bill of Lading

A title document called a bill of lading is issued by a shipping company. It also serves as a formal receipt of the goods and is the contract of carriage between the carrier and the shipper. The holder of the bill of lading has a right to claim delivery of the goods from the shipping company at the port of destination. The most common bill of lading in international transport is the ocean bill of lading. A multimodal transport bill of lading may be used when more than one form of transport is being used.

Letter of Indemnity

This document allows a carrier to release goods to the consignee not yet in possession of the bill of lading. It is a guarantee to indemnify the carrier from all liability related to the release. It is also called a "steamer guarantee."

Export License

This is a document filed with the government of export (general export license). Some export licenses require government approval before the exporting (validated license). Validated licenses are only required for certain commodities (e.g. encryption technology) or when goods are being exported to certain countries (e.g. North Korea).

Dock Receipt

This document certifies the receipt of the goods by a carrier at the port of shipment. A "dock warrant" not only acknowledges receipt but is also a document of title.

Warehouse Receipt

This acknowledges receipt of the goods by a warehouse operator.

Commercial Invoice

This document is prepared by the exporter and lists and describes the goods. It generally also gives the prices, discounts, quantities, and delivery and payment terms. It is used by government customs to place a valuation of the goods for the assessment of tariffs or duties.

Consular Invoice

This is an invoice certified by the consul of the country of import; customs officials use it to verify the value, quantity, and quality of the goods. Also, the consular officer may compare the export price with the market price in the exporting country to determine if the goods are being "dumped" (being sold below market prices or below the cost of production) into the importing country's market.

Figure 12.7 Doing Business Internationally: List of Export Documents.

Certificate of Inspection

An independent inspection company issues a certificate of inspection to assure the buyer of the quantity and quality of the goods being shipped. Preshipment inspection is a requirement for importation of goods into many developing countries.

Certificate of Origin

This is provided by a third party such as an official of the local chamber of commerce or an official of the consular office.

Bill of Exchange or Draft

This is an order addressed to the importer or the importer's bank for the payment of a fixed sum at sight or in the future (time draft).

ATA Carnet

The ATA Carnet or "Merchandise Passport" is an international customs document which allows for the duty- and tax-free temporary import and export of professional equipment, commercial samples, and goods for trade shows and exhibitions. Generally, a bond or cash deposit of 40 percent of the value of the goods is required.

ISO 9000 Certificate

The International Standards Organization has developed standards which certify

Figure 12.7 (Continued)

stated that the carrier's general obligations began upon the initial pickup of the goods in Canada and continued until final delivery in Russia. The court held that the bill of lading did not nullify the lengthy course of negotiations that culminated in the prior freight agreement.

The **electronic bill of lading** has already transformed documentary transactions. Electronic bills of lading enable a more efficient sale or transfer of documents while the goods are in transit. The first electronic bill of lading was developed in conjunction with rail transport (CMI Rules for Electronic Bills of Lading). The Comité Maritime International has also adopted the Rules for Electronic Bills of Lading (CMI Rules). A more expansive system is known as the Bolero Project that allows for electronically transmitting all standard documents. Bolero possesses a core messaging platform that allows electronic transmissions related to bills of lading (corporate-to-bank communications), bank guarantees, standby letters of credit, other documents used in documentary collections, processing of both national and international open account transactions, and expediting bank payment obligations through use of the electronic bill of lading (eBL). Bolero's eBL gives carriers and logistics providers the ability to create, send, amend, and manage bills of lading digitally with greater accuracy, integrity, and speed, which reduces the likelihood of fraud, errors, and the cost of administration.[3]

Characteristics of Bills of Lading

Table 12.1 lists the characteristics of the ocean bill of lading. The standard documentary sales contract requires an **on-board bill of lading.** The on-board bill of lading warrants that the cargo has been placed aboard a named vessel and is signed by the master of the vessel. This type of bill ensures the buyer that the goods are indeed on the ship in transit to the port of destination. A **received-for-shipment bill of lading** recognizes only the delivery of the goods to the common carrier; but it does not warrant that the goods have been placed upon the ship. If the sales contract is silent regarding the type of bill of lading, Article 23 of the UCP 600 (Uniform Customs and Practices for Documentary Credits)[4] states that banks will, unless otherwise stipulated in the letter of credit, accept a document which indicates that the goods have been loaded on board or shipped on a named vessel.

Again, bills of lading are contracts between the shipper of goods and the carrier. They do not affect the contractual relationship between the seller and the buyer. The person or firm named in a bill of lading to which goods are to be turned over is the **consignee.** A **straight bill of lading** is nonnegotiable. Such a bill allows only for delivery to the named consignee in the bill. A negotiable or **order bill of lading** can be bought, sold, or traded while the goods are in transit. The order bill is also used for many types of financing transactions that will be discussed in Chapter 13. The buyer needs the original bill of lading in order to take possession of the goods. A **clean bill of lading** is a receipt for goods issued by a carrier with an indication that the goods were received in "apparent good order and condition." In letter-of-credit transactions, a "Clean, On-Board, Full Set (all copies) Order Bill of Lading" is necessary for the shipper to obtain payment.

Table 12.1 Characteristics of the Bill of Lading.

Nonnegotiable or Straight B/L: only deliverable to Consignee (name on B/L)	*versus*	*Negotiable or Order B/L*
Unclean (Flawed, "Claused"): common carrier writes a notation on B/L indicating damage or count of goods	versus	Clean
Received for Shipment: goods have been delivered to common carrier or shipping terminal, but not yet loaded onto ship	versus	On-board
N/A	versus	Full Set (all copies of B/L)

Air Waybill

Most transport of goods is performed through ocean carriage. In the event of transit by air, the operative transport document is the **air waybill**. The air waybill is a nonnegotiable instrument that serves as a shipping contract and receipt for the shipper. Unlike the ocean bill of lading, the air waybill does not act as a document of title. The front of the air waybill makes a number of important representations. First, unless noted otherwise, the "goods are accepted in apparent good order and condition." Second, the shipper is directed to the reverse of the form for an explanation of the carrier's "limitation of liability." Third, the shipper is provided with notice of his right to increase carrier's liability by declaring a higher value and paying a supplemental charge. Also provided is a space for the "amount of insurance" requested by the shipper. Above the signature line, the shipper is notified that he is certifying that the goods are not dangerous unless described as such. If dangerous by nature, then the shipper certifies that the goods are in "proper condition for carriage by air according to applicable dangerous goods regulations."

Trade Terms

The insertion of a **trade term** into the sales contract allows the parties to designate the point at which the costs and risks of transport are divided between the seller and buyer. The **risk of loss** allocation determines who has the responsibility for any loss or damage to the goods while they are in transit. The generic costs allocated by trade terms include the costs of freight and insurance. As a practical matter the trade term also allocates a number of other responsibilities, including customs clearance, payment of import duties, and the loading or unloading of the goods from the common carrier. The trade term is an element in the contract of sale and can normally be found in the *pro forma* invoice. The importance of the trade term and other **risk-shifting clauses**[5] in the international sales contract is explained in the following excerpt:

Harold J. Berman, *Law of International Commercial Transactions (Lex Mercatoria)*

1 Journal of International Dispute Resolution 245–248, 276 (1988)

Export-Import Contract

The general functions and features of export–import contracts are succinctly described as follows:

> *Many of the risks inherent in an international transaction can be allocated by the importer and exporter through their contract of sale, under familiar principles of contract law. ... Out of the price-delivery term, and*

> *especially out of the term "CIF" [see also, CPT and CIP] which is probably the most widely used term in international trade contracts, has come a great deal of law. The price-delivery term defines the title to the goods, time and place of delivery, time and place of payment, importer's right of inspection, the risk of loss or damage to the goods in transit, and the cost of transportation.*
>
> ***
>
> *An international sales contract typically contains other risk-shifting clauses.* Force majeure *and other contingency clauses are added to escape liability where unforeseen circumstances prevent performance of an assumed obligation. Choice of law, choice of forum, and arbitration clauses seek to avoid the vagaries, uncertainties, and delays of foreign litigation. The tendency to spell out in detail such matters as inspection rights and remedies for breach may also be an attempt to substitute the law of the contract for that of any national legal system.*
>
> ***
>
> ***Destination and Shipment Contracts***
>
> *An importer may ask his foreign supplier to place the goods on board a vessel bound for the country of destination and to bear the risks of the voyage. Such a contract is called a destination contract. Shipment contracts shift the risk of loss to the purchaser from the moment of loading or shipment. The seller typically agrees to place the goods on board or alongside the vessel, but the risks of transit are shifted to the buyer. Typical shipment contracts include FAS, FOB, CIF, and CFR.*

The trade term controls the parties' respective obligations regarding contracting for shipping and insurance services. The trade term is also important in determining the conformity of documents in the documentary transaction. Trade terms are selected from the international trade terms manual, known as **Incoterms 2020** as published by the International Chamber of Commerce. These trade terms use three-letter acronyms that allocate the cost, risk of loss, and responsibilities of transporting the goods between the seller and buyer.

In addition, the trade term affects documentary requirements. For example, the **FOB** (free on board) trade term generally dictates that the bill of lading need not show that the freight has been paid since freight costs and shipping arrangements are delegated to the buyer. There are some variations recognized by most parties. For instance, the buyer can negotiate an additional service clause in a FOB contract. This clause requires the seller to secure liner space and an insurance certificate as agent for the buyer. This type of clause acts as a compromise for the seller who wants to avoid the risk of paying for any escalation in insurance or freight costs. Such a clause benefits the buyer who is willing to incur such costs but finds it difficult to book a ship or obtain insurance at the port of shipment.

In selecting trade terms, the parties should also be concerned with any conflicts between the chosen trade term and other terms in the contract. For example, a CIF contract shifts the risk of loss to the buyer at the port of shipment. If the contract provides that the seller guarantees a certain weight or quality at arrival, then the risks of loss for delivery below that weight shifts back to the seller. The tendency of courts has been to subordinate conflicting terms to the CIF term. A guarantee of quality clause is construed only as a guarantee of "ordinary deterioration, shrinkage, and the like in transportation."[6] Other types of loss or damage remain with the buyer. Furthermore, an occurrence within the "quality clause" does not provide the buyer with a right of rejection but only a right of price adjustment.

The exporter should quote CIF whenever possible, because it has meaning abroad. It shows the foreign buyer that the cost of shipping the product to the port in the country of importation will be borne by the seller. If assistance is needed in calculating the CIF price, an international freight forwarder can help. If at all possible, the exporter should quote the price in its domestic currency. Doing so eliminates the exporter's risk of exchange rate fluctuations and problems of currency conversion.

> *[T]he language used in an agreement is frequently a precautionary, fuller statement of the normal CIF terms and hence not intended as a departure or variation from them. Moreover, the dominant outlines of the CIF term are so well understood commercially that any variation should, whenever reasonably possible, be read as falling within those dominant outlines rather than as destroying the meaning of a term which essentially indicates a contract for proper shipment rather than one for delivery at a destination.*[7]

Nonetheless, it is important for contracting parties not to vary recognized trade terms. The dangers of varying the standard trade terms are illustrated by *Kumar Corp. v. Nopal Lines, Ltd.*[8] Kumar Corporation entered into a contract to sell goods to Nava in Venezuela on a consignment basis. In a consignment transaction, the consignor (seller) retains title to the goods until they are sold in the country of import. The consignee sells the goods for commission and remits the net proceeds to the consignor. The contract trade term was CIF. Unfortunately, the goods were stolen while in possession of the common carrier at the port of shipment. In bringing suit against the common carrier, the exporter-seller would have to overcome the defense that under the CIF term, risk of loss had passed to the buyer and, therefore, the exporter had no standing to sue. Ironically, the exporter's negligence in not procuring insurance coverage enabled it to sue the common carrier. The court held that since the exporter had failed to obtain insurance as required by the CIF term, the risk of loss remained with it. Thus, the exporter had the requisite standing to sue the common carrier.

International sales of goods contracts are defined as either **shipment** or **destination contracts**. The selected trade term allocates the risk of loss. Whether a contract is described as a shipment or destination contract depends on when the risk of loss passes from the seller to the buyer. In a shipment contract, the risk of loss passes to the buyer at the point of shipment. In a destination contract, the risk of loss passes to the buyer at the port or point of destination. The risk of loss refers to which party will suffer the loss of damaged or lost goods. If the risk of loss has passed to the buyer and the goods are subsequently lost at sea, then the buyer will have to pay for the goods it will never receive. If the contract fails to use a trade term, then generally the risk of loss passes at the time the seller delivers the goods to the carrier.[9] Thus, the presumption is in favor of shipment contracts. Again, it is important to examine the interrelationship between the trade term and other terms in the contract. This is especially necessary if other language in the contract can be construed as modifying the trade term. This was the issue in *Warner Bros. & Co. v. Israel*.[10] That case involved the purchase of Philippine sugar for shipment to New York City. The trade term in the contract stated "Philippines—CIF Terms." Another provision in the contract provided that the seller was to deliver sugar of a "net delivered weight." The sugar was delayed entry into the U.S. due to the imposition of a government sugar quota. The buyer attempted to avoid payment by arguing that the "net delivered weight" language converted the contract to a delivery or destination contract since the net delivered weight could only be determined at the port of destination.

The court rejected the argument, holding that it was a CIF contract where the purchaser must pay upon the presentation of documents. It held that the "net delivered weight" language referred to the adjustment of the price based upon the weight of the sugar delivered but was not enough to convert the shipment trade term into a destination contract. It further noted the general proposition that a delivery term (to be delivered to New York City) does not change the meaning of the trade term (shipment to destination contract). The result may be different, however, if the destination term is included in the same provision as the trade term. It is important, therefore, to use the trade term without further explanation. The contract of carriage (bill of lading) should be consistent with the allocation of responsibilities provided by the trade term in the sales contract. A misunderstanding regarding the trade or delivery term is likely to prevent exporters from meeting contractual obligations or make them responsible for shipping costs they sought to avoid.

Incoterms 2020

Incoterms 2020 went into effect on January 1, 2020. See Figure 12.8 "2020 verse 2010 Incoterms." Business parties, courts, and arbitration tribunals have universally accepted Incoterms as the definitive source of interpreting trade terms. It is important that exporters and importers familiarize themselves with the new rules and that new contracts specifically state that trade terms are to be governed by "Incoterms 2020." Incoterms 2020 retain the number of trade terms at 11 with some modifications of the terms and rules. The 11 Incoterms provide a broad range of options regarding the relative responsibilities of the exporter and importer. It is important not to attempt any variation of the terms.

The 11 terms are divided into two groups into those fit for all modes of transport including multimodal transport (EXW, FCA, CPT, CIP, DAP, DAT, DDP) and those that are only intended for ocean transport (FAS, FOB, CFR,

(1) Incoterms 2020 expressly allocates the obligation to obtain "security clearances" in the rules. It deals with this issue in more detail, reflecting the fact that over the last few decades, with the increase of terrorist-like acts, security arrangements have become more important. Unless specified otherwise, the responsibility of arranging security is given to the party responsible for the transport.
(2) Because some users were mistaken in their opinion that DAT Incoterms 2010 could only be used if the goods were delivered to a terminal, it was changed to DPU without any change in substance. As the order of the clauses follows the idea of increasing the obligations of the seller, DPU was placed after DAP.
(3) Increases in insurance coverage for the CIP and CIF terms. Before the seller was required to obtain basic marine insurance (Institute Cargo Clause C). The CIP seller is now required to obtain more extensive insurance coverage (Institute Cargo Clause) The insurance for CIF sellers still only requires a Clauses C policy.
(4) FCA should be combined with the place of delivery at the place of shipment or departure (country of the seller). C-terms have to be combined with the place/port of destination (country of the buyer). D terms must name the place of destination and not the place of departure.
(5) For containerized goods it is recommended that the seller use the FCA term instead of FAS/FOB and CPT/CIP instead of CFR/CIF since under F terms the risk regularly passes to the buyer when the container is delivered ready for unloading from the seller's truck at the container terminal.

Figure 12.8 2020 versus 2010 Incoterms.

CIF). See Figure 12.9 *Focus on Transactions*: "Summary of Incoterms 2020." It is important to note that the ocean transit terms are designed for transport by vessel only and are not appropriate for container shipments.[11]

Incoterms can also be divided in four groups: (1) E-clause (EXW; buyer must arrange shipment from seller's place of business or warehouse); (2) F-clauses (FCA, FAS, FOB; seller must deliver to carrier); (3) C-clauses (CPT, CIP, CFR, CIF; seller must deliver to carrier, and arrange and pay for carriage to destination); and (4) D-clauses (DAT, DAP, DDP; seller must deliver at destination). See Table 12.2 *Doing Business Internationally*: "Incoterm Groups."

Table 12.2 *Doing Business Internationally*: Incoterm Groups.

E Term	*F Terms*	*C Terms*	*D Terms*
Pro-Seller (Costs, Insurance, and Risk of Loss to Buyer)	Costs to Buyer (Risk of Loss to Buyer)	Costs to Seller (Risk of Loss to Buyer)	Pro-Buyer (Costs, Insurance, and Risk of Loss to Seller)
N/A	Shipping Contract	Shipping Contract	Destination Contract

Terms for any Mode of Transport

EXW (Ex-Works)

"Ex-Works" means that the seller delivers when it places the goods at the disposal of the buyer at the seller's premises or at another named place (works, factory, warehouse). The seller does not need to load the goods on any collecting vehicle, nor does it need to clear the goods for export, where such clearance is applicable. The buyer bears all costs and risks involved in taking the goods from the seller's premises to the desired destination. This term thus represents the minimum obligation for the seller. The risk of loss may shift to the buyer before he actually picks up the goods, such as when the seller notifies the buyer that the goods are ready for pick-up. Only an expert importer willing to undertake satisfying export formalities in a foreign country should use this term.

FCA (Free Carrier)

"Free Carrier" means that the seller delivers the goods to the carrier or another person nominated by the buyer at the seller's premises or another named place. The parties are well advised to specify as clearly as possible the point within the named place of delivery, as the risk passes to the buyer at that point. When, according to commercial practice, the seller's assistance is required in making the contract with the carrier (such as in rail or air transport) the seller may act at the buyer's risk and expense.

CPT (Carriage Paid to)

"Carriage Paid To" means that the seller delivers the goods to the carrier or another person nominated by the seller at an agreed place (if any such place is agreed between parties) and that the seller must contract for and pay the costs of carriage necessary to bring the goods to the named place of destination. If subsequent carriers are used for the carriage to the agreed destination, the risk passes when the goods have been delivered to the first carrier.

CIP (Carriage and Insurance Paid to)

"Carriage and Insurance Paid to" means that the seller delivers the goods to the carrier or another person nominated by the seller at an agreed place (if any such place is agreed between parties) and that the seller must contract for and pay the costs of carriage necessary to bring the goods to the named place of destination. The seller also contracts for insurance to cover against the buyer's risk of loss of or damage to the goods during the carriage. The buyer should note that under CIP the seller is required to obtain insurance only on minimum cover. Should the buyer wish to have more insurance protection, it will need either to agree with the seller for additional coverage or make its own extra insurance arrangements.

Figure 12.9 Focus on Transactions: Summary of Incoterms 2020.

DAT (Delivered at Terminal)

"Delivered at Terminal" means that the seller delivers when the goods, once unloaded from the arriving means of transport, are placed at the disposal of the buyer at a named terminal at the named port or place of destination. "Terminal" includes a place, whether covered or not, such as a quay, warehouse, container yard or road, rail, or air cargo terminal. The seller bears all risks involved in bringing the goods to and unloading them at the terminal at the named port or place of destination.

DAP (Delivered at Place)

"Delivered at Place" means that the seller delivers when the goods are placed at the disposal of the buyer on the arriving means of transport ready for unloading at the named place of destination. The seller bears all risks involved in bringing the goods to the named place.

DDP (Delivered Duty Paid)

"Delivered Duty Paid" means that the seller delivers the goods when the goods are placed at the disposal of the buyer, cleared for import on the arriving means of transport ready for unloading at the named place of destination. The seller bears all the costs and risks involved in bringing the goods to the place of destination and has an obligation to clear the goods not only for export but also for import, to pay any duty for both export and import, and to carry out all customs formalities. While the ex-works term represents the minimum obligation for the seller, DDP represents the maximum obligation. This term may be used irrespective of the mode of transport.

Terms for Sea and Inland Waterway Transport

FAS (Free Alongside Ship)

"Free Alongside Ship" means that the seller delivers when the goods are placed alongside the vessel (on a quay or barge) nominated by the buyer at the named port of shipment. The risk of loss of or damage to the goods passes when the goods are alongside the ship, and the buyer bears all costs from that moment onwards.

FOB (Free on Board)

"Free on Board" means that the seller delivers the goods on board the vessel nominated by the buyer at the named port of shipment. The risk of loss of or damage to the goods passes when the goods are on board the vessel, and the buyer bears all costs from that moment onwards.

CFR (Cost and Freight)

"Cost and Freight" means that the seller delivers the goods on board the vessel. The risk of loss of or damage to the goods passes when the goods are on board

Figure 12.9 (Continued)

the vessel. The seller must contract for and pay the costs and freight necessary to bring the goods to the named port of destination (in some countries it is known as C & R).

CIF (Cost, Insurance, and Freight)

"Cost, Insurance, and Freight" means that the seller delivers the goods on board the vessel. The risk of loss of or damage to the goods passes when the goods are on board the vessel. The seller must contract for and pay the costs and freight necessary to bring the goods to the named port of destination. The seller also contracts for insurance to cover against the buyer's risk of loss of or damage to the goods during the carriage. The buyer should note that under CIF the seller is required to obtain insurance only on minimum cover. Should the buyer wish to have more insurance protection, it will need to require that the seller obtain additional coverage or obtain its own extra insurance.

Figure 12.9 (Continued)

Each trade term in the Incoterm Manual provides 10 sets of rules—one each for the buyer and seller—obligations of the seller (A1-10) and of the buyer (B1-10).

Along with selecting the appropriate trade term, the parties must also nominate a specific place that fits the term. For instance, the port of shipment for the FOB term and the port of destination for the CIF term. This nomination should be as precise as possible, such as naming the number of the quay (wharf) or loading or unloading place, in order to avoid problems determining the correct place of performance.

As noted above, the rules for interpreting trade terms are of primary importance in international sale of goods transactions. Along with risk of loss and freight and insurance costs, the rules of interpretation for trade terms also determine who is responsible for dealing with customs agents and payment of tariffs. Incoterms also allocate the obligations of: (1) obtaining necessary export licenses and government authorizations; (2) satisfying import requirements and formalities; (3) giving notice regarding a vessel hired for transport; (4) giving notice of delivery to the common carrier; (5) packaging; (6) marking goods; and (7) obtaining transport and other documents. Beyond selecting an Incoterm, the parties should detail any rights and obligations associated with the shipment of the goods, including any special marking, packaging, inspection, and testing requirements.

FOB and FAS Terms

Under FOB (free on board), the seller must deliver conforming goods on board the vessel named by the buyer at the stipulated time and must give notice to the buyer of the delivery. The seller bears all costs up to the delivery of goods on board the ship at the port of shipment, including exportation fees, the packing and checking of the goods, and the costs of obtaining a document evidencing the loading of the goods. It is also obligated to obtain a certificate of origin at the buyer's request and expense.

The buyer must book the carriage and give notice to the seller of the name, loading berth, and dates for delivery to the vessel. The buyer, along with bearing the costs of freight and insurance, pays the costs of obtaining most documents including the certificate of origin, consular invoice, and in some incidences the bill of lading. It should be noted that if the FOB term is attached to the place of destination, such as "FOB Buffalo (place of destination)" some courts may interpret this as a destination contract whereby the risk of loss would not pass until arrival in Buffalo. In order to prevent this misinterpretation, the place of destination should be placed in a separate clause independent of the trade term. FAS or free alongside ship is essentially the same as FOB except that the seller's responsibilities end when the goods are brought alongside the ship. This is performed when the goods are delivered on the dock or placed in lighters (flat-bottomed barges used to transfer goods to and from moored ships) at the port of shipment. The buyer has to bear all costs and risks of loss, including the loading of the goods onto the ship. The responsibility of obtaining export clearance is also placed upon the buyer. Therefore, this term should not be used by an unsophisticated buyer who is not familiar with the formalities of exporting.

CIF and CFR Terms

Under the CIF term, the seller's responsibilities include obtaining a marine insurance policy and a carriage contract. The seller-exporter also at its expense obtain any export license and arrange for the loading of the goods. The marine insurance policy must be in the amount of CIF value plus 10 percent. The seller must also obtain war risk coverage at the request and expense of the buyer.

The costs of packing and checking the goods are those of the seller. In turn, the buyer is required to pay the cost of unloading. The buyer also pays for the costs of obtaining any necessary import licenses or permits, along with payment of customs duties. In sum, the seller pays all costs (freight and insurance) to the port of destination. The party responsible for customs clearance or delivery should negotiate a *force majeure* or **time-extension clause** in case of delay in clearing customs or making delivery. The CFR term is essentially the same as the CIF term, except that the responsibility to obtain and pay for the marine insurance is shifted to the buyer. It is important to understand that "C terms" are "shipment contracts" and not "arrival or destination contracts" because the risk of loss is transferred, like in the "F terms," at the port of shipment.

CPT, CIP, and FCA Terms

The advent of modern containerization and multimodal transport has resulted in the greater use of the FCA, CPT, and CIP terms, simply because the traditional function of the ship's rail as the dividing point between sellers' and buyers' functions, and in the transferring of the risk of loss from seller to buyer, has been replaced by other points, such as cargo terminals. This has also influenced documentation and reduced significantly the use of on-board bills of lading. Thus, even in the carriage of goods by sea, nonnegotiable sea waybills have replaced bills of lading. Under Incoterms 2020, the FCA term now provides that delivery by the seller is completed when the goods have been loaded on the transport provided by the carrier.

D Terms

The D group is now made up of three multimodal terms—DAT, DAP, and DDP—which can be used for any type of transport, including ocean carriage. These are destination terms, meaning that the risk of loss does not pass to the buyer until some point after the shipment of the goods. The DDP term stands for delivered duty paid. When the DDP term is followed by words naming the buyer's place of business the term represents the seller's maximum obligation under Incoterms. The seller must clear the goods for import into the buyer's country. The DDP term may be modified in the event the buyer and seller want to allocate specific costs associated with the importation. For example, they could modify the DDP term to read "Delivered Duty Paid, VAT Unpaid," which allocates the import costs to the seller, except for the cost of value-added taxes.

Outsourcing and the CIF Term

Companies that outsource materials or component parts commonly use the CIF term. It allows a company to obtain bids from companies throughout the world since the price in all the bids would be for delivery at the same port in the buyer's home country. If instead the buyer receives bids based on a FOB contract, it may be difficult to determine which bid is the best one. For example, a company in Buffalo, New York, receives bids of $38 per unit from a company in Montreal, Canada; $34 per unit from a company in São Paulo, Brazil; and $30.50 from a company in Sabah, Malaysia. It would seem that the lowest bid is from the Malaysian company, but the buyer would have to pay for the costs of freight, insurance, and import tariffs. When those costs are factored in, the cheapest price could easily be the bid from the Montreal company since transport of the goods from Montreal to Buffalo is a much shorter distance and substantially less costly, likely accomplished by trucking transport, and since Canada is a USMCA country, the tariff rate would be less than the rates charged for imports from Brazil and Malaysia.

Multimodal Transport

Before the establishment of multimodal carriers and the multimodal bill of lading, title documents would have to be procured for each segment of the transport. In addition, the different types of common carriers—truck, railroad, ships—are governed by different laws and each type issues bills of lading. In case of damage or loss, it would have to be determined in which segment of the transport the damage or loss occurred in order to determine the applicable law and the culpable party.

For example, a company in Mexico City contracts to sell its goods to a company in Dusseldorf, Germany. The chain of transport would involve a series of common carriers: The seller loads the goods into a shipment container that is then handed over to a trucking company for delivery of the goods to a railroad company for transport to the Port of Altamira and loaded onto a ship. The ship transports the goods to the Port of Rotterdam in Germany where they are transported by a railroad to Dusseldorf. In this scenario, there are four common carriers and could have involved a fifth, such as a trucking company in Germany. In a CIF contract, the seller would first obtain a bill of lading from the trucking company, then one from the railroad company, and finally an "on-board" bill of lading from the ocean shipping company. In a DPP (delivery duty paid), with delivery to Dusseldorf, the seller would also have to obtain a bill of lading from the German railroad company. Instead, the shipper (seller or buyer) may hire a multimodal transport company that will arrange the entire transport and issue a single multimodal bill of lading. Incoterms EXW, FCA, CPT, CIP, DAP, DPU, and DDP apply to any mode of transport (ocean, railroad, trucking) or multimodal transport, where the bill of lading (multimodal bill of lading) covers more than one type of transport.

The FCA (free carrier) term is now preferred over the CIF term. It requires the seller to deliver the goods to the first common carrier or the common carrier designated by the buyer. In the above scenario, either the Mexican trucking or railroad company (assuming the trucking company was hired by the buyer) could be considered the first common carrier.

Standards, Certifications, and Markings

One of the continuing barriers to international trade are differing country products standards. Product standards concern health, safety, quality, and environmental issues. A product may meet the standards in some countries and be insufficient for importation to other countries. Fortunately, there has been a movement toward the harmonization of standards at the supranational level. A producer of goods can obtain recognized certifications that will facilitate importation into other countries. Markings are often required on the products to confirm standards certifications.

EU Standards and CE Marking

Importing to the countries of the EU has been simplified by the creation of a uniform import instrument known as the EU Single Administrative Document (SAD). See Figure 12.10 *Comparative Law*: "Single Administrative Document." This form can be used for entering goods into any of the 27 countries of the

SAMPLE EU SAD (SINGLE ADMINISTRATIVE DOCUMENT)

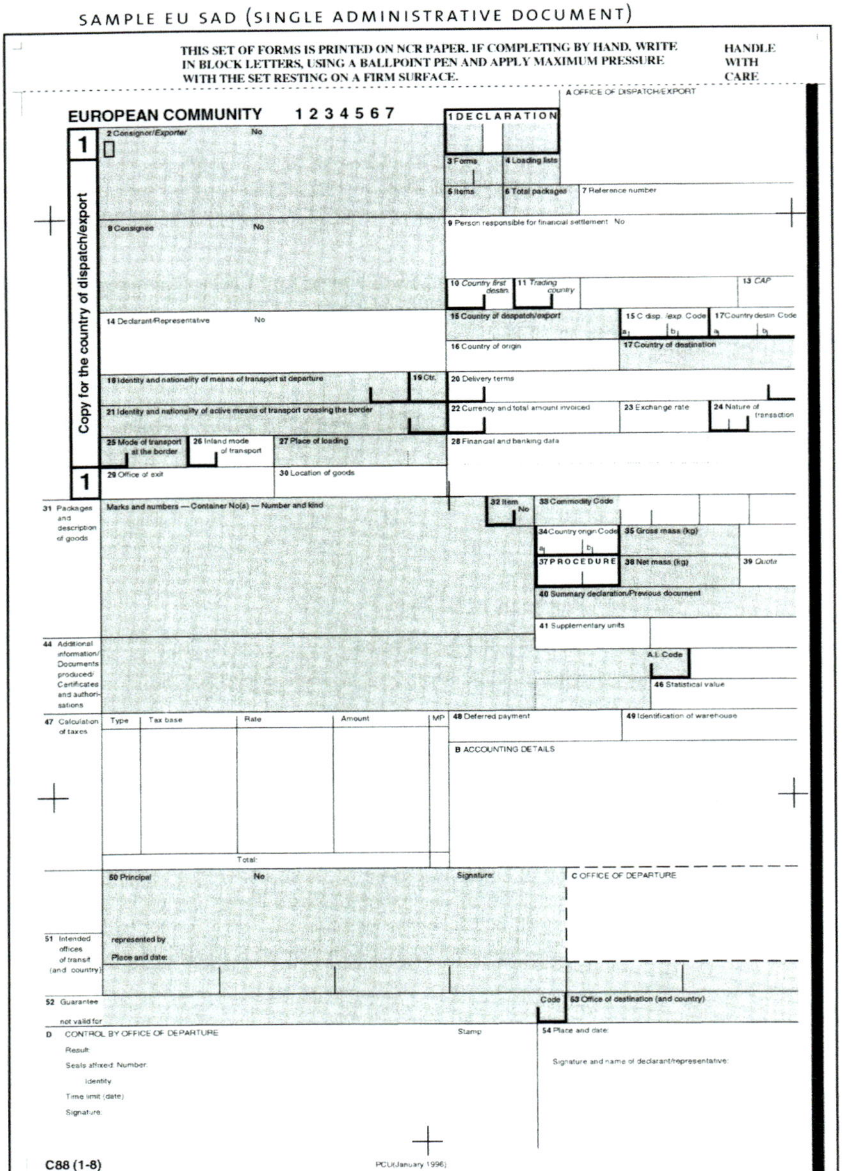

THIS SET OF FORMS IS PRINTED ON NCR PAPER. IF COMPLETING BY HAND, WRITE IN BLOCK LETTERS, USING A BALLPOINT PEN AND APPLY MAXIMUM PRESSURE WITH THE SET RESTING ON A FIRM SURFACE.

HANDLE WITH CARE

A OFFICE OF DISPATCH/EXPORT

EUROPEAN COMMUNITY 1 2 3 4 5 6 7

1 DECLARATION

Copy for the country of dispatch/export

1

2 Consignor/Exporter No

3 Forms

4 Loading lists

5 Items

6 Total packages

7 Reference number

8 Consignee No

9 Person responsible for financial settlement No

10 Country first destin.

11 Trading country

13 CAP

14 Declarant/Representative No

15 Country of dispatch/export

15 C disp. /exp. Code a b

17 Country destin. Code a b

16 Country of origin

17 Country of destination

18 Identity and nationality of means of transport at departure

19 Ctr.

20 Delivery terms

21 Identity and nationality of active means of transport crossing the border

22 Currency and total amount invoiced

23 Exchange rate

24 Nature of transaction

25 Mode of transport at the border

26 Inland mode of transport

27 Place of loading

28 Financial and banking data

1

29 Office of exit

30 Location of goods

31 Packages and description of goods

Marks and numbers — Container No(s) — Number and kind

32 Item No

33 Commodity Code

34 Country origin Code a b

35 Gross mass (kg)

37 PROCEDURE

38 Net mass (kg)

39 Quota

40 Summary declaration/Previous document

41 Supplementary units

44 Additional information/ Documents produced/ Certificates and authorisations

A.I. Code

46 Statistical value

47 Calculation of taxes

Type | Tax base | Rate | Amount | MP

Total:

48 Deferred payment

49 Identification of warehouse

B ACCOUNTING DETAILS

50 Principal No

Signature:

C OFFICE OF DEPARTURE

represented by

Place and date:

51 Intended offices of transit (and country)

52 Guarantee not valid for

Code

53 Office of destination (and country)

D CONTROL BY OFFICE OF DEPARTURE

Stamp

54 Place and date:

Result:

Seals affixed: Number:

identity:

Time limit (date):

Signature:

Signature and name of declarant/representative:

C88 (1-8)

PCU(January 1996)

Figure 12.10 Comparative Law: Single Administrative Document.

EU. Once imported into one of the countries, the goods may be freely shipped throughout the EU.

Prior to exporting, manufacturers have to consider product the suggested or required certifications needed for import to the EU. Certifications relate to conformity (testing and certification) that would comply with EU regulatory requirements. For the majority of exported products, compliance with EU regulations is visibly attested to by the placement of CE marking on the product. The **CE mark** (*Conformité Européenne*) certifies that a product has met EU health, safety, and environmental requirements. A manufacturer only needs to go through the CE certification process once. With appropriate certification, goods travel freely within the borders of the Common Market. The process of obtaining a CE mark is shown in Figure 12.11 *Doing Business Internationally*: CE Marking Step-by-Step.

The CE mark is not required by all European countries. However, manufacturers-exporters voluntarily obtain a CE mark as evidence of conformity to EU standards. Most of the countries within the **European Economic Area** (**EEA**), which includes the EU countries, as well as Iceland, Liechtenstein, and Norway, require CE marking. Switzerland and Turkey also require CE marking.

Phytosanitary Inspection Certificate: A certificate issued by the government of the country of export that certifies that the goods being exported have been inspected and are free of harmful pests or plant diseases.

- Find the applicable EU Directive. For example, the Electromagnetic Compatibility (EMC) Directive (2004/108/EC), which provides a guide through the process for CE certification.
- Determine the essential requirements in the Directive.
- Review the Harmonized European standards produced by the European Standardization Organizations (CEN), European Committee for Electrotechnical Standardization (CENELEC), and the European Telecommunications Standards Institute (ETSI).
- Locate **Notified Bodies** (accredited test laboratories). European countries designate companies certified to perform CE compliance certification. The EEA also has **Mutual Recognition Agreements** (MRAs), which are bilateral agreements that recognize testing and certifications from other countries. Notified Bodies certify that a product meets all the applicable EU requirements. The conformity assessment procedure results in a **Declaration of Conformity**. An example is provided in Figure 12.12 **Doing Business Internationally**: "Declaration of Conformity."

Figure 12.11 Doing Business Internationally: CE Marking Step-by-Step.

Manufacturer: XYZ Corp. 325 Grassy Knoll Garden City, New York Telephone No. (516) 555-3333 Product: Walk-Behind Lawn Mower (3.5 HP) Model No. 3.5L Serial Number 350000-360000 The undersigned hereby declares, on behalf of the XYZ Corp. of Garden City, New York, that the above-referenced product, to which this declaration relates, is in conformity with the provisions of: Council Directive 2006/42/EC (May 17, 2006) on the Approximation of the Laws of the Member States Relating to Machinery; Council Directive 2004/108/EC (December 15, 2004) on Electromagnetic Compatibility;	List European standards used Council Directive 2006/95/EC (December 12, 2006) on Low Voltage Equipment Safety; List European standards used Council Directive 2000/14/EEC amended by Directive 2005/88/EC (June 17, 2006) about noise limits and labelling requirements machines intended for use outdoors. The Technical Construction File required by this Directive is maintained at the corporate headquarters of XYZ, Inc., 325 Grassy Knoll, Garden City, New York. ____________________ Joseph P. Glass Vice President–Design Engineering

Figure 12.12 Doing Business Internationally: Declaration of Conformity.

In sum, CE marking provides product access to 33 European countries (including Turkey) with a population of nearly 600 million. Unfortunately, there is no comprehensive list of the products that require a CE mark. Therefore, it is the manufacturer's responsibility to determine if a product requires a CE marking.

Inspection Certificates

Inspection certificates satisfy import standards and information requirements. The type of certificate varies depending on the type of the good: Certificate of Inspection (verifying amount and description of the goods); Phytosanitary Certificate (plant products); Safety Test Certificate (toys, automobiles, electrical products); Quality Certificate (all sorts of products); Dangerous Goods Certificate; and Sterilization Certificate (packaging materials).

The types and numbers of certificates required vary depending on the product and the country of import. Table 12.3 *Doing Business Internationally*: "Certifications for Import" lists some of the certificates required by countries.

Table 12.3 *Doing Business Internationally*: Certifications for Import.

Certificate	*Description*	*Countries*
Analysis	Food, drugs, & cosmetics	Nigeria, Chile (foodstuffs)
Composition	Used food and clothing	Greece
Disinfection	Coffee sacks; shaving brushes; goods and clothing	Colombia (sacks), Egypt (brushes), Greece (clothing)
Free Sale	Goods are freely sold in country of origin	Argentina, Mexico, Nigeria, Saudi Arabia

(*Continued*)

Table 12.3 (Continued)

Certificate	*Description*	*Countries*
Halal	Certified by Islamic Center	Saudi Arabia, United Arab Emirates
Health	Meat products	Hong Kong, India, Indonesia (fruits & potatoes), Israel & Japan (textiles), Malaysia, Netherlands, Norway (pickled meat), Pakistan (no swine content)
Kosher	Food products	Israel
Microbiological	Products with microorganisms	Mexico
Pharmaceutical	Registration	Hungary
Textile and Footwear	Certify origin	Egypt/Peru
Wood Products	Certifies treatment or fumigation of wood	New Zealand, China (wood packaging), UK, Austria, Belgium, Finland, France, Germany, Egypt, Peru
Wine & Whiskey	Certifies type & country of origin	Austria, Belgium, Finland, France, Germany, Malaysia, Peru, Brazil

Labeling and Marking Requirements

The importer–buyer specifies required marks that must appear on the cargo. Products require numerous markings for shipment. Exporters need to put the following markings on cartons to be shipped: shipper's mark; country of origin; weight (pounds and kilograms); number of packages and size of cases (inches and centimeters); handling marks (international pictorial symbols); cautionary markings (this side up or use no hooks); port of entry; labels for hazardous materials (universal symbols); and ingredients (language of the destination country).

Chapter Summary

1. A number of methods of exporting and importing carry a high risk to one or both of the contracting parties. These include open account, cash in advance, and consignment sales.
2. The exporter often prepares a *pro forma* invoice or price quotation to calculate its selling price. It is vital that this price incorporates all the additional expenses related to the international sale of goods.
3. Many of the risks of exporting–importing—seller's risk of nonpayment and buyer's risk of nondelivery—are mitigated by the documentary collections transaction. Documentary collections change the sale of goods transaction into a sale of documents. The bill of lading is the key title document that

allows for this to happen. The bill of lading is obtained by the exporter and is packaged with other required documents. The documents are then transmitted using commercial banks to the importer in exchange for payment (while the goods are in transit).

4. The standard bill of lading is either an ocean bill of lading or a multimodal bill of lading. The common ocean bill of lading will be "negotiable, on-board, and clean." The buyer should demand delivery of a "full set" (all copies) of the bill of lading.
5. A bank draft (bill of exchange) is one of the key documents since it is the means by which the banks process the payment to the exporter. A collections transaction that requires immediate payment on the delivery of the documents is referred to as a Cash against Documents transaction, which requires the use of a sight draft. If payment is not to be made until sometime after the documents are presented and accepted by the importer, a time draft is required. This type of transaction is referred to as a Documents against Acceptance transaction. The difference between a documentary draft and a regular check is that the exporter is both the drawer and beneficiary of the draft.
6. In negotiating a sales contract, the buyer (importer) will require that the exporter prepare and obtain numerous documents. Some of the more common documents include the bill of lading; bank draft; commercial invoice; export license; inspection certificate; insurance binder; certificate of origin; and packing list.
7. One of the most important terms in international sales contracts is the trade term. Trade terms allocate the costs of freight, insurance, and risk of loss between the exporter and the importer, along with many other responsibilities, such as obtaining export licenses, loading the goods for transport, import clearance and the payment of tariffs, and the loading and unloading of the goods. There are 11 internationally recognized trade terms called Incoterms 2020, which are published by the International Chamber of Commerce.
8. Incoterms 2020 are divided into four groups: ex-works; F; C; and D. The ex-works term is the most pro-seller term, while the DDP (Delivered Duty Paid) is the most pro-buyer term. F and C terms are shipment contracts. F terms allocate the costs and insurance of transport to the buyer, and the risk of loss transfers at the time of shipment. C terms allocate the costs of freight, and sometimes the cost of insurance, to the seller, but the risk of loss passes at the time of shipment. Under the D terms, the seller is allocated the costs of freight, insurance, and the risk of loss to the point or port of destination. The CIF term is often used by importers who are obtaining bids from companies in different places of the world (outsourcing).
9. Other requirements that exporters of goods to foreign countries need to be aware of are product standards, certifications, and markings mandated by that country.

Key Terms

Air Waybill
Anti-Diversion Clause
Bank Draft
Bill of Exchange
Bill of Lading
Cash Against Document
Cash in Advance
CE Mark
Certificate of Inspection
Certificate of Origin
Clean Bill of Lading
Commercial Invoice
Confirmed Letter of Credit Consignee
Consignment Sale
Consular Invoice
Cost, Insurance, and Freight (CIF)
Cost-plus Method
Destination Contract
Destination Control Statement
Documentary Collections Transaction
Documentary Credit Transaction
Documents against Acceptance
Draft
Drawee
Drawer
Electronic Bill of Lading
European Economic Area
Ex-Works
Export License
Free on Board (FOB)
Incoterms 2020
Insurance Certificate
Marginal Cost Pricing
Mutual Recognition Agreements
Notified Bodies
On-board Bill of Lading
Open Account
Order Bill of Lading
Packing Slip
Payment against Acceptance
Payment against Documents
Phytosanitary Certificate
Pro Forma Invoice
Received-for-Shipment Bill of Lading
Risk of Loss
Risk-Shifting Clause
Shipment Contract
Shipper's Export Declaration
Sight Draft
Straight Bill of Lading
Time Draft
Time-Extension Clause
Trade Term

Chapter Problems

1. A buyer and seller entered into a contract for the sale of widgets, "CIF Belin." A further provision stated that delivery was to be at a "factory in Berlin, Hamburg, or Frankfurt" to be designated by the buyer. The widgets were lost in transit. The buyer refused to pay on the presentation of the documents, arguing that the additional provision had converted the shipment contract to a destination contract. What type of contract was this and why? What advice would you give someone regarding the use of trade terms?
2. You are the purchasing agent for a foreign luggage manufacturer. You are asked to outsource some of the components, including steel strips used in the fabrication of the structural frames of the larger pieces of luggage. Your company's manufacturing plant is located in Chicago, Illinois. Your research finds that the companies best able to supply the strips are located in

Windsor, Canada; São Paulo, Brazil; and Padang, Indonesia. In asking for price quotations, what types of documents should you require? From your perspective, which trade term should be used in the price quotations?

3. You are a manufacturer of precision industrial tools and parts based in Edmonton, Canada. You have been contacted by a manufacturer in Budapest, Hungary, to begin supplying it with an assortment of your products. Using Incoterms 2020, prepare a *pro forma* invoice with three different shipping options. For each option (Incoterm), itemize the costs and relative responsibilities of the two parties. Consider how you will get the goods from Edmonton to Budapest. What modes of transport will need to be utilized? Who can you contact for information needed to prepare the invoice?
4. An export contract required that the seller provide: "a full set of three original clean on-board bills of lading." Instead, the seller presented a full set of three clean on-board bills of lading but only one was marked "Original." The other two bills of lading were marked "Duplicate" and "Triplicate." Can the buyer reject the bills of lading as not conforming to the documentary requirements of the contract?
5. A foreign buyer negotiates with a foreign exporter for goods to be shipped out of a foreign port. To protect itself from fraud in the transaction, the buyer requires that the exporter provide an inspection certificate as one of the documents to be presented for payment. When the documents were presented for payment, the buyer noticed that the date on the inspection certificate was later than the shipment date on the bill of lading. The certificate failed to state when the inspection occurred. Can the buyer refuse payment due to this discrepancy?
6. What is the legal status of Incoterms? Is it a law?
7. What are the main differences between the FOB, CIF, and DDP Incoterms?
8. What Incoterms are only used for ocean transport?
9. What right of inspection does a buyer have under the CIF Incoterm?
10. Write out the words for the Incoterms acronyms:

EXW ______________________________

FCA ______________________________

FOB ______________________________

FAS ______________________________

CIF ______________________________

CFR ______________________________

CIP ______________________________

CPT ______________________________

DAP ______________________________

DPU ______________________________

DDP ______________________________

Internet Exercises

1. You are unsure of what trade term to use in negotiating an export contract. You are willing to be responsible for the loading and shipping costs to the port of destination, along with the cost of unloading, but do not want to be responsible for import and customs clearance. What Incoterm would best serve your needs? See http://export.gov/faq/eg_main_023922.asp.
2. Review the charts—"Incoterms 2020: Responsibility Matrix for Contract of Sale" and Incoterms 2020: "Point of Delivery and Transport of Risks"—found at https://oceanair.net/resources_trashed/incoterms-2020.
3. Select a country and research the documentary requirements for the importation of goods into that country. Such information can be obtained from the following sources: (1) U.S. Department of Commerce; (2) foreign government websites, especially consulate sites; (3) *Bureau of National Affairs Export Shipping Manual*; and (4) National Council on International Trade Documentation (NCITD).
4. Check the services and types of e-documents provided through the Bolero Project at www.bolero.net.

Notes

1 *The Delfini*, 1 *Lloyd's Law Report* 252, 268 (1990).
2 2000 U.S. App. LEXIS 11573 (9th Cir. 2000).
3 Bolero at http://www.bolero.net.
4 Uniform Customs and Practices for Documentary Credits as published by the International Chamber of Commerce (UCP).
5 Examples of risk-shifting clauses include arbitration, forum selection, choice of law, *force majeure*, and liquidated damages clauses.
6 UCC § 2-321(2).
7 UCC § 2-320, Comment 14.
8 462 So.2d 1178 (Fl. Ct. Appeals 1985).
9 See CISG Article 67 ("handing the goods over to the first carrier") when the contract envisions carriage of goods and Article 69 (when contract requires buyer to pick up goods at seller's place of business).
10 101 F.2d 59 (2d Cir. 1939).
11 See B. Piltz and U. Magnus, "Trade Terms and Incoterms" in L. DiMatteo, A. Janssen, U. Magnus and R. Schulze, *International Sales Law: Contract, Principles, & Practice* (2d ed. 2020).

Chapter 13

International Trade Finance

The importance of the letter of credit is the main topic of this chapter. Chapter 12's review of the documentary collections transactions showed that the seller's risk of nonpayment and the buyer's risk of nondelivery are minimized because the sale of goods transaction is converted into a sale of documents transaction. However, one risk remains in which the buyer fails to purchase the documents. Although the seller retains title (control of the goods), it receives no payment and will incur the additional costs of returning or transshipping the goods in the event it finds an alternative buyer.

The risk of nonpayment is removed through the use of a **documentary credit**. In such a transaction, the buyer obtains from a bank a letter of credit that guarantees payment to the seller. Substituting the credit or guarantee of a bank for that of the buyer eliminates the risk of nonpayment. This chapter will examine three uses of letters of credit in international sales transactions. First, the letter of credit is used as a device to guarantee the buyer's payment obligation to the seller in a documentary transaction. Second, the **standby letter of credit** is used to guarantee a performance obligation (delivery of goods). Third, the letter of credit is used to help finance the exporting or importing of goods.

Documentary Letter of Credit

Letters of credit have been called the lifeblood of commerce. Their origins in international transactions are traced to the bankers in Imperial Rome, ancient Greece, Phoenicia, early Egypt, and Renaissance Europe. These simple instruments have survived because of their inherent reliability, convenience, economy, and flexibility. In initial transactions with a new or unknown business party,

DOI: 10.4324/9781003469230-16

securing payment is a crucial concern. A letter of credit adds a bank's promise to that of the foreign buyer to pay for the goods. For a list of the terminology relating to documentary credits and their use in trade finance, see Figure 13.1 *Focus on Transactions*: "Definitions of Key Letter of Credit and Finance Terms."

The method of payment and the requirement that the buyer provide a letter of credit to guarantee payment in an international sale of goods is, of course, a matter for the parties to negotiate. Equally important is for the contract to clearly state the parties' intention as to the type of letter of credit to be provided. Figure 13.2 shows a checklist of characteristics of the letter of credit that should be stated in the sales contract.

The letters of credit are presumed to be irrevocable unless stated otherwise. Notice that the title states "documentary credit" instead of letter of credit. This

Account Party: The party requesting or applying for the letter of credit from a bank.
Advising Bank: A bank in the beneficiary's country through which the issuing bank communicates the credit to the beneficiary—sometimes referred to as the correspondent or nominating bank.
Back-to-Back Letter of Credit: This term is used when a third bank agrees to issue a second letter of credit at the request of the beneficiary using the first credit as collateral. The second credit is often used to pay or secure the beneficiary's suppliers.
Beneficiary Party: The party for which favor the letter of credit is issued such as the exporter (seller) in an international sale of goods transaction.
Confirming Bank: The bank in the beneficiary's country that further guarantees the issuing bank's commitment to pay the letter of credit.
Documentary Collection: The use of the banking system for an exporter to transfer documents to purchaser and to receive payment. The bank does not transfer the documents to the purchaser unless the purchaser makes payment or accepts a draft. The bank does not act as a guarantor of payment as in the documentary credit transaction.
Documentary Credit (letter of credit): An instrument requiring a bank to pay a sum of money to the beneficiary against the presentation of documents stipulated in the letter of credit. Used most commonly as a payment mechanism for export sales.
Factoring: The exporter sells its rights to receive payment to a factoring company. The factoring company discounts the amount of the payment owed to the exporter in order to produce the desired rate of return. Used in short-term financing.
Forfaiting: The use of a draft or promissory note given by the purchaser (guaranteed by purchaser's bank) to the exporter to obtain nonrecourse financing. The terms are negotiated in advance so that the exporter is assured of payment before shipping the goods. The importer assumes the costs of discounting the note or draft. Used in long-term financing.
Red Clause Financing: This is where the seller–exporter is allowed to receive an advance on the letter of credit prior to presenting the required documents. The red clause represents a form of unsecured financing offered by the purchaser to a trusted exporter.
Standby Letter of Credit: A type of credit issued as a guarantee against default by one of the parties to the contract. Generally used to guarantee the performance (not payment) of one of the parties and paid only upon default (nonperformance), it acts as a standby. Alternative devices that serve the same purpose are the bank guarantee and the performance bond.
Transferable Credit: The beneficiary party, in whole or part, can transfer a transferable credit to secondary beneficiaries. An exporter may transfer the credit in order to finance the manufacture or purchase of the goods to be exported. The UCP requires that the original credit expressly provide for transferability. If it does not, the credit will be presumed to be nontransferable.
Uniform Customs and Practices for Documentary Credits (UCP): The international rules for letters of credit published by the International Chamber of Commerce in Paris. The current version is known as the UCP 600.

Figure 13.1 Focus on Transactions: Definitions of Key Letter of Credit and Finance Terms.

Confirmed _____ Unconfirmed_____
Place of issue (if applicable): ______ Place of confirmation: _______
Credit available:
Partial shipments: _____ Transhipment: _____
_____By payment at sight
_____By acceptance of draft at _____days
Date on which the documentary credit must be notified to seller ________days before date of delivery

Figure 13.2 Irrevocable Documentary Credit.

phrase is used because the letter of credit in exporting–importing is heavily dependent on the presentation of documents provided by the seller.

The sophisticated seller–exporter will require a confirmed letter of credit, which requires that payment be guaranteed by the issuing bank (buyer's bank) and a bank located near the seller (seller's bank). The second bank is called the confirming bank since it is co-guaranteeing payment along with the issuing bank. This allows the seller to obtain payment sooner upon delivery of documents to the confirming bank and to bring a claim against the local bank in the event the credit is not honored. The credit may also allow for partial payments upon partial shipments.

The credit also must state the time of payment—by payment at sight or a number of days after acceptance. In the first case, the documents are delivered to the issuing bank (at sight) and the documents are given to the buyer upon payment. The second option is used when the seller agrees to give the buyer additional time for payment. In this case, a number is placed in the blank before the word "days"; the buyer is then required to make payment within that number of days after receiving the documents (see Figure 13.2: "Time Draft"). Note, however, that the buyer has to "accept" the documents and the bank draft at sight before receiving the documents. This acceptance creates an independent obligation (a negotiable instrument) to pay so that if the buyer later finds the documents to be nonconforming, it still must honor its independent obligation to pay the draft within the time provided. The final line of the time draft provides the amount of time for the buyer to obtain the letter of credit and for the bank to notify the seller of its issuance. If the buyer delays in obtaining the credit past the time allowed, then the seller may reject the credit and hold the buyer in breach of contract.

The letter of credit (bank guarantee) requirement in an export contract produces a number of contractual relationships. The purchaser enlists the services of its commercial bank by way of a letter of credit application. If the bank accepts the application, it issues the letter of credit. The application forms the basis of the contract between the applicant or account party (buyer) and the **issuing bank**. Once the bank issues the letter of credit to the exporter (**beneficiary party**), the letter of credit itself fixes the issuing bank's obligations to the beneficiary party. Most often an intermediary bank located near the seller or the port of shipment is used to process the documents. If that bank confirms the letter of credit, then two additional contractual relationships are formed: Between the **confirming bank** and the beneficiary and between the confirming bank and the issuing bank. See Figure 13.3 *Focus on Transactions*: "Confirmed Letter of Credit Transaction." If the intermediary bank elects not to confirm or guarantee the letter, then it is referred to as an **advising bank**. It acts merely as a conduit for transmitting documents and payments and has no independent legal obligation to the beneficiary party.

The buyer needs to negotiate in the sales contract all the required documents it will require the seller to obtain and supply. Prior to entering a sales contract, the importer should seek advice from a **customs broker** regarding import regulations and the documents needed for import purposes. It is important for the buyer to carefully list the documentary requirements and the description

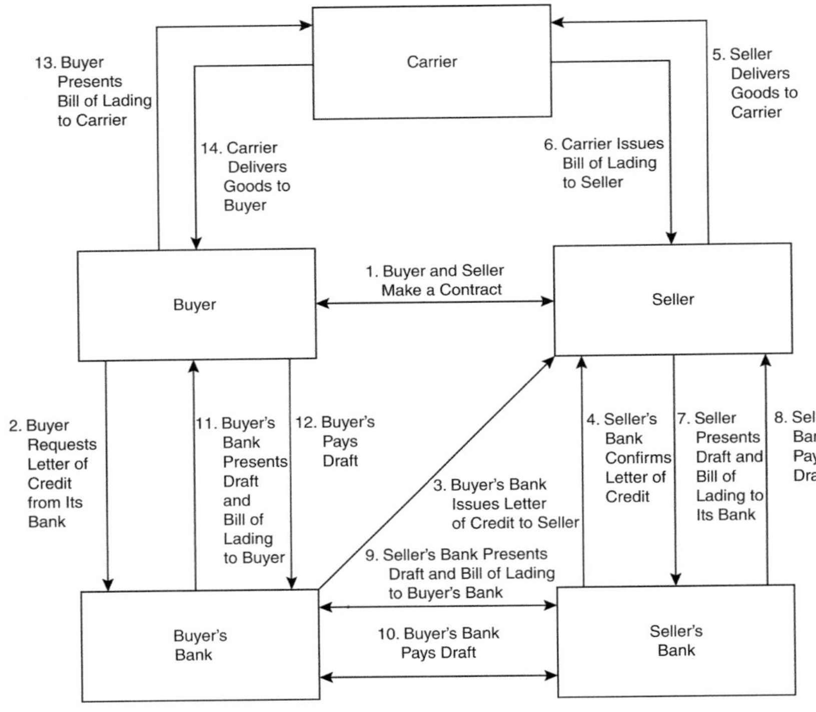

Figure 13.3 Focus on Transactions: Confirmed Letter of Credit Transaction.

of the goods on the letter of credit application. A review of the International Chamber of Commerce (ICC) forms and *Guidance Notes*[1] help the purchaser draft instructions to the issuing bank and the beneficiary (seller) in preparing the stipulated documents.

The typical letter of credit transaction follows a common chronology: (1) seller and buyer enter a sales contract; (2) buyer arranges for its bank to open a letter of credit; (3) buyer's bank prepares and sends to the corresponding bank (seller's bank) an irrevocable letter of credit, including instructions to the seller concerning required documents; (4) buyer's bank confirms the letter of credit; (5) seller arranges with the freight forwarder for the delivery of the goods to the appropriate port; (6) common carrier issues the bill of lading to seller; (7) seller presents documents to the seller's bank (confirming bank); (8) if the documents are conforming, the confirming bank processes the draft and pays the seller; (9) seller's bank forwards the draft and other documents to the buyer's bank (issuing bank); (10) if the documents are in order, buyer's bank reimburses the seller's bank for payment on the draft; (11) buyer's bank presents the documents to the buyer; (12) buyer pays on the draft; (13) buyer presents the bill of lading to the common carrier; and (14) common carrier delivers the goods to the buyer.

The original letter of credit is forwarded through the Society for Worldwide Interbank Financial Telecommunication or SWIFT[2] to the exporter's bank. The exporting bank then advises the exporter (beneficiary party) that the letter of credit has been issued. If required, the exporter's bank may also confirm the letter of credit. In order to ensure that the letter of credit will be confirmed by a local bank, the exporter should negotiate clear language in the contract. The following clause provides for an irrevocable, confirmed letter of credit:

> *The Letter of Credit is to be drawn in IRREVOCABLE form and be subject to the Uniform Customs and Practices for Documentary Credits (UCP) as published and updated from time to time by the International Chamber of Commerce. The Letter of Credit must be advised through and CONFIRMED by a bank located at the port of shipment acceptable to the seller. It must be PAYABLE AT THE COUNTERS OF THE CONFIRMING BANK.*

The above clause expressly makes the UCP the choice of law and requires payment upon presentation of the documents to the confirming bank. This is especially important to the exporter wanting to receive payment quickly. If the letter of credit does not expressly state "payable at the counters of the confirming bank" the confirming bank may withhold payment until the documents are reviewed and approved by the issuing bank. To expedite the receipt of funds, wire transfers are used. The UCP is incorporated by reference into most banks' application and letter of credit forms. Upon receiving a letter of credit, the exporter should carefully compare the letter's terms with the terms of the exporter's *pro forma* invoice or price quotation. The exporter must provide the required documentation, including showing that the goods were shipped by the date specified in the letter of credit, or it risks not being paid. Exporters should check with their freight forwarders to make sure that no unusual conditions have arisen that would delay shipment.

Following approval by the beneficiary (exporter) of the letter of credit, the exporter's freight forwarder books shipment with a common carrier. The **freight forwarder** coordinates the movement of the goods, secures the bill of lading, and completes other documentation as required in the letter of credit. Generally, to initiate a relationship with a freight forwarder, the exporter completes a **power of attorney** form. The power of attorney allows the freight forwarder to complete documents in the name of the exporter.

The original letter of credit and the shipping documents are presented to the advising or confirming bank. If the bank has confirmed the letter of credit, then it will review the documents and pay the exporter. The documents are then sent to the issuing bank with a claim for reimbursement. Upon its approval of the documents, the issuing bank will debit the importer's bank account for the amount of the letter of credit, along with any charges due and remit payment to the confirming bank. Following a review of the documents and payment, the importer may instruct the bank to forward the documents to a customs broker. The customs broker secures the release of the goods by clearing them through customs. The customs broker will require, among other items, a commercial invoice and a properly endorsed bill of lading.

A letter of credit is especially useful when reliable credit information about a foreign buyer is difficult to obtain. Another use of the letter of credit is that it allows the seller to securely defer payment by the buyer. The letter of credit may be used where payment is through a **sight** or **time draft**. A draft is simply a check drawn on the account of the purchaser. A sight draft allows the seller to "cash" the draft immediately on presenting the documents to the bank or purchaser. A time draft, like a post-dated check, can be cashed sometime after the presentation of the documents, most commonly 30, 60, or 90 days. The draft may be sued upon independently under negotiable instruments law.

Payment under a documentary letter of credit is based on documents, not on the terms of sale or the condition of the goods sold. The bank responsible for making payment verifies that the documents conform to the requirements in the letter of credit. When they are not as required, a **discrepancy** exists, which must be cured before payment can be made. Common inconsistencies include different descriptions of the goods or quantities stated in the commercial invoice, packing slips, inspection certificate, and other documents. Inconsistencies may result in the custom authorities performing additional inspections of the goods and delaying the importation of the goods.

Figure 13.4 *Focus on Transactions*: "Documentary Letter of Credit" provides an example of a typical "documentary letter of credit." The important things to note include that it: (1) states an expiration date as required by the UCP 600 (120 days from date of issue; that being September 1, 2015); (2) states that it is irrevocable (would be implied if not stated); (3) states that it is transferable (would not be implied if not stated); (4) notes that payment is at sight (cash against documents); (5) provides a list of six documents, along with the sight draft, to be presented by the seller–exporter; (6) provides for payment by wire transfer; (7) states that the governing regulation is the UCP 600 (would be implied if not stated); and (8) selects the choice of law as the UK.

Importers that repeatedly require the issuance of letters of credit and who have strong banking ties often obtain a **revolving letter of credit**, which offers the convenience of requesting letters of credit without the need to apply for each one individually.

Face Value: $10,000,000 (Ten Million USD)
Date of Issue: September 1, 2015
Place of Issue: Bank of Monrovia
Branch of Issue: 1 Madison Avenue, Danubia, Monrovia
Expiration Date: 120 days from date of issue
Letter of Credit Number: 153676-777789
Beneficiary Party: ABC Exporting, Münsterland, Germany
We, Bank of Monrovia, Branch 1 Madison, Avenue, have opened an unconditional, irrevocable, transferable Letter of Credit Number: 153676-777789 in favor of Beneficiary ABC Exporting in the amount of USD $10,000,000 (Ten Million US Dollars) valid for a period of 120 days from date of issue September 1, 2015. This letter of credit is effective immediately and expires at our office in 120 days of issuance.
Funds under this Letter of Credit against a sight draft drawn on us and demanding payment under "Letter of Credit Number 153676-777789." Along with the sight draft the following documents must be provided:

1 Commercial Invoice (description to be identical to the description provided herein)
2 Clean Ocean Bill of Lading (marked freight prepaid)
3 Certificate of Insurance (in an amount equal to the amount stated on the Commercial Invoice and date prior to the date of the Bill of Lading)
4 Inspection Certificate (issued by the Association of Widget Manufacturers International and dated prior to the loading of the multimodal container)
5 Packing List
6 Consular Invoice issued by the Government of the Country of Monrovia

The Bank of Monrovia will pay under this Letter of Credit with its own funds by wire transfer to the account noted in the Sight Draft. Payment under this Letter of Credit will be free of any fees and charges of any kind. All charges are to be drawn from the account of the Applicant.

This Letter of Credit is governed by the UCP 600 (Uniform Customs and Practices for Documentary Credits) as published by the International Chamber of Commerce in Paris, France. The laws of the United Kingdom shall govern all other matters not governed by the UCP 600. For and On Behalf of the Bank of Monrovia ______________ Authorized Bank Officer.

Figure 13.4 Focus on Transactions: Documentary Letter of Credit.

Revolving Letter of Credit: This arrangement allows the buyer to obtain multiple letters of credit up to a stated limit. After existing letters of credit expire, the amount available for future letters of credit is restored. This arrangement is highly efficient for a buyer who is doing multiple contracts at a time. The buyer can get an immediate issuance of a letter of credit instead of having to apply for each individual letter of credit.

The *Voest-Alpine International v. Chase Manhattan Bank* case that follows describes a typical letter of credit transaction and introduces the **rule of strict compliance.** The rule of strict compliance is the standard by which banks review documents being presented for payment under a letter of credit. The UCP allows a bank to reject any nonconformity or discrepancy between the documents being reviewed and the requirements stated in the letter of credit. The rule of strict compliance should not be confused with the independence principle or **facial compliance rule.** The facial compliance rule refers to the principle that a bank's only obligation in a letter of credit transaction is to review documents. Under the facial compliance rule, a bank is free to disregard any information, such as fraud in the transaction that comes from a source outside of the documents or to review documents not listed in the letter of credit.

Voest-Alpine International v. Chase Manhattan Bank

707 F.2d 680 (2d Cir. 1983)

Circuit Judge. Originally devised to function in international trade, a letter of credit reduced the risk of nonpayment in cases where credit was extended to strangers in distant places. Interposing a known and solvent institution's (commercial banks) credit for that of a foreign buyer accomplished this objective. A typical letter of credit transaction, as the case before us illustrates, involves three separate and independent relationships—an underlying sale of goods contract between buyer and seller, an agreement between a bank and its customer (buyer or account party) in which the bank issues a letter of credit, and the bank's resulting engagement to pay the beneficiary (seller) providing that certain documents presented to the bank conform [strict compliance rule] with the terms and conditions of the credit issued on its customer's behalf.

Significantly, the bank's payment obligation to the beneficiary is primary, direct, and completely independent of any claims that may arise in the underlying sale of goods transaction [independence principle or facial compliance rule]. Viewed in this light it becomes clear that the doctrine of strict compliance with the terms of the letter of credit functions to protect the bank that carries the absolute obligation to pay the beneficiary. Adherence to this rule ensures that banks, dealing only in documents, will be able to act quickly, thus enhancing the letter of credit's fluidity. Literal compliance with the credit is also essential so as not to impose an obligation upon the bank that it did not undertake and jeopardize the bank's right to indemnity from its customer. Documents nearly the same as those required are not good enough.

MSTC, an agency of the Indian government, contracted to buy 7,000 tons of scrap steel from Voest, a trading subsidiary of an Austrian company. MSTC asked the Bank of Baroda to issue two letters of credit—one for $810,600 and the other for $604,950—to Voest to assure payment for the steel. The credits were expressly made subject to the Uniform Customs and Practice for Documentary Credits (UCP). Chase Manhattan Bank (Chase) would serve as a confirming bank, independently obligated on the credit.

The terms and conditions of the credits required proof of shipment, evidenced by clean-on-board bills of lading; certificates of inspection indicating the date of shipment; and weight certificates issued by an independent inspector. The date of shipment was set before January 31. Sometime between February 2 and February 6, the cargo was partially loaded aboard the *M/V Atra* at New Haven. Unfortunately, the *Atra* never set sail for India. A mutiny by the ship's crew disabled the ship and rendered it unseaworthy. On February 13, two days before the expiration date on the credits, Voest presented three drafts with the required documentation to Chase. The bills of lading indicating receipt on board of the scrap metal were signed and dated January 31 by the captain of the *Atra.* The weight and inspection certificates accompanying the drafts revealed, however, that the cargo was loaded aboard the *Atra* sometime between February 2 and February 6. Despite this glaring discrepancy, Chase advised the Bank of Baroda on February 25 that the drafts and documents presented to it by Voest conformed to the terms and conditions set forth in the letters of credit.

The Bank of Baroda apparently looked at the documents with more care than Chase. It promptly advised Chase that the documents did not comply with the requirements of the letters of credit, that it would therefore not honor the drafts, and that it would hold the documents at Chase's disposal. When Voest presented the drafts for payment on July 30, Chase refused to honor them. Voest thereupon instituted the present lawsuit. It asserted that Chase waived the right to demand strict compliance with the terms of the credits and therefore wrongfully dishonored the drafts. Voest alleged that regardless of whether the documents were conforming Chase was liable on the drafts because it accepted them.

Acceptance is the drawee's (bank) signed engagement to honor the draft as presented and that it "must be written on the draft." Requiring written acceptance on the draft is aligned with negotiable instrument law that prohibits oral acceptances. The present record is silent as to whether Chase actually accepted the drafts by proper notation on them. Presentation of fraudulent documents to a bank by a beneficiary subverts not only the purposes which letters of credit are designed to serve but also the entire transaction at hand in particular. Falsified documents are the same as no documents at all. We affirm the judgment in favor of the Bank of Baroda. All parties have acknowledged that the documents tendered to Chase did not conform to the established terms and conditions of the letters of credit. The Bank of Baroda, as the issuing bank, was entitled to a strict compliance review.

Case Highlights

- A typical letter of credit transaction comprises a number of contractual relationships, including between the buyer (account party) and its bank (issuing bank), between the issuing bank and the seller (beneficiary), and between the issuing bank and a corresponding bank (confirming bank)
- A confirming bank owes an independent obligation to the beneficiary party
- The rule of strict compliance protects banks by allowing them to reject documents because of discrepancies
- A bank is liable for payment if it "accepts" a draft. However, legal acceptance of a draft may be done only by a written endorsement on the draft.

A number of expiration dates exist in most international export transactions. First, is the expiration date inserted on the letter of credit. The documents in *Voest-Alpine International v. Chase* were presented before the expiration of the letters of credit. However, the documents were untimely, because the letter of credit requirements stated that an on-board bill of lading had to be acquired on or before January 31. The UCP also provides a second expiration date known as the **21-day rule**, which requires the bill of lading, and accompanying documents, be presented to the bank within 21 days from their procurement. If the exporter obtains the bill of lading and delays presentation past 21 days, then the letter of credit expires even though the written expiration date on the letter has not passed. The UCP rules will be discussed in greater depth later in this chapter.

The second item highlighted in the above case is the **bill of exchange** or **draft**.[3] The draft is a collection instrument that acts very much like a check. It is the mechanism by which a payment is processed through the banking system. When a seller presents documents for payment on a letter of credit, it presents the bank with a draft drawn on the letter of credit. The draft is an order to the drawee (bank) to pay. The difference between a draft and an ordinary check is that in the documentary draft the seller acts as both the drawer and the payee.

As previously discussed, there are two general types of drafts used in export transactions—the sight draft and the time draft. A sight draft requires payment immediately upon the presentation of the documents. A draft in which the time of payment is not specified is deemed payable at sight. If a period of time is entered into the blank (following or after) "Sight Days After," then the draft would be converted into a time draft. See Figure 13.5 *Focus on Transactions*: "Time Draft" for an example of a time draft. Behind Citibank's "Acceptance" stamp there is the number 120, which is part of a line that reads "120 days after SIGHT," meaning payment is due 120 days after delivery of documents to the bank by the seller.

As noted in Chapter 12, electronic bills of lading and letters of credit are technologically possible. In reality, most sellers still prefer a hard copy of the letter of credit. So although entirely paperless letter of credit transactions are possible, in reality they are not common. However, letter of credit transactions between banks (issuing, confirming, advising) have become purely electronic. For example, an issuing bank will electronically send the letter of credit to the confirming bank. The confirming bank will issue to the beneficiary party (seller) a paper letter of credit or a notice that the letter of credit has been issued. Electronic communications between banks are processed through SWIFT system.

If the exporter wants to extend credit to the buyer, a time draft is used, stating that payment is due within a certain time after the buyer accepts the draft and receives the documents. By signing and writing "accepted" on the draft, the buyer is formally obligated to pay within the stated time. When this is done the draft is called a **trade acceptance** and can be either kept by the exporter until maturity. The acceptance can be sold at a discount prior to maturity on the secondary market or sold to one of the banks involved in the transaction. The amount of the discount (value of a trade acceptance) is dependent on the size and creditworthiness of the company (importer-buyer). **Acceptance** creates an independent obligation on the acceptor (drawee). The independence of the acceptance obligation means that the obligation can be enforced by subsequent holders of the instrument without regard to the buyer's rights under the sales contract. In short, the acceptance is considered to be a negotiable instrument. When a bank accepts a draft, the draft becomes an obligation of the bank known as a **banker's acceptance.** A banker's acceptance is easily resaleable by the seller (beneficiary party). The excerpt from the *Interpane Coatings v. Australia & New Zealand Banking Group* case below describes the use of time drafts and the importance of acceptance.

Interpane Coatings v. Australia & New Zealand Banking Group

732 F. Supp. 909 (N.D. Ill. 1990)

District Judge. Interpane (U.S.) and an Australian entity named McDowell Pacific Pty, Ltd. entered into a contract for the sale of goods where delivery and payment were to be made using bills of exchange (drafts) and bills of lading. Interpane delivered goods to McDowell who then did not pay despite having accepted the goods as well as having endorsed the three bills of exchange. In this action, Interpane seeks to hold ANZ, the collecting bank, liable for its failure to obtain the money from the buyer.

The banks involved in the transaction were ANZ and Swiss Bank. Interpane sent ANZ three bills of exchange accompanied by three bills of lading. The bills of exchange were for payment in 60 days from its acceptance (time drafts) in order to distinguish them from sight drafts, which are payable on sight. If acceptance is required, the collecting bank need only obtain the endorsement of the drawee/buyer before releasing the title documents. By accepting the bills of exchange, the drawee (buyer or buyer's bank) acknowledged the debt and is committed to making payment as required by the bill of exchange. As the designated collecting bank, ANZ had a contractual duty to follow Interpane's collection orders. Interpane alleges that ANZ breached this contractual duty by not obeying its special instructions, which it alleges required ANZ to endorse the bills of exchange as a guarantor, thus converting them into banker's acceptances, before releasing the title documents to McDowell. The court holds in favor of the plaintiff (Interpane).

Case Highlights

- Banks play an intermediary role in effecting the transfer of documents and payments relating to the export transaction
- Documentary collection transactions condition the release of documents on acceptance or payment of the documentary draft by the buyer
- Bills of exchange or drafts are the means by which an exporter obtains payment in an international sale of goods transaction
- Bills of exchange or drafts are orders by the drawer (exporter) to the buyer or buyer's bank (drawee) to pay the exporter (payee). It differs from a check only in that the drawer and the payee are the same party (exporter)
- A time draft is a bill of exchange that requires payment sometime after the buyer accepts the documents.

Uniform Customs and Practices for Documentary Credits (UCP)

The UCP is a set of rules published by the ICC, the most recent compilation of which is the UCP 600.[4] The UCP applies to letters of credit used to guarantee payment to an exporter in a documentary transaction. They may also be used in conjunction with **standby letters of credit** used to guarantee the performance of the exporter. Letters of credit used to guarantee payment to an exporter are called **documentary credits**. This name refers to the fact that payment under the letter of credit is contingent upon the presentation of documents by the exporter.

As discussed earlier, banks have the duty to use reasonable care in examining documents for conformity to the requirements of the letter of credit. If the documents are in compliance, then the bank pays the beneficiary party (exporter) through the letter of credit. The conforming and issuing banks must examine the documents within a reasonable time and notify the parties promptly of any nonconformity (discrepancy). Banks are not liable for accepting forged or false documents under the facial compliance rule. The letter of credit instructions of the account party (buyer) generally requires an on-board bill of lading and that insurance documents be dated prior to the loading of the goods on board the ship. The description of the goods in the commercial invoice must be the same as the one contained in the letter of credit.

The sophisticated importer should become familiar with the requirements and rules of the UCP 600. They have a direct bearing on how the applicant (importer-buyer) completes a letter of credit application. If the applicant places a noncustomary term or instruction in the application, the banks will often disregard that instruction in favor of a default rule found in the UCP 600. The

ICC has developed a number of standard documentary credit forms, along with "Guidance Notes" for their proper use. The ICC forms incorporate the requirements of the UCP.

Terminology and Descriptions

The ICC Guidance Notes warn against the use of broad terminology to describe items of value or amounts. The most important point in filling out the letter of credit forms is to be simple, clear, and precise in drafting the instructions to the bank. The use of words like approximate in association with the amount of the credit or the quantity or unit price of the goods will be automatically translated under Article 30(a). The buyer will have to accept documents that vary the amount of goods as stated in the letter of credit in the range of 10 percent. In order to avoid such a variance, the applicant should state a specific number of packing units or words to the effect that the quantity of the goods specified may exceed or not be less than certain amounts.

A balance should be struck between filling out the letter of credit application completely and not using excessive detail. Excessive detail in the letter of credit application may lead to unnecessary confusion given the different countries and cultures represented in many international transactions. The more detailed the letter of credit, the greater the likelihood of banks finding discrepancies in the documents. The currency of the letter of credit should be designated using the ISO Currency Code, such as USD for U.S. dollars or CNY for Chinese yuan or renminbi (RMB). Abbreviations for geographical designation should be avoided. For example, "UK" should be avoided in favor of "United Kingdom."

The applicant should state the latest date for shipment, dispatch, or taking in charge under the space next to the phrase "not later than" on the credit application. Otherwise, the time limit will be the date of expiration as provided in the UCP. If the applicant uses the phrase "on or about," the UCP defines an acceptable period as five days before or after the specified date. The applicant should specify the period of time when the documents need to be presented following shipment of the goods. If a period is not stipulated, then the UCP sets the period as 21 days from the date of obtaining the bill of lading.

The description of the goods should generally be as brief as possible. The UCP requires only that the commercial invoice reflect the description found on the letter of credit. It states that the description of the goods in the commercial invoice must correspond with the description in the letter of credit. In all other documents, the goods may be described in general terms not inconsistent with the description of the goods in the letter of credit. Therefore, it is advisable to keep the description simple and clear. Article 18(c) reemphasizes that: "The description of the goods, services or performance in a commercial invoice must correspond with that appearing in the credit." However, there is no requirement for a mirror image or an identical description between the letter of credit and the commercial invoice. For example, details of the goods may be stated in a number of areas within the invoice which, when collated together, represents a description of the goods corresponding to that in the letter of credit.

The content of insurance documents is addressed under the UCP. If the applicant fails to state the amount of the insurance to be procured, then the UCP requires an amount equal to CIF value plus 10 percent. If the CIF value cannot be discerned from the documents, then the banks require 110 percent of the amount found in the commercial invoice.

Review and Notice

The UCP 600 changes the rule for the time banks have to review the documents and employs a single notice requirement. The old rule stated that the reviewing bank had to review the documents within a "reasonable time" not exceeding five business days. The new rule rejects the flexibility of the reasonable time standard and adopts the fixed rule that a bank has five days to review the documents. The single notice rule states that a bank need only give one notice of the existence of discrepancies in the documents. If the bank sends a notice that the documents are conforming and subsequently finds discrepancies or sends a notice of discrepancies and subsequently finds additional discrepancies, the bank no longer has the right to give notice of those discrepancies even if the second notice is within the five-day review period.

If a bank accepts nonconforming documents, then it may sue the beneficiary party if it proceeds in a timely fashion. This was the issue in *Habib Bank Ltd. v. Convermat Corp.*[5] In that case, the bank paid against documents that included a bill of lading with a discrepancy in the shipping date. The account party (buyer) subsequently rejected the documents. The bank waited a month before making a claim against the beneficiary party for a return of the monies paid. The court held that the claim was not made in a timely fashion and dismissed the action. Article 16(d) requires the bank to give notice "by expeditious means" and such notice "must state all discrepancies in respect of which the bank refuses the documents." In this case, the bank did not refuse or reject the documents, but only sent notice of nonconformity when it learned of the discrepancy from the account party.

Rule of Strict Compliance

Under the rule of strict compliance, banks are authorized to reject documents even if they are technically in conformity. An example of this is the use of abbreviations or acronyms in the description of goods. Abbreviations or acronyms are commonly used by businesspersons in a given industry. However, banks are not required to know or to investigate trade custom or usage. This was the situation in the historically important English case *of J.H. Rayner & Co. v. Hambros Bank Ltd.*[6] in which the bank rejected a bill of lading that used the notation "CRS" in describing the goods. In the nut industry, CRS is the abbreviation for "Coromandel groundnuts." The letter of credit required that the bill of lading state "Coromandel groundnuts."

The accompanying invoice did use the full name. Nonetheless, the court upheld the bank's right to reject the documents. Two rationales were given.

First, "that even though the description of the goods in the bill of lading was correct in accordance with the custom of trade, the bank could not be held to be affected with a knowledge of the customs of the various trades in which its customers might be concerned." Second, even if the bank possessed knowledge of the trade custom or usage, it must do exactly what its customers require it to do. There may be some unknown reason why the account party (importer) wants the documents to be detailed in a certain way. It is not for the bank to impose common sense to abrogate a specific instruction in the letter of credit. The application of the rule of strict compliance is the issue in *Courtaulds North America v. North Carolina National Bank*.

Courtaulds North America v. North Carolina National Bank

528 F.2d 802 (4th Cir. 1975)

Circuit Judge. A letter of credit with the date of March 21, 1973 was issued by the North Carolina National Bank (NCNB) at the request of and for the account of its customer, Adastra Knitting Mills, Inc. It was issued to the benefit of Courtaulds North America, Inc. for "up to" $135,000 at "60 days date" to cover Adastra's purchases of acrylic yarn from Courtaulds. The life of the credit was extended in June to allow the drafts to be "drawn and negotiated on or before August 15, 1973." The Bank refused to honor a draft for $67,346.77 dated August 13, 1973, for yarn sold and delivered to Adastra. Courtaulds brought this action to recover this sum from the NCNB.

NCNB denied liability on the assertion that the draft did not agree with the conditions in the letter of credit that required the draft be accompanied by a commercial invoice stating "100% acrylic yarn." Instead, the accompanying invoices stated that the goods were "Imported Acrylic Yarn." The lower court held the defendant NCNB liable to Courtaulds for the amount of the draft, interest, and costs. It concluded that the draft complied with the letter of credit when each invoice is read together with the packing lists stapled to it, which stated "Cartons marked: 100% Acrylic." After considering the insistent rigidity of the law and usage of bank credits and acceptances, we must differ with the lower court and uphold the Bank's position.

On August 20, NCNB called Adastra and asked if it would waive the discrepancies. Courtaulds on August 27 sent amended invoices to NCNB, which were received by NCNB on August 27. They referred to the consignment as "100% Acrylic Yarn," and thus would have conformed to the letter of credit had it not expired. NCNB informed Courtaulds that the draft remained unaccepted because of the expiration of the letter of credit: "The only issue presented by the facts of this case is whether the documents tendered by the beneficiary to NCNB were in conformity with the terms of the letter of credit." The letter of credit was subject to the Uniform Customs and Practice for Documentary Credits (UCP). Of particular relevance are UCP Articles 7–9.

Article 7. *Banks must examine all documents with reasonable care to ascertain that they appear, on their face, to be in accordance with the terms and conditions of the credit.*

Article 8. *In documentary credit operations all parties concerned deal in documents and not in goods. If, upon receipt of the documents, the issuing bank considers that they appear on their face not to be in accordance with the terms and conditions of the credit, that bank must determine, on the basis of the documents alone, whether to claim that payment, acceptance, or negotiation was not effected in accordance with the terms and conditions of the credit.*

Article 9. "*Banks ... do [not] assume any liability or responsibility* for the description, ... *quality,... of the goods represented thereby. The description of the goods in the commercial invoice must correspond with the description in the credit. In the remaining documents the goods may be described in general terms.*

The UCP states that the drawee bank is not to be embroiled in disputes between buyers and the sellers, the beneficiary of the credit. The drawee is involved only with documents, not with the merchandise. Its duties and liability are governed exclusively by the terms of the letter, not the terms of the parties' sales contract. The beneficiary must precisely meet the terms of the letter of credit in order to get paid. Failing such compliance there can be no recovery from the drawee. "There is no room for documents which are almost the same, or which will do just as well."

At trial, Courtaulds prevailed on the contention that the invoices in actuality met the specifications of the letter of credit in that the packing lists attached to the invoices disclosed on their faces that the packages contained "cartons marked:—100% acrylic." However, the UCP distinguishes between the "invoice" and the "remaining documents," emphasizing that in the latter the description may be in general terms while the invoice must have a description in (strict) conformity with the credit letter. The Bank was not expected to scrutinize the collateral papers, such as the packing lists. Nor was it permitted to read into the instrument the contemplation or intention of the seller and buyer. The Bank was within its powers in rejecting the invoice as nonconforming. REVERSED

Case Highlights

- Article 7 of the UCP requires that banks review the required documents for facial compliance. Banks are not required to know or to research trade custom or usage
- Article 8 (strict compliance rule) allows banks to reject documents that do not comply on their face
- Article 9 requires that the description of the goods in the commercial invoice must strictly correspond to the description in the letter of credit. Descriptions in other documents may be made with more general terms.

(1) Rule of Facial Compliance

Banks are only required to review documents listed on LOC application; banks are not liable for "fraud in the transaction" (even if aware of the fraud)

(2) Banks Not Required to Know Trade Usage or Technical Terms

Banks not required to know or investigate trade usage, customs, or commercial practices; banks not required to know meanings of abbreviations

(3) Rule of Strict Compliance (Standard of Review)

Banks may reject any "discrepancies" in the documents unless discrepancy is de minimis (unreasonable or bad faith rejection)

(4) LOC Must Have Express Expiration Date

If expiration date is missing, then the LOC is unenforceable

(5) 21-Day Rule

Beneficiary party (seller) must deliver documents within 21 days of obtaining the bill of lading (LOC expires even if express date on LOC has not expired)

(6) Bank Has 5 Days to Review Documents

If the bank fails to review within allotted time, the documents are deemed to be conforming

(7) Presumption of Irrevocability

If LOC is silent, then it is presumed to be irrevocable (Period of time affixed by expiration date or by running of 21-day rule)

(8) Insurance Certificate

Must be dated no later than the date of loading of goods (issuance of bill of lading); must be in an amount of 110 percent of CIF value (unless parties agree otherwise)

(9) Commercial Invoice

Must include exact description of goods as provided on LOC application

(10) LOC is Presumed to be Non-transferable (unless LOC states otherwise)

Figure 13.5 Focus on Transactions: Ten Rules Pertaining to International Letters of Credit (LOC).

In the above case, the result would have been different under the UCP if the letter of credit had not specifically stated that the bill of lading should have a particular description. The UCP requires only that the commercial invoice reflect the description found in the letter of credit. Figure 13.5 *Focus on Transactions*: "Ten Rules Pertaining to International Letters of Credit (LOC)" further summarizes the rules governing letters of credit.

Table 13.1 *Focus on Transactions*: "UCP 600 Rules" reviews some of the rules used in determining the conformity of certain documents and the timeliness of the presentation of the documents.

Table 13.1 *Focus on Transactions*: UCP 600 Rules.

UCP Article	*Description and Rules*
17. Original Documents	At least one original document required; letter of credit (L/C) requires only copies.
18. Commercial Invoice	Issued by beneficiary to the Applicant; need not be signed; same currency as L/C; description of goods must match the description in the L/C.
19. Multimodal Transport Document	At least two modes of transport; must name carrier of an agent. Example: XYC Forwarders as Agent of "Master" of Common Carrier; must indicate "trans-shipments" (reloading from one means to another means of conveyance).
20. Bill of Lading	Must be signed by master or agent; state "on-board"; all originals required; transshipment from one ship to another need not be stated as long as both ships are covered by same bill of lading.
21. Road, Rail, or Inland Waterway	Must state the date of issuance or when goods received for shipment; indicate places of shipment and destination as noted in L/C.
22. "Clean" Transport Document	Clean transport document is one bearing no clause or notation declaring a defective condition of goods or packaging; word "clean" need not appear on the document even if L/C requires "clean on-board."
23. Insurance Document and Coverage	Insurance certificate or policy; signed by the insurance company, agents, or proxies; issued no later than the shipment date (must be dated on or before the date on the bill of lading); minimum coverage is 110 percent of CIF or CIP value unless L/C indicates a different value; L/C should state the type of risks covered: if L/C states "customary risks" banks will accept any type of coverage; if L/C states "all risks" then the insurance document must note that it is "all risks."
24. Expiration of L/C	If last day falls on a day the bank is closed, then extended to the next banking day; the latest day of shipment will not be extended.
25. Tolerance in Amounts and Prices	If the L/C uses words such as "approximately" or "about," then amount, quantity, or unit prices stated on the documents may vary 10% more or less.
26. Hours of Presentation	Bank has no obligations to accept documents outside its normal banking hours.

Another ICC instrument aimed at reducing the number of rejections based upon the strict compliance rule is the *International Standard Banking Practice (ISBP)*(ICC Publication 645). These rules have been universally accepted by the world banking system and, therefore, a basic knowledge of their requirements is necessary for all exporters–importers involved in a documentary credit transaction. *ISBP* was conceived as a checklist of procedures for document checkers to follow in examining the documents presented under letters of credit.

International Standard Banking Practice (ISBP)

Uniform Customs and Practices for Documentary Credits–UCP 600.

While not a substitute for the UCP, which remains the guiding text, the *ISBP* demonstrates how the UCP is to be integrated into day-to-day practice. It clarifies ambiguous or unstated provisions of the UCP. For example, UCP 27 requires a clean bill of lading. Rule D25 of the ISBP states that it is not necessary for the word "clean" to appear on the bill of lading even if the letter of credit states "clean bill of lading." Rule D1 of the IBSP states that if the letter of credit does not specify multimodal bill of lading, even though more than one mode of transport is listed in the letter of credit, then the transport documents should be reviewed under UCP 19 (multimodal document). Rule B14 states that when there is a conflict between the amount stated numerically versus in words, the amount stated in words is controlling.[7]

Payment Systems

SWIFT[8] is a member-owned cooperative of more than 10,800 banking organizations, securities institutions, and corporate customers in over 200 countries that processes millions of standardized financial communications. SWIFT sees its role as providing a communications platform, products, and services that allow customers to exchange financial information securely. It also facilitates collaborative efforts by the financial community to shape market practice, define standards, and consider solutions to issues of mutual interest. SWIFT enables its customers to automate and standardize financial transactions, lowering costs and reducing operational risk. SWIFT provides the means for the financial world to conduct business operations with speed and certainty.

Rise of Real-Time Digital Payments

The use of mobile technology for funds transfers has become commonplace. Mobile payment systems offer speed, convenience, and safety. Over the same period, supply chain logistics have also improved, and the delivery of digital and physical goods has become faster. There are two types of real-time immediate payment schemes: closed systems and RT-RPS. A closed system can be either through "on-us" payments within a bank, or in a closed system such as PayPal, Alibaba, or BlueCash. Both the payer and payee must be users of the same closed system. RT-RPS means an immediate transfer, confirmation, and the ability for funds reuse, on a 24/7/365-day basis.

Virtual Currencies

Virtual currency is, generally, a digital unit of exchange that is not backed by a government-issued legal tender. **Bitcoin** has become the most popular example of a virtual currency. The lower cost of Bitcoin assists small businesses by providing an alternative to more expensive credit cards, enabling migrants to make cheaper remittances of payments to their families in developing countries, helping to protect individuals from censorship and capital controls, providing oppressed groups with financial privacy, and facilitating innovation and micropayments.

Countries have increased their regulation of virtual currencies and some countries have not recognized Bitcoin as a legal currency. Virtual currency transactions are investigated for criminal activity, such as laundering money and moving of illicit proceeds from one country to another.[9] FinCEN, a bureau of the U.S. Treasury Department, is charged with the power to investigate financial crimes involving the transmission of currencies and reports to the Office of Terrorism and Financial Intelligence. The FBI established the Virtual Currency Emerging Threats Working Group (VCET).

Standby Letters of Credit

Buyers often worry about the certainty of the seller's performance (supply goods, perform services, construction of a building) and require guarantees, such as performance bonds, which are issued by insurance companies. An alternative to a performance bond is the **standby letter of credit** issued by commercial banks. Banks, by law, are prohibited from issuing performance bonds, so the standby letter of credit was developed as an alternative. The standby letter of credit is distinct from the documentary letter of credit. The latter is based on the proper performance of the parties, while the former is based upon improper performance or nonperformance. The ordinary letter of credit is utilized when the seller performs by the presenting of conforming documents. Payment through a standby letter of credit is less commonly exercised since payment to the buyer is only triggered when there is nonperformance of the seller, service provider, or construction company.

Standby Letter of Credit "represents an obligation to the beneficiary on the part of the issuer: (1) to repay money borrowed by or advanced to or for the account of the customer (account party); (2) to make payment on account of any evidence of indebtedness undertaken by the account party; or (3) to make payment on account of any default by the account party in the performance of an obligation."[10]

The UCP 600 may also be used to govern standby letters of credit. However, the UCP 600 is a poor fit for standby letters of credit. Therefore, specialized rules have been developed for the standby letter of credit, including the UN Convention on Independent Guarantees and Stand-by Letter of Credit and the ICC's International Standby Practices (ISP98).[11] Unlike the numerous documents that are required to effectuate payment through the letter of credit, there is usually only one document that needs to be presented to receive payment under a standby letter of credit. That document is a simple demand by the beneficiary party (buyer) for payment due to nonperformance. The ISP recognizes the simplicity of the document requirement by allowing the demand notice to be made electronically through the SWIFT banking network. It should be noted that the standby letter of credit could require the beneficiary party to present additional documents, such as a third-party certification to the nonperformance.

Standby letters of credit can be used to help secure a variety of contractual obligations associated with the export transaction. They have been used to guarantee warranties, support borrowers under international loans, ensure availability of suppliers, secure countertrade commitments, along with acting as deposits in the sale of goods and as prepayment of fees for services.[12] *Itek Corp. v. First National Bank of Boston* illustrates the use of standby letters of credit to guarantee the performance of a construction project and for the return of monies paid by the foreign buyer.

Itek Corp. v. First National Bank of Boston

730 F.2d 19 (1st Cir. 1984)

Circuit Judge. First National Bank of Boston (FNBB), at the request of Itek Corp., issued several letters of credit running in favor of Bank Melli Iran (Melli). Melli demanded payment on the letters. Itek obtained a court injunction prohibiting FNBB from paying Melli. The basic question that Melli's appeal presents is whether its effort to obtain the money by calling the letters is "fraudulent."

The letters of credit arise out of a contract between Itek and the county of Iran. The contract provided that Itek would make and sell high-technology optical equipment to Iran at a price of $22.5 million. Iran was to make a 20 percent down payment. It would pay Itek 60 percent of the total price ($13.5 million) as work progressed; it would pay the remaining 20 percent upon satisfactory completion. The contract required Itek to provide two types of bank guarantees. The first, *down payment guarantee*, gave Iran the right to obtain return of the down payment until Itek produced work of sufficient value. The second, *good performance guarantee*, was for $2.25 million, 10 percent of the contract price. Its object was to protect Iran against a breach of contract. Iran could call for payment under the guarantees simply by submitting a written request for payment to the bank.

Melli, an instrumentality of the Iranian government, issued the guarantees. Melli required Itek to provide it similar "standby" letters of credit in the same amounts as payment and performance guarantees, issued by an American bank in Melli's favor. The underlying contract provided that if the contract "is cancelled due to *Force Majeure*, all Bank Guarantees of good performance of work will be immediately released (canceled)." The contract defines *Force Majeure* to include termination by the U.S. of necessary export licenses. Itek's work proceeded until Iran's government collapsed. Soon after the collapse, the U.S. suspended Itek's export license. Itek then proceeded to cancel the contract in accordance with the *Force Majeure* provisions. At that point, Melli demanded payment on the letters of credit.

The basic legal question, in this case, is whether the circumstances surrounding Melli's calls on FNBB's letters of credit establish "fraud in the transaction." We answer this question fully aware of the need to interpret the "fraud" provision narrowly. The very object of a letter of credit is to provide a near foolproof method of paying a beneficiary when it complies with the terms contained in the letter itself. In this case, the only requirement was a simple written demand for payment. Despite these reasons for hesitating to enjoin payment of a letter of credit, the need for an exception is apparent. The exception would be the situation in which the beneficiary has no colorable claim that it had done what the contract called for as a precondition to obtaining the money. If Melli has no plausible or colorable basis under the contract to call for payment of the letters, its effort to obtain the money is fraudulent. Court orders that the payment be stopped.

Therefore, the injunction was properly issued.

Case Highlights

- A letter of credit that is used to guarantee a performance or return of a deposit is called a standby letter of credit
- A bank *may* honor a letter of credit when documents comply on their face even if notified that the documents are forgeries or that there is fraud in the transaction
- The account party can enjoin the bank from honoring a letter of credit by obtaining a court order (injunction)
- A *force majeure* clause describes events that allow a party to be excused from performing a contractual obligation.

The *Itek Corp. v. First National Bank of Boston* case notes that under the UCP courts may enjoin a bank from honoring the demand for payment when the bank has been notified of fraud in the transaction. The "fraud" exception to the traditional reluctance of courts to interfere has been liberally construed in the law. However, in most export transactions obtaining an injunction may not be a practical alternative because of the time it takes to obtain such an order.

Alternative Methods of Guaranteeing Performance

Besides the standby letter of credit, there are other methods of guaranteeing a performance or ensuring the return of monies. A **performance bond** minimizes the buyer's risk of nonperformance by the seller in the export transaction or nonperformance by a contractor in a construction project. The performance bond is a guarantee from an insurance company to pay the insured in case of default (nonperformance). It serves the same function as a standby letter of credit. **Bid bonds** insure against the risk that a bidder may not honor its bid. These are usually required to bid on government procurement contracts.

A **credit surety** guarantees repayment to a bank or lender who finances an export transaction or development project. These sureties generally take the form of a payment guarantee from a state agency or a development bank, such as the **World Bank**. A surety may also be in the form of a corporate guarantee from a parent company of the borrowing party. Another technique is the creation of a **retention** fund, which is not a third-party guarantee, but an arrangement between the parties. In large projects or government procurement contracts, a percentage of the monies is deducted from each payment due to the seller or contractor and is retained in a fund pending the completion of the contract or the expiration of the warranty period.

The bank guarantee or **demand guarantee** is a popular means of guaranteeing performance. Like the standby letter of credit, the demand guarantee secures performance of a nonmonetary obligation. It serves as a default device when performance is not satisfactory. Whereas a bank pays a documentary letter of credit only if things go right, a bank will be called upon to pay a demand guarantee or standby letter only if things go wrong. Just as with the standby letter of credit, all the beneficiary is required to do is make a written demand on the bank for payment.[13] Both the ICC and UNCITRAL have developed rules to govern these types of instruments. The ICC publishes the **Uniform Rules for Demand Guarantees** and UNCITRAL has published the **Convention on Independent Letters of Guarantee and Standby Credits**. In order to discourage unfair calls on demand guarantees, Article 15 of the ICC rules require the beneficiary to provide a statement describing the way in which the other party is in breach.

Sources of Trade Finance

The ability to finance export transactions is a critical part of most export and import businesses. Financing can be obtained in one of two ways: The first, external to the transaction, where one of the parties obtains a general loan from a commercial bank or a government agency. The second method, internal to the transaction, is facilitated by two documents found in most export transactions—the bill of lading and the letter of credit. The importance of the bill of lading as a document of title was discussed in Chapter 12. A negotiable bill of lading allows for the transfer of the goods while they are in transit. Because it is negotiable, it can be used as collateral to secure a loan.

Exporters naturally want to get paid quickly, and importers usually prefer to delay payment at least until they have received and resold the goods. Because of the intense competition for export markets, being able to offer good payment terms is often necessary to make a sale. Various financing sources are available to exporters, depending on the specifics of the transaction and the exporter's overall financing needs. A number of variables need to be assessed before deciding on export or import financing: (1) cost of financing; (2) length of the financing; and (3) risks of financing. The impact on price and profit of the different methods of financing should be understood before a ***pro forma* invoice** is submitted to the buyer.

The greater the risks associated with the transaction the greater the costs of financing and the more difficult financing will be to obtain. The creditworthiness of the buyer directly affects the probability of payment to the exporter, but it is not the only factor of concern to a potential lender. The political and economic stability of the buyer's country is also a factor. To provide financing for either accounts receivable or the production or purchase of the product for sale, the lender may require more secure methods of payment, such as a letter of credit or export credit insurance. If a lender is uncertain about the exporter's ability to perform, or if additional credit capacity is needed, a government guarantee program may enable the lender to provide additional financing.

Commercial Banks

Large commercial banks have international banking departments and specialists familiar with specific foreign countries and various types of commodities and transactions. These large banks maintain correspondent relationships with smaller banks throughout the country. Larger banks also maintain correspondent relationships with banks in most foreign countries or operate their own overseas branches. If they are unable to provide direct guidance or assistance, they may be able to refer inquirers to other specialists. Banks frequently provide consultation and guidance free of charge to their clients, since they derive income primarily from loans to the exporter and from fees for special services.

Finally, large banks frequently conduct seminars and workshops on letters of credit, documentary collections, and other banking subjects of concern to exporters. Among the many services a commercial bank may perform for its clients are the following: (1) exchange of currencies; (2) assistance in export financing; (3) collection of foreign invoices, drafts, and letters of credit; (4) transfer of funds to other countries; and (5) credit information on potential sales representatives or buyers overseas.

A logical first step in obtaining financing is for an exporter to approach its local commercial bank. If the exporter already has a loan for domestic needs, then the lender already has experience with the exporter's ability to perform. By using letters of credit, government loan guarantees, or export credit insurance, an exporter can reduce the lender's risk. When selecting a bank, the exporter should ask the following questions: (1) What are the charges for confirming a letter of credit, processing drafts, and collecting payments? (2) Does the bank have foreign branches or correspondent banks? Where are they located? (3) Does the bank have experience with government financing programs that support small business export transactions?

A time draft under an irrevocable letter of credit, confirmed by a local bank, presents relatively little risk of default. To convert these instruments to cash immediately, an exporter may obtain a loan using the draft as collateral or sell the draft to an investor or a bank for a fee. Banks or other lenders may be willing to buy time drafts that a creditworthy foreign buyer has accepted or agreed

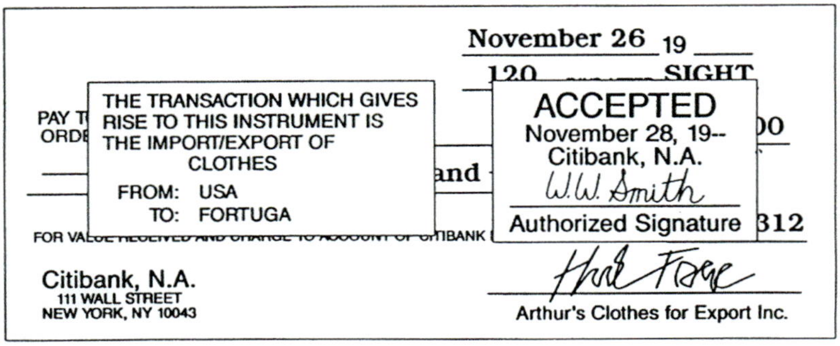

Figure 13.6 Focus on Transactions: Banker's Acceptance.

to pay at a specified future date. The endorsed drafts or bills of exchange are called trade acceptances.

In some cases, banks pre-agree to accept the obligations of paying a draft for a fee. As discussed previously, the banker's acceptance is a draft drawn on and accepted by a bank (see Figure 13.6 *Focus on Transactions*: "Banker's Acceptance"). The acceptance becomes a financial instrument that can be discounted and sold before maturity to third-party investors. The exporter receives an amount less than the face value of the draft so that when the draft is paid at its face value at the specified future date, the investor or bank receives a return on its investment. The difference between the amount paid to the exporter and the face amount paid at maturity is called a discount and represents the fees or interest the investor or bank receives for holding the draft until maturity. The bank often discounts drafts **without recourse** to the exporter in case of default by the drawee. Other drafts may be discounted with recourse to the exporter, in which case the exporter must reimburse the investor or bank if the party obligated to pay the draft defaults.

Factoring and Forfaiting

Factoring is the discounting of foreign account receivables without a draft. The exporter transfers title to its account receivables to a factoring company at a discount. Factoring houses specialize in the financing of account receivables by giving cash at a discount from the face value owed to the exporter. Although factoring is often done without recourse to the exporter, the exporter should verify the specific arrangement. The factoring company assumes the financial risk of nonpayment and handles the collections on the receivables. Export factoring allows an exporter to sell on **open account**, by which goods are shipped without a guarantee of payment such as a letter of credit.

There are two types of factoring schemes—single factor and two-factor systems. The two-factor system involves the use of two factoring companies: an export factor and import factor. The two-factor method is the most efficient and secure. The exporter hires the export factor, and the export factor contracts with an import factor in the country of import. The import factor is useful in assessing the creditworthiness of the importer. Upon delivery of the goods, the import factor issues an invoice to the importer with a copy sent to the export factor. The export factor will then advance 80 percent of the invoice value to the exporter. The import factor also is responsible for the collection of overdue accounts.The two-factor system is more expensive than the single-factor one and should be considered depending on the risks presented by the country of importation.

The single factor scheme involves a single contract in which the exporter sells its account receivable to a factoring company without the knowledge of the importer. The exporter may pursue "disguised or undisclosed factoring" (single factor) in which the importer is not informed that its accounts receivable will be factored. The exporter may not want the buyer to question the financial stability of the exporter's company due to the need to factor.

Forfaiting is the selling at a discount of longer-term account receivables or promissory notes of foreign buyers. This is a form of supplier credit in which the exporter turns over export receivables, usually guaranteed by a bank in the importer's country, by selling them at a discount to a forfaiter. This arrangement is generally agreed to in advance before the conclusion of the sales contract. The exporter is thus able to incorporate the discount (costs) into the selling price. For a comparison of the different characteristics of factoring and forfaiting, see Table 13.2 *Focus on Transactions*: "Comparison: Factoring versus Forfaiting."

Buyer and Supplier Financing

In order to produce the goods under an export contract, the seller will often need to obtain financing. This financing will at times come from the buyer or the seller's suppliers. One form of buyer financing is when a letter of credit allows for progress payments. Under a progress payment, the bank is authorized by the buyer to pay seller on inspection by the buyer's agent or receipt of a statement by the seller that a certain percentage of the product has been completed. This type of partial payment under a letter of credit is known as a **red clause** advance. Under the red clause, the seller may demand a partial payment under the letter of credit before the presentation of documents. It is called a red clause because of the danger associated with it. The buyer is at risk for any red clause payments. If the seller subsequently fails to produce the goods or provide conforming documents, then the buyer must reimburse the bank for any red clause advances. Red clause payments are simply unsecured loans from the buyer to the seller.

Supplier financing is generally obtained through the supplier's selling materials to the exporter on account. Generally, the seller produces the goods needed to fulfill the export contract and pays its suppliers out of the future proceeds from the export contract. Suppliers will want some sort of collateral or security for selling materials on account. Two methods of providing such security are the

Table 13.2 *Focus on Transactions*: Comparison: Factoring versus Forfaiting.

Characteristics	*Factoring*	*Forfaiting*
Types of items used to obtain financing	Low-value, short-term (90–120 days) accounts receivables	Higher-value, medium- to long-term (may exceed 180 days) obligations
Number of instruments or transactions	Numerous and continuous flow of invoices (accounts receivables)	Provides financing for individual transactions
Amount advanced or paid	Generally about 80 percent of the value of the invoices or accounts receivable	Payment given on full invoice price
Type of instruments needed	Unsecured accounts receivable	Requires negotiable instrument such as bank draft (often requires bank guarantee) or promissory note
Rate of discount (fees)	Lower	Higher
Other benefits	Provide risk assessments of prospective buyers and sales accounting services (important for small exporters)	Purchases drafts and notes on a nonrecourse basis; assumes commercial, currency, and political risks

transferable credit and the **back-to-back letter of credit** (see Figure 13.7 *Focus on Transactions*: "Back-to-Back Letter of Credit").

Under the transferable credit arrangement, a supplier accepts assignment of the buyer's letter of credit as collateral for selling on account (without payment). Unless provided for in the letter of credit, it cannot be divided and transferred to numerous suppliers; the exporter is allowed only a single transfer or assignment of the letter of credit.

The best way to deal with the multiple supplier situation is for the exporter–manufacturer to arrange a back-to-back letter of credit without the assistance of the buyer or issuing bank. The seller arranges with a third-party bank to take the letter of credit from the export transaction as collateral for the issuance of new letters of credit in partial amounts to the suppliers of the seller. Thus, unlike the transferable credit arrangement, the back-to-back letter of credit scenario involves separate letters of credit. The documentary letter of credit simply acts as collateral for the issuance of new letters of credit by another bank. The back-to-back letter of credit highlights the importance of the documentary letter of credit in both guaranteeing payments and in financing international trade. Table 13.3 *Doing Business Internationally*: "Features and Risks of Different Types of Drafts and Credits" compares the risks of the exporter–seller and importer–buyer in the use of different types of drafts and letters of credit.

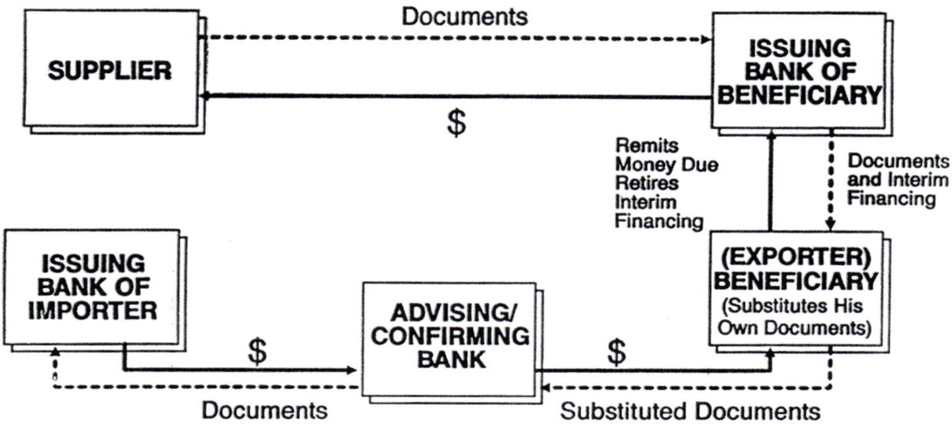

Figure 13.7 Focus on Transactions: Back-to-Back Letter of Credit.

Table 13.3 *Doing Business Internationally*: Features and Risks of Different Types of Drafts and Credits.

Type	*Time of Payment*	*Goods Available*	*Risk to Exporter*	*Risk to Importer*
Irrevocable	At sight (confirming bank)	After payment	Provides most security	Fraud in the transaction
Revocable	At sight	After payment	Provides least security	Easier for issuing bank to cancel in cases of fraud
Sight Draft	Soon after shipment of goods	After payment	Risk on confirming bank	Assured shipment has been made
Time Draft	At maturity of draft	Before payment	Loses control over goods	Assured delivery before payment
Red Clause	Percentage of payment before shipment	After payment	Confirming and issuing banks	Total risk on amount paid in advance
Transferable	At sight	After payment	Payment to creditor or supplier	None
Back-to-Back	At sight	After payment	Payment to secondary beneficiaries	None
Standby L/C	At sight	After payment	Payment to importer for nonperformance	None

Government-Guaranteed Export Working Capital Programs: Some countries provide various grant, insurance, and loan guarantee programs to their nationals to encourage exporting. For example, the U.S. Small Business Administration offers programs that guarantee export working capital facilities granted by participating lending banks.

Export Credit Insurance: Export credit insurance provides protection against commercial losses, such as default, insolvency, bankruptcy of the buyer, and political losses due to events, such as war, nationalization, and currency inconvertibility. Insurance also provides security for banks that are providing working capital and are financing exports.

Export Factoring: Factoring in international trade is the discounting of short- term receivables (up to 180 days). The exporter sells its short-term foreign accounts receivable to a factoring house, or a factor, for cash at a discount from the face value. It allows an exporter to ship on open account and still receive payment immediately. Factors usually work with exports of consumer goods.

Forfaiting: Forfaiting is a method of trade financing that allows the exporter to sell his medium and long-term receivables (180 days to seven years or more) to a forfaiter at a discount, in exchange for cash. The forfaiter assumes all the risks, thereby enabling the exporter to offer extended credit terms and to incorporate the discount into the selling price. Forfaiters usually work with exports of capital goods, commodities, and large projects.

Figure 13.8 Focus on Transactions: Competing Internationally by Offering Open Account Terms.

In order to compete internationally, the exporter may have to sell on open account or through a time draft. The problem is that the exporter may not have the financial ability to wait for payment. In order to provide open account terms, such exporters will need to obtain funding in order to overcome cash flow problems that an open account sale may cause. Figure 13.8 *Focus on Transactions*: "Competing Internationally by Offering Open Account Terms" provides a number of options available to the exporter.

Chapter Summary

1. The letter of credit that calls for payment upon the delivery of the documents is called a Cash against Document transaction and requires a sight draft. The type of transaction that allows the buyer to obtain the documents and make payment in the future is called Acceptance against Documents and requires a time draft.

2. The buyer obtains a letter of credit from a bank to guarantee payment to the seller. The buyer is called the account party, the seller is the beneficiary party, and the bank is referred to as the issuing bank. If the letter of credit is also guaranteed by the seller's bank the letter is referred to as a confirmed letter of credit. If there is no second guarantor, then the seller's bank is simply acting as an advising bank that simply transmits documents and payments.
3. The rules that govern international documentary letters of credit are called the Uniform Customs and Practices for Documentary Credits or UCP 600.
4. The UCP rules state that banks are only required to review the documents listed in the letter of credit (facial compliance rule) and are not required to understand the technical terms used by the contracting parties. Other UCP rules presume that letters of credit are not transferable unless they state so and that they are irrevocable unless they state otherwise.
5. The banks are entitled to reject any document that contains a discrepancy under the strict compliance rule. The arbitrariness of banks rejecting generally conforming documents is regulated by the International Standard Banking Practice (ISBP).
6. The letter of credit is required to expressly state an expiration date. Despite the express expiration date, an implied second expiration date known as the 21-day rule requires the seller to deliver the documents within 21 days after receiving the bill of lading.
7. One form of trade finance is the banker's acceptance in which the issuing or conforming bank guarantees payment by placing a stamp on the time draft. The time draft is then referred to as a banker's acceptance and can be sold on the secondary market.
8. The seller's performance may be guaranteed by a standby letter of credit, bank guarantee, or a performance bond. A set of rules that govern standby letters of credit is the International Standby Practices (ISP98).
9. Other means of trade financing include back-to-back letters of credit, factoring, and forfaiting. Factoring is the discounting and selling of foreign account receivables to another company. Forfaiting is the selling at a discount of longer-term account receivables or promissory notes. A buyer may also allow an unsecured advance to the seller on the letter of credit through the insertion of a red clause into the letter of credit.

Key Terms

21-Day Rule
Acceptance
Account Party
Advising Bank
Back-to-Back Letter of Credit
Banker's Acceptance
Beneficiary Party
Bid Bond
Bill of Exchange
Bitcoin
Confirming Bank
Convention on Independent Letters of Guarantee and Standby Credits
Credit Surety

Customs Broker
Demand Guarantee
Documentary Collections Transaction
Documentary Credit Transaction
Draft
Eximbank
Facial Compliance Rule
Factoring
Forfaiting
Freight Forwarder
International Standby Practices (ISP98)
Irrevocable Letter of Credit
Issuing Bank
Letter of Credit
Open Account
Performance Bond
Power of Attorney
Pro Forma Invoice
Red Clause
Retention Fund
Revolving Letter of Credit
Revolving Line of Credit
Rule of Strict Compliance
Sight Draft
Standby Letter of Credit
Time Draft
Trade Acceptance
Transferable Credit
UCP 600
Uniform Law on Bills of Exchange
Uniform Rules for Demand Guarantees
Virtual Currency
World Bank

Chapter Problems

1. One topic of great interest at a recent global banking conference was dealing with letters of credit in China. As those who use Chinese letters of credit know, the Chinese will reject a letter of credit on the minutest of discrepancies. Several participants now report that in certain instances the scrutiny has gotten even worse. One member related an instance where a letter of credit was rejected because it was signed in blue ink instead of black. Several members theorized that the reason for the increased inspection is the cash flow problems in certain provinces. What can be done to overcome this problem of overly strict review and enforcement of documentary requirements?
2. Should the parties to a documentary credit include a dispute resolution clause in their letters of credit or allow disputes to be resolved through litigation? Are there any alternatives to arbitration that could be used to minimize the time and cost of litigation or arbitration?
3. A company engaging in the manufacture and sale of telecommunications equipment entered into an agreement with the "Imperial Government of Carpathia" to install and maintain certain telecommunications equipment. As a condition of the contract and to secure the advance payment, the company was required to guarantee its performance by obtaining two irrevocable letters of credit in the amounts equal to the advance payments made by Carpathia. Subsequently, a revolution occurred in Carpathia and the company was at least temporarily prevented from finishing the contract. The company was concerned that a new government would "arbitrarily" demand payment on the letters of credit. In light of the foregoing, the

company sought a preliminary injunction preventing the bank from making payment on the letters of credit without first giving the company an opportunity to prove lack of authenticity or the fraudulent nature of the demand. Should the court grant a preliminary injunction? *Stromberg-Carlson Corp. v. Bank Melli Iran*, 467 F. Supp. 530 (SDNY 1979).

4. The terms and conditions of a letter of credit state that the beneficiary party (seller) is to provide a certificate of origin listing the goods as originating from "EU Countries." The certificate of origin did state "EU Countries," but the commercial invoice stated only "EU." The issuing bank rejected the documents because the declaration of origin in the commercial invoice was inconsistent with the declaration in the certificate of origin. The beneficiary party bank sues the issuing bank for wrongfully dishonoring the letter of credit. Under the UCP, who wins? Why?
5. A letter of credit is issued with the following terms and conditions: "(1) The beneficiary party must present a full set of clean-on-board bills of lading evidencing shipment from Port A to Port B and (2) documents must arrive at the offices of the issuing bank before arrival of the ship at Port B." The issuing bank rejected the documents for the following reasons: "(1) The bill of lading does not indicate that the goods were placed on board, but instead states that they were taken in charge at Container Freight Yard and (2) the documents were untimely because they were presented to the bank one day after the arrival of the ship." Were the two discrepancies given appropriate for rejecting the documents?
6. Test your knowledge of trade finance terminology. Match the term with its definition (see answers on the next page).

(A) Irrevocable	(1) A letter of credit that does not require the presentation of specified documents. It is extremely risky for the purchaser in an export transaction.
(B) Negotiable	(2) The letter of credit used in an export transaction that requires the seller to present specified documents in order to receive payment under the letter.
(C) Transferable	(3) A draft or bill of exchange that requires the bank to pay under the letter of credit at the time the documents are presented.
(D) Confirmed	(4) A letter of credit in which the buyer is named as beneficiary. It is used to guarantee performance on a contract and the return of a deposit or installment payments.
(E) Clean	(5) Cannot be revoked without the beneficiary's consent. Most common form used in international transactions because it provides greatest security against nonpayment.
(F) Revolving	(6) The provision in a letter of credit allows for the advancement of monies prior to the seller presenting the required documents. This is a means by which a buyer can provide financing to the seller. It is very risky because it is unsecured, and the buyer is responsible to reimburse the bank whether the seller performs or not.

(G) Documentary Credit	(7) Permits the accompanying drafts or bills of exchange to be transferred. This allows for the negotiation of a draft at other banks. The issuing bank is required to reimburse any bank that negotiates the letter of credit.
(H) Standby	(8) A second bank endorses the letter of credit indicating that it will also guarantee payment upon the presentation of the required documents. In an export transaction, the exporter's bank will generally be that bank.
(I) Sight Bill	(9) Permits the beneficiary to negotiate the letter of credit to secondary beneficiaries. The original letter of credit must expressly state that it is transferable.
(J) Time Bill	(10) The buyer provides the seller with a letter of credit. That credit is used as collateral to obtain a second letter of credit by the seller. The second letter provides a guarantee to the seller's suppliers. The second letter finances the acquisition of the materials needed by the seller to produce the goods.
(K) Red Clause	(11) Generally granted by commercial banks to large importers. The buyer is allowed to reuse the credit after the bank is reimbursed.
(L) Back-to-Back	(12) A draft or bill of exchange that orders the bank to pay on the letter of credit only after passage of a certain amount of time after the presentation of the documents. This allows the buyer to resell the goods or to obtain financing before being required to pay the seller.

Internet Exercises

1. Take a self-guided tour from a Canadian perspective of an international trade transaction at www.royalbank.com/trade.
2. The U.S. Eximbank is America's largest export financing agency. Explore www.exim.gov to see how its programs benefit U.S. exporters.

Other Internet Sources

Dictionary of **banking terms:** www.helpwithmybank.gov/dictionary.

World Bank—links to Multilateral Investment Guarantee Agency (MIGA), International Development Association (IDA), and International Finance Corporation (IFC): www.worldbank.org.

[Answers to Problem 6: A(5); B(7); C(9); D(8); E(1); F(11); G(2); H(4); I(3); J(12); K(6); L(10).]

Notes

1 See ICC, "Guidance Notes for Documentary Credit Formats," http://files-eu.clickdimensions.com/iccwboorg-avxnt/files/simpledocumentarycreditformat.pdf?1576594441752&_cldee=amFrYkBueWtyZWRpdC5kaw%3d%3d&recipientid=contact-4989ca396f30e911a9a7000d3ab38ab1-170a5c429d0e46c8af81523052cb0591&esid=0b682858-d520-ea11-a810-000d3aba77ea. See also, ICC, "Commentary on UCP 600," ICC Publication 600E (ICC Publishing 2007).

2 The SWIFT network, cooperatively owned by more than 1,000 banks, was set up to provide banks with a means of handling interbank transactions, including bank transfers and foreign exchange confirmations.

3 The terms *draft* and *bill of exchange* can be used interchangeably. The term used in the UK is *bill of exchange*. The term used in the U.S. is *draft*.

4 The second edition of eUCP came into force on July 1, 2019. The eUCP are based on the principles of the UCP and standard practices for e-Commerce transactions. The eUCP focuses on the principles of electronic issuance and draws from practice in the paper world in functionally equivalent situations for electronic presentations.

5 554 N.Y.S.2d 757 (1990).

6 112 K.B. 37 (1943).

7 Note, this rule is also found in negotiable instrument law relating to amounts on checks or drafts.

8 www.swift.com.

9 Lawrence Trautman, "Virtual Currencies; Bitcoin & What Now After Liberty Reserve, Silk Road, and Mt. Gox?," 20(4) *Richmond Journal of Law and Technology* 13 (2014).

10 Regulation H, 12 C.F.R. § 208.8(*d*)(1) (1979).

11 The ISP98 can be obtained through the website of the Institute of International Banking Law and Practice at http://iiblp.org/resources/isp98.

12 See Gordon Graham and Benjamin Geva, "Standby Credits in Canada," 9 *Canadian Business Law Journal* 180 (1982).

13 Roy Goode, "Abstract Payment Undertakings in International Transactions," 22 *Brooklyn Journal of International Law* 1, 15 (1996).

Chapter 14

Employment and Sale of Services

The globalization of services is similar to global supply chains in the production of goods, consisting of the coordination of business functions across national borders. Types of services that are outsourced include: technical and business services such as IT, software development, accounting, legal, human resources, engineering, and customer services (contact centers), as well as research and development. Sales of services internationally include private employment and **independent contractor contracts**, which are subject to host country restrictions and regulations. Some countries have developed regulatory schemes that cover such transactions. This chapter provides examples of foreign regulations that pertain to employers and principals, agents, consultants, and employees.

Generic methods for entering foreign markets include employment, foreign sales representation, and commercial agency contracts. The distinction between employment and independent contracting is important in determining applicable regulations. A number of service industries make the sale of goods transactions possible. Service contracts exist in almost all industries and businesses. One way of defining a sale of services is by comparing it to the other two modes of international trade—sale of goods and licensing. A good is something tangible and movable. Licensing involves a less than total transfer of ownership found in the sale transaction. Licenses generally pertain to intangible items such as technology, know-how, trade secrets, and intellectual property rights (trademarks, patents, copyrights). Many transactions are **mixed sales** that include two or all three of the above modes of doing business (sale of goods, licensing, sale of services). A technology transfer, for example, may include a sale of goods (software or computer equipment), a license (right to use the software), and a sale of services (technical assistance and training).

DOI: 10.4324/9781003469230-17

Cross-Border Trade in Services: Temporary Entry

Services are a key component of global value chains as they help to promote value-added commercial activities. Services represent a high proportion of the value of trade, particularly when accounting for services that are embedded in goods, as well as services bundled with goods. Cross-border trade in services includes the production, distribution, marketing, sale, and delivery services. Free trade in services is a core principle of the World Trade Organization (WTO). Free trade agreements also provide protections in the sale or supply of services. For example, the Comprehensive and Progressive Agreement for Trans-Pacific Partnership (CPTPP)[1] includes a chapter entitled Cross-Border Trade in Services (CBTS). The key provisions of the CBTS include:

- **National treatment:** Obligates each country to treat foreign suppliers of services no less favorably than domestic service suppliers.
- **Most-favored-nation treatment:** Each country must treat service suppliers of the other country no less favorably than it treats service suppliers of any other CPTPP country.
- **Market access:** The market access obligation prohibits quantitative limitations on the number of service suppliers, the total value of services transactions or assets, the total number of service operations or the total quantity of service output, or the total number of persons who may be employed in a certain service sector.
- **Local presence:** The local presence obligation prohibits a party from requiring a foreign service of the supplier to establish or maintain a representative office or any form of enterprise, as a condition to supply a service.
- **Standstill mechanism:** The standstill mechanism ensures that countries will not impose future measures that are more restrictive than those that were in place when the CPTPP came into force.
- **Ratchet mechanism:** The ratchet mechanism ensures that any future regulatory or legal change that makes it easier for service suppliers from one country to access another country's market will automatically be locked-in under the Agreement and therefore cannot subsequently be made more restrictive.
- **Exclusions/exceptions:** Countries may exclude types of services such as health, public education, social services, and fisheries, as well as cultural policies and cultural programs.

The CPTPP also provides a degree of mobility for workers and investors across the different countries. Its chapter on Temporary Entry for Businesspersons provides various periods of residency for different categories of workers or persons. These temporary-entry commitments give businesses the ability to move key personnel from one location to another and access highly skilled global talent on a temporary basis. It covers only certain types of businesspersons and requires the country of that person to do the same (principle of reciprocity). The CPTPP describes four categories of businesspersons: business visitors, intra-company transferees, investors, and professionals and technicians. These rights are not connected to persons seeking permanent employment, citizenship, or residency.

- **Business visitors:** Eligible for up to a six-month length of stay with possible extension.
- **Intra-corporate transferees:** Eligible for up to a three-year length of stay with possible extension. Canada took reciprocal commitments for executives, managers, specialists, and management trainees.
- **Investors:** Eligible for up to a one-year length of stay with possible extension.
- **Highly skilled professionals and technicians:** Eligible for up to one-year length of stay with possible extension.
- **Specific commitments** for certain types of professionals and technicians. Persons from specific types of occupations may be given entry but could be subject to additional licensing and training requirements.

It should be noted that the principle of reciprocity means that these periods may vary depending on the country of the persons entering a given CPTPP country.

This chapter is intended to alert the student to the importance of sales of services in international trade. A growing portion of world exports falls in the area of sales of services. Due to the breadth of the topic, this chapter provides cases of different service sectors for illustrative purposes. The focus is on the practical and legal issues that an individual or company faces in hiring foreign personnel, with a focus on European employment law. The chapter also discusses the importance of independent contractor status, especially in the areas of contracting with foreign agents and distributors.

International Sale of Services

The **Organisation for Economic Co-operation and Development (OECD)** has estimated that between 60 percent and 70 percent of the business sector in OECD countries[2] relates to the sale of services. Export growth for services exists in Latin America, Asia, and Central and Eastern Europe. The means for selling services internationally include international consulting, licensing agreements, franchising services, and tourism services. There has been rapid growth in many service sectors, including transport, communications, finance, and business services, along with knowledge-intensive services, such as computing services.

The rules-based multilateral trading system has been expanded to include trade in services. The WTO Agreements' **General Agreement on Trade in Services (GATS)** is targeted at reducing obstacles to trade in services. At the bilateral level, the U.S. and the EU reached a number of **Mutual Recognition Agreements (MRAs)**. These agreements are aimed at reducing trade barriers in specific industries. Trade barrier reduction is achieved through the mutual recognition of other countries' certification procedures. At the nongovernmental level, the **Trans-Atlantic Business Dialogue (TABD)**, which endorses multilateral cooperation in the area of electronic commerce identified five priority areas: protection of personal data and privacy; digital signatures and harmonized legal framework; encryption; tax, tariff, and customs; and intellectual property, protection, and associated liabilities.

There are a number of important features that differentiate exporting services from exporting products. First, services are less tangible than products, providing little in terms of samples that can be seen by potential foreign buyers. Consequently, communicating a service offer is much more difficult than communicating a product offer. Second, the intangibility of services makes financing more difficult. Financial institutions are less willing to provide financial support for service exports than for product exports. Third, selling services is more personal than selling products, often requiring direct involvement with the customer. This involvement demands greater cultural sensitivity. Fourth, services are much more difficult to standardize than products. Service activities are tailored to the specific needs of the buyer.

Demand for certain services is often related to product exports. Exporting of goods is supported by service activities such as banking, insurance, and transportation. For example, the big accounting firms have expanded into the customs compliance area and advising exporters and importers on how to minimize the payment of duties and value-added taxes, as well as handling transfer-pricing and international tax issues. They also offer consulting in valuation, sourcing, trade strategies, logistics, trade process management, and information technology.

General Agreement on Trade in Services (GATS)

Some countries still mandate that only nationals may act as agents and in others, commercial agents must be registered with the government. Also, professionals, such as lawyers, architects, doctors, and so forth cannot practice their services in another country without having to be retrained or recertified. The EU has made some inroads for allowing people certified in one EU country to practice their profession in other EU countries without needing to pursue additional education or training. In recent decades, the rise of the e-service sector has challenged the national barriers to trade in services. Numerous countries have adjusted their regulations to accommodate transborder e-services including e-banking, distance learning, software development, consultant services, and collaborative works.

The preamble in the GATS agreement places the liberalization of trade in services as necessary in helping impoverished and developing countries by allowing them access to services that may not be available in their countries.[3] The transparency principle encourages countries to make available clear and stable rules and regulations for foreign parties who want to provide services in their countries. Liberalization refers to the reducing of obstacles to trade in services. This involves countries recognizing degrees, licenses, and certifications of service professionals earned in other countries and with the harmonization of standards and requirements regionally and internationally.

GATS encourages countries to negotiate specific commitments applying to the movement of people providing services.

The GATS is structured to address the different "modes of supply," which represent how countries permit or restrict foreign participation in the different services sectors. The objectives of the current round of services negotiations fall into two basic categories: First, efforts to remove restrictions and limitations on market access and second, the GATS Council wants to expand the reach of services sectors covered, such as environmental, energy, express delivery, distribution, and health and education services.

Finally, the GATS Agreement places a focus on the liberalization of trade in services that benefits least-developed countries by building domestic service capacities, efficiency, and competitiveness through access to technology; and facilitate access to information, related to their respective markets. This building of capacity includes improving commercial and technical aspects of the supply of services; registration, recognition and obtaining of professional qualifications; and availability of services technology.

Services and the Internet

An evolving issue is the role of e-commerce and how the GATS commitments can be responsive to the new opportunities for providing services over the Internet. In nearly all sectors, there will be increasing pressure to allow services to be provided across borders. For example, in the case of financial services, regulators will be challenged to justify the requirement to provide these services through a local subsidiary, when the service can be provided more efficiently from abroad. However, there is also the possibility that nations and free trade areas will respond with specialized laws aimed at controlling cross-border transactions over the Internet. Consumer protection laws are likely to be tailored to protect nationals engaged in Internet transactions with foreign sellers. An example of such a law is the **EU Directive on Distance Contracts**,[4] which is described in Figure 14.1 *Comparative Law*: "Protection of Consumers in Distance Contracts."

Rights of Consumer

1 Prior to the conclusion of any distance contract, the consumer must be provided with clear and comprehensible information concerning the identity and possibly the address of the supplier; characteristics of the goods *or services* and their price; delivery costs; arrangements for payment, delivery, or performance; existence of a right of withdrawal; period for which the offer or the price remains valid and the minimum duration of the contract, where applicable; and cost of using the means of distance communication.

2 This information must comply with the principles of good faith in commercial transactions and the principles governing the protection of minors. In the case of telephone calls, the caller's identity and commercial purpose must be made clear at the beginning.

3 The consumer must receive written confirmation or confirmation in another durable medium (electronic mail) at the time of performance of the contract. The following information must also be given in writing: arrangements for exercising the right of withdrawal; place to which the consumer may address complaints; information relating to after-sales service; and conditions under which the contract may be rescinded.

4 The consumer has a right of withdrawal. Where the supplier has met his obligations relating to the provision of information, the consumer has at least seven working days to cancel the contract without penalty.

5 Where the supplier has failed to meet his obligations as regards information, this period is extended to three months. The supplier is obliged to repay the amounts paid by the consumer within thirty days.

6 Where the supplier fails to perform his side of the contract, the consumer must be informed and any sums paid refunded. In some cases it is possible to supply an equivalent good or service.

7 Where unsolicited goods are supplied, the consumer's failure to reply does not constitute consent.

8 The use by the supplier of automatic calling devices or faxes requires the prior consent of the consumer.

9 The Member States must ensure that consumers are allowed judicial or administrative redress so that they are not deprived of protection under the law of a non-Member country.

Figure 14.1 Comparative Law: Protection of Consumers in Distance Contracts.

Source: EU Directive 97/7/EC.

The EU Directive on Distance Contracts requires the (foreign) seller to disclose certain types of information. The required disclosure information includes the location of the seller, the price and additional costs, and the minimum length of time that the consumer will be bound to the contract. The Directive allows the seller to solicit over the telephone, but it is required to follow up with a written confirmation. An e-mail confirmation satisfies the writing requirement. The statute recognizes a consumer right of withdrawal within seven days to cancel the contract and receive a full refund. The right of withdrawal is extended to three months in the event that the seller has failed to provide the information required by the Directive. This consumer right is akin to the right of rescission found in some common law countries. Finally, the Directive does not prevent member countries of the EU from enacting more stringent consumer protection legislation. A foreign exporter will not only have to satisfy the dictates of the EU's numerous consumer protection laws but will also have to research the consumer protection requirements of each EU country it chooses to export goods or services.

Hiring Foreign Personnel

Any company seeking to sell its products internationally will need foreign representation. For example, an exporter contemplating an initial entry into a foreign market has three alternatives. First, it may elect to use employees, whether those already in place or new foreign hires. Second, it may elect to hire independent contractors. A common form of service provided by independent contractors is sales representation. Third, it may elect to enter into a distribution relationship with a foreign distributor. It is estimated that over half of world trade is handled through sales representatives and distributors.[5]

A **foreign sales representative** is an agent who distributes, represents, services, or sells goods on behalf of foreign sellers. The agent can be either an employee or an independent contractor. Foreign laws heavily impact the classification of a given relationship. Once a relationship is designated as an employment or independent contractor relationship, a number of host country laws regulate areas such as notice, termination, and remuneration.

The terminology of agency, employment, and independent contractor differs across countries. For example, the general meaning of *agent* varies from country to country. Generally, an agent denotes the person being hired while the party doing the hiring is referred to as the *principal*. The term *agent* encompasses both dependent and independent agents. A *dependent agent* is an employee. A mixture of employment and agency law governs the employer–employee relationship. An independent contractor, such as a consultant, is an *independent agent*. Agency law governs the principal–agent relationship between the hiring company and the consultant.

Employment Relationship

The employer should pay special attention to the last item on the above list. Laws and cultural attitudes vary widely among countries. Therefore, a clear **sexual harassment policy** should be developed with the international employee in mind. At the minimum, a policy should state the company's general policy, provide workable definitions of inappropriate conduct, and provide a user-friendly complaint procedure.

> **Sexual Harassment Policy.** All employees are prohibited from making offensive remarks or engaging in unwelcome overtures, either verbal or physical. Such prohibited conduct includes offensive and unwelcome flirtations, advances, or propositions; verbal abuse of a racial, ethnic, religious, or sexual nature; graphic or degrading comments about an individual or his or her appearance; display of sexually suggestive objects or pictures; or offensive or abusive physical contact. Acts of harassment by any employee are strictly prohibited and will result in disciplinary action that may include termination of employment.

The employment relationship is viewed differently culturally and legally throughout the world. The philosophical foundation of the U.S. employment relationship, the **employment-at-will doctrine**, provides that, except for express employment contracts, the employment relationship can be terminated at will (without notice) by either party. Germany views **employment as a property right** that becomes stronger the longer an employee works for a company. In Germany, hiring a single employee can result in the company being designated as having "permanent status," leading to the taxation of the exporter's German-generated revenues. Thus, designating a German national as an independent contractor in a clearly written contract is prudent.

The decision to hire foreign employees, especially in most EU countries, should be made with full knowledge of European national employment law. In Germany, the notice required to discharge an employee may vary from four weeks to seven months depending on the longevity of the employment. Dismissals are permitted only following consultation with statutorily mandated **Works Councils**. Also, workers can sue for reinstatement and damages if the dismissal is determined to be "unjustified." Furthermore, severance payments can reach as high as a full year of salary or more for long-term employees.

Under the **French Labor Code**, a meeting with the employee being discharged and notice is required, making immediate termination impossible. In order to avoid civil sanctions for breach of contract, the employer must be able to prove that there were serious grounds for the dismissal. The employee also has a right to a severance payment based upon seniority. He may waive this right in favor of a statutorily mandated **conversion contract**. Under the conversion contract, the employee receives, at the cost of the employer, enhanced government unemployment benefits and retraining or educational opportunities. If the ground for dismissal is economic, then the discharged employee has a right to reemployment for a period of one year in the event that the economic factors change.

In France, dismissals for reasons of **redundancy** are allowed under certain conditions. Redundancy is the term for "laying off" workers no longer needed because of restructuring or downsizing. The employer may make such collective dismissals only following consultation with labor unions. Also, the selection of workers to be dismissed must be based upon the criteria established by law that factors in the number of family dependents, seniority, and organizational needs.

In Italy, trade unions are given standing to sue employers under the law for any violations of rules pertaining to union membership or activities. Under Italian law, an employer's freedom to hire is limited. A number of agencies are given the responsibility to place workers. These include the Ministry of Labor and the Central Employment Commission, along with regional and provincial employment offices. The Placement Office selects workers among those registered on its **hiring list.** Unemployed workers are given priority over those wanting to change jobs. This procedure is known as *annunzione numerica* or **hiring by number.**

In the area of termination, the employer must follow a statutory **consultation procedure** that includes the giving of notice. Failure to give notice obligates the employer to pay an **indemnity in lieu of notice.** The indemnity payment is an amount equal to the pay the worker would have received for the period of the required notice. On average, it can take about three months to dismiss an employee. The employee is entitled to up to three years of indemnity (unemployment) paid through contributions by the employer to the National Social Security Institute.

International Labor Standards

Labor regulation has become a controversial issue in both the regional and global contexts. In the global arena, national and international labor groups have criticized the creation of the WTO with its narrow mandate of fostering free trade. Historically, the **International Labour Organization (ILO)** has been associated primarily with the development of international norms applicable to labor issues. The Treaty of Versailles established the ILO in 1919 with the stated principle that "labor should not be regarded merely as a commodity or article of commerce." A common device used to advance labor standards is the inclusion of **labor clauses** in trade agreements.

The **ILO Declaration on Fundamental Principles and Rights at Work** enumerates a number of "core labor standards" including: (1) freedom of association and the right to collective bargaining; (2) elimination of all forms of forced or compulsory labor; (3) abolition of child labor; and (4) elimination of discrimination in respect of employment and occupation. A developing country may lose preferential tariff rates for violating labor rights. The Generalized System of Preferences (GSP) law states that reduced tariff rates are to be removed if a "country has not taken steps to afford internationally recognized worker rights to workers in the country."

The EU has addressed labor standards on a piecemeal basis by incorporating them into agreements on specific activities. For example, EU directives require the insertion of labor clauses in public procurement contracts. Another pro-labor device recognized in Europe is the Works Council. These employee councils require a company to provide information and seek consultation with its workers on plant and workforce relocations.[6]

Independent Contractor Contract

The designation of a foreign agent as an employee, partner (joint venture), or independent contractor is crucial. If the foreign agent is hired as an independent contractor, then the employment regulations discussed above do not apply to the relationship. Furthermore, the principal (company) doing the hiring would not be liable for the acts of the independent contractor, as it would be for acts of an employee or partner.

It is important that independent contractor status be stated in a written contract and in the actual carrying out of the relationship. The independent contractor agreement should include a **nonpartnership clause** to prevent the principal from being vicariously liable under agency principles. A typical nonpartnership clause states that "the party being hired is to perform as an independent contractor and nothing contained herein should be construed as creating a partnership between the parties to this agreement."

In addition, a **work for hire clause** should be inserted into employment and independent contractor agreements in which the employee or independent contractor is being paid to develop new technology or to perform research and development. This clause makes it clear that all rights to the research and intellectual property rights revert to the employer. A typical work for hire clause reads that "all inventions, creations, and research of the employee (or independent contractor) during the term of his employment shall be work for hire and shall be the property of the employer, and that all rights to the intellectual property shall be assigned by the employee to the employer."

Foreign Sales Representative

The most common use of the independent contractor vehicle for transacting business is to hire a foreign sales representative. This relationship has been defined as the hiring of an agent "to prospect for and visit customers with a view to negotiating and concluding sales agreements in the name and for account of the exporter of goods, services, technology."[7] This relationship is also referred to as a **commercial agency** arrangement. The main difference between a representative office and an agent is that the former cannot sell or sign contracts but only market and do research, while the latter can perform all trade activities. To protect the foreign company's interests properly, a comprehensive agreement should be drawn between the parties concerned.

A subsequent determination or conversion by a foreign government of an independent sales agent to employment status subjects the exporter to a wide array of foreign laws, including tax and labor laws. An employment designation may also "establish" the company for purposes of personal jurisdiction in the courts of that country. Thus, the structuring and wording of the services contract as one of the independent agency, and not a dependent agency, is crucial for avoiding such host country laws. The profound differences in the area of agency law between civil law and common law countries require the advice of foreign legal counsel when entering such a relationship.

Logistical Services

An exporter must comply with foreign packing, labeling, and documentation requirements. Because of the complexity of these requirements, most exporters enlist the services of freight forwarders and customs brokers. **Freight forwarders** are agents for exporters and importers and are experts at transporting cargo worldwide. However, the services of the freight forwarder are broader than those offered by a customs broker; freight forwarders provide services pertaining to export requirements, transportation, and importation regulations. A **Customs broker's** expertise is in the government requirements for the importation of goods. Freight forwarders are familiar with import and export regulations, methods of shipping, and documentation requirements. In a documentary transaction, the freight forwarder can be hired to review the bill of lading and other documents. The freight forwarder can also help in packaging and marking goods for transport.

Law of Freight Forwarding

The freight forwarder plays a crucial role in the transportation of products under an international sales contract. In some cases, freight forwarders act as agents for carriers, particularly liner shipping companies for carriage of goods by sea. Freight forwarding services normally include the clearance of goods for export and import. They have cooperating partners in other countries to whom instructions are given for the receipt of the cargo and for customs clearance.

The freight forwarder also plays the important role of **cargo consolidator**. Most exporter shipments require booking only a portion of a ship's cargo space. The freight forwarder obtains reasonable shipment rates by consolidating the cargo of a number of its clients. In addition, the demands of international **multimodal transport** have transformed the freight forwarder from a mere agent of the shipper to that of an operator with carrier liability. The role of the freight forwarder as a common carrier is recognized in Article 19 of the UCP 600. It allows freight forwarders to issue bills of lading if they are acting as a carrier or multimodal transport operator.

Advertising Services and Law

National laws dealing with deceptive advertising vary in scope and enforcement. Because of cultural differences, an advertising campaign that is legal in one country may be illegal in another. Almost all developed countries possess laws that make it illegal to use misleading advertising. There are three means of enforcement—administrative agencies, through private litigation, and via industry self-regulation—that vary dramatically throughout the world.

In the U.S., the **Federal Trade Commission** (**FTC**) regulates virtually all forms of advertising. It is empowered to prevent "unfair and deceptive practices."[8] Section 43(a) of the **Lanham Act**[9] created a private cause of action for anyone injured by false advertising. There are also many examples of industry and media self-regulation. One example is the National Advertising Division of the Council of Better Business Bureaus.

Civil law countries, including Germany, rely on advertising law that authorizes private litigation to control misleading advertising. The Scandinavian countries make use of the consumer ombudsman to enact advertising guidelines and to resolve disputes. Because of the vast differences in advertising law enforcement, it is important for the international entrepreneur to seek local counsel before embarking on a marketing campaign.

Businesses can minimize the risks of false or improper advertising through insurance. Although insurance will not protect against government prosecution, it will minimize exposure to private litigation. The *Heritage Mutual Insurance* case illustrates some of the issues created by the intersection of advertising and insurance law. This case explains the important concepts of **advertising injury** and the **duty to defend**.

Heritage Mutual Insurance v. Advanced Polymer Technology

97 F. Supp. 2d 913 (S.D. Ind. 2000)

Judge. "Advertising injury" describes a type of insurance coverage provided in standard commercial general liability insurance (GCL) policies. Standard policies are published by the Insurance Services Organization (ISO). Heritage Mutual Insurance Company (Heritage) filed a complaint seeking a declaratory judgment (a party to civil litigation asks a court to conclusively rule on its rights or obligations) that it has no duty to defend or to indemnify its insured, Advanced Polymer Technology (APT). The policy at issue was a Commercial General Liability policy.

Coverage "B" of the CGL policy, entitled "Personal and Advertising Injury Liability," insured APT for any "advertising injury caused in the course of advertising APT's goods, products or services." The policy defined "advertising injury" as arising out of one of the following offenses: (a) oral or written publication of material that slanders or libels a person or organization or disparages a person's or organization's goods, products, or services; (b) oral or written publication of material that violates a person's right of privacy; (c) misappropriation of advertising ideas or style of doing business; or (d) infringement of copyright, title, or slogan.

Coverage is excluded for advertising injury arising out of material whose first publication took place before the beginning of the policy period. Additionally, the policy obligated Heritage to "defend any suit seeking those damages." The insured is required to prove that her claims fall within the coverage provisions of her policy, but the insurer bears the burden of proving specific exclusions or limitations to policy coverage.

The insurer's duty to defend is broader than its duty to indemnify (pay on the claim). An insurer must defend an action even if only a small portion of the conduct alleged in the complaint falls within the scope of the insurance policy. When an insurance contract contains an ambiguity, it is strictly construed against the insurance company.

Environ, a patent owner, claims that APT willfully infringed on its patents. It also accuses APT of "federal unfair competition" under the Lanham Act by contending that APT made "false and misleading statements as to the creation or ownership" of the piping product "in its application for a patent." Environ alleges that APT's marketing of its POLY-TECH piping system as "patent pending" creates a cloud on its ownership of the invention, thereby discouraging investment in or purchase of its products.

APT claims that Environ's allegations fall within the "disparagement category" of advertising injury offenses. Direct reference to the competitor's product is necessary to fall within the plain meaning of "disparage." The phrase "patent pending" signifies nothing about the quality or state of Environ's product, and, therefore, does not constitute implied disparagement.

Heritage's reasons for denial of coverage were rational and understandable. We hold that Heritage has no duty to defend its' insured since the allegations do not constitute advertising injury offenses.

Case Highlights

- Insurance Services Organization (ISO) is a trade association that develops standard insurance forms and clauses
- "Advertising injury" is a type of insurance coverage provided in standard commercial general liability insurance policies (CGL)
- Under insurance law, the insured is required to prove that her claims fall within the coverage provision of her policy, but the insurer bears the burden of proving specific exclusions or limitations to policy coverage
- Insurer's duty to defend is broader than its duty to indemnify
- When an insurance contract contains an ambiguity, it is strictly construed against the insurance company.

Cross-Border Security Offerings

Companies raise capital in a number of ways including borrowing from banks and accepting investments by venture capitalists. The most common way of raising capital is to sell either debt instruments (bonds) or equity instruments (stock shares). The advantage of selling shares in the company is that it raises capital without incurring a debt obligation. The internationalization of the capital markets has been one of the major developments in the business world. It is not uncommon for even small or medium investors to allocate a portion of their portfolios to foreign securities. From a legal perspective, this poses questions as to the enforcement and regulation of international securities transactions.

The key issue with the international sale and purchase of securities is how such offerings are to be regulated. Since there is no international policing institution, the regulation comes through the enforcement of national regulatory laws. The extraterritorial application of securities laws follows a standard two-prong test. First, the foreign parties must have the intent of selling their securities in a country's marketplace. Second, the alleged foreign activities are likely to have an *effect* within that country. The second prong is commonly referred to as the **effects test**. The effects test has been used to determine the extraterritorial applicability of numerous American laws such as discrimination, antitrust, and tort law. The effects test stands for the principle that the exercise of jurisdiction is appropriate where the illegal activity, such as fraud abroad, injures someone within another country.

In order to avoid foreign securities laws, a company can take steps to prevent the solicitation of persons within another country. However, the development of securities transactions over the Internet challenges a company's ability to avoid foreign jurisdiction. An offering on the Internet not intended for U.S. investors may still be subject to SEC enforcement actions. The global nature of the Internet can lead to the conclusion that such offers are being made in another country. Those wanting to avoid a country's securities laws in offshore offerings should take reasonable precautions to guard against making sales to persons in that country and to place a disclaimer on the offer stating that it is not intended for persons from that country.

The **International Organization of Securities Commissions** (**IOSCO**) has made it a goal to achieve the comparability of information required under national securities laws in order to facilitate cross-border offerings and listings by multinational securities issuers. In order to achieve this goal, IOSCO continues to develop generally accepted disclosure standards that could be used in a uniform disclosure statement for cross-border offerings and listings. A company planning to sell shares internationally should review these standards when preparing required prospectuses and registration statements.

A problem with international standards is that they fail to provide a definition of **materiality**, which is crucial in determining the accuracy of documents and statements. All countries require that a company or issuer disclose all material information. However, the definition of materiality varies from country to country. In *TSC Industries, Inc. v. Northway, Inc.*,[10] the U.S. Supreme Court defined materiality as a fact where there is "a substantial likelihood that a reasonable shareholder or investor would have considered it important." In Quebec, Canada, materiality is considered as something likely to have significant influence on the value or market price of the securities of the reporting company or issuer. The Stock Exchange of Hong Kong's Listing Rules define *materiality* as the disclosing of information "necessary to enable an investor to make an informed assessment of the activities, assets and liabilities, financial position, management, and prospects of the issuer." In contrast, the EU does not use the concept of "material" and therefore does not provide any definition of materiality.

Internationalization of Accounting and Taxation Services

The internationalization of business has placed pressure upon the accounting profession to provide necessary support services. Accounting services, as with most professional services, have been internationalized. The areas where international accounting services are needed include transfer pricing, currency translation, and joint venture accounting. **Transfer pricing** refers to a method of tax avoidance. In structuring contracts between itself and its foreign subsidiaries, a company will often attempt to recognize or transfer profits to subsidiaries located in low-tax countries. International standards require that such intra-company transactions be calculated using an arm's length method of valuation. Contract prices between affiliated companies are to be set at market prices. Therefore, multinational corporations need to develop a transfer pricing policy that will be generally accepted in the countries in which they do business. This is needed to avoid being subject to double taxation. Guidance can be obtained by using guidelines for transfer pricing produced by the OECD.

One approach for taxing multinational corporations or cross-border business transactions through unitary taxation. This approach apportions corporate profits to the different taxing authorities using a formula based on sales, payroll, and property within each jurisdiction.

The two most influential bodies in harmonizing accounting standards are the International Accounting Standards Committee (IASC), which publishes of **International Accounting Standards (IAS)** and the International Organization of Securities Commissions (IOSC), which focuses on the development of a common international prospectus for securities offerings and listings. The diversity of accounting practices throughout the world is an obstacle to the development of global capital markets. The ability to provide comparable financial statements to be used in cross-border security offerings significantly decreases the number and types of required filings.

Commercial Agents and Distributors

The difference between commercial agency and distributorships is that the first involves the parties: principal (manufacturer–exporter), agent, and third parties (customers). In the agency relationship, the key issue is whether the agent has the power (actual or apparent authority) to bind the principal to contracts with third parties. In the distributor relationship, there are normally two parties: principals and distributors. However, there are different types of distributor relationships including those in which the distributor also acts as an agent.

Under many national laws, an agent can bind the **principal** (manufacturer–exporter) to contracts with third-party customers, either through **actual** or **apparent authority**. However, across countries apparent authority may or may not be presumed in specific situations. In beginning a new agency or distribution relationship, the exporter should not initially give a foreign sales representative the ability to bind it to contracts with third parties. Instead, although inconvenient, the exporter should retain the right to approve or disapprove any such contracts. In some countries, depending on the agent's title and characteristics, apparent authority is often presumed. However, in international practice actual or apparent authority is not presumed. In such cases, the foreign purchaser should ask for proof of the agent's authority to bind the exporter.

Apparent Authority: An agent's power to act on behalf of a principal, even though not expressly or impliedly granted. This power arises if a third party reasonably infers, from the principal's representations and conduct, that the principal granted such power to the agent.

Sales representatives or commercial agents are generally compensated by payment of commissions per contract brokered. If the sales representative receives a salary, then she may be considered an employee under most national laws. A foreign distributor is also independent, especially when it buys goods on its own account and is compensated by making profits on reselling the goods. Distribution sales, independent or not, require the exporter and distributor to cooperate to keep the distribution of the goods efficient and reliable, and the distributor has obligations to the manufacturer–exporter that an ordinary buyer does not. From the perspective of the exporter, using an independent distributor relationship is less risky because the distributor assumes the risks of loss due to not being able to sell the goods at a profit. The risk to the exporter occurs if it selects an incompetent or inefficient distributor and is tied to a longer-term supply contract, resulting in lower sales of its products.

The distribution agreement is a type of commercial agency relationship. It is also an example of a common form of service contract. Successful exporting is dependent upon the strength of the exporter–distributor relationship. It is the job of the foreign distributor to get the goods to market. There are numerous choices that an exporter has in how it markets, sells, and export its goods.

Sales Representative

An overseas sales representative is the equivalent to the manufacturer's domestic representative. The representative uses the company's product literature and samples in presenting the product to potential buyers. The sales representative may operate on either an exclusive or a nonexclusive basis. Sale representatives often represent numerous companies. The sales representative works on a commission basis, assumes no risk or responsibility, and is under contract for a definite period of time (renewable by mutual agreement).

Commercial Agent

The terms *foreign representative* and *commercial agent* are often used interchangeably. A representative commonly acts as an agent for the manufacturer–exporter. The distinction made here is that a foreign representative may either be an employee or an independent contractor, while a commercial agent is an independent contractor. In either case, agency principles apply. Agency and specialized agency law is widely recognized and accepted in common and civil law countries.[11]

In civil law countries such as France and Germany, the rules of agency are based on the Roman law concept of "mandate," which distinguishes, on the one hand, the principal–agent relationship and, on the other hand, the agent–third party relationship ("theory of separation").[12] This is a restrictive approach since the principal will only be bound when he consents to the agent acting on his behalf within the limits defined by the terms of the **mandate**.

In Anglo-American common law, the position is different since the rules are of a general nature and apply to a wide category of agents. There is more of a fusion of the agent and principal as a single personality. The agent can therefore bind the principal even when the latter does not wish to be bound, under apparent authority. This explains why the common law protects the principal in the form of fiduciary duties imposed on the agent, such as the duty to obey, the duty to account, the duty of loyalty (disclosure of conflict of interests), and the duty of care (to act competently). See Figure 14.2 "Sampling of Agency Laws."

UNIDROIT Principles for International Commercial Contracts

- Article 2.2.2(2) (scope of authority): An agent has authority to perform all acts necessary in the circumstances to achieve the proper purposes for which the authority was granted.
- Article 2.2.4(2) (nondisclosure of agency): If, when contracting with the third party on behalf of a business, an agent represents herself to be the owner of that business, the third party, upon discovery of the real owner of the business, may exercise also against the latter the rights it has against the agent.
- Article 2.2.7(2) (conflict of interests): A principal may not avoid the contract if the agent has disclosed the conflict of interests to the principal.
- Article 2.2.10 (termination of authority): Termination of an agent's authority is not effective in relation to the third party unless the third party knew or ought to have known of it.

Principles of European Contract Law

- Article 3.102 (categories of representation): If an agent acts in the name of a principal, the rules on direct representation apply. It is irrelevant whether the principal's identity is revealed at the time the agent acts. If a third party neither knows nor has reason to know that the intermediary acts as an agent, the rules on indirect representation apply.
- 3.207 (ratification): If a person acting as an agent acts without authority or outside its authority, the principal may ratify the agent's act.

Principles of European Law on Mandate Contracts

- Article 2.101 (duty of cooperation): A principal must provide information in so far as it is needed to allow the agent to perform under the mandate contract.
- Article 2.103 (expenses): An agent is entitled to reimbursement of expenses.

Figure 14.2 Sampling of Agency Laws.

EU Commercial Agency Directive

- Article 3 (duties of agent): An agent shall make proper efforts to negotiate and, where appropriate, to conclude the transactions he is instructed to take care of; communicate to his principal all the necessary information available to agent; and comply with reasonable instructions given by his principal.
- Article 17 (indemnity): The commercial agent shall be entitled to an indemnity (after termination) to the extent that the agent has brought the principal new customers or has significantly increased the volume of business with existing customers and the principal continues to derive substantial benefits from the business with such customers. The maximum indemnity is for one year calculated from the commercial agent's average annual remuneration over the preceding five years.
- Article 23 (restraint of trade clause/territorial restrictions): A restraint of trade clause shall only be valid if it relates to the geographical area or the group of customers and the geographical area entrusted to the commercial agent and to the kind of goods covered by his agency under the contract. A restraint of trade clause shall be valid for not more than two years after termination of the agency contract.

German Handelsgesetzbuch (Commercial Code or HGB)

- § 84: An agent is independent if he is essentially free to organize his activities and to determine his hours of work.

French Civil Code

- Article 1154: Where a representative states that he is acting on behalf of another person but contracts in his own name, he alone is bound toward the other contracting party.

French Code de Commerce

- Article L 134-1: Commercial agents are independent professionals permanently entrusted with negotiating and possibly concluding sale, purchase, rental, or service provision contracts.
- Article L 134-4: Contracts concluded between commercial agents and their principals shall be in the common interest of the parties.

United States Restatement (Third) Agency Law

- §2.02(3) (scope of authority): An agent's understanding of the principal's objectives is reasonable if it accords with the principal's manifestations and the inferences that a reasonable person in the agent's position would draw form the circumstances creating the agency.
- §2.06(2) (undisclosed principal): An undisclosed principal may not rely on instructions given an agent that qualify or reduce the agent's authority to less than the authority a third party would reasonably believe the agent to have under the same circumstances if the principal had been disclosed.
- §8.01 (fiduciary principle): An agent has a fiduciary duty to act loyally for the principal's benefit in all matters connected with the agency relationship.
- §8.02: An agent has a duty not to acquire a material benefit from a third party related to the transaction
- §8.08 (duty of care): An agent has a duty to the principal to act with the care, competence, and diligence normally exercised by agents in similar circumstances.

Figure 14.2 (Continued).

Distributors

The foreign distributor is a business that purchases goods from an exporter (at a discount) and resells them for a profit. The foreign distributor generally provides support and service for the product. The distributor usually carries an inventory of products and a supply of spare parts and also maintains adequate facilities and personnel for servicing broken or defective products. Distributors typically handle a range of noncompeting, complementary, products. The distributor often sells to retailers or dealers. In selecting a distributor for the first time, it is prudent to provide a trial period before commencement of the longer time period. Some countries have laws limiting the exporter's ability to terminate the distribution contract.

Exporter–Distributor Relationship

There are numerous reasons that an exporter may use a foreign distributor. First, it lowers the costs of marketing and transporting the goods within a foreign country. Second, the appropriate distributor will already have an established distribution network in the country and will possess the expertise to introduce the goods to the market. Small and medium-sized companies that do not have the capital to adequately advertise, comply with foreign regulations, and distribute their goods are unlikely to penetrate a foreign market without the aid of distributor. Third, the distributor takes on the responsibilities of complying with the foreign country's laws and regulations.

A company should develop a checklist to be used for the selection of a foreign distributor. A company's checklist should be tailored to reflect the types of products or services being sold and the characteristics of the countries targeted for export. See Figure 14.3 *Doing Business Internationally*: "Factors in Choosing a Foreign Distributor." Common duties assigned to distributors include (1) marketing of the product; (2) loyalty to the manufacturer–exporter (noncompetition clause); (3) buying and selling the goods in its own name; and (4) complying with local laws and informing the manufacturer of any changes in the law that impact the legality of its product.

Negotiated duties include requiring the distributor to defend the manufacturer from product liability claims; duty to obey instructions of the manufacturer relating to the distribution of goods; obligation of distributor to provide after-sales services (warranty claims, repair or replacement of defective goods); spending a minimum fixed amount on advertising and promotion; requiring the distributor to purchase a minimum quantity of the goods; and requiring the distributor to assist the manufacturer in protecting the manufacturer's intellectual property rights. In regard to the assumption of liability for product liability

Size of Sales Force

How many field sales personnel does the representative or distributor have?
What is the company's short and long-range expansion plans?

Sales Record

Has its sales growth been consistent over the last five years? What are its sales objectives for next year?

TerritorialAnalysis

What territory does it now cover? Is its coverage consistent with the coverage you desire?
Does it have any branch offices in the territory to be covered?

Product Mix

How many product lines does it represent? Are these product lines compatible with yours?

Facilities and Equipment

Does it have adequate warehouse facilities? What is its method of stock control?
If your product requires servicing, is it equipped and qualified to do so? To what extent will you have to share training costs? Is it willing to inventory repair parts and replacement items?

Marketing Policies

Does it have special incentive or motivation programs for its sales personnel? How does it monitor sales performance? How does it train its sales staff?

Customer Profile

Who are its key accounts? What kinds of customers is it currently targeting?

Principals Represented

How many principals is it currently representing? Would you be its primary supplier?
If not, how does your percentage compare with that of other suppliers?

Promotion

Can it help you compile market research information to be used in making forecasts?
What media does it use, if any, to promote sales? How much of its budget is allocated to advertising?

Figure 14.3 Doing Business Internationally: Factors in Choosing a Foreign Distributor.

claims by the distributor is unenforceable under some national laws. It is important that the manufacturer obtain products liability insurance, as well as requiring the distributor to do so.

Consignment

There is an exception to the general rule of distributors (and commercial agents) as independent contractors that buy on their own account. The exporter and distributor may work under a consignment arrangement. In a consignment arrangement, the ownership or title to the goods remains with the exporter on delivery of the goods to the distributor, instead of the outright sale of goods to the distributor. The first concern is that the risk of loss (damage or theft of the goods) remains with the exporter so appropriate insurance needs to be obtained to cover consigned goods against loss or damage, as well as to mitigate the risk of nonpayment.

Under a consignment contract, the exporter (**consignor**) ships the goods to a distributor in a foreign country (**consignee**). The risk of the goods not selling and being returned remains with the exporter. This is different than a distribution contract where the foreign distributor normally purchases the goods and assumes the risks of not being able to resell the goods. A consignment contract is also different from a commercial agency contract where the agent procures a sales contract and the exporter sends the goods directly to the buyer.

From the perspective of the manufacturer–exporter (consignor), the primary issues of concern that need to be dealt with in the consignment contract are (1) **independent contractor status**; (2) territorial restrictions; and (3) legal compliance in the foreign country. Independent contractor status is important in order for the consignor to avoid the employee protection laws of the country of import, which can be onerous. The EU is noted for **evergreen laws**, which will be discussed later in the section on **commercial agency**. These laws require the exporter to give advance notice and just cause for the termination of an employee or agent, as well as substantial severance and damages payments. Therefore, the contract should state that the consignee is being hired as an independent contractor and not as an employee or partner. The consignor must also treat the consignee as an independent contractor, meaning it should not attempt to exercise control over the consignee's business. These precautions are likely to allow the exporter to avoid the evergreen laws related to the employment relationship, but the consignee may still be considered to be a commercial agent. In some countries, especially in the EU, evergreen statutes also protect agency relationships, but these protections are not as costly as those that pertain to employees and can be limited by a properly drafted agency contract.

The parties should negotiate detailed terms in their contract to govern all matters relating to consignment stocks, such as: (1) whether the principal can take back the whole inventory or part of it; (2) whether the agent is allowed to send back unsold goods; and (3) whether that the agent is to take all necessary safeguards to protect the principal's ownership rights. In some countries, the creation of consignment subjects the principal to being taxed as a resident.

The exporting on **consignment** is somewhat like a partnership between two independent parties. To succeed, the exporter must partner with a reputable and trustworthy foreign distributor. Figure 14.4 *Doing Business Internationally*: "Exporting on Consignment" provides an example of why and how a consignment–distribution arrangement works.

The exporter–consignor will want to assign the obligation for legal and regulatory compliance to the consignee. The consignee should be knowledgeable in its country's regulations (safety, health, and environmental standards) and be able to obtain necessary government permits, licenses, and approvals. The

Manufacturers and suppliers often enter in contracts with clients that require just-in-time delivery (delivery immediately after receiving the purchase order). Just-in-time supply chains reduce the costs of storing and managing inventory for the purchaser. The risk to the exporter–seller is that delays in delivery of the goods exposes it to liability for breach of contract. In order to mitigate the risk, manufacturers enter a consigned inventory arrangement with a foreign distributor who receives and stocks the goods in the foreign country and sells them to the downstream customers. The distributor receives a commission for sales made, and then sends the net proceeds to the manufacturer as the goods are sold. This arrangement allows manufacturers to increase production and increase foreign sales since the delivery and consignment of goods overseas with a distributor allows for faster delivery to the local market.

Figure 14.4 Doing Business Internationally: Exporting on Consignment.

consignment contract should also expressly state that the consignee is responsible for the payment of taxes and fees related to the sale of the goods.

Negotiating a Distribution Contract

Drafting an international distribution agreement is shaped by the law of the distributor's country. The distributor (along with commercial agency) relationship is regulated under some foreign statutes. Some countries require distributors to register as distributors with the government. Some countries, by statute or case law, require that the distribution agreement provide some minimal level of protection to the distributor or agent. In France, judges regularly order additional compensation to be paid by the principal (manufacturer) when severing a distribution relationship. Germany recognizes a "**goodwill indemnity**" that is owed to the distributor upon termination. Finally, foreign competition laws may invalidate territorial restrictions limiting where and to whom the distributor may sell. EU law has been used to challenge territorial restrictions as restrictive trade practices.

The International Chamber of Commerce's (ICC) ***Guide to Drafting International Distribution Agreements*** outlines the underlying risks of the distribution relationship and the ways to deal with such risks in the distribution contract. A brief review of this guide is a good starting point for analyzing this type of contractual relationship. A *distributor* is "not a middleman, but a dealer who buys goods in order to resell them in his own name, even if he is often called an agent." It should be noted that a distributor may act as both an agent and as a distributor so that he may owe fiduciary duties (duty of loyalty and duty of care) to the exporter.

The exporter/manufacturer–distributor relationship is a special kind of sales relationship because: (1) the distributor often deals with the promotion and organization of distribution within its contractual territory; (2) generally the contractual territory is exclusive to the distributor; (3) the contract is for a certain duration; (4) there exists a duty of loyalty (owed by the distributor (obligation to refrain from competing with its principal); and (5) the relationship almost always relates to the distribution of brand-name products. The exporter should include a clause requiring the distributor to use its "best efforts" to achieve maximum sales. Often the manufacturer will want to ensure that each of its distributors offers the same conditions and pricing to their customers. France, Germany, the UK, and the Scandinavian countries, among others, invalidate fixed pricing as illegal retail price maintenance.

If **key personnel** are considered essential, they should be recognized in the contract. The contract can then provide for termination in the event that essential persons cease to be associated with the distributor. In order to avoid the reach of evergreen statutes, the contract should have specific commencement and expiration dates. Setting a fixed term for the agreement will help minimize the chances of large indemnity payments being owed under certain national laws. Also, renewals should be kept to a minimum. In order to minimize the size of indemnity payments, it is better to enter into an entirely new contract at the expiration of the first contract.

Distribution Contract

Contract terms that protect the exporter include best efforts, products liability, and post-termination clauses. The **best efforts clause** requires the distributor to make reasonable efforts to achieve a maximum number of sales. The best efforts clause should provide a measure or benchmarks to determine the level of effort, such as "minimum sales quota" or annual thresholds of the quantity of goods that need to be sold. Failure to meet these benchmarks gives the exporter a just cause to terminate the contract or deny a renewal of the contract. The best efforts obligation can be further detailed by requiring the distributor to spend a minimum amount of money on advertising and sales promotion.

It is beneficial to both parties to allocate the risk of products liability claims. The exporter will want to place a **products liability clause** in the contract assigning the risk of product liability claims to the distributor. However, such a clause may be unenforceable under some foreign laws, which impose joint liability on both the manufacturer–exporter and the distributor.[13] In such cases, the contract should obligate both the parties to obtain a minimum amount of products liability insurance.

Manufacturers often insert **territorial restrictions** limiting the distributor's sales to an assigned territory. One method is to prohibit the distributor from selling goods to customers outside its territory. However, such a provision is invalid under **EU Regulation 1983/83**. The distributor can be prohibited from openly soliciting customers outside its territory but cannot be prohibited from making passive sales—those in which the customer contacts the distributor.

It is important that the contract specify any obligation that will survive or continue after the end of the contract. The contract should provide for the disposition of a distributor's inventory of products or spare parts. It should provide for the price to be paid by the manufacturer if it is obligated to buy back stock, which is required under some national laws. The contract should also terminate the distributor's use of the manufacturer's intellectual property rights and confidential information, such as customers' lists or databases.[14]

A distribution contract with a distributor in a country with evergreen statutes (see the section below on commercial agency) that protect employees and commercial agents at the time of termination should include not only an independent contractor clause, but also a **no agency–no partnership clause**. Such a clause characterizes the distribution relationship as simply one between a seller and a buyer. Furthermore, the contract does not create an implied partnership or joint venture between the parties. To support this characterization, the contract should allocate to the distributor all matters relating to customer credit, billings, and invoices, and that the risk of nonpayment is borne by the distributor. This type of clause seeks to avoid the evergreen protections provided to employees, commercial agents, or distributors.

The duration of the contract should be specified in the contract, along with matters relating to future renewals of the contract. Thus, distribution contracts generally self-terminate at the expiration of the contract term. However, either party may terminate distribution contracts for just cause. It is best to define what would trigger a **just cause termination**. Any type of breach may not be sufficient to justify the termination of the contract. Some courts and arbitration panels make a distinction between a material breach justifying termination and a minor breach leading to a bad faith termination of the contract. From the perspective of the exporter, it is best to include a detailed list of events that allow for termination. This list is placed in either the **default** or **termination clause**. For example, the clause provides that the distributor shall be deemed in default and the exporter has a right of termination upon the occurrence of the following events: (1) if the distributor ceases to operate or otherwise abandons its business with respect to the sale of exporter's goods; (2) if the distributor transfers any rights or obligations under the contract to a third party; (3) if the distributor sells its business or a controlling interest; (4) if the distributor knowingly maintains false books or records, or knowingly submits any false reports to the exporter; (5) if the distributor fails to make timely payments for the goods; (6) if the distributor fails to comply with host country laws and regulations relating to the marketing and selling of exporter's products; and (7) if the distributor markets or sells similar products of a competitor. The longer and more detailed the list of default events, the greater the rights of the exporter to terminate the contract and reasonably argue that the termination was for just cause. Other types of default events include cases where the distributor files for bankruptcy or becomes insolvent or if it fails to meet required sales thresholds or quotas.

Protection of IPR, Trade Secrets, and Confidential Information

It is especially important in international distribution contracts to provide for the protection of intellectual property rights (IPR), trade secrets, and know-how. A common clause is called the **nonchallenge** or **validity clause**, which prohibits the distributor from challenging the validity of the manufacturer–exporter's IPR. For example, a patent or copyright recognized under the country of the exporter may not be enforceable under some foreign laws. The distributor could challenge the validity of the patents and copyrights in its home country. If they are not valid, then there is no reason for the distributor to pay fees or royalties for their use. Even more problematic for the exporter is when a distributor registers for ownership of the patent or copyright in the countries covered by the distribution contracts.

The exporter will want to protect its trademarks by requiring that its products and relevant packaging sold by the distributor display all necessary trademarks. The contract should require that the distributor should not alter or add to such trade names, trademarks, labels, or literature in any way, and not do any act which might injure or dilute, diminish, or otherwise adversely affect the reputation of the exporter and its products. **Dilution of trademark** is a technical term that is discussed in Chapter 15. The contract should also make clear that trademarks and brand names are the exclusive property of the exporter, and that any rights in any new trademarks or copyrights related to the products, such as a new slogan, developed by the distributor, shall be assigned to the exporter.

The manufacturer–exporter should carefully state in the contract that the IPR and confidential information being licensed or shared with the distributor. This description is accompanied by a **reservation of rights clause** that states that any rights not expressly granted to the distributor remain with the exporter. Often the rights given to use such information and know-how are provided on a royalty-free, nonexclusive basis, but for the sole purpose of selling or distributing the exporter's products. The exporter will also want to control how the distributor markets its products by requiring that any sales, advertising, promotional, or related materials directed to the ultimate consumers receive the exporter's prior written approval.

As noted previously, a **confidentiality clause** in the contract should state that the obligations continue after the termination of the contract. The distributor must maintain the confidentiality of the exporter's trade secrets indefinitely after the termination of the distribution contract, except in the cases where the confidential information becomes part of the **public domain**. In order to prevent the distributor from using the exporter's information or know-how to promote a competitor's products, even if not intentionally, the exporter may consider including a prohibition that the distributor shall not manufacture, sell, or distribute any product that is similar to the exporter's products for a period of years following the termination of the relationship. However, such a provision may not be enforceable under foreign competition (antitrust) law, which is the subject of the next section.

Public domain refers to information, images, and creative works that have become part of public information and are freely useable. For example: previously protected intellectual property rights that have expired or have been forfeited; trade secrets that have been leaked or reverse engineered that become part of the public domain.

Competition Law

Most distribution agreements provide exclusive territories to the distributor; the exporter may be prohibited from selling products to customers who are likely to import them into the distributor's territory and the distributor will be prohibited from selling the products outside of its exclusive territory. The developing countries look with skepticism on any such restrictions and generally will not enforce restrictive contract provisions in their courts. Most developed countries allow the contracting parties full freedom to contract and will enforce most restrictive clauses. Under antitrust or competition laws, some forms of exclusivity may be deemed to be anticompetitive, and certain restrictions will be scrutinized.

EU Regulation 1983/83 deals with the legality of exclusive distribution agreements. For example, it generally disfavors clauses that prohibit a distributor from selling within the territory of another distributor. However, certain **block exemptions** can be utilized to defend against such challenges. A block exemption is simply a statutory recognition that certain types of business practices are to be permitted even though they technically violate EU competition (antitrust) law. An example would be exclusive territories pertaining to automobile dealerships. In addition, foreign competition laws need to be researched to see if exclusivity in a distribution agreement will be enforceable. Because of the complexity of foreign competition law, it is advisable to have a specialist review the distribution agreement.

Price-fixing and **tying clauses** are those most likely to be held as illegal. For example, many national laws prohibit the principal or licensor from setting pricing guidelines, especially at the retail level. Tying clauses that require the distributor to purchase other items along with the licensed product are generally unenforceable. One exception is when tying products or services is needed to ensure the quality of the licensed or distributed product. In such cases, a requirement that the licensee purchase materials from certified suppliers is likely to be enforced.

Noncompetition clauses are also susceptible to nonenforcement. Generally, a distribution contract cannot prohibit the agent or representative from also selling the products of another company. The one major exception is that U.S. courts will allow such clauses in cases involving patented property rights where the distributor is given an exclusive license. Thus, one strategy to increase the chances of enforceability is to tie exclusivity to noncompetition. For example, the distributor can be given the right to sell the goods of a competitor but in doing so converts the distribution agreement from exclusive to nonexclusive.

"Just in Case" Distribution

Just-in-time contracting (JIT) has been a popular supply management system for decades. It is an inventory strategy that companies employ to increase efficiency and decrease waste by receiving goods only as they are needed in the production process, thereby reducing inventory costs. JIT supply developed in Japan in the 1960s, most notably at Toyota. It eventually became a mainstream method in supply chain management with its adoption by many Western companies in the 1980s. It aims to reduce costs and waste, such as the costs of warehousing large inventories of supplies or manufactured products. JIT also refers to the ability to quickly respond to changes in the market and the needs of customers and has been tied to **total quality management** (TQM). JIT and TQM are interconnected since JIT depends on making it right the first time (avoidance of defective goods) and on preventive maintenance to avoid shutdowns and disruptions in the supply chain.

Total Quality Management (TQM): After working with industries in Japan after World War II, W. Edwards Deming returned to the U.S. and started the TQM movement. The main insight is that, by consistently looking at lowering costs, manufacturers inevitably lowered the quality of their products. The International Standards Organization (ISO) defines TQM as:

> A management approach of an organisation centered on quality, based on the participation of all its members and aiming at long term success through customer satisfaction and benefits to all members of the organisation and society.

However, there are inevitable disruptions in the supply chain, such as those due to natural disasters. An example was the closing of the ports in New York and New Jersey because of Hurricane Sandy in 2012 and the emergence of the COVID-19 virus in 2020. Even before Sandy, some companies modified their JIT approach by moving to a **"just-in-case" distribution** system.[15] It is interesting to see how thinking changes and ideas are recycled. For many years, companies went to centralized distribution centers by reducing the number of their warehouses and manufacturing plants in order to reduce costs. Just-in-case is based upon bringing the goods closer to the customer, which means increasing the number and strategically placing distribution centers throughout the supplier's market, which strengthens the supplier's JIT capabilities. Previously, it was common to warehouse goods at the major ports and ship the goods based on JIT needs throughout the country. More and more companies are now building distribution centers closer to their customers based upon the goal of being able to deliver materials and goods by truck within 24 hours. For example, Amazon opened three new distribution centers just in Texas. Increasing the proximity of the goods to customers decreases the chances of disruption in the supply chain and reduces transportation costs. It is generally accepted that the last leg of transporting goods is the most expensive since the trucks are often nearly empty in delivering a single order. Shortening the distance of the final leg reduces transportation costs. Furthermore, it reduces the competitive advantage of local supply companies by being able to deliver goods just as quickly.

From a law perspective, JIT shifts the risks of untimely delivery from the buyer to the supplier. When entering into a JIT contract, a manufacturer–exporter should take added precautions in negotiating the distribution or supply contract. Even though just-in-case supply reduces the risk of delay, JIT still provides a great deal of risk to the exporter–supplier of goods when ocean carriage is used. The *force majeure* clause should be expanded to include additional events that may delay the delivery of the goods, such as a shortage of materials needed to produce the goods. A clause requiring the buyer to maintain a minimum level of inventory alleviates the risk of damages for short-term delays in delivery.

Commercial Agency

The most common use of the agency (independent contractor) vehicle for transacting business is the hiring of a foreign sales representative or commercial agent. This relationship has been defined as the hiring of an agent "to prospect for and visit customers with a view to negotiating and when appropriate concluding sales agreements in the name and for account of the principal (exporter of goods, services, technology)."[16] Under EU regulations, the mere supplying of marketing services does not fall within the definition of **commercial agency.**[17] The ICC's *Commercial Agency—Guide for the Drawing up of Contracts* notes that some domestic laws grant special status to the commercial agent.

Therefore, laws of the foreign country of the commercial agent need to be researched "to ensure that nothing contained in a commercial agency contract is repugnant to imperative [mandatory] provisions"[18] of any law applicable to the contract. Even if the contract is enforceable as written, foreign laws will need to be studied in order to avoid their application to the principal. The clearest example of this is the application of foreign tax liability to the principal. In many countries, a nonresident principal will be liable for tax if the agent has, and habitually exercises, a general authority to negotiate and conclude contracts on behalf of the principal. For instance, when a principal appoints an agent in a foreign country with a fixed office therein and with power to make contracts on his behalf, the principal may be deemed to be carrying on business in that foreign country and be taxed accordingly.[19] Clearly, the use of foreign counsel is required in order to avoid such liability traps.

Provisions related to the termination of the agreement are the most important part of an international agency contract.[20] This is because of the existence of host country laws that restrict a foreign company's right to terminate an agency agreement. These laws, popularly referred to as **evergreen statutes**, will be dealt with in the next section.

Evergreen Statutes

The most difficult laws to avoid are national agency termination laws, popularly referred to as evergreen statutes. These laws often impose minimum notice requirements for terminating an agent or require the payment of an indemnity upon termination unless the termination is based upon a just cause. These laws are different than the employment regulations discussed earlier in the chapter. Unlike employment regulations, evergreen statutes do apply to agents acting as independent contractors.

Many European countries grant the agent a right upon the termination of the agency relationship to either an indemnity payment, based upon the length of the relationship and the level of past or anticipated payments, or to a claim for *damages* attributed to the termination. In countries like France, a decision not to renew an agency contract is construed as a termination requiring compensation be paid to the agent. **EU Directive 86/653** provides that agency contracts should provide for a minimum notice of termination. A reasonable notice period is one month per year of service. A commercial agent will be owed an indemnity upon termination to the extent that he has brought new customers to the principal or significantly increased the principal's volume of business.[21]

Article 17(3) of the EC Directive also allows national laws to provide for a damage claim to the agent, especially if at the time of termination, the agent had not completely amortized his costs and expenses relative to the representation. Article 117(5) requires the agent to notify its principal of a claim for indemnity or damages within one year from the date of termination. The best approach is to enter into a fixed-term contract with no renewal options. As stated earlier, the contract should provide a detailed list of performance standards upon which termination for *just cause* may be based. Also, some country laws, as in Belgium and France, presume that the agent is an employee even if the contract designates the agent as an independent contractor. Therefore, the easiest way to avoid this presumption is to deal with agents who are artificial entities (corporations). For example, in Belgium, if the contract subordinates the agent to the authority of the principal, then there is a legal presumption that an employment relationship has been formed. However, this presumption can be overcome if the agent is a corporate entity.

National labor and employment laws will need to be checked for obligations of the principal pertaining to social security and other "employment-related" statutory requirements. Under Italian law, the principal and the agent must pay 5 percent each on all commissions paid to the national agency (ENASARCO) as social security contributions. The principal is legally obligated to withhold the agent's contribution and remit it to the agency, along with an amount to be used toward the severance indemnity. A certain percentage is paid on a sliding scale based on the amount of the commissions paid, ranging from 4 percent to 1 percent.

It is vital to include an **escape clause** that allows for the termination of the agency contract with a fixed period of notice. Some contracts specify that either party may terminate the agreement with written advance notice of 30, 60, or 90 days. Some countries require a minimum notice period. Three months satisfies the requirements of many countries. Other contracts specify a certain term for the agreement (usually one year) but arrange for automatic annual renewal unless either party gives written notice of its intention not to renew. In some cases, escape clauses and other provisions to safeguard the exporter are limited by evergreen protections afforded to the agent under national law. Because of the existence of these statutes, the agency contract should include a default and termination clause in the agreement that allows the exporter or principal to end

- How far in advance must the representative be notified of the exporter's intention to terminate the agreement? (Three months satisfies the requirements of most countries.)
- What is just cause for terminating a representative? (Specifying causes for termination in the written contract usually strengthens the exporter's position; specific causes include the agent's failure to meet a minimum level of sales or a conflict of interest related to agent's sales of a competitor's products.)
- Which country's laws will govern a contract dispute (choice of law)? (Courts in some countries will disregard the contract's choice of law clause and apply the laws of the representative or agent nation's legal jurisdiction.)
- What compensation is due the representative on dismissal? (Depending on the length of the relationship, the added value of the market the representative has created for the exporter, and how termination for just cause is defined by the foreign country, the exporter may be required to pay damages or an indemnity.)
- What must the representative give up if dismissed? (The contract should specify the return of patents, trademarks, name registrations, customer records, promotional, and other confidential materials.)
- Should the representative be referred to as an agent? (The contract may need to specify that the representative is not a legal agent with power of attorney.)
- In what language should the contract be drafted? (English should be the official language of the contract in most cases.)

Figure 14.5 Doing Business Internationally: Legal Issues in Drafting Termination Clauses.

the relationship for just cause termination, which require little if any advance notice. The contract should spell out exactly what constitutes *just cause* for ending the agreement. See Figure 14.5 *Doing Business Internationally*: "Legal Issues in Drafting Termination Clauses."

Negotiating a Commercial Agency Contract

The ICC *Guide* can be used as a checklist in order to draft an agency contract. The following summary of the *Guide* illustrates the types of issues and contract terms that an international agency contract should address. Again, due to the existence of evergreen statutes, it is crucial that the agency contract contain an **independent contractor clause** stating that the agent is an independent entity and is not controlled in any way by the exporter. To make clear the independent nature of the relationship the agent should not be an individual, but a legal entity, such as a limited liability company. The title of the agreement should state that it is an independent contractor contract. For a brief review of other important contract terms, see Figure 14.6 *Focus on Transactions*: "Key Contract Terms."

As noted earlier, foreign laws heavily impact the classification of a given relationship as one of employment or independent contracting. Also, once designated as an employment or independent contractor relationship, a number of host country laws regulate areas such as notice, termination, and remuneration. It is important to note that the terminology of agency, employment, and independent contractor as used in the U.S. often differs in other countries. For example, "the general meaning of *agent* may differ from country-to-country, which emphasizes the need for contractual clarity in defining the relationship."[22] It is important to understand the local terminology and factors used in a host country's law before drafting relevant clauses, such as an independent contractor clause. The heading of the agreement should clearly state that it is a commercial agency contract. In order to be absolutely clear as to the intended contractual relationship, the heading and a provision in the contract should state that it is an independent contractor arrangement.

Assignment: If the parties intend to allow assignment, the contract should state the conditions and procedure for assignments.
Language of the Contract: If the contract is written in two languages, it should state which language is to control in the enforcement of the contract.
Products: The contract should be clear regarding the products that are to be sold on behalf of the principal. If the principal produces different classes of products, then the contract should state which classes are subject to the agency contract.
Agency Territory: The contract should precisely delineate the sales territory that is being given to the agent. A further restriction may be placed upon the sales to third parties who are likely to export the goods to another territory. Such restrictions are needed to prevent the gray market problem discussed in Chapters 18 and 19.
Solicitation of Customers: The parties should agree to the groups to be targeted by the agent as potential customers.
Acceptance of Orders: The agreement should clearly state whether the agent has the authority to bind the principal.
Intellectual Property Rights Infringement: The relative responsibilities of the parties as to infringement of intellectual property rights should be defined. For example, the agent's responsibility to notify the principal of any such infringements should be detailed.
Advertising and Marketing Materials: The contract should stipulate whether the principal is to provide any samples or advertising materials, and which party is to pay the costs of such materials. The contract should make clear whether the principal has the right of prior consent for any materials or advertising produced by the agent.
Best Efforts Provision: The principal will want to negotiate a clause that requires the agent to use "best efforts" in marketing and selling the principal's products. The agreement should attempt to define the meaning of "best efforts" such as tying them to generally accepted business practices.
Noncompetition Clause: This provision prohibits the agent from selling the products of a competitor.
Parts and Service: The obligations of the agent should be detailed with regard to providing after-sales service and spare parts.
Legal Information: A clause may be inserted that the agent must inform the principal of any changes in national laws or regulations relating to technical requirements, labeling, and customs regulations. This should include information regarding any national requirement to register the agency contract.
Confidentiality: The agreement should require the agent to maintain the secrecy of the principal's trade secrets even after the termination of the relationship.
Minimum Sales: The principal may want to negotiate that the agent is required to meet certain minimum sales levels. It should specify the consequences for the failure to meet sales quotas such as termination, reduction of territory, or loss of exclusivity.
Termination: The contract may be for a fixed period or an indefinite time period subject to reasonable notice. Some national laws require that the notice be of a certain length of time. It may be stipulated that certain events, such as bankruptcy, merger, assignment, resignation of a key employee, give a party the right to terminate.

Figure 14.6 Focus on Transactions: Key Contract Terms.

Del credere relationship is generally recognized when the agent guarantees its customer's payments to the principal. The agent acts not only as a salesperson or broker for the principal, but also as a guarantor for the buyer. If the buyer is unable to pay, a *del credere* agent may become liable for the unpaid amount. The contract should explain the extent of the agent's liability.

Consulting Contracts

A **foreign consultant** is a variation of the foreign sales representative or commercial agent. The same issues of host country labor laws and agency termination laws apply to the consulting relationship. The **consulting contract** should be specific as to the scope of the engagement, such as for advertising or technology services, and should emphasize the independent status of the consultant. A separate "independent contractor status clause" should be incorporated into the agreement. The factors often utilized in making the distinction between employee and the independent contractor should be incorporated into this clause, including that the consultant is not an employee; the consultant performs the job based on its own discretion and skills; the consultant is responsible for hiring any subagents or assistants; and the consultant provides its tools, equipment, and materials, and pays its own overhead expenses. The agreement should state that the services are being provided on a nonexclusive basis and that the principal takes no responsibility for the manner in which the consultant performs on the contract. Compensation should be structured to highlight the independent basis of the relationship.

In the negotiation of a commercial agency contract, it is important for the principal (manufacturer) to list detailed reasons or causes for termination, including benchmarks or specific tasks that the agent must perform. The *Schuler v. Wickman Machine Tool Sales* case involved a claim for unjust termination of an agency agreement.

L. Schuler AG v. Wickman Machine Tool Sales Ltd.

[1974] AC 235

L. Schuler, a manufacturer, granted Wickman the sole right to sell their products in the UK. The terms of the agreement required Wickman to visit six of Schuler's major British clients each week for the duration of the four-year contract, which they failed to do. Schuler repudiated (terminated) the contract.

Simply calling something a "condition" in a contract does not necessarily mean that its breach of contract leads to termination without looking at the surrounding circumstances. In *Hong Kong Fir Shipping Co. Ltd. v. Kawasaki Kisen Kasisha Ltd*, Lord Diplock stated that the test does not always depend on whether the thing that was breached was a warranty or a condition. The correct test is to look at the events which occurred following the purported breach and to decide if these events deprived the party attempting to terminate the benefits that it expected to receive from the contract.

LORD REID, writing for the majority, stated that simply calling something a "condition" does not necessarily make its breach one that entitles a party to a right of rescission (termination). In this case, it is clear that it would be practically impossible for Wickman to successfully complete all of the visits. Another clause in the contract required Schuler to inform the distributor of material breaches and demand a remedy, which did not occur here.

The House of Lords (now the Supreme Court of the UK) held that Schuler was not entitled to terminate since that clause requiring a number of visits was not a condition for the contract continuance. In addition, Schuler failed to give the required notice to enable Wickman to remedy the situation before declaring a breach.

Schuler maintains that the use of the word "condition" is in itself enough to allow it to terminate. No doubt some words used by lawyers do have a rigid inflexible meaning. Use of the word "condition" is an indication, even a strong indication, of the parties' intention but it is not conclusive. The fact that a particular construction leads to a very unreasonable result must be considered in determining the parties'intent. In this case, one visit per week amounted to 1,400 visits, implying that some of the visits would be missed for good reason, such as the illness of the sales representative or a customer being unavailable on a given week. Under Schuler's contention, even one missed visit gave grounds for termination of the contract. Thus, the clause is subject to a reasonable, alternative interpretation, that being that only a contractual breach left unremedied can be a basis for termination and that a single breach, however minor, is not grounds for termination of the whole agreement.

LORD WILBERFORCE dissented, holding that Schuler should have been able to terminate, ruling that the clause was a condition. On a matter of construction (interpretation), it is improper to declare a clear clause arbitrary, capricious, or to introduce the reasonable person. To do so is to assume, contrary to the evidence, that the parties adopted a standard of easy-going tolerance rather than one of insistent punctuality and efficiency. This is not an assumption I am prepared to make.

Case Highlights

- It is important to be specific in listing causes or types of defaults that trigger the ability of a party to terminate a contract. However, the case shows that the parties should be cautious not to insert a default clause that, if literally interpreted, results in unjust termination
- The idea that not all breaches trigger a right to terminate was noted by Lord Diplock when he stated that the "correct test is to look at the events, which have occurred as a result of the purported breach and to decide if these events deprived the party attempting to terminate of the benefits that it expected to receive from the contract"
- The battle between Lord Reid and Lord Wilberforce is centered on different approaches to contract interpretation, with Lord Reid taking a contextual approach and Lord Wilberforce taking a formalistic approach. For Lord Reid, the literal or plain meaning interpretation is nonsensical, which leads him in search of an alternative meaning and the idea of "unremedied" breaches—since Wickman's missed visits did not cause any damage to Schuler, and follow-up visits remedied the breach, therefore, the few nonvisits did not give Schuler the right to terminate the agency contract. Lord Wilberforce takes the traditional approach that if the contract language is clear, then the court should ignore the context of the contract and that a clear meaning interpretation would result in an injustice. He begins with using the outdated distinction between ordinary breach (not all breaches lead to a right of termination) and a condition (failure of which terminates the contract). This leads Lord Wilberforce to the conclusion that 100 percent performance is a condition of the contract. Therefore, the termination was appropriate.

Chapter Summary

1. Exporting–importing of services makes up a large part of international trade, along with the exporting–importing of goods, foreign direct investment, and the licensing of intellectual property rights or technology.
2. The importance of trade in services was recognized by the World Trade Organization (WTO) with the adoption of the General Agreement on Trade in Services (GATS). The GATS agreement applies general WTO principles—national treatment, most-favored-nation, and transparency—to the trade in

services. The GATS agreement places a strong emphasis on the liberalization of services to benefit developing countries.

3. Liberalization and harmonization of the trade in services has also been targeted at the national and regional levels. Countries have entered into Mutual Recognition Agreements (MRAs) to recognize each other's certification procedures for industries and professionals that provide services.
4. With the explosion of sales of goods and services via the Internet, the EU has passed numerous directives, such as Directive on Distance Contracts.
5. The sale of goods is intimately connected with the sale of services as exporters hire foreign representatives, commercial agents, freight forwarders, custom brokers, and distributors to move, market, and sell their goods.
6. When hiring foreign personnel such as sales representatives it is preferable to hire them as independent contractors than as employees. Numerous countries, especially in Western Europe have pro-employee laws (evergreen statutes) that provide employee protections and benefits at the time of termination.
7. It is generally accepted that workers' rights, such as a right to be treated with respect, in a nondiscriminatory way, the right to unionize, and the obligation of the employer to provide a safe and healthy workplace, are inseparable from basic human rights. The ILO established a set of "core labor standards" (*Declaration on Fundamental Principles and Rights at Work*).
8. A number of services that have increasingly transcended national borders have been subject to increased scrutiny and regulation, including logistical services and the law of freight forwarding, accounting and tax services, advertising, and cross-border securities offerings.
9. A manufacturer–exporter who does not want to sell directly to ultimate purchasers (consumers) has a number of choices in the type of foreign presence it uses in selling its products abroad. The choices include the foreign sales representative, who may be an employee or an independent contractor; a commercial agent (independent contractor); and a foreign distributor (independent contractor) and it may also elect to sell directly to foreign retailers. These relationships have different characteristics and legal ramifications, especially in places like the EU.
10. One of the exporter's most important decisions is the selection of a commercial agent or distributor to market and sell its products within a foreign territory. The major difference between a commercial agent and a distributor is the former sells the exporter's goods as a representative (goods pass directly from exporter to customer). The distributor buys the goods on its "own account" and sells directly to the customer.
11. A variation on the common distributorship arrangement is exporting by consignment. In such a case, the ownership and title remain with the exporter until the goods are sold to the ultimate purchaser, making the exporter a consignor and the distributor a consignee.
12. In selecting a distributor, the exporter should review foreign law relating to a party's authority to act as a distributor, competition law relating to

territorial restrictions, and evergreen laws relating to the termination of the distributorship.

13. Important provisions in distribution contracts include best efforts, products liability, and termination or default clauses, as well as territorial restrictions. The termination or default clause is the most sensitive due to the existence of evergreen laws. In order to avoid the legal liability to pay an indemnity or damages in terminating the contract, the contract should be for a limited duration and require advance notice to terminate, usually a minimum period of three months. The termination or default clause should list events (nonperformance) that allow the exporter to terminate the contract immediately for just cause.
14. Commercial agency involves a relationship in which the law in some countries provides protection for commercial agents. EU Directive 86/653 requires the exporter to give advanced notice of termination, and in some cases, make indemnity payments or damages.
15. A *del credere* agent is a commercial agent that guarantees its customer's payments to the principal.
16. In distribution and commercial agency relationships that involve the transfer of sensitive information (intellectual property rights, trade secrets, and confidential information), the exporter protects this information by inserting confidentiality, no-challenge or validity, reservation of rights, and post-contractual obligations clauses in the contract.
17. Consulting contracts are, if well written, something less than a commercial agency relationship, where the consultant is an independent contractor, usually hired on a nonexclusive basis for a fixed task or job.
18. The *Schuler v. Wickman* case demonstrated the importance of drafting clear but flexible termination or default clauses, as well as the distinction between a condition and a term and contextual versus formalistic interpretation of contracts.

Key Terms

Advertising Injury
Authority, Actual
Authority, Apparent
Best Efforts Clause
Block Exemption
Cargo Consolidator
Commercial Agency
Compulsory Hiring
Confidentiality Clause
Consignee
Consignment
Consignor
Consultation Procedure
Consulting Contract
Conversion Contract
Default Clause
Del Credere Agent
Dilution of Trademark
Dismissal for Cause
Duty to Defend
Effects Test
Employment as a Property Right
Employment-at-Will Doctrine
Escape Clause

EU Regulation 1983/83
EU Directive 86/653
EU Directive on Distance Contracts
European Works Council Directive
Evergreen Statutes
Foreign Consultant
Foreign Sales Representative
Framework Agreement
Freight Forwarder
General Agreement on Trade in Services (GATS)
Goodwill Indemnity
Guide to Drafting International Distribution Agreements
ILO Declaration on Fundamental Principles and Rights at Work
Indemnity in Lieu of Notice
Independent Contractor
Independent Contractor Clause
International Accounting Standards (IAS)
International Labour Organization (ILO)
International Organization of Securities Commissions (IOSCO)
Just Cause Termination
Just-in-Case Distribution
Just-in-Time Contracting
Labor Clause
Materiality
Mixed Sales
Multimodal Transport
Mutual Recognition Agreements (MRAs)
No-Agency-Non-Partnership Clause
Non-Challenge (Validity) Clause
Noncompetition Clause
Office of Service Industries
Organisation for Economic Co-operation and Development (OECD)
Price-fixing Clause
Products Liability Clause
Public Domain
Recognition Requirements
Redundancy
Reservation of Rights Clause
Securities and Exchange Commission (SEC)
Sexual Harassment Policy
Termination Clause
Territorial Restrictions
Total Quality Management (TQM)
Trans-Atlantic Business Dialogue (TABD)
Transfer Pricing
Tying Clause
Unitary Taxation
Work for Hire Clause
Works Council

Chapter Problems

1. What are the different characteristics of a foreign representative, consultant, commercial agent, and a distributor? What is the importance of independent contractor status in all these relationships from the perspective of the manufacturer–exporter?
2. What are evergreen laws, who do they protect, and what type of protection do they provide?
3. Explain and give an example of the difference between a formalistic and a contextual interpretation of a contract term.
4. Match the left column with the right column (see answers on the next page).

A. Apparent Authority	1. EU Regulation 1983/83
B. Trade Secret	2. No Plain Meaning
C. Finding a Distributor	3. "When Needed" Supply Chain
D. Territorial Restrictions	4. Exporter Retains Title
E. Evergreen Law	5. No Actual Authority
F. Just-in-Time Contracting	6. Agent-Distributor Searches (ADS)
G. Consignment	7. EU Directive 86/653
H. Contextual Interpretation	8. Termination of Agency

5. Match the contract clause on the left with the definition on the right (see answers on the next page).

A. Best Efforts Clause	1. Just Cause Termination
B. Confidentiality Clause	2. Competition Law
C. No Challenge Clause	3. Passive Sales
D. Default Clause	4. Benchmarks for Performance
E. Price-Fixing Clause	5. Intellectual Property Rights
F. Reservation of Rights Clause	6. Manufacturer Liability
G. Territorial Restrictions	7. Perpetual Obligation
H. Products Liability Clause	8. IP Rights Reserved by Manufacturer

6. Review the following consulting agreement. What are the purposes of the different clauses? Would these clauses be enforceable in the U.S. and in the EU? How would you improve this agreement? How would you make this agreement more pro-principal or more pro-agent?

CONSULTING AGREEMENT

This Agreement dated April 11, 2001, is made by and between Joe "Hot Shot" Muldune of Mentone, France ("Consultant"), and Gator Exporting of Gainesville, Florida ("Company"). The above parties agree as follows:

A. *Services*. The Company employs the Consultant to perform certain consulting services. The Consultant will consult with the officers and employees of the Company concerning matters relating to the selling, marketing, and advertising of Company's products in the country of France.

B. *Term*. The agreement shall begin on June 1, 2001 and terminate on May 30, 2004. Either party may cancel this agreement on thirty-day notice to the other party in writing, by certified mail or personal delivery.

C. *Time Devoted by Consultant*. It is anticipated that the Consultant will spend approximately 35 hours per week in fulfilling his obligations under this agreement. The amount of time may vary from week to week. However, the Consultant will devote a minimum of 100 hours per month to his duties in accordance with this agreement.

D. *Place of Services*. The Consultant will perform services at a location of Consultant's discretion.

E. *Compensation*. The Consultant will be paid at the rate of $125 per hour of work performed. However, the Consultant will be paid a minimum of $15,000 per month regardless of the time actually spent. The Consultant will send an itemized statement, on a monthly basis, setting forth the services and time rendered. The Company shall remit payment within 15 days of the receipt of each itemized statement.

F. *Independent Contractor*. The Company and Consultant agree that the Consultant is being hired as an independent contractor. Accordingly, the Consultant shall be responsible for payment of all taxes arising out of the Consultant's activities, including but not limited to income tax, social security tax, and unemployment insurance taxes.

G. *Confidential Information*. The Consultant agrees that any information received from the Company which concerns the personal, financial, or other affairs of the Company will be treated in full confidence and will not be disclosed to any other persons or companies.

H. *Subcontractors*. The Company may from time to time request that the Consultant arrange for the services of third parties. The Company will pay all costs to the Consultant but in no event shall the Consultant employ others without the prior authorization of the Company.

IT IS HEREBY AGREED THIS 5th day of May of 2001
Joe Muldune Gator Exporting

[Answers to Problem 4: A(5); B(8); C(6); D(1); E(7); F(3); G(4); H(2).]
[Answers to Problem 5: A(4); B(7); C(5); D(1); E(2); F(8); G(3); H(6).]

Internet Exercises

1. Review the following website on how to evaluate a foreign distributor: http://www.going-global.com/articles/evaluating_foreign_distributors.htm.
2. Review the following website on how to develop an export strategy: http://www.unzco.com/basicguide/c4.html.
3. Review the following distribution agreement on file with the Securities and Exchange Commission (SEC): http://www.sec.gov/Archives/edgar/data/1423542/000119312511017025/dex1025.htm.
4. The most recognized authority on international labor standards is the ILO. Review the ILO website at http://www.ilo.org and become familiar with its standards and its current activities.
5. Research industry organization websites for information on exporting services in those specific sectors.
   - Management and Public Relations: Public Relations Society of America at http://www.prsa.org; Society for Human Resource Management at http://www.shrm.org.
   - Insurance Services: American Insurance Association at http://www.aiadc.org.

- Information Technology: International Federation for Information Processing at http://www.ifip.or.at; Society for Information Management at http://www.simnet.org.
- Franchising: International Franchise Association at http://www.franchise. org.
- Environmental Technologies: National Association of Environmental Professionals at http://www.naep.org.
- Banking and Financial Services: Financial Management Association International at http://www.fma.org.

Other Internet Sources

Choosing a Distributor: http://www.unzco.com/basicguide/table3.html.

Organisation for Economic Co-operation and Development (**OECD**): http://www.oecd.org.

Review major objectives of the **General Agreement on Trade in Services** (**GATS**): https://www.wto.org/english/tratop_e/serv_e/gatsqa_e.htm and https://www.wto.org/english/tratop_e/serv_e/serv_e.htm.

International Labour Organization: http://www.ilo.org.

American Advertising Federation: http://www.aaf.org.

Association of International Accountants: http://www.aia.org.uk.

Notes

1 CPTPP is a Free Trade Agreement of countries that border on the Pacific Ocean including, Australia, Brunei, Canada, Chile, Japan, Malaysia, Mexico, New Zealand, Peru, Singapore, and Vietnam.

2 OECD member countries include Australia, Austria, Belgium, Canada, Chile, the Czech Republic, Denmark, Estonia, Finland, France, Germany, Greece, Hungary, Iceland, Ireland, Israel, Italy, Japan, Korea, Luxembourg, Mexico, the Netherlands, New Zealand, Norway, Poland, Portugal, Slovak Republic, Slovenia, Spain, Sweden, Switzerland, Turkey, the UK, and the U.S. See http://www.oecd.org/about/membersandpartners/list-oecd-member-countries.htm.

3 WTO Secretariat, *A Handbook on the GATS Agreement* (2005).

4 This Directive applies to sales of both goods and services through distance contracts such as mail order, telephone communications, or other means of telecommunications.

5 See Henry King, "Legal Aspects of Appointment and Termination of Foreign Distributors and Representatives," 17 *Case Western International Law Journal* 91 (1985).

6 The **European Works Council Directive** requires large companies to establish European Works Councils (EWC) (Directive 94/45/EC of 22 September 1994).

7 ICC, *Guide for the Drawing Up of Contracts—Commercial Agency* 5 (1993).

8 15 U.S.C. § 45(a)(1) (1982).

9 15 U.S.C. 1125(a) (1988).

10 426 U.S. 438 (1976).

11 See Séverine Saintier, "Agency and Distribution Agreements" in L. DiMatteo, A. Janssen, U. Magnus and R. Schulze, *International Sales Law: Contract, Principles, & Practice* (2d ed. 2020).
12 Wolfram Müller-Freinfels, "Legal Relations in the Law of Agency: Power of the Agent and Commercial Certainty" (1964) 13 *American Journal of Comparative Law* 193.
13 See EU Directive of July 25, 1985 (Products Liability Directive).
14 See Michala Meiselles, *International Commercial Agreements: An Edinburgh Law Guide* (Edinburgh University Press 2013).
15 Matt Hudgins, "New Hubs Arise to Serve 'Just In Case' Distribution," *New York Times*, B4 (February 12, 2013).
16 ICC (n 7).
17 See EC Directive 86/653/EEC of December 18, 1986.
18 Ibid. (n 1) at 6.
19 Ibid. at 7.
20 The label "agency contract" is broad enough to include a wide variety of contracts including sales representation, distribution, consulting, advertising, and transportation agreements.
21 EC Directive 86/653, Article 17(2).
22 Ralph Folsom and Michael Gordon, *International Business Transactions* (West 1995).

Part IV

Intellectual Property

Chapter 15

Intellectual Property Law

A growing portion of world gross domestic product (GDP) is reflected in the increased value of intellectual property rights (IP). This chapter reviews the basics of intellectual property law, as well as international and regional conventions, and reviews a sample of foreign national intellectual property laws. The major intellectual property law regimes include patents, trademarks, and copyright. The areas of trade secrets, software, and database protections will also be examined. A review of the licensing contract will be provided later in the chapter.

By way of introduction, brief definitions of the recognized areas of intellectual property will be offered here. **Patent law** protects inventions that are "novel, useful, and non-obvious." There are a number of statutory categories of *patentable* subject matter, including machines, manufactured articles, processes, and compositions of materials. The term *trademark* includes any word, name, symbol, or device, used by persons or companies, which they intend to use in commerce to identify and distinguish its goods, including a unique product, from those manufactured or sold by others and to indicate the source of the goods. Other than the traditional trademark, **trademark law** also protects other types of distinctive "marks," including trade dress, service marks, certification marks, collective marks, and geographical indicators (country of origin). A **service mark** is the same as a trademark, except that it identifies and distinguishes the source of a service rather than goods.

Copyright law protects works of original authorship from unauthorized duplication, modification, or distribution. Mere creation of the work results in copyright protection. However, placing a copyright notice on the work and registering it with the Copyright Office provides more complete protection. A **trade secret** is any device or confidential information that is used in a business

DOI: 10.4324/9781003469230-19

and gives its owner an advantage over its competitors. Trade secrets law provides for perpetual protection, unless the protected information becomes publicly known.

The next section will review the major tenets of these areas of IP law for three purposes: first, to highlight major issues and concepts found in intellectual property protection; second, to compare international and national laws; and, third, the shortcomings of intellectual property laws, especially in the international arena, which underscores the importance of transfer and licensing agreements.

Intellectual Property Rights

National and international IP laws recognize a wide range of IP protections for patents, trademarks, service marks, copyrights, trade secrets, and semiconductor mask works. Many businesses, particularly high-technology firms, publishers, chemical and pharmaceutical firms, recording companies, and computer software companies, depend heavily on these protections. This section will review the four major areas of protection found—trademarks, copyright, patents, and trade secrets.

Trademark Protection

A trademark is any word, name, symbol, or device that identifies goods and distinguishes them from those manufactured or sold by others. Trademarks are derived from their *commercial use* in identifying brands and are protected by registration and filing under national laws, as well as international treaties and conventions. There are three prohibited forms of unfair competition related to trademark infringement: (1) false advertising, (2) passing off (counterfeiting), and (3) false designation of place of origin. *False advertising* is the use of a "false or misleading description of fact, or false or misleading representation of fact in commercial advertising or promotion which misrepresents the nature, characteristics, qualities, or geographic origin of a company's goods, services, or commercial activities." A service mark is a name, phrase, or other device used to identify and distinguish the services of the provider.

It is not required that a mark be registered in order to bring a claim of trademark infringement (passing off) or *false designation of origin*. In order to prove passing off, the plaintiff needs to prove that there is a likelihood of consumer confusion between the trademarked good or service and the infringer's good or service. A trademark or service mark registered with a national Patent and Trademark Office remains in force for five to ten years from the date of registration and may be renewed for successive periods, provided the mark continues to be used and has not been previously canceled or surrendered. Another way of losing trademark protection is based on the brand name–generic distinction. A brand name is protected as a trademark. However, if the name is used widely as a generic name, then it is said to have entered the **public domain** and is no longer entitled to trademark protection.

The infringing mark need not be identical to the protected trademark. Under the **doctrine of equivalents**, however, similarity alone may not support a claim for trademark infringement. In *Enrique Bernat F., S.A. v. Guadalajara, Inc.*,[1] the trademark owner "Chupa Chups" (ice cream-flavored lollipops) sued the seller of "Chupa Gurts" (yogurt cone-shaped lollipops) for trademark infringement. The court held that there was no infringement because the key term, *chupa*, is a generic Spanish word. Under the *foreign equivalents doctrine*, courts translate foreign words used as trademarks into their common English meaning in usage to test them for their generic or descriptive meaning. The word *chupa* is a generic Spanish word for lollipop or sucker, so it cannot be protected under trademark law.

To prove trademark infringement, a party must prove that another's use of the registered mark is likely to confuse consumers regarding the source of the product or service. A number of factors are used to determine the likelihood of confusion, including: (1) degree of similarity between the marks; (2) the intent of the alleged infringer; (3) similarity of use of the two products or services; (4) similarity in the marketing of the goods or services; (5) degree of care likely to be exercised by the consumer or purchaser; (6) evidence of actual confusion; and (7) strength of the registered mark.[2]

The *Best Cellars Inc. v. Grape Finds at DuPont, Inc.* case explores the above factors used in making the determination of likelihood of confusion. The case involves the application of trademark protection to **trade dress**. Trade dress refers to the general way a product, service, or business is packaged or presented to the public. The case also serves to highlight the distinction between legally protected trademarks and unprotected **generic marks**.

Best Cellars Inc. v. Grape Finds at DuPont, Inc.

90 F. Supp. 2d 431 (SDNY 2000)

District Judge. Plaintiff Best Cellars, Inc. (Best Cellars) seeks an injunction to stop defendants Grape Finds at Dupont from infringing on various intellectual property rights. This action presents difficult issues relating to the law of trade dress protection. The action involves a unique concept, the retail sale of wine by taste, captured and exemplified in the particular trade dress of the Best Cellars stores. It presents the tension between the protection of certain intellectual property and free and open competition.

Best Cellars developed a new kind of retail wine store where people who knew little or nothing about wine could feel as comfortable when shopping as wine connoisseurs, and in which the "wine by style" concept was implemented. The company spent considerable time before and during the design phase of the first Best Cellars store refining the wine by style concept. It eventually reduced the "world of wine" to eight taste categories: sparkling wines, light-, medium-, and full-bodied white wines, light-, medium-, and full-bodied red wines, and dessert wines. Reducing the world of wine to eight taste categories demystified wine for casual buyers.

The design for the first Best Cellars retail store contained the following elements: (1) each of the eight taste categories had a corresponding color and a graphic image (icon-identifier); (2) a display bottle for each wine stands upright on a stainless-steel wire pedestal so that the label is viewable by the customer; (3) under each display bottle, at eye-level, is a "shelf-talker" or information card providing the name of the wine, vintage, a short description of its taste, the type of grape, place of origin, foods which the wine complement, and price; and (4) the racking system, which was patented, lit from behind, causing the bottles to glow.

The founder of Grape Finds visited the Best Cellars New York store numerous times. Grape Finds opened a store in Washington, D.C. The store possessed many similarities to the Best Cellars store. Wines were organized into eight taste categories, with a corresponding color and icon-identifier. Lights above the racks shone down on the wines, causing them to glow.

Trade dress has a broad meaning and includes "all elements making up the total visual image by which a product is presented to customers as defined by its overall composition and design, including size, shape, color, texture, and graphics." The public policy rationale for trade dress protection is that trade dress, no less than trademarks, "serves the purpose to secure to the owner of the mark the goodwill of his business and to protect the ability of consumers to distinguish among competing producers." To establish a claim of trade dress infringement, a plaintiff must demonstrate (1) "that its trade dress is either inherently distinctive" and (2) "that there is a likelihood of confusion between defendant's trade dress and plaintiff's."

Inherently Distinctive

Trade dress is classified on a spectrum of increasing distinctiveness as generic, descriptive, suggestive, or fanciful. Suggestive and fanciful trade dress is deemed inherently distinctive. A descriptive trade dress may be found inherently distinctive if the plaintiff establishes that its mark has acquired a secondary meaning giving it distinctiveness to the consumer. Under this standard, many trade dresses are likely to be found to be inherently distinctive. The Best Cellars stores, like no other wine stores, are unique with their "wall of wine" and color-coded, iconographic signs identifying eight taste categories.

Substantial Likelihood of Confusion

Courts generally apply an eight-factor test to determine the likelihood of confusion between the trade dress of two competitors: (1) strength of the plaintiff's trade dress; (2) similarity between the two trade dress; (3) proximity of the products in the marketplace; (4) likelihood that the prior owner will bridge the gap between the products; (5) evidence of actual confusion; (6) defendant's bad faith; (7) quality of defendant's product; and (8) sophistication of the relevant consumer group. The inquiry ultimately hinges on whether an ordinarily prudent person would be confused as to the source of the allegedly infringing product. Applying the factors to this case shows that:

- Distinctiveness is the tendency to identify the goods sold as coming from a particular company or source. "Marks that are descriptive are entitled to protection only if they have acquired a 'secondary meaning' in the marketplace." Under this standard, Best Cellars' trade dress is quite strong;
- The dominant visual element in Best Cellars stores is the wall of wine. The evidence demonstrates a significant probability that ordinarily prudent customers will be confused as to the company selling the wine;
- "[T]he 'proximity-of-the-products' factor concerns the extent the two products compete with each other." The products here are indisputably similar: value-priced bottles of wine. The class of customers is nearly identical;
- When the first user sells its products in one field and the second user sells its products in a closely related field, into which the first user might expand, thereby "bridging the gap." Here, there is no gap to bridge since Best Cellars and Grape Finds sell the same products in the same field;
- Best Cellars presented evidence of actual confusion, but no survey or systematic research was conducted. However, the law requires only a likelihood of confusion;
- The defendant adopted its dress with the intention of capitalizing on the plaintiff's reputation and goodwill given the evidence of the extensive copying of so many aspects of the Best Cellars business;
- No evidence was presented that Grape Finds' products were inferior so this factor favors Grape Finds;
- Both stores are specifically targeting the same consumer group—unsophisticated wine purchasers.

In this case, seven of the eight factors weigh in favor of Best Cellars' claim of infringement. Some factors weigh more strongly than others, but there is no doubt that, taken together, Best Cellars has made a substantial showing of a likelihood of confusion between its trade dress and that of Grape Finds. Therefore, it has met the requirements for a preliminary injunction.

Case Highlights

- Trademark law seeks to balance the protection of intellectual property and the need not to deter free and open competition. Protection of trade dress is needed to secure to the owner of the mark the goodwill of his business and to protect the ability of consumers to distinguish among competing producers
- To establish a claim of trade dress infringement, a plaintiff must demonstrate (1) "that its trade dress is either inherently distinctive or that it has acquired distinctiveness through a secondary meaning," and (2) "that there is a likelihood of confusion between defendant's trade dress and plaintiff's"
- Generic marks are not entitled to protection under the Lanham Act

Secondary meaning is the principle that marks that are merely descriptive or generic may still obtain trademark protection if the producer so effectively markets its products with the mark that consumers come to associate the mark with only that producer. For example, a company markets "Sunshine Oranges"; if customers come to recognize Sunshine Oranges as the oranges of that particular company, the company may prohibit others from using the mark "Sunshine" in association with oranges.

Trademark Dilution

An alternative modern cause of action is called **trademark dilution.** The American **Federal Trademark Dilution Act** (**FTDA**)[3] defines dilution as "the lessening of the capacity of a *famous mark* to identify and distinguish goods or services, regardless of the presence or absence of competition between the owner of the famous mark and other parties or likelihood of confusion." A trademark dilution claim entitles the trademark owner to seek an injunction against another person's commercial use of its mark or trade name.

Trademark dilution is defined as dilution by *tarnishment* or by *blurring*.[4] The FTDA defines "dilution by blurring" as an association arising from the similarity between a mark or trade name (**junior mark**) and a famous mark (**senior mark**) that impairs the distinctiveness of the famous mark. The following factors are used in determining whether a mark or trade name is likely to cause dilution by blurring: (1) the degree of similarity between the mark or trade name and the famous mark; (2) the degree of inherent or acquired distinctiveness of the famous mark; (3) the extent to which the owner of the famous mark is engaging in exclusive use of the mark; (4) the degree of recognition of the famous mark; (5) whether the user of the mark or trade name intended to create an association with the famous mark; and (6) any actual association between the mark or trade name and the famous mark. **Blurring** is a diminishing of the selling power and value of the trademark by unauthorized use. The differences between the senior user (trademark owner) and junior user (infringer) marks are blurred to the extent that individuals are prevented from disassociating the two marks.

The FTDA defines "dilution by tarnishment" as an association arising from the similarity between a mark or trade name and a famous mark that harms the reputation of the famous mark. **Tarnishment** generally arises when the trademark is linked to products of shoddy quality or is portrayed in an unsavory context likely to evoke unflattering connotations about the product or service.

The junior mark or user is the party accused of trademark infringement or dilution. The senior or *famous mark* or user refers to the trademark owner that brings the claim of infringement or dilution. The FTDA sets forth a number of factors to consider in determining whether a trademark is a "famous" one, including degree of distinctiveness of the mark, duration and extent of use of the mark, duration and extent of advertising of the mark, geographical extent of the trading area in which the mark is used, and the degree of recognition of the mark in trading areas used by the mark's owner and the person against whom the injunction is sought.

The complex questions generated by the intersection of the Internet and copyright or trademark laws are illustrated by *meta-tag* abuse. Internet browsers use search engines to find relevant websites. For those maintaining websites, a good listing in a search engine index is crucial for obtaining optimum exposure. The search engines index websites through the use of HTML (Hypertext Markup Language) source codes. The HTML consists of "markup" symbols or codes inserted in a file intended for display on a World Wide Web browser. The markup tells the web browser how to display a website's words and images for the user. Meta-tags, a portion of this underlying source code, act as signposts that notify the search engines of the content of websites and facilitate matching search requests to websites.

Meta-tags are embedded and are not seen by the viewer of the page but are readable by the search engines. Thus, a party can link itself to a popular website without overtly using the more popular website's name in its URL (Uniform Resource Locator) or web address. Instead, it can embed in its source code keywords taken from the more popular website. As a result, its website will be found by a search engine in response to a viewer's search request for the more popular site. For example, a pornography site may manipulate metatags that results in its website being listed on searches for the Mattel Company's famous toy "Barbie Doll." The global nature of the Internet indicates that amending U.S.

Figure 15.1 Focus on Transactions: Trademark Dilution and the Internet.

A new source of trademark infringement and dilution claims involves the Internet and e-commerce. See Figure 15.1 *Focus on Transactions*: "Trademark Dilution and the Internet," which provides one example of the intersection between trademark law and the Internet. It discusses the abuse of **meta-tags** to divert web searchers to websites unrelated to a famous name or trademark.

Copyright Protection

Copyright is a form of protection provided to authors of "original works of authorship" fixed in a **tangible form** of expression. Copyright has become increasingly important with the development of digital technology and the Internet in order to protect online content. The eight generic categories of copyrightable works include literary, dramatic, musical, choreographic, pictorial (including graphic and sculptural) works, motion pictures, sound recordings, and architectural works. These categories are interpreted broadly. For example, computer programs may be registered as "literary works." Copyright protection is available to both published and unpublished works and affixes to the work at the time of its creation. A copyright has a term of the author's life plus an additional 70 years. In the case of works made for hire (owned by a business), the duration of the copyright lasts between 95 and 120 years.

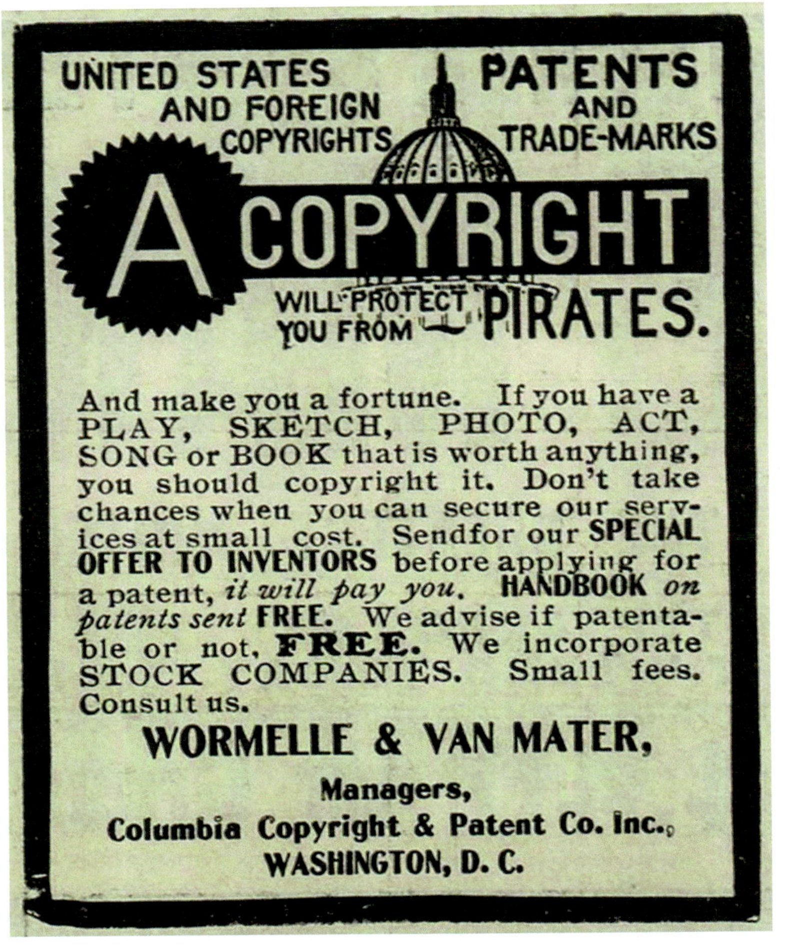

Image 15.1 Copyright Pirate Poster.

Source: Advertisement from the *New York Clipper*, 1906; obtained from the Library of Congress (Author: Columbia Copyright Office).

The copyright owner has the exclusive *right to reproduce* the work in copies; to prepare derivative works; to distribute copies by sale, rental, lease, or lending; and to perform or display the work publicly. It is illegal for anyone to violate any of these rights. However, the rights are not unlimited. A number of exemptions from copyright liability include: (1) first sale doctrine; (2) fair use doctrine; (3) materials that have entered the public domain; and (4) work for hire. See Figure 15.2 *Focus on Transactions*: "Four Exemptions to Copyright Liability."

The **first sale doctrine** terminates the copyright owner's protections over a copy of the copyrighted work once the work is legally sold. The purchaser gains the right to resell the copy.[5] The law allows for certain "fair uses" of copyrighted material without the need to obtain the consent of the copyright owner. In *Quality King Distributors, Inc. v. L'anza Research International, Inc.*,[6] the court held that under the first sale doctrine the owner of copyrighted

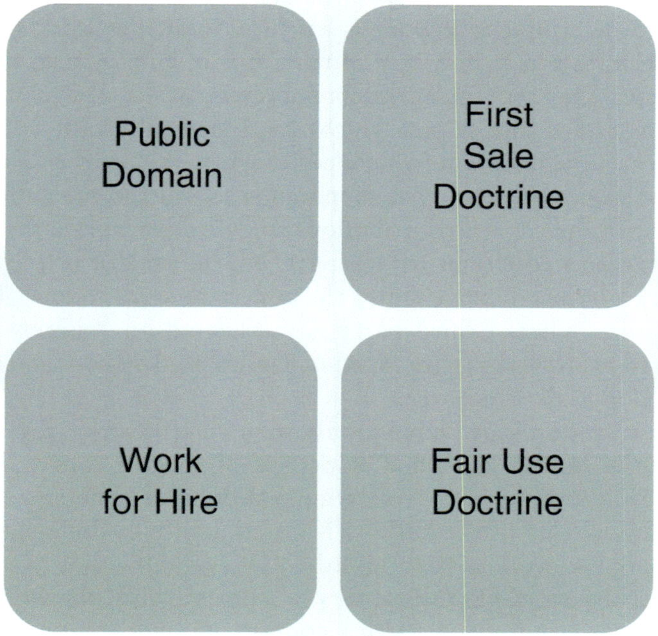

Figure 15.2 Focus on Transactions: Four Exemptions to Copyright Liability.

material is also entitled, without permission of the copyright owner, to sell or otherwise dispose of purchased copyrighted materials, imported or not. The domestic owner of the copyright had entered into a distribution agreement with an English distributor. The distributor sold large quantities of the goods to the defendant–importer, who resold them at discount prices to unauthorized retailers in the U.S. The court held that there was no infringement and resale could not be prevented.

The **fair use doctrine** allows others to use small portions of a copyrighted work in the creation of another work. The most common contexts include criticism of a work, in the course of news reporting, use in teaching, and as part of scholarship or research activities. The factors analyzed to determine fair use include the purpose or character of the use, such as commercial use versus non-profit or educational purposes. The courts will also look at the amount of material taken from the copyrighted work and the effect of the use upon the value or market of the copyrighted work. The material found in the **public domain** is not protected. These materials include government publications and materials whose copyrights have expired.

Authorship of copyrighted works determine who holds the copyright. A work created by an individual vests copyright ownership in that individual automatically upon its creation. **Work for hire** is the major exception. There is a two-pronged test to determine if a work is for hire. First, the work was prepared by an employee or a third party within the scope of employment or within the scope of a contract for hire (independent contractor).

Second, a work for hire is one which was specifically ordered or commissioned for use as a contribution to a collective work or as part of a compilation. The person for whom the work was prepared is considered the author for copyright purposes. In the case of contributions to **collective works**, the contributor of the work retains a copyright for her part, but the creator or producer of the collective work obtains a copyright to the collective work. Some of the factors used to determine when a third party is considered an "employee" for purposes of copyright ownership are listed in Figure 15.3 *Focus on Transactions*: "Factors for 'Copyright Employee.'"

Copyright protection is available for all unpublished works, regardless of the nationality of the author. Published works are eligible for copyright protection under a national law if any of the following conditions are met: first, on the date of first publication, one of the authors is a national or is domiciled of a given country; second, the work is first published in a country that is a party to an international treaty to which the country is a party; third, the work is a sound recording that was first *fixed* in a treaty country. No publication or registration is required to secure a copyright. The mere act of creation and fixing the work in a tangible form automatically creates the copyright. Publication of the work is a way of informing the public that the work is protected by copyright. It also provides evidence as to the date of copyright.

Notice of copyright is no longer necessary when publishing a copyrighted work. The law previously required that copyright notice be affixed when publishing or distributing a copyrighted work. A standard notice looks as follows: "© Jane Doe 2020." In 1989, the notice requirement was eliminated when the U.S. adhered to the **Berne Convention**. Notice is still recommended, however, because it removes the infringer's defense of **innocent infringement**. Under the innocent infringement defense, the infringer is absolved of liability if it can prove that it did not know the work was protected.

Registration of a copyright is not a condition for protection, but registration does provide a number of benefits. First, registration of a copyright establishes a

- hiring party's control over the means and manner by which the work is accomplished
- level of skill required
- source of the instrumentalities and tools used in creating the work
- location of the work
- duration of the relationship between the parties
- whether the hiring party has the right to assign additional projects to the hired party
- extent of the hired party's discretion over when and how long to work
- method of payment
- hired party's role in hiring and paying assistants
- whether the work is part of the regular business of the hiring party
- whether the hiring party is in business
- provision of employee benefits
- tax treatment of the hired party

This is not considered to be an exhaustive list and no one factor is considered to be determinative.

Figure 15.3 Focus on Transactions: Factors for "Copyright Employee."

public record that can be used as evidence to prove the owner's claim in future infringement or ownership disputes. Registration establishes a *prima facie* case of the validity of the copyright and of the facts stated in the registration certificate. Second, registration makes available statutory damages, while at common law the copyright owner is limited to actual damages. Third, registration allows the copyright owner to request that customs authorities bar the importation of infringing or counterfeit copies.

Software Piracy

Types of software piracy include: (1) end-user piracy (users copy software for distribution in violation of their software license); (2) preinstalled piracy (computer manufacturer illegally installs software on numerous computers); (3) Internet piracy (copies are illegally downloaded and distributed); (4) counterfeiting (illegal copies are manufactured and distributed); and (5) online auction piracy (software resold that was marked "not for resale"). The **Business Software Alliance** (**BSA**)[7] is a trade group that represents software makers and is a member of the International Intellectual Property Alliance. Its principal activity is trying to stop copyright infringement of software produced by its members. The BSA, and other nongovernmental organizations (NGOs) such as the International Anti-Counterfeiting Coalition (IACC), lobby governments to toughen and enforce antipiracy laws.

Patent Protection

To achieve patent protection, an invention generally must be of practical use (utility), show an element of novelty, and must have been non-obvious (some new application not known in the body of existing knowledge in its technical field). The invention must show an inventive step (one that could not be deduced by a person with average knowledge of the technical field). The body of existing knowledge is called **prior art**. Finally, its subject matter must be accepted as "patentable" under law. In many countries, scientific theories, mathematical methods, plant or animal varieties, discoveries of natural substances, commercial methods, and methods for medical treatment are generally not patentable. See Figure 15.4 *Focus on Transactions*: "Four Requirements to Obtain a Patent."

It is important to file a patent application before you publicly disclose the details of the invention. In general, any invention that is made public before an application has been filed would be considered prior art. In countries that apply the foregoing definition of the prior art, the applicant's public disclosure of the invention before filing a patent application would prevent him or her from obtaining a valid patent for that invention, since the novelty requirement would not have been met.

Patent law confers on the patent owner the exclusive rights to manufacture, use, and sell the patented product or process within a period of 20 years. In order to be fully protected, the patent holder or **patentee** should serve notice by affixing the word "patent" or the abbreviation "pat." together with the number

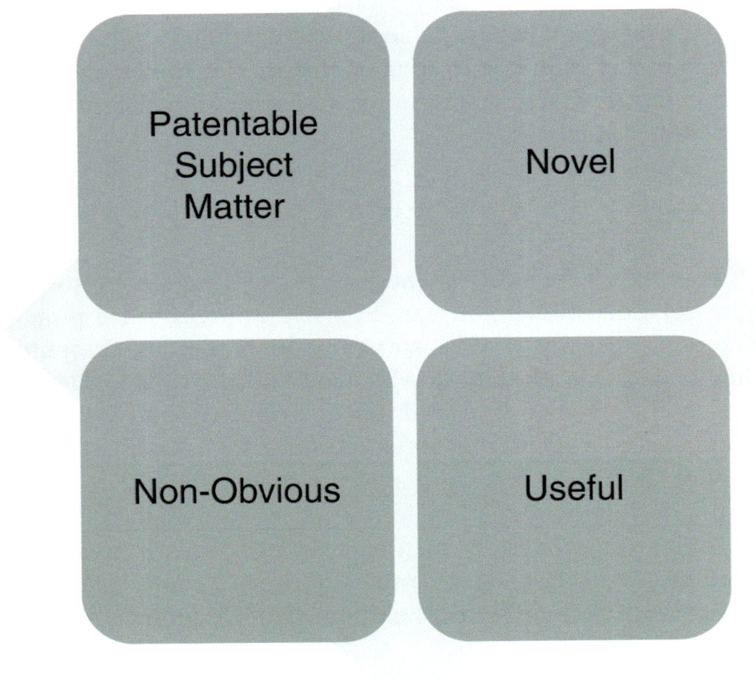

Figure 15.4 Focus on Transactions: Four Requirements to Obtain a Patent.

of the patent to the item or product. An infringer is defined as whoever makes, uses, offers to sell, sells, or imports any patented invention, within the country where the patent is recognized. Furthermore, anyone who falsely marks goods with the name of the patentee "with the intent of counterfeiting or of deceiving the public" is liable for damages.

America Invents Act of 2011: The goal of amending American patent law was to harmonize U.S. patent law with other systems around the world. The significant provisions include (i) changing from a first-inventor to the first-to-file standard, (ii) creating a prior user right, (iii) expanding the content allowed for prior art submissions during examination, and (iv) creating post-grant proceedings for challenging patents before the Patent Trial and Appeal Board (PTAB).

Under the **doctrine of equivalents**, there need not be an exact copying of an invention to prove a case of patent infringement. The patent owner has to show only that there is "equivalence" between the elements of the patented invention and the infringing product. However, if the second invention is an improvement of the first then the patent owner is not likely to benefit from the doctrine of equivalents. In *Warner-Jenkinson Co. v. Hilton Davis Chemical*,[8] the patent owner had developed a process to remove impurities from commercial dyes. Its process operated at pH levels between 6.0 and 9.0. It sought an injunction against the developer of a purification process that worked at a pH level of 5.0. The doctrine of equivalents must be applied to the individual elements of the invention or process and not just the invention as a whole. The fact that both parties had developed a process for the purification of dye did not make them equivalent inventions. Instead, it needs to be determined whether a process that operates at a pH level of 5.0 is equivalent to one that works at 6.0. If the two processes were of equivalent quality, then the owner of the first process was entitled to an injunction under the doctrine of equivalents. If a process that works at a lower pH is qualitatively better, then it is to be considered an improvement and, as such, would be protected as a new invention.

Trade Secrets

Unlike a patent, a trade secret does not entitle its owner to a government-sanctioned monopoly (patent) of its invention for a particular length of time. Nevertheless, trade secrets are protected in private law and through private contracts. Trade secrets law prohibits the misappropriation of trade secrets by theft, bribery, or misrepresentation. Companies protect their trade secrets through confidentiality agreements between them and their employees and by trade secret licensing agreements that prohibit disclosure by licensees. In some countries, the stealing of a trade secret can be considered as a criminal act. The U.S. adopted the **Economic Espionage Act** (**EEA**).[9] The EEA makes it a crime to steal not only government secrets but also business trade secrets (often related to the stealing of technology).

The issue of protecting customer lists or databases as trade secrets was examined in *Nowogroski Insurance, Inc. v. Rucker*.[10] The court held that customer lists or databases, reasonably protected by an employer, were protected under trade secrets law. An insurance agency sued three former employees for soliciting its clients after they went to work for a competitor by using confidential information (customer list). It is the nature of the employment relationship that imposes a duty on employees and former employees not to use or disclose the employer's trade secrets.

Extraterritorial Application of Law

Some countries' laws allow for claims of false designations of origin.[11] It is illegal for any person to affix, apply, annex, or use in connection with any goods or services, or any container or containers for goods, a false designation of origin. In *Scotch Whisky Assoc. v. Barton Distilling*,[12] a court held that trademark law could be applied extraterritorially where a producer supplies false labels to a foreign licensee. In that case, a U.S. company supplied labels designating the product as "Scotch Whisky" to a Panamanian licensee. There was no evidence that the whisky was imported into the U.S. Nonetheless, the court held that "no principle of international law bars a country from governing the conduct of its own citizens."

In *Steele v. Bulova Watches*,[13] a U.S. citizen registered the name "Bulova" in Mexico. He then manufactured watches, using the Bulova name (associated with a Swiss company), for sale in Mexico. There was evidence that some of the watches had been imported into the U.S. The Supreme Court broadly defined "commerce" to include activities of U.S. citizens outside of the country. The court in *Scotch Whiskey* held that the purpose underlying trademark law, to make actionable the deceptive use of false designations of origin, should not be evaded by the simple device of using a foreign license.

Gray Market

The importation of counterfeited goods is prohibited under numerous national laws.[14] There are two areas of counterfeited or pirated.[15] The customs services are authorized to seize such goods at the point of entry into the country. Trademark and copyright owners should *record* their rights with their custom service. The **gray market** problem refers to imports bearing a genuine trademark but imported by a party other than the trademark holder or authorized importer. Also referred to as *parallel imports*, they include goods produced outside a country pursuant to an intellectual licensing agreement, as well as goods licensed in the home country for export that are subsequently reimported. In these instances, a licensor will find its own market territory undercut by identical goods produced under a foreign licensing agreement. The firm that is hurt by gray market imports will often seek to prevent their importation. Trademark law does not prevent the importation of goods legally produced outside of the home country of the trademark owner. This was the situation in *NEC Electronics v. Cal Circuit Abco*. In that case, the defendant had purchased gray market semiconductor chips from a foreign source and imported them to compete against the trademark owner's subsidiary. The court held that the onus is on the licensor (trademark owner) to provide safeguards in its foreign licensing agreements to diminish the chances of parallel importing.

NEC Electronics v. Cal Circuit Abco

810 F.2d 1506 (9th Cir. 1987)

Circuit Judge. A Japanese manufacturer of computer chips, NEC-Japan, assigned its U.S. trademark rights to its California subsidiary, NEC-USA. Defendant, CAL Circuit Abco (Abco), engages in "parallel importation" of NEC-Japan's chips: it buys them abroad at lower prices and then imports and sells them in the U.S. NEC-USA sued for trademark infringement. In 1983, NEC-Japan, owner of the trademark "NEC" assigned all rights to the mark in the U.S. to NEC-USA, and duly registered this assignment with the Patent and Trademark Office. NEC-Japan continues to market its computer chips in other countries at prices substantially lower than those charged by NEC-USA. Defendant Abco buys these so-called "gray market" chips from a foreign source, imports them, and sells them in the U.S. in direct competition with NEC-USA. The parties have stipulated that Abco's chips are genuine NEC products. NEC-USA alleges that Abco's use of the "NEC" trademark confuses consumers who believe that Abco's sales are authorized by or connected to NEC-USA.

Trademark law generally does not reach the sale of genuine goods bearing a true mark even though such sale is without the trademark owner's consent. Once a trademark owner sells his product, the buyer ordinarily may resell the product under the original mark without incurring any trademark liability. If, as NEC-USA alleges, Abco sales agents mislead their buyers about the availability of NEC-USA servicing, then Abco may be liable in contract or tort, but not in trademark. If NEC-Japan chooses to sell abroad at lower prices than those it could obtain for the identical product that is its business. In doing so, however, it cannot look to trademark law to insulate the American market or to vitiate the effects of international trade. Otherwise, trademark law would allow NEC-Japan to establish a worldwide discriminatory pricing scheme. The preliminary injunction is DENIED.

Case Highlights

- Once a trademark owner sells its product, the buyer ordinarily may resell the product under the original mark without incurring any trademark law liability
- If a company sells a good more cheaply in a foreign market or licenses someone who does so, the company cannot look to trademark law to prevent the importation of such legally produced foreign goods into other domestic markets.

The first sale doctrine, highlighted in *NEC Electronics*, protects the importer of trademarked products from an infringement action if the goods were purchased from or produced under a legally valid license held by the importer or a foreign producer of the goods.

There is a history of special statutory protection for music and musical performances. Musicians or performers may enjoy copyright or copyright-like protection in three things: first, a musical composition protected under copyright law; second, the **Sound Recording Act of 1971** extended copyright protection to sound recordings. This means that persons who make unauthorized reproductions of records or tapes can be prosecuted or face civil liability for copyright infringement. Piracy is an unauthorized duplication of a performance already reduced to a sound recording and commercially released; and third, the **1994 Anti-Bootlegging Statute**[16] criminalizes the unauthorized recording or, transmission to the public, and the sale or distribution of or traffic in unauthorized recordings of live musical performances. Bootlegging is distinct from piracy; the former deals with commercially unreleased performances and the latter deals with duplication of commercially released recordings.

Enforcement of Intellectual Property Rights

After IP owners secure rights in foreign markets, enforcement must be pursued diligently through local law. As a general matter, intellectual property rights (IPR) are private rights to be enforced by their owners. Enforcement varies from country to country and depends on such factors as the attitude of local officials, substantive requirements of the law, and court procedures. The availability of criminal penalties for infringement, either as the exclusive remedy or in addition to private suits, also varies among countries.

Exporters with IP concerns should develop a comprehensive strategy for protecting their property. First, they should obtain the available protection provided under laws covering inventions, trademarks, service marks, copyrights, and semiconductor mask works. Second, before entering into a licensing agreement with a foreign party, licensors should research the IP laws of countries where prospective foreign licensees conduct business. Third, the services of foreign legal counsel should be engaged to file an appropriate patent, trademark, or copyright applications or registrations in the licensee's country within priority periods afforded under international conventions. Fourth, entering the foreign licensing agreement should be viewed as only the beginning of the process. The use of licensed rights should be monitored for abuse and infringement. The licensor should be prepared to act promptly to protect its rights in case of a foreign infringement. Finally, trade secrets should be protected through appropriate confidentiality provisions in employment, licensing, marketing, distribution, and joint venture agreements.

The importance of utilizing all the sources of IP protection is illustrated in the *Carell v. Shubert Organization* case, which references domestic, foreign, and international copyright laws.

Carell v. Shubert Organization, Inc.

2000 U.S. Dist. LEXIS 8807 (S.D.N.Y. 2000)

Judge. This action arises out of a dispute concerning the copyright of certain makeup designs created for the cast of the Broadway musical *Cats*. Plaintiff Candace Carell filed this action asserting claims for copyright infringement, false designation of origin, antitrust violations, and an accounting for profits, arising out of defendants' use and publication of her Makeup Designs. The show *Cats* was "the longest running, most financially successful property" in the history of American theater. Her infringement claims are brought under several foreign copyright statutes.

In order for a work to be copyrightable, it must be "an original work of authorship"; that is, it must be (i) original and (ii) fixed in a tangible form. Copyright protection for an original work does not extend to "any idea, procedure, process, system, method of operation, concept, principle, or discovery." There is no disagreement between the parties that Makeup Designs are copyrightable, or that the creator of such Designs is entitled to protection. The Designs contain the requisite degree of originality and are fixed in tangible form on the faces of the actors.

Infringement Claims

A certificate of registration from a Register of Copyrights constitutes *prima facie* evidence of the valid ownership of a copyright, although that presumption of ownership may be rebutted.

Plaintiff asserts her copyright infringement claims are supported by the copyright statutes of Australia, Canada, Japan, UK, and the U.S., and pursuant to the Berne Convention for the Protection of Literary and Artistic Works (Berne Convention).

While acknowledging that extraterritorial jurisdiction may be prohibited under national laws, Professor Nimmer has explained that even a national copyright law is "inoperative with respect to acts occurring outside of its jurisdiction, it does not necessarily follow that courts are without jurisdiction in certain cases. If the plaintiff has a valid cause of action under the copyright laws of a foreign country, and if personal jurisdiction of the defendant can be obtained in an American court, an action may be brought in such court for infringement under a foreign copyright law. This would be on a theory that copyright infringement constitutes a transitory cause of action, and hence, may be adjudicated in the courts of a sovereign other than the one in which the cause of action arose."

Motion to dismiss is denied.

Case Highlights

- Makeup designs are copyrightable as "original works of authorship"
- Copyright law protects works that are "original" and "fixed in a tangible medium"
- National courts will at times exercise jurisdiction over foreign copyright infringement claims.

International Property Rights Protection

Outside of the country of copyright, protection is available through international treaties or foreign intellectual property laws. The relevant international treaties establish minimum standards for protection, but individual national laws and practices can differ significantly. See Table 15.1 *Doing Business Internationally*: "International and Regional Intellectual Property Laws."

The **World Intellectual Property Organization** (**WIPO**) is the official depository of most international intellectual property conventions. WIPO grew out of the 1883 Paris Convention on patents and trademarks and the 1886 Berne Convention on copyrights. Today it serves two main purposes. First, it administers and monitors the enforcement of more than 20 treaties. Second, it promotes the adoption of new intellectual property treaties and conventions. The World Trade Organization's **Agreement on Trade-Related Aspects of Intellectual Property Rights** (**TRIPS**) requires that member countries pass IPR laws that meet certain standards.

Table 15.1 *Doing Business Internationally*: International and Regional Intellectual Property Laws.

Law	*Description*	*Number of Countries*
Berne Convention	Artistic Works	168
Universal Copyright Convention	Copyright	100
WIPO Copyright Treaty	Copyright	93
Paris Convention	Patents and Trademarks	176
Patent Cooperation Treaty	Patents	148
Patent Law Treaty	Patents	36
Trademark Law Treaty	Trademarks	53
WTO Trade-Related Aspects of Intellectual Property Rights (TRIPS)	Copyright, Trademarks, Geographical Indications, Industrial Designs, Patents, Layout-Designs of Integrated Circuits, Trade Secrets	162
USMCA	Copyright, Patents, Trademarks, and Trade Secrets	3
EU Directives	Copyright, Patents, Trademarks, and Database Protection	28

Paris Convention and Patent Cooperation Treaty

To secure patent and trademark rights internationally, a company must apply for patents or register trademarks on a country-by-country basis. Individuals and companies are entitled to a **right of priority** and to **national treatment** in the more than 100 countries that are parties to the **Paris Convention for the Protection of Industrial Property** (**Paris Convention**). The Paris Convention is the major international agreement providing basic protections for patents, designs, and trademarks.

A person who files for a patent or trademark in a member country is given a 12-month right of priority to file patent applications in other countries (six months for trademarks). This right of priority relieves the burden of filing applications in many countries simultaneously. National treatment means that a member country cannot discriminate against foreigners in granting patent or trademark protection. Rights conferred must be the same as those that the country provides its own nationals.

Article 5 of the Convention authorizes member countries to issue **compulsory licenses** to third parties if the patent owner does not use or work their patent. A compulsory license grants patent rights to third parties without the consent of the patent or trademark owner. Compulsory licenses cannot be issued any sooner than four years from the date of the grant of the patent. A compulsory license is not to be issued if the patentee gives legitimate reasons for its failure to work the patent. In addition, the parties granted licenses must pay reasonable royalty fees to the patent owner. Some countries, like the U.S., do not permit the granting of such licenses.

Many countries require that an invention be worked locally to retain the benefit of patent protection. Working a patent requires the manufacture or licensing of the patented goods. In some cases, non-use is seen as the abuse of patent rights, resulting in the grant of compulsory licenses followed by forfeiture of the patent when the grant of a compulsory license is not sufficient to prevent abuses.

Compulsory Licenses: Government grants (licenses) of statutory rights (patents) owned by one party for the use of other parties. Such licenses are found in some countries where owners are required to use or work their patents. If a patent is unused for an unreasonable period of time then a business or person may petition the government for a license to use the patent, without the consent of the patent owner.

The **Patent Cooperation Treaty** (**PCT**) addresses procedural requirements aimed at simplifying the filing, searching, and publication of international patent applications. The PCT entered into force in 1978 and is open to any member of the Paris Convention. The PCT allows companies to file a uniform international application for protection in other member states. Individual national applications must follow within 18 months.

Berne Convention and Universal Copyright Convention

There is no such thing as an international copyright that automatically protects an author's work throughout the world. Protection against unauthorized use depends on the enforcement of national laws on a country-by-country basis. Most countries' laws recognize foreign works due to the enactment of international copyright treaties. Copyright protection is seen as a moral right of authors and artists in their works. The moral nature of copyrights is inscribed in the cupola above the lobby at WIPO headquarters. It states that: "human genius is the source of all works of art and invention. These works are the guarantee of a life worthy of men and women. It is the duty of the state to protect the arts and inventions with care." See Figure 15.5 *Comparative Law*: "Ten Rights of Authors and Artists (Berne Convention)."

In most countries, the place of first publication is an important criterion for determining whether foreign works are eligible for copyright protection. Works first published in a member country of the **Berne Convention for the Protection of Literary and Artistic Works** are protected in more than 80 countries. Some countries are members of the Berne Convention and the **Universal Copyright Convention.** Universal Copyright Convention countries that do not also adhere

Moral Right: The right to preserve the integrity of the work. This is an inalienable right that cannot be assigned to an employer or another.

Reproduction Right: The right over all sound and visual recordings and adaptations of the work.

Translation Right: Right over the authorization of translations into other languages except for the limited right of least-developed countries to grant compulsory licenses.

Public Performance Right: Right over the performance of dramatic, musical, and literary works.

Broadcasting Right: Right over performances including radio and television broadcasts.

Adaptation Right: Indicates that a broadcaster needs to obtain permission of both the original author and the adapter or arranger.

Recording Right: Covers recording of musical or dramatic works.

Author's Film Right: The right of the original author to authorize a film of the work.

Rights of Film Creator: Recognizes the separate rights of the owner and creator of the cinematographic work (film).

Right of Pursuit: Allows national laws to create a right of pursuit to an interest in the secondary and subsequent sales of the work. If the author or heirs sell or transfer rights to the work, they may still claim an interest in the subsequent sale or transfer by the transferee.

Figure 15.5 Comparative Law: Ten Rights of Authors and Artists (Berne Convention).

to the Berne Convention often require compliance with certain formalities to maintain copyright protection. These formalities require that the copyright be registered and that published copies of a work bear copyright notice, the name of the author, and the date of first publication. Countries also enter into bilateral copyright agreements; the laws of different countries may or may not be consistent with the international copyright conventions. Before the first publication of a work in a country it is advisable to investigate the scope of and requirements for maintaining copyright protection in that country.

The Berne Convention, originally enacted in 1886, has been amended numerous times. A review of the Convention and its amendments, discussed below, illustrates the evolution of copyright protections.

The Berne Convention firmly established the rights of authors as an international principle but left it to national laws to determine the degree of protection to be given. Once a type of work is afforded protection, then a country is required to extend to foreign authors the same protections granted to national authors. However, if a country's domestic law grants a longer term of protection than the laws of the author's country of origin, then that country need only grant a term of protection equivalent to the law of the author's country.

Subsequent amendments to the Convention expanded the scope of its reach, created additional rights, and recognized new technological developments. These amendments include the Berlin Act of 1908, the Rome Act of 1928, the Brussels Act of 1948, the Stockholm Act of 1967, and the Paris Act of 1971. The **Berlin Act of 1908** recognized copyright protection for photographic works. These rights included the right to authorize the adaptation of an original work and the right over subsequent public performances of recordings of the work. This was a response to the emerging technologies of sound recording, cinematography, and photography.

The **Rome Act of 1928** recognized the moral rights of authors and the authors' broadcast rights in their works. The moral right allows an author to object to any distortion or other modification of their works. The moral rights of authors are now recognized in Article 6*bis* of the Berne Convention, which states that: "even after the transfer of rights, the author shall have the right to object to any distortion, mutilation, or other modification of the work, which would be prejudicial to his honor or reputation." Thus, an author could sell the right to reproduce or display their work but retain the ability to reject a modification of the work. The Rome Act, through Article 11*bis* established a broadcast right in response to the development of public radio.

The **Brussels Act of 1948** extended copyright protection to motion pictures. It is left to national law to determine the author or owner of the copyrights to a film. English law places that right with the producer of a film. In contrast, civil law countries of Europe grant the rights to creative individuals such as the author of the original story or the writer of the screenplay. The Brussels Act also extended the broadcast right recognized in the Rome Act from sound broadcasting to television. The **Stockholm Act of 1967** and the **Paris Act of 1971** allowed less-developed countries to impose compulsory licenses for works out of print or for the translation of works not available in the language of their countries.

A relatively new area of copyright has been the recognition of traditional or **indigenous rights**. Indigenous peoples possess unique information and resources, which in some cases have been used, without the permission of the originators, without any economic return or recognition. Indigenous rights refer to "traditional knowledge" (agriculture and medicinal plants) and "traditional cultural expressions" (handicrafts, dances, songs, and stories).

Agreement on Trade-Related Aspects of Intellectual Property Rights (TRIPS)

TRIPS is divided into three parts, which provide: general provisions, scope of intellectual property rights, and enforcement provisions. The following review will furnish an understanding of TRIPS and aims to reinforce the reader's knowledge of the basic principles of IP protection.

General Principles

The "General Provisions" restate the foundational tenets of the WTO system, including the national treatment, most-favored-nation, and transparency principles. Transparency states that a country's "laws and regulations, and final judicial decisions and administrative rulings of general application, pertaining to the availability, scope, acquisition, enforcement, and prevention of the abuse of IPR shall be published." Countries are required to transmit copies of their laws and regulations to the **Council for Trade-Related Aspects of Intellectual Property.** The Council, along with the WIPO, are resources for those interested in intellectual property protection.

Copyright and Related Rights

The TRIPS Agreement requires all WTO members to accede to the Berne Convention, which extends copyright protection to computer programs, whether in source or object code. Copyright protection is also expressly extended to "compilations of data or other material, whether in machine-readable or other form, which by reason of the selection or arrangement of their contents constitute intellectual creations." Thus, databases or customer lists are protected under copyright. The minimum **term of protection** for photographic work or a work of applied art is no less than 50 years from its authorized publication or, failing such authorized publication, within 50 years from the making of the work.

Trademark Protection

The TRIPS Agreement provides a broad definition of trademarks, including that such signs made up of particular words including personal names, letters, numerals, figurative elements, and combinations of colors, as well as any combination of such signs, which are eligible for registration as trademarks. Article 17 recognizes the fair use concept found in copyright law and applies it as an exception to trademark protection. The period of protection for trademarks and renewals is set at a minimum of seven years, which can be renewed indefinitely.

The TRIPS Agreement recognizes the principle that trademark rights can be lost through abandonment or nonuse but rejects the notion of compulsory licensing found in some national laws. Article 19 allows a country to cancel a trademark registration if it is unused for a period of three years. Article 9 recognizes Article 6*bis* of the Paris Convention, giving the owner of a *well-known* trademark the right to block or cancel an unauthorized registration of its marks in a foreign country.

Patent Protection

Article 27 of the TRIPS Agreement defines *patentable* as something that is "new, involves an inventive step and is capable of industrial application." The rights conferred on the patent owner last for 20 years and include the right to prevent third parties from the acts of making, using, offering for sale, selling, or *importing* the patented product or process. Interestingly, the TRIPS Agreement recognizes integrated circuit designs as a *sui generis* type of IP and provides for a ten-year period of protection. It requires members to agree to provide protection for the layout and design of integrated circuits pursuant to the **Treaty on Intellectual Property in Respect of Integrated Circuits.**

Trade Secrets

Trade secrets are recognized under Section 7 of the TRIPS Agreement. It states that the purpose of recognizing trade secrets is the "protection of undisclosed information." Trade secret is defined as information having commercial value that is not commonly known and for which reasonable steps have been taken to maintain secrecy. Article 40 is of special importance to licensors of IPR since it recognizes a country's right to prohibit certain contractual restrictions that have "adverse effects on trade and *may* impede the transfer of technology." It allows member states to single out for scrutiny contractual restrictions, to be discussed later in the chapter, found in exclusive grant-back clauses and clauses that prohibit challenges to the validity of the licensor's rights.

Remedies and Penalties

The TRIPS Agreement provides a menu of penalties and remedies to parties seeking the enforcement and protection of their IPR. Countries are required to provide civil and criminal remedies, along with procedures for seizing and destroying illegal goods. Civil remedies include damages for lost profits and attorney's fees, along with the granting of injunctions to prevent imported goods from entering "the channels of commerce." The owner of IPR may petition the government or customs authority to suspend the importation or exportation of infringing goods. The administrative or judicial authority may require the petitioner to supply security (guarantee), to indemnify a party whose goods are wrongfully enjoined or suspended.

Foreign Intellectual Property Laws

The countries with the largest number of patent filings are China, U.S., and Korea, with the Chinese patent office becoming the largest patent office. Therefore, it is important to research the different national laws relating to IP.

Regional Patent Treaties

Regional patent treaties have served to advance stronger IP protections. There are two types of regional organizations. The first type establishes a regional patent system. The second attempts to harmonize existing patent systems within a region. Five regional treaties have offices that issue regional patents: (1) African Intellectual Property Organization (OAPI); (2) African Regional Intellectual Property Organization (ARIPO); (3) **Eurasian Patent Office** (EAPO); (4) **European Patent Office** (EPO); and (5) Gulf Cooperation Council Patent Office (GCC).

The OAPI consists of 16 French-speaking countries of Africa. None of the 16 countries has a national patent system and, therefore, OAPI patents are automatically effective in all the countries. ARIPO created a regional patent office for 17 English-speaking countries in Africa. After the issuance of an ARIPO patent, the member countries have six months to deny the patent's applicability in their countries. Also, the patent is subject to the compulsory licensing laws of the individual countries. The EAPO issues a regional patent for Russia and eight other countries (Azerbaijan, Belarus, Kazakhstan, Tajikistan, Turkmenistan, Kyrgyzstan, Moldova, and Armenia). Upon issuance, the patent owner selects the countries for which the patent will be effective.

The *European Patent Convention* (EPC) established the European Patent Office (EPO). All 27 members of the EU, as well as an additional ten other European countries (not including the UK), are parties to the EPC. An EPC patent is equivalent to a national patent in each of the member countries and is enforced in the same manner as national patents. Some countries require the patent owner to have the patent translated into the country's language. In order to acquire the **Single European Patent**, an application needs to be submitted to the EPO in Munich. In the area of trademarks, the EU Trademark Office in Alicante, Spain, issues a single **EU Trademark** that is valid in 15 EU countries. It should be noted that national trademarks continue to coexist alongside the EU trademark. In 2013, the EU created the Unified Patent Court, which is able to hear patent infringement cases, as an alternative to filing a claim in a national court system.

Foreign Trademark Law

National trademark laws need to be researched for substantive differences. For example, a trademark owner should not only research the requirements of registering a trademark in a foreign country, but also for preserving the trademark. Three of the common areas for concern include: (1) term of the trademark and the requirements for renewal; (2) preventing infringement of the trademark; and (3) preventing it from being labeled as an abandoned trademark due to nonuse.

In most countries of the world a trademark is recognized and protected only on the registration of the mark. Article 2 of the **Russian Trademark Law** states that "legal protection of a trademark within the Russian Federation shall be granted upon its registration with the State." The system that allocates rights based upon the **first to register principle** is referred to as an **attributive system**. That is, all rights stem from the registration of the trademark or patent. A registration of a trademark is valid for a period of ten years. In the event that a registration or a renewal request is rejected, the applicant has three months to appeal the decision to the Chamber of the Patent Authority. An applicant may appeal the decision of the Patent Authority, within six months, to the Supreme Patent Authority.

Most countries, however, as required by international trademark conventions, are required to reject the registration by third parties of internationally recognized or **famous trademarks. Brazilian Industrial Property Law** grants protection for well-known marks. In determining whether a trademark is well-known, the law refers to Article *6bis* of the Paris Convention. However, the rightful owner or a licensee has only 60 days from the time it contests a trademark registration to apply for its own trademark. In accordance with the Paris Convention and the Stockholm Revision, whether the trademark is used or not, protection continues as long as the trademark is registered.

Trademark laws are relatively uniform regarding the treatment of a trademark with the general rule being that a trademark that is used generically loses its trademark protection. Alternatively stated, if a trademark or trade name is used to refer to all goods of a certain type and not just to a particular brand name, then all trademark rights are expunged. The *Comité Interprofessionnel du Vin de Champagne* case explores the generic–brand name distinction. Note that, in an international setting, a trademark may be considered generic in one country and a protected brand name in another.

Comité Interprofessionnel du Vin de Champagne v. Wineworths

2 NZLR 432 (1991)

Comité Interprofessionnel du Vin de Champagne (CIVC) is a semi-official body created under French law whose purpose is the protection of the name Champagne. It is challenging Australian wine companies exporting sparkling white wine, labeled as Champagne, into New Zealand. The main dispute is over whether, in New Zealand, the word "Champagne" had crossed the divide from a distinctive (brand) name to a generic word. The process of making Champagne was developed in the 19th century by Dom Perignon of the Benedictine Abbey near Epernay, France. The two features of Champagne of prime importance are the soil and climate in which the grapes are grown, and the method of manufacture by skilled personnel.

The essence of the *methode champenoise* is that the process of second fermentation takes place in the bottle in which it is sold. That requires an operation for shifting the yeast by gradually turning the neck of the inverted bottle for its removal. The plaintiffs' view is that the uniqueness of Champagne is its avowedly alcoholic nature and readily capable of producing a pleasurable effect in the stomach. Champagne is appropriate as a wine with which to celebrate; characteristics are that it palpably agitates in the glass, that it is reinforced by exotic origin (France), and its costs. The plaintiffs recognize that for Australia, like Canada and the U.S, there is no legal protection available to them over the use of the appellation *champagne*.

In 1987, Penfolds (Australia) reached an agreement with Wineworths (New Zealand) to export to New Zealand a sparkling wine bearing the label

"Australian Champagne." Plaintiffs brought suit claiming that the defendants were guilty of the charge of passing off.

Is Champagne a Generic Term?

The Court's central task is to determine the perception of New Zealanders of the word *champagne*. The following categories of evidence are used in making that determination: (1) dictionaries and linguistic experts; (2) market research; (3) wine expert witnesses; and (4) restaurant wine lists and newspaper advertisements. Based on this evidence, the Court held that the word champagne in New Zealand is not generically used to describe any white sparkling wine.

Law of Passing Off (Deceit)

The cause of action is not of the classic form whereby one manufacturer seeks to disguise its goods as those of another by imitating name or style of packaging so as to pass off or deceive a buyer as to the true nature of the purchase. This case involves a new type of passing off, which is characterized by inconspicuous attachment, and invalid sharing, of a reputation. This type of passing off makes the identification of the misrepresentation or deceit an indispensable ingredient for liability. The plaintiffs concede that there is no attempt by the defendants to sell the wine as French wine but argue that the buyers thought they were buying sparkling wine with all the attractive attributes of Champagne because the product is described by the word.

The essentials of a claim of passing off are: (1) to establish sufficient reputation or goodwill in the name Champagne; (2) to show that the challenged actions are likely to cause or have actually caused deception; and (3) that the plaintiffs suffered or are likely to suffer damage or injury to their business or goodwill. First, there has already been a finding that the word *Champagne* retains a distinctive reputation and goodwill and has not become a generic word in New Zealand. Second, the court held that the marketing of the wine as Champagne was deceptive. Third, the plaintiffs will suffer damage if the word champagne is used on any sparkling wine sold in New Zealand. It follows that the ordinary purchaser in New Zealand without special knowledge of wines is likely to be misled. Judgment for Plaintiffs.

Case Highlights

- "Passing off" is a form of trademark infringement characterized by inconspicuous attachment and invalid sharing of a reputation
- The crucial factor in passing off is the distinctiveness of the trademark and whether it has become generically used
- The standard for making the brand name–generic distinction is the perspective of the "ordinary purchaser" or consumer
- For purposes of conversation at future cocktail parties, note the distinction between champagne that is fermented in "the" bottle versus in "this" bottle. The *methode champenoise* requires that the champagne

remain in the bottle while impurities are removed during the second fermentation process. Experts turning the bottle over a prolonged period of time "magically" remove the impurities. This is an expensive process and is referred to as in "this" bottle. The cheaper method involves pumping the champagne out of the bottle, removing the impurities by a machine process, and then returning the future champagne by pumping it into another bottle for the second fermentation. This second method is referred to as in "the" bottle. If used adeptly, this bit of trivia can help earn you a cosmopolitan reputation.

Obligation to Use Trademark

A large number of countries require the owner of a trademark to use the mark or lose protection under trademark law. Russian Trademark Law allows the Supreme Patent Chamber to terminate a trademark registration if there has been a nonuse of the trademark for a period of five years unless, failure to utilize the trademark was for reasons beyond its control. If, for example, the sale of trademarked goods was prevented due to import or export controls, then the owner will retain its trademark rights.

The People's Republic of China views the purpose of IP law in a unique way. Besides the traditional purposes of protecting private property and encouraging technological development, the Chinese see trademark law as a mechanism for quality control and consumer protection. The Chinese Trademark Law allows the government to revoke a registered trademark if the trademarked good is not of reasonable quality. The trademark owner that produces goods of inferior quality is seen as deceiving consumers. This deception assumes that if a good is trademarked, then it is of reasonable quality.

People's Republic of China

In the area of what types of inventions are protected under patent law, there is a great deal of uniformity among national legal systems. Chinese patent law mimics American law in defining a "patentable" invention as one that possesses *novelty*, *creativity*, and *utility*. Article 22 of the **Patent Law of the People's Republic of China** describes novelty as an invention that has previously not been published or publicly used. Creativity is defined as a substantial progress over existing technology. Utility requires that the invention be capable of being manufactured or producing a "positive effect." In the *Honda Motor Co. v. Beijing Xuyang Hengxing Trade Co.* case, a Higher People's Court explores the concepts of primary and secondary liability, as well as the remedy of disgorgement of profits of the infringing parties.

Honda Motor Co., Ltd v. Beijing Xuyang Hengxing Trade Co., Ltd

Beijing Higher People's Court (2010) GMZZD No. 2556

Issue: Where a party entrusts another to produce components and assemble the components into a completed product, if the components are patent infringing who assumes liability for paying compensation for the infringement?

Primary and Secondary Liability

Article 11(2) of the Patent Law of China provides that the patentee (owner) of a design patent has the exclusive right to exploit the patent. Honda is the owner of the patent for a particular car bumper. The alleged infringing products are similar in design. Jiangsu Kawei Motor Accessories Co., Ltd. (Kawei) produces parts for a car manufacturer based on drawings provided by the car manufacturer, namely Shijiazhuang Shuanghuan Motor Inc. (Shuanghuan).

The court held that Shuanghuan and Kawei infringed upon Honda's patent rights. It held that Shuanghuan as the designer and manufacturer of the car had primary liability. Kawei is the hiree of the infringing designer, and his degree of fault is less than Shuanghuan. Therefore, Kawei had secondary liability. Furthermore, Beijing Xuyang Hengxing Trade Co., Ltd. (Xuyang) is enjoined from selling cars with the infringing bumpers.

Calculation of Damages

Article 21 (1) and (3) of the *Provisions of the Supreme People's Court on Issues Concerning the Trial of Patent Controversies* provide that, when ascertaining the infringer's liabilities, the court may fix the amount of compensation in light of the losses suffered by patentee or the benefits obtained by the infringer. Benefits obtained by the infringer may be ascertained in light of the total amount of sales multiplied by the reasonable profits made from each infringing product (remedy of disgorgement). We may ascertain the costs and profits of car sales and amounts of sales, the bumper's unit price, and calculate the proportion of the back bumper to the whole car. Accordingly, this court ascertains that the interests obtained by Shuanghuan and Kawei's infringement are RMB 1.72 Million Yuan. Shuanghuan and Kawei shall undertake **joint and several liabilities** for such damages.

Case Highlights

- The owner–patentee of a design patent may prevent any entity or individual, without permission of the patentee, from exploiting the patent; that is, to make, sell, or import any product incorporating its patented design
- More than one party may be sued for infringement of patents in a given case, with each party deemed to be jointly and severally liable (each liable for the entire damages). However, the infringement damages may

be allocated between the primary infringer (car designer) and a secondary infringer (parts manufacturer)

- In calculating liability, damages may be based on the profits obtained by the infringing parties in violating the patentee's patent rights.

Chinese patent law adopts the notion of compulsory licensing found in a large number of countries, especially in European and developing countries. Chinese patent law requires the patent holder to *work* the patent in China. To satisfy the work requirement, a foreign patent holder will need to produce the good in China, enter into a joint venture to produce the good in China, or license someone in China to produce the good. If the patent holder fails to work the license for a period of three years, the State Patent Bureau is authorized to grant compulsory patent licenses to third parties. Holders of the compulsory licenses must pay a reasonable royalty to the patent holder. Compulsory licenses are also granted to parties who have improved on a previous invention. Often the government will grant a **reciprocal license** to the prior patent holder to be able to use the improvement or new invention.

European Union

In the area of trademarks, a person or company may obtain a single EU trademark; however, national trademarks continue to coexist with the EU trademark. Figure 15.6 *Comparative Law*: "EU Regulation on the Community Trademark" provides excerpts from Regulation 2868/95 implementing the EU Trademark. This regulation is binding in its entirety and directly applicable in all EU countries. Among other things, it calls for uniform forms for applying, contesting, and renewing trademarks, along with the option of converting a community trademark application into a national application. The regulations also provide for the registering of licenses by licensees.

This Regulation contains the necessary provisions for a procedure leading to the registration and administration of Community trademarks.

Rule 22: Proof of Use

A party has to furnish proof of use or show that there are proper reasons for nonuse. If an opposing party fails to provide such proof before the time limit expires, the Office shall reject the opposition.

Figure 15.6 Comparative Law: EU Regulation on the Community Trademark.

Rule 23: Registration of the Trademark and Rule 85: Community Trademarks Bulletin

The registration shall be published in the Community Trademarks Bulletin. The Community Trademarks Bulletin shall also contain publications of applications.

Rule 34: Special Provisions for the Registration of a License

A license in respect of a Community trademark shall be recorded in the Register as an exclusive license if the proprietor of the trademark or the licensee so request

Figure 15.6 (Continued)

EU Database Protection

The EU is unique in adopting a legal regime for the protection of databases through the adoption of the 1996 Database Directive, which grants the maker of a database a *sui generis* right to control the uses of its contents. The Directive confirms the availability of copyright-like protections for authors of databases. According to the Directive, legal protection is attached to each element incorporated in the database if its creation is sufficiently original to be qualified as the "author's own intellectual creation." The *sui generis* right is accorded if the database maker can demonstrate that it made a qualitatively or quantitatively *substantial investment* in the obtaining, verification, or presentation of the contents of the database.

The concept of substantial investment has come under close scrutiny in the European Court of Justice (ECJ). The ECJ has given a restrictive interpretation, thus curtailing the availability and scope of the database *sui generis* protection. The ECJ made a distinction between "creating" and "obtaining" the data. In its view, "creating" the data to be gathered in the database does not qualify as a relevant investment for the granting of database protection. Conversely, obtaining or collecting existing data may qualify as an investment under the Database Directive. The investment may not be substantial enough if the collection is made with standard hardware, software, or Internet tools.

IPR Infringement in Transitional and Emerging Economies

Protection of IPR in many countries is hampered by inadequate enforcement of laws and regulations. The **U.S. Trade Representative** (**USTR**) maintains an IPR "**watch list**" under Section 301 of the U.S. Trade Act of 1988.[17] This list should be examined prior to making the decision to license in another country. Some IPR owners, in protecting their products from IPR infringement, choose to file claims in the foreign legal system against infringers, but cases may take years before they are finally resolved. Occasionally, foreign companies work with local law firms and law enforcement officials to conduct police raids of counterfeiters. Others conduct periodic seminars on the adverse effects of IPR infringement on the local economy, one of which is reduced investment by foreign companies.

Some companies pursue an IPR strategy of identifying the counterfeiters and then proceed to work with them by signing them to license contracts. Some computer software companies provide free training and sell their software at competitive prices, while warning that copies of their product may contain damaging viruses. In general, acquiring a strong local partner or agent can help in protecting IPR.

The general patent principle is that the owner of a patent is the party who is "first to register" at a national patent office.[18] Thus, a patent holder may find it difficult to prevent infringement unless it takes the necessary steps to register its patent in foreign countries. The best approach is to secure the services of a **patent agent**[19] in order to obtain the necessary patents (and trademarks) within a foreign country. A second issue is the ownership and protection of inventions created by an employee. Employee inventions belong to the employer, but in some countries, the employer must pay the employee for the invention and in other countries, the employer must file a patent application within a certain period of time or risk losing ownership to the employee. In such countries, a written employment contract should provide for a formal notification procedure, establish the obligation of the employee to cooperate in the filing of a patent application, and detail the amount of remuneration that will be paid to the employee.

If a third party makes an improvement on a patent, then the patent holder must grant the improvement owner a (compulsory) license to use the underlying patent or technology. The junior patent holder must first show that it cannot use its patent without infringing on the rights of the other senior patent holder. The danger of this law is that a minor improvement by a second inventor theoretically gives him the right to a license without a reciprocal requirement to license the improvement in return.[20] For this reason, it is important to periodically use or work patents in order to preclude the creation of second inventor rights.

A number of tangential issues should be explored by the licensor (IPR owner) before entering into a licensing agreement. First, all protections provided by international conventions should be explored. Second, in some countries, it is important to pay periodic maintenance fees. Failure to pay such fees can result in a termination of the patent. Third, in some countries, a licensor is required to record any license, transfer, or assignment of property rights for instruments to be enforceable. Fourth, the licensee should be required to enter into employment contracts with its employees, which clearly delegate ownership of rights to any improvements made to the licensed technology. Fifth, a "best efforts" clause should be incorporated into any transfer agreement to prevent claims of abandonment and to prevent the issuance of compulsory licenses. Sixth, any regional intellectual property regime should be used, such as the EU Community Mark or the Eurasian patent.

Chapter Summary

1. The value of intellectual property rights and the licensing of those rights have become a substantial percentage of international trade. The core intellectual property protections relate to patents, trademarks, copyrights, and trade secrets. Databases and software have been increasingly recognized as deserving of legal protection.
2. Trademarks protect the brand names and symbols related to a company's products or services and include the trademark for goods, trade dress, service marks, certification marks, and designations of the place of origin. Trademarks are effective for a fixed period of time, usually ten years, but can be perpetually renewed unless the trademark is not protected and becomes a generic term. In order to bring a claim for trademark infringement, the claimant must show a likelihood of confusion (by consumers) between the senior mark and the junior or infringing mark. A claim can also be brought when there is no likelihood of confusion if a trademark is harmed due to blurring or tarnishment.
3. Copyrights protect creative works, which extend from literary works, collective works such as movie and television productions, and live performances to computer programs. The major exceptions to copyright infringement include the first sale doctrine, fair use doctrine, public domain, and work for hire. Copyright protection is good for a period of 70 years after the death of the author or in cases of work for hire, 120 years.
4. Patents protect inventions, as well as processes and compositions of materials. In order to obtain a patent, the creation must be within one of the above patentable categories, as well as be useful, novel, and non-obvious. A patent's duration is 20 years. One of the major differences between American patent law and those of some other countries is the issuance of compulsory licenses for patents not being used by their owners. The U.S. does not grant or recognize compulsory licenses.
5. Trade secrets include confidential information that gives a company a competitive advantage over its competitors. They can include business know-how, secret ingredients or formulas, and customer lists or databases. Trade secrets are protected from theft or unauthorized usage as long as the owner keeps them secret.
6. The major international intellectual property conventions include the Berne Convention (copyright), Uniform Copyright Convention, Paris Convention (patents and trademarks), Patent Cooperation Treaty, as well as the WTO's Agreement on Trade-Related Aspects of Intellectual Property Rights (TRIPS).
7. At the regional level, EU law provides for a Community Trademark, Single European Patent, and a unique intellectual property law regime that protects databases. Another regional intellectual property protection regime is the Eurasian Patent Convention.

Key Terms

Agreement on Trade-Related Aspects of Intellectual Property Rights (TRIPS)
Anti-Bootlegging Statute
Berne Convention for the Protection of Literary and Artistic Works
Blurring
Brussels Act of 1948
Collective Works
Compulsory License
Council for Trade-Related Aspects of Intellectual Property
Dilution of Trademark
Doctrine of Equivalents
Economic Espionage Act of 1996
Electronic Agent
Electronic Records
EU Trademark
Eurasian Patent Office (EAPO)
European Patent Office (EPO)
Fair Use Doctrine
First Sale Doctrine
First to Register Principle
Generic Marks
Gray Market
Indigenous Rights
Inducement to Infringe
Innocent Infringement
International Patent Searching Authorities (ISA)
Junior Mark
Lanham Act
Meta-tags
National Treatment Negotiations
Opinion Letter
Paris Act of 1971
Paris Convention Patent Agent
Patent Cooperation Treaty (PCT)
Patent Law of the People's Republic of China
Public Domain
Right of Priority
Rome Act of 1928
Secondary Meaning
Senior Mark
Service Mark
Single European Patent Sound Recording Act of 1971
Statute of Frauds
Stockholm Act of 1967
Tangible
Form Tarnishment
Technology Transfer Laws
Trade Dress
Trade Secret
Trademark Dilution
Treaty on Intellectual Property in Respect of Integrated Circuits
Uniform Trade Secrets Act
Universal Copyright Convention
Work for Hire
World Intellectual Property Organization (WIPO)

Chapter Problems

1. *Conflicts of law rules* play an important role in the application of national intellectual property laws. Courts determine which national law is to be applied in the case by applying conflicts of law rules. They are applied when the parties are from different countries or the activities at issue transpired in different countries. The court must decide whether the law of the country of the plaintiff or the defendant or of some other country, should be applied. In a recent case, Itar-Tass Russian News Agency sued *Kurier*, a Russian-language newspaper in New York that copied articles originally

published by Itar-Tass, for copyright violation. Itar-Tass claimed *Kurier*'s publication of its articles violated the Berne Convention and the Universal Copyright Convention. Under what law is the ownership of the articles to be determined? Does the Russian copyright owner have the standing to sue for infringement in U.S. courts? *Itar-Tass Russian News Agency v. Russian Kurier, Inc.*, 153 F.3d 82 (2d Cir. 1998).

2. L'Oreal applied for a patent on a sun protection factor (SPF) product in Luxembourg on April 13, 1987. It applied in the U.S. on April 12, 1988. Estée Lauder applied for a patent in the U.S. on the same SPF on December 21, 1987. Assuming that the Paris Convention and Patent Cooperation Treaty applied, who is entitled to the U.S. patent? *Estée Lauder, Inc. v. L'Oréal, S.A.*, 129 F.3d 588 (Fed. Cir. 1997).
3. McCoy hired Mitsuboshi to make and supply shrimp knives covered by McCoy's patent and trademarks. When Mitsuboshi produced the knives, McCoy refused to pay for them. Mitsuboshi resold the knives to Admiral Craft. McCoy sued Mitsuboshi Cutlery, Inc. for patent and trademark infringement in violation of U.S. federal law. Is Mitsuboshi guilty of patent and trademark infringement? *McCoy v. Mitsuboshi Cutlery, Inc.*, 67 F.3d 917 (Fed. Cir. 1995).
4. "Green River" is the trademark under which Sethness-Greenleaf, Inc. sold to bottlers a soft drink according to a formula that was Sethness-Greenleaf's trade secret. Sethness-Greenleaf sold the Green River business, including the trademark and the trade secret, to Green River Corp. The purchase price was to be paid in installments. When the price was paid in full, the secret formula for the manufacture of Green River beverage and syrup, till then held in escrow, would be released to Green River Corp. Green River Corp. fell behind in its payments and Sethness-Greenleaf declared a default, stopped supplying Green River Corp., and demanded the return of the formula from the escrow agent. Unwilling to stop doing business under the "Green River" name, Green River Corp. procured a green soft drink from another producer and sold it under the "Green River" name, precipitating this suit by Sethness-Greenleaf. Green River Corp. counterclaimed that it is not guilty of infringement because Sethness-Greenleaf's failure to continue to supply it with the product was a breach of contract. Assuming that Sethness-Greenleaf is guilty of breach, is Green River Corp. correct? *Green River Bottling Co. v. Green River Corp.*, 997 F.2d 359 (7th Cir. 1993).
5. The premier German manufacturer of compact discs decides to export its discs to markets in Eastern Europe. Because of the economic realities of these emerging-economy countries, the manufacturer is forced to sell the discs at a lower price than it sells them in the German market in order to obtain market share. A wily entrepreneur purchases large quantities of the exported discs and reimports them into the higher-priced German market. What is the likely result under EU law of the German manufacturer's attempt to prevent the importation of the discs?

Internet Exercises

1. Research the activities of the World Intellectual Property Organization by reviewing its website at www.wipo.org.
2. Review the websites of the U.S. Patent and Trademark Office (www.uspto.gov), European Patent Office (www.epo.org), and Japanese Patent Office (www.jpo.go.jp). Also, through these websites, research the work of the Trilateral Office. The U.S. PTO, EPO, and JPO established the Trilateral Office to facilitate cooperation in the administration of their patent functions (www.trilateral.net/index.html).
3. Review the website of The Cyberspace Law Institute for information on how the Internet interrelates with intellectual property law: http://www.cli.org.

Notes

1 210 F.3d 439 (5th Cir. 2000).
2 See *First Savings Bank v. First Bank System, Inc.*, 101 F.3d 645 (10th Cir. 1996).
3 15 U.S.C. § 1127 (1996).
4 15 U.S.C. § 1125.
5 17 U.S.C. § 109(a).
6 118 S. Ct. 1125 (1998).
7 See www.bsa.org.
8 117 S. Ct. 1040 (1997).
9 18 U.S.C. § 90.
10 971 P.2d 936 (Sup. Ct., Wash., 1999).
11 15 U.S.C.A §§ 1125(a) and 1127.
12 489 F.2d 809 (7th Cir. 1972).
13 344 U.S. 280 (1952).
14 19 U.S.C. Section 1526(e).
15 15 U.S.C. § 1114(1).
16 18 U.S.C. § 2319A. See *U.S. v. Ali Moghadam*, 175 F.3d 1269 (11th Cir. 1999).
17 For the 2015 USTR Report, see www.stopfakes.gov/news/ustr-releases-2015-special-301-report.
18 It should be noted that Russia is a signatory of the Paris Convention. Therefore, the true inventor should have 12 months from the filing date in another country to file for a patent in Russia.
19 Russian patent agents are certified under the Statute of Patent Agents enacted in 1993.
20 Marina Portnova, "Ownership and Enforcement of Patent Rights in Russia: Protecting an Invention in the Existing Environment," 8 *Indiana International and Comparative Law Review* 505, 516 (1998).

Chapter 16

Licensing of Technology

Intellectual Property Licensing

The above review of foreign and international IP law (Chapter 15) showed some of their shortcomings. These shortcomings mean that the licensor–patentee of technology and IPR needs to negotiate added protections in international licensing agreements. This chapter will analyze the contractual arrangements used in the field of intellectual property transfer and licensing, including a review of common clauses used to protect the rights of the licensor (owner) and how best to protect the confidentiality of the licensor's property rights.

Developing an Intellectual Property Protection Strategy

Before entering a foreign market, an intellectual property owner or licensor should develop a strategy or checklist to protect its IP rights. The following is an example of such a strategy, using Russia as the target market: (1) explore the protections provided by international conventions. Russia is currently a party to the Patent Cooperation Treaty, the Madrid Protocol, the Berne Convention, and the Universal Copyright Convention, along with the Paris Convention. These treaty commitments supersede domestic patent law; (2) use a patent agent to obtain a Russian patent, along with any necessary copyrights and trademarks; (3) determine duties or fees payable during the patent term. After obtaining a Russian patent (or Eurasian patent), periodic maintenance fees need to be paid. Failure to pay such fees can result in a termination of the patent; (4) be sure to satisfy all notice and registration requirements. In Russia, a licensor is required

DOI: 10.4324/9781003469230-20

to record any transfer or assignment of IP rights. For example, patent transfers or licenses must be registered with the Patent Office; (5) define ownership rights for employees. In Russia, licensees should be required to enter into contracts with their employees that clearly delineate ownership of rights to any improvements made to the licensed technology; (6) explore enforcement options; (7) protect against compulsory licenses. In Russia, a best efforts clause in licenses should help prevent claims of abandonment and the issuance of compulsory licenses; and (8) the Eurasian Patent Convention should be utilized when appropriate to expand the reach of the patent to other countries near Russia.

Finally, the licensor should enlist the services of **International Patent Searching Authorities** (**ISA**) when filing foreign patent applications. A number of national patent offices, including the U.S., Japan, and the EPO recognize patent search certificates, which confirm that there are no existing patents equivalent to the patent being requested.

Companies frequently license their IPR to foreign companies who manufacture and sell products abroad.[1] Licensing, from the licensor's perspective, provides an inviting means of generating revenues without committing large amounts of capital. A technology or IPR licensing agreement enables a company to enter a foreign market quickly, and it poses fewer financial and legal risks than foreign direct investment (FDI). The **licensor** or owner of the technology and IPR can avoid the costs and time of exporting and importing goods across national borders, as well as avoid tariff and nontariff barriers. The licensing company also avoids the variety of host country laws, such as tax, labor, and environmental laws that would apply to FDI. Licensing can be attractive for small companies or companies with little international trade experience.

Technology transfer covers different types of agreements, such as highly complex agreements to conduct research and development abroad, to provide technical assistance to a subsidiary or joint venture, or to perform other activities under direct commercial licensing agreements between a manufacturer or IPR owner and a foreign entity. Technology licensing is a contractual arrangement in which the licensor's patents, trademarks, service marks, copyrights, or know-how are sold or otherwise made available to a **licensee** for compensation. The licensee compensates the licensor by paying **royalties** as a percentage of sales or a lump sum royalty.

IP licensing in the narrowest sense involves the sale or assignment of statutorily recognized rights of patents, trademarks, and copyrights to a foreign licensee or buyer. IP also includes trade secrets. Technology transfer in its widest sense includes more than the licensing of IPR. It may include the transfer of technical know-how and skills, along with managerial processes and technical services or assistance.

IPR licensing may also be used to acquire foreign technology through **cross-licensing** agreements. With some patented inventions, opportunities may exist for cross-licensing across areas or broader fields of invention, where each party grants a patent license to the other party, effectively allowing both parties to combine resources to exploit the full field of the patented technology. Cross-licensing arrangements also relate to the creation of **patent pools** where multiple patent owners pool their patents covering a certain field for licensing to one another. However, cross-licenses that are exclusive raise a risk of antitrust scrutiny from government authorities or challenges by other competitors excluded from the cross-licensing arrangement.

As a method of doing business, licensing has drawbacks; most importantly, the licensor loses control over its confidential information, know-how, and trade secrets. It risks losing its competitive advantage over competitors if the licensee or its employees disclose its information to others. As discussed previously, the importation of licensed goods into the licensor's market is popularly known as the **gray market** problem. A gray market problem exists when goods produced under a foreign license agreement are imported into the sales territory of the licensor or other licensees. The IP licensing agreement must deal with the gray market issue (grant and termination of license clauses).

The law as applied to international IP licensing is multilayered and complex.[2] Four areas of applicable law need to be analyzed: (1) home country law (law of licensor) may apply extraterritorially; (2) international conventions can be used in protecting the IP being transferred; (3) foreign or host country IP laws; and (4) host country laws that regulate the content of licensing agreements. The fourth area of law becomes especially important when the host country is weak in protecting foreign IPR. In such countries, the restrictions placed in the licensing agreement may be the only means by which a licensor can protect its IP.

Protecting Intellectual Property Rights

In considering the licensing of IPR, it is important to remember that foreign licensees may attempt to use the license to manufacture products to be marketed in third-party countries in direct competition with other licensees. In many instances, licensors will wish to impose territorial restrictions on their foreign licensees if permitted by foreign competition (antitrust) law. Competition law, as a general rule, prohibits international IPR licensing agreements that unreasonably restrict imports of competing goods or technology. In instances when significant competition law issues are presented, licensors may consider applying for a review from the relevant government agency for an **opinion letter**.

The *Farrel Corporation v. International Trade Commission* case illustrates the use of parallel proceedings to protect IPR rights. The Farrel Corporation uses both public and private means against the infringing party. Its only strategic failure was improperly pursuing private litigation instead of arbitration as required by the licensing agreement.

Farrel Corporation v. International Trade Commission

949 F.2d 1147 (Fed. Cir. 1991)

Farrel manufactures heavy machinery used in mixing plastics. Pomini, an Italian company, also sells imported plastics processing machinery in competition with Farrel. Farrel and Pomini entered into a series of licensing agreements allowing Pomini to manufacture, using Farrel's technology, a line of plastics mixing machines worldwide, except for the U.S., UK, and Japan.

The agreements included provisions requiring that Pomini return all designs, specifications, and other materials on the expiration of the contractual relationship. Each of the licensing agreements contained an arbitration clause requiring that "all disputes arising in connection with the present Agreement shall be finally settled by arbitration" through the International Chamber of Commerce.

Subsequently, Farrel terminated Pomini's rights to use Farrel technology. Pomini announced that it planned to supply American customers with internal mixing devices. Farrel alleged that Pomini had misappropriated its trade secrets. Farrel filed a complaint against Pomini in the Tribunal of Busto Arsizio, alleging the misappropriation of trade secrets and infringement of various patents and trademarks registered in Italy. A similar suit was filed in the Scottish Court of Session, in which Farrel alleged that Pomini infringed its patents and trademarks registered in the UK. In both suits, Pomini asserted the affirmative defense that the parties had agreed to binding arbitration.

Meanwhile, Farrel filed a complaint against Pomini with the U.S. International Trade Commission (ITC). It alleged that Pomini violated American law by importing machines made by the misappropriation of trade secrets, trademark infringement, and falsely representing the manufacturer's source. Farrel petitioned for an immediate cease and desist order forbidding entry into the U.S. of Pomini's mixing devices. The administrative law judge terminated the investigation due to the existence of the arbitration clauses in Farrel's technology licensing agreements.

The ITC has exclusive authority to investigate allegations that foreign importers are engaging in unfair methods of competition and unfair acts in the importation of products. We conclude that the administrative law judge acted contrary to law by terminating its investigation without first determining whether a violation existed. REVERSED AND REMANDED.

Case Highlights

- This case shows the dangers of co-licensing with a competitor and the need to pursue multiple infringement claims under national patent laws
- The U.S. **International Trade Commission (ITC)** has exclusive jurisdiction over the issuance of *cease and desist orders* preventing infringing foreign goods from being imported.

Some countries have IP specific laws that intervene into private licensing contracts including government approval of the licensing agreement and prohibitions on royalty payments that exceed a certain rate or contractual provisions barring the licensee from exporting products embodying the licensed technology to third countries. The prospective licensor should review the host country's patent, trademark, and copyright laws; exchange controls; product liability laws; antitrust and tax laws; and restrictions on the repatriation of royalties. The existence of a tax treaty or bilateral investment treaty between the home and host countries is an indicator of whether the foreign country is investment and trade friendly. In many instances, licensors should retain legal counsel in the host country in order to obtain advice on applicable laws.

Due Diligence

In contemplating the exportation of IPR, the licensor should undertake a **due diligence** review. Due diligence should provide answers to the following questions: (1) what formalities are needed to register or protect IP rights in the host country? (2) Will the transfer agreement or license need to be registered and approved by government authorities? (3) What types of clauses are likely to be disapproved or violate foreign competition (antitrust) laws? (4) Are there other mandatory legal rules that specifically apply to cross-border IP licensing? For an example of a preventive law checklist, see Figure 16.1 *Doing Business Internationally*: "Due Diligence Checklist for Intellectual Property Transfers."

Intellectual Property Review Team

Assemble an intellectual property review team. This team should include representatives from management; local and foreign legal counsel; technical personnel, such as representatives from research and development, engineering, and production; sales and marketing; human resources; and finance.

Patents

- What are the terms remaining on the patents?
- Have patents been used in countries that require *working*?
- Identify all patents associated with the transfer.
- Search foreign patent office records for title and payment of all necessary fees.
- Identify other research and development projects, which may be exposed to competition in the event of a transfer.
- Identify procedures for protecting inventions, including procedures for determining whether an invention should remain a trade secret, making foreign filing decisions, and ensuring the timeliness of patent filings.
- Determine which patents cover which products.
- Identify all markings to be used in conjunction with the production of the licensed product.
- Identify all existing and pending agreements dealing with the patents.
- Whether a licensor or licensee, always ask: Are the patents or licenses transferable? Are improvements included in the transfer?
- Are there any non-compete provisions? What are the termination dates on the patents and licenses? Are there any security interests (liens) on file with Patent Offices and have applicable state records been reviewed?
- Review all correspondence relating to patent disputes, claims of infringement, and letters threatening lawsuits or other notices received by licensor or licensee.
- What steps have been taken to insure patent rights in the foreign country of the licensee or the geographic area of the license grant? Has the patent been registered under the appropriate foreign national law?

Figure 16.1 Doing Business Internationally: Due Diligence Checklist for Intellectual Property Transfers.

Source: See generally, Mary Ann Tucker, "Checklist for Due Diligence in Intellectual Property Transactions," 14 *Corporate Counsel's Quarterly* 68 (1997).

Trademarks

- Identify all federal, state, and foreign trademark registrations and pending applications.
- Check title and payment of renewal fees.
- Identify all procedures for protecting trademarks, including procedures for deciding whether to seek registrations.
- Determine the products on which each trademark is used. Provide licensee with sample of the proper use of the trademarks.
- Review copies of all product advertising and promotional materials.
- Check use of the trademark on the Internet.
- Has there been any period of nonuse of the trademarks?
- Have there been any previous assignments of the trademarks? Have these assignments been recorded?
- Are the trademarks and any licenses pertaining to them transferable or assignable? Are there any restrictions or limitations in the licenses?
- Review renewal dates on trademarks.

Copyrights

- Identify all copyrighted materials associated with the transfer or license.
- Check title to copyrights and payment of renewal fees for copyrights by searching the Copyright Offices.
- Review procedures for identifying "copyrightable" material including procedures for deciding whether to mark materials or to register them.
- Review all agreements dealing with the copyrights. Are they assignable or transferable? Are there any restrictions or limitations on their use or transfer?
- Check for security interests by searching the Copyright Offices.
- Have the licensor and licensee enforced their copyrights in the past?
- Does any action need to be taken in the country of the licensee to protect foreign copyrights?

Miscellaneous

- What procedures should the licensee be required to undertake in order to protect the rights being licensed? (site security, employee access, and monitoring).
- Review employment agreements relating to IP and confidentiality.
- What responsibilities should the licensee be required to undertake in relationship to third-party infringements?

Figure 16.1 (Continued)

Copyright is recognized globally, but patents and trademarks are territorial. Therefore, before entering any licensing agreement, the licensor should register its trademarks and patents under the appropriate foreign national laws. The rights to use the licensor's trademark should be expressly limited to the duration of the agreement. The rights should also be limited to the territory of the license grant and used only in reference to specific products.

A trademark holder should also investigate the local connotation of a trademark or trade name before licensing with a foreign entity. A different language or culture may have unfavorable meanings for words or symbols with neutral or favorable meanings. Even packaging colors may connote different meanings in different countries. For example, white is the color of mourning in most of the Far East.

Special attention should be given to the protection of **trade names**. The problem is that trade names are not well protected under some foreign incorporation laws. In a number of countries, there is no explicit prohibition against a new company using or modifying the name of a pre-existing company. Therefore, the license agreement should address the issue of the licensee's use or modification of the licensor's trade names.

More and more companies are taking aggressive, self-help approaches to deterring the counterfeiting and piracy of their IP. One approach is to establish **Brand Protection Units** (BPU) inside the country where the piracy and counterfeiting is being done. This strategy has become common for companies doing business in China. These units are essentially private investigators who work with the Chinese authorities. The manager of the BPU comes from the corporate security department. The BPU coordinates their activities with Chinese authorities. The goal is to identify and locate sources of counterfeited goods. The location of counterfeiters is not revealed to Chinese authorities until the raid is in progress. A member of the BPU or company should be present at the raid in order to identify the illegal goods. Another strategy has been to find the counterfeiters and enter into licensing agreements with them. It is often the best practical solution due to the costs and uncertainty in pursuing legal actions.

Once a patent, copyright, or trademark is obtained, the holder is free to assign, transfer, or even mortgage those rights. The licensing agreement is the most common means of transfer. The IP agreement or license takes on added significance in international transfers as compared to purely domestic transfers. Most jurisdictions require *exclusive copyright licenses* to be in writing, typically signed by at least the licensor. Nonexclusive licenses, on the other hand, typically need not be in writing and many jurisdictions recognize open and Creative Commons-style licenses. A few jurisdictions require copyright licenses to be filed or registered. Different jurisdictions have different requirements about whether a *trademark license* agreement must be in writing.

The IP agreement or license takes on added significance in international transactions as compared to purely domestic transfers. The wide variety of IP protections offered by foreign laws requires the exporter of technology to take added precaution in drafting its licensing. It is important that the contract provide avenues for lawsuits for breach of contract where an infringement claim is unlikely to be sustained under a foreign IP law regime.

Following the identification of the parties, the generic licensing agreement will have a number of **recitals** and a definitional section. The recitals will often list the rights being licensed. Any untruthful recitals can become the basis for lawsuits asserting breach of warranty or misrepresentation. The licensor should verify the status of all its trademarks, copyrights, patents, and any patents pending. Extra care should be taken in defining terms in the definitions section. Given the differences in language, culture, and national IP laws, the agreement should contain a carefully negotiated and drafted list of definitions. For example, the meaning of terms such as "net sales" or "gross sales" for the purposes of calculating royalties is often at the center of disputes if they are not carefully defined.

The core element of IP transfer agreements is the **grant clause**, which describes the rights, trade secrets, and know-how being transferred, along with any restrictions or limitations on their use. The grant clause should itemize all IP rights and know-how being transferred. The grant should make clear whether the license is exclusive or nonexclusive. The difference is fundamental to issues regarding the degree of competition that may be expected by the licensee and in setting the royalty rate. The grant clause will be examined in more detail later.

Exclusivity is interconnected with issues dealing with infringement. In an exclusive license, the licensee can negotiate the duty of the licensor to bring suit against any third-party infringer or be given the right to sue in the name of the licensor for any infringements in the license territory. A nonexclusive license grant may include a **most-favored-license clause** in which the licensor is required to amend the license to include more favorable terms negotiated in subsequent licenses given to other licensees. This ensures that earlier licensees are not placed at an unfair competitive disadvantage.[3] The problem with such clauses is the difficulty in determining the relative values of different terms. All things being equal, the negotiation of a more favorable royalty rate would be considered to be subject to a most-favored-license clause. A well-written most-favored-license clause requires the licensor to provide a copy of any such licenses so that the licensee can determine if the terms are more favorable. Finally, the clause should provide that if the licensee demands an amendment to its license in order to incorporate any more favorable terms, it must also accept the less favorable terms included in the subsequent license.

Common Licensing Clauses

Because the licensing of IPR is a private contract, the parties are free to formulate their contract as they wish. In case of a subsequent dispute, the courts and arbitration panels will look initially to the contract to determine the respective duties and rights of the parties. It is important to note, however, that the licensing agreement is regarded as a *sui generis* or unique type of contract. Competition (antitrust) laws, for example, will preempt the operation of overly broad territorial restrictions or tying provisions in a licensing agreement.

In most developing countries, certain license clauses are limited by a variety of specific **technology transfer laws**. Unlike competition law, the aim of technology transfer laws is not to protect competition, but to improve the bargaining strength of the licensee and to promote local technological development. The government approval authorities will examine the contract to see if they are too one-sided in favor of the licensor. The clauses that are most closely examined include the confidentiality, grant back, choice of law, export restrictions clauses, and clauses limiting the licensee's use of the technology after the termination of the license. For example, a **duration clause** will often prohibit the use of know-how after the termination of the term of the contract. A technology transfer law may eliminate such a restriction and convert the so-called license into an outright sale. A **grant-back clause** that requires any improvement of the technology made by the licensee to be assigned back to the licensor is considered invalid under some technology transfer laws. Most countries will allow a grant-back clause that is reciprocal or nonexclusive. In a reciprocal grant-back clause, improvements made by either the licensor or licensee are to be shared with the other party. The grant-back clause will be examined in more detail later in this chapter. A **confidentiality clause** restricts access to the technology to a limited number of **key personnel** of the licensee and prohibits any further disclosure of confidential information to third parties. Many licensors will require licensees to have all their employees sign separate confidentiality agreements. Most developing countries will insist on a broader dissemination of the technology to their citizens. Therefore, they will often limit the scope of confidentiality clauses and agreements. A **choice of law clause** and **forum selection clause** that designate the law of the licensor and the licensor's country as the place of dispute resolution are likely to be disregarded by the courts in a developing country. The courts in a developing country will generally decide that the transfer agreement be subject to the jurisdiction and law of the host country.

In addition, most licensors will desire strict territorial provisions limiting the licensee to selling only in the territory specified in the license. An *export restriction clause* is generally inserted to prevent a gray market problem from developing. Such restrictions on export may be invalidated under foreign competition law, such as in the EU, or under technology transfer laws found in many developing countries. Generally, developing countries aggressively promote the export of goods in order to acquire hard currencies and to improve their balance of trade. See Figure 16.2 *Focus on Transactions*: "Explanations of Common License Clauses" for examples and purposes of some other common license clauses.

Foreign competition, technology transfer, and consumer protection laws cannot be avoided through a contractual agreement. For example, some foreign contract or consumer laws limit the scope of disclaimers or limitation of liability

Compliance with Export Laws

"The licensed products shall not be exported, directly or indirectly, in violation of the export regulations of the United States or be used for any purposes prohibited by the export regulations." In this clause, the licensee agrees to comply with the export regulations of the licensor's country.

Merger or Integration Clause

"This contract supersedes the terms of any purchase order or ordering document, along with the terms of any unsigned or 'shrinkwrap' license included in any product package." This clause is especially important where the individual products being transferred come with their own licenses. The licensor would want to supersede such "individual licenses" only if it has provided adequate terms in the master license or transfer agreement.

Limitation of Liability

"The provisions of this Agreement allocate the risks between the licensor and licensee. The licensor's pricing reflects this allocation of risk and the limitation of liability hereto specified." The parties will generally want to exclude liability for indirect, incidental, special, or consequential damages. The licensor may want to limit the extent of its liability to an amount no greater than the total fees paid by the licensee.

Exclusive Remedy Clause

"The licensee's exclusive remedy and the licensor's total liability shall be the correction of defects in the licensed product or the reperformance of services rendered. Upon failure by the licensor to correct the defects within a reasonable period of time, the licensee may terminate the license and recover any fees paid for the product or for the unsatisfactory services." An ancillary clause to the limitation of liability clause is one that limits the types of remedies available to the parties.

Infringement Indemnity Clause

"Licensor will defend and indemnify licensee against claims of infringement of patent, copyright, or other intellectual property rights provided that (a) the licensee notifies licensor in writing within 45 days of receiving the claim, (b) the licensor shall have full control over the defense of the claim, and (c) the licensee shall assist the licensor in defending the claim. The licensor shall reimburse the licensee for reasonable expenses incurred in providing such assistance. The licensor shall have the option to (a) modify the licensed products to make them noninfringing or (b) obtain a valid license for the licensee. If the licensor determines that it is not commercially reasonable to perform either (a) or (b), then the licensor may terminate this license and refund the license fees. This shall be licensor's entire liability and the licensee's exclusive remedy for third-party claims of infringement." The licensee will want assurance that the licensor will defend it against any infringement claims. In turn, the licensor will want to limit its exposure to defending such claims.

Most-Favored License Clause

The licensor is required to notify and offer more favorable terms given to other licensees in the future to ensure that the favored licensee remains on an equal competitive footing with other licensees. Such a clause requires the licensor to provide the same royalty rate and terms to the licensee that he subsequently gives to another competitive licensee. Such a clause is likely to place the burden in future litigation on the licensor to prove that the most-favored licensee's competitor was not given a license at a more favorable or lower royalty rate.

Figure 16.2 Focus on Transactions: Explanations of Common License Clauses.

clauses. Thus, it is imperative that the international licensor determine how such laws, along with differences in customs and trade usage, will impact the operation of their standard licensing agreements. The following sections focus upon some of the standard clauses found in intellectual property agreements.

License Grant and Limitations

As noted previously, the single most important clause in any intellectual property, technology, or software licensing agreement is the **grant clause**. It describes the rights and know-how being transferred, along with any restrictions or limitations on their use. The licensor will want to emphasize that it is granting to the licensee only the right to use the items being transferred. The grant clause should limit or prohibit the licensee's right to copy the licensed material; clearly state that the licensor retains all title, copyright, patents, and other proprietary rights; and require the licensee to cease using the information upon termination and for the return or destruction of all copies.

The grant clause should also define the grant in terms of its geographic scope, as well as its duration. If the license is for the right to produce, sell, and use the rights in the U.S., then the Patent Act implies that the grant territory is the entire U.S., along with its possessions and territories.[4] If the license is silent as to duration, then a court may imply that it was intended to grant rights for the entire statutory term of the patent, copyright, or trademark.[5] The grant clause may also restrict the nature of the rights being transferred. For example, for technology with different **fields of use**, the grant clause may restrict the type of use for which the transferred rights are to be utilized. For example, the patent owner of laser technology may elect to license the technology separately in the fields of medicine, industry, and government armament or defense. The *Mallinckrodt, Inc. v. Medipart, Inc.* case that follows provides an example of a field of use restriction. It also demonstrates that the licensor has the right to sue not only the licensee for violating a grant restriction, but also a third party who assists the licensee in committing the violation. The third party that assists a licensee in the violation of a patent license can be sued for **inducement to infringe**.

Mallinckrodt, Inc. v. Medipart, Inc.

976 F.2d 700 (Fed. Cir. 1992)

Circuit Judge. This action for patent infringement and inducement to infringe relates to the use of a patented medical device in violation of a "single use only" license. Mallinckrodt sold its patented devices to hospitals, some of which, after initial use, sent them to Medipart for servicing in order to use the device again. Mallinckrodt claimed Medipart directly infringed the patent and induced infringement by the hospitals. The device is marked with the appropriate patent numbers and bears the trademarks "Mallinckrodt" and the inscription "Single Use Only." The package instructs that the entire contaminated apparatus be disposed of in accordance with procedures for the disposal of biohazardous waste. Instead, the hospitals shipped the used manifold-nebulizer assemblies to Medipart, Inc. The "reconditioned" units, as Medipart calls them, are shipped back to the hospitals from where they came.

Restrictions on use are judged in terms of their relation to the patentee's right to exclude from all or part of the patent grant, and where an anticompetitive effect is asserted, the rule of reason is the basis of determining the legality of the provision. To sustain a misuse of patent defense involving a licensing arrangement, a factual determination must reveal that the overall effect of the license tends to restrain competition unlawfully. The appropriate criterion is whether Mallinckrodt's restriction is reasonably within the patent grant, or whether it ventured beyond the patent grant and into behavior having an anticompetitive effect. We conclude that the lower court erred in holding that the restriction on reuse was, as a matter of law, unenforceable under the patent law. REVERSED.

Case Highlights

- A license grant may restrict the licensee to a "single patent use"
- A third party that provides a service that allows a licensee to avoid restrictions found in its patent license is guilty of "induced infringement"
- A patent owner has the right to exclude others from using its invention. Therefore, it has the right to place use restrictions on licensing its patent, unless the restrictions have an unreasonable anticompetitive effect.

In addition to the field of use and territorial scope issues, parties to a patent license may agree to divide the scope of the grant into the various rights granted under the patent laws. For example, a patent licensor may grant one licensee the exclusive right to manufacture the patented invention, while granting another licensee the right to sell the invention to retailers or end users.[6]

A major issue that should be addressed in the license is the right of the licensee to export goods from the licensed territory (gray market problem). If the mobility of the goods being produced is a concern for the licensor, then it should place restrictions in the license in order to prevent gray market imports. The license can prohibit the licensee from exporting goods to other markets. Such a prohibition may not be enforceable under competition law. Another method for minimizing gray market risks is for the licensor to place caps on the maximum number of units of the licensed product the licensee can produce in a given year. The overall cap could be determined by calculating an estimate of sales expected for the licensed territory. The licensor could also limit the number of units that the licensee can sell to individual purchasers. This should include placing a "due diligence" duty upon the licensee to investigate a third-party purchaser, especially in large-volume sales. In addition, the license should state that the licensee is precluded from selling to anyone who is known to export goods into other markets.

In attempting to describe the scope of uses granted by a license, the grant clause may fail to anticipate future unforeseen uses of its IP. This was the issue addressed by the court in *Cohen v. Paramount Pictures Corp*. In such cases, the court must determine whether the unforeseen use comes within the spirit of the license grant.

Cohen v. Paramount Pictures Corp.

845 F.2d 851 (9th Cir. 1988)

Circuit Judge. This case involves a novel issue of the copyright law of whether a license conferring the right to exhibit a film "by means of television" includes the right to distribute videocassettes of the film. We hold it does not. Herbert Cohen is the owner of the copyright in a musical composition. Cohen granted H & J Pictures, Inc., a "synchronization" license, giving the right to use the composition in a film called *Medium Cool*. H & J then assigned to Paramount Pictures all of its rights in the movie. Paramount hired a manufacturer to produce videocassette copies of the film—including a recording of the composition.

Cohen filed suit against Paramount alleging copyright infringement. Cohen contended that the license did not confer the right to use the composition in a reproduction of the film in videocassettes distributed for home display. To resolve this case, we must examine the terms of the license, in order to determine whether the license conveyed the right to use the composition in making videocassette reproductions. The license grant gives the licensee "authority to record, in any manner, medium, form or language, the words and music of the musical composition and to make copies of such recordings and to perform said musical composition everywhere." It further states: "The license herein granted the right to: (a) exhibition of said motion picture to audiences in motionpicture theatres and other places of public entertainment; and (b) exhibition of motion picture by means of television, including pay television and subscription television." Finally, another provision states that the license reserves to the grantor "all rights and uses in and to said musical composition, except those herein granted to the Licensee" (reservation of rights clause).

Although the language of the license permits the recording and copying of the movie, nothing in the express language of the license authorizes distribution of copies to the public by sale or rental. Thus, the right to distribute copies of the videocassettes by sale or rental remained with the grantor (licensor) under the *reservation of rights provision.*

It is obvious that the distribution of videocassettes through sale and rental to the general public for viewing in their homes does not fit within the purpose of the license grant that is restricted to showing in theaters and other similar public places. Paramount argues that the distribution of videocassettes for showing in private homes is the equivalent of "exhibition by means of television." Distribution of individual videocassettes to the general public for private "performances" cannot be found in that language.

Moreover, the license must be construed in accordance with the purpose underlying copyright law. We would frustrate the purposes of copyright law were we to construe this license—with its limiting language—as granting a right in a medium that had not been introduced to the domestic market at the time the parties entered into the agreement. WE HOLD that the license did not give Paramount the right to use the composition in connection with videocassette production and distribution.

Case Highlights

- In determining the scope of the grant clause, courts will examine any relevant terms of the license for guidance

- The copyright law reserves all rights, whether or not they existed at the time of the creation of the work, to the creator of the work (copyright owner)
- Expanding a license grant to include the application of the licensed property to a medium that had not been developed at the time of the execution of the license would frustrate the purpose of the Copyright Act.

Review of Typical License Agreement

A number of contract provisions are found in most generic IP licensing agreements. Sample clauses are provided in Figure 16.3 *Doing Business Internationally*: "Examples of License Clauses." When reading these clauses and other clauses discussed in this section, bear in mind the following questions: (1) What issues are being dealt with in these clauses? (2) What issues are being neglected? (3) How can the clauses be rewritten for added clarity? (4) How can the clauses be made more pro-licensor or pro-licensee? See Problem 4 of the Chapter Problems ("License Writing and Review Problem") for another opportunity to review and re-draft license clauses.

In a **licensed territory clause**, the licensor defines the appropriate sales areas or distribution channels for the licensed product. "Licensed product" refers to the products to be produced or sold under the authority granted by the agreement. If the license grants "exclusive" territory, then the licensor cannot grant other licensees the right to sell in the exclusive territory. The licensor will want to restrict the licensee's ability to sell products outside the licensed territory.

Another clause that attempts to limit the licensee's ability to compete against the licensor is the **covenant not-to-compete**. Courts highly scrutinize and limit these types of clauses. The licensor will often require such a clause in order to prevent the licensee from competing against it after the termination of the license agreement. Article 2596 of the Italian Civil Code typifies the restrictions placed upon covenant not-to-compete clauses. It requires that such clauses be in writing, be limited to a certain geographical area and activity, and not exceed five years in duration. Italian courts generally favor the licensee in narrowing the restrictions pertaining to area and activity.

In the **reservation of rights clause**, the licensor reserves any IP or contractual rights not expressly transferred by the license. This reservation should always be inserted, even if the license is intended to be exclusive (see above, *Cohen v. Paramount Pictures Corp*).

The improvements or **grant-back clause** attempts to reserve to the licensor future rights of any subsequent improvements made by the licensee in the licensed property. The licensor will want to stipulate that any modifications or improvements made by the licensee shall revert (assigned) to the ownership of the licensor. The grant-back clause should deal with two distinct issues: (1) ownership of the improvement; and (2) the right to use the improvement. A one-sided, nonreciprocal grant-back clause gives all rights, title, and the right to use any improvements made by the licensee to the licensor. This type of clause

Royalties

"Guaranteed Consideration": The sum of $________ is payable upon the following dates: _____________. These sums as set forth above shall be applied against such royalties as become due to the licensor. No part of such Guaranteed Consideration shall be repayable to the licensee. "Royalty Payments": The Royalty Rate shall be five percent (5%). The licensee shall pay a sum equal to the Royalty Rate of all "net sales" by the licensee of the Licensed Product. The term "net sales" shall mean gross invoice price billed customers, less actual quantity discounts and actual returns (actual returns not to exceed 5%).

Accounting and Record-keeping

Within thirty days of the end of every month, the licensee shall furnish to licensor complete and accurate statements certified by an officer of the licensee with respect to the number of units sold, their gross sale prices, and itemized deductions from the gross sale prices.

The licensee shall maintain and preserve records pertaining to the license at its principal place of business for at least two years following termination or expiration of the license term or any renewals. These records shall include, without limitation, purchase orders, inventory records, invoices, correspondence, banking and financial records, and any other records pertaining to the Licensed Products. Such records and accounts shall be available for inspection and audit at any time during or after the license term during reasonable business hours and upon at least three (business) days written notice by the licensor.

Indemnification

The licensor shall indemnify the licensee and hold it harmless from any loss or liability arising out of any claims brought against the licensee by reason of the breach by the licensor of the warranties and representations stated within this License Agreement. The licensee shall indemnify the licensor and hold it harmless from any loss or liability arising out of any claims brought against the licensor by reason of the licensee's breach of any provision of this License Agreement including any unauthorized use by the licensee, any improper use of trademarks, copyright, patent, design, or process not specifically granted or approved by the licensor, any noncompliance by the licensee with laws or regulations, and for any defects attributable to the licensee's production of the Licensed Products.

Quality Control

The licensee agrees to strictly comply and maintain compliance with the quality standards, specifications, and rights of approval of the licensor in respect to any and all usage of the Licensed Property. Any modification of the Licensed Product must be submitted in advance for the licensor's written approval as if it were a new product.

Licensor Warranties

The licensor warrants that it possesses the right to license the Licensed Products, including any patents, copyrights, or trademarks, in accordance with the provisions of this License Agreement. The making of this License Agreement does not violate any agreements or rights of any other person, firm, or corporation.

Licensee Warranties

The licensee warrants that it will not harm, misuse, or bring in disrepute the Licensed Property. The licensee will manufacture, sell, and distribute the Licensed Products in accordance with the terms of this License Agreement, and in compliance with applicable government regulations and industry standards. Upon reasonable notice, the licensee shall permit the licensor to inspect testing records and procedures with respect to the production and sales of the Licensed Products for compliance with applicable quality standards provided in this License Agreement and for compliance with applicable governmental, regulatory, industry, and certification standards.

Confidentiality

The licensee warrants that it will use its best efforts to maintain the confidential nature of all proprietary information and to prevent unauthorized access, reproduction, use, or disclosure of that information. It will restrict access to key employees on a need-to-know basis. In furtherance of this obligation it shall: (a) maintain all copyright notice, trademark notice, and other proprietary markings and (b) not copy or reproduce the proprietary information except as authorized under this agreement.

Copyright and Trademark Protection (Infringement)

The licensee shall cause to be imprinted on each Licensed Product sold under the License Agreement, and on all advertising, promotional, and packaging material, the proper copyright notices and trademarks as instructed by the licensor. The licensee shall promptly notify the licensor in writing of any infringements by others of the Licensed Property. The licensee shall assist the licensor at the licensor's expense in the procurement, protection, and maintenance of the licensor's rights in the Licensed Property. The licensee agrees to cooperate with the licensor in connection with any claims or suits relating to infringements on the licensor's property rights.

Assignment and Sublicensing

This License Agreement is personal to the licensee. The licensee shall not sublicense, franchise, assign, or delegate to third parties any of the rights acquired hereunder. Neither this License Agreement nor any of the rights hereunder shall be sold, transferred, or assigned by the licensee.

Independent Contractor

The licensee is an independent company. Nothing in this agreement is intended to represent that the licensee is to act as an agent or partner of the licensor. The licensee is not granted any rights or authority, express or implied, to bind the licensor in any manner.

Termination

The licensor shall have the right to terminate this Agreement without prejudice to any rights which it may have upon the occurrence of any of the following events: (1) The licensee fails to deliver or maintain the required product liability insurance policy, (2) The licensee becomes delinquent on any payments due under this License Agreement, (3) The licensee fails to provide access to the premises or access to the records required to be maintained under this License Agreement, (4) The licensee fails to comply with applicable laws, regulations, or industry standards, (5) The licensee does not commence in good faith to manufacture, distribute, or sell the Licensed Products throughout the Licensed Territory, and (6) The licensee delivers or sells Licensed Products outside the Licensed Territory or knowingly sells Licensed Products to a third party who the licensee knows intends to or reasonably should suspect intends to sell or deliver such Licensed Products outside the Licensed Territory.

Figure 16.3 Doing Business Internationally: Examples of License Clauses.

is not enforceable in some countries.[7] Depending upon the country, it may be necessary to provide for reciprocity or sharing within the grant-back clause; any subsequent improvements made by the licensor also have to be made available to the licensee.

One technique for increasing the likelihood that a grant-back clause will be enforced is to provide for reasonable compensation for the grant back of the licensee's improvements. Also, the grant back can be made nonexclusive. A nonexclusive grant back allows the licensee to continue to use its improvement within the geographical scope of the license.

The licensee generally pays for the licensed property through royalty payments. The **royalty clause** is negotiated along three general parameters: royalty rate, guaranteed consideration, and momentum royalties. A generic royalty rate is based upon a percentage of sales, determined in one of two ways: gross sales (favors licensor) and net sales (favors licensee). The distinction, however, between gross sales and net sales is not always significant. A net sales definition that allows for very few offsets or deductions will result in a figure very close to a gross sales amount. Conversely, a gross sales definition that allows for a liberal number of setoffs or deductions can result in an amount close to a net sales figure.

Guaranteed consideration may be a schedule of payments, including a good faith deposit, not connected with sales by the licensee. Guaranteed consideration ensures that the licensee will make reasonable efforts to produce, market, and sell the licensed product. The licensee should negotiate that any advance payments ("Guaranteed Consideration") are to be credited against future royalties. **Momentum royalties** are paid when the licensee sales of other product lines are expected to increase due to the introduction of the licensed product. These royalties are based upon increases in the licensee's overall sales. Momentum royalties are negotiated in licenses of marquee products that are likely to draw customers to the licensee's other products.

One type of license that creates problems in drafting a royalty clause is the **hybrid license**. A hybrid license includes patent use rights, along with other IPRs with different durations to that of the patent being licensed. The U.S. Supreme Court in *Brulotte v. Thys Co.*[8] held that an agreement that extends royalties beyond the life of a patent is *per se* unenforceable. Therefore, royalty clauses must be carefully written to avoid invalidation because of post-expiration royalties. In order to avoid invalidation of royalties in a hybrid license, the license should allocate royalties between the patent right and the other rights. It should provide for a reduction in royalties upon the expiration of one of the patents or other rights.

A **best efforts clause** is vital in an exclusive license agreement since the licensor depends on the licensee to generate sales and royalty payments. Courts have implied such clauses in exclusive licenses, but the licensor would be better served by negotiating a specific best efforts clause with appropriate timetables or benchmarks for production and sales, amount of monies to be expended by the licensee in promoting sales, and minimum royalty levels. The best efforts clause should provide "penalties" for failure to reach stated goals and for the termination of the license.

Another purpose of the best efforts clause is to prevent a foreign country from issuing compulsory licenses of the licensor's technology to third parties. Some countries require a patent owner to use the patent in order to avoid losing the exclusive rights to exploit that patent in the country. Granting a license to a national of that country usually satisfies these so-called "working requirements." The threat remains, however, if the licensee fails to work the license; in that case, compulsory licenses may be granted to third parties. A best efforts clause requires the licensee to "work" the license.

Transparency in the licensing relationship requires the insertion of accounting and record-keeping requirements. The accounting provision should call for periodic statements of sales and royalty payments. It should also provide for certification and audit by an independent accounting firm. The licensor should specify payment of interest on delinquent payments and assurances in case of default.

Indemnification clauses work both ways between the licensor and licensee. The licensee generally wants to be indemnified for any liability stemming from the licensor's title or product warranties. The licensor seeks to be indemnified for any misuse of the license. The licensor should also protect itself through a **disclaimer** or limitation of warranty applicable against the ultimate purchaser or consumer and require the licensee to obtain customer signatures agreeing to the disclaimer or limitation. In conjunction with the indemnification clause, the licensor should require the licensee to obtain a product liability insurance policy. Also, the licensor will want to ensure that the licensee complies with quality standards and specifications by negotiating inspection rights.

Warranties and **representations** made in the license are important in liability claims for negligence, misrepresentation, and breach of warranty. The licensor should insert language disclaiming warranties implied in law (goods that are merchantable, satisfactory, or for a particular purpose). To further prevent the implication of warranties, the licensor should insert **negations**. An example of a negation is a statement that the license does not grant the licensee the rights to any subsequent know-how or to additional technical support. Another negation precludes the licensee from using the licensor's trade name. The problem with negation clauses is that a licensor cannot assume that the negation clause will be enforced under foreign law.

The licensee should be required to take all reasonable measures to protect the licensor's copyrights and trademarks. The licensee's duties in this area are detailed in an **infringement clause**. These duties include affixing the appropriate marks and patent numbers to the products being licensed. Failure to affix the patent numbers may prevent the licensor from collecting damages for infringements.[9] The court in *Yarway Corp. v. Eur-Control USA, Inc.*[10] held that a licensor has a cause of action for damages against the licensee's failure to mark goods as required under the license.

In the area of third-party infringement, the infringement clause places a number of obligations upon the licensee. First, the licensee should be made to act as the "eyes and ears" of the licensor since it is in the best position to uncover infringement. The licensee is then required to notify the licensor of acts of infringement by third parties. Second, the licensee's cooperation in any infringement proceeding should be required under the license. The licensee would in exchange want protection from third-party infringement lawsuits with a covenant requiring the licensor to defend and indemnify the licensee against such title claims. A compromise would be an agreement to share the costs of defending any third-party infringement claims.[11]

The licensee's right in the license agreement to sue third parties for patent infringement may not be sufficient protection. Some countries require the licensor–patentee to be joined in infringement lawsuits.[12] The rationale for this rule is that a license grants to the licensee merely a privilege that protects him from a claim of infringement by the owner. As such, he has no ownership interest in the patent. The courts have also held that granting the licensee the right to sue for third-party infringement does not imply any obligation on the part of the licensor to assist in such actions. Courts have, however, recognized the right of an exclusive licensee to join the licensor as an involuntary plaintiff to an infringement action.[13] In order to protect its interests, the licensee should negotiate a clause requiring the licensor to sue third-party infringers or to join the licensee in any such actions. The *Abbott Laboratories v. Diamedix Corp.* case reviews the law regarding whether a licensee has the *standing to sue* for the infringement of IPR included in its license.

Abbott Laboratories v. Diamedix Corp.

47 F.3d 1128 (Fed. Cir. 1995)

Circuit Judge. Abbott Laboratories held a license from Diamedix and brought a claim of patent infringement against Ortho Diagnostic Systems. Abbott received a worldwide license to make, use, and sell products incorporating the inventions claimed in the patents. The license was exclusive to Abbott but was subject to the rights previously granted to Diamedix's other licensees. The agreement contained a clause addressing the rights of the parties in suits against third parties for infringement of patent rights: "If any patent rights are infringed, Abbott shall have the right, but not the obligation, to bring suit to suppress such infringement against any unlicensed third party."

Ortho denied the allegations of infringement and asserted an affirmative defense that the patents were invalid. Because Abbott did not join Diamedix as a party to the lawsuit, Diamedix filed a motion to intervene as a plaintiff–intervenor. Diamedix argued that Abbott has an incentive not to defend the validity of the patents with vigor, since a decision invalidating the patents would free Abbott from its royalty obligations.

Patent law provided that a civil action for infringement may be brought only by "a patentee." If the patent owner grants only a license, the title remains in the owner of the patent; and suit must be brought in its name and not in the name of the licensee alone. The Supreme Court recognized an exception to that rule for cases in which the owner of a patent refuses to be joined as a co-plaintiff with the exclusive licensee. However, the law still requires that before the exclusive licensee can sue in the patent owner's name, the patent owner must be given an opportunity to join the infringement action. Abbott, therefore, does not have an independent right to sue for infringement as a "patentee." Diamedix retained the right to make and use, for its own benefit, products embodying the inventions claimed in the patents. In light of the various rights that Diamedix retains under the agreement, Abbott must be considered a licensee, not an assignee. Diamedix's motion to intervene is GRANTED.

Case Highlights

- The invalidity of a patent is an affirmative defense against a claim of patent infringement
- An assignment of the entire patent, unlike a license of the patent, makes the assignee the owner and gives it standing to sue against third-party infringement
- An exception to the rule that a licensee does not have independent standing to sue a third-party infringer is made for an exclusive licensee, as long as the patent owner is given an opportunity to join the infringement action.

Validity or no-challenge clauses prohibit the licensee from challenging the exclusiveness or validity of the licensor's IPR. Such clauses may be invalid in some foreign countries, where they are viewed as illegal restrictions on trade. They are also often prohibited in the transfer-of-technology codes found in developing countries.

The license agreement should define the licensee's rights to assign or sublicense its license rights through the insertion of **assignment** and **sublicensing clauses.** The license will generally state that it cannot be sublicensed or assigned without the consent of the licensor. The **non-partnership and independent contractor clause** states that the licensee is not acting as an agent or partner of the licensor, to insulate the licensor from liability to third parties under agency law principles. Specific termination rights are detailed in the **termination clause**. The termination clause provides specific grounds upon which the licensor may unilaterally terminate the license. Under some foreign laws, the unilateral termination of a licensing agreement may require the payment of an indemnity. For this reason, the licensor should specify the types of causes that can automatically trigger a termination without indemnity. For example, the failure of the licensee to meet prescribed sales quotas results in an automatic termination of the license.

The *Paramount Pictures Corp. v. Metro Program Network, Inc.* case examines a typical termination clause and the remedies available to the licensor against a licensee that violates the default provisions of the clause. The case also examines post-termination use by the licensee.

Paramount Pictures Corp. v. Metro Program Network, Inc.

962 F.2d 775 (8th Cir. 1992)

Circuit Judge. Metro, owner of television station KOCR-TV, signed eight interim license agreements with Paramount to broadcast episodes of *Happy Days*, *Mork and Mindy*, and *Taxi*, and a package of movies. Under the interim agreements, Metro was to pay Paramount 10 percent of the license fees on January 14, and the remainder in 36 equal monthly installments. The agreements contained the following language: "The license arrangement is subject to the provisions in Paramount's Standard Series Contract and Paramount's Standard Terms and Conditions, copies of which are available on request, and will be fully set forth in a formal written contract." Metro tendered a check to Paramount dated January 14 in the amount of $26,000. This check was dishonored on March 19 because Metro's account was closed. Prior to March 19, Paramount delivered the episodes of *Happy Days*, *Mork and Mindy*, and *Taxi* to Metro and Metro began to broadcast them.

Paramount sent Metro a letter terminating the contracts pursuant to the bankruptcy and default provision of the Standard Terms and Conditions and reserving their rights to collect the sums due under the licenses. It brought a claim for breach of contract and willful copyright infringement damages. Metro argued that the lower court award for breach of contract and infringement damages constituted an impermissible award of double damages. Under copyright law, the copyright owner is entitled to either actual damages or statutory damages. Actual damages are defined damages suffered as a result of the infringement, and any profits of the infringer that are attributable to the infringement. Statutory damages are defined as a sum of not less than $250 or more than $10,000 as the court considers just.

The lower court found that Metro broadcast 47 episodes of the three sitcoms and awarded statutory damages of $500 per infringement, totaling $23,500, as well as breach of contract damages for failure to make the upfront payment of $26,000. Metro claims that the breach of contract damages was an award of actual damages and, therefore, Paramount was not entitled to statutory damages.

We find that the breach of contract damages award is not an award of actual damages for copyright infringement. The breach of contract claim relates solely to events prior to the broadcasts of the shows. Metro was liable for these damages even if they had not broadcast any of Paramount's products after the contracts were terminated. In contrast, the copyright infringement claim relates to events that occurred afterwards, when Metro broadcast the shows following the termination of the licenses.

Because the damage awards for breach of contract and copyright infringement were for completely separate injuries, the lower court correctly awarded both breach of contract and copyright infringement damages. AFFIRMED.

Case Highlights

- A well-worded termination clause allows the licensor to quickly cancel the licensee's rights
- A licensee who continues to use licensed property following the termination of its license is susceptible to actual damages for breach of contract and statutory damages for infringement.

International licenses should provide for dispute resolution. This is done through choice of law and forum selection clauses. Given the unevenness of foreign IP law protections, a licensor should select the law of a country that rigorously protects IPRs. However, a host country court is unlikely to honor a choice of law that avoids its competition, IP transfer, consumer protection, and termination laws. Therefore, the most common forum selection clause in international licensing agreements is the arbitration clause. To enhance one's ability to obtain and enforce a foreign arbitral award, the place of arbitration should be in a country that has ratified the Convention on the Recognition and Enforcement of Foreign Arbitral Awards ("New York Convention") and where the courts have a reputation for not interfering with arbitration proceedings.

Law of Licensing

In the event that a licensing agreement fails to resolve a disputed issue, what body of law will be used to interpret and enforce the contract? If a court determines that a license is essentially a sale of goods, then the Convention on Contracts for the International Sale of Goods (CISG) could apply. This has generally been the case involving the sale of software or licensing of some information products. But, for more complicated licensing contracts, it is likely that a national civil law or the common law would apply unless a country has specialized rules dealing with licensing.

Some transactions have a mix of subject matter, such as the sale of goods, sale of services, and licensing of IPR. The **mixed sale** article of the CISG indicates that software sale contracts are to be considered sales of goods unless a "preponderant part of the obligations consists of labor or services" or the purchaser supplies "a substantial part of the materials." Off-the-shelf software is considered as a good. One view of the licensing of information sees the license as a "sale" of the exclusive rights to use that particular copy of the information. But, in most cases, IPR and information licensing would fall outside the concept of a "sale of goods" because the licensor retains title to the IPR and proprietary information. The next section will briefly review a model law dealing with some types of licensing contracts.

Uniform Computer Information Transactions Act

A series of rules that may be applied to licensing transactions are found in the American **Uniform Computer Information Transactions Act (UCITA)**. A brief review of its provisions is useful for two reasons. First, UCITA highlights some of the issues that confront licensors of IPR, technology, and information. Second, its provisions can be used in the negotiation and writing of a license agreement. UCITA is a model law for regulating the formation, performance, and enforcement of computer information transactions. *Computer information transactions* are defined as agreements "to create, modify, transfer, or license informational rights." "Information" is defined as "data, text, images, sounds, or computer programs, including collections and compilations." License means "a contract that authorizes access to, or use, distribution, performance, modification, or reproduction of information including, access contracts, lease of a computer program, and a consignment of a copy." UCITA provides rules pertaining to contract formation, authentication, duties and rights of performance, breach, remedies, and warranties.

EU Digital Services Act

The Digital Services Act (DSA) regulates online intermediaries and platforms such as marketplaces, social networks, content-sharing platforms, app stores, and online travel and accommodation platforms. Its main goal is to prevent illegal and harmful activities online and the spread of disinformation. It ensures user safety, protects fundamental rights, and creates a fair and open online platform environment.

As of 17 February 2024, the DSA rules apply to all platforms. Since the end of August 2023, these rules had already applied to designated platforms with more than 45 million users in the EU (10% of the EU's population), the so-called Very large online platforms (VLOPs) or Very large online search engines (VLOSEs). All online intermediaries offering their services in the single market, whether they are established in the EU or outside, will have to comply with the new rules. The DSA includes rules for online intermediary services, which millions of Europeans use every day. The obligations of different online players match their role, size, and impact on the online ecosystem. Figure 16.4 shows the type of online actors that are subject to the DSA including, (1) **VLOPs and search**

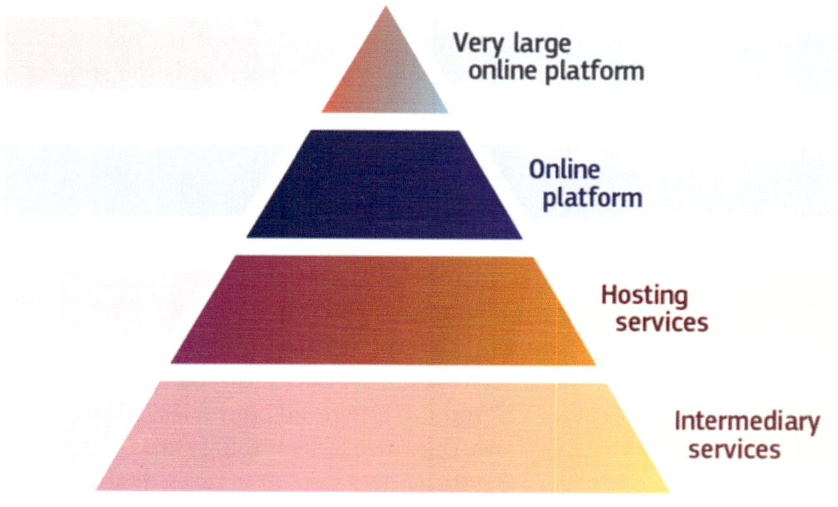

Figure 16.4 Scope of Digital Services Act.

Source: European Commission, https://commission.europa.eu/strategy-and-policy/priorities-2019-2024/europe-fit-digital-age/digital-services-act_en.

engines (risks in the dissemination of illegal content and cause societal harms), (2) **Online platforms** that provide a conduit for sellers and consumers (online marketplaces, app stores, and social media platforms), (3) **Hosting services** such as cloud and web hosting services, and other online platforms, (4) **Intermediary services** offering network infrastructure such as Internet service providers (ISPs) and domain name registrars.

Formation of a License Contract

The formation or offer-acceptance rules mimic those found in the common law; however, the dispatch or *mailbox rule*[14] is modified for electronic acceptance. Under UCITA, an electronic acceptance is effective upon receipt. Another model law, the **Uniform Electronic Transactions Act (UETA)** states that the acceptance is received when it enters the e-mailbox of the other party (offeror). Section 15 (b) of UETA states that "an electronic record is received when it enters an information processing system that the recipient has designated for the purpose of receiving electronic records or information." The obtaining and giving of an e-mail address satisfies the designation requirement.

Another issue is whether a license can be formed between computers or between a human and a computer. UCITA answers in the affirmative on both questions. It defines an **electronic agent** as "a computer program, or electronic or other automated means, used by a person to initiate an action, or to respond to electronic messages or performances, on the person's behalf without review or action by an individual." Therefore, placing an order through a website or voicemail creates a contract. Is an offeree able to make a counteroffer when dealing with an electronic agent? No, because electronic agents are unable to evaluate and respond to counteroffers or acceptances with additional terms. The counteroffer will be construed as an acceptance if it causes the electronic agent to perform, provide benefits, or allow the use or access that is the subject of the counteroffer.

Foreign Transfer Restrictions: EU

EU Regulations, although restrictive, offer the importer of technology or the licensor of IP a degree of harmonization throughout the EU. The regulations of the People's Republic of China on the importation of technology will also be examined. In Europe, a foreign licensor must understand the restrictions posed by the competition laws of the EU and its individual countries. Many European countries have strict antitrust laws that affect technology and IPR licensing. The EU Regulations control the legality and scope of clauses dealing with parallel or gray market imports, infringement, tying clauses, royalties, and term or duration of the license. The EU's block exemption regulation—Commission Regulation (EC) No. 772/2004 of April 27, 2004, dealing with the application of Article 81(3) of the Treaty of Rome to categories of technology transfer agreements—governs patent, information transfer, design, and software copyright licenses.

EU competition law incorporates the following restrictions. First, a licensing clause cannot prohibit gray market or parallel importing of goods legally produced. It can, however, prohibit a licensee from using the license outside the licensed territory, or more specifically, in the territory of the licensor. Second, no-challenge or **validity clauses** are void by law. A licensee cannot be prohibited from challenging the validity of the licensor's IPRs that are the subject of the license.

Third, a **tying clause** often requires that a licensee purchases its supplies of unlicensed materials from the licensor or a designated supplier. This requirement is allowed only if the licensor justifies the tying to issues of quality control. Patent owner–licensors often attempt to "tie" the license grant for a patented invention to use of tangential or related items—not covered by the patent—that inure to the benefit of the licensor. Licensors also may try to "tie" negative obligations, namely requirements to refrain from making or selling items related to the invention. As with patent pools, tying is not necessarily anticompetitive or impermissible; the legality of such arrangements often depends upon the parties' relative market power. In some jurisdictions, negative tying is prohibited outright, regardless of market power. Fourth, the license can require the payment of a minimum royalty amount regardless of actual sales, but it cannot require payment of royalties for rights or know-how that subsequently become unprotected or become public information. Fifth, the term of the license may not extend beyond the expiration of the latest patent or IP right that is subject to the license.

In general, a licensor may grant exclusive territories but is prohibited from limiting competition. It may prohibit its licensees from soliciting sales from outside their exclusive territories but cannot prohibit unsolicited or passive sales. Gray market sales or parallel imports are therefore permitted under EU law. This prohibition against limiting competition prevents a licensor from compartmentalizing territories and artificially setting different prices based on the market conditions in particular countries. EU competition law allows one licensee to purchase licensed products from another licensee.

EU law on gray market sales prevents the licensor from completely prohibiting sales or movement of licensed products outside the licensee's exclusive territory. A clause may, however, prohibit the licensee from selling the products of a competitor of the licensor. Despite the fact that exclusivity is a natural characteristic of most licensing, franchising, and distribution agreements, some foreign courts presume an agreement is nonexclusive if it does not expressly state that it is an exclusive grant of rights. Figure 16.5 "White-Listed Clauses" shows clauses that are expressly allowed under EU law.

EU Regulation 240/96 impacts joint ventures between competitors involving technology transfers. However, to benefit from the block exemption provided by the Regulation, the parent companies of the joint venture may not have a

(1) Confidentiality provisions prohibiting the licensee from disclosing licensor's know-how;
(2) prohibition of the continued use of the licensor's technology after the expiration or termination of the license;
(3) nonexclusive grant-back clauses; however, the licensor may be required to grant an exclusive license to the licensee for subsequent improvements made by the licensor;
(4) best efforts clauses requiring the licensee to fully work the technology in the licensed territory;
(5) clauses giving licensor the right to terminate the license in the event that the licensee challenges the validity of the licensor's patents;
(6) field-of-use restrictions;
(7) production limitations when the licensed product is a component part of another product; and
(8) obligations to pay royalties on sales of non-licensed products (momentum royalties), a practice which was formerly unenforceable and is now permitted.

Figure 16.5 White-Listed Clauses.

Source: See Commission Regulations 556/89, Article 3(3) and 2349/84, Article 3(4).

combined market share of more than 20 percent in a production joint venture or 10 percent in a distribution joint venture. Another extension of the Regulation is in the area of software licensing. Software licensing agreements based on copyright are protected under the Regulation if patents or know-how accompanies the software. Thus, the lists of exempted and prohibited contract clauses are applicable to most types of technology transfer agreements.

Chapter Summary

1. The licensing of intellectual property rights (IPR) and technology has become a substantial part of the world economy. Licensing contracts provide the licensor with the opportunity to include clauses to protect the IPR it is licensing. IPR licensing is subject to numerous laws, such as home country laws (law of licensor) that are applied extraterritorially; international IPR conventions; foreign host country's laws that provide protection; and host country laws that regulate the content of the licensing agreement.
2. The gray market is one of the major risks of licensing IPR for the production of goods in other countries. Some of these countries have lower costs of production, which leads to the temptation to export licensed goods to higher priced markets, including the markets of the licensor and other licensees. It is crucial that the license contract combat the exportation of goods through territorial restrictions, maximum quantities of production, and maximum

sales to individual purchasers. However, under some laws, such as EU competition laws, these provisions may be invalid.

3. The most important clause in a license is the grant clause, which states the IPR rights, trade secrets, and know-how that are being licensed. The license may be exclusive or nonexclusive and include other restrictions, such as field of use. The grant-back clause deals with the ownership and right to use any improvements made by the licensee.
4. Any exporter (licensor) of IPR should make sure it follows all necessary formalities, such as the registration of licenses in pertinent countries, as well as inserting clear duration and territorial provisions in its license so that ones will not be implied later by a court.
5. Common licensing clauses include the reservation of rights, royalties, best efforts, quality control, confidentiality, most-favored-licensee, infringement, and termination clauses.
6. In the U.S., the applicable law for licensing contracts is the common law of contracts. Other countries like China have specific rules that relate to licensing and technology contracts. The EU has strict regulations invalidating some pro-licensor clauses that violate EU competition law.
7. The Uniform Computer Information Transactions Act (UCITA) is a non-binding model law that provides useful rules that can be applied to some licensing contracts.

Key Terms

Assignment Clause
Best Efforts Clause
Brand Protection Units
Business Software Alliance (BSA)
Choice of Law Clause
Confidentiality Clause
Covenant Not-to-Compete
Cross-Licensing
Disclaimer
Due Diligence
Duration Clause
Exclusive License
Field of Use
Grant Clause
Grant-Back Clause
Guaranteed Consideration
Hybrid License
Indemnification Clause
Independent Contractor Clause
Infringement Clause
Licensed Territory Clause
Licensee
Licensor
Mixed Sale
Momentum Royalties
Most-Favored License Clause
Non-partnership Clause
Parallel License
Patentee
Patent Pools
Reciprocal License
Recitals
Reservation of Rights Clause
Royalties
Royalty Clause
Sublicensing Clause
Termination Clause
Tying Clause
Uniform Computer Information Transactions Act (UCITA)
Uniform Electronic Transactions Act (UETA)
Validity Clause

Chapter Problems

1. What can a licensor of intellectual property rights do to prevent a gray market problem?
2. Your company produces a quality component product that is used in the manufacture of high-end stereo equipment. The component is manufactured through the use of special software developed by your company. The component and associated software are covered under a number of U.S. patents and copyrights. In addition, your company holds a federally registered trademark that stereo manufacturers are allowed to use in the marketing of their products. Your company has made it a strategic goal to expand the production and sale of the components overseas. It is considering licensing the technology in exchange for royalties; however, it wants to protect the market of its domestic manufacturers. What steps should be taken to maximize the protection of the company's intellectual property rights? What license terms should your company insist upon?
3. Your company, a technology company based in the U.S., holds a number of patents on Internet-related business applications. It is negotiating a licensing agreement with a major French innovator of Internet technologies. Your company's standard grant-back clause provides a nonreciprocal reversion of all licensee improvements. The French company is refusing to execute the agreement because of the one-sided nature of the clause. Your job is to draft a fair grant-back clause that provides reciprocal rights to the licensor and licensee. How should such a clause deal with the questions of ownership and use? What will be the status of these rights after the termination of the license?
4. *License Writing and Review Problem*: You represent an American manufacturing company whose products are based upon an assortment of patents, copyrights, trademarks, trade secrets, and know-how. The company has a very popular line of electronic products that has only been marketed and sold in the U.S. and Canada. The company is considering licensing the rights to produce the products to companies in other markets. Your company has been approached by a manufacturer–distributor from Nigeria who wants to negotiate a contract for the central African market. The Nigerian company had entered into such licensing agreements before and provided a "prototype" license agreement. Your company's major concerns include: How will it be able to control the quality of the products being manufactured by the licensees and the impact of the relevant host country laws, including laws relating to intellectual property rights, competition (antitrust), currency control, and taxation? Your job is to review the license below and determine if the clauses adequately protect your company's interests. How would you make the relevant clauses more pro-licensor? Additional questions are given at the end of the Licensing Agreement.

Licensing Agreement

Licensing agreement between "American Tech Products Company" (licensor–patentee) and Nigerian Manufacturing Limited (licensee). The Parties hereby agree to enter the following Agreement:

Operative Clauses

8. *License Grant*
   Licensor hereby grants to the licensee an exclusive, nontransferable license and right to manufacture and sell the product within the countries of Nigeria under the licensor's trademark, along with the rights to use related patents, information, and know-how that will be provided by the licensor. The licensor will provide all necessary data, specifications, technology, and marketing information relating to the product and its manufacture.
9. *Future Improvements (Product and Process)*
   During the duration of this license, the licensee shall supply to the licensor any improvements and know-how to the process of manufacture (process) or product developed subsequently to the signing of this agreement at no additional costs (royalty).
10. *Grant Back*
    The licensee shall promptly notify the licensor of any improvements it has made or developed relating to the product or process. The licensee will provide a cross-license to the licensor to use the improvement without paying royalties. The licensee shall have the right to patent the improvement.
11. *Confidentiality*
    Licensee shall treat all information and rights provided by licensor as "secret and confidential," except to the extent that the information becomes part of the public domain. Licensee shall divulge the information to only key personnel and to third parties on a need to know basis.
12. *Support*
    If the licensee requires additional assistance the licensor shall use its best efforts to comply with the requests for assistance. The licensee shall pay additional remuneration for the additional services.
13. *Royalty*
    The licensee shall pay a six percent (6%) royalty fee to the licensor on licensee's net sales. Any income tax on the licensor's royalties claimed by the host countries listed in Clause 1 shall be paid by the licensee and deducted from the royalty due to the licensor.
14. *Reports*
    Accrued royalties shall be due no later than 45 days after the end of each quarter. Each payment shall be accompanied by a report that includes an itemized list of products sold and at what prices. The licensee's senior accountant and Chief Financial Officer shall certify each report.
15. *Payment*
    The royalty payment shall be in U.S. dollars at the conversion rate posted on the date of remittance. The costs of conversion shall be to the account of the licensor.

16. *Audit*
    Licensee shall maintain accurate records of all sales, which shall annually be audited and certified by licensee's auditor. The cost of the audit and certification shall be paid by licensor.

17. *Patent and Trademark Protection*
    Licensor shall take all action needed to maintain its patents and trademarks in the host countries including renewing all necessary registrations. Licensee shall display licensor's trademarks at all times to make clear to all third parties of licensor's ownership and in order to prevent the trademark from becoming generic.

18. *Third-Party Patent Claims*
    Licensor warrants that it has clear title and ownership to all intellectual property rights being licensed and that their use will not infringe on any third-party rights. Licensor shall defend and "hold harmless" against any third-party claims against license for infringement.

19. *Infringement of Licensor's Patents*
    Licensee shall promptly notify licensor of any infringements by third-parties on licensor's patent and trademarks. Licensor may, at his discretion, take legal steps to enforce its rights.

20. *Duration and Expiration*
    The license shall continue in force until the expiration of the last patent related to the product or needed to produce the product unless the license is terminated "for cause" as provided in Clause 14 and Clause 15. Upon termination of the license, the licensee shall cease to manufacture and sell the licensed products, as well as the licensor's trademark. Licensee shall maintain the confidentiality of licensor's information and know-how unless they become a part of the public domain.

21. *Cause and Notice*
    The licensor may terminate this license by giving three months' written notice for the following reasons:
    a. If licensee fails to begin production within four months of receiving all necessary information from the licensor;
    b. If licensee fails to start marketing and sales of the product within three months of the production of the products;
    c. If licensee fails to pay royalties within 12 months of the time provided under Clause 8 unless the delay is due to a *force majeure* event;
    d. If licensee sells or transfers a controlling interest in its company, becomes insolvent, or files for bankruptcy.

22. *Momentum Clause*
    In consideration for the marketing value of licensor's product and its likely positive impact on other products sold by the licensee, licensee shall pay a 2% royalty on net sales of any increases in the sale of the other products for the period of this license.

23. *Applicable Law*
    The Law of the Country of the United Kingdom shall govern this contract, and any claims or disputes related to it.

24. *Arbitration*
    In the event of a dispute over a breach of this contract or any related claims, the dispute shall be submitted for arbitration. The arbitration panel shall consist of

three arbitrators, each party shall nominate one arbitrator. The two arbitrators shall select the third arbitrator. The arbitration proceeding shall be conducted under the Arbitration Rules of the International Chamber of Commerce.

Questions:

1. Which of the above clauses are one-sidedly pro-licensee?
2. How would you change the clauses to be more pro-licensor?
3. What terms are ambiguous? What words should be defined in the agreement?
4. What terms are missing? Are there terms missing that would better protect the interests of the licensor?
5. What "generic terms" are missing? How would you make the contract more comprehensive?

Internet Sources

World Intellectual Property Organization (WIPO): www.wipo.org.
Eurasian Patent Office: www.eapo.org.
International Patent Searching Authorities: www.wipo.int/pct/en/access/isa_ipea_agreements.html; www.uspto.gov/web/offices/pac/mpep/s1840.html.
Licensing Digital Information (Yale Library) provides examples of and commentary on a number of important licensing clauses: http://www.library.yale.edu/~llicense/remcls.shtml.
Text of UCITA: http://www.ucitaonline.com.

Notes

1 U.S. Commercial Service, *Basic Guide to Exporting* (D. Barry ed., 11th ed. 2015).
2 For a brief review on issues in licensing and standard see Raymond T. Nimmer, "Issues in Licensing: An Introduction," 42 *Houston Law Review* 941 (2005–06).
3 Most-favored-license clauses were held to be enforceable in *Carpenter Tech. Corp. v. Armco, Inc.*, 800 F. Supp. 215 (E.D. Pa. 1992).
4 35 U.S.C. §§100, 271(a) (1994).
5 See *U.S. v. Radio Corp. of America*, 117 F. Supp. 449 (D. Del. 1954).
6 ICC, *ICC Intellectual Property Roadmap* (12th ed. 2014).
7 In contrast, nonreciprocal grant-back clauses are generally enforced in American courts unless they are held to violate the antitrust laws. *See Santa Fe Pomeroy, Inc. v. P. & Z. Co.*, 569 F.2d 1084 (9th Cir. 1978).
8 379 U.S. 29 (1964).
9 35 U.S.C. §287.
10 775 F.2d 268 (Fed. Cir. 1985).
11 See *Ortho Pharm. Corp. v. Genetics Institute, Inc.*, 52 F.3d 1026 (1995).
12 See *Yarway Corp. v. Eur-Control USA, Inc.*, 775 F.2d 268 (Fed. Cir. 1985).
13 See *Rite-Hite Corp. v. Kelly*, 56 F. 3d 1538 (Fed. Cir. 1995).
14 The irrational common law rule that a contract is formed at the moment the acceptance is sent or dispatched and not when it is received by the other party.

Part V

Foreign Direct Investment, E-Commerce, and Digital Economy

Chapter 17

Foreign Direct Investment

The era of free trade in goods and services, beginning in the post-World War II era with the creation of the General Agreement on Tariffs and Trade (GATT), is also an era of the opening of capital markets and the free flow of investment funds throughout the world. The interconnectedness of the financial markets and the proliferation of **foreign direct investment** (**FDI**) shows that the world economies grow and falter due to economic shocks that can happen any place in the world. We also live in an era of climate change where unchecked development and pollution of air, land, and water have harmed the environment to the extent that it challenges the quality of life throughout the world.

FDI is the category of international investment made by a company or person (direct investor) in order to acquire a lasting interest in an entity operating in another country (**direct investment**). The World Bank defines FDI as the net inflows of investment to acquire a lasting interest (10 percent or more) in a foreign enterprise operating. Net FDI is the sum of equity capital, reinvestment of earnings, other long-term capital, and short-term capital flows as reflected in a country's balance of payments. The opposite of FDI is **disinvestment** or the *outflow* of money by foreign investors.

Host Country Laws

Countries vary in openness to foreign investment and in the ease in doing business. The two are interconnected in that the easier it is for a foreign company to do business in a foreign country the more likely they will invest, and the greater will be the amount of the investment. See the World Bank's 2020 "Ease of Doing Business Rankings" in Table 17.1. Countries need inflows of capital to increase

DOI: 10.4324/9781003469230-22

Table 17.1 *Doing Business Internationally*: Ease of Doing Business Rankings.

Country	*2019*	*2010*	*2006*	*Starting a Business*	*Enforcing Contracts*
New Zealand	1	2	1	1	23
Singapore	2	1	2	4	1
Hong Kong	3	3	7	5	31
Denmark	4	6	8	45	14
South Korea	5	19	27	33	2
U.S.	6	4	3	55	17
Georgia	7	11	100	2	12
UK	8	5	9	18	34
Norway	9	10	5	25	3
Sweden	10	18	14	39	39
Lithuania	11	26	15	34	7
Malaysia	12	23	21	126	35
Mauritius	13	17	23	20	20
Australia	14	9	6	7	6
Taiwan	15	46	35	21	11
Germany	22	25	21	125	13
China	31	89	91	27	5
Poland	40	72	54	128	55
Montenegro	50	71	92	101	44
Mexico	60	51	73	107	43
India	63	133	116	136	163
Vietnam	70	93	99	115	68
South Africa	84	34	28	139	102
Philippines	95	144	113	171	152
Brazil	124	129	119	138	58
Nigeria	131	125	94	105	73
Bangladesh	168	119	65	131	189

Source: World Bank Group.[1,2,3]

economic growth. Attracting FDI is affected by numerous macroeconomic, geopolitical, and regulatory issues. This chapter will sample some of these factors, ranging from regulatory factors controlled by foreign governments, self-inflicted government decisions that retard FDI, and factors outside of the control of a national government. Thus, the ease in doing business in a country is one factor among others that affect the flow of FDI and capital into and out of a country. The example of foreign laws that make FDI difficult is seen in equity participation requirements in India. Russia's decision to invade Ukraine and subsequent Western sanctions produced large capital outflows from the country and a dramatic decrease in the gross domestic product (GDP). Finally, the global financial crisis in 2008 and the coronavirus pandemic, beginning in 2020, are examples of factors outside the control of individual countries.

India has a history of imposing **equity participation requirements** (**EPR**), as well as varying the percentages of ownership allowed, for FDI. This produces a great deal of uncertainty for foreign investors, discouraging them from investing. EPR limit the percentage ownership in a company that can be held by foreign interests. The percentage of ownership allowed to foreign investors has ranged between 51% and 49%, the difference between the rates means the ability to control or not control the enterprise. For example, at the time of the **Bhopal Disaster** in 1984, the maximum equity ownership for foreign investors was 51 percent and at other times the maximum was set at 49 percent. Union Carbide, an American company, was seen as the responsible party for a chemical plant explosion that killed thousands. But in fact, by agreement with the Indian government, it was not in direct control and did not manage the Union Carbide plant in Bhopal, India. The other majority owners of Union Carbide of India were Indian nationals and the Indian government. Indian engineers designed the plant (Union Carbide's design was rejected), all the workers and managers at the plant were Indian, and all safety inspections were the responsibility of the Indian government. Furthermore, the lack of zoning restrictions allowed the building of residential housing (shanty towns) adjacent to the plant—a major factor in the harm caused to the population. The disaster was a public relations problem for Union Carbide, and despite India's inability to bring a lawsuit in the U.S. due to jurisdictional grounds—Union Carbide India Limited was an independent company incorporated under the laws of India for which Union Carbide was a mere shareholder—Union Carbide still paid $470 million in damages. Subsequently, it sold its interests to Eveready Industries India.

> **Bhopal Disaster:** On the night of December 3, 1984, an explosion at a Union Carbide plant in Bhopal, India resulted in the release of methyl isocyanate (MIC), a toxic chemical that injured about a half-million people and killed an estimated 3,000 people.

FDI flows generally in the direction of large, untapped markets (emerging markets) and stable economies. This can be seen in the fall of FDI in Russia due to the perception of political and economic instability caused by Russia's invasion of Crimea in 2014 and 2022 invasion of Ukraine. In addition, the Russian regulatory laws became more unpredictable due to the Russian response to Western financial and economic sanctions. FDI in Russia decreased dramatically and the Russian economy contracted 4.6 percent the following year. This demonstrates the importance of legal and **macroeconomic stability** in attracting FDI. Russia is an example of a country in which FDI inflows were on the rise, but is now seen as an unstable economy, where the risks of FDI are greater than the expected rewards. This instability not only caused a decrease in the inflow of FDI, it also resulted in *capital flight* (outward FDI) to more stable countries.

A stark comparison is seen in the FDI inflows and Singapore. Singapore, as a city state with a much smaller population, benefited from large amounts of FDI, about ten times more than Japan. Why is this so? Both countries rate high on stability. However, Japan has a history of being insular and not open to FDI. Japan also has seen little growth over the last few decades. In contrast, Singapore has had high rates of growth and has been friendly toward FDI.

FDI is highly dependent on the ease of doing business in a given country. Table 17.1 shows the top-rated countries for ease of doing business, as well as a selection of other countries. The ease of doing business score helps assess the absolute level of regulatory performance over time. The overall ranking is a summation of numerous ranking categories, which include ease of establishing a business (number of procedures required), ease in obtaining construction permits, legal protections afforded to minority investors, and severity of taxation.

Table 17.1 shows that Western and Central Europe (especially the Nordic countries) are considered to be secure places for FDI. It also shows that from 2006 to 2019 some countries instituted major regulatory reforms to improve the ease of doing business in their countries. Georgia moved from 100 to 7 in that course of time. China continued to improve its ranking from 91 to 31. Other countries moved in the wrong direction, such as Nigeria, from 94 to 131 and Bangladesh, from 65 to 168. In sum, most obstacles to FDI are created by countries that are most in need of FDI due to regulatory complexity and corruption.

Types of Foreign Investment

FDI comes in numerous forms of doing business, such as the purchase (merger or acquisition) of a foreign company, establishing a company or foreign presence, or entering into a joint venture with another party in a foreign country. All three forms of FDI are commonly used, but the establishment of foreign presence is the most common vehicle for a company wanting to enter a foreign market.

Greenfield Investment

Instead of purchasing or merging with a foreign company, foreign investors may elect to begin a new business. **Greenfield** or ***de novo*** **investment** is when the investor creates and capitalizes a new company in a foreign country. The new company is incorporated under the foreign country's incorporation or company law. Greenfield investment entails establishing a company, purchasing land, and building a manufacturing plant. This type of investment is highly preferred by the host country because it creates value, employs workers, and adds to the national tax base. However, as discussed in the India case above, some countries place restrictions on the degree of ownership allowed to non-nationals. These restrictions on the amount of ownership interest allowed to foreign parties are referred to as **equity participation requirements**. These restrictions vary widely across countries. Most countries have more specific restrictions that only apply to ownership in vital industries, such as industries related to national security.

Portfolio Foreign Investment

FDI needs to be distinguished from other forms of foreign investment, such as **portfolio foreign investment** or **indirect foreign investment**. FDI involves conducting a business or business operations in a foreign country, while portfolio investment refers to passive investments, such as the purchase of stocks and bonds of foreign companies. Passive investments mean that the investor does not partake in the active management of the company. Investments that acquire 10 percent or more of a foreign entity are considered to be "controlling" interests by government regulators and as a type of FDI. A controlling interest subjects the investor to a wider range of the foreign country's laws. This chapter focuses on FDI in which a domestic business seeks to expand its business into foreign markets and not merely to invest in foreign companies.

FDI Strategy and Methods

Depending on the industry sector and type of business, FDI may be an attractive and viable option. However, companies often pursue a long-term strategy when entering foreign markets. They pursue a graduated risk approach by first pursuing a lower risk market entry strategy such as exporting or licensing and move then to FDI.[4] A company may primarily use the export method, but also hire employees in the foreign country to market and sell their goods to wholesalers or large companies.

FDI is vital to many economies, especially lesser-developed and emerging economies, because it can provide the financial, technological, and managerial skills, information, goods, and services that promote growth and make a country more competitive internationally. For a company seeking to enter foreign markets, FDI provides a means to gain access and avoid trade barriers, especially disguised ones (such as unfounded safety and health standards). FDI is also a means of increasing production capacity as a company expands. Often because of the risks of FDI (government regulations, corruption) companies elect to hedge those risks by pursuing coproduction, joint venture, licensing, and joint marketing arrangements with a company in the foreign country.

Often it becomes necessary to follow the expansion of competitors, especially if a company's major customers are also expanding overseas. The overwhelming majority of FDI is made in setting up or acquiring foreign companies in order to build, manufacture, or sell directly to the ultimate consumers. This type of investment is accomplished through mergers and acquisitions of existing companies.

Instead of large companies' FDI, high-tech start-ups are small companies that have grown out of research and development projects, including products such as software programs, digital online platforms, apps, and technology-based processes. High-tech types of companies, especially those that produce intellectual property-type products, take a long time to develop and may go through many changes and capital before the product is marketable. Thus, the capital investment in such enterprises is unknown as compared to traditional manufacturing, where the costs of equipment and machinery are known. Nonetheless, the expanded role of technology and intellectual property has changed the nature of FDI.

When the costs of production and marketability of products in a foreign country are uncertain, companies may elect to lower their risks through licensing or technology transfer arrangements that shift production and marketing costs to another company. Another alternative is the use of strategic or global alliances, such as **reciprocal distribution agreements**, in which two companies in the same industry agree to act as distributors of each other's products in their home countries. In this way, instead of having to build a foreign distribution network, each company gains access to the other company's distribution system. The distributors may also elect to agree to piggyback marketing of the other party's products alongside its own products.

> **Piggyback Marketing** is a cost-effective marketing strategy where two or more companies represent the other firm's non-competing product in various promotions and referrals. It is a strategy in which two or more businesses work together to market their complementary products. Sometimes lesser-known goods may piggyback successfully on better-known brands.

Another method of hedging risks in FDI is through **joint venture** arrangements with a foreign company. The common joint venture is between two companies, although more than two companies may form an alliance or syndicate. Alliances or **syndicates** are usually compiled for major construction or public works projects that require a wide variety of expertise and resources. The primary reason for a joint venture is to share the costs and risks of FDI. Other reasons include to gain access to **proprietary information** (intellectual property rights, know-how, trade secrets, and other types of confidential information); to gain access to foreign channels of distribution; and to exchange core competencies (innovation, marketing, production, and so forth).

Franchising as Alternative to FDI

For companies wanting to expand their core competencies (production of goods or sale of services), **franchising** has been a popular alternative to traditional FDI. There are different types of franchising arrangements: (1) direct franchising; (2) **area development agreements**; and (3) **master franchising.** Direct franchising involves a contractual relationship between the franchisor and each franchise location. In an area development agreement, the franchisor grants exclusive rights to a developer. The developer establishes multiple franchise locations within its assigned geographical area and remains directly bound by contract to the franchisor; there are no third parties (sub-franchisees). Area developers are larger companies that have the financial ability to develop an entire area rather than a single location. Such agreements are generally easier to terminate than a master franchise agreement.

A master franchise agreement creates a chain of contractual relationships: franchisor to franchisee/subfranchisor to subfranchisees. In the master franchise arrangement, the master franchisee-subfranchisor has the power to grant franchise rights to other parties (subfranchisees). Master franchise agreements are most commonly used internationally to rapidly penetrate and expand in foreign markets. Such arrangements require less involvement by the franchisor, but at the same time, the franchisor loses direct control of the franchise locations. Also, in cases where the subfranchisor does not perform to expectations, it is more difficult to terminate a master franchise agreement than it is to terminate a direct franchise or area development agreement.

Emerging Economies

FDI varies dramatically from one country to the next based upon the combination of risks and rewards related to a given country. On the benefits side, factors include the size of the foreign economy and its population. Risk factors include lack of government guarantees relating to FDI, instability of government, high levels of corruption, weakness of the country's currency, and weakness of the judicial system and the rule of law. Given the volatile nature of the international economy and the instability of some foreign countries, FDI can vary drastically over time.

Brazil's growth has seen a severe decline in the past decade and India has experienced slower than expected growth rates. However, India, being the most populated country in the world, has the potential to become an economic power. The Russia case study will show how economic and political developments, including war and hostilities, currency rate fluctuations, fluctuations in **world commodity prices**, and the failure to restructure inefficient economies, impact FDI and capital flows, and overall economic growth.

With its full-scale invasion of Ukraine in 2022, the Russian Federation plunged into a financial and economic crisis. The crisis was exacerbated by underlying structural problems of the Russian economy, mostly due to overreliance on revenues from oil and gas production and the failure to use those revenues to diversify the Russian economy. Russia became an example of a country with enormous scientific and technological abilities failing to use its oil and gas revenues to transform that potential into a more developed economy. Even more disastrous, numerous Western companies have closed their stores in Russia and foreign direct investment in Russia dissipated resulting in capital outflows.

The Russian crisis and the decline of Brazil's economy exposes the structural vulnerabilities of emerging economies. Russia's crisis is a lesson to other emerging economies that they must use their new revenues to restructure (diversify) their economies, to continue to privatize their industries, open their markets, and invest in education and research.

Managing the Risks of FDI

This section looks at ways FDI has been made safer through public and private means. It reviews the WTO's **Agreement on Trade-Related Investment Measures (TRIMs)**, country-to-country FDI protection agreements known as **bilateral investment treaties (BITs)**, to private–public (company to the government) **concession agreements**, and the management of investment risks through joint ventures, before concluding with a brief discussion of competition (antitrust).

WTO's Agreement on Trade-Related Investment Measures (TRIMs)

The **Agreement on Trade-Related Investment Measures (TRIMs)** provides a general framework of rules and standards for national laws and regulations relating to the treatment of foreign investors. Policies such as local content requirements, which have been used to protect the interests of domestic industries are prohibited. TRIMs prohibit national rules that give preferences to domestic firms to better compete against foreign companies. The result has been a substantial increase in world FDI beginning in the late 1980s. However, some countries continue to place restrictions on FDI, such as limiting the repatriation of investment profits in order to prevent the outflow of foreign exchange reserves.

Other types of restrictions include: (1) local content requirements and manufacturing requirements (require the use of domestically manufactured materials and components); (2) domestic sales requirements; (3) technology transfer requirements; (4) export performance requirements (require the export of a specified percentage of the goods produced); (5) local equity restrictions; and (6) employment restrictions (minimum percentage of local workers). Many of these restrictions are prohibited under WTO rules. Nonetheless, the foreign investor should research the existence of such restrictions before investing in a foreign country.

Bilateral Investment Treaties (BITs)

BITs are the successors to the 19th century Friendship, Commerce and Navigation Treaties (FCN) that were used to open Asian ports to Western commerce. A BIT is an agreement establishing the terms and conditions for private investment or FDI by nationals and companies of one country in another country. Most BITs grant foreign investors from the other BIT country a number of guarantees, which typically include fair and equitable treatment, protection from expropriation, and free transfer of capital. The distinctive feature of many BITs is that they allow for an alternative dispute resolution mechanism, whereby an investor whose rights under the BIT have been violated has recourse to international arbitration, commonly through the **International Centre for Settlement of Investment Disputes (ICSID)**, rather than being forced to litigate using the host country's courts.

The ICSID is an international arbitration institution that settles investment disputes between foreign investors and host countries. As well as arbitration, it offers conciliation services. The ICSID is a member of the World Bank. It was established in 1966 as an independent, specialized institution to encourage the international flow of investment and mitigate non-commercial risks. It has over 160 member countries. Member states agree to enforce and uphold arbitral awards in accordance with the ICSID Convention.

> **Alternative Dispute Resolution (ADR)** includes mediation, conciliation, and arbitration. *Conciliation* is a process in which parties to a dispute use a conciliator who meets with the parties both separately and together in an attempt to resolve their differences. Conciliation differs from arbitration in that the conciliation process, in and of itself, has no legal standing, and the conciliator usually has no authority to seek evidence or call witnesses, writes no decision, and makes no award. A significant difference between conciliation and mediation lies in the fact that conciliators possess expert knowledge of the area in which they conciliate. The conciliator can make suggestions for settlement terms and can give advice on the subject of the dispute, while a mediator simply acts as a conduit for negotiations.

BITs are a way for countries to ensure the safety of inward FDI in order to attract much needed foreign capital. The U.S. Department of State lists the six core principles of its *Model BIT*. First, BITs provide that investors and their **covered investments** (investments of a national or company in the other BIT country) are entitled to be treated as favorably as the host country treats its own investors. Second, BITs establish clear limits on the expropriation or taking of investments and provide for prompt payment of adequate and effective compensation when expropriation takes place. Third, BITs require the free transferability of funds into and out of the host country. Fourth, BITs limit the scope of **performance requirements**, such as local content requirements or export quotas. Fifth, BITs give investors the right to submit an investment dispute to international arbitration. Sixth, BITs give covered investments the right to engage the top managerial personnel of their choice, regardless of nationality.

Core Principles

BITs adopt the core principles of GATT—national treatment principle, most-favored-nation principle, and the principle of transparency.

- **National Treatment Principle:** Each country shall accord foreign investors treatment no less favorable than that it accords to its own investors with respect to the establishment, acquisition, expansion, management, conduct, operation, and sale or other disposition of investments in its territory.
- **Most-Favored-Nation Principle:** Each country shall accord to foreign investors' treatment no less favorable than that it accords to investors of any other country.
- **Minimum Standard of Treatment Principle:** Each country shall accord to covered investments treatment in accordance with customary international law, including **fair and equitable treatment** and full protection, security, and due process, as embodied in the principal legal systems of the world.
- **Transparency Principle:** Each country shall ensure that its laws, regulations, procedures, and administrative rulings, as well as its judicial decisions, are promptly published or otherwise made publicly available.

A key component of the Model BIT deals with the issues of **expropriation** and foreign country regulations. In the area of expropriation and compensation, the three core concepts include: (1) conditions in which expropriation or nationalization are deemed appropriate (expropriated for a public purpose or for the public welfare); (2) prompt payment of compensation; and (3) calculation of just compensation. First, expropriation or nationalization is only appropriate under the following conditions: it is taken for a public purpose; in a nondiscriminatory manner; and with payment of prompt, adequate, and effective compensation. The taking of property for a public purpose is similar to the taking of private property under the *eminent domain* power in the U.S. Constitution. By nondiscrimination, a country should not specifically take property from companies from certain countries and not others.

The condition of prompt compensation means that payment should be made without delay; be equal to the fair market value of the expropriated investment (property); and be realizable and freely transferable. Furthermore, the payment must be made in a hard or usable currency.

> **Expropriation and Nationalization:** The process of expropriation occurs when a public agency takes private property for a purpose deemed to be in the public interest. International law recognizes the right of countries to seize private property to further national welfare, but it requires the payment of prompt, adequate, and effective compensation. **Nationalization** is the process of taking by a national government of an entire private industry into public ownership. In the past, industries commonly subject to nationalization included transport, communications, energy, banking, and natural resources. The opposite of nationalization is *privatization*, which involves the sale of government property or assets. Privatization of public assets is a prime target for foreign investors.

The Model BIT also recognizes two types of expropriation—direct and indirect or **creeping expropriation**. Creeping expropriation involves a country taking a series of actions, such as passing laws that diminish the value of an investor's investment or control over its investment, such as severely increasing regulations, taxes, and equity participation requirements, that has an effect equivalent to direct expropriation.

Protection of Environment and Workers' Rights

The Model BIT states that FDI should not be conditional on reducing environmental and workers' protections. Each country is obligated not to waive its environmental laws and in the area of workers' or labor rights, BITs obligate countries to comply with the International Labour Organization's (ILO) **Declaration on Fundamental Principles and Rights at Work**, which recognize freedom of association; right to collective bargaining; elimination of forced labor; abolition of child labor; elimination of discrimination in employment; and acceptable conditions of work (minimum wages, hours of work, and occupational safety and health).

Dispute Resolution

In an investment dispute, between an investor and government, a disputing party may submit the dispute to arbitration, after six months have elapsed since the time of the event that gave rise to the claim. If both parties are members of the ICSID Convention, a claim may be filed under the ICSID Rules of Procedure for Arbitration Proceedings. If only one of the parties is a member of the ICSID Convention, then a claim can be brought under the ICSID's **Additional Facility Rules.** Also, a claim may be brought under the UNCITRAL Arbitration Rules or the parties may agree to institutional arbitration, such as through the International Chamber of Commerce.

The large role of BITs in increasing FDI is due in large part to the existence of the ICSID.[5] It is the "model of commercial style arbitration for investor–country disputes." In *Asian Agricultural Products Ltd (AAPL) v. Republic of Sri Lanka*,[6] an ICSID arbitration panel held that the right to arbitrate is not found in the parties' contract but is found in the BIT. The panel reasoned that the BIT serves as an ongoing offer by the country to arbitrate and the investor's filing of a notice of arbitration serves as an acceptance. Thus, instead of needing the country to voluntarily agree to an arbitration submission, a company may directly file a claim with the ICSID.

Additional Facility Rules authorize the Secretariat of ICSID to administer certain categories of proceedings between states and nationals of other states that fall outside the scope of the ICSID Convention, including fact-finding proceedings; conciliation or arbitration proceedings; and conciliation and arbitration proceedings between parties at least one of which is a Contracting State (ICSID member) or a national of a Contracting State for disputes not arising directly out of an investment.

Parallel Proceedings

Large foreign investors may lobby their home government (country of the investor) to file a claim against the host country for violating the WTO Agreements, while at the same time pursuing investment arbitration, under a BIT or a free trade agreement (FTA). The difference is the government pursues a WTO **trade claim**, while the individual company pursues an **investment claim**. This approach provides the investor two chances at winning relief from the action or inaction of a foreign government and is referred to as **parallel proceedings**. Examples include:

- An import ban on goods or services gives rise to a claim of an indirect expropriation under an investment treaty (BIT) and a quantitative restriction in violation of GATT.
- An improper denial of a license to establish business results in a market access violation under GATS, as well as an arbitration claim under an FTA.
- The imposition of performance requirements may give rise to a claim under the TRIMs and a BIT claim.
- Disguised trade barriers (inappropriate quality, safety, licensing standards) may lead to a WTO national treatment claim or a BIT claim for fair and equitable treatment.[7]

For a further analysis of the concept of parallel proceedings, see Figure 17.1.

Concession Agreement

A **concession agreement** is a negotiated contract between a company and a government that gives the company the right to operate a specific business within the government's jurisdiction, subject to certain conditions. For example, a government that is looking to attract mining companies to an impoverished area may offer significant inducements, such as tax breaks and a lower royalty rate. The term "concession agreement" is used in two slightly different ways in the business world. Both refer to a type of negotiated contract, which gives a company the right to do business, with some specific requirements and protections. In one sense, it refers to a contract between a foreign company and a government in which the government signs a concession agreement to provide guarantees to the investing party, such as no increases in income tax rates applicable to the foreign company. In a second sense, this type of agreement may include the foreign company (concessionaire) the exclusive right to do business in a particular area or venue in exchange for some carefully negotiated terms.

In sum, concession agreements occur when a foreign government wants to incentivize a foreign investment by lowering taxes, relaxing restrictions, and offering protections against expropriation. In cases where the government is not as enthusiastic, the company may need to make some concessions such as ceding some of the profits to the government or paying a special tax rate which may be higher than that of domestic businesses. Once the agreement is negotiated and

A claimant filed parallel claims under the WTO Agreement and a BIT relating to an Australian law (**Australian Tobacco Plain Packaging Act**) that prohibits the branding of tobacco products and regulates almost every aspect of the appearance, size, and shape of the packaging, with civil and criminal penalties for importing, packaging, or manufacturing noncompliant products. Such measures have prompted both trade and investment litigation. The countries of Ukraine, Honduras, and the Dominican Republic have filed claims under the WTO's TRIPS Agreement, arguing that the law: (1) unjustifiably diminishes the value of trademarks; (2) prevents owners from enjoying the rights conferred by trademark; and (3) fails to provide effective protection against unfair competition with respect to geographic indications (country of origin). At the same time, tobacco company Philip Morris brought a BIT claim in arbitration against Australia alleging that the law constitutes an unlawful expropriation of its intellectual property, violates fair and equitable treatment, guarantees of full protection and security, and umbrella clause guarantees.

Umbrella Clauses (in BITs) protect investments by bringing obligations or commitments, such as independent investment contracts between a foreign company and a host country, within the protective umbrella of the BIT. Investors often rely on an umbrella clause as a catch-all provision to pursue claims when a host state's actions *do not* otherwise breach the BIT. For example, is a simple breach of contract claim between a country and a foreign company within the scope of a BIT? This is a controversial issue on which courts have made contradictory decisions. A second issue is, even if the contract comes within the BIT, should a contract dispute be arbitrable under the BIT in conflict with a forum selection clause found in the contract?

The tobacco industry also filed suit in the Australian courts. The Australian Supreme Court ruled that "the mere restriction on a right of property or even its extinction does not necessarily mean that a proprietary right has been acquired by another." The WTO Agreements incorporate general exceptions to protection of property rights, relating to the protection of human health and safety, but many BITs do not include such exceptions.

The tobacco industry acted strategically to find countries willing to initiate WTO proceedings on its behalf. It funded the Ukraine WTO proceeding. Win or lose, the tobacco companies successfully delayed the enactment of plain packaging laws in the EU, Canada, and New Zealand. Further, since there is no precedent (*stare decisis*) in trade litigation or investment arbitration even if it loses the Australian proceedings, the tobacco industry can re-litigate the same question against other countries that enact plain packaging laws.

Figure 17.1 Comparative Law: Tobacco Packaging in Australia.

Note: For an in-depth study of the issues related to umbrella clauses in BITs and information posed by the question in the textbox defining the umbrella clause, see Jarrod Wong, "Umbrella Clauses in Bilateral Investment Treaties," 14 *George Mason Law Review* 137 (2006) and pages 48–50.

signed, the company has the right to do business locally under the terms of the agreement.

Joint Ventures

International joint ventures are used in a wide variety of manufacturing, mining, and service industries, and they frequently involve technology licensing by one company to the joint venture. Host country laws may require that a certain percentage of the company be owned by nationals of that country (**equity participation requirements**) or that a percentage of the materials and labor be from within that country (**local content requirements**). Despite such legal requirements, a foreign company may find it desirable to enter into a joint venture with a domestic company to help spread the high costs and risks associated with foreign operations. The local partner brings to the joint venture its knowledge of the customs and tastes of local consumers, an established distribution network, and valuable business and political contacts.

There are disadvantages to international joint ventures. A major potential drawback, especially in countries that limit foreign companies to minority participation, is the loss of effective managerial control. As a result, the foreign investor may experience reduced profits, increased operating costs, inferior product quality, exposure to product liability, and environmental litigation and fines.

Strategic Joint Venturing

Joint venture agreements are highly customized contracts.[8] The structure and content of such arrangements may make one partner susceptible to the other party gaining a strategic advantage. This is especially true when the joint venture involves otherwise competing companies. The interfirm collaboration anticipated by the partners in a joint venture can be threatened when one of the partners attempts to gain additional benefits, often not in the interest of the other partner or the joint venture. For example, one partner may provide confidential information to assure joint venture success. The fear is that the contributed information will be taken by the other partner to gain competitive advantages outside of the joint venture. This is especially a concern in high-technology international joint ventures where there is a substantial exchange and use of proprietary (confidential) information. If the purpose of the joint venture is the promotion of mutual interests through the joint venture enterprise, then it is vital that the joint venture agreement provide means to deter one party from taking advantage of the other or taking the confidential information produced by the joint venture for personal use.

The joint venture should include a carefully worded *purpose clause*, which defines the scope of the venture. Whether the clause should be tightly or narrowly drawn or whether it should be open and flexible in its mandate depends on the nature of the enterprise. A single project venture (building a highway) is aligned with a narrow clause. The joint venture agreement should also include "incentive schemes" to encourage venture-enhancing conduct by individual partners, such as structuring rewards for partner conduct that confers benefits on the joint venture. The incentive may consist of an additional portion of the profits or being granted extended licensing privileges of the joint venture's products.

Proprietary Information: Information that is not public knowledge, such as financial data and product test results. The information is viewed as the private property of the creator or holder. Therefore, someone who receives the information, such as a subcontractor or joint venture partner is under a duty to keep the information confidential and not make unauthorized use of the information. The term *proprietary information* is often used interchangeably with the term *trade secret*.

Other methods or techniques to increase collaboration and deter bad behavior by partners include: (1) substantial mutual investment; (2) creation of an interlocking board of directors; and (3) assignment of key personnel to the joint venture. If both parties have substantial sunk costs invested in the venture, then they will be more willing to collaborate in order to recoup their investments. When one party invests substantially more capital than the other party, the other party may use that imbalance (hostage scenario) to renegotiate more favorable terms. The benefits of a board of directors made up of representatives or managers from the parent companies leads to trust-building and greater cooperation. Finally, companies often hesitate to allocate their best personnel to a joint venture project. In order to increase the likelihood of success, however, it is important for both partners to assign key personnel to the venture.

Finally, a strategically drafted joint venture agreement addresses the issue of dispute resolution. A well-worded dispute resolution clause provides a problem-solving framework to deal with disputes internally. For example, an internal dispute resolution committee made up of managers that come from the different parent companies should be tasked to resolve disputes through negotiations and consensus. If this fails, then the agreement should provide for an amicable method of terminating and unwinding the business through good faith negotiation, mediation, and arbitration. The next section deals with the important issue of the joint venture agreement providing strategies for partners to exit the joint venture.

Exit Strategies for International Ventures[9]

It is important to pre-plan for the termination of the joint venture agreement or the withdrawal of a partner. Dissolution of a joint venture can lead to prolonged litigation. It makes business sense for the parties to consider exit strategies at the time of the formation of the venture. There are various types of exit strategies. See Figure 17.2 "Joint Venture Exit Strategies."

There are associated rights linked to some exit strategies, such as the drag-along and tag-along rights. **Drag-Along** strategy benefits majority owners. Typically, in a drag-along provision, the majority owner, if it decides to sell its ownership interest in the venture, can require the minority owners to sell their interests to the buyer on the same terms. The **Tag-Along** strategy is a co-sale right that benefits minority owners. In a tag-along provision, the minority owners (partners) have the option of requiring the selling owner to include their ownership interests in the sale on the same terms.

- **Russian Roulette or Mexican Shoot-Out** allows one partner to name a price at which the partner is willing to sell its interest in the joint venture to the other partner. The other party must either agree to buy at the offered price or has to sell its interest at the offering price.

Downside: The problem with this strategy is that a partner that really wants to exit the joint venture does not want to be faced with the possibility that it will be forced to buy the other partner's interest and have to take over the entire venture.

- **Right of First Refusal** is the most commonly used exit strategy. There are a number of variations of the right of first refusal depending on how many partners are included. The right is triggered when one of the partners receives an offer from a third party to buy its ownership interest. The partner, before accepting the offer, must first offer to sell its interest to its joint venture partner or partners at the offered price. If the other partners decide against buying the other partner's interest, then that partner is free to sell its interest to the third party. Often, this strategy is teamed with the drag-along or tag-along provision discussed below.
- **Right of First Offer** allows a partner wanting to exit the venture to make an offer to sell to the other partners at a price and terms which it deems appropriate. If the partners cannot reach an agreement, the partner is free to sell its interest to a third party, however, if the partner reaches an agreement to at a lower price, then it is required to give the other partners another opportunity to buy its interest.
- **Forced Dissolution** or **Forced Sale** is where the partners have contractual rights to require the dissolution or liquidation of the joint venture for certain reasons. The most common reason that triggers the right to dissolution is a deadlock in the management of the venture. The forced sale is similar, but instead of having a right to dissolve the venture, the contract requires the venture to be sold. The forced sale is the less drastic strategy and likely to be more profitable to partners than a forced dissolution.

Figure 17.2 Joint Venture Exit Strategies.

Competition Law

The proliferation of international trade, FDI, and privatization has led to an increase in the importance of competition (antitrust) law. The existence of **competition law** and the proclivity of its enforcement vary depending on the level of economic development of the countries of concern. Countries with developed economies use competition law to combat anticompetitive activities while developing countries see competition law as a means to eliminate barriers to attract foreign capital and investment in order to spur economic growth. The result has been the passage of competition laws in many countries where they did not previously exist; however, enforcement is often minimal.[10,11,12,13,14,15,16,17,18]

Due to the constant innovations in the business world, competition law is constantly evolving. It is important for companies to be alert to such changes when purchasing or merging with a foreign company, franchising, licensing, and in other company-to-company arrangements. Countries and companies need to stay abreast of changes in competition policies and best practices in enforcing or complying with competition law. A number of international organizations that study these issues include the International Competition Network (ICN), the Organisation for Economic Co-operation and Development (OECD), and the United Nations Conference on Trade and Development (UNCTAD).

New Bilateral Investment Treaties

Model bilateral investment treaties (BITs) have evolved to be more than guarantees of foreign investor rights, including labor and environmental protections. The Model BIT defines environmental harm as follows: "[Environmental law are those whose] primary purpose is the protection of the environment, or the prevention of a danger to human, animal, or plant life or health, through the: (a) prevention, abatement, or control of the release, discharge, or emission of pollutants or environmental contaminants; (b) control of environmentally hazardous or toxic chemicals, substances, materials, and wastes, and the dissemination of information related thereto; or (c) protection or conservation of wild flora or fauna, including endangered species, their habitat, and specially protected natural areas." BITs should be revised to include not just the "do not harm" obligations described above, but also proactive obligations that investors are required to pursue to aid sustainable development and fight climate change.

Government Procurement and Programs

One of the major buyers of goods are governments. As such, governments through their procurement power can advance the environmentally friendly production of goods. **Green procurement** has played a major role within European procurement mechanisms. The 2014 EU Public Procurement Directive has been used to make the "case for sustainable public procurement linking minimisation of social and environmental risk with enhanced cost-saving (life-cycle costing methodologies) and the creation of markets for products and services that enrich sustainability."

Another area to promote sustainability is the implementation of government policies and programs that incentivize private contractors to make contracts that take into account sustainability goals. These include government programs to incentivize the construction of energy efficient or green buildings. The criteria for earning such certifications include the use of locally sourced sustainable materials, reduction in water usage, energy efficiency, quality of indoor air, and minimization of environmental pollution. In addition, such programs incentivize the use of products constructed with recycled materials. Such criteria should be used to draft clauses in public and private contracts.

Chapter Summary

1. Just like the international trade of goods and services, the amount of foreign direct investment (FDI) has proliferated since the creation of the WTO in 1994, making national economies more interdependent.
2. Different types of FDI include greenfield investments and portfolio investments. Greenfield investing involves the establishment of a business in the host country, sometimes through mergers and acquisitions of existing companies. A number of methods can be employed to mitigate risks of FDI, such as a joint venture, alliances or syndicates, reciprocal distribution agreements, and franchising. Portfolio investments, or indirect foreign investment, consist of acquiring shares in a foreign company, which do not rise to the level of FDI.
3. The ability of a foreign country to attract FDI will depend on a number of factors, including size of economy, existence of natural resources, and the stability of the government and the macroeconomic environment. Investors are uncomfortable with uncertainty. The "Russian crisis" is used to show how a government through the decisions it makes can seriously disrupt the inward flows of FDI, as well as the overall health of its economy. Russia failed to use the wealth generated from its past oil and gas revenues to restructure and diversify its economy and build much needed infrastructure.
4. There are a number of risks associated with FDI including expropriation and nationalization. Expropriation in the free trade era has become a rare occurrence; instead, the trend has been toward the privatization (selling) of government-owned industries and resources. The more relevant risk is that of creeping expropriation. In creeping or indirect expropriation, the value of a foreign investment is reduced by increases and changes in host country regulations, such as increases in equity participation requirements (maximum percentage of foreign ownership); increases in local content requirements (minimum percentage of materials or component parts that need to come from the host country); export requirements (minimum required exports to ensure inflow of currency into host country); and capital and exchange controls (limiting the ability to exchange host country currency for hard currency and limiting the ability to repatriate hard currencies from the country).
5. The WTO's Agreement on Trade-Related Investment Measures (TRIMs) provides basic protections for FDI that must be adhered to by WTO countries. Countries also insure the FDI of their citizens by entering bilateral investment treaties (BITs) with other countries. In large investment projects, companies and investors should negotiate a concession agreement with the foreign government that would ensure certain rights and protections including protections against creeping expropriation. Companies also mitigate risks by entering joint ventures, alliances, and syndicates. The most common form is joint venturing with a domestic company of the host country in order to share the costs and lessen the risks of conforming to the country's laws and regulations.

6. The most important development in FDI protections is the ability of an investor to bring a claim against a foreign government in arbitration instead of being forced to use the foreign government's court system. The most common venue for investor–government arbitration is the International Centre for Settlement of Investment Disputes (ICSID). Most BITs require that disputes be arbitrated at the ICSID.
7. The Model BIT provides these basic FDI protections: fairness of treatment under the national treatment, most-favored-nation, and transparency principles; limiting the grounds for expropriation; prohibiting the use of performance or local content requirements; free transferability of funds; and the right of investors to submit an investment dispute to international arbitration. BITs also provide for environmental protection and workers' rights.
8. Another method that the foreign investor can use to shift risks is through franchising. In such a scenario, the investment costs are greatly diminished, as well as the risks of doing business with a foreign government. There are variations of franchising that should be considered, such as direct franchising, area development agreements, and master franchising.
9. In response to the proliferation of FDI, most countries have enacted competition (antitrust) laws. These laws may protect the foreign investors from unfair business practices of host country companies. At the same time, the investor must become aware of the requirements and restrictions of foreign competition law, especially in the case of mergers and acquisitions.

Key Terms

Agreement on Trade-Related Investment Measures (TRIMs)
Alternative Dispute Resolution (ADR)
Area Development Agreement
Australian Tobacco Plain Packaging Act
Bhopal Disaster
Bilateral Investment Treaties (BITs)
Competition Law
Concession Agreement
Covered Investments
Creeping Expropriation
Declaration on Fundamental Principles and Rights at Work
Direct Investment Enterprise
Disinvestment
Drag-Along Provision
Equity Participation Requirements
Emerging Economies
Expropriation
Fair and Equitable Treatment
Forced Dissolution
Forced Sale
Foreign Direct Investment (FDI)
Franchising
Greenfield Investments (*De Novo* Investment)
Green Procurement
ICSID Additional Facility Rules
Indirect Foreign Investment
International Centre for Settlement of Investment Disputes (ICSID)
Investment Claim
Joint Venture
Local Content Requirements
Macroeconomic Stability
Master Franchising
Minimum Standard of Treatment Principle
Model Bilateral Investment Treaty

Most-Favored-Nation Principle
National Treatment Principle
Nationalization
New York Convention
Parallel Proceedings
Performance Requirements
Piggyback Marketing
Planned Foreign Investment
Proprietary Information
Reciprocal Distribution Agreements
Right of First Offer
Right of First Refusal
Russian Crisis
Russian Joint Venture Syndicates
Tag-Along Provision
Trade Claim
Transparency Principle
Umbrella Clause
Warranty Law
World Commodity Prices

Chapter Problems

1. Why might a company consider investing abroad?
2. In what respects is foreign direct investment riskier than the sale of goods (exporting)? What are the different means of minimizing those risks?
3. What role do international institutions play in the protection of FDI?
4. What are the differences between the following:
   a. greenfield investment
   b. merger and acquisition
   c. joint ventures

   What are the advantages of each of these forms of foreign direct investment? What are the unique concerns and issues for each form?
5. Have foreign regulations of FDI become more or less restrictive over the last few decades? Why?
6. In what ways can a company mitigate the risks of FDI?
7. What legal standards must a host country meet in expropriating (nationalizing) a foreign investment?
8. What is the importance of bilateral investment treaties (BITs) to a party considering FDI?
9. What are the key issues in establishing and operating an international joint venture?
10. How is international franchising different from purely domestic franchising? How is franchising different from licensing?
11. What benefits does international franchising provide the franchisor and the franchisee?
12. What factors should a franchisor consider in determining who, where, and how it should enter a franchise agreement?
13. What types of provisions should a franchisor negotiate to protect itself?
14. Explain the difference between:
    a. area development agreement
    b. direct franchising
    c. master franchise agreement
    d. subfranchisee

Internet Exercises

1. Review the U.S. Model Bilateral Investment Treaty available at http://www.state.gov/documents/organization/188371.pdf.
2. Review the website of the Asia-Pacific Economic Cooperation (APEC) to see the many different working groups, areas, and projects that it undertakes: http://www.apec.org.

Other Internet Sources

Global foreign investment trends: country investment guides, investment reviews, and analysis: www.oecd.org.

A joint venture between the **World Bank and WTO**, this site contains links to a wide range of country and regional reports, and information on local government agencies: www.itd.org.

Notes

1 The World Bank Group Rankings can be found at http://www.doingbusiness.org/ rankings.

2 International Monetary Fund (IMF) and World Bank, "Foreign Direct Investment, Net Inflows (% GDP)," https://data.worldbank.org/indicator/BX.KLT.DINV.WD.GD.ZS.

3 World Bank at https://data.worldbank.org/indicator/NY.GDP.MKTP.CD?locations=RU.

4 See generally, U.S. Commercial Service, *A Basic Guide to Exporting* (2015).

5 Joost Pauwelyn, "Rational Design or Accidental Evolution? The Emergence of International Investment Law" in *The Foundations of International Investment Law* 27 (eds Z. Douglas, J. Pauwelyn and J. Vinuales, Oxford University Press 2014).

6 ICSID Case No. ARB/87/13 (June 27, 1990).

7 Ibid.

8 See Larry A. DiMatteo, "Strategic Contracting: Contract Law as a Source of Competitive Advantage," 47 *American Business Law Journal* 727 (2010).

9 This section benefited from material provided by Andrew J. Markus, Carlton Fields, P.A., 100 SE 2nd Street, Suite 4000, Miami, Florida 33131.

10 H. Vedia Jerez, *Competition Law Enforcement and Compliance across the World: A Comparative Review* 389 (Wolters Kluwer 2015).

11 Countries adopted the Paris Agreement, effective November 1, 2016 in order to limit global temperature rise to below 2 degrees centigrade. As of April 2018, 175 parties had ratified the Paris Agreement.

12 *Gabčíkovo-Nagymaros Project (Hungary v. Slovakia)* (Judgment) [1997] ICJ Rep 7, (1998) 37 ILM 162 (September 25, 1997).

13 Permanent Court of Arbitration: In the Arbitration Regarding the Iron Rhine ("Ijzeren Rijn") Railway, between the Kingdom of Belgium and the Kingdom of the Netherlands (May 24, 2005) at 59, 114, Award of the Arbitral Tribunal,

Permanent Court of Arbitration, http://www.pca-cpa.org/ENGLISH/RPC/BENL/ BE-NL%20Award%20240505.pdf.

14 Brussels, 11.12.2019 COM(2019) 640 final.

15 See European Green Deal, p. 3, https://ec.europa.eu/info/sites/info/files/european-green-deal-communication_en.pdf.

16 See European Commission, "Ecolabel for Consumers," available at http:// ec.europa.eu/environment/ecolabel/eu-ecolabel-for-consumers.html, 23.09.2019.

17 Larry A. DiMatteo and Stefan Wrbka, "Planned Obsolescence and Consumer Protection: The Unregulated Extended Warranty and Service Contract Industry," 28 *Cornell Journal of Law & Public Policy* (2019) Stefan Wrbka and Larry A. DiMatteo, "Comparative Warranty Law: Case of Planned Obsolescence," 21 *University of Pennsylvania Journal of Business Law* (2019).

18 Latent or hidden defects are not visible (patent defects) upon a reasonable inspection of delivered products. They only appear sometime after delivery and often after the warranty period has expired.

Chapter 18

E-Commerce

The growth of international Internet sales of goods, services, and digital content has been stunning. It has had a major impact in facilitating commercial (business-to-business or B2B) transactions but has especially reshaped the marketplace for consumer sales (business-to-consumer or B2C). Retail e-commerce sales continue to grow exponentially from $1.3 trillion in 2014 to $2.4 trillion in 2017, $3.5 trillion in 2019, $4.2 trillion (estimated), and were projected to be $6.5 trillion by 2023.

As Internet marketing and sales transformed the international marketplace, they have raised numerous regulatory issues because of the Internet's transborder nature and position within the public domain. The scope of e-commerce issues touches upon many different areas of business and law. An EU Council Resolution on the Consumer Dimension of the Information Society outlined the areas of concern: (1) accessibility and affordability; (2) transparency, including in quantity and quality of information; (3) fair marketing practices and contract terms; (4) protection of children; (5) security of payment systems; (6) privacy and the protection of personal data; and (7) access to efficient systems of dispute resolution.

Despite the technological nature of the Internet, the same issues that are found in more traditional international business transactions apply to Internet transactions. For example, does an Internet transaction bring the seller within the scope of the laws and jurisdiction of the country of the buyer? Will the seller be liable for foreign income, sales, and value-added taxes? Is the transaction subject to foreign consumer protection laws? See Table 18.1 *Focus on Transactions*: "Legal Issues Relating to the Internet" for a list of legal issues posed by the Internet and e-commerce.

DOI: 10.4324/9781003469230-23

Table 18.1 *Focus on Transactions*: Legal Issues Relating to the Internet.

Issue	*Area of Law*	*Solution*
Posting material that harms another's reputation (jurisdiction)	Tort law (defamation)	Long-arm statute
Liability of Internet service providers (ISPs) for digital content	Tort law (secondary or vicarious liability); Digital Millennium Copyright Act (DMCA)	ISPs have liability protection, but must disclose the source of information and are liable if they fail to remove offensive material after being notified of its existence
Spam and other Internet abuses	Tort law (nuisance law)	Injunction
Misrepresentation	Tort-contract law	Use of disclaimers of not doing business in certain states or countries
Defective products and services (online sales)	Product liability and consumer protection laws	Litigation and government regulation (use of disclaimers of not doing business in certain states or countries)
Internet contracting	Contract formation	Uniform Electronic Transactions Act (UETA) Electronic agents
Online securities	Securities law	Extraterritoriality; offshore exemption
Employee e-mails	Privacy law	No expectation of privacy; Canada's Personal Information Protection and Electronic Documents Act
Discovery of company and employee e-mails	Federal Rules of Civil Procedure	May subpoena employee's home computer for business-related evidence
Unauthorized downloading	Copyright and trademark law	Injunction
Domain names and metatags	Anti-cybersquatting law	Internet Corporation for Assigned Names and Numbers (ICANN)
Criminal and fraudulent activities	Criminal law	Encryption of data

This chapter begins with a brief look at how questions of jurisdiction are applied to electronic transactions. It then focuses directly on issues specific to e-commerce, such as trademark infringement, privacy, database protection, and liability related to digital or electronic platforms. An analysis of legal issues related to e-contracting is undertaken, as well as the rise of smart contracts and blockchain technology. Finally, a review of the impact of legal technology on the practice of law, and the benefits and risks of artificial intelligence in business is discussed.

Personal Jurisdiction

A key issue in e-commerce is whether persons and companies become amenable to the jurisdiction of a foreign court. Does advertising or processing an order over the Internet give a foreign court personal jurisdiction over a seller? Jurisdiction means the power of a court to hear a case. **Personal jurisdiction** pertains to the power or authority of a court to require a defendant to defend itself in that court. A court gains personal jurisdiction over a defendant only if the defendant has had **minimum contacts** with the forum (foreign) state.

A number of American court decisions offer some guidance regarding personal jurisdiction in Internet transactions. In *Bensusan Restaurant Corp. v. King*,[1] the court held that the mere creation of a website did not constitute transacting business in a foreign jurisdiction. The court reasoned that the plaintiff had to prove that the defendant had sufficient intent to do business in the state.

Bensusan Restaurant Corp. v. King

126 F.3d 25 (2d Cir. 1997)

Circuit Judge. Bensusan Restaurant Corp. alleges in its complaint that it is the creator of a successful jazz club in New York City called The Blue Note, which was registered as a federal trademark. King owns a club in Missouri called The Blue Note. King hired a website design company to create a website on the Internet for King's cabaret. Bensusan seeks a "cease and desist" order to prevent King from using The Blue Note name.

Bensusan brought suit in the Southern District of New York, alleging violations of the Federal Trademark Dilution Act of 1995, as well as common law unfair competition. The website described King's establishment as "Mid-Missouri's finest live entertainment venue." The website expressly stated that it should not be confused with the jazz club, Blue Note, located in New York's Greenwich Village.

New York law (long-arm statute) states that a New York court may exercise personal jurisdiction over a nonresident who "in person or through an agent" commits a tortious act within the state or who commits a tortious act outside the state, causing injury to person or property within the state. However, the exercise of jurisdiction is limited to persons who expect or should reasonably expect the tortious act to have consequences in the state and in addition derive substantial revenue from interstate commerce.

The court held that the Blue Note's business operations were of a local character and that it did not earn substantial revenues from interstate commerce. As such, the courts of New York do not have personal jurisdiction over the Blue Note. Case is dismissed.

Case Highlights

- The "minimum contacts" standard for establishing personal jurisdiction over a defendant must be applied to Internet activities
- A long-arm statute grants jurisdiction where a tort (such as trademark infringement) that occurs outside the state causes injury in another state
- Mere creation of a website containing trademark-infringing material does not satisfy the long-arm statute's requirements for personal jurisdiction
- Personal jurisdiction does not attach to a tort committed outside of a state unless the defendant purposely directed its activities inside the foreign other state and derived substantial revenue from those activities.

A case on the opposite end of the jurisdictional spectrum from *Bensusan Restaurant Corp. v. King* is *CompuServe, Inc. v. Patterson.* The case involves the method of licensing software known as **shareware.** In that case, a person transmitted his product from Texas through CompuServe's system in Ohio. The question is whether Patterson purposefully availed himself of the privilege of doing business in Ohio to establish personal jurisdiction in the Ohio courts.

CompuServe, Inc. v. Patterson

89 F.3d 1257 (6th Cir. 1996)

Circuit Judge. CompuServe is a computer information service headquartered in Columbus, Ohio. CompuServe operates as an electronic conduit to provide its subscribers computer software products. Computer software generated and distributed in this manner is referred to as "shareware." Shareware makes money only through the voluntary compliance of an "end user," another CompuServe subscriber who pays the creator's suggested licensing fee if she uses the software beyond a specified trial period. The "end user" pays that fee directly to CompuServe in Ohio, and CompuServe takes a 15 percent fee before remitting the balance to the shareware's creator.

Defendant Patterson subscribed to CompuServe and placed items of "shareware" on the CompuServe system for others to use and purchase. When he became a shareware "provider," Patterson entered into a "Shareware Registration Agreement" (SRA). This Agreement expressly provides that both parties entered into the contract in Ohio, and that it is to "be governed by Ohio law." CompuServe subsequently began to market a similar product with markings and names that Patterson alleged to be too similar to his own. CompuServe filed this declaratory judgment action (legal determination of a court that resolves legal uncertainty for the litigants) hoping the court would declare that it had not infringed any common law trademarks of Patterson. Patterson responded with a motion to dismiss for lack of personal jurisdiction.

The "purposeful availment" requirement is satisfied when the defendant's contacts with a State "creates a 'substantial connection' with the forum

State," and due to that connection, a person should reasonably anticipate being sued in a court of that state. Patterson chose to transmit his software from Texas to CompuServe's system in Ohio, others gained access to Patterson's software via that system, and Patterson advertised and sold his product through CompuServe's system. Moreover, this was a relationship ongoing in nature.

We deem it important to note what we do not hold. We do not hold that Patterson would be subject to suit in any state where his software was purchased or used. We also do not have before us an attempt by another party from a third state to sue Patterson in Ohio for, say, a "computer virus" caused by his software. Finally, we do not hold that CompuServe may sue any regular subscriber to its service for non-payment in Ohio.

We do hold that Patterson had sufficient contacts with Ohio to support the exercise of personal jurisdiction over him.

Case Highlights

- Shareware is a way of selling software where the user is permitted to download and use that software for a trial period, after which the user is asked to pay a fee to the author for continued use
- Due process considerations for purposes of personal jurisdiction are satisfied if the defendant "purposely avails" itself of the laws of the forum state
- Mere advertising on a passive website does not subject one to the jurisdiction of foreign courts, but repeatedly selling your product through a website located in another state is grounds for jurisdiction.

The *Bensusan* case involved the use of a *passive website*, while the Internet user in *CompuServe* specifically targeted Ohio by entering into an agreement to sell its software over the Internet to out-of-state purchasers. The *Zippo Manufacturing Co. v. Zippo Dot Com, Inc.*[2] case established a sliding-scale approach to the establishment of personal jurisdiction for Internet activities. In that case, the defendant's web advertisement was followed by the sale of services to more than 3,000 subscribers in the foreign state. The number of contacts and sales within a given state is a major factor in the determination of personal jurisdiction.

Zippo Manufacturing Co. v. Zippo Dot Com, Inc.

952 F. Supp. 1119 (W.D. Pa. 1997)

Judge. This is an Internet domain name dispute. Domain names serve as a primary identifier of an Internet user. Internet companies commonly use their business names as part of their domain names (e.g., IBM.com). The designation ".com" identifies the user as a commercial entity. We must decide the permissible reach of Pennsylvania's Long-Arm Statute (personal jurisdiction over the defendant) through cyberspace. Zippo Manufacturing Corporation (Zippo) filed a complaint against Zippo Dot Com, Inc. (Dot Com), alleging trademark dilution, infringement, and false designation under the Trademark Act. Dot Com has moved to dismiss for lack of personal jurisdiction.

Zippo is a Pennsylvania corporation with its principal place of business in Bradford, Pennsylvania. It makes the well-known "Zippo" tobacco lighters. Dot Com, a provider of financial services, is a California corporation with its principal place of business in Sunnyvale, California. Dot Com operates an Internet website and obtained the exclusive right to use the domain names "zippo.com," "zippo.net" and "zipponews. com."

Dot Com's contacts with Pennsylvania occurred exclusively over the Internet. Dot Com's offices, employees, and Internet servers are located in California. Dot Com maintains no offices, employees, or agents in Pennsylvania. Dot Com's advertising to Pennsylvania residents involves posting information about its service on its web page, accessible via the Internet. Dot Com has approximately 3,000 subscribers located in Pennsylvania.

The Due Process Clause of the American Constitution governs the extent to which a state court may exercise authority. Pennsylvania's long arm jurisdiction statute permits the exercise of jurisdiction over nonresident defendants doing business in the state or committing a tort that impacts the state. General jurisdiction permits a (forum) court to exercise personal jurisdiction over a nonresident defendant for non-forum related activities when the defendant has engaged in "systematic and continuous" activities in the forum state. The defendant can be sued in the state for any wrongdoing whether or not the wrongdoing was in the forum state.

In the absence of general jurisdiction, specific jurisdiction permits a court to exercise personal jurisdiction over a nonresident defendant for forum-related activities, where the defendant's activities reach the level of "minimum contacts." A three-pronged test has emerged for determining whether the exercise of specific personal jurisdiction over a nonresident defendant is appropriate: (1) defendant has sufficient "minimum contacts" with the state; (2) claim asserted against the defendant arises out of those contacts; and (3) exercise of jurisdiction is reasonable ("purposely avails standard" in which a party, due to its commercial activities, expects it could be subject to lawsuits in the foreign state).

The Supreme Court noted that "as technological progress has increased the flow of commerce between States, the need for jurisdiction has undergone a similar increase." The likelihood that personal jurisdiction can be constitutionally exercised is directly proportionate to the nature and quality of commercial activity that an entity conducts over the Internet. At one end of the spectrum are situations where a defendant clearly *does business* over the Internet (virtual store). If the defendant enters into contracts with residents of a foreign jurisdiction that involve the knowing and repeated transmission of computer files over the Internet or sending of goods personal jurisdiction is proper.

At the opposite end are situations where a defendant has simply posted information on an Internet website that is accessible to users in foreign jurisdictions. *Passive websites* are those that do little more than make information available to those who are interested, which is not grounds for the exercise of personal jurisdiction. *Interactive websites* where a user can exchange information with a host computer occupy the middle ground. In these cases, the exercise of jurisdiction is determined by examining the level of interactivity and commercial nature of the exchange of information that occurs on the website.

First, we must note that this is not an Internet advertising case. Dot Com has not just posted information on a website in Pennsylvania. This is not even an interactivity case since Dot Com has done more than create an interactive website through which it exchanges information. We are not being asked to determine whether Dot Com's website alone constitutes the purposeful availment of doing business in Pennsylvania. We are being asked to determine whether Dot Com's conducting of e-commerce with Pennsylvania residents constitutes the purposeful availment of doing business in Pennsylvania.

Dot Com's e-commerce activities included 3,000 fee paying subscribers. We conclude that this Court may appropriately exercise personal jurisdiction over the Defendant.

Case Highlights

- A sliding scale is used to determine if an Internet activity is sufficient to qualify as "minimum contacts" for purposes of attaching personal jurisdiction to a defendant
- A company that clearly does business over the Internet is amenable to the personal jurisdiction of a foreign state in which it transacts business
- A person or company that merely maintains a "passive" website is not subject to the jurisdiction of a foreign court
- Personal jurisdiction based upon an interactive website will depend on the level of interactivity and the commercial nature of the site.

In order to avoid being amenable to suit in a given jurisdiction, it is advisable to place clear **disclaimers** (e.g., this offer does not extend to persons or entities located in the countries of Canada and Mexico or offer is intended only for those persons and entities residing in France) within a website that your intent is not to engage in transactions with residents in certain jurisdictions.

Figure 18.1 *Comparative Law*: "EU Regulation on Jurisdiction, Recognition, and Enforcement of Judgments" provides excerpts from an EU regulation that requires an Internet retailer to defend itself in the courts of a consumer located in an EU country. This statutory intervention makes the minimum contacts analysis required in the U.S. unnecessary. EU regulations also void forum selection clauses in licenses or web pages whose intent is to avoid the consumer protection laws.

The EU regulation brings up a crucial issue of whether a court's exercise of personal jurisdiction over a foreign defendant will be recognized and enforced by a foreign court system.

Under the international law principle of *comity*, countries are expected to honor the judicial judgments and orders of foreign courts. However, this recognition is sometimes denied. The *Braintech, Inc. v. Kostiuk* case demonstrates that even closely aligned legal systems, such as the U.S. and Canada, will not enforce the judgment of the other if they determine that the exercise of personal

EU Regulation on Jurisdiction, Recognition, and Enforcement of Judgments

Jurisdiction over Consumer Contracts

In matters relating to a contract concluded by a person, the consumer, for a purpose which can be regarded as being outside his trade or profession, jurisdiction shall be determined by this Section, if: (1) it is a contract for the sale of goods on installment credit terms; (2) it is a contract for a loan repayable by installments, or for any other form of credit, made to finance the sale of goods; or (3) in all other cases, the contract has been concluded with a person who pursues commercial or professional activities in the Member State of the consumer's domicile or, by any means, directs such activities to that Member State or to several countries including that Member State, and the contract falls within the scope of such activities.

Article 16

A consumer may bring proceedings against the other party to a contract either in the courts of the Member State in which that party is domiciled or in the courts for the place where the consumer is domiciled. Proceedings may be brought against a consumer by the other party to the contract only in the courts of the Member State in which the consumer is domiciled.

Jurisdiction over Individual Contracts of Employment
Article 18

Where an employee enters into an individual contract of employment with an employer who is not domiciled in a Member State but has a branch, agency, or other establishment in one of the Member States, the employer shall, in disputes arising out of the operations of the branch, agency, or establishment, be deemed to be domiciled in that Member State.

Article 20

An employer may bring proceedings only in the courts of the Member State in which the employee is domiciled. The provisions of this Section shall not affect the right to bring a counterclaim in the court in which, in accordance with this Section, the original claim is pending.

Figure 18.1 Comparative Law: EU Regulation on Jurisdiction, Recognition, and Enforcement of Judgments.

jurisdiction was improper. This case involved the posting of defamatory information on an Internet bulletin board.

Braintech, Inc. v. Kostiuk

British Columbia Court of Appeals (1999)

Justice. The Plaintiff was a technology company incorporated in Nevada and doing business in various jurisdictions. It brought an action in Texas against a resident of British Columbia, Canada alleging the Defendant had published defamatory information about the corporation on an Internet bulletin board. The Plaintiff obtained a default judgment in Texas and commenced an action on that judgment in British Columbia. British Columbia is obligated to recognize foreign judgments according to principles of reciprocity and comity. However, there is a constitutional limitation in the U.S. on the exercise of personal jurisdiction that requires the Defendant to have sufficient minimum contacts with the jurisdiction. The Defendant's only connection to Texas was a passive posting on an Internet bulletin board. To enforce recovery of the default judgment would encourage a multiplicity of actions wherever the Internet is available.

The issue in this case is whether there was a real and substantial connection between Texas and the wrongdoing alleged to have taken place. In the circumstances, British Columbia is the only natural forum and Texas is not an appropriate forum. Comity does not require that the courts of this province recognize the default judgment. DISMISSED.

Case Highlights

- Countries are obligated under international law's principle of comity to recognize the judicial judgments of foreign courts
- Any exercise of personal jurisdiction must satisfy the requirements of due process
- Passive postings of defamatory statements on Internet bulletin boards do not establish a "real and substantial" connection with a foreign state for purposes of personal jurisdiction.

Trademark Infringement and Dilution

Trademark protection is "the law's recognition of the psychological function of symbols." Two goals of trademark protection are the protection of consumers who have formed particular associations with a mark and the protection of the investment in a mark made by the owner. An early problem in Internet commerce was the misappropriation of names by so-called *cybersquatters*. Cybersquatters are parties that register famous brand names or trademarks as their Internet domain name. The cybersquatter then attempts to extort payments from the trademark owners for their registered domain name.

Famous Trademarks: Trademark law provides the following factors in determining whether a mark is distinctive and famous: (1) degree of inherent or acquired distinctiveness of the mark; (2) duration and extent of use of the mark in connection with the goods or services with which the mark is used; (3) duration and extent of advertising the mark; (4) geographical extent of the trading area in which the mark is used; (5) channels of trade for the goods or services with which the mark is used; (6) degree of recognition of the mark in the trading areas and channels of trade used by the mark's owner and the person against whom the injunction is sought; and (7) nature and extent of use of the same or similar marks by third parties.

Courts have held that the registering of a domain name for the purpose of selling it to a trademark owner is illegal under trademark law. Unlike infringement and unfair competition laws, evidence of a likelihood of confusing consumers is not required. Injunctive relief is available when a plaintiff can show: (1) its mark is famous; (2) defendant is making commercial use of the mark; (3) defendant's use began after the plaintiff's mark became famous; and (4) defendant's use presents a likelihood of weakening or diluting the distinctive value of the mark. In this classic "cybersquatter" case, the court needs to determine that the infringer's intent was to "arbitrage" the registration that included another's trademark. **Blurring** is a type of trademark dilution where the infringer's use of the mark still may dilute the uniqueness of the more famous mark (see Chapter 15).

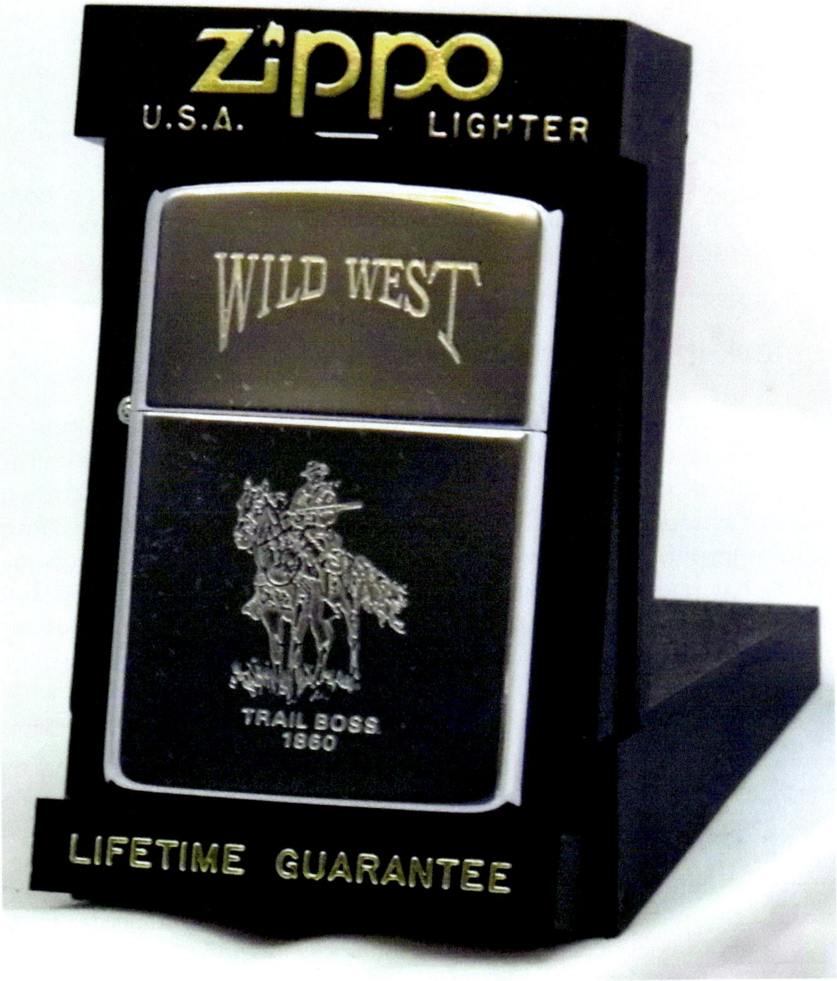

Image 18.1 Zippo Lighters.

The idea of tarnishing or blurring a trademark is the issue in *Mattel, Inc. v. Internet Dimensions*.

Mattel, Inc. v. Internet Dimensions, Inc.

2000 U.S. Dist. LEXIS 9747 (S.D.N.Y. 2000)

District Judge. Plaintiff Mattel, Inc. (Mattel), commenced this action against defendants Internet Dimensions, Inc. (Internet Dimensions), asserting causes of action for (1) trademark infringement, (2) trademark dilution (tarnishes or harms a trademark), and (3) violation of the Anticybersquatting Consumer Protection Act of 1999 (ACPA). One of Mattel's products is the trademarked "Barbie" doll.

The "Barbie" doll is the bestselling toy doll in the world. Internet Dimensions owns Internet domain names for sites that provide, among other things, "adult" entertainment. One of its domain names is "barbiesplaypen.com." Mattel's primary claim in this action violated the American ACPA, which provides that "a court may order the forfeiture or cancellation of a domain name or transfer of the domain name to the owner of the mark."

The ACPA provides a claim for civil liability when a person or entity:

> (1) has a bad faith intent to profit from an existing mark and (2) registers, traffics in, or uses a domain name that: (a) is identical or confusingly similar to a registered mark that is distinctive; (b) in the case of a famous mark, is identical or confusingly similar to or dilutive of that mark.

The distinctiveness of the name "Barbie" was acquired through four decades of exposure in the American consumer market. The name "Barbie" and the font normally used to advertise BARBIE products are widely recognized throughout the world. The Court finds that the trademark BARBIE is both "distinctive" and "famous." The next question is whether the domain name "barbiesplaypen.com" is "identical or confusingly similar to" the BARBIE mark. The similarities are as follows:

(1) both use the name "Barbie;" (2) the name "Barbie" appeared on the front page of the website with approximately the same font, slant, and size; (3) BARBIE and "barbiesplaypen.com" are inextricably associated with the verb "play." Hence, the above similarities make the website "barbiesplaypen .com," and its domain name, "confusingly similar," though not "identical" to the BARBIE mark.

We find that the defendants did engage in a "bad faith attempt to profit" from the BARBIE trademark by maintaining the infringing domain name and website. It is expected that consumers searching under the word BARBIE using an Internet search engine would be directed to defendants' pornographic "barbiesplaypen.com" site. The diversion of Internet users to a site containing pornographic images *tarnishes* the image of Mattel's BARBIE products in the minds of consumers.

Under the ACPA, Mattel is entitled to an order directing defendants to transfer the registration of the domain name "barbiesplaypen.com" to Mattel and a permanent injunction barring defendants from the commercial use and infringement of any of Mattel's BARBIE trademarks. Finally, the plaintiff is entitled to statutory damages and attorneys' fees.

Case Highlights

- A party can be liable for trademark infringement even if it sells a product dissimilar to the products sold by the trademark owner, if the infringing use of the trademark "tarnishes" the image of the trademark owner, resulting in trademark dilution

- Cybersquatting is the bad faith registration of distinctive trademarks as Internet domain names
- The Anticybersquatting Consumer Protection Act (ACPA) protects trademark owners from the bad faith use of their trade name by others who register infringing domain names.

Internet Privacy and Database Protection

Justice Brandeis once stated that: "the right to be left alone is the most comprehensive of rights, and the most valued by civilized persons."[3] Internet privacy involves the need to balance the individual's right to privacy with the proprietary right to develop, transfer, and sell databases compiled with personal data. One issue is when information that an individual believes to be submitted confidentially to one party is transferred to other parties for different purposes. Many of today's most popular websites serve as data collection instruments.

Personal information given by a visitor to a website is collected for future use, sometimes covertly through the use of *cookies* or tags. Cookies are used to identify visitors to a website. They allow the website to obtain the visitor's e-mail address, name, the specific pages of the website that were visited, and what electronic transactions were made. This personal information can then be used for future marketing purposes or sold to others by the website owners.

The U.S. and the EU have elected two different approaches to this problem. Europeans are more restrictive in regulating the way companies collect and process personal data. The U.S. has not enacted a broad data protection law, instead protection is provided by a patchwork of different laws and relies on the Internet industry to self-regulate. See Figure 18.2 *Comparative Law*: "American Privacy Laws."

- **Fair Credit Reporting Act** governs the use of data by the credit reporting industry;
- **Privacy Act of 1994** restricts government agencies from releasing personal information found in its documents and records;
- **Telephone Consumer Protection Act** is directed at the abuse of telemarketing activities through telephone and bulk e-mail solicitations or **spamming**;
- **Electronic Communications Privacy Act of 1986** extends federal wiretap requirements to new forms of electronic communications such as e-mailing and service providers' transmission and storage of electronic communications.
- **Telecommunications Act of 1996** restricts the disclosure by telecommunications companies of information about subscribers' use of their services.

Figure 18.2 Comparative Law: American Privacy Laws.

In contrast to the American approach, the EU has enacted comprehensive legislation to deal with personal privacy (data) on the Internet, as reflected in the **EU's General Data Protection Regulation of 25 May 2018** (GDPR).[4] The GDPR is the strictest privacy law in the world. It imposes obligations on any company or organization that targets or collects data related to individuals in the EU (processes the personal data of people in the EU including tracking on websites). It requires organizations to safeguard personal data and uphold the privacy rights of persons in EU territory. The regulation includes seven principles of data protection and eight privacy rights that must be given. It also empowers EU Member State-level data protection authorities to enforce the GDPR with sanctions and fines. See Figure 18.3 *Comparative Law*: "EU General Data Protection Regulation."

Key Definitions

Personal data—Personal data is any information that relates to an individual who can be directly or indirectly identified. Pseudonymous data can also fall under the definition if it is relatively easy to ID someone from it.
Data processing Action performed on data, whether automated or manual, such as: collecting, recording, organizing, structuring, storing, using, and erasing.
Data subject Person whose data is processed, such as customers or website visitors.
Data controller Person who decides why and how personal data will be processed.
Data processor A third party that processes personal data on behalf of a data controller.

Seven Basic Principles

- *Lawfulness, fairness, and transparency* processing must be lawful, fair, and transparent to the data subject;
- *Purpose limitation* process data for the legitimate purposes specified explicitly to the data subject;
- *Data minimization* collect and process only as much data as absolutely necessary for the purposes specified;
- *Accuracy* keep personal data accurate and up to date;
- *Storage limitation* only store personally identifying data for as long as necessary for the specified purpose;
- *Integrity and confidentiality* processing must be done in such a way as to ensure appropriate security, integrity, and confidentiality (encryption);
- *Accountability* data controller is responsible for being able to demonstrate GDPR compliance with all of these principles.

Figure 18.3 Comparative Law: EU General Data Protection Regulation.

Eight Data Subject Rights

- *access to information* about the processing of personal data;
- *access to the personal data* being held;
- *correction* of inaccurate or incomplete personal data (*blocking right*);
- request that personal *data be erased* (*right to be forgotten*);
- *object* to the processing of your personal data for marketing purposes;
- *restriction* of the processing of your personal data in specific cases;
- receive your personal data in a machine-readable format to send to another controller (*data portability*);
- request that decisions based on automated processing are *reviewed by natural persons*.

Figure 18.3 (Continued).

Given the difficulty of verifying foreign countries' compliance with the GDPR, the EU entered **safe harbor** agreements in order to prevent a total shutdown of data transfers from Europe. One such safe harbor provision was the "EU Commission Decision 2016/1250 on the adequacy of the protection provided by the EU-US Data Protection Shield." This Decision allows the outflow of data from the EU to the U.S. based upon EU data exporters certifying that appropriate safeguards are in place. They can do this simply by inserting standard data protection clauses, adopted by the Commission, into their data transfer contracts. In this way, the cost of formal certification of a company in the U.S. and detailed compliance with the GDPR are avoided. In some ways, this acts like the block exemptions found in EU competition law.

However, in a landmark 2020 decision of the European Court of Justice, the court invalidated the 2016 EU-US Data Protection Decision in *Data Protection Commissioner v. Facebook Ireland and Maximillian Schrems* (Schrems II).[5] The case involved an Austrian Facebook user, whose personal data was sent to Facebook servers in Ireland and then subsequently sent to servers in the U.S. pursuant to standard data protection clauses. The claimant sought a court order prohibiting the data transfer to the U.S., alleging that the law and practices in the U.S. did not offer sufficient protection against access by public authorities. An example is the vast powers granted to the American National Security Agency (NSA) under the Foreign Intelligence Surveillance Act or FISA.

The court held that despite the Commission Decision 2016/1250 that enables transfers to countries outside the EU using data protection clauses the Irish supervisory authority was empowered to do an independent inquiry to determine that in fact the foreign country's laws provide the data protection required by the GDPR. The court then invalidated Decision 2016/1250 since U.S. law did not provide an actionable cause of action to EU citizens against American surveillance authorities. It reasoned that Decision 2016/1250 did not fulfill the requirements mandated by the GDPR or the EU Charter of Fundamental Rights.

The court did uphold the safe harbor provisions found in Decision 2010/87,[6] asserting that it contained "effective mechanisms" to ensure compliance with EU law. Unlike Decision 2016/1250, Decision 2010/87 "imposes an obligation on a data exporter and the recipient of the data to verify, prior to any transfer, whether that level of protection is respected in the third country concerned and requires the recipient to inform the data exporter of any inability to comply with the standard data protection clauses." In August 2020, Ireland's Data Protection Commissioner sent Facebook a preliminary order to stop transferring data from the EU to the U.S., signaling a potential crackdown on big tech companies' data sharing practices. Failure to do so could subject Facebook to a $2.8 billion fine. The impact of the preliminary order is not likely to be great. Only time will tell, after additional litigation and inter-government negotiations, the extent to which Schrems II affects bulk data flows from the EU to the U.S.

Article 17 of the GDPR establishes the fundamental right of erasure or **right to be forgotten.** This right is not absolute and must be based on one of the following grounds: (1) personal data are no longer necessary for purposes for which they were collected; (2) data subject withdraws consent; (3) data subject objects to the processing because there are no overriding legitimate grounds for the processing; (4) personal data was unlawfully processed; (5) personal data has to be erased for compliance with a legal obligation; and (6) personal data had been collected in relation to the offer of information society services. The exceptions to the right to be forgotten include exercising the right of freedom of expression and information; compliance with a legal obligation; reasons of public interest in the area of public health; archiving purposes in the public interest, for scientific historical research, or statistical purposes; and the establishment, exercise, or defense of legal claims. Whether someone can be truly forgotten will depend on technology's ability to expunge all copies of that information and whether technology will be able to retrieve supposedly erased information. Companies' unwillingness to "forget" makes it difficult to exercise the right to erasure.

GDPR Compliance

Companies seeking to comply with the GDPR may find it cost-effective to hire a GDPR consultant or appoint a Data Protection Officer (DPO). Failure to comply with the requirements of the GDPR can lead to substantial fines. In 2019, the largest GDPR fine of €50 million was assessed against Google. The French data protection watchdog, CNIL, concluded that the search engine was breaking GDPR rules related to transparency and not having a valid legal basis when processing people's data for advertising purposes.

There are a number of core requirements for GDPR compliance that apply regardless of where the data is processed or where the company is located. GDPR rights also apply against non-EU companies operating in the EU. Obligations of companies or organizations include the duty to respond to requests without undue delay and no longer than one month. Another important duty is found in the principle of "data protection by design and by default." This means that a data processor or controller must consider the data protection principles in the design of any new product or activity.

- Perform an information audit to determine the information you process and who as access to it;
- have a legal justification for data processing;
- provide clear information about data process activities and legal justifications in company's privacy policy;
- encrypt, pseudonymize, or anonymize personal data;
- create an internal security policy;
- conduct periodic data protection impact assessments;
- create processes to notify authorities and data subjects of data breach;
- designate employee to ensure compliance with GDPR; consider hiring an expert Data Protection Officer;
- sign data processing agreements with any third parties that you hire to process data;
- make it easy for customers to make requests and receive information; to correct inaccurate or incomplete information; to stop the processing of their data; to receive a copy of their data in a transferable format; to object to processing;
- organizations that use automated processes to make decisions must have a procedure to protect the rights of data subjects such as the ability to request human intervention into automated decisions and to challenge decisions.

Figure 18.4 GDPR Compliance Checklist.

Suppose, for example, a company launches a new app. It must first consider the personal data the app will collect from users, then consider ways to minimize the amount of data collected and how it will be secured by using the best available technology. In other words, data collectors and processors have to consider data protection from the beginning of their development of data collection and processing operations. The design must include the incorporation of technical safeguards, such as encryption,[7] and organizational measures, such as limiting the amount of personal data collected and deleting data that is no longer needed. Figure 18.4 "GDPR Compliance Checklist" provides the elements for a strong compliance system.

Part of a company's data privacy policy should provide information relating to a customer's or data subject's right to see their personal data, how it is being used, length of time that the data will be stored, and the reason for keeping it that length of time. Upon request, the data processor must send a copy of the data information to the data subject.

Database Protection

The EU has a law dealing with database protection. **Directive 96/9/EC on the Legal Protection of Databases** defines the term *database* as "literary, artistic, musical, or other collections of works or collections of other material such as texts,

1 The making of databases requires the investment of considerable human, technical, and financial resources while such databases can be copied or accessed at a fraction of the cost needed to design them independently;

2 This Directive protects collections, sometimes called *compilations*, of works, data, or other materials, which are arranged, stored, and accessed by means which include electronic processes;

3 No criterion other than originality, in the sense of the author's intellectual creation, should be applied to determine the eligibility of the database for copyright protection, and in particular no aesthetic or qualitative criteria should be applied;

4 Works protected by copyright and subject matter protected by related rights that are incorporated into a database remain, nevertheless, protected by the respective exclusive rights and may not be incorporated into, or extracted from, the database without the permission of the right holder or his successors in title;

Article 3: Object of Protection

1 In accordance with this Directive, databases, which by reason of the selection or arrangement of their contents constitute the author's own intellectual creation, shall be protected as such by copyright.

2 The copyright protection of databases provided for by this Directive shall not extend to their contents and shall be without prejudice to any rights subsisting in those contents themselves.

Article 10: Term of Protection

The right provided for in this Directive shall run from the date of completion of the making of the database and shall expire 15 years from the first of January of the year following the date of completion.

Figure 18.5 Comparative Law: Directive 96/9/EC: Legal Protection of Databases.

sound, images, numbers, facts, and data systematically or methodically arranged and that can be individually accessed." The EU Directive provides special protections to databases that are a product of "considerable investment of human, technical, and financial resources" (see Figure 18.5 *Comparative Law*: "Directive 96/9/EC: Legal Protection of Databases"). If a database is a product of such investment, then the Directive grants its creator or owner a 15-year term of protection.

U.S. law, in contrast, does not protect databases other than by prohibiting the verbatim copying of databases under copyright law. An alternative means of protecting a database in the U.S. is through trade secrets law. However, it is difficult to maintain a database or customer list as a trade secret if it is accessible by a large pool of employees. It is strategically prudent for U.S. companies to review Directive 96/9/EC in order to afford the Directive's protections for its European operations.

E-Commerce and E-Contracting

Doing business on the Internet has become so commonplace that traditional "brick-and-mortar" retail stores have had to aggressively go online or suffer diminished sales. There are three basic types of commercial websites: informational, transactional, and e-marketplaces. *Informational websites* generate sales by promoting corporate awareness rather than facilitating online transactions. They function much like a brochure that provides information about the product or service, as well as contact information needed to purchase. **Transactional websites** are electronic storefronts for brick-and-mortar retailers or catalog businesses. They act as showrooms for manufacturers to sell directly to the public. Transactional websites conduct full "end-to-end" transactions through the website, allowing customers to search for, order, and pay for products online, and obtain after-sales services. The more sophisticated websites integrate online sales with internal systems such as accounting, inventory, service, and sales.

E-Marketplace websites or digital platforms bring buyers and sellers together to facilitate transactions. Participation in a brokerage-style website provides the ability to obtain customers and at the same time avoid the costs of building a proprietary transactional website. Types of brokerages include auctions, virtual malls, and matching services. Popular third-party marketplaces or platforms include eBay, Amazon, and Alibaba. They are price competitive because they make bulk purchases from suppliers and arrange logistics (shipment of goods).

The first generation of electronic contracting was performed through the use of **electronic data interchange (EDI)**. EDI is the computer-to-computer (direct party-to-party) communication of information. For example, in the documentary sales transaction, contracts are electronically formed, electronic bills of lading are sent by third-party record-keeping services, letters of credit can be based upon pre-existing templates, and other necessary documents like insurance certificates will be transmitted electronically. The rules governing EDI transactions are provided in contracts known as **trading partner agreements** or interchange agreements. This form of contracting makes sense in long-term contractual relationships with a relatively modest number of contracting parties.

E-Contracting Law Issues

The open nature of the Internet calls for a legal framework to ensure the security and integrity of Internet transactions. The three major concerns for international electronic contracting are authenticity, enforceability, and confidentiality. Authenticity involves the verification of the identity of the party one is dealing with electronically. Enforceability includes the legal scope of the license granted or the warranty given under a national law. It also includes the provability and verification of the contractual terms of an online transaction.

Confidentiality revolves around the protection of sensitive information such as payment information and trade secrets. The public nature of e-commerce makes such information susceptible to fraud and misappropriation by third parties. The minimum level of due diligence pertaining to these three concerns demands a workable knowledge of the legal requirements of forming and proving a contract through the Internet.

Electronic contracting poses a number of questions about the application of contract law to this medium for transacting business. For example, when and where does an electronic acceptance reach the offeror—upon placement in the offeror's mailbox or when the offeror opens their mailbox? The better answer would seem to be the former because the offeror is inviting acceptance by e-mail and is thus under an implied duty to retrieve their mail in a timely fashion. Such answers depend on the type of communications and information being provided. A non-interactive web page is more like an advertisement or an invitation to make an offer. The next section will review a model law that attempts to provide answers to these and other contract formation questions.

Uniform Computer Information Transactions Act

Uniform Computer Information Transactions Act (UCITA) is a model law enacted to cover the creation, transfer, and licensing of computer information and software. UCITA provides rules for sales of software and the licensing of information. The formation of a contract under UCITA depends on the receipt of the acceptance by the offeror. This is opposite to the common law's acceptance-upon-dispatch or mailbox rule. Receipt of an electronic notice is defined as "coming into existence in an information processing system or at an address in that system in a form capable of being processed by or perceived from the system of that type by a recipient, if the recipient uses, or otherwise has designated or holds out, that place or system for receipt of notices." Thus, a contract is formed even if the receiving party fails to open or read the message of acceptance.

UCITA provides the following rules: (1) downloading of information or *clicking* approval to terms constitutes acceptance. Internet sites must give the licensee an opportunity to review the terms of the license (click-wrap contract); (2) additional terms (standard terms or general conditions) found in the shrink-wrapped license become a part of the contract if the purchaser or licensee is able to review them prior to being obligated to pay; (3) **electronic agents**, such as a computer or voice ordering system can form contracts through the interaction of two electronic agents or by the interaction of an electronic agent and an individual. The contract is formed if the individual takes actions or makes statements that he knows will cause the electronic agent to perform. Additional terms incorporated into the acceptance by the individual do not become a part of the contract if the individual "had reason to know that the electronic agent could not react to the inclusion of additional terms."

Shrink-Wrap Contracts

Computer software is generally sold encased in plastic wrappers. Inside the wrapper are the terms of the contract, including warranty provisions. A **shrink-wrap contract** (license) provides that the purchaser accepts all terms of the license upon opening the package. The purchaser does not see the license terms until after purchasing and taking possession of the software. At issue is whether the parties have actually agreed to the terms provided in the shrink-wrapped package. In *Arizona Retail Systems v. Software Link*, the court concluded that, at best, the license agreement was "a proposal to modify the contract between the parties." Thus, unless expressly agreed to by the purchaser, the standard terms do not become a part of the contract since the license was delivered after the contract had already been formed. An alternative rule would deny the formation of a contract on the shrink-wrap terms unless the buyer has a right to return the goods for a full refund (after reading the terms).

International E-Commerce Developments

Developments in e-commerce and Internet law are ongoing at both the national and international levels. One of the first documents on the subject was the International Chamber of Commerce guide **General Usage for International Digitally Ensured Commerce** (**GUIDEC**) that addresses some of the definitional and legal aspects relating to e-commerce. GUIDEC gives a general framework for ensuring (authenticating) and certifying digital messages. The stated goals of GUIDEC are "to enhance the ability of the international business community, to execute secure digital transactions."

Germany enacted a broad Multi-Media Law, Federal Act Establishing the General Conditions for Information and Communications Services or "Information and Services Act." One of its provisions provides for liability for **Internet service providers** (**ISPs**) for the content of materials accessed through their services. Liability extends only if the ISP knew of the content and had the technical means to prevent its dissemination. The law provides a reasonableness standard when determining if the ISP is jointly liable with the creator or provider of the material. Similar limitations of liability for ISPs are found in the American Digital Millennium Copyright Act.

United Nations Model Law on Electronic Commerce

The United Nations Commission on International Trade Law (UNCITRAL) adopted the **Model Law on Electronic Commerce** (Model Law).[8] The law serves three purposes: it can be used as a model or guide in drafting national legislation, used as a source for the drafting of contracts, and courts and arbitration panels may use it "in interpreting existing international conventions and other instruments as far as they impede electronic commerce."

The United Nations also published a **Guide to Enactment** (Guide) to be used in conjunction with the Model Law.[9] Article 15 provides that an offer or acceptance is received when the message enters the information system of the addressee. Under Article 15(4) of the Model Law, the place of dispatch is the place of business of the sender, making it the choice of law when there is no express choice of law. In contrast, Europe's **Brussels Convention** establishes the domicile of the defendant as the fundamental ground for jurisdiction.[10] Regarding the choice of law, the **Rome Convention** on law applicable to contractual obligations provides that the contract, in the absence of a choice of law clause, is to be governed "by the law of the country with which it is most closely connected." Article 4(2) provides a presumption in favor of the performing party's principal place of business.

Free Trade Agreements

The importance of international e-commerce is recognized by the newer generation of free trade agreements. See the excerpts presented in Figure 18.6 *Comparative Law*: "Korea–U.S. Free Trade Agreement," which are the operative

The Parties recognize the economic growth and opportunity that electronic commerce provides, the importance of avoiding barriers to its use and development, and the applicability of the WTO Agreement to measures affecting electronic commerce.

Article 15.3: Digital Products
Neither Party may impose customs duties, fees, or other charges on or in connection with the importation or exportation of: (a) a digital product fixed on a carrier medium; or (b) a digital product transmitted electronically. Nothing in the agreement precludes a Party from imposing internal taxes or other internal charges on digital products (such as a sales tax).

Article 15.4: Electronic Authentication and Electronic Signatures
Neither Party may adopt or maintain legislation for electronic authentication that would: prohibit parties to an electronic transaction from mutually determining the appropriate authentication methods for their transaction or deny a signature legal validity solely because it is in electronic form.

Article 15.5: Online Consumer Protection
The Parties recognize the importance of maintaining and adopting transparent and effective measures to protect consumers from fraudulent and deceptive commercial practices when they engage in electronic commerce.

Article 15.6: Paperless Trading
Each Party shall endeavor to make trade administration documents available to the public in electronic form.

Article 15.7: Access and Use of the Internet for E-Commerce
To support the development and growth of electronic commerce, each Party recognizes that consumers should be able to access and use services and digital products of their choice and have the benefit of competition among network providers, application and service providers, and content providers.

Article 15.8: Cross-Border Information Flows
Recognizing the importance of the free flow of information in facilitating trade, and acknowledging the importance of protecting personal information, the Parties shall refrain from imposing or maintaining unnecessary barriers to electronic information flows across borders.

The FTA ensures that digital products that are exported or imported between the two countries will pass duty free, whether they are delivered in a fixed medium or electronically transferred. The final provision is a reaction to the EU's imposition of privacy laws aimed at regulating the flow of such information.

Figure 18.6 Comparative Law: Korea–U.S. Free Trade Agreement.

Source: Free trade agreement between the United States of America and the Republic of Korea, U.S.–South Korea, June 30, 2007, Office of U.S. Trade Representative, http://www.ustr.gov/trade-agreements/free-trade-agreements/korus-fta/final-text.

provisions relating to e-commerce. The Parties recognize the economic growth and opportunity that electronic commerce provides, the importance of avoiding barriers to its use and development, and the applicability of the WTO Agreement to measures affecting electronic commerce.

The FTA ensures that digital products that are exported or imported between the two countries will pass duty-free, whether they are delivered in a fixed medium or electronically transferred. The final provision is a reaction to the EU's imposition of privacy laws aimed at regulating the flow of such information.

Internet and Small Businesses

The Internet has facilitated transborder transactions by individuals and small and medium-sized enterprises (SMEs). Before exporting goods through an Internet sale, the exporter needs to classify the product for purposes of export and import regulations. The determination of the classification should be made in consultation with the importer. This is because the classification of the goods will determine the tariff rate charged by the country of import. Shipping companies, custom brokers, and government customs agents also use product information in the transport and importation of the goods. The classification of goods is done using the harmonized tariff schedule (HTS) in which a ten-digit number is assigned to the product. It is a harmonized schedule because the first six digits are the same in all countries. Based on this number, the importing country assigns a tariff rate to collect duties (see Chapter 5).

Figures 18.7 and 18.8 provide brief case studies of two companies' first entries into exporting their goods and the lessons learned. The first case study highlights the importance of properly classifying exported goods and the use of suppliers to provide the necessary information. The second case study illustrates the use of export management consultants to facilitate a company's export function.

ABC, a manufacturer and wholesale stocking distributor, generates significant sales through its website. All international orders go through a single export manager who reviews each order individually, ensures that the order has been paid for, and then forwards it to shipping company. ABC relies on its suppliers to provide much of the information needed for export documentation. However, a nonexpert, using this information, may not properly classify the goods under the HTS. The HTS is a highly detailed code, meaning it is somewhat common to misclassify goods and to conform to the HTS country of origin rules. Such misclassifications may lead to higher import duties and fees, and in some cases, the importation may be barred by the country of import. Any company that wants to expand its international ecommerce sales must budget time and money for export-requirements training and request its shipping company to help with documentation.

Figure 18.7 Focus on Transactions: Case Study: Exporting for the First Time.

A hobby store, Games and Things, restricted it sales to the U.S. market, but recognized that there was a large international market for its products.

Business Challenge

Games and Things decided that exporting to Canadian customers would be the safest and easiest first step. But it soon found out that it had to educate itself on the costs charged by customs brokers, tariffs, and Canadian sales taxes. Games and Things also realized there were other concerns it had to manage, such as credit card fraud and hiring an exporting consultant to handle compliance with export and import regulations.

Approach

Games and Things hired International Export Managers LLC (IEM), a third-party service provider that they interviewed at a retailer trade show. IEM integrated Games and Things' online "shopping cart" to provide the international buyers a U.S. address for order shipment. Once the order arrives at this U.S. address, the orders are packed, the proper documents are completed for international delivery, and the item is shipped to buyers at their international address. IEM also verifies the buyer's credit information and credit card details, provides analysis on potentially fraudulent orders, and forwards the information to Games and Things to determine whether the buyer is likely to be a credit risk. In the end, IEM provided Games and Things the expertise and confidence to market its products internationally.

Figure 18.8 Doing Business Internationally: Case Study: Export Management Consultants.

Payment Methods

Companies that use the Internet to reach overseas customers use websites to process orders and accept payments. The available options include credit card payments, account-to-account transfers, person-to-person transfers, and escrow transactions. Most overseas customers use credit cards for online purchases. *Card verification numbers* (*CVNs*) are three- or four-digit security codes found on credit cards. It is a number only available to the cardholder; the seller requests the CVN to reduce the chance of fraud. However, such numbers could also be stolen, reducing the CVN's effectiveness as a fraud-prevention tool. *IP geolocation* is a service that is available from various companies enabling a seller to identify a prospective buyer's geographic location (country, region, ZIP/postal code) based on the IP address of the computer being used. If the country or region of the buyer's credit card address doesn't match that of the IP address, the seller should investigate or reject the order.

Account-to-account (A2A) transfers involve the electronic transfer of money between a customer's and a seller's bank. A2A transactions occur in real time and offer the additional advantage of reducing the potential for fraud. A person-to-person transfer is when payment is sent electronically to a third party, which in turn deposits the funds in the seller's account. PayPal has become one of the most popular P2P service providers. PayPal lets anyone with an e-mail address use a credit card or bank account to securely send and receive online payments. PayPal will also calculate currency exchange rates. An escrow service is a long-standing payment method now used for export. By definition, an escrow service reduces the potential risk of fraud as the escrow agent acts as a trusted third party that collects, holds, and disburses funds according to the exporter's and importer's instructions.[11]

Electronic Documentation

In the documentary transaction that is central to the exportation of goods, "paper" is becoming less vital. Cost savings are generated by using electronic transmission of documents: "In the transport industry, the cost of using conventional paper documents and the attendant delays involved in their issuance and verification constitute about 10 to 15 percent of total transportation costs."[12] These costs can be reduced by electronically formed contracts, electronic bills of lading, letters of credit issued based upon pre-existing templates, and other necessary documents like insurance certificates being transmitted by computers. The realization that a bill of lading need not be in writing in order to transfer title led the Comité Maritime International (CMI) to produce the Rules for Electronic Bills of Lading.

Bolero Project

The Bolero "concept" is based on a central "registry" for all trade-related documents of title and ensures that documents sent through Bolero would have the same legal meaning as the paper document. Bolero entered into an agreement with SWIFT (bank owned co-operative that secures interbank transmissions) and TT Club (international transport provider of insurance and related risk management services) to create a joint venture company to build, market, and support Bolero infrastructure. In 2010, the operation of the Bolero services was successfully transitioned from SWIFT to a leading-edge commercial hosting facility with full SAS 70 compliance.

> **SAS 70** is the Statement of Auditing Standards. SAS 70 certification is based upon an audit that assesses the quality of a service association's internal controls. Service organizations are entities that provide outsourcing services that impact the control environment of their customers.

Bolero is now a cloud-based platform that links trade with trade finance by providing corporate customers with access to a community of trade enablers, from banks to ocean carriers; users are able to manage their complete financial and trade processes including the use of electronic bills of lading. All Bolero applications are built on the Bolero Exchange, which is a collaborative platform that supports all trade flows between parties across locations. Each Bolero member has access to all other community members. Bolero also provides an **Electronic Bill of Lading** (eBL) approved by the International Group of P&I (Protection and Indemnity) Clubs. Finally, Bolero offers a full range of electronic document templates for all types of transactions, including open account and letters of credit issued under eUCP 600.

> **International Group of P&I (Protection and Indemnity) Clubs** is the umbrella organization of 13 insurance underwriter clubs that provide insurance for about 90 percent of international ocean carriage. P&I covers a wide range of ocean carrier liabilities, such as injuries to crew, cargo loss, oil pollution, and dock damage.

Internet Securities Offerings

There has been a recent trend to offer investment information and securities over the Internet. This has become possible in the U.S. because the American Securities Exchange Commission (SEC) has relaxed a number of regulatory requirements, openly authorizing **direct public offerings** (**DPOs**) over the Internet. Thus, companies may make investment information available directly to prospective investors, prospectuses can be posted online, and sales may be processed over the Internet. A major problem with electronic securities transactions is fraud. Numerous instances of illegal Ponzi and pyramid schemes have been reported, as well as more traditional misrepresentations, such as using the opinion of well-known "investment advisors" who are compensated by the offering party. The SEC established the **Office of Internet Enforcement** to investigate and prosecute cases of Internet securities fraud. The most common is the "pump and dump," where promoters make false claims to artificially drive up the price of a stock in order to sell their own shares at a profit.

E-Commerce Ethics

Along with the need for an adequate legal support structure, electronic commerce carries numerous ethical concerns. The United Nations Educational, Scientific, and Cultural Organization (UNESCO) has raised a number of themes focusing on the ethical, legal, and societal aspects of e-commerce and the information society. UNESCO has noted that while industry and business provide the infrastructure for access to information resources and content, the challenge is to define the concepts of public domain and **universal access** in a global context. Another theme addressed by UNESCO is the special plight of developing countries, especially the inability for many of its citizens to obtain Internet access. This problem is referred to as the **digital divide**.

UNESCO's plan of action states that the following elements need to be addressed within a global context: (1) broader and fairer access to information and communication networks and services; (2) application of legal exceptions to copyright for developing countries through international conventions; and (3) promotion of freedom of expression while protecting privacy on global networks.

Advertising and Marketing Ethics

The International Chamber of Commerce has developed **Guidelines on Advertising and Marketing on the Internet** (**Guidelines**). The Guidelines' purpose is to encourage advertisers and marketers "to create an electronic environment which all the world's consumers can fully trust." Article 1 states that "all advertising and marketing should be legal, decent, honest, and truthful." This core principle requires that: (1) advertisers and marketers should identify themselves and the nature of their connection to any commercial messages placed on the Internet; (2) addressees of commercial messages should be clearly informed of the cost of accessing the message or service; (3) advertisers and marketers should take reasonable precautions to safeguard the security of their files; and (4) advertisers and marketers should post a **privacy policy statement** on their online sites.

Another issue of Internet ethics is the obtaining and monitoring of user information without the consent of the user through the use of "cookies" to store information about the user's Internet use, including frequency, as well as files and pages accessed by the user. The key fear about cookies is that they give a company the ability to link a user's Internet browsing habits to the user's name and provide that information to other companies. The use of uninvited bulk e-mails (spamming) is considered an unethical business practice. Receipt of unwanted e-mail solicitation (spamming) continues to plague Internet users.

Chapter Summary

1. The Internet has transformed the international marketplace by facilitating commercial transactions, seizing at least one-half of the consumer sales market, and creating a larger person-to-person sales market. Internet sales and licensing are regulated by the same laws that apply to storefront sales, but also pose a number of new issues, such as determining the proper forum to settle disputes (personal jurisdiction); spamming and an assortment of Internet abuses, such as fraud and criminal activities; cybersquatting and trademark dilution; privacy of personal information; and the protection of electronic databases.
2. Personal jurisdiction refers to the ability of a court to hear a legal dispute based on whether or not it has authority over the defendant. Court decisions have used numerous factors to make this decision including, type of website (passive, interactive, electronic storefront); commercial or non-commercial website; and the type of claim or injury caused. The EU has enacted regulations that require Internet retailers to defend themselves in the courts of a consumer who is located in an EU country.
3. The U.S. has passed a number of laws that are applicable to trademark infringement and dilution via the Internet, such as the Federal Trademark Dilution Act and the Anti-cybersquatting Consumer Protection Act.
4. The EU's General Data Protection Regulation aggressively deals with the issues of the privacy of personal information collected via the Internet and the protection of electronic databases. Non-EU companies have to conform to this Regulation, but their ability to do so has been made easier through a Safe Harbor Agreement.
5. EU Directive 96/9/EC on the Legal Protection of Databases creates a *sui generis* or new category of intellectual property law that provides a 15-year protection period for databases that meet certain requirements.
6. For long-standing business relationships, Electronic Data Interchange (EDI) is the oldest and most secure form of electronic transactions. The basis of

this relationship is a trading partner agreement entered into by the contracting parties.

7. General contract or sales law applies to electronic transactions on the Internet or through a blockchain (smart contracts). There is a great deal of uncertainty relating to the time of contract formation, contracting with or between electronic agents, and the enforceability of shrink-wrap contracts. A number of hard and soft law legal instruments have been created to provide solutions to issues specific to electronic transactions, such as the Uniform Computer Information Transactions Act (UCITA), the International Chamber of Commerce's General Usage for International Digitally Ensured Commerce (GUIDEC), the United Nations' Model Law on Electronic Commerce, and the Convention on the Use of Electronic Communications in International Contracts.
8. The Internet has allowed small businesses to enter the international marketplace, but this can be a dangerous proposition for the unsophisticated businessperson. Issues that present themselves include the proper classification of the products being exported, payment methods, tax law, and privacy law.
9. Electronic documentation related to the transport of goods, documentary collections transactions, and transfer of funds has increasingly become reality. Examples include the Bolero Project, electronic bills of lading, and eUCP 600.
10. The EU's General Data Protection Regulation (GDPR) provides a comprehensive list of protections and rights to individuals. These rights include the data subject's right to be forgotten (right to have all personal data erased). Data collectors and processors, such as online websites, must be GDPR compliant including non-EU countries that transfer data into or out of the EU.
11. The liability of owners or operators of digital platforms that act as a medium to match supplier-sellers and buyers remains uncertain. The EU Online Platforms Regulation of 2019 provides a legal framework for the regulation of platform liability.

Key Terms

Acceptable Use Policies (AUPs)
Access Contract
Anti-cybersquatting Consumer Protection Act
Authentication
Blocking Right
Blurring
Bolero Project
Brussels Convention
Click-Wrap License
Digital Divide
Digital Platforms
Direct Public Offerings (DPOs)
Directive 96/9/EC on the Legal Protection of Databases
Disclaimer
Electronic Agent
Electronic Bills of Lading (eBL)
Electronic Data Interchange
Federal Trademark Dilution Act
General Usage for International

Digitally Ensured Commerce (GUIDEC)
Guidelines on Advertising and Marketing on the Internet
Minimum Contacts
Model EDI Agreement
Model Law on Electronic Commerce
Notaries
Online Dispute Resolution (ODR)
Online Platforms Regulation of 2019
Personal Jurisdiction
Privacy Policy Statement
Right of Access
Right of Correction
Right of Objection
Right to be Forgotten
Rome Convention
Shrink-wrap License
Spamming
Trading Partner Agreements
Uniform Computer Information Transactions Act (UCITA)
Websites, passive, interactive, doing business

Chapter Problems

1. Marobie released copyrighted clip art. The National Association of Fire Equipment Distributors (NAFED) used the clip art on its webpage so that any web user could download it. Marobie sued NAFED for infringement. Is the Internet service provider liable for infringement? *Marobie-FL, Inc. v. Natl. Assn. of Fire Equipment Distributors* (1997 WL 709747 (N.D. Ill. 1997)).
2. E-Data Corporation (E-Data) is an American corporation with a business office in Connecticut. West Stock, a French corporation with its principal place of business in Paris, licenses stock photography to commercial users. It has no offices, property, or employees in Connecticut. West Stock operates "Muse," an Internet-based stock photography service through which purchasers may electronically select a photograph, license and pay for its use, and download the image—all via the Internet. E-Data claims that West Stock has infringed on its patent. The patented invention is a system for reproducing information embodied in material objects, such as recordings, video games, motion pictures, books, and the like, at point-of-sale locations with the permission of the owner of the information. Specifically, plaintiff claims that defendant West Stock infringes the patent when it offers consumers the opportunity to purchase photography images via the Internet by paying a licensing fee to unlock and instantly download photography images. West Stock moves to dismiss, contending that the court lacks personal jurisdiction over it in Connecticut. Does the Connecticut court have personal jurisdiction over West Stock? *E-Data Corp. v. Micropatent Corp.*, 989 F. Supp. 173 (D. Conn 1997).
3. Employees may send personal e-mails at work just as they may have personal phone conversations. Do employees have a right of privacy in the e-mails? Do employers have the right to monitor employee e-mail? Does an employer have to notify its employees of its intent to monitor? Can an employer monitor e-mail after stating that it would not monitor? *Smith v. Pillsbury Co.*, 914 F. Supp. 97 (E.D. Pa., 1996).

Internet Exercises

1. Explore the various online dispute resolution websites. Assess their benefits and pitfalls. Research the framework and workings of Chinese Internet Courts.
2. Review the EU General Data Privacy Regulation (GDPR) to determine your rights as a data subject. Assume you are constructing a new website which will collect data and determine what steps you should take to comply with the GDPR.
3. Visit the website of the Cyberspace Law Center at http://www.cyberlaw.com. Prepare a report on recent developments in the area of international piracy and patent infringement.
4. Visit the website of Internet Legal Services at http://www.legalethics.com. This site covers legal issues dealing with advertising on the Internet and the confidentiality of e-mail. Report on employer and employee rights pertaining to e-mail privacy.
5. Review the directory of firewall and computer security information at http://www.firewall.com.
6. Review the German Multi-Media Law at http://www.iid.de, http://www.iukdg.de, or http://www.bmbf.de.

Notes

1 126 F.3d 25 (2d Cir. 1997).
2 952 F. Supp. 1119 (W.D. Pa. 1997).
3 *Olmstead v. United States*, 277 U.S. 438, 478 (1928).
4 Implementation date of May 28, 2018, superseding the Data Protection Directive 95/46/EC.
5 Court of Justice of the EU, Case C-311/18 (16 July 2020) (Press Release No 91/20), available at https://curia.europa.eu/jcms/upload/docs/application/pdf/2020-07/cp200091en.pdf.
6 Commission Decision of 5 February 2010 on standard contractual clauses for the transfer of personal data to processors established in third countries.
7 Article 45 of the GDPR provides guidance as to the types of technical measures a company is required to implement: "Taking into account the state of the art, the cost of implementation and the nature, scope, context and purposes of processing as well as the risks and severity for rights and freedoms of natural persons posed by the processing, the controller shall, both at the time of the determination of the means for processing and at the time of the processing itself, implement appropriate technical and organisational measures, such as pseudonymisation, which are designed to implement data-protection principles, such as data minimisation, in an effective manner and to integrate the necessary safeguards into the processing in order to meet the requirements of this Regulation and protect the rights of data subjects."
8 UNCITRAL Model Law on Electronic Commerce: http://www.un.or.at/uncitral; U.N. Doc. A/51/17 Annex I (1996), reprinted in 36 I.L.M. 200 (1997).

9 United Nations Commission on International Trade, UNCITRAL Model Law on Electronic Commerce with Guide to Enactment (Guide No. 3) (1997).

10 See Christopher Glatt, "Comparative Issues in the Formation of Electronic Contracts," 6 *Journal of Law and Information Technology* 34, 61–63 (1996).

11 See, e.g., escrow.com.

12 See Amelia H. Boss, "The International Commercial Use of Electronic Data Interchange and Electronic Communications Technologies," 46 *Business Lawyer* 1787 (1991).

Chapter 19

Digital Economy and Acceleration of Technology

Smart Contracts and Blockchain Technology

Smart contracts are literally computer code that is placed on a blockchain, an open, distributed ledger technology (DLT) that runs on the computers of thousands of users, and which has no central authority. "Smart" refers to the self-performing, self-enforcing quality of smart contracts. These so-called contracts are immutable, meaning that the code cannot be changed, thus ensuring performance. Smart contracts present a particular challenge to contract law and regulation in general.

The idea of smart contracts is inviting to the libertarian notion of small government and little regulatory intervention. Central to this revolution is the idea of "contracting without the state" by entering smart contracts based on blockchain technology. Smart contracts represent mechanisms for enforcing promises, allowing us to make credible commitments with each other on a blockchain. The fundamental question becomes whether we can trust the technology and the people using it without the support of the law and courts.

The core questions pertaining to smart contracts include: (1) Are smart contracts legal contracts or a means to form, perform, or enforce contracts? (2) If they are not "real" contracts, should they be regulated by contract law or otherwise? (3) If deemed to be a type of contract, how does contract law apply to this new form of contracting? (4) Can a form of contracting be truly autonomous, self-enforcing, and independent of the legal system? (5) Is general contract law sufficiently adaptable to regulate smart contracts or will specialized rules be needed?[1]

Smart contracts self-execute (perform the parties' obligations) without the need for human intervention. Smart contracts have recently received tremendous

DOI: 10.4324/9781003469230-24

attention because they are capable of not only automating a contract's execution but also because they are being used in more and more industries. For instance, smart contracts can automate compliance by digitalizing lien and judgment filings and automating renewal and release of liens and licenses. In sum, "a blockchain is a type of database that takes a number of records and puts them in a block (rather like collating them on to a single sheet of paper). Each block is then 'chained' to the next block, using a cryptographic signature. This allows block chains to be used like a ledger, which can be shared and corroborated by anyone with the appropriate permissions."[2]

> The idea of **smart contracts** originated in the mid-1990s, when programmers and legal scholars published a series of papers explaining their potential. Smart contracts are literally computer code that runs on a blockchain, an open, distributed ledger (linking of thousands of computers), and which has no central authority. "Smart" refers to the self-performing, self-enforcing quality of smart contracts. These so-called contracts are immutable (breachless contracts), meaning that the code by default cannot be changed, ensuring performance.

As with earlier Internet contracting, is the smart contract simply a means to contract or a contract in and of itself? In very simplistic contracts, such as the execution of a payment for goods delivered or repayment on a loan, the parties can to an agreement, but instead of going to a lawyer to write the contract they go to automators (lawyer or nonlawyer) to code the agreement. In this case, the coded contract is the equivalent to a written contract. In more complicated agreements, the smart contract is best described as a smart function of a larger written contract. This is why smart contracts are actually "dumb contracts."[3] Flexibility built into contracts through terms that are vague or standard-like, such as a duty to renegotiate due to a change of circumstances, cannot be replicated in code.

In the securities market, smart contracts can facilitate the automatic payment of dividends, stock splits, and liability management, while reducing counterparty and operational risks. In trade finance, smart contracts can facilitate international transfers of goods through faster transmissions of letters of credit and trade payment initiation, while increasing the liquidity of financial assets. Other than that, smart contracts have been proposed for various uses, such as in the areas of derivatives, government record-keeping, auto insurance, and supply chain management. Figure 19.1 "Blockchain Technical Terms" provides definitions of terms related to blockchain technology.

Image 19.1 "Blockchain Transaction: Payment" provides an example of a blockchain transaction. The simplicity of the transaction illustrates the efficiency and security of the blockchain in sending a payment. Smart contracts are used in industries in which the rules of law are fixed and formal (negotiable instrument law and secured transactions law), and the transactions are straightforward. This is why most smart contracts are increasingly used in financial

Blockchain: A distributed ledger taking the form of an electronic database that is replicated on numerous nodes (computers) spread across multiple countries or the entire world. Records in a blockchain are stored sequentially in the form of blocks.
Distributed Ledger Technology (DLT): Identical copies of each record are held on numerous computers (nodes) across countries.
Node: A node is a single computer involved in processing a message in order to reach consensus. Nodes are connected to each other via the Internet. Every transaction is broadcast across the network to all nodes, which through consensus add blocks to the blockchain.
Permissioned/Permissionless: Permissionless blockchains are open, do not have access controls, and reach decentralized consensus through proof-of-work calculations; permissioned blockchains limit participation and do not depend on proof-of-work.
Proof-of-Work: To create a block and append it to the blockchain, each mining node (participant in the network) must provide a proof-of-work (solution to a mathematical problem).
Proof-of-Stake: The whole mining process described above as proof-of-work is inefficient due to the time required for validation and energy consumed by the many nodes. Researchers are working on a different validation mechanism called proof-of-stake, which is an algorithm but, unlike the proof-of-work, it delegates the validation to selected nodes.
Public/Private Blockchain: Blockchains can be private, which means it is only accessible for the selected participants, or public, as in the Bitcoin system, where any party is able to inspect the input parameters and detailed execution of any on-chain smart contract.
Cryptography: Blockchain transactions rely on cryptography, which involves the use of public and private keys. The keys are generated together by a complex algorithm, which guarantees that it is impossible to derive the private key from the public key.
Wallet: It is a software program that allows users to buy, sell, and check the balances of their digital currency.
Consensus Rule: More than 50% of nodes conclude that a proposed block message is authenticated and verified to allow a block to be appended to the chain.
Hash/Hashing: Process by which a grouping of digital data is converted into a single number, called a hash. The number is unique (digital fingerprint) and the source data cannot be reverse engineered.
Mining: A blockchain is made of interconnected blocks. Each block contains a list of all prior transactions. The creation of each block requires a significant amount of computation (mining). Miners are incentivized to add new blocks by earning a virtual currency.
Oracles: Oracles are agents who connect the smart world to the real world; this allows smart contracts to refer to facts in the real world, such as when a contract pays out if a stock exceeds a certain price on a certain date or a price needs to be imputed into the smart contract from a commodity price index.

Figure 19.1 Doing Business Internationally: Blockchain Technical Terms.

transactions and in the transfer of title or liens. Image 19.1 shows how the blockchain works in a simple transaction involving the payment of money. Alice wants to send 20 units of virtual currency to Bob. Alice sends her request to the network of nodes (computers) that authenticate the message from Alice and that Alice has sufficient funds in her account to cover the payment. To add the payment transaction to a block (which has other payment instructions, such as a payment from Jane to Mark) the nodes must solve a complex mathematical

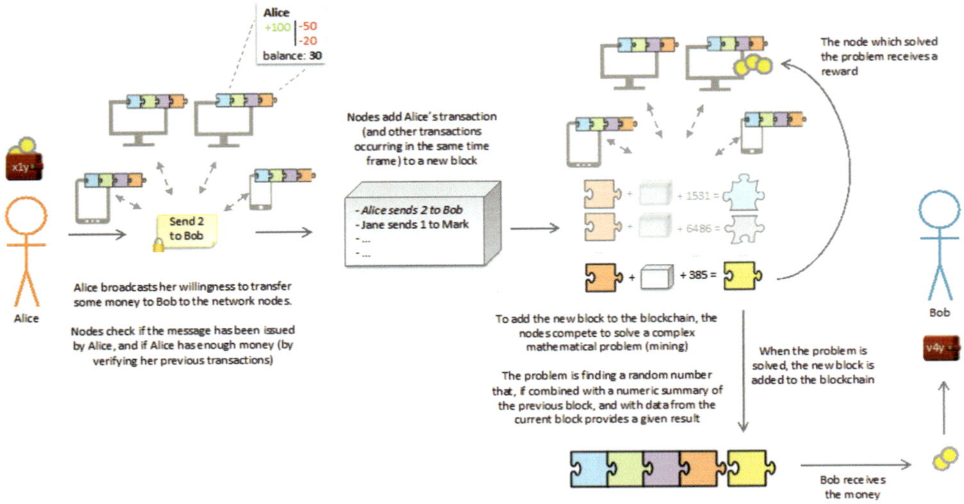

Image 19.1 Blockchain Transaction: Payment.

problem, with the first node to solve the problem receiving an award. At that point, a new block authorizing payment to Bob is added to the blockchain.

Image 19.2 "Blockchain Last Will and Testament" shows the use of the blockchain to record a last will and testament. Alice instructs that her estate is transferred upon her death to her nephew Bob, but only when Bob graduates from college. Therefore, the payment of the inheritance is triggered when two events occur—the death of Alice and Bob's graduation from college. Oracles are used to verify the death of Alice (search and input of death certificate) and of Bob's graduation (input of diploma or graduation certificate).

A bit of caution: smart contracts should not be analyzed through the lens of replacing the existing contract law system. Smart contracts can play an instrumental role aimed in serving the contract law system, such as effectuating payment, but not as an alternative to contract law or the court system. As noted above, smart contracts have been focused on simplistic payment, financial, and transfer of title transactions. These are the most formalized areas of law populated by "if-then" rules that lend themselves to computer coding. However, in more complex, long-term, relational, and ambiguous contract types coding is problematic if not impossible.

In very simplistic contracts, such as the execution of a payment for goods delivered or repayment on a loan, the parties can agree on the contract and have it coded by a third-party technician. In this case, the coded contract is the equivalent to a written contract. In more complicated agreements, the smart contract can at best provide a function or be part of the written contract, such as transferring title to property. Some smart contracts meet the requirements of a fully enforceable contract and others do not.

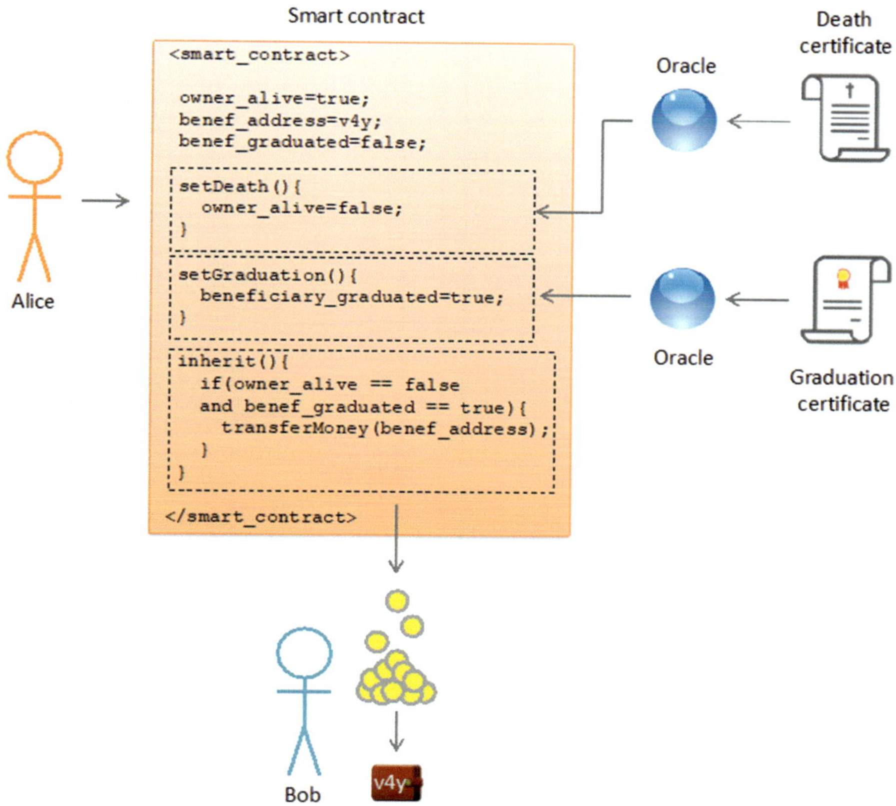

Image 19.2 Blockchain Last Will and Testament.

Other Issues Related to Blockchain and Smart Contracts

One scholar famously claimed that "code is law," based on the premise that codes work outside of law and can act as an alternative to the court system. In fact, code is not law and the law is not *the* code. In simple transactions where the contract is in code, and all the legal requirements of contract formation are met, then the smart contract is a legally enforceable contract. But such contracts, despite being immutable and self-performing, are subject to all the regulatory principles found in contract law such as unconscionability, mistake, misrepresentation, fraud, good faith, and hardship. They are also subject to consumer protection law, subject to interpretation, and the subject for litigation.

The fact that smart contracts are tamper-proof presents another issue. A faulty smart contract could continue to operate. Furthermore, coded contracts, as in most ordinary contracts, cannot anticipate all possible events. Therefore, they will be incomplete and not subject to modification during their lifetimes. More complicated contracts, in which all terms are not framed as if-then propositions, pose translation and interpretation problems that will persist. Put simply, when natural language contracts (wet code) are translated into computer language (dry code), a smart contract code will not completely reflect the natural language contract. From a technical point of view, this could happen because the programmer was not able to code all the information reported in the legal contract. The solution may be that lawyers need to possess coding skills or work closely with programmers in converting contract language into code.

There are a number of legal issues that are unsettled. For example, can each node in the blockchain be considered a data controller and subject to the privacy protections required by the General Data Protection Regulation (GDPR)?[4] The relationship between blockchain and the GDPR is unclear. The European Court of Justice (ECJ) in the case of C-131/12 *Google v. Agencia Española de Protección de Datos*, noted that the GDPR introduced the right to be forgotten (Art. 17), which provides that data subjects have the right to obtain the deletion of their personal data. The problem is that once a piece of data is inserted in the blockchain, it is almost impossible to delete it. The best answer is that since the blockchain decentralizes data it does not fit into the definition of a data controller.[5]

Technology as Regulator

Smart Transactional Technologies (STTs) can have regulatory effects by designing the architecture to modify human behavior. For example, a risk management approach to law would mandate **privacy by design** to control the use and access of personal data. Producers or innovators should be required to design their smart products and services according to privacy standards (as required by the GDPR).

In more general terms, "law by design" can allow for a better allocation of risks, act as a tool for regulatory authorities, and improve legal services delivery. It can also incentivize access to justice by engaging and educating people about the law and providing low cost access to dispute resolution. It can be a dynamic regulatory tool in the service of law. Regulators can learn from best practices using design and technology products to better regulate the acceleration of technology.

Liability Related to Digital Platforms

Digital or electronic platforms provide the means through the Internet by which consumers and other customers can conclude contracts with suppliers of goods, services, and digital content. The EU's **Online Platforms Regulation of 2019** (**Platform Regulation**) is a recognition that liability exemptions for Internet providers should not necessarily apply to all digital intermediaries. Approaches to regulating digital platforms (such as Uber and Airbnb) include general regulations that cover all platforms and sector-specific regulations (e.g., airline ticket or hotel reservation aggregators). The EU Package Travel Directive is an example of sector-specific regulation. The Platform Directive provides general rules and a framework that could be made to apply to other types of all digital platforms. The scope of the proposed Directive is broad: "Directive applies where contracts for the supply of goods, services or digital content are concluded between a supplier and a customer with the help of an online intermediary platform (OIP)."

The general principles of the Platform Directive include transparency, duties of platform operators, and liability of operators. Any posting on the platform must disclose that the supplier paid for a better placement on the platform and reveal the corporate links between the supplier and the platform. Also, a platform operator who provides a reputational feedback system (customer ratings or reviews) on its online intermediary platform must provide information about the methods of collection, processing, and publication of ratings and reviews. The platform operator must verify that reviews are based on a confirmed transaction and if the review had been solicited in exchange for any benefit. If a review is rejected, the reviewer must be informed without undue delay about the rejection. The reviews must be posted in chronological order and if reviews are consolidated into an overall rating, the total number of reviews on which the rating is based must be indicated.

Platform operators owe duties to customers and suppliers. A platform operator must inform the customer that the customer will be entering into a contract with a supplier and not with the platform operator. The operator must also take adequate measures for the protection of platform users if it obtains credible evidence of criminal conduct on the part of suppliers or customers to the detriment of another platform user. Before concluding the platform-supplier contract, the platform operator has a duty to inform the supplier: (1) supplier will supply goods, services, or digital content under contracts with customers and not with the platform operator; (2) fees due to the platform operator; (3) whether the platform operator selects customers for the supplier; and (4) whether the supplier has the right to reject a proposed customer.

The liability of a platform operator is based on a number of grounds, including failure to remove misleading information. The operator also has the duty to customers who reasonably rely on the predominant influence of the platform operator over suppliers to correct misleading statements made on the platform. The platform operator is liable for damages caused by the misleading information unless the platform operator takes appropriate measures to remove or rectify the misinformation.

A platform operator who presents itself to customers and suppliers as an intermediary is not liable for non-performance under supplier-customer contracts. However, the operator may be held jointly liable with the supplier for nonperformance (of the supplier–customer contract) based on the following criteria: supplier–customer contract is concluded exclusively through facilities provided on the platform; platform operator can withhold payments made by customers under supplier–customer contracts; terms of the supplier–customer contract are essentially determined by the platform operator; price to be paid by the customer is determined by the platform operator; platform operator provides a uniform image of suppliers or a trademark; marketing is focused on the platform operator and not on the suppliers; and the platform operator promises to monitor the conduct of suppliers.

Legal Technology (Legaltech)

New technology has had many positive effects but can also be disruptive of pre-existing ways of doing business. Law practice is one business that has been and will be impacted as legal technology (legaltech) continues to accelerate. The digitalization and the development of automated systems, as well as the evolution of artificial intelligence (AI), has and will change the practice of law. The wide range of existing **legaltech** applications include: contract drafting software, data case law mining, algorithmic predictions of litigation outcomes, electronic discovery (e-discovery), legal tech in the courtroom, legal tech enhancement of arbitration, and creation of smart online dispute resolution platforms (ODR), as well as legal advice and services platforms. It is important for the legal community to have a framework for analyzing the benefits and costs of new technology and computer programs before implementing them into legal practice. The costs of using new technologies include potential legal and business risks, as well as ethical concerns and technological problems.

Recent initiatives include using AI to help build legal briefs and using blockchain-related technology in real estate transactions. E-discovery is the electronic aspect of identifying, collecting, and producing electronically stored information (ESI) in response to request for production in a lawsuit or investigation. ESI includes, but is not limited to, e-mails, texts, documents, presentations, databases, voicemail, audio and video files, social media, and website usage. Among all AI developments, its application in legal research is the most significant. It uses machine-learning algorithms to conduct natural language searches to retrieve the most relevant cases related to a legal issue or topic and then ranks the cases.

Online Legal Services

Online legal products and services allow ordinary people and small businesses to find affordable legal help. However, their services are limited to simple types of transactions, such as establishing a business organization and writing a will. So far, online pseudo-law firms have not developed as a substitute for traditional legal services. Law firms with sound reputations are better structured with respect to their legal teams and resources to provide qualified legal services.

Internet and Digital Courts

Online Dispute Resolution (**ODR**) has been used for decades, established by trade associations, arbitration institutes, and other private entities. ODR includes online mediation, arbitration, and customer complaint systems. The next generation of online dispute resolution includes the development of public (government) established ecourts. E-courts or "intelligent courts" have been defined as the use of technologies, such as the Internet, cloud computing, big data, and AI to promote the modernization of trial systems and judgment capability, so as to achieve a highly intellectualized operation and management of the courts.

The development of online courts has evolved from purely informational or passive websites that provide information about the judicial process to interactive court websites where a party may contact the court for updates on specific procedures, receive a consultation, and file a complaint. The next generation court will fully integrate information communications technology into the daily operations of the courts. China has begun to create an e-court system. At this time, it is limited to online sales on certain digital platforms. But it provides a template for future advances in online court systems. Its features include: (1) compulsory online pretrial mediation; (2) registration through Alipay-Alibaba; (3) evidence based on records archived on online platform systems (immediately available); (4) enforcement of judgments through payment order confirmed by the e-court; and (5) e-court record-keeping through data storage and cloud computing services. The future will see the advent of AI or robotic judges, initially engineered to handle simple types of complaints.

Internet courts are dedicated to resolving Internet-related disputes through online litigation platforms. With Internet courts, the entire litigation process can be conducted online, including filing a case, service of process, mediation, exchange of evidence, pretrial preparation, court hearing, verdict, and execution of judgment. In 2017, China launched three Internet courts in Hangzhou, Beijing, and Guangzhou. The appearance of Internet courts and the use of technologies, especially tamper-proof technologies, to store and authenticate evidence benefits lawyers in two ways. The first benefit is that having trials online offers more flexibility in time and space for lawyers. Lawyers will not need to spend time traveling to courts. They can instead spend more time doing legal research or preparing defense strategies, bringing higher-quality legal services to customers. Another benefit is that using tamper-proof technologies to store and authenticate evidence reduces the lawyer's burdens to prove the authenticity of evidence. For example, pictures, texts, or transaction histories stored on the blockchain are tamper-proof.

Legal Ethics

Legal practice has confronted new ethical challenges in the digital age; those challenges will only become more complicated in the future, with the use of advanced AI and other emerging technologies. These technologies may compromise the lawyer's duties of competence, diligence, and confidentiality. With AI, "one of the most notable issues is known as the **black box** challenge: A lawyer submits a query to an AI-powered tool, it goes into a black box, and the AI-based solution provides an answer. AI-powered tools provide one answer to the legal enquiry, but lawyers often need to have numerous answers to different questions in order to meet the ethical requirements of competence and diligence." In addition to ethical issues caused by delegating legal work to an AI-powered tool, lawyers face the problem of underutilizing AI, resulting in less efficient services for clients. Lawyers also bear the burden of understanding the benefits and risks associated with legaltech tools and of further determining whether and how to use them to properly meet their ethical obligations. The exponential growth of data and the risk of data breaches is the other area of difficulties lawyers encounter in upholding their ethical duty of confidentiality. Data security will become a core task for law firms.

Notaries and the Blockchain

The blockchain has the potential to enhance and disrupt the work of the notary profession in Europe and elsewhere. Unlike in the U.S., where a non-professional notary public verifies signatures often without being paid a fee, **notaries** in Europe have expanded duties and are considered professionals, alongside lawyers.

> **European notaries** are legal professionals who act as public officers, whose services are required for certain legal transactions. European-style notaries provide impartial advice and authentication of legal documents. Notaries possess exclusive competence to draw up legal instruments incorporating and modifying enterprises, in addition to certifying many legal instruments, such as minutes of corporate meetings. In the area of real estate, notaries are given exclusive competence to draw up sales contracts and monitor the legal certainty of transactions. Notaries provide impartial advice to sellers and buyers. They are real estate specialists and, in authenticating the final contract, give it probative value and enforceability. Notaries also provide answers to legal and tax questions raised by families with respect to their estate: marriage contracts, registered partnerships, donations, wills, and succession settlements. The Council of the Notariats of the European Union (CNUE) is the official body representing the notarial profession in the 22 EU Member States based on Latin civil law.

The blockchain can provide a traceable history of any document recorded and, more easily than a notary, it can verify that there have been no alterations to a document. Once the recipient receives a signed document and checks the unchanged history of this document on the blockchain, he or she can be confident that this document is the same as what the notary witnessed. Luxembourg has launched the first European notary blockchain system. The system allows the following: registering certain kinds of documents, ensuring their integrity over time, and providing a time stamp for the registration. It optimizes the security and collaboration of notarization processes while reducing costs and guarantees the immutability of records. Therefore, the blockchain is likely to transform notary services.

Acceleration of Technology

The acceleration of technology, most noticeably the innovation of Advanced AI and **Generative AI** (AI that creates original content), raises numerous legal and ethical issues. Advanced AI will create disruption in almost all sectors of the economy and society. Image 19.3 "Deep Learning" shows the advancement of AI from its earlier form as a means to automation, to self-learning algorithms, to deep learning that includes generative AI and neural networks. Generative AI is not to be confused with general intelligence since it creates based on human instructions known as prompts. General intelligence currently only exists in the human brain. The ultimate advancement of AI is likely to be what has been called superintelligence or **Artificial General Intelligence** (**AGI**). This type of AI would match or surpass human capabilities across a wide range of cognitive tasks including human reasoning.

The bleakest vision is that AI poses an existential threat to humanity with the potential of replacing human control and decision-making. In response, there

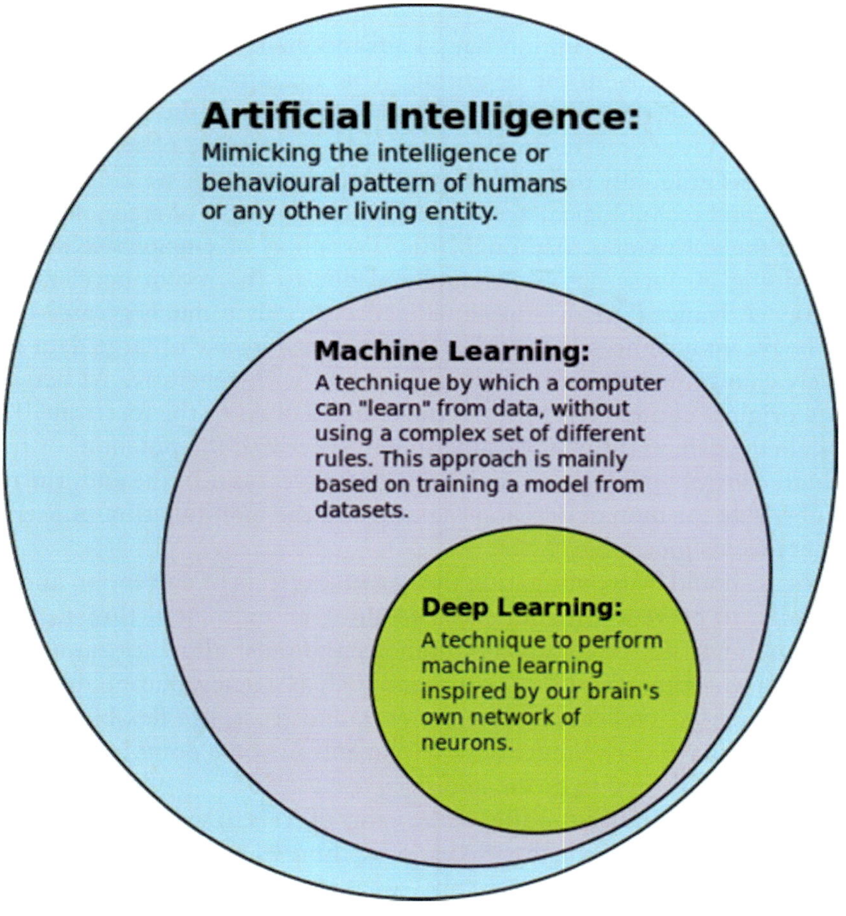

Image 19.3 "Deep learning is a subset of machine learning and machine learning is a subset of artificial intelligence (AI)" (Author: Original file: Avimanyu786; SVG version: Tukiiaaliwa, 12 May 2020, https://commons.wikimedia.org /wiki/File:AI-ML-DL.svg.)

is the belief that the benefits of AI are too great and its development is an inevitability. Therefore, the most prudent approach is to foster the development of **Responsible AI** that seeks certain beneficial outcomes but not at the expense of harm to human rights, human dignity, and democratic values. Thus, the issue becomes one of determining the best approach to governing AI. The best approach is likely to consist of a layered scheme that includes self-regulation by AI companies, hard law (government regulation), soft law (ethical codes), and standardization (regulation by design). Standardization is the notion that AI will need to be designed to regulate itself. The following sections further examine these different facets of the regulation of AI.

AI as Disruptive Force

Societal and economic disruption due to advancements in technology has been a part of humankind from the beginning. One example is the transition from a mostly agrarian economy to the industrial age toward the end of the nineteenth century. Over time stalwart career paths were made obsolete. The need for blacksmiths gradually diminished, while the demand for welders arose. The information and technological age is just another example of technological disruption of the status quo. Although, the disruption of employable skills and ways of doing business has been amplified due to the recent acceleration of technology. Advanced AI or superintelligence promises much greater disruption.[6] The recent advances in machine learning with its use of large data sets to effectively change human created algorithms and with generative AI being able to create original content has brought the dangers of AI to the forefront. This is the so-called existential threat of superintelligence with the potential of replacing human control and decision-making with its creation. In the end, the use of AI to substitute for human decision-making and the manipulation of users and consumers seems inevitable.

The focus should be on mitigating the negative effects of disruption and using smart design to prevent AI from ever becoming an existential threat. AI decision-making must not be totally autonomous and must allow for human intervention. Current legal and ethical concepts, such as agency, autonomy, fairness, contract, property, intellectual property (IP), and trust, are flexible enough to regulate abuse in the early stages of development. At some point in time specialized regulation will need to be created.

The most positive understanding of the value of AI is to see it as a public good: "One area of great optimism about AI and machine learning is their potential to improve people's lives by helping to solve some of the world's greatest challenges and inefficiencies."[7] On the negative side, AI can manipulate people into decisions that are not in their best interests. This manipulation is referred to as **dark patterns** where user-consumer choice and free will are effectively eliminated. Examples of types of AI manipulation that would be considered dark patterns include: (1) *nagging* (repeatedly asking users to consent to cookies although they have already refused), (2) *obstruction* (making a process needlessly difficult to dissuade actions such as restrictive consent to cookies), (3) *sneaking* (hiding or delaying relevant information), (4) *interface interference* (manipulating the user interface to privilege certain actions over others), and (5) *forced action* (requiring a certain action to access functionality).[8]

The European Commission, in June 2018, established the High-Level Expert Group on Artificial Intelligence which began work on *Ethics Guidelines on Trustworthy AI* (Trustworthy AI). Subsequently, in 2020, the Council of Europe (COE) Ad hoc Committee on Artificial Intelligence (CAHAI) published *Towards a Regulation of AI Systems* (Towards Regulation). Towards Regulation lists a number of ethical themes and related issues as shown in Figure 19.2 *Comparative Law:* "Towards Regulation of AI."

There is generally a feeling that AI brings both risks and benefits. There, the benefits of personalization (targeted advertising) must be balanced against the risks, such as discrimination and manipulation. The autonomous car, for instance, has the potential to be safer and deliver us faster to our destinations than traditional vehicles. Data protection regulation relies on disclosure and consent, but consent fatigue reduces its effectiveness. At minimum, regulation is needed to protect fundamental rights in the AI context and also to consider whether psychological harm should be claimable in court. AI also has implications for the enforcement of consumer protection law.[9] There are also concerns about opacity (blackbox effect), potential bias, and cyber-security risks from the transfer of data.

1. *Justice* is mainly expressed in terms of fairness and prevention (or mitigation) of algorithmic biases that can lead to discrimination; fair access to the benefits of AI (designing AI systems especially when compiling the training datasets).
2. *Nonmaleficence and privacy*: misuse via cyberwarfare and malicious hacking (privacy by design frameworks).
3. ***Responsibility and accountability:*** includes AI developers, designers, and the entire industry sector.
4. *Beneficence*: AI should benefit "everyone," "humanity," and "society at large."
5. *Freedom and autonomy*: freedom from technological experimentation, manipulation, or surveillance (pursuing transparent and explainable AI, raising AI literacy, ensuring informed consent).
6. *Trustworthiness*: control should not be delegated to AI (processes to monitor and evaluate the integrity of AI systems).
7. *Dignity*: prerogative of humans but not of robots; protection and promotion of human rights; not just data subjects but human subjects

Figure 19.2 Comparative Law: Towards Regulation of AI (Council of Europe, Ad hoc Committee on Artificial Intelligence).

Regulation of AI

"EU consumer law pivots around the principles of protection of the weaker party, regulated consumer autonomy, non-discrimination and consumer privacy. However, core legislation, such as the Unfair Commercial Practices Directive (UCPD) fails to protect consumers from AI-related risks,"[10] while the Digital Services Act only applies to companies that operate platforms and not when they supply directly. Nonetheless, its scope could be expanded to cover AI systems in general. Article 30 of the DSA provides:

> Providers of online platforms allowing consumers to conclude distance contracts with traders shall ensure that traders can only use those online platforms to promote messages on or to offer products or services to consumers located in the Union if, prior to the use of their services for those purposes, they have obtained the following information, where applicable to the trader:
>
> (a) the name, address, telephone number and email address of the trader;
> (b) a copy of the identification document of the trader or any other electronic identification as defined by Article 3 of Regulation (EU) No. 910/2014 of the European Parliament and of the Council;
> (c) the payment account details of the trader;
> (d) where the trader is registered in a trade register or similar public register, the trade register in which the trader is registered and its registration number or equivalent means of identification in that register;
> (e) a self-certification by the trader committing to only offer products or services that comply with the applicable rules of Union law.

Furthermore, Article 54 of the DSA provides a right of private action by an aggrieved consumer seeking compensation.

The EU Digital Content Directive's (DCD) main use is directed at consumers that deal with an unreliable, fraudulent, or even fictitious traders contacted through AI-driven platforms. Another issue is the applicability of the right of withdrawal from distance contracts given to consumers by Article 9 of the Consumer Rights Directive (CRD). One solution to the risk of consumers falling victim to fraudulent or even fictitious merchants is to place a duty on AI platforms "to vet potential merchant participants and accept to the marketplace only those that meet certain criteria of creditability, and verifying their identity and payment account details."[11] Article 25 of the Digital Services Act (DSA)[12] states that: "Providers of online platforms shall not design, organise or operate their online interfaces in a way that deceives or manipulates the recipients of their service or in a way that otherwise materially distorts or impairs the ability of the recipients of their service to make free and informed decisions."

Advanced AI, including generative AI and the metaverse (see below), poses challenges to the law and to society as a whole. The proper governance of AI is unresolved but a multi-pronged approach will be needed to regulate AI as is the case with any new method or way of doing business. This would include the application of existing laws on standard terms, data protection, privacy, and human or fundamental rights. It will also require new regulatory rules specific to the risks that AI presents. But given the uncertainty of what those risks may entail, and the fluidity of risk assessments given the changing nature (intrusiveness) of AI systems, a general regulatory apparatus is an essential ingredient for managing the danger and risks of AI in the present and future (see AI Act below).

Standard terms regulation applicable to AI contracts is the **EU Unfair Contract Terms Directive** (**UCTD**).[13] The difference being that standard terms regulation relating to the creation, licensing, and use of AI systems should apply to commercial (B2B) and consumer contracts (B2C). The EU is initiating the trend of controlling standard terms in both B2B and B2C contracts in digital markets. The EU's **Artificial Intelligence Act** (**AI Act**) was enacted into law on May 13, 2024. Commentary on the Regulation has focused on its risk-based approach and failure to adequately protect consumer interests. The review here does not take a position on the sufficiency of the AI Act but on what it states about the role of ethical principles in the regulation of AI. Recital 6 states that "as a prerequisite, artificial intelligence should be a human-centric technology. It should serve as a tool for people, with the ultimate aim of increasing human well-being." The nefarious use of AI manipulation—use of biometric data (Recitals 14 and 15), emotion recognition systems (Recital 18), and facial recognition (Recital 43)—allows operators of AI to nudge users into making decisions that are not in their self-interest or are not true expressions of free choice. Recital 29 prohibits such uses.

The placing on the market, putting into service or use of certain AI systems intended to distort with the objective or the effect of materially distorting human behavior, whereby significant harms occur, in particular having sufficiently important adverse impacts on physical and psychological health, or financial interests. Psychological harms are particularly dangerous and should therefore be forbidden.

The role of ethical principles is noted in numerous places in the AI Act. Recital 25 requires that "any research and development activity should be carried out in accordance with recognised ethical and professional standards for scientific research." The role of ethics is most evident in the AI Act's call for the voluntary creation of **Codes of Conduct** guided by the EU's new **AI Office**: "to ensure that the Codes of Practice reflect the state of the art and duly consider a diverse set of perspectives, the AI Office should collaborate with relevant national authorities, and could, where appropriate, consult with civil society organisations and other relevant stakeholders and experts."[14]

EU Artificial Intelligence Act

The EU AI Act is the first law that provides a framework for the general regulation of AI. The general scope of the AI Act will be reviewed here, along with its shortcomings. The AI Act's stated purpose is to ensure "a high level of protection of health, safety and fundamental rights." Although it is not considered a consumer protection law, it is likely to be used to address the abuse and manipulation of consumers since it is the only law that deals with the risks of AI.[15]

Banned Applications

The new rules ban certain AI applications that threaten citizens' rights, including biometric categorization systems based on sensitive characteristics and untargeted scraping of facial images from the Internet or CCTV footage to create facial recognition databases. Emotion recognition in the workplace and schools, social scoring, predictive policing (based solely on profiling a person or assessing their characteristics), and AI that manipulates human behavior or exploits people's vulnerabilities are also forbidden.[16]

Obligations for High-Risk Systems

Obligations under the AI Act depend on the degree of risk attributed to a given AI system. The AI Act categorizes AI uses as Unacceptable Risk (banned applications), High-Risk, Limited Risk, and Minimum Risk. Figure 19.3 *Comparative Law:* "Risk-Based Focus of AI Act" shows the different designated levels of risk and regulation incorporated into the AI Act. Obligations of AI creators and platforms are clearest for high-risk AI systems (due to their significant potential for harm to health, safety, fundamental rights, environment, democracy, and the rule of law). Examples of high-risk AI uses include use in critical infrastructure, education and vocational training, employment, essential private and public services (e.g., healthcare, banking), certain systems in law enforcement, migration and border management, justice and democratic processes (e.g., influencing elections). Such systems must assess and reduce risks, maintain use logs, be transparent and accurate, and ensure human oversight. Citizens will have

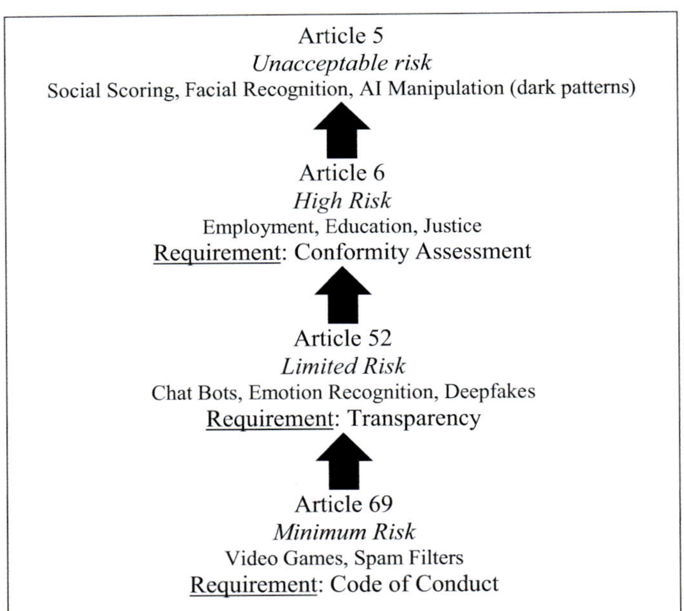

Figure 19.3 Comparative Law: Risk-Based Focus of AI Act.

a right to submit complaints about AI systems and receive explanations about decisions made by high-risk AI systems that affect their rights.

The AI Act primarily aims to regulate high-risk AI systems that create adverse impact on people's safety or their fundamental rights. The draft text distinguished between two categories of high-risk AI systems. First, systems used as a safety component of a product or falling under EU health and safety harmonization legislation (e.g., toys, aviation, cars, medical devices, lifts). Second, systems deployed in eight specific areas specified in Annex (e.g., law enforcement), which the Commission could update as necessary through delegated acts. Such high-risk AI systems would have to comply with a range of requirements particularly on risk management, testing, technical robustness, data training and data governance, transparency, human oversight, and cybersecurity before being placed on the market or put into service. AI systems that conform to new harmonized EU standards would benefit from a presumption of conformity with the AI Act's requirements.

Providers of a high-risk AI system must perform a conformity assessment before making the system available. Article 3 of the AI Act defines conformity assessments as the process of verifying and/or demonstrating that a high-risk system complies with certain requirements laid out in the Act. These requirements include the implementation of: (1) risk management system; (2) data governance; (3) technical documentation; (4) record keeping; (5) transparency and provision of information; (6) human oversight; and (7) accuracy, robustness, and cybersecurity. The process of performing a conformity assessment is seen in Image 19.4.

AI systems presenting limited risk, such as systems that interact with humans (chatbots), emotion recognition systems, and AI systems that generate or manipulate image, audio, or video content (deepfakes), would be subject to a limited set of transparency obligations. Finally, all other AI systems presenting only low or minimal risk could be developed and used in the EU without conforming to

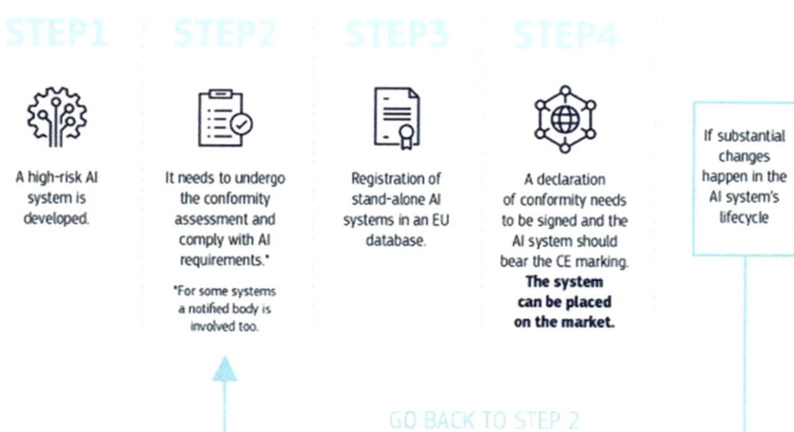

Image 19.4 Conformity Assessment Process.

Source: European Commission, "AI Act," https://digital-strategy.ec.europa.eu/en/policies/regulatory-framework-ai

any additional legal obligations. However, the AI Act envisaged the creation of codes of conduct to encourage providers of non-high-risk AI systems to apply the mandatory requirements for high-risk AI systems voluntarily.

Transparency Requirements

General-Purpose AI (GPAI) systems must meet certain transparency requirements, including compliance with EU copyright law and publishing detailed summaries of the content used for training. The more powerful GPAI models that could pose systemic risks will face additional requirements, including performing model evaluations, assessing and mitigating systemic risks, and reporting on incidents. Additionally, artificial or manipulated images, audio, or video content (**deepfakes**) need to be clearly labelled as such.

It prohibits the placing on the market, putting into service, or use of an AI system that:

(a) deploys subliminal techniques beyond a person's consciousness or purposefully manipulative or deceptive techniques, with the objective to or the effect of materially distorting a person's or a group of persons' behavior by appreciably impairing the person's ability to make an informed decision, thereby causing the person to take a decision that that person would not have otherwise taken in a manner that causes or is likely to cause that person, another person, or group of persons significant harm;

(b) exploits any of the vulnerabilities of a person or a specific group of persons, including characteristics of such person's or such group's known or predicted personality traits or social or economic situation, age, physical or mental ability, with the objective or to the effect of materially distorting the behavior of that person or a person pertaining to that group in a manner that causes or is likely to cause that person or another person significant harm.

A key issue in claims of being harmed by AI is which party has the burden of proof. The burden of proof is about how or why an AI system reached a certain harmful output. In the case of a claim for damages against a provider of a high-risk AI system pursuant to Article 4(5) of the AI Act, national courts would presume that noncompliance of the requirements of the AI Act was the cause of the harm to support a claim for damages. When the damages have been caused by a non-high-risk AI system under the AI Act, the presumption would only apply where the national court considers it excessively difficult for the claimant to prove the causal link between the AI system and the harm or damages claimed. Furthermore, the presumption of causality does not apply if the defendant proves that the claimant has sufficient evidence and expertise to prove the causal link between the fault of the defendant and the output produced by the AI system or the failure of the AI system to produce an output that gave rise to a relevant damage.

Consumers must be informed when they interact with an AI system or when their emotions or characteristics are recognized through automated means.[17] To ensure proper enforcement, several governing bodies are set up: An **AI Office** within the Commission to enforce common rules across the EU, **Scientific Panel of Independent Experts** to support the enforcement activities, **AI Board** with member states' representatives to advise and assist the Commission and member states on consistent and effective application of the AI Act and an **Advisory Forum for Stakeholders** to provide technical expertise to the AI Board and the Commission.

Rise of Non-Fungible Tokens (NFTs)

Tokens held and transferred on the blockchain are generally associated with cryptocurrencies like Bitcoin and Ethereum. Such tokens are fungible in that they are all the same—one Bitcoin is identical to another. More recently **non-fungible tokens** (**NFTs**) have drawn interest creating NFT marketplaces. NFTs leverage blockchain technology to certify the authenticity and ownership of unique digital objects. His Majesty Treasury's Consultation on the Future of the Financial Services Regulatory Regime for Cryptoassets distinguishes NFTs from other types of cryptoassets in stating that: "NFTs are cryptoassets which confer digital ownership rights of a unique asset, such as a piece of digital art (see Image 19.5), using a technology such as digital ledger technology or DLT (blockchain) to support the recording and storage of data."

One of the popular NFT marketplaces uses the **Ethereum** blockchain where the token keeps a record of who owns the file, but the art is stored in a file that exists off the blockchain. NFT stands for ownership of something not directly stored on the blockchain such as a piece of digital art. A token representing digital art might contain a URL pointing to the art and a hash of the art file.[18] This presents the problem of whether ownership of an NFT is the same as ownership of the underlying asset. Under traditional concept of property law this may not

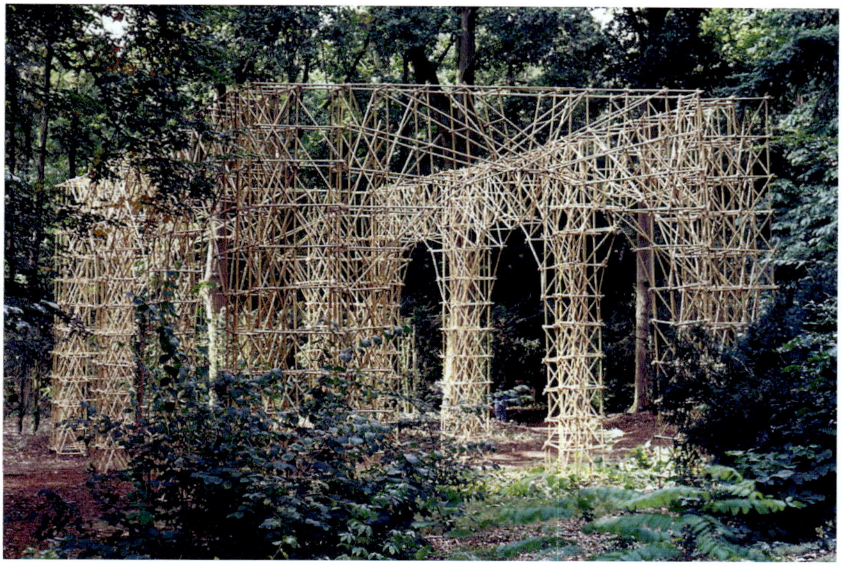

Image 19.5 NFT of Transient Wood Structure.

be the case. First, the NFT is restricted by the terms and conditions of the smart contract. Second, the creator of the underlying asset often retains certain ownership rights such as the right to commercialize the asset. Third, there are other bodies of law that could be used to classify NFTs, such as intellectual property law, contract law, and securities law. None of these other laws are good fits for NFTs in protecting the interests of the purchasers of NFTs.

Blockchains and smart contracts are the backbone of the NFT ecosystem. But this fact is not pivotal in determining how an NFT should be characterized as a matter of law. As noted above, various views see NFTs as legal titles to a digital asset or personal property, as a type of financial instrument or security, a license given by the creator of the asset (contract rights), or as a type of intellectual property. The development of NFTs shows that not all crypto or digital assets are the same. Personal property generally requires that the property be tangible (physical and movable). In this sense, an NFT does not qualify as property. Image 19.6: "NFT Ownership Diagram" shows the features of an NFT (smart contract). Note the statement that it is not copyrightable but can be owned. It is transferred through a smart contract but the underlying asset (example: digital art) is separate from the NFT. The description of the diagram states: "A diagram illustrating the ownership of NFTs, which may not guarantee the ownership of the asset itself." It has been argued that despite these failings the best approach is to treat NFTs as a form of digital property.

The common and civil law traditions share a past, before the advent of the digital age, in which property law was divided into two categories—real property (land) and personal property. The major categories of personal property were ownership of raw materials or of goods. However, the common law has been more willing to expand the notion of property beyond the need for tangibility.

Image 19.6 NFT Ownership Diagram.

Author: Alhadis, commons.wikimedia.org/wiki/File:NFT_ownership _diagram .svg (public domain).

In short, the common law applies the term property to both a physical thing and rights: "In English the word 'property' is used interchangeably to describe an object of property (the actual thing), as well as the relationship between a person and a thing, and the rights which the person has over things."[19] For example, the rights to royalties, although intangible, are viewed as a type of property that can be used as collateral to obtain a commercial loan.

Thus, the common law has a more diverse view of property that covers tangible and intangible things, while the civil law retains an older view of property needing to have a corporeal or physical dimension. The civil law concept of *numerus clausus* principle means that there is a limited number of forms of property. Therefore, parties are not free to create new forms of property and instead other forms are best handled under contract law. In this way, the common law view is more flexible and easier in applying property concepts to digital assets. The incorporeal nature of digital assets makes the categorization of NFTs as personal property almost impossible under civil law. Nonetheless, there has been a recent tendency to apply property law rules to tokens, which has been the case in Germany, that probably has the strictest approach where only "things" can be owned. According to § 903 and § 90 of the German Civil Code (BGB), "things" (*Sache*) are physical objects. However, although NFTs are not physical, they have other characteristics common with personal property—their uniqueness (one of a kind) and permanence (on the blockchain). Because of these attributes, NFTs can be viewed as things within the meaning of Section 90 BGB. Thus, the application of property law rules to NFTs would allow them to be capable of being owned within the meaning of Section 903 BGB. In the case of ownership of virtual land or buildings in video games or a metaverse, the use of real property law may prove useful. This is plausible because the blockchain operates as a type of clerk of records equivalent to physical land record offices.

Even though the property law approach to NFTs seems best fitted to protect NFT purchasers and create a robust NFT marketplace, other approaches have been suggested. In the U.S., certain cryptocurrencies and initial coin offerings (ICOs) come within the reach of securities law, but NFTs due to their uniqueness and lack of an investment contract makes it difficult to argue that they are part of a common enterprise. In sum, NFTs are not securities.

Another approach is to view NFTs as within the domain of intellectual property law and believe they should be protected by trademark and copyright law. But this is also not a good fit since digital creations, such as a composite digital artwork or personal avatars (sold as NFTs) have not been subject to trademark or copyright protection. The problem of viewing NFTs as the transfer or licensing of intellectual property rights is that the underlying asset would have to be recognized as a form of intellectual property. At the present, NFTs and their underlying assets do not meet the threshold of originality or creativity required under trademark and copyright law.

Finally, NFTs can be viewed merely as representing contract rights and within the scope of contract law. Contracts play a major role in the creation of an NFT through the "terms and conditions" set by the NFT platform and transferred through smart contracts (minted by the creator or seller and sold to a purchaser). The relationship between property and contract is that property has intrinsic value, while contracts serve as the means to transfer property. The fact that property is sold or leased through a contract, and includes restrictions on the use of the property, does not support an argument that contract law preempts the application of property law.

The ownership of NFTs and the meaning of that ownership will depend on whether they are recognized as a contract (license), intellectual property, security, or as personal property.

The most rational approach is to recognize NFTs as a type of personal property. It is through the application of property law to NFTs that the emerging NFT market can best be protected. A major benefit of viewing NFTs as personal property (goods) is the applicability of the well-developed area of sales law to regulate the transfer of NFTs. The property designation also clears the way to recognize NFTs as collateral for the purpose of securing loans and allows them to be subject to inheritance.

Law and the Metaverse

It is difficult to give a definition of the metaverse. The literal meaning of metaverse is "beyond the universe." At most, we can simply state its main characteristics: it is an online service that allows access to a virtual world, in 3D, in real time, and which is persistent and shared. At present, some metaverses are non-immersive, while others are immersive and require the use of virtual reality headsets.[20] Major tech companies are investing large amounts of money in an attempt to create fully immersive virtual realities. Users will create their own personas known as **avatars** to experience the virtual world and interact with other avatars. A fully immersive metaverse is still in the future, but the legal issues that it will elicit can be studied in the present. The purpose of this section is to review the areas of law and society that will be most impacted.

The metaverse is often connected to the term Web 3.0, which is a combination of recent technological advancements including the blockchain, cryptocurrencies, and non-fungible tokens (NFTs). The legal response to a combination of these technologies in creating a metaverse or metaverses is two-fold—what existing causes of action will apply to metaverse activities and how and what types of new law will be needed to regulate against harm caused to users? First, the building and content of the metaverse is inherently creative, the law of intellectual property (patent; copyright; trademark; right of publicity; contracts, especially those related to licensing) will be front and center in real-world disputes. Second, a group of legal actions will center on the relationship between users and platform operators (violation of privacy, use of personal data, torts causing psychological harm). The third group of actions will focus on interactions between users (torts and crimes).[21]

Tort and criminal law may have to separate real wrongs (against individuals) from virtual wrongs (against virtual persons). This necessitates the separation of real harms from virtual harms, and finally distinguishing between real remedies and virtual remedies. Real remedies are used and enforced in real life, while virtual remedies can be used in the metaverse, such as terminating user access.[22]

There is a growing trend to transacting business in current virtual worlds. The metaverse is a world where users' avatars interact with one another and enter virtual shops, allowing them to engage in social and contractual relationships. The result has been the emergence of virtual shopping. This includes the purchase of real goods in the physical world and virtual goods, such as clothing for an avatar, to be used in the metaverse. Metaverse-commerce or **m-commerce**, while digital will mimic physical experiences. A key component of this new marketplace will be the impact of the Digital Services Act (DSA) on virtual shops in virtual worlds. The DSA only applies to **very large online platforms** (VLOPs). Future metaverses are likely to qualify as VLOPs. If they are not so characterized, then the DSA should be amended to apply to all metaverse platforms.[23]

EU consumer law is premised on the belief that consumers are the weaker party to most transactions and need an increased level of protection in order to level the playing field. The reasonable consumer (person) standard is used in contract and tort law in determining if a claim for damages can be brought. The reasonable person standard requires the law to judge a matter not from the actual consumer involved in the case but from the view of an objective reasonable consumer. It has been suggested that due to the potentially greater manipulation of users posed by the metaverse and AI, this longstanding standard may need to be replaced by a more protective standard known as the **vulnerable user** (consumer) standard.

In the end, the dangers and harms possible in the metaverse may be beyond the law to directly regulate. Along with law and courts, human-implemented technological management will be needed. This type of regulation will come in two forms. First, one *ex ante* or before a technology or platform is implemented. This type is referred to as technology by design or **regulation by design**. The second type is *ex post* involving the use of technology to monitor and regulate after the implementation of an AI system, metaverse, and other advanced technology.

Chapter Summary

1. Smart contracts are digital agreements written in computer code, run on blockchain or similar distributed ledger technology (DLT), which is immutable, anonymous, and self-performing, essentially creating a breachless contract. Despite these features, smart contracts cannot escape the reach of contract law, consumer protection law, or the court system.
2. Legal Technology (legaltech) holds the potential of transforming the practice of law by enhancing the work of lawyers. It is also highly disruptive to the traditional ways of law practice since much of legaltech aims to replace some of the tasks traditionally performed by lawyers. It also presents ethical issues for lawyers who use it and those that neglect to use it.

3. The use of AI in law practice must conform with the lawyer's Professional Code of Conduct such as the duty of competence and the duty of confidentiality. It is important that lawyers receive consent from clients before using client data in an AI application and to take precautions to secure the safety and anonymity of that data. If lawyers ignore the use of AI systems that are more accurate than human work and are less costly to clients, then they would violate the duty of competency. If the lawyer uses an AI System that proves to be faulty, then again the lawyer would violate the duty of competency. The lawyer must perform due diligence in implementing an AI system and maintain human oversight. The lawyer should never use AI as a substitute for the lawyer's own judgment and experiences. In the end, it is important to distinguish AI systems that enhance the practice of law and those that are meant to act as lawyer substitutes.
4. The acceleration of technology disrupts existing ways of doing business and continues to place stress on the legal system on how best to apply existing law to disputes related to AI and online activities. The EU's Online Platforms Regulation of 2019 (Platform Regulation) is a recognition that liability exemptions for Internet providers should not necessarily apply to all digital intermediaries.
5. Recent developments in advanced and generative AI hold numerous benefits but also pose risks of manipulation and abuse of users and consumers. AI's creation of dark patterns manipulates users' autonomy and free will. Often the AI system can influence users into purchasing things that they don't want or doing things not in their best interests.
6. The 2024 EU AI Act is the first general law that attempts to regulate AI. It approaches AI regulation based on a risk assessment system. Providers of higher risk types of AI are required to meet more stringent requirements such as performing a conformity assessment.
7. Technology has created a new category of things known as digital assets. One such type are non-fungible tokens (NFTs), which have developed their own marketplaces. The regulation of such assets depends on how they are categorized (intellectual property, license contract, security, or personal property).
8. The anticipated creation of the metaverse poses numerous issues for law to prevent the potential abuse and harm to users. Users through their avatars may suffer psychological harm from immersion into virtual worlds. The law will have to determine whether virtual harm is actionable in the real world.

Key Terms

Advisory Forum for Stakeholders
Artificial Intelligence (AI)
Artificial General Intelligence (AGI)
Artificial Intelligence Act
AI Board
AI Office
Avatars
Banned Applications
Bitcoin
Black Box

- Blockchain Technology
- Codes of Conduct
- Conformity Assessment
- Dark Patterns
- Deepfakes
- Digital Content Directive (DCD)
- Digital Services Act (DSA)
- Ethereum
- EU AI Office
- EU Platform Regulation
- General-Purpose AI
- Generative AI
- High-Risk AI
- High-Risk Systems
- Internet Courts
- Legal Technology (legaltech)
- M-Commerce
- Metaverse
- Non-Fungible Tokens (NFTs)
- Personal Property
- Privacy by Design
- Psychological Harm
- Regulation by Design
- Responsible AI
- Scientific Panel of Independent Experts
- Smart Contracts
- Smart Transactional Technologies
- Unfair Contract Terms Directive (UCTD)
- Very Large Online Platforms (VLOPs)
- Vulnerable User

Chapter Problems and Internet Exercises

1. Review the Artificial Intelligence Act to understand its core elements. See https://www.europarl.europa.eu/topics/en/article/20230601STO93804/eu-ai-act-first-regulation-on-artificial-intelligence. Also, research commentary on the Act to determine its shortcomings.
2. Report on the use of Internet Courts in China. See Duke University, "Judicature" at https://judicature.duke.edu/articles/chinas-e-justice-revolution.
3. See examples of NFTs and read a brief discussion of NFTs. See Linda Xie, "Beginner's Guide to NFTs," https://linda.mirror.xyz/df649d61efb92c910464a4e74ae213c4cab150b9cbcc4b7fb6090fc77881a95d.
4. Read about the metaverse—its meaning and varied characteristics. Do you see any dangers or risks to individual users? See, for example, *NY Times*, "Are We in the Metaverse Yet?" at https://www.nytimes.com/2021/07/10/style/metaverse-virtual-worlds.html; Pew Research Center, "The Metaverse in 2040" at https://www.pewresearch.org/internet/2022/06/30/the-metaverse-in-2040.
5. Review amazing catalogue of the European Council on "Responsible AI: Ethics and Regulation" (https://consilium-europa.libguides.com/c.php?g=690732&p=4948483) with access to reports and papers on AI such as:
   - Ethical guidelines on the use of artificial intelligence (AI) and data in teaching and learning for educators
   - Humans and societies in the age of artificial intelligence
   - Artificial intelligence in healthcare
   - Digitalization of justice
   - Law enforcement and the challenge of deepfakes

Notes

1 Larry DiMatteo, Michel Cannarsa, and Cristina Poncibò (eds.), *The Cambridge Handbook of Smart Contracts, Blockchain Technology and Digital Platforms* (CUP 2019), 5.

2 UK Government Chief Scientific Adviser, "Distributed Ledger Technology: Beyond Block Chain," 2016, 17, at https://assets.publishing.service.gov.uk/government/uploads/system/uploads/attachment_data/file/492972/gs-16–1-distributed-ledger-technology.pdf.

3 Jeffery Lipshaw, "The Persistence of 'Dumb' Contracts" (2019) 2 *Stanford Journal of Blockchain Law & Policy* 1.

4 Regulation (EU) 2016/679 of the European Parliament and of the Council of 27 April 2016 on the protection of natural persons with regard to the processing of personal data and on the free movement of such data.

5 Riccardo de Caria, "Definitions of Smart Contracts: Between Law and Code" in DiMatteo, Cannarsa, and Poncibò, *Cambridge Handbook of Smart Contracts*, 35.

6 Larry A. DiMatteo, Cristina Poncibò, and Michel Cannarsa (eds.), *The Cambridge Handbook of Artificial Intelligence: Global Perspectives on Law and Ethics* (CUP 2022), 3.

7 National Science and Technology Council, "Preparing for the Future of Artificial Intelligence" (October 2016), 2.

8 Eric Tjong Tjin Tai, "Using AI to Influence Consumer Choice" in *Cambridge Handbook of AI and Consumer Law*, Ch. 6.

9 Geraint Howells, "AI and Consumers" in *Cambridge Handbook of AI and Consumer Law*, Ch. 1.

10 Mateja Durovic, "AI and Existing Consumer Law" in *Cambridge Handbook of AI and Consumer Law*, Ch. 5.

11 Christiana Markou, "Substituted Consumers: Digital Content Directive and Damages" in *Cambridge Handbook of AI and Consumer Law*, Ch. 3.

12 EU Regulation 2022/2065.

13 Council Directive 93/13/EEC of 5 April 1993 on unfair terms in consumer contracts [1993] OJ L 95/29. See Philip Hacker, "Regulating the Economic Impact of Data as Counter-Performance: From the Illegality Doctrine to the Unfair Contract Terms Directive," in S. Lohsee, R. Schulze, and D. Staudenmayer, *Data as Counter-Performance—Contract Law 2.0?* (Nomos 2020) 47.

14 Larry A. DiMatteo and Francisco de Ezalde, "Governance of Lawyering and Lawyering Governance of AI" in Roger Brownsword and Larry A. DiMatteo, *Governance of AI: Discontent, Disruption and Doubts* (CUP 2025).

15 Martin Ebers, "EU Consumer Law and the Artificial Intelligence Act" in *Cambridge Handbook of AI and Consumer Law*, Ch. 14.

16 EU Parliament News, https://www.europarl.europa.eu/news/en/press-room/20240308IPR19015/artificial-intelligence-act-meps-adopt-landmark-law.

17 Eliza Mik, "Algorithmic Exploitation of Consumers" in *Cambridge Handbook of AI and Consumer Law*, Ch. 13.

18 However, in some cases the digital asset is stored on the blockchain. The SuperRare platform stores a hash of the digital art piece directly in the token on the smart contract.

19 Matteo Alessandro, "Non-Fungible Tokens: An Argument for the Ownership of Digital Property?" (2023) *International Journal of Law in Changing World*, 171 (Special Issue on NFTs).
20 Tristan Girard-Gaymard, "Role of NFTs, Cryptocurrencies and Blockchain Technologies" in Larry A. DiMatteo and Michel Cannarsa, *Research Handbook on Metaverse and Law* (EE Elgar 2024), Chapter 3.
21 Larry A. DiMatteo and Michel Cannarsa, "Into the Metaverse" in DiMatteo and Cannarsa, *Research Handbook on Metaverse and Law*, Chapter 1.
22 In the context of smart contracts see Larry A. DiMatteo and Cristina Poncibó, "Quandary of Smart Contracts and Remedies: Role of Contract Law and Self-Help Remedies" (2019) 26 *European Review of Private Law*, 805.
23 Cristina Poncibò and Luigi Cantisani, "E-Commerce in Virtual Worlds: Digital Services Act" in DiMatteo and Cannarsa, *Research Handbook on Metaverse and Law*, Chapter 15.

APPENDIX

APPENDIX: UNITED NATIONS CONVENTION ON CONTRACTS FOR THE INTERNATIONAL SALE OF GOODS (CISG; 1980)

(Part IV Final Provisions, Articles 89–101, have been deleted)

THE STATES PARTIES TO THIS CONVENTION,

BEARING IN MIND the broad objectives in the resolutions adopted by the sixth special session of the General Assembly of the United Nations on the establishment of a new International Economic Order,

CONSIDERING that the development of international trade on the basis of equality and mutual benefit is an important element in promoting friendly relations among States,

BEING OF THE OPINION that the adoption of uniform rules which govern contracts for the international sale of goods and take into account the different social, economic and legal systems would contribute to the removal of legal barriers in international trade and promote the development of international trade, HAVE AGREED as follows:

PART I: Sphere of Application and General Provisions

Chapter I: Sphere of Application

ARTICLE 1

1 This Convention applies to contracts of sale of goods between parties whose places of business are in different States:

a when the States are Contracting States; or
b when the rules of private international law lead to the application of the law of a Contracting State.

2 The fact that the parties have their places of business in different States is to be disregarded whenever this fact does not appear either from the contract or from any dealings between, or from information disclosed by, the parties at any time before or at the conclusion of the contract.

3 Neither the nationality of the parties nor the civil or commercial character of the parties or of the contract is to be taken into consideration in determining the application of this Convention.

ARTICLE 2

This Convention does not apply to sales:

a of goods bought for personal, family or household use, unless the seller at any time before or at the conclusion of the contract, neither knew nor ought to have known that the goods were bought for any such use;
b by auction;
c on execution or otherwise by authority of law;
d of stocks, shares, investment securities, negotiable instruments or money;
e of ships, vessels, hovercraft or aircraft;
f of electricity.

ARTICLE 3

1 Contracts for the supply of goods to be manufactured or produced are to be considered sales unless the party who orders the goods undertakes to supply a substantial part of the materials necessary for such manufacture or production.

2 This Convention does not apply to contracts in which the preponderant part of the obligations of the party who furnishes the goods consists in the supply of labour or other services.

ARTICLE 4

This Convention governs only the formation of the contract of sale and the rights and obligations of the seller and the buyer arising from such a contract. In particular, except as otherwise expressly provided in this Convention, it is not concerned with:

a the validity of the contract or of any of its provisions or of any usage;

b the effect which the contract may have on the property in the goods sold.

ARTICLE 5

This Convention does not apply to the liability of the seller for death or personal injury caused by the goods to any person.

ARTICLE 6

The parties may exclude the application of this Convention or, subject to article 12, derogate from or vary the effect of any of its provisions.

Chapter II: General Provisions

ARTICLE 7

1 In the interpretation of this Convention, regard is to be had to its international character and to the need to promote uniformity in its application and the observance of good faith in international trade.

2 Questions concerning matters governed by this Convention which are not expressly settled in it are to be settled in conformity with the general principles on which it is based or, in the absence of such principles, in conformity with the law applicable by virtue of the rules of private international law.

ARTICLE 8

1 For the purposes of this Convention statements made by and other conduct of party are to be interpreted according to his intent where the other party knew or could not have been unaware what that intent was.

2 If the preceding paragraph is not applicable, statements made by and other conduct of a party are to be interpreted according to the understanding that a reasonable person of the same kind as the other party would have had in the same circumstances.

3 In determining the intent of a party or the understanding a reasonable person would have had, due consideration is to be given to all relevant circumstances of the case including the negotiations, any practices which the parties have established between themselves, usage and any subsequent conduct of the parties.

ARTICLE 9

1 The parties are bound by any usage to which they have agreed and by any practices which they have established between themselves.

2 The parties are considered, unless otherwise agreed, to have impliedly made applicable to their contract or its formation a usage of which the parties knew or ought to have known and which in international trade is widely known to, and regularly observed by, parties to contracts of the type involved in the particular trade concerned.

ARTICLE 10

For the purposes of this Convention:

a if a party has more than one place of business, the place of the business is that which has the closest relationship to the contract and its performance, having regard to the circumstances known to or contemplated by the parties at any time before or at the conclusion of the contract;
b if a party does not have a place of business, reference is to be made to his habitual residence.

ARTICLE 11

A contract of sale need not be concluded in or evidenced by writing and is not subject to any other requirement as to form. It may be proven by any means, including witnesses.

ARTICLE 12

Any provision of article 11, article 29 or Part 11 of this Convention that allows a contract of sale or its modification or termination by agreement or any offer, acceptance or other indication of intention to be made in any form other than in writing does not apply where any party has his place of business in a Contracting State which has made a declaration under article 96 of this Convention. The parties may not derogate from or vary the effect of this article.

ARTICLE 13

For the purposes of this Convention "writing" includes telegram and telex.

PART II: Formation of the Contract

ARTICLE 14

1 A proposal for concluding a contract addressed to one or more specific persons constitutes an offer if it is sufficiently definite and indicates the intention of the offeror to be bound in case of acceptance. A proposal is sufficiently definite if it indicates the goods and expressly or implicitly fixes or makes provision for determining the quantity and the price.
2 A proposal other than one addressed to one or more specific persons is to be considered merely as an invitation to make offers, unless the contrary is clearly indicated by the person making the proposal.

ARTICLE 15

1 An offer becomes effective when it reaches the offeree.
2 An offer, even if it is irrevocable, may be withdrawn if the withdrawal reaches the offeree before or at the same time as the offer.

ARTICLE 16

1 Until a contract is concluded an offer may be revoked if the revocation reaches the offeree before he has dispatched an acceptance.
2 However, an offer cannot be revoked:
  a if it indicates, whether by stating a fixed time for acceptance or otherwise, that it is irrevocable; or
  b if it was reasonable for the offeree to rely on the offer as being irrevocable and the offeree has acted in reliance on the offer.

ARTICLE 17

An offer, even if it is irrevocable, is terminated when a rejection reaches the offeror.

ARTICLE 18

1 A statement made by or other conduct of the offeree indicating assent to an offer is an acceptance. Silence or inactivity does not in itself amount to acceptance.

2 An acceptance of an offer becomes effective at the moment the indication of assent reaches the offeror. An acceptance is not effective if the indication of assent does not reach the offeror within the time he has fixed or, if no time is fixed, within a reasonable time, due account being taken of the circumstances of the transaction, including the rapidity of the means of communication employed by the offeror. An oral offer must be accepted immediately unless the circumstances indicate otherwise.

3 However, if, by virtue of the offer or as a result of practices which the parties have established between themselves or of usage, the offeree may indicate assent by performing an act, such as one relating to the dispatch of the goods or payment of the price, without notice to the offeror, the acceptance is effective at the moment the act is performed, provided that the act is performed within the period of time laid down in the preceding paragraph.

ARTICLE 19

1 A reply to an offer which purports to be an acceptance but contains additions, limitations or other modifications is a rejection of the offer and constitutes a counter-offer.

2 However, a reply to an offer which purports to be an acceptance but contains additional or different terms which do not materially alter the terms of the offer constitutes an acceptance, unless the offeror, without undue delay, objects orally to the discrepancy or dispatches a notice to that effect. If he does not so object, the terms of the contract are the terms of the offer with the modifications contained in the acceptance.

3 Additional or different terms relating, among other things, to the price, payment, quality and quantity of the goods, place and time of delivery, extent of one party's liability to the other or the settlement of disputes are considered to alter the terms of the offer materially.

ARTICLE 20

1 A period of time for acceptance fixed by the offeror in a telegram or a letter begins to run from the moment the telegram is handed in for dispatch or from the date shown on the letter or, if no such date is shown, from the date shown on the envelope. A period of time for acceptance fixed by the offeror by telephone, telex or other means of instantaneous communication, begins to run from the moment that the offer reaches the offeree.

2 Official holidays or non-business days occurring during the period for acceptance are included in calculating the period. However, if a notice of acceptance cannot be delivered at the address of the offeror on the last day of the period because that day falls on an official holiday or a non-business day at the place of business of the offeror, the period is extended until the first business day which follows.

ARTICLE 21

1 A late acceptance is nevertheless effective as an acceptance if without delay the offeror orally so informs the offeree or dispatches a notice to that effect.

2 If a letter or other writing containing a late acceptance shows that it has been sent in such circumstances that if its transmission had been normal it would have reached the offeror in due time, the late acceptance is effective as an acceptance unless, without delay, the offeror orally informs the offeree that he considers his offer as having lapsed or dispatches a notice to that effect.

ARTICLE 22

An acceptance may be withdrawn if the withdrawal reaches the offeror before or at the same time as the acceptance would have become effective.

ARTICLE 23

A contract is concluded at the moment when an acceptance of an offer becomes effective in accordance with the provisions of this Convention.

ARTICLE 24

For the purposes of this part of the Convention, an offer, declaration of acceptance or any other indication of intention "reaches" the addressee when it is made orally to him or delivered by any other means to him personally, to his place of business or mailing address or, if he does not have a place of business or mailing address, to his habitual residence.

PART III: Sale of Goods

Chapter I: General Provisions

ARTICLE 25

A breach of contract committed by one of the parties is fundamental if it results in such detriment to the other party as substantially to deprive him of what he is entitled to expect under the contract, unless the party in breach did not foresee and a reasonable person of the same kind in the same circumstances would not have foreseen such a result.

ARTICLE 26

A declaration of avoidance of the contract is effective only if made by notice to the other party.

ARTICLE 27

Unless otherwise expressly provided in this Part of the Convention, if any notice, request or other communication is given or made by a party in accordance with this Part and by means appropriate in the circumstances, a delay or error in the transmission of the communication or its failure to arrive does not deprive that party of the right to rely on the communication.

ARTICLE 28

If, in accordance with the provisions of this Convention, one party is entitled to require performance of any obligation by the other party, a court is not bound to enter a judgement for specific performance unless the court would do so under its own law in respect of similar contracts of sale not governed by this Convention.

ARTICLE 29

1 A contract may be modified or terminated by the mere agreement of the parties.
2 A contract in writing which contains a provision requiring any modification or termination by agreement to be in writing may not be otherwise modified or terminated by agreement. However, a party may be precluded by his conduct from asserting such a provision to the extent that the other party has relied on that conduct.

Chapter II: Obligations of the Seller

ARTICLE 30

The seller must deliver the goods, hand over any documents relating to them and transfer the property in the goods, as required by the contract and this Convention.

Section I: Delivery of the Goods and Handing Over of Documents

ARTICLE 31

If the seller is not bound to deliver the goods at any other particular place, his obligation to deliver consists:

a If the contract of sale involves carriage of the goods—in handing the goods over to the first carrier for transmission to the buyer;

b if, in cases not within the preceding subparagraph, the contract relates to specific goods, or unidentified goods to be drawn from a specific stock or to be manufactured or produced, and at the time of the conclusion of the contract the parties knew that the goods were at, or were to be manufactured or produced at a particular place—in placing the goods at the buyer's disposal at that place;
c in other cases—in placing the goods at the buyer's disposal at the place where the seller had his place of business at the time of the conclusion of the contract.

ARTICLE 32

1 If the seller, in accordance with the contract or this Convention, hands the goods over to a carrier and if the goods are not clearly identified to the contract by markings on the goods, by shipping documents or otherwise, the seller must give the buyer notice of the consignment specifying the goods.
2 If the seller is bound to arrange for carriage of the goods, he must make such contracts as are necessary for carriage to the place fixed by means of transportation appropriate in the circumstances and according to the usual terms for such transportation.
3 If the seller is not bound to effect insurance in respect of the carriage of goods, he must, at the buyer's request, provide him with all available information necessary to enable him to effect such insurance.

ARTICLE 33

The seller must deliver the goods:

a if a date is fixed by or determinable from the contract, on that date;
b if a period of time is fixed by or determinable from the contract, at any time within that period unless circumstances indicate that the buyer is to choose a date; or
c in any other case, within a reasonable time after the conclusion of the contract.

ARTICLE 34

If the seller is bound to hand over documents relating to the goods, he must hand them over at the time and place and in the form required by the contract. If the seller has handed over documents before that time, he may, up to that time, cure any lack of conformity in the documents, if the exercise of this right does not cause the buyer unreasonable inconvenience or unreasonable expense. However, the buyer retains any right to claim damages as provided for in this Convention.

Section II: Conformity of the Goods and Third Party Claims

ARTICLE 35

1 The seller must deliver goods which are of the quantity, quality and description required by the contract and which are contained or packaged in the manner required by the contract.
2 Except where the parties have agreed otherwise, the goods do not conform with the contract unless they:
    a are fit for the purposes for which goods of the same description would ordinarily be used;
    b are fit for any particular purpose expressly or impliedly made known to the seller at the time of the conclusion of the contract, except where the circumstances show that the buyer did not rely, or that it was unreasonable for him to rely, on the seller's skill and judgement;
    c possess the qualities of goods which the seller has held out to the buyer as a sample or model;
    d are contained or packaged in the manner usual for such goods or, where there is no such manner, in a manner adequate to preserve and protect the goods.
3 The seller is not liable under subparagraphs (a) to (d) of the preceding paragraph for any lack of conformity of the goods if at the time of the conclusion of the contract the buyer knew or could not have been unaware of such lack of conformity.

ARTICLE 36

1 The seller is liable in accordance with the contract and this Convention for any lack of conformity which exists at the time when the risk passes to the buyer, even though the lack of conformity becomes apparent only after that time.

2 The seller is also liable for any lack of conformity which occurs after the time indicated in the preceding paragraph and which is due to a breach of any of his obligations, including a breach of any guarantee that for a period of time the goods will remain fit for their ordinary purpose or for some particular purpose or will retain specified qualities or characteristics.

ARTICLE 37

If the seller has delivered goods before the date for delivery, he may, up to that date, deliver any missing part or make up any deficiency in the quantity of the goods delivered, or deliver goods in replacement of any non-conforming goods delivered or remedy any lack of conformity in the goods delivered, provided that the exercise of this right does not cause the buyer unreasonable inconvenience or unreasonable expense. However, the buyer retains any right to claim damages as provided for in this Convention.

ARTICLE 38

1 The buyer must examine the goods, or cause them to be examined, within as short a period as is practicable in the circumstances.

2 If the contract involves carriage of the goods, examination may be deferred until after the goods have arrived at their destination.

3 If the goods are redirected in transit or redispatched by the buyer without a reasonable opportunity for examination by him, and at the time of the conclusion of the contract, the seller knew or ought to have known of the possibility of such redirection or redispatch, examination may be deferred until after the goods have arrived at the new destination.

ARTICLE 39

1 The buyer loses the right to rely on a lack of conformity of the goods if he does not give notice to the seller specifying the nature of the lack of conformity within a reasonable time after he has discovered it or ought to have discovered it.

2 In any event, the buyer loses the right to rely on a lack of conformity of the goods if he does not give the seller notice thereof at the latest within a period of two years from the date on which the goods were actually handed over to the buyer, unless this time limit is inconsistent with a contractual period of guarantee.

ARTICLE 40

The seller is not entitled to rely on the provisions of articles 38 and 39 if the lack of conformity relates to facts of which he knew or could not have been unaware and which he did not disclose to the buyer.

ARTICLE 41

The seller must deliver goods which are free from any right or claim of a third party, unless the buyer agreed to take the goods subject to that right or claim. However, if such right or claim is based on industrial property or other intellectual property, the seller's obligation is governed by article 42.

ARTICLE 42

1 The seller must deliver goods which are free from any right or claim of a third party based on industrial property or other intellectual property, of which at the time of the conclusion of the contract the seller knew or could not have been unaware, provided that the right or claim is based on industrial property or other intellectual property:
   a under the law of the State where the goods will be resold or otherwise used, if it was contemplated by the parties at the time of the conclusion of the contract that the goods would be resold or otherwise used in that State; or

b in any other case, under the law of the State where the buyer has his place of business.

1. The obligation of the seller under the preceding paragraph does not extend to cases where:
2. a at the time of the conclusion of the contract the buyer knew or could not have been unaware of the right or claim; or
3. b the right or claim results from the seller's compliance with technical drawing, designs, formula or other such specifications furnished by the buyer.

ARTICLE 43

1 The buyer loses the right to rely on the provisions of article 41 or article 42 if he does not give notice to the seller specifying the nature of the right or claim of the third party within a reasonable time after he has become aware or ought to have become aware of the right or claim.

2 The seller is not entitled to rely on the provisions of the preceding paragraph if he knew of the right or claim of the third party and the nature of it.

ARTICLE 44

Notwithstanding the provisions of paragraph (1) of article 39 and paragraph (1) of article 43, the buyer may reduce the price in accordance with article 50 or claim damages, except for loss of profit, if he has a reasonable excuse for his failure to give the required notice.

Section III: Remedies for Breach of Contract by the Seller

ARTICLE 45

1 If the seller fails to perform any of his obligations under the contract or this Convention, the buyer may:
  a exercise the rights provided in articles 46 to 52;
  b claim damages as provided in articles 74 to 77.

2 The buyer is not deprived of any right he may have to claim damages by exercising his right to other remedies.

3 No period of grace may be granted to the seller by a court or arbitral tribunal when the buyer resorts to a remedy for breach of contract.

ARTICLE 46

1 The buyer may require performance by the seller of his obligations unless the buyer has resorted to a remedy which is inconsistent with this requirement.

2 If the goods do not conform with the contract, the buyer may require delivery of substitute goods only if the lack of conformity constitutes a fundamental breach of contract and a request for substitute goods is made either in conjunction with notice given under article 39 or within a reasonable time thereafter.

3 If the goods do not conform with the contract, the buyer may require the seller to remedy the lack of conformity by repair, unless this is unreasonable having regard to all the circumstances. A request for repair must be made either in conjunction with notice given under article 39 or within a reasonable time thereafter.

ARTICLE 47

1 The buyer may fix an additional period of time of reasonable length for performance by the seller of his obligations.

2 Unless the buyer has received notice from the seller that he will not perform within the period so fixed, the buyer may not, during that period, resort to any remedy for breach of contract. However, the buyer is not deprived thereby of any right he may have to claim damages for delay in performance.

ARTICLE 48

1 Subject to article 49, the seller may, even after the date for delivery, remedy at his own expense any failure to perform his obligations, if he can do so without unreasonable delay and without causing the buyer unreasonable inconvenience or uncertainty of

reimbursement by the seller of expenses advanced by the buyer. However, the buyer retains any right to claim damages as provided for in this Convention.

2 If the seller requests the buyer to make known whether he will accept performance and the buyer does not comply with the request within a reasonable time, the Seller may perform within the time indicated in his request. The buyer may not, during that period of time, resort to any remedy which is inconsistent with performance by the seller.

3 A notice by the seller that he will perform within a specified period of time is assumed to include a request, under the preceding paragraph, that the buyer make known his decision.

4 A request or notice by the seller under paragraph (2) or (3) of this article is not effective unless received by the buyer.

ARTICLE 49

1 The buyer may declare the contract avoided:
   a if the failure by the seller to perform any of his obligations under the contract or this Convention amounts to a fundamental breach of contract; or
   b in case of non-delivery, if the seller does not deliver the goods within the additional period of time fixed by the buyer in accordance with paragraph (1) of article 47 or declares that he will not deliver within the period so fixed.

2 However, in cases where the seller has delivered the goods, the buyer loses the right to declare the contract avoided unless he does so:
   a in respect of late delivery, within a reasonable time after he has become aware that delivery has been made;
   b in respect of any breach other than late delivery, within a reasonable time:
      i after he knew or ought to have known of the breach;
      ii after the expiration of any additional period of time fixed by the buyer in accordance with paragraph (1) of article 47, or after the seller has declared that he will not perform his obligations within such an additional period; or
      iii after the expiration of any additional period of time indicated by the seller in accordance with paragraph (2) of article 48, or after the buyer has declared that he will not accept performance.

ARTICLE 50

If the goods do not conform with the contract and whether or not the price has already been paid, the buyer may reduce the price in the same proportion as the value that the goods actually delivered had at the time of the delivery bears to the value that conforming goods would have had at that time. However, if the seller remedies any failure to perform his obligations in accordance with article 37 or article 48 or if the buyer refuses to accept performance by the seller in accordance with those articles, the buyer may not reduce the price.

ARTICLE 51

1 If the seller delivers only a part of the goods or if only a part of the goods delivered is in conformity with the contract, articles 46 to 50 apply in respect of the part which is missing or which does not conform.

2 The buyer may declare the contract avoided in its entirety only if the failure to make delivery completely or in conformity with the contract amounts to a fundamental breach of the contract.

ARTICLE 52

1 If the seller delivers the goods before the date fixed, the buyer may take delivery or refuse to take delivery.

2 If the seller delivers a quantity of goods greater than that provided for in the contract, the buyer may take delivery or refuse to take delivery of the excess quantity. If the buyer takes delivery of all or part of the excess quantity, he must pay for it at the contract rate.

Chapter III: Obligations of the Buyer

ARTICLE 53

The buyer must pay the price for the goods and take delivery of them as required by the contract and this Convention.

Section 1: Payment of the Price

ARTICLE 54

The buyer's obligation to pay the price includes taking such steps and complying with such formalities as may be required under the contract or any laws and regulations to enable payment to be made.

ARTICLE 55

Where a contract has been validly concluded but does not expressly or implicitly fix or make provision for determining the price, the parties are considered, in the absence of any indication to the contrary, to have impliedly made reference to the price generally charged at the time of the conclusion of the contract for such goods sold under comparable circumstances in the trade concerned.

ARTICLE 56

If the price is fixed according to the weight of the goods, in case of doubt it is to be determined by the net weight.

ARTICLE 57

1 If the buyer is not bound to pay the price at any other particular place, he must pay it to the seller:
   a at the seller's place of business; or
   b if the payment is to be made against the handing over of the goods or of documents, at the place where the handing over takes place.

2 The seller must bear any increase in the expenses incidental to payment which is caused by a change in his place of business subsequent to the conclusion of the contract.

ARTICLE 58

1 If the buyer is not bound to pay the price at any other specific time, he must pay it when the seller places either the goods or documents controlling their disposition at the buyer's disposal in accordance with the contract and this Convention. The seller may make such payment a condition for handing over the goods or documents.

2 If the contract involves carriage of the goods, the seller may dispatch the goods on terms whereby the goods, or documents controlling their disposition, will not be handed over to the buyer except against payment of the price.

3 The buyer is not bound to pay the price until he has had an opportunity to examine the goods, unless

4 the procedures for delivery or payment agreed upon by the parties are inconsistent with his having such an opportunity.

ARTICLE 59

The buyer must pay the price on the date fixed by or determinable from the contract and this Convention without the need for any request or compliance with any formality on the part of the seller.

Section II: Taking Delivery

ARTICLE 60

The buyer's obligation to take delivery consists:

a in doing all the acts which could reasonably be expected of him in order to enable the seller to make delivery; and
b in taking over the goods.

Section III: Remedies for Breach of Contract by the Buyer

ARTICLE 61

1 If the buyer fails to perform any of his obligations under the contract or this Convention, the seller may:
  a exercise the rights provided in articles 62 to 65;
  b claim damages as provided in articles 74 to 77.
2 The seller is not deprived of any right he may have to claim damages by exercising his right to other remedies.
3 No period of grace may be granted to the buyer by a court or arbitral tribunal when the seller resorts to a remedy for breach of contract.

ARTICLE 62

The seller may require the buyer to pay the price, take delivery or perform his other obligations, unless the seller has resorted to a remedy which is inconsistent with this requirement.

ARTICLE 63

1 The seller may fix an additional period of time of reasonable length for performance by the buyer of his obligations.
2 Unless the seller has received notice from the buyer that he will not perform within the period so fixed, the seller may not, during that period, resort to any remedy for breach of contract. However, the seller is not deprived thereby of any right he may have to claim damages for delay in performance.

ARTICLE 64

1 The seller may declare the contract avoided:
  a if the failure by the buyer to perform any of his obligations under the contract or this Convention amounts to a fundamental breach of contract; or
  b if the buyer does not, within the additional period of time fixed by the seller in accordance with paragraph (1) of article 63, perform his obligation to pay the price or take delivery of the goods, or if he declares that he will not do so within the period so fixed.
2 However, in cases where the buyer has paid the price, the seller loses the right to declare the contract avoided unless he does so:
  a in respect of late performance by the buyer, before the seller has become aware that performance has been rendered; or
  b in respect of any breach other than late performance by the buyer, within a reasonable time:
    iv after the seller knew or ought to have known of the breach; or
    v after the expiration of any additional period of time fixed by the seller in accordance with paragraph (1) of article 63, or after the buyer has declared that he will not perform his obligations within such an additional period.

ARTICLE 65

1 If under the contract the buyer is to specify the form, measurement or other features of the goods and he fails to make such specification either on the date agreed upon or within a reasonable time after receipt of a request from the seller, the seller may, without

prejudice to any other rights he may have, make the specification himself in accordance with the requirements of the buyer that may be known to him.

2 If the seller makes the specification himself, he must inform the buyer of the details thereof and must fix a reasonable time within which the buyer may make a different specification. If, after receipt of such a communication, the buyer fails to do so within the time so fixed, the specification made by the seller is binding.

Chapter IV: Passing of Risk

ARTICLE 66

Loss of or damage to the goods after the risk has passed to the buyer does not discharge him from his obligation to pay the price, unless the loss or damage is due to an act or omission of the seller.

ARTICLE 67

1 If the contract of sale involves carriage of the goods and the seller is not bound to hand them over at a particular place, the risk passes to the buyer when the goods are handed over to the first carrier for transmission to the buyer in accordance with the contract of sale. If the seller is bound to hand the goods over to a carrier at a particular place, the risk does not pass to the buyer until the goods are handed over to the carrier at that place. The fact that the seller is authorized to retain documents controlling the disposition of the goods does not affect the passage of the risk.

2 Nevertheless, the risk does not pass to the buyer until the goods are clearly identified to the contract, whether by markings on the goods, by shipping documents, by notice given to the buyer or otherwise.

ARTICLE 68

The risk in respect of goods sold in transit passes to the buyer from the time of the conclusion of the contract. However, if the circumstances so indicate, the risk is assumed by the buyer from the time the goods were handed over to the carrier who issued the documents embodying the contract of carriage. Nevertheless, if at the time of the conclusion of the contract of sale the seller knew or ought to have known that the goods had been lost or damaged and did not disclose this to the buyer, the loss or damage is at the risk of the seller.

ARTICLE 69

1 In cases not within articles 67 and 68, the risk passes to the buyer when he takes over the goods or, if he does not do so in due time, from the time when the goods are placed at his disposal and he commits a breach of contract by failing to take delivery.

2 However, if the buyer is bound to take over the goods at a place other than a place of business of the seller, the risk passes when delivery is due and the buyer is aware of the fact that the goods are placed at his disposal at that place.

3 If the contract relates to goods not then identified, the goods are considered not to be placed at the disposal of the buyer until they are clearly identified to the contract.

ARTICLE 70

If the seller had committed a fundamental breach of contract, articles 67, 68 and 69 do not impair the remedies available to the buyer on account of the breach.

Chapter V: Provisions Common to the Obligations of the Seller and of the Buyer

Section 1: Anticipatory Breach and Installment Contracts

ARTICLE 71

1 A party may suspend the performance of his obligations if, after the conclusion of the contract, it becomes apparent that the other party will not perform a substantial part of his obligations as a result of:

a a serious deficiency in his ability to perform or in his creditworthiness; or
b his conduct in preparing to perform or in performing the contract.

2 If the seller has already dispatched the goods before the grounds described in the preceding paragraph become evident, he may prevent the handing over of the goods to the buyer even though the buyer holds a document which entitles him to obtain them. The present paragraph relates only to the rights in the goods as between the buyer and the seller.

3 A party suspending performance, whether before or after dispatch of the goods must immediately give notice of the suspension to the other party and must continue with performance if the other party provides adequate assurance of his performance.

ARTICLE 72

1 If prior to the date for performance of the contract it is clear that one of the parties will commit a fundamental breach of contract, the other party may declare the contract avoided.

2 If time allows, the party intending to declare the contract avoided must give reasonable notice to the other party in order to permit him to provide adequate assurance of his performance.

3 The requirements of the preceding paragraph do not apply if the other party has declared that he will not perform his obligations.

ARTICLE 73

1 In the case of a contract for delivery of goods by installments, if the failure of one party to perform any of his obligations in respect of any installment constitutes a fundamental breach of contract with respect to that installment, the other party may declare the contract avoided with respect to that installment.

2 If one party's failure to perform any of his obligations in respect of any installment gives the other party good grounds to conclude that a fundamental breach of contract will occur with respect to future installments, he may declare the contract avoided for the future, provided that he does so within a reasonable time.

3 A buyer who declares the contract avoided in respect of any delivery may, at the same time, declare it avoided in respect of deliveries already made or of future deliveries if, by reason of their interdependence, those deliveries could not be used for the purpose contemplated by the parties at the time of the conclusion of the contract.

Section II: Damages

ARTICLE 74

Damages for breach of contract by one party consist of a sum equal to the loss, including loss of profit, suffered by the other party as a consequence of the breach. Such damages may not exceed the loss which the party in breach foresaw or ought to have foreseen at the time of the conclusion of the contract, in the light of the facts and matters of which he then knew or ought to have known, as a possible consequence of the breach of contract.

ARTICLE 75

If the contract is avoided and if, in a reasonable manner and within a reasonable time after avoidance, the buyer has bought goods in replacement or the seller has resold the goods, the party claiming damages may recover the difference between the contract price and the price in the substitute transaction as well as any further damages recoverable under article 74.

ARTICLE 76

1 If the contract is avoided and there is a current price for the goods, the party claiming damages may, if he has not made a purchase or resale under article 75, recover the difference between the price fixed by the contract and the current price at the time of avoidance as well as any further damages recoverable under article 74. If, however, the party claiming damages has avoided the contract after taking over the goods, the current price at the time of such taking over shall be applied instead of the current price at the time of avoidance.

2 For the purposes of the preceding paragraph, the current price is the price prevailing at the place where delivery of the goods should have been made or, if there is no current price at that place, the price at such other place as serves as a reasonable substitute, making due allowance for differences in the cost of transporting the goods.

ARTICLE 77

A party who relies on a breach of contract must take such measures as are reasonable in the circumstances to mitigate the loss, including loss of profit, resulting from the breach. If he fails to take such measures, the party in breach may claim a reduction in the damages in the amount by which the loss should have been mitigated.

ARTICLE 78

If a party fails to pay the price or any other sum that is in arrears, the other party is entitled to interest on it, without prejudice to any claim for damages recoverable under article 74.

Section III: Exemptions

ARTICLE 79

1 A party is not liable for a failure to perform any of his obligations if he proves that the failure was due to an impediment beyond his control and that he could not reasonably be expected to have taken the impediment into account at the time of the conclusion of the contract or to have avoided or overcome it or its consequences.
2 If the party's failure is due to the failure by a third person whom he has engaged to perform the whole or a part of the contract, that party is exempt from liability only if:
  a he is exempt under the preceding paragraph; and
  b the person whom he has so engaged would be so exempt if the provisions of that paragraph were applied to him.
3 The exemption provided by this article has effect for the period during which the impediment exists.
4 The party who fails to perform must give notice to the other party of the impediment and its effects on his ability to perform. If the notice is not received by the other party within a reasonable time after the party who fails to perform knew or ought to have known of the impediment, he is liable for damages resulting from such non-receipt.
5 Nothing in this article prevents either party from exercising any right other than to claim damages under this Convention.

ARTICLE 80

A party may not rely on a failure of the other party to perform, to the extent that such failure was caused by the first party's act or omission.

Section IV: Effects of Avoidance

ARTICLE 81

1 Avoidance of the contract releases both parties from their obligations under it, subject to any damages which may be due. Avoidance does not affect any provision of the contract for the settlement of disputes or any other provision of the contract governing the rights and obligations of the parties consequent upon the avoidance of the contract.
2 A party who has performed the contract either wholly or in part may claim restitution from the other party of whatever the first party has supplied or paid under the contract. If both parties are bound to make restitution, they must do so concurrently.

ARTICLE 82

1. The buyer loses the right to declare the contract avoided or to require the seller to deliver substitute goods if it is impossible for him to make restitution of the goods substantially in the condition in which he received them.
2 The preceding paragraph does not apply:

a if the impossibility of making restitution of the goods or of making restitution of the goods substantially in the condition in which the buyer received them is not due to his act or omission;
b if the goods or part of the goods have perished or deteriorated as a result of the examination provided for in article 38; or if the goods or part of the goods have been sold in the normal course of business or have been consumed or transformed by the buyer in the course of normal use before he discovered or ought to have discovered the lack of conformity.

A buyer who has lost the right to declare the contract avoided or to require the seller to deliver substitute goods in accordance with article 82 retains all other remedies under the contract and this Convention.

ARTICLE 84

1 If the seller is bound to refund the price, he must also pay interest on it, from the date on which the price was paid.
2 The buyer must account to the seller for all benefits which he has derived from the goods or part of them:
  a if he must make restitution of the goods or part of them; or
  b if it is impossible for him to make restitution of all or part of the goods or to make restitution of all or part of the goods substantially in the condition in which he received them, but he has nevertheless declared the contract avoided or required the seller to deliver substitute goods.

Section V: Preservation of the Goods

ARTICLE 85

If the buyer is in delay in taking delivery of the goods or, where payment of the price and delivery of the goods are to be made concurrently, if he fails to pay the price, and the seller is either in possession of the goods or otherwise able to control their disposition, the seller must take such steps as are reasonable in the circumstances to preserve them. He is entitled to retain them until he has been reimbursed his reasonable expenses by the buyer.

ARTICLE 86

1 If the buyer has received the goods and intends to exercise any right under the contract or this Convention to reject them, he must take such steps to preserve them as are reasonable in the circumstances. He is entitled to retain them until he has been reimbursed his reasonable expenses by the seller.
2 If goods dispatched to the buyer have been placed at his disposal at their destination and he exercises the right to reject them, he must take possession of them on behalf of the seller, provided that this can be done without payment of the price and without unreasonable inconvenience or unreasonable expense. This provision does not apply if the seller or a person authorized to take charge of the goods on his behalf is present at the destination. If the buyer takes possession of the goods under this paragraph, his rights and obligations are governed by the preceding paragraph.

ARTICLE 87

A party who is bound to take steps to preserve the goods may deposit them in a warehouse of a third person at the expense of the other party provided that the expense incurred is not unreasonable.

ARTICLE 88

1 A party who is bound to preserve the goods in accordance with article 85 or 86 may sell them by any appropriate means if there has been an unreasonable delay by the other party in taking possession of the goods or in taking them back or in paying the price or the cost of preservation, provided that reasonable notice of the intention to sell has been given to the other party.
2 If the goods are subject to rapid deterioration or their preservation would involve unreasonable expense, a party who is bound to preserve the goods in accordance with article

85 or 86 must take reasonable measures to sell them. To the extent possible he must give notice to the other party of his intention to sell.

3 A party selling the goods has the right to retain out of the proceeds of sale an amount equal to the reasonable expenses of preserving the goods and of selling them. He must account to the other party for the balance.

Index

Note: Page numbers in *italics* indicate figures, and page numbers in **bold** indicate tables in the text